Folktales Told around the World

Edited by Richard M. Dorson

Folktales Told around the World

The University of Chicago Press
Chicago and London

The University of Chicago Press, Chicago 60637
The University of Chicago Press, Ltd., London

© 1975 by The University of Chicago
All rights reserved. Published 1975
Paperback edition 1978
Printed in the United States of America

99 98 97   11 10 9 8 7

Library of Congress Cataloging in Publication Data

Main entry under title:

Folktales told around the world.

   Includes bibliographical references and indexes.
   1.   Tales.   I.   Dorson, Richard Mercer, 1916–
GR15.F63   398.2   74–33515

ISBN: 0-226-15874-8 (paperback)

♾ The paper used in this publication meets
the minimum requirements of the American
National Standard for Information Sciences—
Permanence of Paper for Printed Library
Materials, ANSI Z39.48–1984.

Contents

x   Contents

Illustrations

Acknowledgments

The following permissions to reprint published materials are herein gratefully acknowledged:

"Origin of the Enmity between Dog and Leopard," "Trapper, Gatherer-of-Honey, and Cultivator," and "How Nturo Rejected Mpaca" from Daniel P. Biebuyck and Kahombo Mateene, *Anthologie de la littérature orale nyanga*, © 1970 by Académie Royale des Sciences d'Outre-Mer, Brussels, pp. 87–93, 173–75, 187–89. The French texts given there have been translated especially for this volume by Brunhilde Biebuyck.

"The Gungutan and the Big-Bellied Man," reprinted from *Philippine Social Sciences and Humanities Review*, © 1961 by the University of the Philippines, vol. 26.

"Agkon, the Greedy Son" reprinted from *Unitas*, © 1966 by the University of Santo Tomas, vol. 39.

"Paree at the Carnivalle" from R. M. Dorson, "Dialect Stories of the Upper Peninsula," © 1948 by The American Folklore Society. Reprinted from the *Journal of American Folklore*, vol. 61, no. 240, pp. 121–23, by permission of The Society.

"The Myth of Fuusai" from Elli Köngäs Maranda, "Five Interpretations of a Melanesian Myth," © 1973 by The American Folklore Society. Reprinted from the *Journal of American Folklore* vol. 86, no. 339, pp. 4–7, by permission of, and by arrangement with, The Society.

Selection from R. M. Dorson, "Tales of a Greek-American Family on Tape," reprinted from *Fabula*, vol. 1 (1957), nos. 1–2, pp. 121–22, by permission of the editor, Kurt Ranke.

Introduction to R. M. Dorson, "Polish Wonder Tales of Joe Woods," and text of "The Two Brothers," © 1949 by The California Folklore Society. Reprinted from *Western Folklore*, vol. 8, no. 1 (January 1949), pp. 25–28, 50–52.

"The Flood," reprinted from pp. 41–48 in R. M. Dorson, *Bloodstoppers and Bearwalkers*, © 1952 by the president and fellows of Harvard College.

"The Legend of Yoho Cove" by R. M. Dorson, © 1959 by The California Folklore Society. Reprinted from *Western Folklore*, vol. 18, no. 4 (October 1959), pp. 329–31, by permission of The Society.

"The Mass of Saint Joseph," "Santa Catalina," and "The Unbeliever and the Skull" from Aurelio M. Espinosa, *Cuentos populares españoles*, published in Madrid by Consejo Superior de Investigaciones Scientíficas, Instituto "Antonio de Nebrija" de Filología, vol. I, nos. 74, 78, 79, pp. 135–36, 138–39, 140–41, by permission of Manuel Espinosa. The Spanish texts have been translated especially for this volume by Merle E. Simmons.

The story of the *witranalwe*, reprinted from *Hawks of the Sun: Mapuche Morality and Its Ritual Attributes* by L. C. Faron, pp. 72–73, by permission of and arrangement with the University of Pittsburgh Press.

"The Origin of Maui," "The Theft of Fire," "Snaring of the Sun," and "Earth-Fishing" from Katharine Luomala, "A Dynamic in Oceanic Maui Myths," reprinted from *Fabula*, vol. 4 (1961), nos. 1–2, pp. 155–58, by permission of the editor, Kurt Ranke.

Also I wish to thank my faithful research assistant Inta Carpenter for valuable aid in assembling and indexing the manuscript, and the skilled collectors and talented narrators who have made the volume possible.

The following contributors wish to indicate special acknowledgments:

Hafizullah Baghban
     Teachers, including the mullah in my native village and the folklore scholars at Indiana University, for my training; the Afghan male and female narrators and performers for letting me collect their treasures; and Teachers College, Columbia University, and Indiana University for giving me grants to study and do fieldwork.

Daniel P. Biebuyck
     Académie royale des Sciences d'Outre-Mer (Brussels), publishers of *Anthologie de la littérature orale nyanga*.
     Brunhilde Biebuyck for translating the texts.

Barbara Kirshenblatt-Gimblett
     Canada Council and the Folklore Division, National Museum of Canada, who funded the fieldwork.

Deirdre La Pin
     Foreign Area Fellowship Program for their grant for dissertation research from January 1972 through June 1974.
     Francis Speed, Senior Research Fellow at the Institute of African

Studies, University of Ife, for his assistance with the filmstrips which accompany James Olá's narrative.

Luc Lacourcière
The Archives de Folklore, Laval University, Quebec, who are in turn grateful for the valuable financial support of the Killam Foundation, administered under the auspices of the Canada Council.

Katharine Luomala
The Wenner-Gren Foundation for Anthropological Research, Guggenheim Foundation, National Science Foundation, Smithsonian Institution, University of Hawaii, and Bishop Museum, for support of my Gilbert Islands Research.

Jean MacLaughlin
Foreign Area Fellowship Program, New York (now administered by the Social Science Research Council), who financed the field research in Peru (1971–72).
Merle E. Simmons for reading the translations and making suggestions.

Georgios A. Megas
Research Center for Greek Folklore of the Academy of Athens, for the unpublished material from which some texts have been drawn.

Philip A. Noss
The Foreign Area Fellowship Program, whose grant (1966–68) made possible the original recording and research; and the African Studies Association and American Philosophical Society (1970), whose grants made possible additional work on the tales.

Paul S. Powlison
Laureano Mozombite for his contribution both as narrator and interpreter of the tales he told.

Sean O'Sullivan
The Irish Folklore Commission (now the Irish Folklore Department), University College, Dublin.

Hazel Wrigglesworth
Si Juanitu for narrating the Ilianen Manobo tale "The Seven Young Sky Women"; and the Summer Institute of Linguistics, under whose auspices the tale was collected.

Introduction
Choosing the World's Folktales
Richard M. Dorson

Serving up a selection of folktales from around the world in one volume is a tall order. Many questions at once present themselves to the folklore scholar. How can the compiler fairly represent the geographical and culture areas of the globe? Should he try to do justice to the many forms of traditional narrative? What aesthetic criteria should he employ in culling his choices? How may he balance the requirements of scholarship with the demands of reading entertainment? Where will he find trustworthy sources, faithful to the spoken word? What evidence can he produce that a given tale truly represents the storytelling tradition within a particular country—especially if it enjoys widespread international currency? Or should he better de-emphasize the tale's association with a nation or people and group his choices according to themes, plots, and characters?

These kinds of questions have not deterred anthologists from assembling volumes of the world's folktales. In 1930 F. H. Lee brought together *Folk Tales of All Nations*, in 1949 Milton Rugoff produced *A Harvest of World Folk Tales*, in 1953 James R. Foster offered *The World's Great Folktales*, and in 1968 Stith Thompson chose *One Hundred Favorite Folktales*. The compendiums vary in their principles of selection and organization, but in common they perpetuate certain stereotypes about the nature of folktales. Equally they slight the oral narrators, who are not even named, select tales from previously published volumes whose contents reveal a high literary gloss, and emphasize readability. They follow the notion of the Grimm brothers that a literary hand should improve the rude oral utterance of the peasant. So Lee complimented one of his sources by saying, "Mr. Parker Fillmore has rendered the somewhat stiff, bald, and monotonous wording of these Finnish tales in captivating language."[1] Fairy tales should be charming, delightful, beautiful, touched with an aura of magic and mystery befitting the childlike minds of peasants and savages. They were meant to be read for pleasure by a public far removed from the cultures that bred the tales, and quite uninterested in scholarly analysis. Even Stith Thompson, great scholar of the folktale, reinforced these erroneous conceptions in his own compendium.

Any attempt today to present a meaningful and representative sampling of the world's folktales to the reading public should reflect the now commonly held views of folklore scholarship. The first great correction that needs to be made concerns the nature of the folktale itself, which should be indicated as a spoken performance, rather than as a literary text. Yet in the eyes of the trade publishers, the public, the reviewers in the mass newspapers and magazines, the librarians and schoolteachers, and many academics, the folktale is a specimen of written literature, supposedly emanating from an unlettered peasantry but a fixed and smooth-flowing text nonetheless. Because anthologists draw from collections that themselves often draw from previous publications, the printed folktale grows ever farther from an original word-of-mouth delivery. Today's anthologist should seek fresh oral texts, from collectors or from archives, and avoid previously printed and translated tales. Coverage of the world should be determined not by the attempt to blanket the earth's surface but by the availability of trustworthy collectors, even though a handful are scattered over vast continents. Because it is much simpler to go to books on the library shelves, usually out of date and unreliable to begin with, certain tales are anthologized to death—to the death of their traditional character. Joseph Jacobs's rewritten English and Celtic fairy tales, for example, are fair game for the second-hand tale-gatherer, and so are the old nineteenth-century collections from Africa and Asia made by missionaries and colonial administrators.

A second revision should provide for background information on the tales. If professional folklorists still often fail to obtain adequate data on the narrators, the stature of the teller has steadily increased until now he occasionally shares the title page with the collector. Our world anthology should pay some tribute to its tale-tellers. To do this means that space must be allowed for more than just the tales. And somehow the public must be persuaded that a book of folktales should contain information about the stories, that the stories by themselves are virtually worthless and valueless without commentaries.

Indeed, the point can be argued that the comparative note illuminating the pedigree and diaspora of a tale-family possesses greater interest than the individual tale-variant it serves. Of course the folklorist must learn to write his note, and not simply string together hieroglyphics referring in cryptic abbreviations to titles, types, and motifs. A satisfying note can explain customs, values, and beliefs embodied in the tale, perhaps gloss allusions to historical events and personalities, say something about other forms in which the tale is told and the localities where it is most popular, consider reasons for its appeal, and mention literary versions if they exist as well as describe the technique of the narrator. The notes of Linda Dégh in *Folktales of Hungary*, for example, become informative little essays. They light up the legends about the herdsman who, at the close of the nineteenth century when the Hungarian plains were drained, emerged as an independent idolized figure, friend of outlaws, protector of the flocks, trusted minion of the squire, a Jack-of-all-trades, tough fighter and gay dancer, and a practitioner of magic arts.[2] In Sean O'Sullivan's *Folktales of Ireland* a note to "Sean Palmer's Voyage to America with the Fairies" places this account of a countryman's overnight sail from Ireland to New York within a narrative pattern of aerial journeys to foreign countries by a lucky lad whom the fairies befriend. Sean Palmer tells of visiting his rich relatives and old sweetheart in America, and returns next morning all duded up with dollars in his pocket as proof of his trip. By itself the tale, which I heard myself in County Kerry told by Tige Murphy, might seem a wish-fulfillment fantasy, but the note pointing to a cabinet of variants in the archives of the Irish Folklore Commission attests its debt to a traditional formula.[3] Or again in *Folktales of China* is Wolfram Eberhard's clarifying note to "Chu the Rogue," whose adventures involve him with plague deities, punishments of the ten hells, and creatures serving the king of hell. Without some information on these traditional concepts in Chinese folk religion, the reader could never properly appreciate Chu's rascality in outwitting and escaping from such captors.

A third major corrective for our volume concerns the kinds of folktales offered repeatedly to an apparently receptive public. The one genre that becomes almost synonymous with the folktale is the European magical fiction or Märchen, usually called the fairy tale. Other large genres of folk narrative in the western world, particularly the legend, anecdote, and joke, become the left-out Cinderellas of the popular storybooks, and yet these are predominantly the tales of our times. Folk narrative forms run from the one-line joke to the half-million-word romance. If we wish to represent contemporary storytelling, we must downgrade the fairy tale, even though the market for editions of Grimm continues unabated. After visiting the major European folktale archives in preparation for his 1955 revision of the *Types of the Folktale*, Stith Thompson reported that their largest accessions since the first edition lay in jokes and anecdotes. In compiling *Folktales of Norway*, Reidar Christiansen devoted over half the contents to legendary traditions of kings, the devil, and water, forest, mountain and household spirits, taken largely from twentieth-century oral sources, but for Märchen he had to turn to the rewritten nineteenth-century stories of Asbjörnsen and Moe. England has long been considered virtually barren of wonder tales, and by the same token, of all folktales, but Katharine Briggs demonstrated in *Folktales of England* —and subsequently in the four volumes of her *Dictionary of British*

Folk-Tales—that legendary and humorous narratives have flourished on English soil. The great Victorian folklorists concentrated too heavily on survivals to pay much attention to modern stories, and to Dr. Briggs's credit she includes contemporary urban legends, shaggy dog stories, and jocular anecdotes that form much of the staple folktale fare in the modern world. But these forms are slow to find their way into the tale anthologies.

Part of the explanation for this lag lies in the scholarly as well as the popular conception of the folktale. Frequently the term "folktale" is opposed to the term "legend," to differentiate between a fiction and a happening. In *The Folktale* Stith Thompson intended to deal with all forms of traditional prose narrative, and this is the sense of the word I have applied to the Folktales of the World series. A joke, if it is told often enough to endure, becomes a folktale, although jokes seem somehow a little disreputable to keep company with Aesop and Grimm. The legend has only recently begun to attract the attention of comparative folklorists. In spite of all the popularity of the Grimms' Märchen, their Sagen have never been translated into English. For the most part legends are too local, too allusive and unstructured, too fragmentary and incomplete, to compete successfully with Märchen for scholarly attention or public acclaim.

How does the collector present in a book for general reading several separate episodes told about a landmark or a notable character? For instance, the brief historical legend of "The Altarpiece in Ringsaker Church" in *Folktales of Norway* tells first of a God-fearing minister from Ringsaker in Norway who some centuries ago exorcised the Devil from an English princess, whereupon she gave him a splendid altarpiece for his congregation. The scene then shifts to the war of 1567 between the Norwegians and the Swedes, when a Swedish company invaded and looted Ringsaker, used the church as a stall for their horses, and attempted to carry off the altarpiece. One horse alone could not budge the wagon on which the altarpiece was loaded, and finally a team of twelve horses with difficulty pulled it as far as Sveinhaug. But a yearling foal easily pulled the wagon and altarpiece back to Ringsaker for the Norwegians.[4] The two halves of this tradition could stand apart, in terms of time period and actors, but the teller united them through the link of the magic altarpiece.

Or again, the much longer narrative in *Folktales of China* entitled "The Bridge of Ch'uan-chou" begins, "There are innumerable tales in Fukien about this bridge, but I will only relate the best known." There follows an intricate account of how in 1025 Ts'ai Hsiang with the help of the Eight Immortals, the monk I-po, and the goddess Kuan Yin built the bridge over the Loyang River. The narrator then turns to a tradition dated seven hundred years later, recounting how Li Wu participated in a wholly different set of adventures with rogues, deities, and hidden treasure, and rebuilt the bridge.[5] This legend too violates the Aristotelian unities, and so probably disturbs the expectations of readers accustomed to a consecutive story line, but it is true to folk tradition.

A direct case in point is the legend of mountain treasure collected in Arequipa, Peru, and published here for the first time by Jean Mac-Laughlin. The collector considered this one of her most striking and representative narratives. But the tape transcript of the legend, delivered in the conversational manner characteristic of legend telling, would not excite a reader unfamiliar with the unspoken givens of the culture. The Quechua in Peru believe that spirits of the mountains themselves possess and guard the treasure, and hence the treasure quest takes on a very different character from a treasure hunt in the United States. MacLaughlin's explicit cultural explanations form a necessary complement to the legend text proper.

While some kinds of narratives, particularly those of distant cultures, require editorial prefaces to explain their values and allusions, others resist print because of their dependence on verbal effects.

Unknown to the reading public as a folktale genre is the so-called dialect story, especially fertile in the United States because of the mingling of nationality groups. During a field trip to the Upper Peninsula of Michigan I kept encountering funny tales told by "dialecticians" at social occasions or by people on the street corner, who mimicked the accents, intonations, and malapropisms of the dominant ethnic groups in the area, the Finns, French Canadians, Cornish, and Swedes. These stories ranged from brief anecdotes to lengthy recitals, but they all shared the same humorous features, the reproduction of the immigrant's broken English and the description of his mishaps in an alien culture. Investigation proved that these yarns met all the criteria of folktales, for they traveled by word of mouth and existed in numerous oral variants.[6] Other cycles of dialect stories dealing with Jewish, Italian, and Mexican characters circulate in regions of the United States where those population elements congregate. The Pat and Mike jests, which must have developed after the mid-nineteenth-century Irish immigration to America, clearly belong to the same narrative pattern. But dialect stories do not readily lend themselves to print. The collector must endeavor to simulate phonetically the speaker's word-mangling, and a reader unfamiliar with their sounds may find the tales meaningless. Yet to those who have grown up among Old Country people in the New World, hearing and reading the dialect stories is an hilarious experience. Jewish publishing companies in New York and Chicago have issued popular collections of Jewish jokes, demonstrably drawn from oral currency, for their clientele.

Allied to but distinct from the dialect story is the bilingual narrative, whose tellers and audiences must possess familiarity with two tongues. The dialect story will be told in broken English (or other language) but the bilingual story is told in both English and the second speech, with the narrator shuttling back and forth between his vehicles. In North America the mingling of European mother tongues with American English produces jocular hybrid narratives involving Pennsylvania Dutch, Cajun French, Mexican Spanish, and above all Yiddish sentences, phrases, and expressions. Above all Yiddish, because Yiddish is already a hybrid, and possesses its own irresistibly comic nuances, as Leo Rosten has demonstrated in *The Joys of Yiddish*. In our volume, Barbara Kirshenblatt-Gimblett offers bilingual English-Yiddish tales from the Toronto Jewish community, whose theme as well as expression depart from conventional folktale specimens. The theme is the funny-sad saga of the immigrant newcomer and his trials and misadventures as he enters a new life.

A device employed by oral performers in various tribal societies to heighten and intensify the action, mood, and color of their narratives is the ideophone. As rendered into English, the ideophone appears as a meaningless word, possibly onomatopoeic, yet it is essential to the rhythm and imagery of the original presentation. The Gbaya of Cameroun are adept in the use of ideophones, and Philip Noss takes pains to indicate their presence in the texts he publishes here, and he has effectively explained them elsewhere.[7]

Our fourth point of redress calls for recognition of the narrator, a recognition now demanded by folklorists but as yet untransmitted to the folktale-reading public. Several tale-tellers who have emerged as personalities in their own right are represented in the Folktales of the World series. Known as the "queen of Gaelic storytellers," Peig Sayers (1873–1958) lived most of her life on Great Blasket Island off the southwest coast of Ireland, where she was discovered by collectors for the Irish Folklore Commission and scholars of Gaelic. One collector secured 375 tales from her, of which forty were long wonder tales and forty-four songs, which she had learned mainly from her father. "It was a great pity," mused Peig, "that these gadgets and horns and machines weren't there then to take down his speech and conversation. . . ."[8] But the machines have recorded Peig. A close student of Gaelic, Robin Flower, has written of Peig: ". . . she has so clean and finished a style of speech that you can follow all the nicest articulations of the language on her lips without any effort; she is a natural orator, with so keen a sense of the turn of phrase and the lifting rhythm appropriate to Irish that her words could be written down as they leave her lips, and they would have the effect of literature with no savour of the artificiality of composition."[9] Any reader of her dictated reminiscences, translated and published as *An Old Woman's Reflections*, will appreciate both the literary quality and the narrative artistry of Peig's spoken words. These reminiscences belong to the province of folk narrative fully as much as do her Märchen, although folklorists have tended to slight such local and family sagas and traditionary incidents. The world of Peig Sayers and the island folk comes clearly into view in the *Reflections*, a world largely bounded by the sea and confined to the island life, where a quarrel over a hen or the theft of a fish furnish the stuff of fireside talk.

Tiny incidents grow into dramas in Peig's telling, and her tellings take the shape of tales, constructed around the jealous fits of a milk-woman against her lover's wife or the near-swamping of a boat coming in to Blasket with a load of turf. Even in translation from the "sweet, tasty Gaelic," the ring of folk speech and folk metaphor and the abundance of proverbs scattered throughout the quoted conversation convey the flavor of oral narration. The account of a day's pilgrimage to Wethers Well includes a telling to Peig by a local woman in Dingle of the legend behind the well, but this, the only folklore text in her *Reflections*, arises naturally within the rhythms of a remembered day's outing.

Cut from a different cloth is the English workingman W. H. Barrett, narrator of three volumes of personal saga, *Tales from the Fens* (1963), *More Tales from the Fens* (1964), local traditions he heard, told, and wrote down, and the autobiography he penned, *A Fenman's Story* (1965). Born in 1891 in the Fenland country of Cambridgeshire and Norfolk counties, until recently an ingrown marshland region, Barrett absorbed tavern tales from master Fen chroniclers and gives an oral source for each one. Although Barrett has written out his narratives, and Enid Porter, curator of the Folk Museum in Cambridge, has edited them—matters of regret for the folklorist, especially since she does not describe her methods—Katharine Briggs in *Folktales of England* has tape-recorded four of his recitals. Barrett, who relates no fictions, is a storytelling genius in a vein hitherto ignored or misunderstood by folklorists, local historical traditions and sagas. Some may deal with personal adventures of daily life, such as the journey to London Barrett's dad took as a ten-year-old lad in 1864, suggestive of Peig Sayer's one-day pilgrimage, save that Barrett paints a far different world, peopled by laborers, gypsies, brigands, Cambridge dons, monks, tarts, parsons, witches, one-horse farmers, Norman invaders, French prisoners, and German mercenaries who lived in or came through the fens. Other tales stretch far back in time, to events of the nineteenth, eighteenth, and seventeenth centuries, such as the flight of Charles I through the Fens in 1646. Thus in 1904 Barrett heard a history from an old sailor who heard it from his father, born in 1805, who in turn had heard it from *his* father born in 1770, a time "when a chap could be hung for stealing sixpence."[10] Still other tales fall within the conventional rubrics of the folklorist and can be labeled place legends or witch legends, but these too all bear Barrett's stamp in the close details of scene and setting, the wry humor, and the wealth of personal associations. In "The Gipsy's Curse," which Katharine Briggs recorded directly from Barrett, he reveals only in the last sentence that the man on whom the gypsy laid the curse that he and his children would never die in bed, a curse later borne out, was his own father. All Barrett's narrations concern the Fen country and its folk and represent the traditional history of that countryside.

A very different repertoire, though of commensurate artistry, is offered by Mrs. Zsuzsanna Palkó, the Szekler narrator recognized as Master of Folklore by the Hungarian government in 1954. Linda Dégh not only published seventy-two of her tales in two volumes in the original Hungarian text, but in *Folktales and Society* examined Mrs. Palkó's techniques, sources, style, and morality with the care literary critics reserve for novelists and poets. Here is the Märchen-teller supreme, the peasant woman specializing in complex magic tales. Knowing her over a fourteen-year period, Dégh became familiar with her routine and her circle and makes them known to us. This is an unlettered, unworldly woman, startled at seeing a full-length mirror on her first visit to Budapest at seventy-four, a toiler throughout her life, pious and modest, but sensitive to the conditions of the poor. "When she was narrating, her accusing voice was like a whip, her judgment hard and implacable, her justice often without pity, even brutal at times."[11] But Mrs. Palkó is no revolutionary; true to the conservative instincts of the Bucovina peasant, she looks to God's will rather than to a people's revolt to right wrongs. At the same time she accepts the peasant's work ethic without complaint. Alongside the suffering but triumphant heroines of her Märchen appear shiftless females in her humorous realistic tales (such as "Lazybones," Mrs. Palkó's contribution to *Folktales of Hungary*), who reap deserved punishment for idleness or vanity. In all her narratives, as Dégh demonstrates, Mrs. Palkó maintained the detached epic manner and a consistent story-line, no matter how considerably she might expand a text when the mood struck her.

In Willowvale District of the Transkei, thirty miles from the Indian Ocean in South Africa, a Xhosa woman named Nongenile Masithathu Zenani narrates *ntsomi*—the Xhosa word for traditional tales—with comparable skills. According to Harold Scheub, who met and recorded her tales in 1967–68, tall and regal Mrs. Zenani captures her audiences with subtle facial and bodily expressions and verbal delineation of character. Scheub compares her rendering of a tale episode in which a boy drinks a pregnancy-inducing medicine and grows breasts with versions from two other Xhosa tellers. Where their tellings each occupy nine lines of print, Mrs. Zenani's text requires fifty-three lines. She introduces a scene in which the boy returns the bottle of medicine to his mother after drinking from it, elaborates on the boy's reactions to the budding breasts, and presents details of the boy's birthing of a baby girl.[12] Mrs. Zenani amplifies the bald statements of the briefer texts into dramatic tableaux. "Sikhuluma," a version told by Mrs. Zenani of the international tale type 313 *The Girl as Helper in the Hero's Flight*, runs to thirty-two printed pages and exhibits the narrator's gift for dialogue and cultural details.[13]

These are some of the narrators who deserve tribute in our volume of the world's folktales. Others too will receive recognition in the following pages.

The format of this work follows the pattern of the Folktales of the World series. In addition to selections from the twelve published volumes, some thirty new countries and culture areas are represented by authentic field-collected texts, many previously unpublished. Since collectors present their supporting data in differing ways, I have not striven for complete uniformity in editing the collection. Collectors, like narrators, have their styles. The materials in *Folktales Told Around the World* result from the joint contributions of sophisticated fieldworkers and talented oral performers.

Notes

1. F. H. Lee, *Folktales of All Nations* (New York: Tudor Publishing Co., 1946), p. 411.
2. Linda Dégh, *Folktales of Hungary* (Chicago: University of Chicago Press 1965), pp. 335–36.
3. Sean O'Sullivan, *Folktales of Ireland* (Chicago: University of Chicago Press, 1966), pp. 278–79.
4. Reidar Christiansen, *Folktales of Norway* (Chicago: University of Chicago Press, 1964), pp. 18–19.
5. Wolfram Eberhard, *Folktales of China* (Chicago: University of Chicago Press, 1965), pp. 103–10.
6. Richard M. Dorson, "Dialect Stories of the Upper Peninsula," *Journal of American Folklore* 61 (1948): 113–50.
7. Philip A. Noss, "Description in Gbaya Literary Art" in *African Folklore*, ed. R. M. Dorson (Bloomington: Indiana University Press, 1972), pp. 75–79.
8. Peig Sayers, *An Old Woman's Reflections* (London, 1962), p. ix.
9. Ibid., p. x.
10. W. H. Barrett, *More Tales from the Fens* (London, 1964), p. 66.
11. Linda Dégh, *Folktales and Society* (Bloomington: Indiana University Press, 1969), p. 199.
12. Harold Scheub, "The Art of Nongenile Mazithathu Zenani, a Gcaleka Ntsomi Performer" in *African Folklore*, pp. 118–20.
13. Ibid., pp. 528–61.

Europe

Ireland

Fionn in Search of His Youth

From Sean O'Sullivan. *Folktales of Ireland* (Chicago: University of Chicago Press, 1966), pp. 57–60.

Irish Folklore Commission Vol. 984; 227–34. Recorded on Ediphone cylinders about 1930 by Dr. Robin Flower, Keeper of Manuscripts in the British Museum, from Peig Sayers, then fifty-six, Blasket Islands, Dingle, county Kerry. The present tale and many others recorded by Dr. Flower were transcribed in 1947 by Seosamh Ó Dálaigh, collector, by which time Peig had left the island and gone to live on the mainland near Dunquin. Peig helped the transcriber to fill in unintelligible gaps in the original recording.

The narrator, Peig Sayers, who died in December 1958 at the age of eighty-five, was one of the most celebrated of Irish storytellers. The Irish Folklore Commission holds in its archives more than 5,000 manuscript papers of hundreds of tales, songs, prayers, proverbs and items of local lore she recorded for them. For more on Peig see the editor's Introduction, pp. xxii–xxiii.

This tale belongs to the mythological cycle of the Fenian warriors, led by Fionn mac Cumhaill, who are believed to have flourished in the third century A.D. Fionn and his men performed mighty deeds of valor against giants, hags, and sorcerers. The discovery that Irish peasants in the twentieth century still related legends about the Fenians or Fionna astonished scholars. This allegorical Fionn legend is represented by 33 orally collected versions in the Irish Folklore Commission and by 8 published versions. For the references see O'Sullivan, p. 263.

Motifs include D1209.6 "Magic thong"; D1355.13 "Love-spot"; D1840 "Magic invulnerability"; D2061.2.1 "Death-giving glance"; F863.1 "Unbreakable chain"; K1886.2 "Mists which lead astray"; T466 "Necrophilism: sexual intercourse with dead human body"; Z111 "Death personified"; and Z126 "Strength personified."

One fine day, Fionn mac Cumhaill and fourteen of his men were hunting on the top of Muisire Mountain. They had spent the whole day since sunrise there but met no game.

Late in the evening, Fionn spoke, " 'Tis as well for us to face for home, men. We're catching nothing, and it will be late when we, hungry and thirsty, reach home."

"Upon my soul. We're hungry and thirsty as it is," said Conán.

They turned on their heels and went down the mountainside, but if they did, they weren't far down when a dark black fog fell on them. They lost their way and didn't know whether to go east or west. Finally they had to sit down where they were.

"I'm afraid, men, that we're astray for the evening," said Fionn. "I never yet liked a fog of this kind."

After they had sat for a while talking and arguing, whatever look Diarmaid gave around, he saw a beautiful nice lime-white house behind them.

"Come along, men, to this house over there," said he. "Maybe we'll get something to eat and drink there."

They all agreed and made their way to the house. When they entered, there was nobody before them but a wizened old man who was lying in a bent position at the edge of the hearth and a sheep which was tied along by the wall. They sat down. The old man raised his head and welcomed Fionn and his men heartily.

"By my soul," said Diarmaid to himself. " 'Tisn't very likely that our thirst or hunger will be eased in this hovel."

After awhile, the old man called loudly to a young woman who was below in a room telling her to come up and get food ready for Fionn and his men. Then there walked up the floor from below, a fine strapping handsome young woman, and it didn't take her long to get food and drink ready for them. She pulled a long ample table out into the middle of the floor, spread a tablecloth on it, and laid out the dinner for the Fianna. She seated Fionn at the head of the table and set every man's meal in front of him. No sooner had each of them put the first bite of food into his mouth than the sheep which was tied along the wall stretched and broke the hard hempen tying that was holding her and rushed towards the table. She upset it by lifting one end of it and not a scrap of food was left that wasn't thrown to the floor in front of the Fianna.

"The devil take you," cried Conán. "Look at the mess you have made of our dinner, and we badly in need of it."

"Get up, Conán, and tie the sheep," said Fionn.

Conán, looking very angry at the loss of his dinner, got up against his will and walked to the sheep. He caught her by the top of the head and tried to drag her toward the wall. But if he broke his heart in the attempt, he couldn't tie her up. He stood there looking at her.

"By heavens," said he. "As great a warrior and hero as I am, here's this sheep today, and I can't tie her. Maybe someone else can?"

"Get up, Diarmaid, and tie the sheep," said Fionn.

Diarmaid stood up and tried, but if he did, he failed to tie her. Each of the fourteen men made an attempt, but it was no use.

"My shame on ye," said the old man. "To say that as great as your valor has ever been, ye can't tie an animal as small as a sheep to the side of the wall with a bit of rope."

He got up from the edge of the hearth and hobbled down the floor. As he went, six pintsful of ashes fell from the backside of his trousers, because he had been so long lying on the hearth. He took hold of the sheep by the scruff of the head, pulled her easily in to the wall, and tied her up. When the Fianna saw him tie the sheep, they were seized with fear and trembling, seeing that he could do it after themselves had failed, brave and all though they were. The old man returned to his place by the fire.

"Come up here and get some food ready for Fionn and his men," he called to the young woman.

She came up from the room again, and whatever knack or magic she had, she wasn't long preparing new food to set before them.

"Start eating now, men; ye'll have no more trouble," said the old man. "This dinner will quench your thirst and hunger."

When they had eaten and were feeling happy with their stomachs full, they drew their chairs back from the table. Whatever peering around Fionn had—he was always restless—he looked toward the room and saw the young woman sitting on a chair there. He got a great desire to talk to her for a while. He went down to the room to her.

"Fionn mac Cumhaill," said she; "you had me once and you won't have me again."

He had to turn on his heel and go back to his chair. Diarmaid then went down to her, but he got the same answer; so did each of the rest of the Fianna. Oisín was the last to try, but she said the same thing to him. She took him by the hand and led him up the floor till she stood in front of the Fianna.

"Fionn mac Cumhaill," said she; "ye were ever famous for strength and agility and prowess, and still each of you failed to tie the sheep. This sheep is not of the usual kind. She is Strength. And that old man over there is Death. As strong as the sheep was, the old man was able to overcome her. Death will overcome ye in the same way, strong and all as ye are. I myself am a planet sent by God, and it is God who has placed this hovel here for ye. I am Youth. Each of you had me once but never will again. And now, I will give each of you whatever gift he asks me for."

Fionn was the first to speak, and he asked that he might lose the smell of clay, which he had had ever since he sinned with a woman who was dead.

Diarmaid said that what he wanted was a love spot on his body, so that every young woman who saw it would fall in love with him.

Oscar asked for a thong which would never break for his flail.

Conán asked for the power of killing hundreds in battle, while he himself would be invulnerable.

On hearing this, Diarmaid spoke.

"Alas!" said he. "If Conán is given the power of killing hundreds, for heaven's sake, don't let him know how to use it. He's a very strong, but a very vicious, man, and if he loses his temper, he won't leave one of the Fianna alive."

And that left Conán as he was ever afterward. He never knew how to use this power that he had, except once at the Battle of Ventry, when he looked at the enemy through his fingers and slew every one of them.

Each of the Fianna in turn asked for what he wanted. I don't know what some of them asked for, but Oisín asked for the grace of God. They say that he went to the Land of Youth and remained there until Saint Patrick came to Ireland, so that he would get the proper faith and knowledge of God and extreme unction when he died. He got them too, for when he returned to Ireland, Saint Patrick himself baptized him and anointed him before he died.

The Cold May Night

From Sean O'Sullivan, *Folktales of Ireland* (Chicago: University of Chicago Press, 1966), pp. 15–18.

Type 1927 *The Cold May Night.* Irish Folklore Commission Vol. 1009, 289–98. Recorded in February, 1946, by Liam MacCoisdeala, collector, from Mícheál Ó Coileáin (70), Carn Mór, Claregalway, county Galway. Mícheál heard the story more than fifty years before from his father, Tomás (60), of the same townland.

Forty-three manuscript and published versions of this tale have been recorded in Ireland. For printed versions, see D. de Híde, *Celtic Review* 10 (December, 1914–June, 1916): 116–43. It was republished by de Híde in *Legends of Saints and Sinners*, pp. 40–55, 56–62 and *Béaloideas* 14 (1944): 207–8. A study of the tale against its literary background has been made by E. Hull, "The Hawk of Achill, or the Legend of the Oldest of the Animals," *Folk-Lore* 43 (1932): 376–409.

Achill is a large island off the Mayo coast. Assaroe is the name of a waterfall on the River Erne in county Donegal. Old May Night has been the traditional name for the night of 11 May, ever since the calendar was changed in 1752.

Motifs include B124.1 "Salmon as oldest and wisest of animals"; B841 "Long-lived animals"; R322 "Eagle's nest as refuge"; and X1620 "Lies about cold weather."

There never was as cold a night as Old May Night long, long ago. It was the eleventh of May.

Hundreds of years later, there came a very cold evening. The Old Crow of Achill was alive at the time, and he felt the great cold. He didn't know how he would survive the night; so he flew off to a wood some distance away. He hovered about, and what should he spy on top of the highest tree in the wood but a bird's nest. He decided to pass the night in it.

When he went to it, he found an eagle's fledgling inside. The mother eagle was away, looking for food; so the old crow took hold of the fledgling in his beak and carried it off and killed it somewhere in the wood. He threw the body into some bushes and flew back to the nest.

It wasn't very long until the old eagle returned with a big lump of meat from somewhere. Night had fallen, and she thought that it was her fledgling that was in the nest. She dropped the meat, and the old crow began to eat it with joy. Then the old eagle lay down on top of him. She spent the whole night rising up and jumping about and complaining—for it is said that birds and animals could talk at that time—that she had never felt a colder night.

The Old Crow of Achill was covered with sweat during the night, fearing that when day came and the eagle saw him, she would kill him. The eagle kept complaining about the cold, and at last the old crow remarked that there had been a colder night.

"How do you know that," asked the eagle, "seeing that you only came out of the shell a month ago?"

"Yes, there was a colder night—Old May Night," said the old crow.

"I find it hard to believe you," said the eagle.

"Such a night did come," said the old crow. "If you don't believe me, go to an old blackbird in a certain forge. She'll be there before you, and you'll find that she will tell you that a colder night than last night came one time."

The old eagle got angry. She flew off and never stopped until she came to the Blackbird of the Forge. The blackbird was inside before her, standing on an iron rod. The blackbird welcomed her.

"This is what brought me here," said the eagle. "A young fledgling of mine came out of the egg a month ago. Last night was the coldest I ever experienced, and I spent it rising up out of the nest with the cold.

When dawn was near, my young one said to me that there had been a colder night, but I can't imagine how it could know, and it only a month old. It told me if I didn't believe it to go to the Blackbird of the Forge to find out."

"Well, I'm the Blackbird of the Forge, and last night was the coldest I ever felt. I was put into this forge when I was young. This iron rod on which I am standing was so many inches long and so many inches thick at that time. Once every seven years, I used to rub my beak to it; and if I rub it once more, it will break. I have been here that length of time, and last night was the coldest I ever felt; but," said the blackbird, "you must go to a certain bull in a certain field. If he can't tell you, I don't know where you'll find out about it."

The eagle flew off and never stopped until she reached the field. The bull was there.

"What brought me here," said the eagle, "is that a month ago a young fledgling of mine came out of the egg. Last night was the coldest night I ever felt, and I spent the whole night rising up out of my nest to try to keep myself warm. Then when the dawn was near, my young one told me that there had been a colder night. I can't imagine how it could know, and it only a month out of the egg. It told me if I didn't believe it to go to you. Have you ever heard of a colder night than last night?"

"No, I haven't," said the bull. "I have been here for thousands of years, and two horns have fallen off me each year. They have been used to make a fence around this one-acre field, and only the two horns on my head now are wanting to complete the fence. That shows how long I have been here. And still, last night was the coldest night I ever experienced. But the Blind Salmon of Assaroe is older than I am, and he might be able to give you some account of it."

"Where is the Blind Salmon of Assaroe?" asked the eagle.

"In a certain river," said the bull, naming it. "That's where he always is."

Anger came over the eagle, but she flew off and never stopped until she reached the river. She watched the part of the river where the bull said the salmon might be, and what did she see below her but the salmon swimming in the river. She spoke to him, and he replied.

"Are you the Blind Salmon of Assaroe?"

"I am."

"Did you feel cold last night?" asked the eagle.

"I did," replied the salmon.

"I never felt a night so cold," said the eagle. "What brought me here to you is that I have a young fledgling, and I spent all of last night, jumping up and down in the nest, trying to keep it and myself warm. Toward morning, the fledgling, which is only a month out of the egg, said to me that there had once been a colder night. I had never heard of it. It told me if I didn't believe it to go to the Blackbird of the Forge at a certain place, and he might know. I went to the Blackbird of the Forge, and he told me that he had been perched on an iron rod so many inches long and so many inches thick since he was young. Once every seven years, he rubbed his beak against the iron rod, he said, and one more rub would cut it through. He said that last night was the coldest he had ever experienced. He advised me to go to a certain bull in a certain field, because he might know. I went to the bull, and he told me that last night was the coldest he had ever felt. He had been in the field for thousands of years; a pair of horns had fallen from him each year; and the fence around the one-acre field was made of these horns; only the two horns on his head were needed to complete the fence. That was his age. But he told me to go to the Blind Salmon of Assaroe, so that he might tell me about it, and you are that salmon."

"I am," said the Blind Salmon of Assaroe. "A night colder than last night came without any doubt. I was here on Old May Night, the eleventh of May, long ago. It was freezing. I was jumping up and down in the water. It was freezing so hard that when I jumped up one time, the water had frozen when I came down. I was frozen into the ice and couldn't free myself. About two hours after daybreak, what should be passing but the Old Crow of Achill. He saw me frozen in the ice. Down he flew and started pecking at the ice with his beak. He made a hole in the ice and picked out my eye and ate it. That's why I have had only one eye ever since, and that's why I'm called the Blind Salmon of Assaroe. But look here," said the blind salmon, "as sure as I am here, it was the Old Crow of Achill that was in your nest last night and not your young one!"

"Ah, it can't be," said the eagle.

"It was," said the blind salmon. "Only he could have told you about Old May Night."

The eagle returned angrily home, but when she reached the nest, neither her fledgling nor the old crow was there. The old crow had left, and it was well for him. If she caught him, his days would be ended.

Scotland (Lowlands)

The King of England

Collected by Hamish Henderson. Forthcoming in *Folktales of Scotland*.

Told by an Aberdeenshire traveling tinker (gypsy), Andrew Stewart, in August 1954 in Causewayend, Aberdeen, in the home of Jeannie Robertson, the famed ballad singer and herself once a traveling tinker. Hamish Henderson notes: "This was the great summer when Jeannie's wee house was always full of friends, relatives, and casual visitors, all eager to record ballads, stories, rhymes, fiddle music, etc., for my ferrograph. The personnel in the house changed like a perpetually mobile Commedia dell'Arte. Children stayed awake as long as possible, then stretched out on the floor and slept like puppies. Andrew, a man in his fifties, came in while Jeannie's Aunt Maggie was singing "The Forester in the Wood" (a version of Child 110), waited while she continued with "Bogie's Bonnie Bell" and "The Dewie Dens o' Yarrow," and then launched into "The King of England." Asked where he learned the story, Andrew replied, "From my own brains."

This long wonder tale contains some of the key motifs for type 303 *The Twins or Blood Brothers*, which appears in two variants in the Grimms' *Household Tales*. The German folktale authority Kurt Ranke studied 770 versions of the Märchen in *Die Zwei Bruder* (Folklore Fellows Communications 114). It is well distributed throughout Europe and densely reported from Finland, Ireland, Germany, France, and Hungary.

Motifs that correspond to the Aarne-Thompson type outline are as follows: E761 "Life token. Object has mystic connection with the life of a person, so that changes in the life-token indicate changes in the person, usually disaster or death"; T15 "Love at first sight"; L161 "Lowly hero marries princess"; G263 "Witch injures, enchants or transforms"; E761.1.3 "Life-token: track fills with blood"; F577.2 "Brothers identical in appearance"; Z210 "Brothers as heroes"; T685.1 "Twin adventurers"; D700 "Person disenchanted"; K1311.1 "Husband's twin brother mistaken by woman for her husband."

In addition a number of other motifs can be noted. Indeed Andrew Stewart's narrative constitutes a treasury of magical themes. T55.1

"Princess declares her love for lowly hero"; F852.1 "Glass coffin";
D765.1.2 "Disenchantment by removal of enchanting pin (thorn)";
D2070 "Bewitching"; T24.1 "Love-sickness"; M200 "Bargains and
promises"; D1931.2 "Magic sword always inflicts mortal wound";
F530 "Exceptionally large or small men"; N821 "Help from little man";
D1254.1 "Magic wand"; D5 "Enchanted person"; D6 "Enchanted cas-
tle"; D1980 "Magic invisibility"; D1065.2 "Magic shoes"; D1552
"Mountains or rocks open and close"; D114.1.1.1 "Transformation:
girl to deer (fawn) (by druid)"; D7 "Enchanted valley"; D191 "Transformation: man to serpent (snake)."

Well, there were once in times on the side of a mountain there was an
old man and an old woman lived, and they had two sons, one called
Jack and the other called William. So William one day said to his
brother, Jack, "Jack," he says, "there's too little here," he says, "to
keep us. I maun go," he says, "to make," he says, "push my fortune
to keep my father and my old mother."

So Jack, he says, "Oh, brother," he says, "don't be like that," he
says—" 'cos there's as much in the little croft," he says, "now, as kep
hiz from our boyhood upward to manhood," he says, "and we never
wantit."

"That's quite all right," he says, "but I never see the world," he
says, "stayin' at the fuit of this mountain."

So William prepared he would go and push his fortune. So he said
to his mother, "Now, mother," he says, "bake me a bannock and roast
me a collop," he says—"I'm away to push my fortune."

His mother says, "Oh, William," she says, "ye're not going to leave
us, surely. We've been living here since ever you were born," she says,
"till now, and what is the reason," she says, "you're leavin'?"

"Well," he says, "mother, I've made my mind up," he says, "to push
my fortune," he says, "let it be right or let it be wrong," he says, "I'm
goin'. So you can roast me a bannock and toast me a collop, for I'm
goin'."

So his mother roastit him the bannock and toastit him the collop,
and he sets off and before he gaed he says, "Now John-Jack," he said
—"if you see that thing changin' its color," he says, "I'm in danger and
if not," he says, "I'm quite safe."

"Very well," Jack says, "I'll keep watchin' it by night and by day."
So Jack, steady day after day, Jack watches this figure.

So William he's pushin' on over hedges, ditches, gates, and stiles—
there was rest for the birds, but none for Jack. So one night he was
persuaded to lie at the fuit of a tree. So he says, "My gracious! if I lie
here," he says, "I'll be eaten with animals," he said, "or stung with
snakes," he said, "or something," he said; "the best plan that I can do

is move on—keep on my feet." And as he was travelin' along in the dark, he happened to slip his fuit and he fell down a precipice. So fallin' down this precipice he thought as he was fallin' he saw light. When he landed at the fuit, he says, "My-oh," he says, "I could ha' sworn," he says, "I saw light as I was fallin'." So when he thought he saw the light, he climm'd up the other side, unhurt, and he foond wi' his hands a little fuit-path. So he got on to this little fuit-path, and he's travelin' on—he says, "This is the direction," he says, "I saw this light" (speakin' to himself), and when he comes round the small bend of the rocks he looks in, and here was a very old gentleman sittin'. "Well," he says, "I wonder," he says, "can I go in here? I wonder," he says, "would that man," he says, "interfere with me by any means or any manner? Well," he says, "I'm pushin' my fortune, and when you are pushin' your fortune you must face the strong as well as the weak." And so he took courage and he walks in.

"Good-evenin'! my old man."

"Good-evenin', son!" this old man replied to him.

Now he's seen by this the old man is for no harm. "Come in and sit down," he says.

When he cam in and sat down, this old man was toastin' and roastin', hitherwise and titherwise, a lump of a sheep.

"Now, son," he says, "you'll be hungry?"

"Well, tell you the truth," he says, "Dad, I'm not very full."

So he catches a sheep and he divides it oot in two shares. He said, "There is a part for you and one for me."

So he lived there all night with this old man—very piercin'-lookin' gentleman he was—William couldn't keep from lookin' at him now and again, he was so wild. And William one dead-night he says to himself, "Noo I wonder," he says, "would that creature," he says, "if a man," he said, "he's very fearsome. I wonder," he says, "would he be for harm or good? But I shall not risk it," William says, "I shall try an' just get out."

Very well, that night, Jack, when he got the old man asleep, he skins out. So he's away up this mountains and glens as far as I could tell you or you could tell me, over hedges, ditches, gates, and stiles, till daylight came in in the mornin'. So when daylight cam in in the mornin', sir, he's about twenty to twenty-five miles from this old man's home by now, and he says, "Now I am here," he says, "and seein' I am here," he says, "am as hungry and as weak," he says, "I don't think I can go much further," he says, "with the travelin' and the bite of supper that I got," he says, "was very, very small," he says.

So he decided to have the lie-down at the dike-side here, restin' himself. So he did so and when he waked he rises up and he looks around him and he's seein' like a house away at the distance. "Well, well," he

says, "this is a house—will it be," he says, "good people or bad people," he says, "I must gae there for the purpose of gettin' a bite of
bread or something."

So he goes on, pushes on to this house, and when he comes to the
house he raps at the door and oot comes a very old lady.

"Well," she says, "my man. What do you want?"

"Well," he says, "mother, I want" he says, "something to eat," he
says, "because I am very weak with hunger."

"Well, come in, son," she says, "I have very little here," she says,
"tell you the truth what we live on here," she says, "I don't suppose
you would eat it," she says—"it's what they call 'birds' feet.' "

"Birds' feet," he said, "well," he said, "I'd eat a very small trifle."

But, howanever, he got served wi' this birds' feet, an' during the
time he was at his meal in comes two as pretty girls as ever his eyes
ever lookit upon, in fact, he'd never seen a girl before—this was the
first as ever he saw, an he didn't know really was it men or was it
women? Because he saw nothing of the kind. And he says, "Well, my
old woman," he says, "what is this people," he said—"are they he or
are they she?" he said.

"They're she—that is two of my daughters," she says.

"Oh me," he said, "they're two lovely creatures."

"Yes, and will you not live with us?" one of them replied to Jack.

"No, no," he says, "I'm pushin' my fortune, my girl," he says, "an'
I see by this little house, you're needin' a fortune yourself, never mind
sharin' with me. Where do you work?" he replies.

"I work," she said, "at the King's castle down."

"Oh," he said, "thir a King's castle here, are they?"

"Yes," she says, "thir a King's castle, an' a very savage brute I may
tell you he is, 'cos doesn't matter anything flyin', creepin', or walkin',
he either destroys, or beheads by some means."

"Well," William said, "that's my opportunity," he says, "if he destroys me it'll be my end, an' if I succeed," he says, "I'll have a job."

So he decided to gae down to this King's castle. Comin' to the castle,
he saw it was a right, nice, big sort of a buildin'—he says, "This is as
nice a buildin' 's ever I saw," he said, "this wud make my mother's
hoose twenty times over," he says, "the little small moat of a house
that we have."

So it doesn't matter—he goes to the door an' he raps an' out comes
the butler.

"Well," the butler says, "my man, what d'you want?"

He says, "I want," he said, "to see the King an' try an' get a job anywhere," he says. "I'm a single man," he says, "no married or nothin'
like this, an' I want to see, can I get a job."

"Well," the butler replies, "if this King has a job for ye, good an' well, an' if he hasn't, it's jist too bad for you. I can't help it," he says. "If I was you," the butler says, "I wud quit it."

"Oh, no," he says, "I shall not quit it," he says, "I shall see the King, let it be right or let it be wrong."

So the King came at the finish an' seen him. He says, "Now, William," he says, "listen. If I've a job for you," he said, "I shall give it to ye, but you'll give me time to consider," he says, "and look over," he says, "my books." So he lookit over. "Well," he said, "you are a lucky man," he said, "you may thank your lucky stars."

"Why, sir?" said William, says he.

He says, "Well, I have a job into the nine-stall stable, where there never was a man breathin' or born from his mother," he says, "could live five minutes."

"Ah," William says, "that's very strange," he says, "and what may be in it?" he says.

"It's horse, and there havena been a livin' soul go near that horses this last fifty years, and so they werenae young."

So, howanever, William he took the job and he was showed down to this nine-stall stable. When he gaed down to the nine-stall stable, he seen there was no ways of gettin' in—the doors was barricaded up with muck and dung and rubbidge of all sorts. "Well," William said, "I'll have to get in," he said, "to see thaim beasts." And when he got in, there were a skylight on the top of the building, so he lowers himsel' down from the skylight and he comes into the hay-loft! "Well," he says, "my gracious," he said, "this is terrible," he says, "the like of that I never saw in my life," he says, "animals," he says, "bein' so bad," he says, "for fifty years," he says, "it's very, very wild. "But," he says, "I'll do my best."

So he got doon through the blow-hole, as we call the hay-hole, and lookit at his horses. The horses smelt him, in fact their heads was almost through holes. He hadn't far to go down. But anyway he fed his animals, as any man wud do. Seein' he fed his animals, the beasts smelt him from the sole of the feet tae the crown of the head.

"Well, well," he said, "it may be bad horse, but I don't think it," he says, and he startit the cairtin' out from the back of the door till he got the door of this stable opened.

"Now," he says, "it's for the barriein' out of this dung." So it took him three weeks to barrie this dung out of this place, till he got it anything like a stable. But it doesn't matter—he was finished wi' that now, and he started reddin' up his stable, cleanin' his harness, dressin' his horses up, combin' them, and dressing their hair up to the best of his abilities.

"Well," he said, "they dae nae harm, I don't know in the world of goodness," he says, "why is the King so severe to these animals," he says, "nice beasts; in fact," he says, "I could do with them all my life."

But each horse jist looked at him and nickert at him. "Well," he said, "they're very hamely animals."

But it doesnae matter—he's sittin' cleanin' his harness one day, and this harness that the King had at one time of life happent to be gold-mounted, but you wouldnae ken were it brass, copper, or silver by this time. So he stopped his cleanin' and he seen what he had, he seen it was very valuable harness. So he cleans them, and his stable and his harness, he had them spotless.

"Well," he said, "that's Number One," and he's sittin' cleanin' away on to a stone at the door—who happent to pass, but the King's daughter? Well, she looks at this man, she says, "What a puir man that is—as puir a man as ever I saw." So she gaed home and when she gaed home she took bedfast, if you understand what that means—took bedfast and she was gaed to bed and she was breakin' her heart now for this gentleman. But her father asked her what was ado, what happent—he couldn't tell what happent.

"Well," he says, "I'll send for all the doctors," he says, "that I can get, and professors, till I'll find out what's ado with you, my lady," he says. "There's something far worse with you." But he sent for an old Scottish doctor. "Well," this doctor replied, "now King," he says, "I want to be in this room alone with this girl and alone only," he says. "I want to ask her things I don't wish you or no other man to hear."

"Well," the King says, "you can have," he says, "your demand, come out everyone," he said, "come out bar the two soldiers, to see if you're gonnae do any good or not."

"Now," he says, "my girl, listen," he says, "you're in love."

"Yes," she says, "I'm in love."

"And who in the world," he says, "are ye in love with?"

"Well," she says, "I'll tell ye," she says, "doctor," she says, "seein' you found out I'm in love. I'm in love," she says, "with our own groom," she says, "in the nine-stall stable."

"Oh," he says, "you weren't long," he says, "of makin' love—he's only there about six months yet, as I'm led to believe."

"Yes," she says, "it doesn't matter though it was only six days," she says, "I'm in love with him," she says, "and if I don't get him I'll die."

So the doctor called in her father and her mother, and the doctor said she was in love.

"Who on earth," they says, "in this world can she be in love with?"

"Well," he says, "she can tell you."

"And who are ye in love wi'?" he says, "my daughter. Let it be gentle, simple," he says, "let it be what it likes, tell me," he says.

"Well," she says, "father," she says, "I'm in love with your groom in the nine-stall stable."

"Is that man alive yet?" he says.

"Yes," she says, "father, alive and alive—like," she says, "as live as what you are."

"But," he says, "my daughter, if he's a man that can work with them horse, I don't know very well—like," he says, "if a gentleman of that kind should have anything to do with ye." He says, "He must be more than a mortal man," he says, "or he wouldnae be there all this time."

"Can't help it," she says, "that's the man that I want, and if I don't get him," she says, "I'm goin to die—I'll break my heart."

"Right, I'll ask him."

So down he goes. When he cam down, there was William sittin' cleanin' away at his straps as usual.

"Well," he says, "William, you're busy?"

"I am," he says, "my noble King"—bows to the King—he says, "I am."

"Well, I've come down here to ask you a question," he says, "dinna be insulted," he says, "when I ask you," he says, "this question," he says—"in fact, if I'd ha' been a woman," he says, "instead of a man," he says, "I wud hae married you myself."

William looks at him. He says, "My goodness gracious!" he says, "what's gone wrong?"

"My daughter," he says, "is almost dyin' for you."

"For me!" he says, "why is she dyin' for me?" he says—"I never saw her in my life."

"Yes," he says, "she saw you," he says, "for you did not see her."

"So very well," he says, "if I can save your daughter's life," he says.

So William he washed himsel' up and made hissel' as tidy as possible to see this young girl. So up he goes, approaches the big house, and raps at the hall door.

Out comes the butler. "Well, my man," he says, "what are you after?"

He says, "I want to see the King as usual."

"All right," he says, "I'll bring him for ye."

"Come in," he says, "William," he says, "and see my girl."

So he took William in, climm'd up this stairs, tae the topmost room of the palace. When he gaed up there, there was the fairest lady lyin' in bed he ever saw in his life.

"My goodness gracious," he says, "girl," he says, "I am led to believe," he says, "you are dyin' for me," he says. "I never happent to see you," he says, "or fixed eyes before."

"That's all right," she says, "William," she says, "I have learnt your name," she says, "since I lay down."

"But howanever," he says, "and what can I do for ye?"

"Well," she says, "if I don't get you tomorrow," she says, "I'll die."

"You'll die," he says, "for me?"

"Yes," she says, "for you, you only."

Well, he consented. He says, "Well, to save a life," he says, "I'll marry you," he says, "only to save your life."

"Very well!"

So the marriage preparations got on to the best of abilities. For about a month it lasted, day and night it lasted, aye on ahead, no stop. And at the finish they had a dance out on the open fields, with all his tenants and natives of his place. So he danced along there with everyone, man, female, and every sort, and the hinmost ones he danced with was the young women in the old house where he got his dinner, ye remember that, yes, well, they were the last dance that he had, and durin' the time one of those that danced wi' him flippit this that they call a sleepin'-pin at the back of his ear, and he danced away dead.

Now William, he was dead, and the safiest uproar got into this castle that you've heard in your life, about the good-son now bein' dead and only a few days married.

"Very well," this lady says, "he is dead, and he shall not be buried —I will not allow him to be buried. He'll be put into a lead coffin and a glass lid as I can see him night and by day, I can look at him."

"Very well," that was replied to.

Now I leave off o' there and I go straight back to his brother Jack. This is where the fun comes in.

So Jack rose one morning at home, and he looks at this mark that his brother made, and he see'd it was red. He ran to his mother. He said, "Mother, mother!" he said, "my brother's in danger," he says. "Will you roast me a bannock," he says, "for I'm away to push my fortune too."

"Silly man," she says, "what are you goin' to do," she says, "pushin' your fortune," she says, "after your brother," she says—"a clever man and a better man and a stronger man every way," she says, "nor what you are," she says.

"I cannot help it hoo clever he may be, or hoo strong," he says, "I'm goin' to follow him," he says, "and nothing will stop me, and if you don't bake me your bannock," he says, "and roast me my collop," he says, "I'll go without it."

"Well, well," she says, "I'll bake your bannock," she says, "and I'll roast your collop."

So she bakes the bannock and she roasts the collop, and Jack says, "Well, mother," he says, "and father," he says, "good-bye!" he said. "If ever I come back I'll see you and if I never come back ye shall never see me."

So he set sail after his brother. Day and night he's wanderin' on, day after day and night, the same direction and the same road as his brother gaed, and almost the same words passed through his lips: "If I lie down here at night, I'll be eaten with wild animals, and if I sleep," he says, "God knows what'll happen to me, and if I climm a tree and faa asleep," he says, "I'll faa doon and probably be killed, and the best thing I can do is keep wanderin' on." So Jack he wanders on, and he made the same mishap that his brother made—he slippit down this precipice the same way in the dark. So at the slippin' down he noticed the same light in the same way as his brother saw, but landed unhurt. "Well," he says, "thank God for that—that's a miracle," and he bended down to this little burn and took a drink of water and he says, "Well, that refreshens me," he says, "most champion."

So he climbs up this steep hill (as you would call it) up till he come to a little fuit-path, and when he comes to this little fuit-path he gropes in the dark with his hands—and he found it was a path, and on this path with his feet and he follows it on for about maybe a quarter of a mile, and he lookit round this corner of the rock, the same light and the same man that his brother saw.

"Now, I wonder," he said, "was this his culprit or not, or I wonder," he said, "was this man on his good side or not?" But he says, "I'll see." So he gaed steppin' in—an auld man, very rough and hard-toned talkin', a brave-lookin' hero, his way. So the auld man lookit roond quite coolly and says, "Well," he says, "good-evenin'," he said, "son." (For I may tell you this two brothers was very like one another.) "Son," he said, "have you come back?"

"I have come back," he says, "father."

"And where have you been?" he said, "or where were you wanderin' to?"

So he made up some scheme of his own of some sort that I do not know and told the old man. So the old man said, "Well," he said, "there's never such a thing will happen again," he said, "you'll be wi' me," he said, "for one month," which he was, and during that month he learned to be the cleverest swordsman that ever traveled Scotland or England.

"Well," he said, "thank God," he says, "I've learned something during my month's holidays wi' this old man, but," he says, "this hasnae been fetchin' me my brother." So that night he considered himself. "Well," he says, "tonight" he says, "I'll make my escape, unseen to that old hero." And when he waked through the middle of the night, this old man he was sleepin', snorin' and sleepin', and when he gaed out he'd an armory to pass, and when he gaed in here there was swords, guns, bow an' arrows—there was every sort of things ye could mention in this world, so he armed himself up with a sword, and he set off. So he's goin' on all night, all the same direction as his brother gaed and by good luck he just drappit on the same road as his brother drappit, and he says, "Well," he says, "I'll go and have a rest here," he says, "for I am very weariet, hungry and tired. And so whatever comes ahead. . . ." So he fell fast asleep and when he wakened, as usual as his brother, he lookit around him and he saw the samne little house. "Well," he said, "there is a house," he says, "perhaps," he says, "I might get some," he says, "word or whatever if my brother cam' this way at all," he says. "He'd be in there sure enough," he says, "and," he says, "they'll be able to tell me about his whereabouts."

So, it doesn't matter, he made to this little house, and whenever he gaed to this house it happent to be dinner-time, and the young girls and the old missis was busy at dinner and when he raps at the door the young woman comes out and looks at him, she cries "Murder!" she says—"a ghost!" she says. And when the old one heard her she made a race to the door—she's out through the window and everyone braks oot of the back windae and they're away for their livin' life—auld man, auld wumman, and the two girls—he stood mesmerized, lookin' after them.

So it doesnae matter anyway. He says, "I back you," he says, "this is the culprit," he says, "was the end of my brother. That shows," he says, "William and I," he says, "is very like one another," he says (they were like twin brothers), "and that shows," he says, "this is the lot," he says, "that has been the death of my brother. Well," he says, "if I can't get him," he says, "I'll plunder the house," and he plunders the house and all the bits of scrap eatables he could get, he ate them, 'cos he was very hungry, and he lookit onto the mantelshelf, and he saw a purse and seven gold sovereigns in it. "Well," he says, "this will come with me too." So he put that in his pocket and he strolls out of the door, and he heppent to look down to the direction of the castle and there he spies this large castle.

"Aha!" he says, "what is this down here?" he says—"I never happent to see that when I came in about," he says. "Who in the world," he says, "lives here?" So he made his way down to this castle, as his brother done. So he came to the back door, and he raps, and out comes the butler. When the butler looks at him, he cries, "Ah, murder!—the ghost!" and he fainted and he picked hisself up and he goes back in and tells the rest of the servants. "Oh!" says he—"William's at the door—the dead man's spirit's at the door."

"Nonsense!" the old cook said, "whatever good I done William," she says, "I done him no harm in this world, and," she says, "I'll go!" and she took a bundle of Bibles in her oxter—readin' all the road. She says, "Now, William," she says, "what do you want?" she says, "back on this earth again?" she says. "I thought when a man parted he parted for ever."

He says, "My old lady," he says, "I'm afraid you are makin' a great mistake," he says—"I am not William," he says, "I am Jack, happen to be, to you," he says.

"Jack," she says, "you are a spirit-man," she says, "you think I don't know a spirit—you'd think I don't know," she says, "my own king when I see him?" she says—"don't pull curtains over my eyes like that."

"Well," he says, "feel me—I am mortal." So she felt him, she found out that he was mortal.

"What like a man," he says—"how is that William?" he says, "you're shoutin' about," he says, "what like a man is he?"

"He's our King," she replied.

"Your King?"

"Yes."

"Well," he says, "I'll give the world," he says, "if I saw your King."

"Oh, there's no one allowed," she says, "up" she says, "where he is buried," she says. "He is buried," she says, "into the topmost room of the castle. And," she said, "he's buried in," she says, "to his wife's room."

"Good heavens!" he says, "that's a funny place to have a grave-yard," he says, "intae a room," he said, "a human being," he says, "alive."

"Well," he says, "I've seven gold sovereigns here," he says, "I'll distribute them among you," he says, "if you take me up and only gie me one glimpse of him," he says, "because I want to see is it the man that I'm after or not."

Well, seven gold sovereigns in those days was like a hundred pound nowadays. She says, "Well, I'll see what the butler says." So she inquired of the butler; well, the butler says, "It's a great salary to us," he said, "seven gold sovereigns," he says, "we only get a sovereign in a year, and that's seven year's wages we're getting all at once," he says, "and we'll let him see if he takes off his shoes."

"Very well," Jack replies, "I'll take off my shoes."

So he took off his shoes and the butler guides him up the stair. When he cam to the door he says, "Cannie!—don't talk or hardly breathe," he says, 'cos she might hear you." "But I won't do that," he says, "I'll be very cautious." So he got to the door and opent it a small bit. He was lookin' at a lead coffin and glass lid, and his own brother lyin' in it.

He catcht the butler by the chest and he threw him—very near broke his neck—down the stair.

"Get out of my way, man!" he said, "This is the man I've been lookin' for so long."

So he traveled over the room and gaed to the coffin. When he gaed to the coffin he kicked the lid right off—he hadn't time to loose it with his hands—and he picked his brother out in his arms.

"Good heavens!" he says, "William," he says, "what has come over you?" he says. "Down here, man!" he says, "till I gie ye a thorough examination." So there wasn't a bit aboot his body but what he lookit, and he saw this, like a thorn, black thorn, at the back of his ear.

He says, "What's this?" he says, "I never saw this in your ears before," he says, "and you and I's been thegither," he says, "for twenty years."

So he picks out this black thorn, and the moment he pickit that out, his brother startit rubbing his eyes as if nothing had happened to him. So, howanever, he says, "Now, brother," he says, "this is where you were lyin'," he says "that I know of. You're not dead," he says, "man," he says, "ye're only at rest for a day or so," he says. "Pick yoursel' together, man." An' his brother rubbed his eyes. He says, "Hullo Jack," he says—"you here?" "Yes," he says, "I'm here," he says. "Where wad I not be," he says, "if I wouldn't follow you?"

"Well," he says, "you're the last man," he says, "in this world I expected here."

"Ah, but," he says, "I happen to be the first one instead of the last one."

"I can see that," he says, "and what's come over me?" he said.

"I don't know," he says. "You'll be able to tell me all them stories," Jack replies. He said, "That's what I'm waitin' on."

"Well," he says, "Jack, I'm married."

"Are ye?" Jack says, "Well, ye're a lucky man," he says, "for I'm not. And who are you married on?"

"Well," he says, "I'm married on," he says, "the King's daughter here" he says.

"Oh, you are!" he said. "Well," he says, "you're lucky, therefore," he says, "you're comin' in to be our young King."

"Well, I hope so," he says, "John."

"So it doesnae matter, Jack," he says. "Now," he says, "William," he says, "I found you," he says. "You know," he says, "you weren't dead," he said, "but you were like a trance," he says, "wi' this pin they'd put at the back of your ear."

"Pin," he says, "back of my ear?" he says.

"Yes," he says, "there is the pin," he says, "a very dangerous weapon it is."

"Well, my-oh," he says, "look at me yet."

"And you know who you danced with last?" he says. "I suppose that's the person that pit it in."

"I know," William replied, he says, "that is the girls," he says, "the servants" he says, "of this house," he says, "that's why they're tellin' me now," he says, "I've been a-missin'."

"I can see that," Jack says, "ye've gone a-missin' for a long time," he says, "I can see that."

It doesn't matter anyway, this girl when she seen what she had, she raise now out of the bed, nothing wrong with whatever.

"Oh dear me!" she says, "which of you two men?" They were that like one another, she didn't know one by the t'other. And she rose— instead of catching William round the neck and kissing him, it happent to be Jack she kissed.

"Oh, my dear beloved," she says, "I'm glad," she says, "you're alive again."

"But," he says, "you are making a grave mistake, my lady," he says, "that is your husband. I'm only his brother."

"It doesn't matter," she says, "which of you I kiss," she says. "The two of you is as like to me."

"Well," he said, "if you say it."

So it didn't matter. She says, "Now Jack," she says, "I hope," she says, "you're not in the intentions of going home, or nothing like that."

"Oh no," he says, "I'll no go home. I'll stay a month at the least anyway, with you," he says, "to see everything goes right."

"Very well."

And the next thing now was the old King, he comes on the scene. When he looks at one, he says, "Good-son," he says, "my good gracious!" he says, "my good-son." (The wrong gaed to again, as his daughter done—the wrong man.)

So he says, "I beg your pardon," he says, "my noble King," he says —am not your son-in-law," he says. "Your son-in-law's standing there," he says, "that is him."

"Well, well!" he says, "if ever I seen two men in this world," he says, "two as one I never say," he says—"as like one another," he says—"as two green peas is," he says—"and tha's like enough."

"Well," Jack says, "if that's the case," he says, "we're very like one another."

"You are," he says. "Now daughter," he says, "what have you to say about Jack?"

"Well, it's I'm goin to make a bargain with Jack," she says, "Father," she says, "and the bargain is this—Jack's not going to leave this castle," she says, "till such time as I have a baby boy."

Jack replies, "That might be never," he says, "and it might be sooner than you expect."

"Well," she says, "that is the bargain," she says, "Jack. If I've a baby boy," she says, "you can leave at any time, but if I haven't got that," she says, "you will remain here for the remainder of your life. There's as much gold," she says, "as much wealth," she says, "in this castle, that'll keep you and I," she said, "and my husband and my father and my mother," she said, "for the remainder of your life," she says, "with abundance for everybody."

"Very well," Jack says, "I can seal your bargain," he says, "I'll stay here till you have the first baby boy."

"Very well," she says.

So Jack stays on, sir, but he wasn't very well suited to the place, but he just stayed on. He would like to go and push his own fortune. "This is my brother's fortune," he said, "this is not mine," he says, "but that's doing me no good," he says, "don't want share," he says, "I'm thinkin' about my father and mother," he says, "at home, how they're going to get on." So that is all very well, so he goes and seen his brother William and he explained his case to William.

"Well," says William, "you made the bargain," he says, "with the young Queen," he says, "till such time as she'd a baby boy," he says, "surely, surely," he says, "Jack, you're no going," he says, "to break what you promised," he says, "your promise," he says. "You stay," says he, "to such time as she's a baby boy."

"Well," he says, "I'll stay on," he says, "I never said I would break my promise," he says, "but I'll stay on." But behold, by that time sooner nor Jack was thinkin' aboot the first year, he seen a difference. He says, "If your land's not agreeing with her," he said, "there some other thing is," he says. "But," he says, "time'll tell."

But, behold, in the nine months, this girl has a baby boy.

"Well," Jack says, "thank God!" he says, "I get a release now," he says, "that I push my own fortune." So Jack says (she was up now on her feet goin' about as usual), "Now," Jack says, "sister," he says, "I made my promise," he says, "to you, I would stay to such time as you had a baby boy." She says, "Yes, you did." "Well," he says, "this baby boy," he says, "happent to come to the world," he says, "and now it's my time to go."

"Oh, no," she says, "not yet," she says, "John. You'll wait," she says, "my dear chap," she says, "to such time," she says, "as I bake you seven little oatmeal bannocks."

"Well," he says, "that won't be long. It won't take ye hours," he says, "to bake them."

"But," she says, "you will stay tonight, and by tomorrow mornin'," she says, "you will have," she says, "your bannocks, and then you can please yourself where you go."

"All right," Jack says, "I'll do that."

She went to the scullery, and she collected the meal and she put it intae her bakin'-bowl, and she said, "Now, what am I gin a mix this bannocks with—jist the one thing and the one thing only." She says, "I'm goin' to mix them with, and that's goin' to be the milk oot of my own breast." She milks her own breast and she collects as much milk from her breast as she could manage to bake this seven little bannocks. After she fired them and made them ready, she wrapped them up carefully and coolly intae a little small box.

And so in the morning when Jack wakens up, he says, "Well," he says, "I'm released—I go today."

"Now," she says, "Jack. Listen. Before you go," she says, "I am gonnae give you a present. This present's not much to look at," she says, "but it is a lot to think about."

"And what is that?" he says.

"This present is seven little oatmeal bannocks."

"Seven little oatmeal bannocks!" he replied. "What am I to do with bannocks?"

"They're not for you," she said, "they're for others. Anyone in this world," she says, "wants to do ye onie harm, all that ye've got to say, 'Taste of my bread.'"

"Well," he says, "I'll do that."

And William replies, "Now Jack," he says, "you're gonnae push your fortune, he says, "bare-handed."

"Oh, but," he says, "I'm not—I've a sword," he says.

"Ah, but," William said, "that sword that you've got is no use, the road that you're going to go. Here is my one," he says. "Doesn't matter where you are—doesn't matter," he says, "where you may be, whatever you point this sword at," he says, "is instant death."

"Well," he says, "if that's the case," he says, "I'd better take hit," he says—"it's a very valuable sword," he says, "if it's instant death," he says, "to everything," he says, "I point it at."

So Jack took the sword and bid his sister-in-law farewell and also his brother and the old King and Queen syne, bids them farewell and he sets on his own hookum. Travelin' here and travelin' there for days and days and nights and nights—there was rest for the birds in the trees, but there was no rest for Jack—he jist keepit travelin' ahead. So one day by another, he found hissel' up on the top of a green hill.

"Well," he said, "I'll sit down here," he says, "and I'll have a piece of my bread. (But not the bannocks; he didn't eat them, for they were some of the warning.)

So it doesn't matter—he took his bread and he ate it, and durin' the time he's at his meals, he happent to look doon and he seen a line of trees at both sides of a road (that's what he thought it was).

"Well," he says, "there's been a road down there," he says—"perhaps it might be done away with now, but," he says, "where I belong to," he said, "if there's two lines of trees," he says, "together like that, it's a road or a river or something—there's something of that descriptions about there. And," he says, "when I get my dinner," he says, "I'll gae down," he says, "and investigate that road."

So he set sail after dinner now, and he heads along for this trees. When he came to where this trees were, there was a large gate. "Good heavens!" he says—"there's a gate here," he says, "I never expected a gate to be in a road of this kind—an old God-forgotten road like this," he says, "it's unpossible. There must be human habitants here somewhere."

So he opens the gate and he walks in and he says, "I'll hold on this road," and there's a voice at his back says, "You'll hold on no road!" And here a little man, about three and a half feet high, with a bonnet on him like an ordinary large meal-mill wheel on his head. When he looks at him, "Good heavens!" he says, "my little man, who has brung you here?"

"I've been here," he said, "this last three hundred years," he says, "and you are the first mortal man," he says, "ever come this way, and there's nothing creepin' or walkin'," he says, "flyin'," he said, "or beneath the grund," he said, but what I can catch and kill. If you see all these bones lyin' there, it's human bones," he says, "animals' bones, birds' bones, every kinnae bones that you could mention," he says, "even to the very worms of the earth lies dead there," he says, "and you can see that."

"I do see that," Jack replies.

"Well," he says, "I'm afraid you shall lie among the remainder. You're what they call," he says, "in forbidden lands now."

"Forbidden lands!" Jack says. "I never knew of no lands be forbidden tae man," he says. "I thought every lands was alike, you could go whaur ye like or please yoursel' where ye gaed."

"Well, but," he says, "youse cannae do thaim things," he says. "I'll fight for it."

"Well," says Jack, "I'm not a fightin' man," he says, "far from that. But if it comes to be," he says, "I've got to fight for my rights," he says, "and I'll do so, the same as my brother done."

So this little customer of a man, he drew to he's sword, so Jack drew to he's. And where it was heich, it was laich, they both was at it, but this little man could use his sword and use it to perfection and Jack could do the same. It didn't—he's sword did not need usin' by him—it could use itself. For it was heich, it was laich, they were goin' at it for aboot four hours, and one couldn't make a hair of the t'other; one man was as good as the t'other, but Jack he happent to nip the sword oot of this little man's hand, accidentally more than anything else.

"Hold on," this little man says, "Jack," he says, "you are very clever indeed," he said, "I maun say. And seein'," he says, "you've beat me, my dear fellow," he says, "this sword that you've beat me happent to be my own one," he says, "and that's the sword that you're carrying—belonged to me," he said. "First and foremost in this world, it was mine," he said, "I got that from my father," he said, "that's three hundred years ago."

Jack says, "I don't care," he said, "who ye got it from," he says, "or who ye didn't get it from, or who made it or who didn't make it," he says, "it's mine now and I mean to keep it," he says. "I got it from my brother," he said, "and I'll deliver it back whenever I return, if I live to that time."

"Well," the little man says, "I am conquered," he says, "and if I can do ye good now," he says, "Jack, in this world," he says, "I'll do it to ye," he says. "I'm not a man of that kind," he says—"if a man beats me, I'm beat, and if I beat a man," he said, "he's beat," he says, "and that's where he goes," he says, "on that bing that ye see there," he says, "wi' the remainder. I don't spare no life," he says, "for you haven't to spare mine."

"Well," Jack says, "I am not bloodthirsty," he says, "far from that, and you'll help me."

"Well," he says, "I'll help you wherever you be," this little man says to Jack. "Wherever you be in this world, all you've got to say," he says, " 'where are ye, my little man with the broad bonnet?' and I'll be there—the word's not out of your mouth," he says, "till I'm staunan beside you."

"Very well," says Jack, "ye're a very handy sort of a man."

Now the little man says to Jack, "When you go on that green avenue," he says, "there," he says, "you go on for aboot the matter of three miles," he says, "and you turn to your right. And when you turn to your right," he says, "ye'll see a forgotten castle—there's not a living human being about it in this world," he says. "They're all what they call enchanted."

"Enchanted!" Jack says. "What is that in the world?" he says. "What do you mean by enchanted?" He didn't know what enchanted meant.

"Well," he says, "enchanted means," he says, "at one time of life," he says, "not now—we don't use it," he says. "I'm enchanted myself," he says, "and I wisht I knew the way to get out of it. Enchanted, means, at one time," he says, "it's what they call a magic wand," he says, "and if you could find that magic wand," he says, "well," he says, "ye could liberate thoosands in that castle," he says, "and there was as nice a King in that castle as ever the world produced."

"Oh!" says Jack. "Well," he says, "I will mind your words, and if I want your help," he says, "which I don't think I will want," he says, "if I want your help," he says, "I'll call on you, and if I don't want it," he says, "I shall not call on you."

"Very well," the little man says, "but remember, always remember on me."

"Very well," Jack says. So they bid each other good-bye, and Jack sets sail for this road.

Now he's travelin' down this road for this three miles, or four miles, or whatever it may be, till he came to this gate in this road going down to the right, so he turned to the right. "Well," he said, "that little man really is true," he says, "that's the fairest castle," he said, "ever I saw in my life." So he said, "My-oh!" he said, "isn't this terrible?" he said —"places of that kind," he says, "for me and my old father," he says, "and my old mother wad be glad to live within, besides a house that I made myself with heather," he says, "going to waste," he says, "isn't that a sin? But," he says, "I'll explore this castle and I'll see what's within it."

So Jack he goes to the hall door and he opens it and he walks in. "Anyone there?" No reply, no kind or another, so he says, "There's no one here, right enough—the little man is quite correct," and he climbs the stair to the very topmost room of the castle, and when he opent the door of the topmost room of the castle, there was a lady lyin' in bed.

"Good heavens!" this lady says. "Man or mortal?" she says. "What has brung you here?" she says, "or what way in the world did ever you get here?"

"I got here," he says, "my fair lady," he said, "with my two feet, which I expect to get away from't again."

"Well," she says, "you are a brave man by words," she says, "but perhaps maybe not so brave by action."

He said, "I've all those things to meet yet," he says, "my fair girl," he says, "I never met one of those things yet that could trip me."

"Well," she says, "if you take my word of honor," she says, "what is your name?"

"My name is Jack," he says, "it's all the name that I gaun under."

"Well," she says, "Jack," she says, "if you take my word of honor," she says, "you may," she says, "look at the back of that door," she says, "and see what you will see."

So Jack he looks at the back of this door, and all he could see was an old topcoat. He said, "There's nothing here," he says, "my fair princess," he says, "but an old topcoat."

"Well," she says, "you keep that. You look again," she said, "and see what you see."

So he looked again and there's a pair of old shoes, all cut and scollopt to pieces. He said, "There's nothing here, my old girl," he says, "but a pair of auld shoes, all cut and torn," he says, "since hundreds of years."

"Well, you keep that," she says, "too as well. That is," she says, "the

Cloak of Darkness you have got," she says—"that coat, as you call it," she says "and that is the Shoes of Swiftness you have got, that cut and scollopt shoes," she says. "When you put that on your feet," she says, "that coat on your back, you're unvisible. No one can see you."

"Ha," he smiled—laughted. "Un-visible!" he says, "with an old topcoat!"

"Well," she says, "don't you believe me," she says—"you try and see."

"Very well!" he says, "I shall try it, my fair girl."

But he couldn't go out of this room—he bended down and he kissed this girl. "My dear little lover!" he cries. And he set sail and he's off, travelin' on and travelin' on for miles and miles, and his feet was so sore. "Daggit!" he says—"my shoes of swiftness, ye talk about. Now I'll see the virty—where the virty bits comes in." He put on this shoes and he was like a fly when he put on those shoes—he was jumpin' aboot everywhere—he couldn't be at peace one minute no place, and he put on this coat and whenever he put on the coat, he's in the air like a bird. "Good heavens!" he says—"she is quite correct," he says —"this is the cloak of darkness and the shoes of swiftness. My-oh!" he said, "it's lovely to be flying." Oot over the tops of trees, rocks, hills, and dales, he's goin' ahead, about sixty miles an hour, and he's so light. So all in a minute he looks down in a glen and he seen a very old man cuttin' rushes with a scythe.

"Good heavens!" he says, "I'll see now," he says, "can the people see me or not," he says, "here's an old gentleman down here," he says, "I'll go down an' see, can he see me?" So he lowers down to where this old gentleman was cuttin' those rushes.

"Good evenin! my old man!" He looks all round about—not a livin' soul to be seen.

The old man replies, "I could hae thought I should hae heard some-one talkin'."

"So ye do," Jack replies, "I'm here."

"Well," he said, "if you're there, whatever you may be, you are not mortal!" he says.

"I am mortal," he says, "I'm alive like yourself. I'm breathing hu-man breath," he said, "like yourself," he says, "my man, I'm alive."

"Well," he says, "I fail to see you."

"Well," he says, "you'll see me in a minute." And he unfastens the old coat and took it off and there Jack was standin' beside him.

"I see ye now," the old man replies, "I see ye now," he says, "and a nice handsome man," he says, "you are indeed," he says, "you're as pretty a man as I've seen for a long time!" So this old man says, "No one," he says, "stays here," he says, "bar me."

"And where do you stay?" Jack says.

"I stay here steady, where you see me staunin' here," he says. "I've cut rushes this two hundred years back. I've been cuttin' rushes here and as quick as I can cut those rushes, as quick as they grow behind me," he says. "I'll never get away frae here."

"Did ever you see anyone," he says, "in the world," he says, "here before?"

"Yes," the old man says. "There is a man comes here," he says, "about oncet every seven years," he said, "and that is the Black Knight."

"The Black Who?" Jack asked.

"The Black Knight."

"And what does he do here?" Jack says.

"Well, he goes up," he says, "the top of that hill. Did you see a bush on the top of that hill?"

"I do," Jack says.

"Well, in that bush," he said, "there's a deer," he says, "they call the White-Milk Deer," he says, "in that bush, and he tries to catch her. And bear in mind," he says, "my man," he says, "that White-Milk Deer is his own daughter."

"His own daughter," he says. "How can that be?"

"Well," he says, "you've heard aboot enchantment, haven't you?"

"I've read about it," he says, "but I never happent to come across any of it yet."

"Well," he says, "ye're in the midst of it this minute," he says, "if ye only knew."

"Good heavens!" Jack says, "I never knew that. And is that deer there now?"

"She's there," he says, "I'll guarantee she's there, because I saw her goin' in."

"Well, here's faith for the deer, my auld man," he says, "Ta ta! I'm off!"

So he goes on to this hill, but oh, the deer saw him—cloak of darkness an aa, hit seen him. So whenever he approached the bush the deer's up and hit's away, and Jack, he after it; as hard as he could go, he's after this deer, and this deer wasn't missin' the road, I tell you. So he's goin' on after this deer, sir, over hills and dales and mountains and rivers, tae he lands in what they caa the Chain of Rock Mountains —no way in the world of gettin' out of the face of this rocks but the one way—that's the way he come. "Aha!" he cries, "I have ye trapped now, my lady," he says. "They call you the White-Milk Deer," he says, "but ye'll be my deer in two, three minutes." But as he approached the rock, the rock opent in front of him—she was cuttin't with a knife.

"Ah!" he says. "Damn that!" he says. And so the identical same . . . afore his sword was the rock opent the same way, and he follows on, for about three miles, and when he comes to the ither end of this hill, this is this deer lyin' pechin', done out.

"Aha!" he said. "You think you'd get away from me, do ye? There never was a bird," he said, "there never was an animal ever run," he says, "ever was made," he says, "once he got in front of me," he says, "any distance, I wad catch him," he says, "at the long run."

"Well," she says, "ye've catcht me," she says, "Jack."

"And you can talk too," he says.

"Oh yes," the deer replies, "I can talk."

"Well," he says, "ye're the first animal in the world," he says, "ever I talked to."

She says, "I beg your pardon," she said, "I am not an animal," she says, "I am only enchanted in this shape, as you were told by the old man among the rushes."

"Well," he says, "I love you better now than what ever I did," he says.

"But there's one thing," she says, "Jack, you must do."

"And what is that?" he says.

"Well," she says, "there is a block at your back."

When he looks round there was a block.

"And also," she said, "there's an ax."

When he lookit again, there was an ax.

"Now," she said, "you catch my head and my body and put it owre that block, and if you cannot separate my head from the body," she says, "with one blow of that ax," she said, "I'll be very sorry for you."

"Eftir me," he says, "runnin'—I don't know hoo far I've run eftir you," he says—"I'll guarantee I've run a hundred miles, and say I wad cut the head off o' you!"

"Yes," she said, "and after ye've cut the head off o' me," she said, "ye throw it doon in that well," she says, "at your back again."

When he looks round at his back again, there was a well.

She said, "Now, you pit my head, and also my body, down that well."

"Well," she said, "if you don't do it to me," she says, "I've got to do it to you. What is it goin' to be—one or the other?"

"Ah well," he says, "I don't want to die young," he says, "I'll do it to you."

So he puts her head on the block and with one blow the head fell separate. So he catcht the head and also the body and he throwed them down the well. So he sat for a while thinkin'. "Well, I was a fool," he says; "if ever there was a fool in this world, I am one," he says, "and a real one. To say an animal would catch an ax, and put my head on a block and cut my head off, that hadn't got hands for a go-off; hit had feet, but it hadn't hands—why could hit use an ax?" he says. "I never seen the like of that in my life," he says, "to be such a stupid, silly man," he says, "as I am. So," he says, "I wouldn't gied the deer," he says, "that I catcht," he says, "for all the ladies," he says, "that ever," he says, "were made. I wouldn't give my deer," he says, "for the lot."

"Surely, surely," a voice said at his back, "you must be in an awful state for that deer, Jack!"

When he lookit round, this was the loveliest lady that ever he saw in his life.

"I come from the well where you put me," she says. "You put me in there, didn't you—you cut my head off, you put me in there," she says. "Well, here I am," she says, "back to you," she says, "in my natural state as I used to be once before. And remember," she said, "that is three hundred years ago."

"Well," he says, "you've lived a long time after your mother," he says.

"Now," she says, "Jack, how are we going to get oot of here?"

"Well," Jack says, "I do not know; I can't get back," he says. "I was tryin' my sword agen the rocks, but," he says, "they're as hard as granite."

"Well," she says, "one word of my mouth," she says, "will open the rocks. Where there is rock," she says, "let it be level land," she says, "and where there is level land," she says, "let it be hills, and where there's no roads, let roads be, and where there's no carriage let one be now."

And no sooner she said it, there was a carriage standing beside them.

"Now," she says, "in over here," she says, "Jack, and we'll drive home."

So Jack he jumps in over this carriage, him and this fair lady, and he says, "Well," he says, "I never thought," he says, "for one moment," he says, "would see a lady," he says, "in a carriage here."

"Aha!" she says, "Jack, ye'd wonder what is here," she says, "there's things here," she says, "I doot, that you never saw in your life," she says. "You come here," she says, "and you'll be seeing them richt sometime, but not just now."

So they're goin' on, goin' on with this pony as far as they could, mile after mile, passin' hill after hill and all of a suddent this girl looks; she says, "Here ye are," she says, "Jack" she says, "now's the time to test yourself," she says. "Here is my father comin'," she says, "one of the deadliest men," she says, "on the face of the earth," she says.

"Oh," he said, "he is, is he?"

"Yes," she said, "he is."

"Well," he says, "I'll test him in a very quiet way."

So he comes on him with a horse and a spear and when he approaches the carriage, he says, "One minute to pray for your souls!"

"Don't be in a hurry," Jack replies. He says, "My man," and he pit his hand in his pocket and he pulls oot this small little packet of oatcakes, and he said, "You taste of my bread, sir," he says. And so gently he put out his hand and tasted his bread. He says, "Curse," he says, "on me," he says, "the day I was born," he says, "if I did kill the man that is goin' to dae me good."

"You'd better eat anither piece," he says, "my man," he says.

So he ate anither piece, but he ate many pieces, till he ate the whole lot by this time.

"Well, well," he says, "Jack," he says, "I am as proud now," he said, "I've met you and my daughter, one of the fairest queens," he says, "in the world. And" he says, "I was gaun to kill the man," he says, "was gaun to do me all the good," he says, "in the world," he says. "The castle that you've seen," he says, "unoccupied, is mine," he says. "I am the King of that place," he says, "one of the largest estates," he says, "in the world and one of the valuablest estates in the world."

"Well," Jack says, "I'm proud to hear so."

"And for saving my daughter," he says, "now, Jack," he says, "breaking her enchantment," he says, "she's goin' to be," he says, "your wife," he says, "you'll get her at the morning."

"Well," Jack says, "it'll always be something," he says, "for my luck."

So they rid on and rid on. "But there's one thing," he says, "Jack, before we go much further, I must tell you," he says. "I've to meet yet," he says, "one of the dangerousest snakes," he says, "on earth, and this dangerous snake, I call him," he said, "is a human being like us, but he's very, very dangerous," he said—"he's worse than a snake," he says, "and we'll meet him, because he knows we're comin', by this time."

So Jack's goin' on wondering what the man was talkin' about—didn't know what this man was talkin' about, no more than what I do. "And but he's fiendish," he said, "he'd soon learn," he said, "what he was talking aboot—here was a man comin', like the Devil himself, if there was such a thing in this world, he's comin'. Here he is!" this man replies, "he's comin'," and he crouches on the corner of this machine, and he darts forrit like a bullet from a gun, and the both of them, what was hills, they were makin' it level lands, and what was level lands, they are makin' it hills and they fought for aboot four hours.

But Jack's father-in-law supposed-to-be is the winner.

"Well," Jack says, "listen," he says, "my King," he says, "you are," he says, "the cleverest man ever I saw," he says, "I never saw a man doin' things like that," he says, "in my life."

"Yes," he says, "Jack—you've mentioned the words," he says, "quite

right, when you said your father-in-law—that is the real word for it,"
he said. "But ye're unmarried yet," he said, "but I guarantee you
there's not monie days till you'll married."

So Jack and his sweetheart gaed home and his father-in-law—they
managed to get home and lived for six weeks.

Now there used to be mountains and rivers and great precipices as
no man—it practically took a bird to cross this mountains to get to his
brother's place from here—took him days and days to travel, and you
could have traveled it all in a quarter of an hour, when the roads was
straightened out properly as they should be. So Jack and his wife was
married, and his brother and his sister-in-law and the other King was
there and all got married together, and so they lived there happy all the
days of their life, and the last time I played at that big hoose wi' my
auld bagpipes, he gied me tuppence, and he gied me a crust of a pie for
tellin' a lie, and the skin of a red herrin'.

Johnnie in the Cradle

Collected by Hamish Henderson. Forthcoming in *Folktales of Scotland.*

Told by Andrew Stewart (but not the narrator of "The King of England"), nicknamed Andra Hoochten because of his expertise in singing mouth-music, of the Stewarts of Blairgowrie. Andra was forty-
three in August 1955 when Henderson recorded this legend in the
Standing Stones berry field on the road to Essendy. These "tinker"
(Scottish gypsy) families in the evening would gather 'round the bon-
fires and sing songs and tell stories. Andra possessed a vivid storytelling style, and rendered the "nyaa, nyaa" of the changeling baby
and its whispered commands to the tailor with dramatic change of
voice.

Printed in *Von Prinzen, Trollen und Herrn Fro* (Jahresgabe 1958
der Gesellschaft zur Pflege des Märchengutes der europäischen Völker,
Rheine in Westfalen), pp. 115–27 (Scots and German), and issued as
a recording in 1960 by the School of Scottish Studies, Edinburgh, disc
A.001/2.

This family tradition deals with the well-known phenomenon of the
changeling (motif F321.1). Submotifs are F321.1.1.2 "Changeling plays
on pipe and thus betrays his maturity"; and F321.1.4 "Disposing of a
changeling." The idea of the changeling, held throughout Great Brit-
ain and so reported for the motif by Baughman, is that a fairy has

stolen the baby and left in its place a fairy-substitute that looks like a child but behaves like an adult. Baughman lists a number of strategies used by the parents to recover their child and get rid of the changeling.

It was a man in a farm, and . . . a man and his wife . . . they werenae long married, ye see, and they'd a wee kiddie, and they christened its name Johnnie, see? But it was a very crabbit wee baby this, it was always goin' "nyaaa, nyaaa, nyaaa," jist that way a' the time, ye see. So here, there was another neighbor man, the tailor, used to come up and visit this farmer, ye see (he'd a small croft). And when they come up tae the farm, they used always to have a wee drink o' whiskey between them, ye see, and a bit talk and a game o' cards, and somethin' like that, ye see. So anyway, it was the day o' the market (I think in them days, if I can mind, it's every six month, or every year, there was a market day); they went away—they loaded up their van wi' pigs or anything, cattle, they went away tae the market with them. So, it was a very warm day, and just as usual, Johnnie wasnae growin', it was aye about the same size nae gettin' oot o' the bit, and it was aye goin' "nyaaa, nyaa," greetin' away.

So here, they were in the . . . down in the byre. The man was cleanin' oot the byre, ye see, an' the man says . . . the tailor says to the farmer, he says, "You're awfy worried-lookin'," he says. "What's wrong wi' ye?"

"Och," he says, "it's market day the morn," he says; "my wife," he says "me and the wife had a bit o' a row," he says. "And . . . she wanted to come wi' me tae the market. She's been . . . stayed closed in the hoose, watchin' the wean," he says, "and that," he says, "she's gettin' kin' o' fed-up. She wants to go tae the market, she wants tae buy some things. And she's naebody to watch the wean."

"Oh, but," says the tailor, he says, "I'll no see naebody . . . wee Johnnie wantin' a nurse. I'll nurse the wean—see? so—if she wants to go."

So the man says, "No, no" he says, "I dinnae think she wad let ye doe that, but we'll gae roon an' see anyway."

So he went roon wi' the tailor, and he asked his wife if she wad let the tailor watch Johnnie till they would get a day at the market. So the woman was pleased, you see, and the next morning come (to make a long story short). The next morning come, and they packed up their van, yoked up the horses—I think it was two horses they had in them days—and away they went to the market. So the man was in, and he was doin' somethin', the tailor, sewin' at a pair o' trousers or makin' a suit, or somethin' at the side o' the fire, finishin' off a job, and he hears a voice sayin':

"Is my mother and faither awa?" See?

So the tailor looks roond, and didnoe think but for one minute it was the baby that was talkin'. See? So he looks roond, he goes over tae the windae, he looks oot the windae, and he could see nothin'. He goes back and sits in the chair again. He thought the baby was sleepin'; it had stopped cryin'.

So he hears the voice sayin' again, "Is my mother and my faither awa tae the market? Are they awa?"

So he looks roond, and this was the baby haudin' wi' its wee hands at each side the pram; it was sittin' up. And it says. . . .

Of course, the tailor was a wee bit . . . he got kin' o' feared like, an' he looks at the baby and he kin' o' kep' hissel', an' he says, "Yes," he says, "they're away tae the market, Johnnie," he says. "What is it?"

He says, "If you look in the boddom press," he says, "there's a bottle o' whiskey," the baby says, "take it oot an gie me a wee taste." See?

So he takes the bottle o' whiskey oot. . . . He went and sure enough the tailor he opened up the boddom o' the press, and here was the bottle o' whiskey, and teemed oot some for the wee baby—the wee baby took the whiskey an' drunk it. See? So it says, "Are there ony pipes . . . hae ye got a set o' pipes in the hoose?" "No' me," says the tailor, he says. "I cannae play the pipes," he says, "but," he says, "I like to hear the pipes."

"Well," he says, "go oot to the byre and bring me in a strae, and I'll play ye a tune."

So of course the tailor got up, and oot he went, brings in a strae. (It wisnae a bashed strae, it was a roon straw, it had to be roon, so that the fairy could blow through it, ye see?) Takes the straw in, and hands it tae Johnnie, and the tailor's watchin' everythin', see? He was worried, the tailor, noo; he was thinkin' aboot the mother and the faither, and this wee Johnnie bein' the fairy, see? Didnae know what to say aboot it. . . . He sat doon and he's watchin'. He says, "Can ye play a strae?" the tailor said.

So the fairy says, "Ay," he says, "I'll play ye a tune on the pipes." Sat doon, and it played the loveliest tune on the pipes that ever ye heard—through a strae! The greatest pipe music—he says he heard lots o' pipers in them days, the MacCrimmons an a' them, pipin', ye see?—but he says he never heard the like o' it in his life, this wee baby in the pram. He knew it was a fairy then, ye see, it was playin' the pipes.

So they had a good talk together, this fairy and the tailor, ye see, so it says, "Is it time for my father and mother to come hame yet?"

So he says, "Ay", he says, "they'll be hame in aboot half an 'oor."

So he says, "Well," he says, "ye'd better take a look an' see if they're comin'."

So the tailor he went oot, and looked oot the windae, and he says, "Ay, here they're comin' up the lane." Ye see?

So of course, the wee fairy, he says, "I'll have tae get back into my pram again." And it lay doon on its back and it's goin' . . . and when the mother come to the door the wee bairn started goin' again "nyaaa, nyaaa," greetin' away, ye see?

So here noo the tailor was worriet. But he broke the news off to the fairmer, ye see, and tellt the fairmer.

"Well," he says, "I don't know," he says, "what I'll dae."

But in them days, what they done wi' a fairy, they got a girdle, ye know a girdle for bakin' scones. They put thon on the fire, and they took—in them days, to put away a fairy—they took horse's manure off the road, or a anywhere at all, ye see, and they put it in a pan and burned it in a pan, and the fairies seen that, they took fear and they disappeared. Ye see? Put it on the top o' the pan. My mother used to tell us this.

So here—the fairmer asked him what was wrong. So he tells the fairmer.

"Well," he says, "I'll have to break it to my wife," he says. "But," he says, "I don't know how I'm goin' tae dae it, it'll break her hairt," he says. "I can hardly believe this."

"Well," says the tailor, he says, "I'll tell ye what I'll dae. You and your wife," he says, "go . . . wait for a while, and go tae another market. Let on there's another market, that the stuff wasnae half sellt, there's two days' market. And go through . . ."

In them days, there was a hole fae the byre right to the kitchen, ye could look through a hole in the wall, through to the byre. Ye see? Ye could see the cattle, and everything.

"Go into the byre, and lift the curtain back, and listen tae everything that's goin' on. Ye can see what I'm tellin' ye," says the tailor, "is true. It's a fairy ye've got for a wan." See?

So, anyway, the next mornin' come, and they packed up their things as usual, lettin' on that they were goin' tae another market. And they went through tae the byre. And here, they're sittin'. An' it heard . . . the mother an' the farmer heard the wee fairy sayin' tae the tailor, "Is my mother and father away tae the market?" So the tailor spoke kin' o' loud, ye see, to let them hear him.

"O yes," he says, "they're away tae the market," he says. "Johnnie," he says, "you'll be wantin' a drink."

"Ay, get the whiskey oot," he says, "and gie me a drink."

Well, the woman nearly fainted when she heard the fairy speakin' . . . her ain baby speakin' tae the tailor, ye see? Soon efter this went on, the next mornin' they never said nothin' when they found oot it was a fairy.

The farmer come in . . . the baby's father come in . . . got the girdle . . . and the fairy looke wi' its eyes wild, watched the mother . . . the father pittin' the girdle on the fire, seein' nae flour or nothin' on the table . . . wi'oot any bread gettin baked, ye see?

Next thing come in, was wi' a bit o' a half o' a bag full o' the horse manure on tap o' the girdle, like that. And the fairy begun to get feared noo, its eyes kin' o' raised up, and it was gettin' feared when it seen the girdle. And just as the farmer was comin' forward to reach for wee Johnnie in the cradle he just made a dive like that, and made a jump up the lum—went up the lum itsel', and it cries doon the chimley:

"I wish I had 'a kent my mother—if I had 'a been longer wi' my mother," he says, "I would have like to ken her better."

Ye can take that meaning oot o' that, what the fairy said, back doon the chimley, when it disappeared.

That was a story my mother told me, years ago.

Applie and Orangie

Collected by Hamish Henderson. Forthcoming in *Folktales of Scotland*.

Told by Andrew Stewart (Andra Hoochter), narrator of "Johnnie in the Cradle," in conjunction with his sister Bella and her son Donald Higgins, in August 1955 in Bella's house in Blairgowrie, Perthshire. Bella was a "settled" or urbanized tinker who had given up the itinerant life. Her home became a notable "ceilidh house" where family and friends engaged in night-long sessions of singing and tale-telling. Andra had just finished a rendition of "The Demon Lover" (Child ballad 243) when he offered this cante-fable. Bella too sang Child ballads and was a skilled piper who could play on the great Highland war-pipes.

The dialogue between the three speakers portrays the reality of folktale narration.

This is type 720 *My Mother Slew Me; My Father Ate Me*. Motifs present are S31 "Cruel stepmother"; G61 "Relative's flesh eaten unwittingly"; E607.1 "Bones of dead collected and buried. Return in another form directly from grave"; E613.0.1 "Reincarnation of murdered child as bird"; N271 "Murder will out"; Q211.4 "Murder of children punished"; Q412 "Punishment: millstone (axe) dropped on guilty person."

This version stops with the revenge on the cruel stepmother, but other versions conclude with the transformation of the bird back into the child. The bird's song, here rendered in Anglo-Scots dialect, is the heart of this tale. Type 720 is a Grimm tale with a broad European distribution, especially in France, but with scant popularity in Ireland, so often the numerical leader in tale-type counts.

Henderson: Tell us, Andra, what was this story your mother was tellin' ye?

Stewart: The story of Applie and Orangie. It was two girls, two little girls. The man—this was his second wife, and his first wife's kiddie was either called Applie or Orangie—I don't know which o' the names they were called, but we'll just say Applie an' Orangie, see?

So one day—the stepmother was very bad to one of the little girls. One day she says tae the good little girl: "Applie," she says, "I want ye tae go," she says, "an' get me milk. This is my golden jug—take this, an'," she says, "if ye break it," she says, "I'll murder ye," she says, "when ye get back." She used that word, ye see?

So anyway, away they went, an' the bad girl tripped her up, an' broke the jug. So, when they come home, the father was away workin'. And when he come home, for two or three (wasn't it?), he missed the girl. She was a-missin'.

Higgins: The stepmother said she was outside, playin' with skippin' ropes.

Stewart: Ay, playin' with skippin' ropes, an' that. But this went on too long, there was no signs o' the wee girl, see? But here, the mother had murdered the wee girl—boiled her, pit parts o' her body in a pot, an' made soup, an' got the husband tae eat it, ye see.

Higgins: He came across the wee pinkie in amongst the soup.

Stewart: He took the bones, a' the little bones thegither—an' he give the wife a good layin'-on at that time—an' he took the bones an' buried them.

Higgins: No, he give them tae the ither sister, an' the ither sister took them oot an' put them atween twa marble stones . . .

Stewart: He put them in marble stones, an' as time goes on, they grew intae a pigeon.

An' one day—he didnae know that wee girl was murdered, though, until the pigeon told him.

Higgins: No, he knew by pinkie.

Stewart: Ah, but . . .

Bella Stewart (Andrew's sister, Donald's mother): Yes, he knew by the pinkie; he got the pinkie in his soup.

Higgins: The wee lassie took the bones, and put them between twa marble stones, ye see. Well, as time goes on, this wee pigeon grows oot, ye see. So it's fleein' aboot, an' it's thinkin' aboot revenge, ye see, on the mother. So it flees aboot . . .

Stewart: An' it lands on the street . . .

Higgins: An' it goes in this shop . . .

Bella Stewart: . . . near Christmas time . . .

Higgins: Near Christmas time, for to buy a present, ye ken. An' it goes intae the first shop, an' it stands on the coonter, an' it says:

> My mammy killed me,
> My daidy ate me,
> My sister Jeannie pickit my banes
> An' put me atween twa marble stanes
> An' I growed intae a bonnie wee doo-doo.

So the shopkeeper, he's listenin' tae this, ye see, an' the shopkeeper says, "Now," he says, "if ye say that again," he says, "I'll give ye the biggest doll in the shop," he says, "the best doll in the shop." So it starts doon again, an' says:

> My mammy killed me,
> My daidy ate me,
> My sister Jeannie pickit my banes
> An' put me atween twa marble stanes
> An' I growed intae a bonnie wee doo-doo.

The man says, "That's marvelous, that's marvelous!" So he gies it the big doll, an' away it goes, an' it goes tae the jeweler's shop—ye see? It flies in the door o' the jeweler's shop, an' it sits on the coonter, an' it does the same thing again:

> My mammy killed me,
> My daidy ate me,
> My sister Jeannie pickit my banes
> An' put me atween twa marble stanes
> An' I growed intae a bonnie wee doo-doo.

So the man in the shop says, "Now," he says, "if ye do that again," he says, "I'll give ye the best watch in the shop." Ye see?

However, tae cut a long story short, she says it again, an' she gets the watch, an' goes on again, an' flies tae the next shop. An' it's an ironmonger's an' it stands on the coonter, an' it says:

> My mammy killed me,
> My daidy ate me,
> My sister Jeannie pickit my banes
> An' put me atween twa marble stanes
> An' I growed intae a bonnie wee doo-doo.

So the man in the shop says, "Now," he says, "if ye say that again," he says, "I'll give ye the sharpest ax in the shop." So she says it again, an' gets the sharpest ax in the shop, an' away she goes flyin' through the air—the wee doo—an' it comes tae the chimney, ye see? An' it shouts doon the chimney the same again, ye see?

> My mammy killed me,
> My daidy ate me,

My sister Jeannie pickit my banes
An' put me atween twa marble stanes
An' I growed intae a bonnie wee doo-doo.

So the wee lassie hears it, an' she pits her heid through the windae, an' it draps the doll doon, ye see, an' the wee lassie catches it.

"O mammy, mammy, mammy," she says, "daddy! Look whit I got —fae Santae Claus!" (She thought it was fae Santae Claus, ye see.)

An' the man says, "My God," he says, "whit's this?" So he pits his heid through—down comes the watch—the gold watch, ye see?

So he says, "O my goodness, wife! Look at that!" he says; "look at that." Ye see?

She says, "Wait a minute, mebber there'll be somethin' for me!" An' she dives forrit, an' she pits her heid under, and the ax comes doon wheek, and wips the heid off her.

The Aberdonians and the Chocolates

Collected by Hamish Henderson. Forthcoming in *Folktales of Scotland*.

Told by Donald MacLean of Tobermory when a student at Edinburgh University in 1965. MacLean frequently contributed humorous tales to the convivial group frequenting Sandy Bell's pub (the Forrest Hill Bar). He subsequently returned to the West Highlands as a teacher at Oban.

Scots' stinginess is proverbial, and the residents of Aberdeen are reputed the most close-fisted of Scotsmen. Type 1704 *Anecdotes About Absurdly Stingy Persons*.

It was told by one of the lecturers at this youth camp in Perthshire, and it's a fairly typical sort of joke but it appealed to me in that I am sure it was a minister who told it.

And it was about this Aberdonian couple, both reputed even in Aberdonian circles for their miserliness. And the pair of them got married and they were going on their honeymoon to Edinburgh. And just as the train was pulling out of the station at Aberdeen, after the wedding reception, somebody threw a two-pound box of chocolates into the compartment shouting—"Best of luck."

So the train had traveled about twenty miles out of Aberdeen when the wife asked if she could have a chocolate. Very grudgingly, the husband opened the box of chocolates and said, "There you are, have one." So the wife had the one chocolate, ate it, but still kept an eye on the box of chocolates. Obviously she would have liked to have eaten more. As they were crossing the Tay Bridge she again asked if she could have a chocolate. Same answer from the husband, "There you are, have one." And as the train was traveling through Fife for to come to the Forth Bridge she again asked if she could have a chocolate. Three she'd eaten during the course of the journey. The husband said to the wife, "Hang on, lassie, I think you're eating far too many; we'll need to keep some for the bairn."

The Lone Highlander

Collected by Hamish Henderson and printed in *Scottish Studies* 2 (1967): part 2, pp. 237–38.

Told by Donald MacLean of Tobermory when a student at Edinburgh University, on 15 March 1965. Henderson printed the text with supplementary notes. There he writes: "International anecdotes that cross political and language frontiers are sometimes hard to place in categories of type and motif, but they frequently illustrate, as nothing else can, the mental attitudes of the communities in which they take root. The following version of an anecdote found all over Scotland, and variously set in the days of the Roman invasion, the Wars of Independence, and the Jacobite rebellions, gives native chauvinistic expression to the 'guid conceit o' himself' not seldom exhibited by the Scottish soldier."

Well, this refers to an incident that took place after the '45 Rebellion in Scotland, when the English were sending troops of Redcoats through the Highlands, partly to police the Highlands, but mainly to put on a great show of strength—subdue the natives. And they were going through this glorious glen in Perthshire—beautiful summer morning, great show of strength, the sun glistening on their bayonets; musket, fife, and drum playing. Everything was grand until they got to the far end of the glen, and standing up on one of the hills was this lone Highlander, who was breaking every rule in the book by brandishing a claymore, wearing a kilt, drinking out of a bottle of whiskey. This was bad enough in itself until he started shouting insults at the regiment below, and started calling them Sasunnach [English] so and so's, and told them all to get home, that they were no use anyway. So the colonel in charge of the regiment rather took offense at this, and delegated a corporal and a private, you see. He said to them, "Corporal, take a man with you, get up there, I want that man." So the corporal and the private disappeared over the hill, and the lone Highlander had of course disappeared over the skyline beyond. And great sounds of battle were heard over the skyline. Half an hour elapsed and the battle still raging. A few minutes later the Highlander himself appeared—no signs of the corporal or the private. He was still brandishing his claymore and saying that was great fun, send some more.

So the colonel thought, "Well, this has just gone too far altogether. Sergeant, take a platoon with you—thirty men. Get up there, I want that man, dead or alive." Too much altogether, sort of. The sergeant and a platoon of thirty men charged up the hillside. The little Highlander disappeared over the skyline as before. Tremendous battle altogether this time that lasted for about an hour. And at the end of the hour the little Highlander appeared again completely unscathed, but his sword dripping blood, you see. By this time he was in grand form altogether and he challenged the whole regiment shouting "Come on, come on, the lot of you—I'm just in trim."

So the colonel: "This is it. It's gone beyond a joke now. Bugler, sound the general advance." So the bugler sounded the advance, and the whole regiment, five thousand, charged up the hillside. The Highlander disappeared over the skyline as before. Just as the regiment arrived at the top of the hill, they were confronted with the original corporal, or at least what was left of him, and he was dying obviously and making a dying attempt to save the regiment. He was shouting, "Get back, get back, it's a trap, it's a trap, there are two of them."

[Postnote by Henderson]

This story is not exclusively Scottish, however. On 26 June 1967, the Hamburg weekly, *Der Spiegel,* printed (on p. 66) the following version in an article describing the Israeli Blitzkrieg:

> Hinter einer Düne entdeckten die Ägypter einen israelischen Scharfschützen. Zwei Nassersoldaten sollten ihn erledigen, aber keiner kam zurück. Daraufhin schickte der Kompaniechef zwölf Männer vor und—als auch die nicht wieder kamen—die ganze Kompanie.
>
> Zwei Stunden später kroch ein zerfledderter Ägypter in den Gefechstand. "Wir sind in eine jüdische Falle geraten," stammelte er. "Das war nicht ein Scharfschütze. Es waren zwei."

(*Translation:* The Egyptians discovered an Israeli sniper behind the sand-dune. Two Nasser soldiers were told off to silence him, but neither of them came back. The company commander then sent twelve to do the job, and finally—when these didn't come back either—he sent the entire company.

Two hours later a torn and tattered Egyptian crept back to Company H.Q. "We fell into a Jewish trap," he stammered. "It wasn't just one sniper. There were two of them.")

Der Spiegel's comment was: "This Jewish front-line joke is the latest variant of the old story of tiny David who put paid to the giant Goliath."

The variant quoted by the German weekly is clearly brand-new, at any rate as far as the modern state of Israel is concerned, but it has emerged from a community of culture and tradition with ancestral memories of a fight against the big battalions. One of the leading military figures of the war that led to the creation of the Israeli state has been conducting the excavations at Masada, where a Jewish garrison defied the Romans, and was massacred to the last man. The Israeli public has apparently taken very great interest in this archaeological reminder of the nation's military prowess in ancient times. Also, that the story has in fact earlier roots among the Jews than might at first seem likely is suggested by the fact that—as Professor D. K. Wilgus of the University of California, Los Angeles, informed me on 1 September 1967—the same anecdote was circulating among students of his university immediately after the end of the four-day Israel-Arab war in June.

The story continues to be popular in Scotland. In 1966 the Glasgow folk-singer Matt McGinn wrote a popular song on the same theme; it is entitled "The Hielanman," and the period of the exploit is in this case the Roman invasion of Pictland; the moral of the story is stated to be "Hadrian's Wall." The text of Matt's song was published in *Chapbook* Vol. 3, No. 3, and his performance of his own song is recorded on a Transatlantic LP (Xtra 1045) issued in December 1966.

The Minister to His Flock

Collected by Hamish Henderson. Forthcoming in *Folktales of Scotland*.

Told by Alan Jackson, a young Scottish poet, in 1965. An old joke in a new variant, treating humorously motif Q560 "Punishments in hell" and the barbaric black humor of Calvinist Scotland.

Aye, ye're enjoyin' yoursels noo wi' yer drinkin' and yer women an' yer nights oot at the pictures, and never a thought given to the Word of God, and his great and terrible laws.

But ye'll change your tune when ye're doon below in the fiery pit, an' ye're burnin' an' ye're sufferin', and ye'll cry: "O, Lord, Lord, we didna ken, we didna ken." And the Lord in his infinite mercy will bend doon frae heaven, and say "Well, ye ken noo."

Scotland (Highlands)

The Blacksmith's Son

Contributed by John MacInnes. Forthcoming in *Folktales of Scotland*.

This novella was recorded in 1946 by the noted Scots' collector Calun I. Maclean on Barra in the outer Hebrides. Maclean described the narrator as follows:

> In the Island of Barra today there survives only one storyteller of the type that both (John Francis) Campbell and (Alexander) Carmichael found quite common in the years 1860–80 . . . he is the last of the old storytellers, and he is now nearing eighty-six years of age. He is an old fisherman named Seumas MacKinnon. I still remember the first evening I went to visit him, one wet September evening in 1946. He was busy repairing shoes when I entered the kitchen of his house. He raised his head to greet me. His eyes were mischievous, his face weatherbeaten, and his features were beautifully chiseled. He wore the peaked blue cap of fishermen and blue dungarees. His life of eighty years had been spent almost as much on sea as on land. At eighty he was still a very handsome old man.
> . . . His diction was crisp, concise, and clear. Every sentence was short and perfectly balanced. His style was, of course, that of the real traditional storyteller. By modulation of tone and gesture he brought considerable dramatization to bear on his telling of a tale. He acted the part of characters and showed that he had mastered an art that had taken centuries to develop. His voice was beautifully clear and pleasing. He stamped his personality on every story he told, and his lively sense of humour enhanced his storytelling considerably [from *Arv* 8 (1952): 124–25. Cf. also *Gwerin* 1 (1956–1957): 21–33].

In the herring fishery Seamus MacKinnon found appreciative audiences for good storytellers. In the evening when the nets were set, the fishermen went aboard the boats of outstanding narrators and listened the night to their tales. MacKinnon could neither read nor write and spoke little English. He narrated some forty pieces: wonder tales, romantic tales, jokes and anecdotes, legends illustrating fairy belief.

The present narrative represents a class of novellas and historical legends in Scottish Gaelic reflecting Scottish-English hostility. In these chauvinistic tales the Gael, by accident or design, always succeeds. For a stirring account, supposedly historical but clearly patterned on the David-Goliath combat, of a sword duel between a Highland stripling and a burly English champion whom he kills, see "After the Battle of Culloden" in R. M. Dorson, *Folklore, Selected Essays* (Bloomington, Indiana, 1972), pp. 85–88, reprinted from *The Dewar Manuscripts*, ed. John MacKechnie (Glasgow, 1964), pp. 233–36. Motifs: D1711.0.1 "Magician's apprentice (son outdoes father)"; D1719.1 "Contest in magic"; D1183 "Magic scissors, shears (scythe)."

Some time or other long ago, when it was winter—just as it is now— a ship went ashore down there at Isinish Point and became a total wreck; she broke up completely. There was a tremendous load of wood in her, and the people of the place bought every scrap of it. They bought it in lots. Any man who had a piece of wood with a lock on it —they were very valuable locks except that they didn't have keys in them, the keys had got lost—any man who had a piece of wood with a lock on it took out the lock and went to the blacksmith to have a key made.

There was a smith somewhere down in Uist who had only one son. When the people had all the locks off the wood, they collected them and gave them to the smith; but the smith was unable to make keys for them. Then, one winter's day, the smith's son—he was only a young lad—went out to the smithy to ask his father to come in for dinner. When his father had gone, the boy began to look around the smithy and saw all these locks, and not one of them with a key in it. He realized that his father had failed to make the keys. So he said to himself that if he could manage to make the keys he'd have the money for himself—whatever the charge was for making keys—for Christmas and New Year. He shut the door and set to work and turned out the keys as well as if they'd been made in a mold. When he had finished them all he sent word for people to come and fetch their locks, because the keys were ready; so they came along, and the boy got a lot of money for the keys.

One day his father said to the boy that he'd have to give him a bit of money—he had too much money just to blow at Christmas. But the boy wasn't willing to hand it over. When his father saw this he put him out of the smithy and shut the door on him. "Don't you ever dare come through that smithy door again!" he said.

"You can keep it tight shut for long enough before I come to open it!" said the boy.

And he left home and went and joined the army. It was to England that he was sent for training; so there he was, living in barracks there. Now, their commander used to go around in the company of Englishmen a lot, and one of them said to him that there was never a blacksmith in Scotland who could beat an Englishman at the smith's trade. The commander said he didn't know—that might be true; all the same, there were good blacksmiths in Scotland. "Well," said the Englishman, "we'll bet you five hundred pounds."

"I won't take you up on that right now," said the commander, "but I will if I see you tomorrow."

When he paraded the soldiers next day he began to ask each of them in turn, "Can you do blacksmith's work?" At last he came to the blacksmith's son and asked him the same question.

"What kind of blacksmith's work do you want, exactly?" said the soldier.

The commander told him how the Englishmen were betting five hundred pounds that there was never a smith in Scotland to beat an English smith at his trade. "Whatever kind of blacksmith's work you want," said the boy, "I can do it for you."

"Well, then, a good gun is the first thing I want made," said the commander.

The soldier went off and found a smithy for himself, set to work, and made the gun. The gun was to have an iron plate on the stock. He fixed this plate on in such a way that it could be lifted off; and he put his own name on the underside of it. When the plate was fixed on the stock you couldn't see the name. Now the Englishmen were to get a gun made too, to see which of them had the better craftsman.

The night the commander was going off with the gun, the soldier said to him, "Now when you get at the hotel where you're to meet, don't take the gun inside at all; leave it at the outer door and make the Englishmen leave their gun out beside it. Otherwise, you'll never prove to them that your gun's the better one. But you ask their man to go out and bring in the better of the two guns; if it's yours that gets brought in, all you have to do is lift this plate and you'll see my name on the underside."

Anyway, they arrived at the hotel and the commander left his gun outside. The Englishman came and left his gun beside it. They went in.

"Well, now," said the commander, "one of you go out and bring in whichever is the better made of the two guns."

They went out and brought in the Scotsman's gun.

"Now you go and bring in your own gun," said the Englishman, "this is mine."

"Is this the better one?" the commander asked him.

"Yes," said the Englishman.

"Then I'm all right," said the commander, "I don't need to go out—

it's my gun you've brought in! Not that I'd go, anyway—I have a servant."

"This isn't your gun!" said the Englishman.

"It is," said the commander.

"It is not!" said the Englishman.

The commander picked up the gun and lifted off the plate on the stock and said to the Englishman, "What Englishman ever had a name like that to put on it?"

The Englishmen were beaten, and they were forced to pay five hundred pounds. The commander went home and told the soldier what had happened. They wanted him, he said, to put up another five hundred on which of them was better at making a peacock and a peahen of iron.

"I won't take you up on that till tomorrow," the commander had said.

Anyway, when he went home he told the soldier what the Englishmen wanted. "You go and put up the money," said the soldier. "If you have to pay them you'll only be giving them their own back."

The soldier went off to the smithy, set to work, and made an iron peacock and peahen, and the commander went off with them. When he got to the hotel, the Englishmen were all there with a peacock and peahen, also of iron. The two pairs were placed on a table. When the men had looked their fill at the two pairs, the Scotsman made the cock tread the hen. The Englishmen couldn't do that with theirs, so they lost the bet again that night.

"We'll bet you another five hundred pounds, then," they said, "that there was never a man reared in Scotland who could match an Englishman at scything."

"I can't say until tomorrow," said the commander, "but I'll know tomorrow if I can take you up on it."

He went to the soldier and told him that the next bet they wanted was to put five hundred pounds on a scyther.

"Well, if you can find a man in the company who says he can use a scythe," said the soldier, "I'll make a scythe for him."

The commander went to the soldiers and asked each of them in turn if he could use a scythe till he found one who said he could. At this, the Englishmen began to praise the scythe that their man had, and to say that its like couldn't be found in Scotland. But when the blacksmith's son heard that, he said, "Go to the Englishmen and tell them that you've got a man here who'll make the geese of England shit a scythe as good as theirs is!"

Anyway, the commander put up his money, and on a given day the scythers were to hold their competition. The commander asked the blacksmith's son if the scythe was finished. "Good Lord, no!" said he, "the geese of England haven't shit the scythe yet! You go and fetch me three bars of steel and two bolls of oatmeal."

The blacksmith's son got the three steel bars and the two bolls of meal. Then he got two dozen geese and tethered them in a corner of the smithy. He ground the steel bars into fine dust and mixed this into the oatmeal and kept doing this until the geese had eaten the two bolls of meal and the three steel bars. When they had finished he got a cauldron and put it on the fire. Then he began to put the geese's dung in the cauldron; as he drained off the water the steel stayed on the bottom. When he had recovered all the steel of the three bars he put it in the fire and set to work to make a scythe. When it was finished he got a calfskin and spread it out on a table and drew the scythe across it. Here and there the blade left a few hairs of down standing. The blacksmith's son broke it into fragments and began to make it all over again. When it was finished this time he spread out another calfskin for the scythe. This time again the blade left a few hairs standing. He broke it up a second time and began to make it yet again. When it was finished a third time he spread out a new calfskin; and unless you could make out from the look of it which side the flesh had been on, you couldn't tell the inside from the outside.

The commander came and asked if the scythe was finished. "Yes, it's done now," said the soldier, "but it hasn't been set on a handle yet. Send up whoever's going to be using it so that I can set it to suit him —the same set doesn't suit everyone."

The scyther came to the smith and the smith set the blade on a handle. And when that was done he said, "Off you go now with it, and if there was enough silver or gold in England to buy it, you could have it sold before you came back. But if you do sell that scythe, you'll sell your life along with it. Whatever you do—no matter what you're offered for it—don't dare sell it without first bringing it back to me!"

The man went off with the scythe and he and the English scyther began to mow side by side. That evening the commander and some high-up from the English group went to see which of the scythers was the better. The Englishman was still at the edge of the meadow, while the Scotsman was in the middle. The English gentleman strode across to where his man was.

"Are you only this far?" said he.

"I am," said the man, "but if you had brought me a scythe from Hell where that fellow got his, I'd be just as far on as he is."

"Is that where the scythe came from?" said the gentleman.

"That's the only place it could have come from," said the man. "A scythe like that couldn't be found on earth—it can carry on without rest or sharpening or anything else!"

"Ah, well, so we've lost the bet anyhow," said the gentleman. "But why don't you go over to the scyther and buy the scythe from him—it doesn't matter what he wants for it. You've lost the bet today, but you might win it another time."

The English scyther went to the Scotsman and began asking him to sell the scythe; but the Scotsman put the scythe on his shoulder and made straight for the smithy with it to see the smith. The Englishman followed him there and started asking the smith to sell it. The smith seized a hammer and chisel and broke the scythe into little bits.

"There you are!" he said. "No English son-of-a-bitch can say of this one that he won a bet with the work of a Gael's hands!"

So the Englishmen had to pay five hundred pounds on every bet they'd made and lost. That's how I heard it.

Black Patrick's Bowshot

Contributed by John MacInnes. Forthcoming in *Folktales of Scotland*.

Recorded in May 1953 from Duncan MacDonald (1883–1954), Peninerine, South Uist, Outer Hebrides, by the storyteller's son, Donald John. Duncan had heard the story from his own father, himself a noted storyteller in his day, fifty years before that.

This historical legend, a version of the William Tell story, is known in North and South Uist in slightly variant forms. For another South Uist version see Angus MacLellan and John Lorne Campbell, *Stories from South Uist* (London, 1961), pp. 78–81.

Black Patrick is said to have been a historical character.

The storyteller was first recorded in the 1930s by Donald MacDonald, the schoolmaster of Eriskay; later by K. C. Craig, Calum I. Maclean, and John L. Campbell. In the last year of his father's life, Donald John MacDonald recorded from him and transcribed over 1,500 pages of prose and verse.

Duncan MacDonald was one of the greatest tradition bearers of modern times in Gaelic Scotland. Writing about him in Gaelic, Calum Maclean describes his extraordinarily rich and varied repertoire, his deep interest in the form of a tale, his love of good style; and adds, "His Gaelic was the best, the most polished and eloquent, that I have ever heard. Everything he uttered he adorned."

(From *Aonghus agus Donnchadh* in the Gaelic quarterly *Gairm*, no. 10, pp. 170–74). F661.3 "Skillful marksman shoots apple from man's head" (William Tell).

See the discussion in Frances James Child, *The English and Scottish Popular Ballads* 3: 16–21 of similar legendary marksmen.

The Rent House Point is the name of the place at Loch Eynort where MacDonald of Clanranald had a rent house in which his tenants paid their yearly rent in grain. When rent day came, people would come from all parts with panniers of grain. Clanranald had a man in the rent house who measured the grain with a peck measure. Well, this year, when rent day came, who appeared but Black Patrick (Dark Servant of Saint Patrick) with two panniers of grain. The man in the rent house started to measure the grain, and the last peck was less than full. "Oh, you're short here," said the man, "You haven't got enough grain to fill it—and it ought to be full according to the rent you owe."

"Wait a minute," said Black Patrick, "it'll soon be full," at the same time grabbing the man by the back of the neck and drawing his dirk. He ran it across the man's throat and held his head above the peck till it was full of his blood. Then he got himself ready and went home.

Now, when Clanranald heard in Ormaclett what Black Patrick had done to his rent collector he was at a loss to know how he could get his revenge on him. He didn't like to fall out with him, because Black Patrick was a renowned bowman, and such a man was more than useful to him if ever enemies threatened to attack.

But what he did was this: he sent word to Black Patrick to come and visit him in Ormaclett and bring his son, Iain Dubh. He had a guest from the mainland there, he said, and he had a bet on with him that he had a bowman on his estate who could shoot an egg off the top of his own son's head, at such and such a distance, without doing the boy any injury.

Well, when the day came, Black Patrick got ready and he and his son left the Gearrachan, where he lived, and the two of them came to Ormaclett. You may be sure there were hands extended in friendship to them there; they were warmly greeted and given food and drink. Then they discussed what they had to do and went outside.

Black Patrick picked a place and made his son stand opposite him, while Clanranald and his lady, and their guest, stood on a threshing platform to get a good view. Black Patrick took an arrow from the quiver and stuck it under his garter on his right leg; then he took another arrow and stuck it under his garter on his left leg. They now placed the egg on his son's head.

"Come, my son," said Black Patrick, "turn your back to me."

"I don't need to, father," said his son; "if you harm me, it won't be your fault."

Then Black Patrick took the third arrow from the quiver. He fitted the arrow to the bow, took careful aim, and shot. The egg smashed into little bits!

"Very good!" said Clanranald. "I'm glad you did that in front of our guest from the mainland—I know he hasn't got anyone on his estate who could do the same. But will you tell me why you first of all stuck an arrow under each garter?"

"If I had done my son any injury," said Black Patrick, "you'd have had one of these through you, and your lady'd have the other!" "Oh, be off with you!" said Clanranald. "I can't do a thing with you!"

Black Patrick and Clanranald parted good friends then, and Black Patrick and his son went back home to the Gearrachan. No more attempts were made to make him pay for his murder of the man in the rent house at Loch Eynort.

England

Annie Luker's Ghost

From Katharine M. Briggs and Ruth L. Tongue, *Folktales of England* (Chicago: University of Chicago Press, 1965), pp. 62–63.

Recorded from Ruth L. Tongue, September 27, 1963, to whom the experience was told in 1963 in Somerset by the widow of the old man in the story, who more than hinted that her husband was a witch as well.

Relevant motifs are E401.1.2 "Footsteps of invisible ghost heard" (many references in E. W. Baughman, *A Type and Motif-Index of the Folktales of England and North America*) and E247 "Ghost kills man who had had ghost exorcised for too short a time," for which Baughman cites a 1904 reference from Northumberland. The belief that a ghost will come to fetch one of the living away is fairly widespread, but perhaps best known in the corpse-candle beliefs investigated by Richard Baxter and John Aubrey in the seventeenth century (see Baxter, *The Certainty of the World of Spirits*, London, 1691 and Aubrey, *Miscellanies upon Various Subjects*, 5th ed., London, 1890, pp. 165–67, "Corps-Candles in Wales"). The accusation of taking the form of a rabbit or hare is commonly leveled against witches in England (G211.2.7).

I know what you say about ghosts is quite true. We 'ad one to our cottage. Oh, yes! We come down to cottage arter it were empty, like, and I got Vicar to come and bless cottage. You see, it did belong to old Annie Luker, and she wasn't well liked. Everybody said she 'ad dark dealings; could turn 'erself into a rabbit. Well, arter she died, there weren't no one as 'ud go near. But my 'usband 'e was a clever man, bit too clever, if you ask me, 'e say, "We'll go to cottage." So us took it.

Folk in village didn't like it very much, and they come and say to me, "Does 'ee know 'twas Annie Luker's cottage?"

I says, "Yes, I'll get Vicar to come and bless it."

So we did, and we went there, me and my 'usband, and our daughter Mary. Well, us 'ad been there about three months, when all of a sudden, one night, I 'ears a girt bang. I sits up in bed, and I listens, and

53

someone come in! I could 'ear 'en downstairs. I nudges 'usband, see.

"Bob," I says, "wake up, will 'ee? What be it?"

Well, we sat up in bed, and then we could 'ear someone coming up-stairs—bump, bump, and kerflop, kerflop.

'Usband, 'e got proper cross, and 'e calls out, "Mary, what be 'ee about? Coming in this time o' night!"

Then us 'eard our Mary, from 'er bedroom next to ours, by the pas-sageway, and she say, "Dad, oh! Dad, I've been 'ome hours. Whatever is it?" And then 'er goes under blankets like I did.

My 'usband 'e listened, and then we 'eard 'en again, thump, thump, kerflop, kerflop coming along up the stairs toward our door, and all of a sudden, my 'usband—'oo nothing much worried 'im—'e say, "Oh! 'Tis old Annie Luker!" And 'e come under blankets too.

Well, sometimes she'd come and sometimes she 'ouldn't. Never see 'er, but 'ear 'er, yes. And then, my 'usband, 'e was took ill, and not long ago 'e died. 'Aven't 'eard Annie since. Folks say she knew what she wanted, and she come for 'im.

The Grey Goose Feathers

From Katharine M. Briggs and Ruth L. Tongue, *Folktales of England* (Chicago: University of Chicago Press, 1965), pp. 84–86.

Recorded from the now celebrated Fen narrator W. H. Barrett, 11 Oc-tober 1963. Mr. Barrett heard this tradition of the Cambridgeshire Fens from Chafer Legge in 1900. His written version, edited by Enid Porter, is in *Tales from the Fens* (London, 1963), pp. 148–49, and is close to the oral text. The grey goose feathers also enter into another unusual tradition in the same book, "French Prisoners in the Fens," pp. 73–84.

Identifiable motifs are M202.0.1 "Bargain or promise to be fulfilled at all hazards"; M205 "Breaking of promises or bargains"; and K1812 "King in disguise."

Thousands and thousands of years ago, the Fenmen, living in their desolate wastes, bonded themselves into a secret society. This society was called "The Brotherhood of the Grey Goose Feathers," and any-one who was initiated into that brotherhood, and possessed a grey goose feather, was sure that whenever they was in trouble or distress, help would immediately be given by the whole Fenmen. When King

Charles the First escaped from Oxford, he made his way into the up-lands of Norfolk, and stayed at a place called Stowe Hall, just outside of Downham Market.

And in passing, I may remark that I saw the chamber where, in case Cromwell's men came to look for him, he did hide. This chamber was aside of a great big chimney; it was hidden by old paneling.

Well, after Charles had consulted with his advisers, he decided to rejoin his troops just outside Oxford. The safest route in those days, for a fugitive, was through the desolate trackless Fens. There was one man, named Porter, who kept an inn at Southery. He used to guide travelers across the trackless waste. So he was sent for, and asked if he would take a very important personage to Huntingdon, and he said, "Yes, I will." So they brought the important personage to see what sort of a man the old Fenman was, and some of the King's advisers didn't think it was safe for him to go that long journey with only one man. But Porter said if that was what was worrying them, he would initiate the important personage into the Brotherhood of the Grey Goose Feathers. So they brought a feather, and Porter severed it down the center, and gave half to the important personage, and retained half himself. As he did so, he said, "Whilst fishes have scales, and birds have feathers, I will do all I can for you, and so will every other man who belongs to the Brotherhood of the Grey Goose Feathers."

Well, the King's advisers seemed quite satisfied to let Porter take him across the Fens alone. When they arrived at Saint Ives, they had to cross the river by a ford. Guarding this ford was two of Cromwell's soldiers. But when Porter produced the grey feather, they said, "Pass, all is well." They were Fenmen. So eventually King Charles arrived at the Bell Tavern, in Huntingdon, and he gave a reward to Porter for taking of him over, but he retained the grey goose feather. Some time afterwards, the king was taken prisoner, but before that happened, one of the officers in charge of the troops in Cromwell's army heard about how the sentry let them through, and he brought them along to Cromwell. But Cromwell was a Fenman too; so he said to that officer, "It is better for a king to escape than for the Fenmen to go back on a man who carries the split goose feather."

The Five-Pound Note

From Katharine M. Briggs and Ruth L. Tongue, *Folktales of England* (Chicago: University of Chicago Press, 1965), pp. 101–2.

Katharine M. Briggs heard this anecdote from a friend from London, Percy Robertson, in 1912 in Perthshire. Baughman assigns it motif N360 (a), on the basis of a newspaper story in the Indianapolis *Sunday Star*, 3 March 1946, "The $50 Bill," written by Frederick W. Gillett, *This Week Magazine*, pp. 3–4.

An elderly brother and sister lived together, and one day the sister wanted to go to town to do some shopping. So her brother gave her a five-pound note, and she set out. She traveled third class, and the only other passenger was a shabby old woman who sat opposite her and nodded. Miss M—— was sleepy too, after her early, hurried start, so she dozed a little too. Then she woke up, and thought it wasn't very safe to go to sleep in a railway carriage, alone with a stranger. She opened her bag to make some notes of what she had to buy, and the five ›ound note wasn't there. She looked at her neighbor, who was sleeping heavily with a big old shabby bag beside her. Miss M—— bent forward and, very cautiously, she opened the bag. There was a new five-pound note on top of everything.

"Old scoundrel!" thought Miss M——. Then she thought, "She's poor and old, and I oughtn't to have put temptation in her way." She wondered what she ought to do. It would cause a great deal of delay and bother to call the police, and it seemed cruel to get an old woman into trouble, but she must have her money. So, in the end, she quietly took the five pounds out of the bag, and shut it up again.

At the next stop, the old woman got out, and Miss M—— got to town and did her day's shopping, and came home loaded with parcels. Her brother met her at the station. "How did you manage?" he said, "I expected to find you up a gum tree. You left your five-pound note on the dressing-table."

France

Cinderella

From Geneviève Massignon, *Folktales of France* (Chicago: University of Chicago Press, 1968), pp. 147–49.

Recorded in the spring of 1961 from a seventy-three-year-old peasant woman, Mme Joly, at Saint-Maurice des Lions (Charente).

Type 510A *Cinderella*. This variant of type 510A, which is generally known in France by the name of *Cendrillon*, is of this area.

The motifs of the food-providing animal—in this case, the milking cow which the little girl strikes with a hazel wand as the Virgin Mary, her godmother, told her to—and of the magic tree that bends down to feed the disinherited girl, are considered by Paul Delarue characteristic of a related type which he calls type 511A, while he reserves the classification type 511B for another type, *Le Petit Taureau Rouge* (cf. his commentaries in *Contes du Nivernais et du Morvan* [Paris, 1953], p. 268). On the other hand, the ugly sister who trims down her foot in order to be able to slip on the shoe, and the animal which reveals the place where the pretty sister is hidden, are both typical of type 510A. The transformation of the two jealous women into stones flanking the staircase or into doorjambs is found in other folklore themes as the punishment for jealousy.

Once there was a widower who remarried, and the stepmother did not like the husband's daughter by his first wife. This stepmother had a daughter of her own.

As for the husband's daughter, the stepmother called her *la Cendrouliée* (Cinderella) because she was always to be found in the ashes in the hearth. Now the stepmother's daughter was called "Ram's balls" by everyone because she was so ugly.

The old woman and her daughter did not like the husband's daughter. The stepmother was always cross with Cinderella, and the other girl was no better to her.

One day the stepmother had said to her, "Go on off and look after the milking cow." Cinderella led the milking cow into the meadows to graze, but she had been given only dry bread to eat, so the Holy Virgin, who was this girl's godmother, gave her a hazel wand and said to her, "Give your milking cow a tap with this hazel wand, and she will give you something to eat." Then Cinderella took the hazel wand, tapped the cow's behind with it, and out fell bread and cheese.

From then on, Cinderella was well fed. The stepmother was very surprised. "How is it that Cinderella always has such a fresh complexion? All I give her is dry bread."

So then the stepmother's daughter watched to see what Cinderella did with the milking cow and then one day "Ram's balls" also took a wand to hit the milking cow, but the cow only presented her with a cowpat!

The Holy Virgin came along. So then what did the old hag and the girl do? They had the milking cow killed.

Poor Cinderella had no more bread and cheese. This time the Holy Virgin had an apple tree brought to Cinderella so that she could eat apples off it. The stepmother said once more, "How is it that Cinderella still has such a fresh complexion? She certainly hasn't any milking cow to give her food now."

So the stepmother's girl watched Cinderella once again. She saw her picking up apples. The apple tree would lower its branches to give her fruit, and then it would spring back up again. In this way the stepmother's girl could not get hold of these apples, and Cinderella went on having a lovely complexion. But the stepmother said, "You will not leave the house."

She gave her a mixture of millet seed and ash to sort out, but poor Cinderella had nothing to pull them out with. The old hag and her daughter went out for a walk, leaving her, by way of amusement, the ashes to sort out.

So the Holy Virgin brought her a hazel wand to sort out the ashes, and, quick as a flash, the millet seeds were separated from the ash. That evening the stepmother was more than surprised to see the ashes sorted out and the millet seed set aside.

Another time there was a ball in that part of the country. The old hag and her daughter went to it, but Cinderella looked after the house. She wished, however, that she could have gone, too.

So the Holy Virgin gave her a carriage drawn by two shining horses and a coachman to take her to the ball, and Cinderella had a beautiful dress and beautiful shoes. She climbed into the carriage and soon she went past the old hag and her daughter, who were on foot.

There was a Prince at this ball. When he saw this lovely girl, he wished to dance with her.

When the old hag and her daughter were still on their way home on foot, Cinderella had already reached the house in the carriage.

They told her, "If you only knew what a beautiful girl there was at the ball!"

"No fairer than Cinderella," said the girl.

Another time there was again a ball. Once more the Prince danced with the beautiful girl, but this time he wanted to know her name. So then Cinderella tried to run away, and one of her shoes slipped off her foot. The Prince was quick to pick it up while the beautiful girl was on her way home.

The next day the Prince said, "The girl who can slip this shoe on shall be my bride."

When the old hag and her daughter saw the Prince coming to their home, the woman said to her daughter, "Trim your foot, for heaven's sake! Then you will be able to slip the shoe on."

However, although "Ram's balls" tried hard to trim her foot, she could not slip on the shoe. Then the Prince noticed Cinderella, and he wanted to make her try it on. Well, the shoe was hers. She slipped it on at once.

When the stepmother saw that the Prince wished to marry Cinderella, she had her put in an attic, where she was locked up and no one could see her any more.

Now there was a little dog who started yapping because Cinderella was shut up in this attic.

The Prince followed the dog and let Cinderella out of the attic.

Then the hag and her daughter were turned into stones. There was one on each side of the stairway in that house.

And so Cinderella married the Prince.

The Scalded Wolf

From Geneviève Massignon, *Folktales of France* (Chicago: University of Chicago Press, 1968), pp. 205–7.

Recorded by Charles Joisten in 1958 from a thirty-seven-year-old farmer, Gaston Trépier, in Aillon-le-jeune, a mountain village of the department of Savoy.

The landmarks of this village—La Fraissette, the Replat, the Col des Prés, the Croix de Fornet—provide the setting for the story, which presents types 121 and 1875 as though they were the successive episodes of a true narrative.

Type 121 *Wolves Climb on Top of One Another to Tree* (motif
J2133.6), and type 1875 *The Boy on the Wolf's Tail.*

Aarne-Thompson does not mention any versions of type 121 in
France. However, Delarue cites a charming variant from French Lor-
raine in the journal *Arts et Traditions Populaires* (1, 1953, pp. 42–43).
The story Joisten recorded in Savoy also bears witness to the fact that
this theme, which is rather common in Nordic folklore and which is
also known in Spain (including Catalonia) is found in southeastern
France. Paul Delarue has written several commentaries on type 1875
(see his *Contes du Nivernais et du Morvan* [Paris, 1953], no. 21, p.
292; the *Contes de Gascogne* by Antonin Perbosc and Suzanne Cezerac
[Paris, 1954], no. 45, p. 289), for which 29 versions are listed in France;
and he has devoted a comprehensive study to it in the journal *Arts et
Traditions Populaires* (1, 1953, pp. 33–58), in which he remarks on
how often this theme is presented as an authentic adventure, especially
in literary adaptations, notably that of Mistral.

There was an old woodcutter who lived with his wife at La Fraissette.
Now his wife was called Jeannette. They were the only ones to live
there all the year round. They would spend the winter there.

One night they were going to have their soup. The woodcutter was
making up a basket. As it was hot, they had opened the door. Coming
back to the table to put down her pot, Jeannette let out an "Ah!" of
surprise as she stared through the half-open door. Her husband turned
round, and what did he see? There stood a wolf, a huge one. This wolf
was as big as a donkey. Jeannette was standing there with her tureen
in her hand. Her husband shouted at her, "Pour away, Jeannette!" So
then his wife tipped the pot over the wolf. The animal gave one howl
and fled into the depths of the forest. He was steaming all over. They
quickly closed the door, and that night they went without soup, but
they were only too happy to have rid themselves of the wolf.

Some time later, when it was fine, our woodcutter went off to the
forest. He went to the Replat to make a few faggots. His wife had
packed his game bag. He began making a faggot, and he did not notice
the time going by. Dusk came and he found he had strayed a bit in the
forest. It took him quite a while to find his game bag. Well, by the
time he had finished roaming around looking everywhere, night had
fallen and he could hear the howling of the wolves. He set off for home
as fast as he could, but the howling began again and he climbed up a
fir tree. Now what did he see coming out from a corner of the clearing?
There was a huge wolf. It was their wolf, the scalded one! The woodcutter recognized him. His coat had not yet grown back. The wolf
stopped at the foot of the tree. He sniffed the air and he, too, recognized the woodcutter, and with his wolf's brain he worked out: "This

is it. This time I have him." He let out a terrifying howl and called his brothers. A few seconds later the whole pack arrived. There were ten, fifteen, twenty. There was a whole pack! They formed a circle round the tree. Then at a given moment the wolves stood aside and held a meeting. After a minute or two they came back to the foot of the tree. The scalded one placed himself at the foot of the tree, and the wolves made themselves into a ladder. One climbed up, then another, then a third, and a fourth. The woodcutter, who could see them coming, climbed higher, too. In this way they reached the top of the fir tree. Our poor woodcutter felt that he was caught, and he saw the wolf climbing and climbing and knew that he could be reached. Then the woodcutter shouted, "Pour away, Jeannette!" The scalded one, remembering the words referring to the tureen of boiling soup, took off at once, but it was he who was holding up the column of wolves, and so down they all came. They fell at the foot of the fir tree and, limping as they went, they ran back to the depths of the forest. The woodcutter went home.

Soon it was Christmas, and there was a little snow. One day Jeannette said to her husband, "Next week it will be Christmas. We must go down to Chambéry to buy some food. You'll take the small sledge to cross the Col des Prés, and you'll put a small barrel on the sledge."

She gave him a snack and a little wine, and the woodcutter left, drawing his barrel along on the little sled. He went by the Col des Prés and went down the other side. When he reached the Croix de Fornet, he met half a dozen brigands, who asked for his money. Afterward they said, "What are we going to do with this man?"

The leader said, "We've only to bring him down and throw him into the ravine." But one of the younger brigands said, "After all he is an old man. We are thieves, not murderers. We must let him live."

Then the leader said, "We've only got to put him in his barrel and then we'll run away."

They took out the bottom of the barrel and put the woodcutter into it. They put back the bottom and the bands, and then they left it. The leader sent the barrel rolling down into the ravine.

The barrel came to a halt against a bush, and our woodcutter came to. He wondered how he was going to get out of the barrel. He tried calling through the bunghole, but no one answered. Night fell. He felt cold, but luckily he had his little bottle of wine to keep him going. The night was followed by another day spent in the same manner. A second night fell. Our woodcutter felt all was lost. He said to himself, "This time this is the end."

There was a moon, and the cold was even more intense. Now, in the middle of the night he heard a noise. He glanced through the hole, and what did he see? The scalded one!

The scalded one came up to the barrel and sniffed at it, and then he began to scratch around it a little, growling. In the end he went right round it. Now at one point the wolf stopped, and the woodcutter saw the wolf's tail swinging in front of the hole. He put his hand through the hole and grabbed the end of the tail and pulled it in. Then he shouted, "Pour away, Jeannette! Pour away!" Our wolf at once imagined the kettle of boiling soup hanging overhead. He set off as fast as he could, dragging the barrel and the woodcutter after him. He climbed up the ravine in this fashion, and helter-skelter they went over the Col des Prés again. Then he reached the chalets of La Fraissette.

When the woodcutter saw the smoke from the chimney of his house, he let go of the wolf's tail and came to a halt in front of his home. He called his wife, "Jeannette! Jeannette!" Jeannette came up to the barrel. She saw that it was her husband shut up in there and she set him free.

The scalded one was never seen again.

Spain

The Unbeliever and the Skull

Selected and translated by Merle E. Simmons from Aurelio M. Espinosa, *Cuentos populares españoles*, 3 vols. (Madrid: Consejo Superior de Investigaciones Scientificas, Instituto "Antonio de Nebrija" de Filologia, 1946–47), 1, no. 79, pp. 140–41.

This religious legend has been known in Spanish literature since Tirso de Molina as the legend of Don Juan in his celebrated play, *El burlador de Sevilla o el convidado de piedra* ("The Deceiver of Seville or the Guest of Stone"). In earlier versions the unbeliever, who was also a seducer and renegade, was condemned and not, as in the present text, saved by relics. Dorothy Epplen Mackay has made the fullest investigation of "The Double Invitation in the Legend of Don Juan" (Stanford University dissertation, 1943). The key elements are the blasphemous man, the offended skull, the double invitations, and the death or condemnation of the protagonist.

Motifs are: D1719.6 "Magic power of holy cross"; V140 "Sacred relics"; V254.1 "Saying of 'Aves' obliterates sin"; V222.1.4 "Lights show where the body of saint is buried."

From Damiel, Cuidad Real.

A man who was an unbeliever was passing once by a cemetery and he saw a skull and he kicked it and said, "Tonight you will come to eat at my house."

And then he went home.

At midnight that night there is a knocking at his door. And his servant goes out to see who is knocking and he comes back and says to his master, "Oh, sir, there is someone from the other world, a skeleton, nothing but bones."

And the man remembered and he says, "Tell him to come in."

And he comes in and says to him, "Well sir, you invited me yesterday and I have come."

And he stayed there having dinner with him, and then he says, "Tomorrow you will come to eat at my house. You already know where it is; yesterday you passed by there."

Then they said good-bye.

And the next day the man confessed and he told the priest "The night before last I went to the cemetery and I saw a skull and I gave it a kick and I invited it to have dinner with me and last night it was at my house to eat with me and it has invited me to eat tonight at its house, which is in the cemetery, and I don't want to go alone."

And then the priest gave him a cross and some relics and said to him, "Put on this cross and those relics and go. And when you get to the place where the cemetery is say 'Hail, Purest Mary!' three times, and the gates of the cemetery will open and there you will see the dinner. Pretend that you are eating but don't eat anything."

And the man left and he went up to the gate of the cemetery and said three times, "Hail, Purest Mary!"

And immediately the gates of the cemetery opened and a voice said to him, "Come in."

And he answered, "I can't. I can't."

And then the skeleton itself came out and said to him, "God be with you!"

And showing him the knife he said to him, "If it weren't for that cross and those relics you would have met your end here. Do you believe in God and the Virgin?"

And the man answered, "Yes."

"Well, go on your way," the skeleton answered him.

And the man left and became a hermit in a cave and lived on herbs there for many years. And one day the bells were ringing in a town and the people asked, "What is it? What is it?"

And they went to see and found the old man dead in the cave, and they found that he had died as a saint, and there was light all around in the cave.

Santa Catalina

Selected and translated by Merle E. Simmons from Aurelio M. Espinosa, *Cuentos populares españoles*, 3 vols. (Madrid: Consejo Superior de Investigaciones Scientíficas, Instituto "Antonio de Nebrija" de Filología, 1946–47), 1, no. 78, pp. 138–39.

This saint's legend is well known in modern tradition and has been classified as type 804 *Peter's Mother Falls from Heaven*. Bolte and

Polívka have gathered a copious bibliography of versions from all parts of Europe. The present text uses the mother of Santa Catalina rather than the mother of Saint Peter as the protagonist, perhaps because of confusion with the traditional Spanish ballads that treat the martyrdom of Santa Catalina.

From Jaraiz de la Vera, Caceres.

Santa Catalina as a child was a saint, and the Lord and the Virgin loved her very much. But Santa Catalina's mother was a real sinner, and her sin was that she was a gossip. She always said bad things about people and she slandered everybody.

And Santa Catalina died before her mother did and she went to heaven in all her glory. And there in heaven she was praying all the time that her mother would also become a saint like her. But the mother stayed as bad as ever. And when her mother died Santa Catalina went to beg the Blessed Lord and the Holy Virgin to take her mother with them into heaven. And Santa Catalina's mother arrived and told the Lord to weigh her sins and the good that she had done in the world. And the scales came down to the ground on the side of the sins. And Saint Peter said that the mother had to go to hell.

And then Santa Catalina went to beg the Holy Virgin to let her mother come into heaven. And the Virgin told her to go see the Lord. And Santa Catalina went to see the Lord, and the Lord told her that whatever the Virgin said was all right. And Santa Catalina went again to see the Virgin and told her that the Lord had said to do whatever she said. And then the Virgin told the saint, "What do you think is best, for you to go to hell with your mother or for her to stay here?"

And the saint told her, "Whatever the Holy Virgin decides."

And then the Virgin went to see the Lord and begged him to let the saint's mother get out of hell and enter heaven. And the Lord said that whatever the Virgin wanted was all right. But the Lord said that when she left hell to enter heaven all the souls that could hang onto her should also get out and enter heaven.

And the angels then went to hell to bring back Santa Catalina's mother along with all the souls that could hang onto her as she came out. And she was about to leave and many souls grabbed hold all around her.

And she when she saw them hanging on yelled at them angrily, "Get away! Get away! If you want to go up to heaven have a daughter who is a saint like the one I had."

And because of that the Lord punished her and refused to receive her into heaven and the angels left her in hell.

And Santa Catalina then went again to beg the Virgin and the Lord to take her mother out of hell. And the Lord told her, "Your mother is to blame for being condemned and she doesn't repent. Do you want to go to hell with her if she can't come into heaven?"

And Santa Catalina said that she wanted to go be with her mother. And Santa Catalina went to hell with her mother.

The Mass of Saint Joseph

Selected and translated by Merle E. Simmons from Aurelio M. Espinosa, *Cuentos populares españoles*, 3 vols. (Madrid: Consejo Superior de Investigaciones Scientíficas, Instituto "Antonio de Nebrija" de Filología, 1946–47), 1, no. 74, pp. 135–36.

Although this saint's legend seems rare in Hispanic and European tradition, it contains recurrent religious motifs: M414.3 "Saint cursed"; N848 "Saint as helper"; V223 "Saints have miraculous knowledge" and especially J225.0.1 "Angel and hermit" (type 759 *God's Justice Vindicated*), in which the angel explains why he does many seemingly unjust things.

From Villanueva del Campillo, Avila.

There was once a widower who had three sons. And he had the custom of paying for a Mass to Saint Joseph every year on his day. And when his three sons were grown and many years had passed since the mother had died, the oldest son died right on the afternoon of Saint Joseph's day. And the poor father was very displeased with Saint Joseph and for several days he was so sad and so grieved that he didn't remember any more to pray to Saint Joseph.

But when Saint Joseph's day came again he remembered the custom that he had of saying Mass on his day and he went to see the priest and he paid him for the Mass for Saint Joseph. And that same afternoon the second of his three sons died. With that the poor father was in despair and he was so disgusted with Saint Joseph that he refused to say any more masses for him.

And once again the day of Saint Joseph came and he didn't pay for his Mass. He was praying to all the saints in heaven except Saint Joseph. And since he saw that his youngest son had not died on Saint Joseph's day he no longer remembered Saint Joseph for anything.

So one night when he was praying in his room Saint Joseph appeared to him and said, "I have taken your two older sons away from you because they were going to dishonor you and were going to condemn themselves."

And he told him to look through the window. And the man looked through the window and saw his two sons, now full-grown men, hanging from a tree. And he told him then to look through another window and the man looked and saw his two sons burning in hell. And Saint Joseph then told him, "That's what was going to happen to your sons, and that's why I have taken them away from you. And I leave the youngest one for you because he is going to be a saint and an archbishop."

And then Saint Joseph disappeared. And the poor father now saw that Saint Joseph had done him a favor instead of harm and he again said Mass to Saint Joseph every year until he died. And his youngest son studied to be a priest and he became a bishop and then an archbishop and he died a saint.

Italy

Bertoldino

Collected and translated by Carla Bianco in Palombara, Lazio, Italy, in 1968 from an illiterate farmer, Mariucca Rossi, age sixty-two.

This is type 675 *The Lazy Boy*, one of the Grimms' *Household Tales*, collected throughout Europe, most frequently in Finland, and reported in the New World in the French and Spanish traditions and among West Indies Negroes and American Indians. This text contains the distinctive motifs of the tale type such as D1523.1 "Self-propelling wagon"; T513 "Conception from wish"; S141 "Exposure in boat"; D1131.1 "Castle produced by magic"; and L175 "Lowly successful hero invites and humbles king."

The rollicking style of the narrator enlivens this Märchen.

They used to call him Bertoldo, that is, Bertoldino. They say that this guy used to go picking wood, he was a wood gatherer. He was a plain-looking fellow, see? A simple soul, and he used to go for wood. One day he was carrying a big bundle of dry wood—but he wasn't really carrying it, he was actually riding on that bundle, like a horse, see? And you know why? Because he had met a fairy one day and, as he had been very nice to that fairy, she had given him a magic gift in return for his kindness. The gift was a magic sword, a big sword, and the fairy had said to him, "Whenever you need something, Bertoldo, just order this sword and you will have anything you want. Whatever you will mention will come true." So this poor guy thought, "Well, what can I ask for? Let's see: that this heavy bundle of wood may walk by itself and carry me on it!" That's what Bertoldino said, and soon the wood was walking and he was riding on it!

Now, it happened that he had to pass under the windows of the King's palace every day and every day he used to see the young Princess at her window and she was very sad, very—like when you don't smile and feel unhappy, see? She was unhappy and she never smiled. Now, Bertoldo was passing under her window this day, too, but now he was riding that funny thing of wood, see? And you should have seen how the King's daughter laughed when she saw him. The minute she spotted him from up there, she started laughing and laughing and pointing at him, like this, see? But Bertoldo didn't like that at all, he was offended and cried back at her, "What're you laughing about? What's the matter with you? You fool!" And, boy, he was angry! He shouted at her "That you may be pregnant now, with this thumb of mine!" and he made this gesture at her, see? With his thumb like this? And he said that and, of course, we know that he had that magic sword, see? Anything he asked was going to happen, just as he said it, see? And so, that's what happened: she was pregnant, at once!

And her father, the King, when he found out that, he started wondering, "But how could it be? How could this daughter of mine do this to me? Who is the father? Who was it?" Nothing, this was impossible to find out, it was impossible to find out who the father was. She kept on saying, "I don't know it, I don't know it." And the father said, "That's because you don't want to tell me! And now I'll show you what I'll do!" And so, one day the Princess delivered a pretty baby with a golden straw in his hands! See, this is things of magic, things of fairies, see? Well, so he had this golden straw in his hands, and there were words written on it, and the words said, "He to whom the baby will give this straw is his father." That was going to be the father, this is how they would know, see? Well, the poor King had nothing else to do but to give a huge banquet and invite all the Princes on earth, but not just the Princes, he had to invite all the men in his kingdom, too. And so all men in this kingdom went into this palace and they ate and drank and there was so plenty of all. And they say that all those young Princes who went there were hoping to be the father; each one said, "Who knows if I am not the father?" The poor men, especially, hoped to be the father, see?

And then, here come this Bertoldo with a jacket which was all torn, a pair of old pants, and a pair of dirty shoes, and he was ugly and looked more like an animal than a man, really! "Get out of here!" these men shouted, "they hardly want us and you have the arrogance to come here? As ugly as you are! Get out! Get out!" But Bertoldo didn't listen, he shouted back, he said, "Let me pass! Give me room, call the King for me!" Well, the others thought he was a madman and they all laughed; but they let him pass and so he came in and he was told to go to the King and the Princess. They said, "Go, go there, you'll see for yourself, you poor fool!" He went there and then everybody saw that the little baby, the little creature that is, just gave him the golden straw, he gave the straw to Bertoldino, see?

Well, the King almost fainted and fell to the ground. He said, "But with these many men and Princes, we had to bump into this beggar, this piece of garbage? What a disgrace! And you (to his daughter), you ungrateful dirty rascal!" And he insulted her, and you can't imagine what went on there, the words they said, the shouting, the confusion of everybody! But there was nothing to do and they had to realize that Bertoldino was the Princess's lover. And so the King ordered his servants to make a chest and to put them in it and to throw the chest into the sea: "Throw them away, in the sea!"

Well, now this girl, you know, she had the baby and she took some dry figs with her for the baby, you know, in those days we used to love them. They were sweet. We still eat them now, but not like before. Well, the Princess gave them to the baby, one by one, and the baby just sucked them because they were sweet, and this way he didn't die. And so, the chest was thrown into the sea and the chest went floating, so they didn't drown, because the chest was floating, see? And they floated. . . . Then, she started asking Bertoldo, this poor girl asked, "But, tell me, where did I ever see you before? Did I ever see you before? How come I am with you now in this disgrace? When did I ever see you before?" And he didn't want to answer, he said, "Shut up, shut up!" "But you won't tell me that you are the father of this creature of mine!"

And finally, Bertoldo said, "What will you give me if I tell you?" "What can I give you? I can give you a dry fig, what else do I have here in this chest with you?" "Well, all right, give me this fig." And he ate that fig, because, of course, he was hungry by now, they didn't have anything there, see? Then he said, "Do you remember that day, when I was passing by with the bundle of wood and you laughed at me?" She said, "Yes, so what?" He said, "Well, what did I tell you then?" "Why, what did you tell me then?" Bertoldo said, "I said, 'that you may become pregnant with this thumb of mine!' and you became pregnant! That's what happened!" The poor girl said, "My God! But is it that whatever you say comes true?" "Sure!" he said, "whatever I say comes true!"

Then the girl said, "Well, then, why don't you say that we are rescued from the sea?" Bertoldo said, "And what will you give me if I say that?" "Well," she said, "I can give you another fig, that's all I have here!" And Bertoldo sucked and ate that fig and then he said, "That we may come out of the ocean!" And they saw that the chest came out of the water and landed on the shore. "Now, why don't you say that the chest may open?" "And what will you give me?" The girl gave him another fig and she didn't give him all the figs at once, see? Because she was afraid he would not do anything else, see? Then Bertoldino ate this other fig and then said, "That this chest may open!" and the chest was open and they came out of there, and she was happy to see light again! And then she said, "Now, why don't you say that you want to have a palace in front of my father's palace? And more beautiful than that one? I give you another fig." And so, Bertoldo ate another fig and he asked for another palace, he said, "That we may have a palace, just in front of the royal palace, and be it much more beautiful than that!" And, my dear! in the morning, when the King got up, he saw that fantastic palace there, and he said, "Boy! Whose palace is that now? Whose is it?" And he sent his servants to look at it from outside, and all around, but they could not find out anything.

Meanwhile, his daughter was inside that palace, see? And she said to Bertoldo, "Now, why don't you say that you want to become a *Signore*, a lord, the most handsome man in the world, full of money and education and intelligence?" Bertoldo was not sure of that, but he said, "What can you give me if I do this?" She said, "Listen, I've got only one more fig and once this is gone, I won't have any more figs. So, take it." And then Bertoldo said all that she wanted and he added, "And I want to remain like that forever." And you should have seen! He got so handsome: he was the seven beauties of the world! Honestly! And she was happy to look at him like that, she said, "Oh, now it's better, this will do!" And so, he went into his study in the palace, he had a writing desk there and everything there was fine and complete and there was everything under the sun in those rooms, a real splendor! And he sat and he wrote things and he read other things, because he was educated now and he liked to read and write, see?

The next day, the King sent his guards all dressed up in high uniforms to knock at this new palace, and Bertoldo sent his servants to open the doors, which were gold and silver. And the guards said that the King had sent them because he wanted to get acquainted and see who were these new neighbors. And so, Bertoldo said, "Yes, let him come in, let the King come in." And then, of course, once the King came to their house, he recognized his own daughter and he fell on his knees, he wanted to be forgiven for sending her away and all that terrible story, see? And he had to excuse himself with this beautiful Prince who was Bertoldino now and so, after all those excuses, they decided to forgive the old King and they invited everybody to a fantastic banquet, with hundreds of tables and chairs and candles.

I was hidden under the table and every once in a while I could get some pieces of cake, and it was so good that I still remember the taste now! Well, I guess that's all for Bertoldino.

The Tale of Sister Cat

Collected and translated by Carla Bianco in Rossano Calabro, Calabria, Italy, in 1962 from an illiterate farmer, Concetta Aloi, age fifty-nine.

This is type 2023 *Little Ant Finds a Penny, Buys New Clothes With It, and Sits in Her Doorway*, a cumulative tale with animal actors involving a death. It has been reported in Italian, French, Spanish, and Turkish traditions.

There was a cat who wanted to get married and so, one day, she bought herself some makeup that was red and white and she painted her face with that. Then she went to the window and waited there to see if she could find herself a groom. After a while, a huge number of cows went by and they said to her, "What's the matter, cat? What are you doing up there at the window?" "Well," she said, "don't you know? I'm going to get married, I am going to find a husband." So, one of the cows said, "Would you like me for a husband?" And the cat said, "First, I want to hear your voice." And the cow went like this, "Moooh! Moooh!" And the cat was scared and she shouted, "Get out! Stay away from me! Your voice is terrible!"

And she waited at the window and after another while there passed a number of goats and one of them said, "Hello, sister cat, what are you doing at the window?" "Don't you know? I am going to get married and I am looking for a husband." "Oh, and would you like me for a husband?" The cat said, "First, I want to hear your voice." The goat went like this, "Mbeeeah! Mbeeah!" and the cat said, "Oh, no, no! You scared me. Go away from here."

After another while there passed a group of rats and one of them said to her, "Hello, sister cat, what are you doing up there at the window?" "Well, don't you know? I am a pretty girl and I am going to get married. I'm looking for a husband." And the rat said, "So, how would you like to have me for a husband?" "First, let me hear your voice." The rat went like this, "Aoo, zoo, zoo!" And the cat said, "Your voice scared me, I don't like it. Go away from me!"

And she waited another while until a group of little mice went by and the smallest one said to her, "Hello, sister cat, what are you doing up there at the window?" "Why, don't you know? I am a pretty girl and I am going to get married. I'm looking for a husband." The little mouse said, "How would you like to take me for a husband?" "First let me hear your voice," said the cat. The little mouse went like this, "Teeetee, teetee, teetee!" And the cat said, "Come upstairs, 'cause you suit me well, come upstairs, for you suit me well!"

So he goes upstairs and they eat and all goes well and all that and then, next morning, the cat says, "Look after the soup, while I am gone to Mass!" And she went to Mass. The mouse, at home, went to look at the pot and went so close to it that he fell into it and died. Now, when the cat came back home after Mass, he was all cooked up, and she didn't know it. She started calling for him, "Brother mouse! Brother mouse!" and she looked under the table and he wasn't there, and she looked behind the door and he wasn't there, and she looked under the bed and he wasn't there! And finally she went to look into the pot and found the mouse well cooked there!

She took him out and started crying, "Poor brother mouse, poor brother mouse!" And the window answered back, "Why do you cry, sister cat?" "I cry because brother mouse is dead!" And the window started mourning and rattling loud.

Then the door heard this and asked, "Window, why do you mourn?" "Don't you know? Brother mouse is dead and the cat is crying and since I am a window, I rattle for mourning." And the door said, "And since I am a door, I'll open and close all the time for mourning."

Then a tree heard and said, "Door, oh, door, why do you mourn?" And the door said, "Don't you know? Brother mouse is dead, the cat is crying, the window is rattling, and since I am a door I close and open all the time." And the tree said, "And since I am a tree I shake off my leaves for mourning."

Then a dog went by and said, "Tree, why are you shaking off your leaves?" The tree said, "Because brother mouse is dead, the cat is crying, the window is rattling, the door is closing and opening, and since I am a tree I shake off all my leaves." "And, since I am a dog, I keep on running."

There was a fountain there and the fountain asked the dog, "Dog, why are you running so?" The dog said to her, "Oh, don't you know? Brother mouse is dead, the cat is crying, the window is rattling, the door is opening and closing, the tree is shaking off all its leaves, and since I am a dog I keep on running." And then the fountain said, "And since I am a fountain, I won't give any water."

The servant of the King was passing by with her bucket and asked the fountain, "Fountain, why don't you have any water?" "Oh," the fountain said, "don't you know? Brother mouse is dead, the cat is crying, the window is rattling, the door is opening and closing, the tree is shaking off its leaves, the dog is running, and since I am the fountain I don't give any water." And the servant said, "And, since I am the servant, I'll break my bucket." Then, the servant went to the Queen without water and bucket, and the Queen asked, "Why did you break the bucket?" "Well," the servant said, "don't you know? Brother mouse is dead, the cat . . . and, since I am the servant, I broke my bucket."

Then the Queen said, "And, since I am the Queen, I'll throw myself on the flour bag." So, in came the King and said, "Why, my Queen, are you on the flour bag?" The Queen said, "Don't you know? Brother mouse is dead, the cat is crying . . . and, since I am the Queen, I threw myself on the flour bag."

"Very well," said the King, "and since I am the King, I'll throw myself on the Queen!" And this is why all Psalms end up in Gloria!

The Dove and the Fox

Collected and translated by Carla Bianco in 1966 in Roseto Valfortore from Mrs. Lucia Sbrocchi, age fifty-five, an illiterate farmwife. Emigrants from this community founded Roseto, Pennsylvania.

The first half of this tale is type 9 *The Unjust Partner*, in which one animal of two farming together does all the work in the field while the other makes excuses and then cheats on the crop division. Kaarle Krohn, the famous Finnish folklorist, wrote a monograph on this tale type, *Bär (Wolf) und Fuchs* (Helsingfors: Druckerei der Finnischen Litteratur-Gesellschaft, 1888), and 183 versions have been collected in Finland. The second half deals with tasks of the sort ordinarily found in Märchen rather than animal tales such as type 571 *Making the Princess Laugh*.

Once there was a dove and a fox. This fox said to the dove one day, "Shall we become godmothers?" And so they did become godmothers. One day the fox went to see his godmother dove. He said, "You know? I wish we could cultivate some land together! Why don't we?" "And why not?" said the dove, "let's do it." And so they found a piece of land and decided that they would work it together.

Now the day came that they had to go and sow the field with wheat, see? And the dove went by the fox and said, "Well, godmother, tomorrow morning we must sow the field, will you come with me?" "Oh, sure I will! Tomorrow morning I will come." But the next day the dove went by the fox and started yelling to wake him up. She said, "Godmother Fox! Hei! Godmother Fox!" She was yelling by the door, see? She had to call a lot of times, she had to shout a lot. Finally, the fox was up and came to the window. He said, "What's the matter, Godmother Dove? What is it?" "Why," said the dove, "I've been here for ages! I've been knocking and calling you; you surely sleep hard!" And the fox, you know? He said, "Well, godmother, don't you know? I had such a high fever! The fever was so high that I couldn't hear anything, see? Now, how can I come with you out in the fields? With this fever? How can I? You go! Let's decide that you'll go sowing and the next job will be mine, all right?" This poor dove was good, see? She said, "All right, I'll do that."

And she went to work in the field. She went sowing all day on their field, see? And, little by little, she had to do all the sowing. Then, a few months later, the wheat was growing nicely in their field, but it needed some cleaning. Because the wheat was all right, but, you know, there were weeds and other things that had to be taken out, see? This had to be done. And so the dove went to see the fox because this job had to be done.

The fox said, "Yes, of course! I'll go there on Saturday. This coming Saturday I'll go," and the dove was happy, see? She believed the fox! When Saturday came, the dove saw that the fox was not going to the field. It was late, and the godmother had not showed up yet. So she had to hurry there and call the fox from down street. She called, "Godmother! Godmother Fox! Aren't you going to the field. Aren't you going to do that job?" But the fox, he said, "Oh, poor me! Godmother Dove, don't you know? I have such a bellyache today! But such a strong bellyache I don't know how I stay alive! You go do this little job now, and I promise that I'll do all the harvesting. I'll reap the field all alone, you'll see."

And the poor dove, what could she do? She went to work for several days all by herself, and she cleaned up the whole field from those ugly weeds and stones, see? And then the field looked really nice and clean. Then June came, and the wheat was tall and blond and it had to be cut, see? The field had to be reaped, and the dove went to see the fox, she said, "Godmother Fox." "What?" said the fox. "But, you know, we must go reap the wheat. Thursday we must go!" "But sure! Thursday I'll go." And, of course, Thursday came and the dove went to see the fox, she said, "Godmother Fox, hurry! Hurry up, it's Thursday, and we must go to the field today! Hurry up." But, you know, the fox said, "Oh, dear! If you only knew what a pain I have here in my legs! My legs feel like broken, I don't see how I can go to the field today. I'm afraid you must go this time." And the poor dove said, "All right," and she went to the field and cut all the wheat and tied it up nicely in bunches and put them all in rows there and the field looked so beautiful, you know?

After all that work the dove was exhausted and she went to the fox, she said, "Godmother Fox, now you should go there to carry the wheat home, 'cause if it rains on it, we lose all our wheat there! Will you go now?" "Oh, sure!" the fox said, "When do you want me to go?" And the dove said, "Well, you can go on Monday." But then, when Monday came, the fox wasn't going. The dove had to go there and carry all the wheat by herself. What a heavy job for a little dove! But the dove thought that the fox would help with the weighing of the wheat and so she carried all the wheat home. But the day came and the dove went by the fox, she called, "Hello! Ha! Godmother Fox! Well, now it's the time to weigh the wheat. Won't you do this job, now?" But the fox said, "Oh! I wish I could go! But, look, I broke my arm yesterday while I was running after a chicken, see? Oh, it aches!" And so, he promised he would go help when they had to divide the wheat, see? So, the poor dove had to weigh all that wheat and she had done such a beautiful job; she had weighed the wheat and she had put all the grain on one side and the straw on the other see? A nice job. All it was needed now was to divide the crop so that each would have his part, see?

So the dove went to the fox. She said, "Well, Godmother Fox, the wheat is ready, won't you come and help me with the division now?" "What? What division? I've already divided the wheat. You get the straw and I get the grain!" See? See what the fox said to the dove? And the poor dove started crying. She was desperate and she cried, "Poor me! After all this work, Godmother Fox is going to take all the grain and I'll be left with the straw! Poor me! What shall I do now?" And she went away across the fields, crying like that, see?

At a certain point, she met the wolf, and the wolf asked why she went crying like that. So, the dove said to the wolf, she said, "Oh, Godfather Wolf, don't you know? I've done all the work, all the jobs there were in the field to be done, since we had an agreement with Godmother Fox. Now that we had to divide the crop, you know what he decided? I get the straw and he gets the grain!" Then the wolf said, "If you can make me laugh hard, if you help me get clean—'cause he was full of burrs all over his fur—and if you make me eat a lot of macaroni, I'll fix this problem for you." And the dove thought this was a good proposal, see?

And so she told the wolf to go to Mass that Sunday and to watch the Mass, and wolf went. The dove, meanwhile, she went to dance off the priest's head, see? To pick on his head, to tickle him right here on the tonsure, see? And the priest tried to send her away, but she continued and he had to say Mass and had to stand that torture and, so, the wolf had a good time and laughed heartily, see? So, that was one thing the dove could do for him, right?

Then, she told the wolf to go after her in the road. And the dove was flying and the wolf followed her on the road. At a certain point they met a mule that was carrying two leather bags full of oil: one for each side, see? The oil poured out from the holes that the dove made in the bags, and the wolf rolled himself around in that oil until he was all soaked and finally he was as clean as new, see? Shining, his hair was shining and clean now. This was the second thing the dove did for the wolf, see?

Now, the third was the macaroni, right? Well, there was a poor woman who had her children out in the country. Now, she went to the village to cook for them, see? And she cooked a lot of fresh macaroni, with lots of tomatoes and cheese, see? Then, she put the pot inside a basket and started walking on the road, back to the country where her children were waiting, see? Now the dove went close to the woman, so close, that the woman started saying "Oh, what a nice dove! I can take it to my children, I'll try to catch her." And, you know what she did? She put the basket down on the road and went after the dove. Because the dove didn't fly far, see? On purpose, she didn't. She stayed close, so that the woman thought she could catch her, see? But, of course, the wolf was eating up all the macaroni from the basket, right? He ate them all! And the poor woman had to go back home and cook more macaroni for the kids!

Now the wolf was happy that he had received the three favors and he went to see the fox, as he had promised the dove, right? He went there and he said to the fox, "Listen, if you don't give the dove her grain, all the grain, I'm going to eat you up in a minute!" And so, the fox had no choice now, because the wolf was too strong for him, see? He had to give the dove all the wheat, and the dove used the straw for the nest and the grain for food throughout the winter. See how smart the fox was? But the wolf was strong, and for this time the fox had to give in, see?

Switzerland

Summoned into the Valley of Josaphat

Contributed by Robert Wildhaber. Forthcoming in *Folktales of Switzerland*.

Collected by Josef Müller, in the period 1910 to 1925, from three women and one man, then seventy-five, in the canton Uri. Müller, a priest, was curator in the cantonal hospital of Altdorf in the canton Uri. He had to take care of all the old and poor people in the hospital, and he asked them to tell him all the legends they knew. These he wrote down directly after hearing them, partly in dialect and partly in German. His collection of legends of a small Alpine canton is unique; it covers all the villages and small valleys of the canton, because all the inhabitants came to this hospital when they were ill. The canton in those times was almost 100 percent Catholic.

Printed in Josef Müller, *Sagen aus Uri*, 3 volumes, edited by Hanns Bächtold-Stäubli and Robert Wildhaber as *Schriften der Schweizerischen Gesselschaft für Volkskunde* (Basel, 1926, 1929, 1945, with index), 1 (1926), pp. 62–65, no. 93, versions *a* and *c*. Translated by Agnes Freudenberg Hostettler.

This legend has its foundation in old conceptions of right and wrong. When somebody was fully convinced that injustice had been rendered to him by an earthly jury and verdict, he summoned his adversary to appear at God's trial in the Valley of Josaphat. Everybody was much afraid of this summoning, which was even severely punished by the authorities. In the canton Wallis we hear of it for the first time in 1567. It was well known in the Catholic Alpine cantons Uri, Wallis, Lucerne, Zug, Saint Gallen, and Appenzell. Petzoldt (see below) gives an example from German settlers in Hajos, Hungary. As a rule, somebody was summoned to appear and answer for his doings or sayings within three days or within a year and a day. He died within this term if he could not find help from a godchild who died immediately after being baptized without eating any earthly food; these children are called *Westerkinder* or *Wesperchinder*. Our legend sometimes is connected with the motif of the *Westerkinder*; in other cases a hanged man on the gallows is jeered at and calls for vindication in the Valley of Josaphat. The first part of version *a* has the motif of a man being sent on from somebody holy (old, wise) to somebody still holier and holier. The legend seems to be influenced by the mentioning of the "Tal Josaphat" (Authorized Version: "Valley of Jehoshaphat") in the Book of Joel (Authorized Version 3:12), where it is said: "Let the heathen be awakened, and come up to the valley of Jehoshaphat: for there will I sit to judge all the heathen round about." It seems that the legend has grown out of this biblical verse and the belief in this judgment. The folk belief probably goes back to the times when newborn children received holy communion right after baptism; from that custom comes the emphasis on worldly food in contrast to the holy food of the communion.

Literature: Louis Carlen, "Die Vorladung vor Gottes Gericht nach Walliser Quellen" in *Schweizerisches Archiv für Volkskunde* 52 (1956): 10–18; Siegfried Hardung, *Die Vorladung vor Gottes Gericht* (Buhl-Baden, 1934); Leander Petzoldt, *Der Tote als Gast: Volkssage und Exempel* (Helsinki, 1968), pp. 33–35; Robert Wildhaber, "Die Sage vom Westerkind" in *Schweizer Volkskunde* 37 (Basel, 1947): 102–7; *Schweizerisches Idiotikon* 3 (1895): 75, *Handwörterbuch des deutschen Aberglaubens* 4: 770–74. Further Swiss examples of the legend: J. Kuoni, *Sagen des Kantons St. Gallen* (Saint Gallen, 1903), p. 145, no. 269; *Walliser Sagen* (Brig, 1907), 1, p. 231, no. 215; Josef Müller, *Sagen aus Uri* 3 (Basel, 1945), p. 231, nos. 1375 and 1376 (where Müller says that when he was a schoolboy, 1877–84, the Valley of Josaphat was still a general folk belief in the canton Uri); Theodor von Liebenau, *Das Alte Luzern* (Lucerne, 1881), p. 97: in 1559 a man was executed; he summoned his adversary into the Valley of Josaphat; this man died a day after the execution.

Someone had just been hanged when three young men sat down in an inn that was near the gallows. They started to drink and play a game of cards. Soon a fourth man entered the room. They knew him well, and one of them held up his glass to him and asked him to drink with them. "To your health," the last one called out, "to the rogue on the gallows!" Then he sat down and kept the other three company.

A few minutes had passed when a fifth man entered. He went straight to the fellow who had offered the toast and said to him dead seriously: "Three days from today, you have to be in the Valley of Josaphat and give account whether I am a rogue or not." No sooner said than he disappeared.

The man who had been called to the Valley of Josaphat thought it over at home and was taken by a deadly fear. He wandered around in his room restlessly and finally went to the priest to ask for his advice and help.

"My dear," he said after he had heard the story, "my dear, there is not much that I can advise or help. Go to the cloisters of the Capucines; there is a holy father who might be able to help." Without delay, the poor man ran to the cloisters and asked for the holiest father.

"We have two holy fathers here," he was told, "a younger one and an old one." He wanted the old one, he quickly decided. And he was led to him. "I can't advise you," said the old father, "go to the younger father, he is above me." But the younger father, a pale, slender man, shook his head and said with a mild expression: "I can't help you. Go find the Jesuits, perhaps one of them can help you, they are wise and well learned in all theology. If none of them can help you, you have to go to the Valley of Josaphat in the Lord's name. But I tell you, if you are wrong, you are lost forever."

Fear wouldn't let the poor man rest, so he went to the capital to find the Jesuits. He tells his trouble to the superior of the cloisters, who sends him to the wisest and devoutest father of the house. But even this father shakes his head seriously and after reflecting for a long time, he declares: "Your case is very difficult, it is not in my power to help you. But, tell me, do you have godchildren?"

"Yes, about twenty of them," says the poor man. "Did one of them die right after his baptism without receiving any earthly food?" "Yes, one of my godchildren died directly after being baptized and I think he had not eaten any earthly food." "Go to his grave immediately and pray there and I shall pray too. The child will appear and, if you ask him, perhaps he will go in your place to the Valley of Josaphat. Be patient, he will surely come."

Much relieved and full of new hope, the young man rushed to the grave of his godchild, kneeled down, and prayed with all his heart. On the third day the child appeared and asked his godfather in a friendly way what was wrong. He (the child) promised him to go in his place into the Valley of Josaphat because the godfather described his trouble so earnestly and begged him so urgently. The little child told him to wait at his grave until he would return, and disappeared. The young man continued his prayers. Hour after hour went by and the child did not return. The young man almost gave up his prayers and his hope. Finally the child came back but he did not smile any more. He shook his finger at him and said: "Godfather, godfather, this once, but never again. How I had to fight for you over there! If I had taken the smallest bite of earthly food, both of us, you and I, would have been lost forever." With those words he disappeared.

Old people tell us that those children who have died directly after having been baptized without having taken the smallest bite of earthly food will be the most beautiful angels and have the greatest joy in heaven. Yes, there were mothers and perhaps there still are some who will not give their newborn children any food for twenty-four hours because of this belief.

This tale is being told in Ursern. The child says, "Godfather, godfather, once I have fought for you but not a second time! I almost lost out, I almost went with you to be lost forever."

About the Black Spider

Contributed by Robert Wildhaber. Forthcoming in *Folktales of Switzerland*.

Collected by Melchior Soodor in Rohrbach (canton Bern), about 1920, from inhabitants in Rohrbach. Translated by Regula Meier. Motif S211 "Child sold (promised) to devil." Printed in *Schweizerisches Archiv für Volkskunde* 25 (1925): 51–53, no. 16; and afterward in M. Sooder, *Sagen aus Rohrbach* (Huttwil, 1929), pp. 125–27.

The legend has become famous because Jeremias Gotthelf (1797–1854), a country clergyman and one of the best Swiss writers (his real name was Albert Bitzius), has written a tale "Die schwarze Spinne" ("The black spider"). He has taken the idea from the legend, but it is certain that on the other hand his short story has revived—or kept alive —the legend. Sooder has given two versions of the legend, which we also reproduce. The black plague is shown here in the form of a spider. As for the belief in spiders (bringing illness, etc.) see *Handwörterbuch des deutschen Aberglaubens*, p. 270. Well known is the idea to plug an illness, a wart, etc., into a tree (into wood) with a peg; see Wayland D. Hand, ed., *Popular Beliefs and Superstitions from North Carolina* (*The Frank C. Brown Collection of North Carolina Folklore* 6–7, Durham, N. C., 1961 and 1964), nos. 303, 328, 1145, 2341, 2583 (hole in tree). There exist a great many legends about the plague in Switzerland. Very often there are only two people still living in a village, always a man and a woman. In our story they give each other a sign with a white rag, in other stories it is bed linen, or they give a signal with a horn. In some regions the midwife had the right to baptize a child in an emergency; here she cheats the devil by doing so.

Legends about the personification of the Great Plague are classified in Reidar Christiansen, *The Migratory Legends* (Helsinki, 1958), no. 7085.

An evil tyrant had a huge castle built on Barhege. And the people had to work for him and lend him their oxen team when they needed them most themselves and they were so busy anyway that they didn't know how to get all their work done. Some of them had to transport a heavy pine tree uphill; maybe you know how awfully steep it is there. Underway the horses collapsed, and they couldn't get them on their legs again, no shouting and beating whatsoever helped. Suddenly, a little green man emerged from the woods and said he could fix them. If they promised to bring him an unchristened child, he would transport tree after tree for them. He would take care of everything.

What should they do? They knew that something was wrong with this deal. But there was no way out and so they let him take over. Afterward the little green man put a cock in front of the trees and let him pull them up the hill one after another in a very short time. After a while the little green man was informed that he could come after the child he had been promised. An unmarried girl was supposed to have a baby. But the minister must have heard something and he prevented the deal. He christened the baby when it was hardly born.

The little man came behind him and, smiling as if there was nothing to worry about, said the mother was going to get a kiss anyway, so he kissed her on her cheek. Soon the woman in childbed had a badly swollen cheek with a black blister on it. She suffered very much and finally she died. But a frightening black spider came out of the blister and crawled onto someone else. This person got the same blister and died soon afterward. And it went on like this, without missing a house. There is a house on the outer part of Hornbach where the people drilled a hole into a beam, put the spider into it, and sealed it with a plug. Later on the house needed rebuilding, and when they did over the beams of the dining-room, they didn't touch the one beam, but made the others a little bit longer.

On the Barhegechnubeli lived a tyrant who had a new road built. Oak trees were to line both sides, and his tenant was supposed to transport them. But he was afraid that it might be too steep; his wife was pregnant, he had no strong help, and he didn't know how to get the job done.

One day a gentleman came to see the tenant and told him that he would not only transport the oak trees, but also see to it that the tyrant didn't bother him any more in exchange for the child his wife was going to give birth to. The tenant agreed with everything.

Now the stranger pulled the oak trees uphill with three jades and he also replanted them. The tyrant was happy. As soon as the last oak tree was set, the distinguished carrier called the tyrant; he was very excited about the excellent job that had been done. But soon he stopped smiling; the stranger looked at him with poisonous eyes and lifting his finger said: "Look, the job is done, but now I want to tell you something. It is enough. I warn you, don't torture your tenant any more. Look here, this tombstone is your great-grandfather's, and that one over there is your grandfather's, and one is your father's. And if you don't change your mind, you will dwell next to him soon."

Soon afterward the midwife had to be called. But the tenant didn't like the whole deal after thinking it all over and he was anxious to get out of it. But how? He told the midwife about his trouble. She was a wicked wife; she knew how to delay the birth and how to christen the child. The devil, the stranger, was too late. He had been waiting for the child in vain. In his anger he beat the midwife on her head when he saw that his calculation was wrong and took off. But the midwife got a blue blister on her head and it got swollen. When it broke, a horrible big black spider came out of it. The midwife had to suffer quite a bit before she died.

And the spider visited many houses. Wherever people talked about it, it appeared. Nobody knew where it came from. Nobody was safe, and the ones it touched got blue blisters and died like the midwife. On the Schonegg, at Trachselwald, and at Sumiswald people died like flies. But at Hornbach a farmer was dwelling in the first house to the left hand when one climbs over the Fritzeflue. He drilled a hole into the window beam, caught the spider in there, and sealed it with a cork. Now people lived in peace again.

But after a while the farmer's son had grown up. He wanted to get married. Because of the beam and the spider everybody teased him, so finally he decided to build a new house. The carpenters tore down everything, the window beam as well, and the spider was out again. It was worse than before. At the Hornbach only a man and a woman survived. They made the tour of the barns and let the cattle out so that they wouldn't starve in the stables. Every morning they waved to each other with a white rag to show that they still were alive.

Sennentunscheli on the Wyssenboden

Contributed by Robert Wildhaber. Forthcoming in *Folktales of Switzerland*.

Collected by Josef Müller, in the period 1910 to 1925, from Johann

Stadler, who was then thirty years old. About Müller see the note to "Summoned into the Valley of Josaphat."

Printed in Josef Müller, *Sagen aus Uri*, 3 volumes, edited by Hanns Bächtold-Stäubli and Robert Wildhaber as *Schriften der Schweizerischen Gesellschaft für Volkskunde* (Basel, 1926, 1929, 1945, with index); 2 (1929), p. 248, no. 874, version 1. Translated by Regula Meier.

Tunsch (diminutive Tunscheli) refers to a puppet the size of a man, used for blasphemous purposes; on being baptized it comes alive.

This is one of the most typical Alpine legends. It is found in the Swiss Alpine cantons Uri, Wallis, Graubünden, Bern, Saint Gallen (Sarganserland), less often also in Austria and Südtirol, and a few cases occur in Bavaria and Böhmerwald. In Finland skinning a live man is known too, but here the devil skins a late sauna-goer; see Lauri Simonsuuri and Pirkko-Liisa Rausmaa, *Finnische Volkserzählungen* (Berlin, 1968), nos. 320, 321 and Simonsuuri, *Typen- und Motivverzeichnis der finnischen mythischen Sagen* (Folklore Fellows Communications 182, Helsinki, 1961), motifs E261, E266. The names Zurrimutzi or similar names (Müller has about ten of them) are usually given to daughters of "wild men" who serve herdsmen. Mostly the names are used in connection with the motif of Pan's Death, F442.1, and type 113A *King of the Cats Is Dead*. In fact they all are cats' names or deformations of them.

Literature: Gotthilf Isler, *Die Sennenpuppe* (Basel, 1971), is a good monograph on the legend. Leopold Schmidt, *Pygmalion in den Alpen* in *Antaios* (Stuttgart) 11 (1969): 209–25, wrongly connects the classic Pygmalion-motif with the Alpine motif; the psychology and background are completely different.

The three servants at the pastures of Wyssenboden in the community of Burglen one day talked to each other and said, "We should have a woman up here, too." They scooped out a puppet from leftovers of wood and baptized it Zurrimutzi. When they were eating ricemeal, they smeared some of it on its face, saying "Here, eat some too!" Finally the puppet started eating. She became the housewife, cooked, washed, mended, and helped taking care of the cattle. She even was talking, but to the milker only. They made all sorts of jokes with Tunscheli and alternately took her to bed. When fall was approaching, they agreed to leave the puppet there. On the day for clearing the pasture, she helped them drive the cattle together. But when the cowboys wanted to leave without paying attention to her, she got her voice back, put herself in front of them, placed her hands on her hips, and said angrily: "I have been working for you all summer long and now I want to have a glimpse of joy, too. I have to stay here and so will one of you."

They were shocked and lost all color in their faces. But there was no mercy. One of them had to stay. They drew lots and it fell to the milker. The other two were dismissed and were not allowed to turn around until they had left the grounds. When they had crossed the border, they turned around for a last look.

Their eyes meet a scene that made their hearts tremble in their bodies. On the roof of the hut Zurrimutzi and the milker are fighting. After a long hard fight the puppet proves to be stronger, throws down the milker, who is yelling so desperately that it makes them shiver, seizes her knife, kneels on him, skins him while he is still alive, and then spreads his bloody skin on the roof of the hut.

The Knife in the Hay

Contributed by Robert Wildhaber. Forthcoming in *Folktales of Switzerland*.

Collected by Josef Müller, about 1910 to 1925, from David Imhof in Seedorf, a village in the canton Uri. About Müller see the note to "Summoned into the Valley of Josaphat." Printed in Josef Müller, *Sagen aus Uri*; 3 volumes, edited by Hanns Bächtold-Stäubli and Robert Wildhaber as *Schriften der Schweizerischen Gesellschaft für Volkskunde* (Basel, 1926, 1929, 1945, with index) 1 (1926): 144, no. 206, version 2a. Translated by Agnes Freudenberg Hostettler. Motif G242.2 "Witch flies as whirlwind."

The legend has a close connection with the folk belief about the whirlwind. Usually there is a witch in the whirlwind, or she has caused it. The *Bohemian Chronicle* of Hajek (1547) already mentions the witch in connection with the whirlwind. The devil as cause of the whirlwind is found in *Tundalus* of Alberus, in the beginning of the thirteenth century. About 1400, Bernhardin of Siena preached against the sorcerers as creators of whirlwinds and said one had to fight against them with strokes of the sword ("strokes of the sword" is found in some versions of the legend). For protection against whirlwinds iron objects are best, especially a knife thrown into it. When the man who protects himself meets the person who is responsible for the whirlwind, the belief is told as a legend. It is found in most countries of Europe where whirlwinds arise; for Switzerland legends are known from the cantons Uri, Bern, Graubünden, Wallis; for the

United States see George D. Hendricks, *Mirrors, Mice and Mustaches* (Austin, 1966), p. 84; Wayland D. Hand, *Popular Beliefs and Superstitions from North Carolina* (Durham, 1964), no. 5770. In Finland the legend has been enlarged and the new motif of the "black ox" added (D2121.8 "Magic journey by throwing knife into whirlwind"; cf. Simonsuuri's index, D1101, D1121, D1331). Archer Taylor has treated the black ox story in a monograph, in which he says the story "was borne to Finland, where it attained a characteristic, highly elaborated form"; more than 100 black ox versions are known in Finland. In former times the inhabitants of the canton Uri had been oriented toward the south, to canton Tessin and Italy; therefore many of their stories have to do with Lugano, Venice, or Milan.

Literature: Robert Wildhaber, "Volkstümliche Auffassungen über den Wirbelwind in Europa" in *Mitteilungen der Anthropologischen Gesellschaft in Wien* 100 (1970): 397–415 (a monograph about the belief and the legend). Archer Taylor, *The Black Ox: A Study in the History of a Folktale* (Helsinki, 1927).

In Erstfeld (a village in Uri) a farmer was occupied with haying. Suddenly a windstorm blew into his hay and almost carried away the whole load. The farmer quickly takes his pocketknife and throws it with all his might in the middle of the bundle blowing away. The wind storm ceased immediately, but the knife never came back and could not be found, although one of the farmhands had watched where it had fallen on the ground.

A year later, our farmer, who also traded with cattle, took a trip to the canton Tessin and went to an inn where he had often gone before. When the innkeeper opened the cupboard to take out a glass, he saw inside his pocketknife which he had lost in the windstorm. He recognized it well from certain marks on it, but he did not let on that it was his.

In the years past the pretty daughter of the innkeeper had always waited on him. He had exchanged many teasing words with her and had fought many friendly fights over her, sometimes losing, sometimes winning them. He did not see her this time and therefore he asked for her. The innkeeper took the fatal knife out of the cupboard, showed it to his guest, and said with a black look: "See here, this little knife has killed my daughter. She understood Sympathy (harmless witchcraft, white magic) and while she was whirling just for fun some hay of a farmer in Uri, the dirty stinker stuck his knife into her heart so that she had to die. Should the owner of this knife come by here one day, I am surely going to kill him."

You will understand that the farmer did not claim his knife. He did not say much but left very quickly.

Germany

The Swineherd Who Married a Princess

From Kurt Ranke, *Folktales of Germany* (Chicago: University of Chicago Press, 1966), pp. 121–24.

Type 850 *The Birthmarks of the Princess*. No. 135048 in Zentralarchiv für deutsche Volkserzählungen, Marburg/Lahn, Germany.

Recorded in 1928 by the teacher Hermann Galbach in Gross Jerutten, district of Ortelsburg, East Prussia.

Sixteen German versions are recorded of this novel-tale, which is narrated throughout Europe as well as in North and South America (see Ranke, *Schleswig-Holsteinische Volksmärchen*, vol. 3, Kiel, 1962, pp. 151–58).

In 1938, Mr. Schütt, a teacher in the Industrial School in Reinbeck, Schleswig-Holstein, sent me an extremely rude version of this novel-tale. In a letter he had added a remark that is most interesting for the teacher as well as for the folklorist concerning the impression such rude stories made on him when he was a child. "Sitting on the bench near the back door, we were delighted to listen to old Jule. Whenever she could not resist any longer our urgent demand: 'Jule, tell us a story,' she would open her toothless mouth and tell one story after the other. Later on I found many of these in other tale collections. But I still remember two of them that will probably never be printed anywhere, for the simple reason that they were told with such originality, in such a direct, rough manner, that a brain glossed with the polish of modern civilization would turn away with a shudder, exclaiming: 'How could you?' I cannot remember that we were shocked. But I still hear the monotonous voice of old Jule. We did not 'understand' the stories any better than we understood the two hundred biblical verses and the twenty psalms we had to learn by heart at school. But I think that we should not hesitate for reasons of popular psychology to record these kinds of popular stories and to classify them among 'Tales for Adults.'"

I did not have this tale from Schleswig-Holstein translated here, for it really is too rough. I give instead the "tamer" version from East Prussia, which might still be rather tough for a reader with delicate feelings.

Once upon a time there was a King who had a very pretty daughter. No day passed without Princes from far and near who wanted to marry her riding to court. The King was delighted about it, but he did not want to make it easy for the suitors. The Princess had a peculiarity on her body. He who could divine it should become his son-in-law. Now this was serious! Of course, the Princess was much more beautiful to look at than other girls, but anything special that was characteristic only of her could not be seen.

In the King's realm there lived a swineherd who was a very strange fellow. He had cut himself a flute and let his pigs dance to it. As he was not stupid at all, he thought: I think the Princess will be mine! Thus on a fine day he drove his herd along to the castle. Not far from the Princess's window he stopped his pigs, sat down in the grass, played the flute, and let the animals dance. After a short while the Princess came to the window. She never had seen such a thing. And before the maidservants could ask where she was going, she was downstairs.

The swineherd let his pigs go on dancing tranquilly. But the Princess did not look at this for a long time. "Listen, you, give me one of your pigs," she said, patting his shoulder.

"Why not? But as a gift? Lift your skirts to the knee, and you may choose one." The Princess did not hesitate; she lifted her skirts to the knee and took a pig.

The swineherd had been watching carefully, but he had not seen anything peculiar. "Well, if it doesn't work this time, it will work the next time." He consoled himself and drove his herd away.

Who could have been happier than the Princess? She had a flute cut, sat down in the middle of the castle yard, and wanted her pig to dance. But however hard she tried, the animal would not dance. Sadly, she went upstairs and went to bed. But at night she dreamed of the swineherd and of his dancing herd. Therefore she was delighted when, waking up, she heard him playing his flute again. She went to the window, and there he was. The pigs were merrily dancing! She quickly put on a skirt and threw a coat over her shoulders. Then she hurried downstairs.

Again the swineherd did not stop playing. "Hey, listen! The little pig of yesterday does not dance at all!" the Princess complained.

"Look here. I might have told you right away. My pigs only dance in society," the rascal told her.

"Well, then give me another one!" the Princess begged.

"A second one? Well, why not? Lift your skirt to your navel, and you may take one." The Princess did not hesitate this time either. She lifted her skirt to her navel and took a little pig.

This time the swineherd seemed to be satisfied. He leaped with joy and drove his herd away. "This certainly is the peculiarity," he thought, "for there certainly is no other girl with three golden hairs on her belly."

At the royal court, however, there was a merry scene to be observed. The Princess was leaning against a tree, playing her flute, and now the pigs danced. The King and the Queen, the whole suite, and the suitors were laughing.

The next morning there was a good deal of movement at the royal court. It was crammed with Princes. They were standing around all deep in their thoughts, for in the afternoon they were to divine again. "Well, what can there be peculiar about the Princess?" one of the Princes, who was standing alone, asked himself.

"What is peculiar about the Princess?" somebody who was standing nearby asked.

"I am sure to know."

"You'd better go back to the wood with your pigs," the Prince rebuffed the speaker, who was nobody else than the swineherd of whom I have told you before. "But wait! Here are one hundred talers if you tell me what you know," the Prince corrected himself.

"With pleasure," replied the sly fellow. "She's got two golden hairs on her body." He took the money and went to town. He ate and drank in an inn, bought some chocolate, sweets, and marzipan. And when it was time, he went back to the royal castle.

And it was just the right moment. The swineherd was hardly in the hall when the doors were closed. The King was sitting on the throne and the Princess was by his side. Then they started divining. One said a honey mouth. The next one eyes as shining as stars. The third one cheeks like pomegranates, and so on. But the King laughed and the Princess shook her head. Then it was the Prince's turn. When he mentioned the two golden hairs, the King stopped laughing and the Princess did not shake her head any more.

Just wait, you will be even more surprised when I tell you what the Princess has, the swineherd said to himself. And truly, the King and his daughter looked at each other not knowing what to say when the man in the shabby clothes talked of the three golden hairs.

"You have guessed it," the King finally announced, and beckoned the swineherd to the throne. "And you have counted wrong by one hair!" This was to the Prince who went to the throne as well.

But who was to marry the Princess? The King thought it over and over. Of course, he would have preferred the Prince to the swineherd. But a King has to keep a promise, and thus he decided as a wise sovereign and as an impartial judge. "You two will sleep tonight beside my daughter, and her husband will be the man she is facing in the morning."

And so it was. The Princess lay in the middle and to her right and left lay the swineherd and the Prince. Being very tired, the Princess soon fell asleep. She dreamed of the swineherd with the dancing pigs. The two suitors lay awake and could not sleep. What am I going to do to make the Princess turn to my side? the swineherd asked himself and could find no rest. But while he was thinking it over, the Prince grew fidgety. Suddenly he jumped up, ran to the corner of the room, and let his trousers down to relieve himself. "You want to be a Prince and you shit in the King's room!" cried the swineherd. The Prince, who was afraid the Princess might wake up, pulled his trousers up in a hurry and lay down again. "I think luck is on my side," chuckled the swineherd. Then he took the sweets out of his pockets and ate chocolate, toffees, and marzipan.

Finally it grew light. And when the Princess woke up, she perceived a frightful stench on her right side. She turned round, and there it smelled nicely like a marzipan shop. But the King was standing in the room. He had the stinking Prince shut up in jail and prepared a great wedding for the swineherd and his daughter.

Where have I it all from? Well, the swineherd was my friend, and I was the King's coachman.

The Ox as Mayor

From Kurt Ranke, *Folktales of Germany* (Chicago: University of Chicago Press, 1966), pp. 185–86.

Type 1675 *The Ox (Ass) as Mayor*. No. 40256 in Zentralarchiv für deutsche Volkserzählungen, Marburg/Lahn, Germany.

Recorded in 1958 by Eva Kautz in Ahausen, Hannover, from the storyteller Heinrich Intemann.

The first version of this joke is given in a satirical poem by Thomas Murner, printed in 1515 in Strasbourg (see Bolte in *Zeitschrift für Volkskunde* 7 [1897]: 93–96). The story is widespread in Europe and is also found in the Arabian collection of *A Thousand and One Nights* (Chauvin, 7: 170, no. 445) as well as in the old jokes about the Turkish Eulenspiegel *Hodscha Nasreddin* (ed. Wesselski, nos. 63, 385, 395). It is known today in the whole Orient, in India, in North Africa, and in Canada. Thirty-four German versions are reported. In the *Folktales of Israel*, edited by Dov Noy (Chicago, 1963), no. 66, "The One-Eyed Cadi," the dupe believes his one-eyed ass has become a judge.

There once lived a peasant. He had an ox with which he used to work in the fields. When he was plowing, his wife brought him his lunch. They had no children. While the two ate their lunch together, the ox went on plowing tranquilly. It was a very clever animal. One day as they were having their meal, the peasant said to his wife, "Our ox is so clever that it would be a pity to let him go on working in the field. Let's send him to school so that he can learn something." His wife agreed.

The next morning the peasant went to town with his ox. On his way he met a group of young fellows who were wearing colored caps. They asked the peasant where he wanted to go with his ox. "Well," he said, "my ox is so clever that I want him to go to school to learn something." The fellows said that they were going to school, too, and that they would take the ox with them. But he would have to give them some money for the books and material the ox would need. The peasant gave them the money and was glad that everything went so smoothly.

The boys took the ox with them and sold it right away. But once in a while they wrote to the peasant that the ox needed more books, for he had read the old ones to pieces, and to send some money. And the peasant always sent the money. After some years the boys wrote that the ox had now finished his studies and that he had become mayor. He might come and call on him.

The peasant went to town. By chance the mayor's name was Ox. The peasant found his way by asking and was admitted to the mayor's office. He had to go up some stairs. When he entered, the mayor was sitting behind his table with a sullen face and big glasses. "Well," thought the peasant, "he has changed a little. But there is still some resemblance." The mayor addressed him gruffly and asked what he wanted. The peasant said, "Well, now you pretend not to know me any more. And in former days you used to shit on my spring bar!"

Norway

The Drinking Horn Stolen from the Huldre Folk at Vallerhaug

From Reidar Christiansen, *Folktales of Norway* (Chicago: University of Chicago Press, 1964), pp. 117–21.

Motif F352 "Theft of cup (drinking horn) from fairies"; R. Christiansen, *The Migratory Legends*, 6045, "Drinking Cup Stolen from the Fairies." This is one of the commonest Norwegian legends, collected in some 140 variants from all parts of Norway. North and west European traditions about thefts of drinking cups from fairies are treated by E. S. Hartland in *The Science of Fairy Tales* (London, New York, 1914), pp. 148–58. Often a celebrated drinking horn in a village is said to have been stolen from the fairy folk.

This story is from Bishop Jens Nielsen's visitation reports from Telemark in the year 1595 while he was traveling in the vicinity of Aase Farm in Hjartdal. He recorded it in his *Visitatsbog* (Kristiania, 1893), p. 393.

"There we went up to the farm and had a talk with the farmer's wife about a horn which was supposed to have come from a mound just north of the farm called Vallerhaug (Valler Mound). The woman said that after the dividing of the inheritance the same horn was now to be found at a farm called Östenaa in Kvitseid. Here is the story about this horn:

"In days gone by there was a farmer named Gunder Giesemand. On Christmas Eve he set out from Hjartdal on his way home to his farm. When he came to Vallerhaug, he shouted:

" 'Listen, *draug* in Vallerhaug, get up and give Gunder Giesemand a drink!'

"Then, from inside the mound, came the answer: 'Yes!' And to the boy: 'Tap and give him a drink, not of the best and not of the worst!'

"When Gunder heard this, he drove on with the horse. And then someone came out of the mound and threw the horn after him, and it struck the horse on the back between the reins. After that, both hair and hide fell off. The same horn fell on the road, and then Gunder fished it up with a kind of ax, the woman said, and took the horn with him to his farm. And since then, whenever they drank from this horn and struck it on the table, everyone in the room always came to blows.

"Afterwards we journeyed north from the above-mentioned Aase Farm, by way of Vallerhaug, which lies on the right. Big birch trees stand around this mound."

The Drinking Horn Stolen from the Huldre-Folk at Vellerhaug

This story was collected by Moltke Moe in Böherad (Telemark) in 1878 and printed in *Norsk Folkeminnelag* 9 (1925): 63. Note the persistency of the tradition since 1595.

Between Böherad and Nesherad lies a mound which is called Vellerhaug (Veller Mound), and where *draugs* are supposed to live. A man from Gjernes, named Gunnar Gjernes, had heard this, and he wanted to find out if it was true.

So one night, as he rode past this mound, he stopped his horse and said, "Get up, *draug* in Vellerhaug, and give Gunnar Gjernes a drink!"

"Yes, now you'll get it!" came the answer from the mound.

But then Gunnar grew frightened and whipped up the horse with all his might. But the *draug* set out after him, and it was not until they came to Griviveien that the *draug* had to give up. Then he hurled the horn at Gunnar and hit the horse's back, and everything in the horn ran out and singed both hair and hide off the horse.

But at the same moment Gunnar turned and grabbed the horn—or else he picked it up on his way home, I don't remember which—but he got it. And as far as I know, the big golden horn is to be found at Gjernes to this very day.

The Drinking Horn Stolen from the Huldre-Folk at Hifjell

This variant was collected by Karen Sollie in Rissa (Tröndelag) in 1935. It appeared in R. Christiansen, *Norske Sagn* (Oslo, 1938), p. 92. Christiansen cites a reference to a similar variant of legend type 6045 reported in 1883.

This is the legend about the way they got the chalice in Reins church. At the time the church was going to be built, an old troll was living in Hifjell mountain. A hatchet-faced man had promised to get a chalice for the altar. He knew that the troll in Hifjell had a big silver goblet, but the hatchet-faced man needed special skis to get up there, so he had to make some very swift skis. He worked on them for seven Christmas Eves in a row while the trees from which he cut them were standing on their roots. On the seventh Christmas Eve all that was left was to put on the bindings and saw them down.

When the skis were ready, he set out for Hifjell and knocked with his ski pole. The Hifjell troll came out. When he saw who it was, he told him to wait a bit. Then he fetched the big silver goblet, which had been filled to the brim, and offered the hatchet-faced man a drink.

But he was a sly one, this man, and instead of drinking, he emptied the goblet over his shoulder. And it was a good thing too, for the drink in the goblet was so strong that it ate through the skis, and the pieces flew off behind him. Then the hatchet-faced man set out on his skis down the mountain, with the goblet in his hand.

"Hey! Wait a minute until I can get on my rolling breeches!" shouted the Hifjell troll. "Then I'll catch up with you again!"

Now the hatchet-faced man understood that it was a matter of life or death, and he set out as fast as he could. The Hifjell troll did not take long to put on his rolling breeches, and came after him so the sparks flew!

As they went by Aalmo, a cock crowed, and the troll shouted:

"The white cock doth crow!
Soon the man I shall throw!"

But down at Modalen, the skis went very fast, and the troll was left far behind. Uphill to Aasen the going was slower, and the troll began to catch up with him again. But on the marshes beyond Aasen, the man was again in the lead.

As they rushed past Solli, a cock crowed again. Then the troll shouted:

"There crowed the red!
Soon he'll bleed 'til he's dead!"

On they went, past Berg and Vallin and on to Rissa, and then the troll started catching up with him again.

But then the hatchet-faced man shouted, "Look at that maiden who's coming behind you!"

At the same moment, another cock crowed, and the old troll of Hifjell mountain shouted:

> "There crowed the black!
> Now, my heart must crack!"

At the same moment the sun came up, and the troll burst asunder. The man hurried to Reins and delivered the goblet to the church, where they used it for a chalice.

The Altarpiece in Ringsaker Church

From Reidar Christiansen, *Folktales of Norway* (Chicago: University of Chicago Press, 1964), pp. 18–19.

R. Christiansen, *The Migratory Legends* (Helsinki, 1958), 7070ff., "Legends about church-bells." A cycle of Norwegian legends deals with sacred objects such as church bells that refuse to be removed from their location. This variant was collected by P. Chr. Asbjörnsen in Ringsaker (in eastern Norway) in 1835 and printed in *Hedmarks Historie*, I (Hamar, 1957), p. 427.

In the old days, hundreds and hundreds of years ago, there was once a Princess in England who was so badly tormented by the Devil that at last she was completely possessed by him. Her father, the King, sent for clergymen from every land and kingdom. Yes, he sent his messengers almost the world over to get hold of the most God-fearing minister, and one who was best trained in the use of the Black Book. But they could not find anyone who was able to drive out Old Erik. One day they managed to draw it out of the Evil One himself that at Ringsaker, in Norway, there was a minister who was so God-fearing and so experienced in black magic that he was the only one who could drive him out. They sent for the Ringsaker minister at once, and when he came he cast out the Devil on the spot.

"Now you can wish for whatever you'd like," said the Princess. She was so happy that she did not know how to repay him.

"I desire nothing for myself," said the minister, "but, with your permission, I would like an altarpiece for my congregation."

"Oh to hell with it!" said the Devil. "If that minister had asked for something for himself, I'd have rushed in and tugged and clawed at both body and soul!" he said, and then away he flew.

The Princess sent word to Holland and ordered the finest altarpiece that was to be had, and it is hanging in Ringsaker church to this very day. The minister is buried in the cellar, and looks as fresh as if he'd been buried yesterday.

During the wars with the Swedes, in 1567, the cathedral at Hamar was destroyed. A company of Swedes also went up to Ringsaker, ravaging and burning on the way, and they used the church as a stall. They thought of taking the altarpiece along with them, but when they had loaded it onto a wagon and were going to leave, the horse could not pull it. They harnessed horse after horse to the wagon, but it was no use; and not until they had harnessed twelve horses did the wagon begin to move. But when they came to Sveinhaug, it stood quite still again. Then they gave up. A yearling foal was all that was needed to pull the load back to the church again.

Finland

The Hunter's Joke

Collected by Pirkko-Liisa Rausmaa, 6 August 1970, in Kiuruvesi, Finland. Translated by Felix J. Oinas.

Type 1092 *Who Can Shoot an Unheard-of Bird* (motif K31.1). Narrator Johannes Allinen, farmer, born 8 October 1908 in Suistamo, Hovinaho. Tape Kn34–35/1970 in the Folklore Archives of the Finnish Literature Society.

Johannes Allinen is the best of the living tale tellers in Finland today. His tales were recorded on tape many times during the years 1966–71. About eighty hours of his narratives have been recorded and the total number of his tales and jokes is about 130. In his repertoire are 49 long Märchen and novellas, the longer ones of which last as much as two hours, 56 jocular tales and jokes, 7 legends, and 27 local legends, some of which have been told in the manner of Märchen. Allinen has learned the bulk of his repertoire from a single person, the shoemaker Mikki Issakainen, in his home area of Suistamo in his youth. He has appeared as teller mainly in the night lodgings of forest workers.

The tale given here is one of Allinen's jocular tales; he himself calls it a joke (*kasku*). Allinen's favorite stories are long, exciting adventure and hero tales, but his usual listeners, forest workmen, have mostly requested to hear jolly, perhaps somewhat obscene jocular tales, and thus Allinen has added a whole bunch of them to his repertoire, although he himself has no specially high opinion of them.

Type 1092 is quite common in Finland: at least 123 variants of it have been collected. It is reported only sparsely elsewhere, from neighboring countries.

One hunter's joke was as follows:

Several times a man went hunting in the forest—he had a wife and he may also have had other family members—and one fall he had quite bad luck. From time to time he would get some game but very little and some days he would have no luck at all, he wouldn't get anything. And he thinks that now he has completely lost his good luck since he doesn't get anything. He had heard it said that if one promises himself to the bad man—formerly it was said—then the bad man would help him. He thinks that if the bad man would come to his help his hunting luck would soon change.

So then the bad man appeared, comes, looks, and goes to meet him. He comes: "Hunter what were you thinking?" "I wasn't thinking of anything." "You were thinking," he said, "I surely know. Just tell!" Then he said: "Lo, I was thinking since my hunting luck has been so bad then I was thinking to myself that they say the bad man will help if all else fails."

He said: "If you would make an agreement with me, for three years we would make the agreement, then for three years you can go to an island in the swamp. You will have to do nothing else but sit there and shoot, I will drive the game there. But after three years then you must shoot for me a bird that I have never seen before. If you are not able to shoot such a bird then I will go on my way, such is the agreement."

The man thinks that it's good, the three years are good, and maybe in three years he will be able to find a bird that the bad man will not recognize. So he says, "Let's make an agreement," and they began making the agreement. He took a piece of paper and said, "Here a mark must be made on the tree, some blood from the little finger must be dripped on the paper, then the agreement is binding." And this is the way the agreement was made.

Well, after the man had made the agreement he just went to a little island. It wasn't necessary to stay there for the whole day; whenever he was there he got several loads of birds or however much forest game there is. All the time he could kill them. They came there, and he goes there three years and he gets so much game that he becomes rich. He gets money and everything that he has—a very good life now, but he doesn't tell his secret to anybody. He doesn't even tell his wife what kind of deal he has.

Now three years go by, and they went quickly, it was not necessary for him to do any slash and burn or anything. He bought with money when he had become so rich. Well, now, the last time he becomes quite nervous and his old woman [wife] always asks, "What has happened to you now that you are like this?" "Nothing has happened." "So we now have a good life and everything." "It's like that."

Now the end of the three years is approaching, there is only three days, and then he thinks it is necessary for him to leave here. There is nothing else to do and so finally he says to his old woman that things are so and so and such and such. He has made such an agreement. He doesn't know the man and doesn't know about him but he was one that could read one's thoughts. That this bad man could help him, that he would help when he would come, and he came and he made the agreement and blood from the little finger had to be put on the tree to mark the agreement. The old woman said, "Ho, what kind of agreement is it, is it necessary for you to go on this trip?" "In this case it wouldn't be necessary for me to go if I had shot a bird that he couldn't recognize, but he knows all of them. No, I cannot do that, I cannot shoot such a thing and I don't know if there is such a bird as he himself drives them and he knows all of them." The old woman said: "Oh, oh, you are really stupid! Here is a bird for him that he doesn't know!" "How is it here?" "Well, when do you have to show him this bird?" "In three more days." "Well, when we go the last morning, then if you tar me well and if I get into this feather basket and turn myself around, well then he will not recognize me."

Thus the last morning she was well tarred; the old woman tarred herself front and back and he tarred her all over. And he noted: when she went to the feather basket and turned herself around there, then it was impossible to consider her a human being or whatever. Every place was covered with feathers. They go to the forest and there the old woman says: "Just go to a place, and I will go to another place. Then when he comes and asks, then just say that you shot it. 'This morning I shot it, there it is on the turf. Go and look.' He surely will not recognize it."

And thus it was. The bad man came again: "Well, are you now ready to go for the trip?" "Wasn't the agreement that if I shoot a bird that you did not recognize?" "But have you shot it?" "Well, I really shot it this morning. I don't know it, but I don't know whether you recognize it or not." "Where is it?" "There it is over there on the turf." And the man takes him to it and it is on the turf. The bad man looks at it, examines it, and goes around: "Well I have known . . . I have recognized all the birds, but this is surely a bird that I do not know, no, no, by no means!" And he looks: "How have you managed to kill such a big one?" Then he looks: "Aha, you have shot it with two bullets." "Yes, that is the way I shot him." "Yes, it seems that one has gone straight and the other has just made a flesh mark." "Yes, exactly like that." "Well, if you once saw such a bird, then for three more years I will drive the game your way. Go to the same island to kill them, since you were so ingenious as to kill a bird that I have never seen and have not been able to recognize."

So, everything is well. So the bad man went away. The man and his wife went home and had quite a job getting her clean. It was necessary to heat the sauna several times and scrub her, and finally she was clean. For three years he brought the game from the same place, so then they finally had enough money and everything to last them a lifetime. So they lived for the rest of their lives. And the old woman said, "Look, didn't I say so!" The old woman was more intelligent, wiser, than the man. "Didn't I say that he doesn't know, and he didn't know! How could he recognize it when he had never seen it? He saw it for the first time." Such was this tale.

Poland

All the following Polish tales were told by Sabała, the only peasant narrator in nineteenth-century Poland to achieve individual recognition. A statue of him stands in Zakopane showing him at the foot of the doctor who discovered him. As guide and singer in the Tatra Mountains, born as Jan Kozeptowski but nicknamed Sabała, he worked for men of letters who came to Zakopane, the well-known southern health resort, for their summer holidays. While employing him as guide they recognized the storytelling genius of the illiterate mountaineer. The writer and painter Stanisław Witkiewicz devoted an entire chapter in his brilliant book *On the Pass* to the "Homer of the Tatras" as he dubbed Sabała. To his intellectual friends Sabała told wonderful stories of his own hunting adventures. For his peers he opened a repertoire of witty jokes.

Henryk Sienkiewicz, the famous Polish novelist whose *Quo Vadis* became an American bestseller when translated into English by the folklorist Jeremiah Curtin, knew and appreciated Sabała. In one of his short stories he inserted a narrative called "Sabała's Tale," which he rendered in the old man's dialect. He took it down on a summer night at Czarne Jezioro, near Zakopane, and in the prologue he thus described the aged raconteur: "We were seated round the campfire, listening intently to the stillness of the mountains ringing in our ears. The hour of rest was coming, when all of a sudden Sabała raised his wrinkled face that resembled both the head of an old vulture and the face of Milton. With his glassy eyes he looked upon the fire and began to talk."

Old Fakla and the Sleeping Knights

Contributed by Julian Krzyzanowski. Collected from Sabała in Zakopane before 1895 and printed by A. Stopka in *Sabała* (1897), p. 111.

The catalogue of Polish folktales by Julian Krzyzanowski, *Polska bajka ludowa* (Warsaw, 1962–63), enumerates some 50 variants under T8256 "The Sleeping Knights." This is the celebrated legend of the Returning Hero, attached to various heroes, sleeping armies, and mountains in Europe, and discussed at length by Edwin Sidney Hartland in *The Science of Fairy Tales* (1891). Walter Scott, who had heard the tradition localized in Highland glens and Northumberland coal mines, once considered developing it into prose fiction (Richard M. Dorson, *The British Folklorists*, London, 1968, page 110).

In the present text the hero is not identified. Motifs are D1960.2 "Kyffhäuser. King asleep in mountain [Barbarossa, King Marko, Holger Danske, etc.] will awake one day to succor his people"; E502 "The Sleeping Army. Soldiers killed in battle come forth on occasions from their resting place [hill, grave, grotto]"; C549.2 "Tabu: touching soldiers of enchanted [sleeping] army and their horses."

In the valley of Kościelisko on the way to Smytnia meadow is a high peak called Pisana—hey! In olden days it was called differently, but today tourists have renamed it as is written on that peak—hey! People tell different stories about it: that inside the mountain is a pond from which the Dunajec River flows and that on that pond swims a golden duck that lays diamond eggs, but only one a year—hey!

Once a shepherd set out to get the duck but didn't make it because the water was awfully cold and the mountain crack from which the water flowed was so narrow that he almost drowned—hey! Nymphs guard the pond and don't let anyone get near by seducing and amusing them and in so doing lead them astray—hey!

However, old Fakla, who was afflicted with paralysis, told me the story of an army that is asleep in that peak—hey! It happened like this.

Once I went to Fakla when the old fellow was lying in bed barely alive. I sat down on the bed next to him and asked if there wasn't something he needed. He spoke to me like this:

"Dear God Almighty! It's all over with me, lad. God punished me, and as you see I've been lying here now for many years. Child, you're young and have your life before you, while I'll die any day now. Listen to me and I'll tell you how I made my living. I was once a sturdy fellow for work. I had a smithy and made whatever anyone needed. I was a crack blacksmith so I always had plenty of work—hey!

"Once it was getting toward evening and I was still working when a person came into the forge. He greeted me nice and polite in the name of the Lord God and I answered him. But when I looked up I was struck dumb for I'd never seen such a person in my life. He was dressed as if he were a soldier for he had armor on his body and a helmet on his head. His beard reached down to his belt and his face was as beautiful as an angel's in heaven. He asked me if I'd make golden horseshoes for him.

"I answered, 'Why not, after all, I'm a blacksmith.'

"And so we set to work. I forged while he worked the bellows and so the work progressed. After we made a lot of horseshoes and nails for them, the soldier told me to put everything in a sack and go with him. I said that I would since he looked like an honest person. Since we're to go, let's go. A hunter has to be quick for the kill. We set out with him in front and me behind carrying the horseshoes. And so we passed through Kiry glade to Kościelisko Valley.

"As we were approaching Pisana peak, he turned around and said: 'Don't be afraid. Just walk as quietly as possible and God keep you from cursing once we enter.'

"We climbed along a mountain groove into a hole and it was as if the peak opened up before us. We went and went until we came to the center. I looked around and saw a lot of people with beards down to their belts lying with their heads on their saddles—hey! I asked quietly who they were. The soldier said that it was a sleeping Polish army that will wake up when the time comes to go fight for the faith in a war that will begin somewhere far away and end on the steel bridge in Kuźnice.

"We began to shoe the horses. I fitted the horseshoes to the hooves and hammered in the nails while he held their legs. After I had repaired everything necessary, the soldier took the shavings of the hooves and put them into my sack, saying, 'Here's your pay.'

"I thought that he was mocking me but didn't dare oppose him although I was awfully sad at wasting a whole day. As I was leaving I poured out the shavings from the bag. But when I got outside and looked in the bag, I saw that they hadn't been shavings but ducats—for a few had stuck to the bag. There were quite a few of them. If I hadn't poured out all the shavings, I would have made out quite well. But I was unworthy. I thought to myself, 'A beggar doesn't deserve a horse, but a sack and a stick.'

"I went and when I arrived at my hut, my wife greeted me with snapping teeth: 'What kept you so long that you weren't home for three days?'—hey!

"I didn't know where the time had flown for it seemed but a moment to me. However, I thought to myself 'I'm not going to argue with a stupid woman, for her hair may be long but her reason is awfully short'—hey!

"I continued to forge axes or whatever other work I got until a few years later the soldier came again. I made horseshoes for him and, after I had made enough, went with him back to the same place. I thought to myself that this time I wouldn't be so stupid as to throw away the shavings. We continued to work until I cut myself in the finger and cursed loudly—hey! What happened but all around the soldiers began to get up. I was seized with fear.

"One of them asked: 'Brother, is it time?'

"But the soldier said to him: 'Not yet, sleep on!' He gave me a dirty look and shook his finger at me. When we finished working, he again poured a handful of shavings into my sack!—hey!

"I left. When I got outside I looked in the bag to see how much money I got but found the chips from hooves unchanged. I became angry for I was sorry to have wasted so much time, but then I said to myself, 'I won't become a beggar because of it.' I poured out the chips and left. At Kiry glade I stopped by the Jew's for a while to have a drink. When one greases one's tongue, one walks more smoothly. However, I blurted out everything to the Jew who told the whole world —hey!

"Now the years fly by and the horses remain unhoofed for they won't let just anyone in to do it now. It has to be a lad who doesn't go after girls—hey! As punishment I immediately took ill and so I've been lying here ever since. One can't play games with God—hey!"

That's just how it was told to me by Fakla as the tears rolled down his cheeks.

The Holy Figure in Szaflary

Contributed by Julian Krzyzanowski. Collected from Sabała in Zakopane by A. Stopka and printed by him in *Sabała* (1897), p. 70. The story is not registered in the Polish catalogues of folktales. Motif V120 "Images."

In olden times it wasn't so close to church as it is now. There was a church only in town (Nowy Targ), Szaflary, and in Czarny Dunajec. So from time to time we went to church either in Dunajec or in Szaflary. The people discussed and discussed to which church they should make an offering and finally decided to make a present to the church in Szaflary because they went there more often. They didn't want to go to church for nothing. At that time people were very poor for those were awfully hard years—hey!

So the head of the village sent out a call for a meeting. When the town council got together, he asked them what they wanted to offer. They deliberated and deliberated and finally decided to make an of-

fering of the figure of Saint Andrew, the patron saint of Szaflary—
hey! And so two fellows, one from the Bankowki settlement and the
other from Piton family, were sent to Jaworzynka Valley to pick out
a spruce from which to make the holy figure. They found an awfully
big one, cut it down, and trimmed it. They hewed and carved until they
made a holy figure out of it. Only it was an awfully poor figure—hey!
Where he should have eyes, they put two pebbles—hey! They were
poor sculptors. Then they didn't have such sculptures as we have today for they didn't know how to make such wonders—hey!

And then they thought how they could get it the two miles to church.
Finally they decided that it couldn't be put on a wagon for it was a
holy object—hey! Although it wasn't yet blessed, it was holy and had
to be carried and not carted—hey! But where could they find a fellow
strong enough to carry such an offering—hey! After deliberating and
deliberating they finally decided to offer a hundred days' indulgences
to the person who would carry it to Szaflary. They thought that they
would certainly find someone who would be tempted by the indulgences. Finally Johnny from Hrube was tempted and set out with it.
He carried it to Bankowki but couldn't carry it any further. A great big
woman came along.

Since she was of those overly pious village women he said to her,
"If you help me carry this holy figure to Szaflary, twenty-five of my
hundred days' indulgences will be yours—hey!"

The woman pulled and tugged so that the bones in her back cracked
and she ruptured herself—but she couldn't move the holy figure from
the spot—hey! After the fellow rested, he put the holy figure on his
back and continued on. In Biaty Dunajec he asked a fellow to help him
carry the holy figure, but when the latter looked at it he just shook his
head. He didn't want any part in it. He even offered him all the indulgences but he didn't want to—hey! He just shook his head.

"I've been carrying you so long," Johnny said to the holy figure,
"and haven't yet earned any indulgences. Since you're not blessed,
you're certainly not holy!"

He looked more closely at it and said, "They told me, 'Saint Andrew
Saint Andrew.' But here I see it's not Saint Andrew but just some old
horse's trough—hey!"

He then threw it into the water and since it was a little rotted out on
the inside it floated to Szaflary where they fished it out and hung it in
the church—hey!

And that's how they thought up a big offering except that they
couldn't carry it out—for a sinful person won't carry a holy figure
very far—hey!

The Ages of Man

Contributed by Julian Krzyzanowski. Collected about 1894 in Zakopane from Sabała by A. Stopka and printed in his *Sabała* (1897), p. 55. The Polish Catalogue of Folktales lists 3 variants under T2462 "Human Span of Life." This is a variation of type 828 *Men and Animals Readjust Span of Life* (motif A1321), reported infrequently, but a Grimm tale and an Aesop's fable.

There are all kinds of people made of flesh and blood—hey!

When the Lord Jesus created animals, he called the lion to himself and said, "You will rule over animals, while I will rule over man."

What happened then? It so happened that an ox, donkey, calf, and dog got together and decided to oust the lion from power so that they could rule themselves—hey! They collaborated together. The dog delivered telegrams. The calf was told to bleat pitifully as if it were hungry, while the ox walked behind and explained why it was bleating—for a calf is a very stupid animal. They thus explained that the lion didn't give them anything to eat and only beat them. The donkey raised and lowered its ears to show how the lion always was at odds with him.

It so happened that the lion found out what was going on and called everyone to his hut and said, "You know—you all acted very stupidly. Who put you up to it?" They all pleaded innocent and no one would confess to any part in it.

"The devil must have gotten into you since you acted so stupidly—hey! Do you think that it's fun to rule? The Lord Jesus commanded me and I must obey—hey! Since you have sinned you must take your medicine. I'll mete out your punishment straightaway."

But it so happened that the lion didn't want to punish them all himself because it didn't pay to mess around with them. He therefore ordered the ox to eat the dog and the donkey to eat the ox, and the calf to eat the donkey. But the calf had trouble eating the donkey because it had hard bones. The calf gnawed and gnawed and broke all its teeth but finally ate the donkey except for the head, which was left aside with the others. The lion finally was to eat the calf (because it was the best and softest) but was afraid to eat the head because it was—pardon the expression—damn stupid. The lion ate the calf and left the head with the others—hey! He then buried the skins and heads in the ground and so they rotted. The years flew by and the heads and skins continued to rot.

Finally the Lord Jesus decided to create man. He took some mud and formed man. But alas, he created him on the very spot where those stupid animals were buried—hey!

For that reason man—even the wisest farmers—comes from those beasts. When he is young he is stupid as a calf. When he grows up he chases like a dog and won't settle down. When he marries he works like an ox, and when old age arrives he becomes stupid as a donkey—hey!

But only men are like that for women were created later—hey!

Song of the Thief

Contributed by Julian Krzyzanowski. Collected in Zakopane from Sabała by A. Stopka and printed in his *Sabała* (1897), p. 87. The Catalogue of Polish Folktales gives nine variants under T1525Q* "The Dance of the Thief." This cante-fable resembles type 1360C *Old Hildebrand* (motif K1556) in which a priest and his paramour joke in rhyme about the presumably absent husband, who from his hiding place answers in rhyme. In the present text, the trickster-thief signals his men in rhyme but the tavernkeeper dupe does not catch on.

In Orawa there was a large tavern run by a rich tavernkeeper's wife whose husband was good for nothing. Although he sat quietly at home with her, they didn't like each other—hey! As it was, he was very watchful. He kept his money in the pantry and guarded it very carefully.

It so happened that Bert Mateya found out about it and began to hover about the tavern and pantry—hey! But neither he nor his comrades were able to fool the tavernkeeper. Whenever they were about to make a move for the money, he caught on right away and chased them away.

What did Mateya do but say to his men, "Let's try once more for I'll be damned if we don't get the money after knowing that it's here and where it is. Let's go. I'll keep the tavernkeeper's wife busy, while you go after the money. There's a lot of it hidden in the pantry—hey!"

And so they went to the tavern. Bert brought a lot of smoked *gomulka* [sheep cheese] and treated the tavernkeeper, his wife, and the musicians to it. But the tavernkeeper was suspicious and carefully watched that Mateya shouldn't kiss his wife—hey! Bert appealed to her because he was handsome, but the tavernkeeper was afraid of him. The music began. Mateya jumped up to dance and the tavernkeeper's wife went after him. She kissed him. While they danced his comrades dug their way into the pantry. But the moss began to fall from between the beams so that they could be seen through the wall. Mateya continued to dance but when he saw one of them through a crack, he told them what to do in song—hey! Neither the tavernkeeper nor his wife suspected that he would fool them like that—hey! At first he sang like this:

"Dance, my fat little hostess,
    without a care
    For tomorrow your pantry
    will be completely bare."

When he saw a cap through a crack he sang like this:

"Bend down, Joe,
    your cap is out.
    If the tavernkeeper sees it
    our luck is out."

When they had already taken everything and were leaving, he sang to them like this:

"Hey, fill your sacks
    and quickly flee,
    In Kiry gorge
    wait for me."

Then he sang a last refrain that went like this:

"Oh, his wife is glad,
    she danced out her feet.
    But the tavernkeeper's sad,
    he'll have nothing to eat."

And he went after them.

That's how they succeeded in doing what they wanted for Mateya was always terribly bold—hey!

Hungary

The Magic Calk

From Linda Dégh, *Folktales of Hungary* (Chicago: University of Chicago Press, 1965), pp. 243–47.

The legend cycle that developed around the figure of the coachman endowed with supernatural knowledge is a specific type of Hungarian folk tradition. No analogies have yet been found in the oral literature of neighboring countries or anywhere else in Europe. The central hero of these legends is the head coachman, in the service of the squire, proudly sitting on the box of the coach in his richly corded and silver-buttoned black livery. A small round hat with a cockade adorned his head. The head coachman was counted among the house servants; he lived with his family in the servants' quarters attached to the manor house. The coachman took the squire wherever he went and enjoyed his master's confidence. The squire would always use his coach if he was called into the town on some business or if he went there to amuse himself. There was ceaseless competition between one squire and another as to which could boast a finer coach, better horses, and a more adroit coachman. The liveried coachman and coach were indispensable for stylish living, so much so that up to the 1930s coaches were preferred to automobiles on most estates. The coachman who was good at driving and took good care of the horses was held in esteem by his master, and for the same reason he won the respect of the simple folk.

The coachman legend cycle is chiefly attached to the figure of a manor coachman famed for some extraordinary quality. It tells of a series of adventures connected with such coachmen. These legends, while having become popular in the villages around the manor estates, have been reported only sporadically from villages where the majority of the villagers belong to a small freeholder peasantry, and they are unknown among the descendants of the landed peasants. Evidently the factors that played a decisive role in giving rise to the coachman legends must be sought in the feudal land system. But we must look back for even more far-reaching motifs that may be considered as cultural survivals from the pre-conquest times of the ancient Magyars.

Generally there are two main themes around which the coachman legends are built: how the coachman obtains his extraordinary knowledge and what marvelous deeds he performs in possession of this knowledge.

Usually the interest of a young and inexperienced coachman is awakened when he sees that his older mate is possessed of some secret knowledge, a knowledge that enables him to keep the horses perfectly groomed without work and perfectly fit for driving without their being fed and watered. He obtains this secret knowledge in any number of ways; he may go to the crossroads; he may be carried off; he may learn it while in deep sleep; or he may acquire his knowledge through the aid of some helping spirits who live in ordinary objects, e.g., a brush, a scraper, a whip, or the like. Sometimes he obtains possession of magic power by paying half a deciliter of brandy to an older coachman who wishes to get rid of his secret knowledge. Incidents occurring most frequently are: driving home with a dead horse; flying with the horses over the river; or making an artisan fall from the roof of a house for having stopped the coachman's horses. But the coachman has to pay dearly for his extraordinary knowledge; he cannot die unless he passes this knowledge on to someone else, and even then the evil spirit with whom he had associated himself will not let him go and keeps tormenting him until his death.

Motif D1209 "Miscellaneous utensils and implements"; motif D1654.12 "Horse magically becomes immovable"; and motif D2072.0.2.1 "Horse enchanted so that he stands still."

Narrator, János Nagy, fisherman of Sára, Zemplén County. Collected by Linda Dégh, 1959.

The two legends linked together in this narrative have been found in a considerable number of variants attached to various figures, all coachmen, but interestingly enough, in most of them the dialogue has been repeated almost word for word. The stopping of the horse is a frequent magic feat, but the figure of the artisan (usually a carpenter or a mason) endowed with superhuman knowledge has not been found in any other connection save as an adversary of the coachman, who overcomes him by his superior magic power. The second story emphasizes the fact that by means of his magic knowledge the coachman has his master in his power and could have taken his revenge on him by destroying his fine horses. Such a story explains how the coachman could win the sympathy and respect of the common people. It is characteristic that while the coachman's son denies that the extraordinary knowledge of his father may have come from the devil or from evil spirits, he willingly admits to magic practices of a different kind.

There was a head coachman in the service of the count living at Berkesz

Manor. Some thirty good horses, to be used only for the count's coach, were under his care. But he never even so much as touched any of them because there were a lot of grooms whose duty it was to look after the horses. They fed and curried the horses and harnessed them to the coach when the count drove out. The coachman had nothing else to do but get on the box and drive the horses. Now the coachman was a man possessed of secret knowledge.

There was a man once who was working on the roof of his shed. He was covering the roof with thatch. One day when out driving the count, the coachman—called Mihály Dajka—had to pass this shed on his way, and the four horses suddenly stopped dead and stood as if nailed to the spot. The coachman tried everything to get his horses to move on, but they wouldn't stir. Wondering what was the matter, the coachman looked up at the man working on the roof of the shed. He called up to him, "I say, my friend, let us pass on our way."

But the man up there pretended not to hear him.

Again the coachman called up to him, "I say, my friend, let us pass on our way."

The man then looked down and said, "What's that? What's the matter with me? To be sure, I'm not holding your horses to keep them from going on. Or do you mean, perhaps, that I should be pushing on your coach?"

"Not at all. You needn't push my coach. Just let us pass on our way."

"Well, go on, if you can."

The coachman listened to him without saying a word. He always carried in his pocket a spare calk so that he might fix it onto one of the horseshoes, to prevent the horse from slipping. He drew forth the calk from his pocket and fixed it to the end of one of the four lashes of his whip. Cracking his whip, he lashed out at the horses. At once the horses began to pull, going off at a steady trot. The very minute that he lashed out with the whip, the man fell from the roof. The calk had knocked out one of his eyes, though the coachman had not touched him with his whip. The count was in the coach, and he saw it all with his own eyes.

Here is another story about Mihály.

This happened on a Saturday in Easter week. The count was called away by a telegram. The telegram had been delivered late, so he gave orders to Miska Dajka, the head coachman, to drive up to the manor house at once as he wanted to catch the eight o'clock train at the station of Kisvárda. It was a good eight miles' distance from the manor house at Gégény to Kisvárda. The count rang up the stationmaster to ask him about the train.

"Well, sir, it has just pulled out," the stationmaster told him.

The count got into the coach. "Well, Miska, we've just missed the morning train."

"Never mind, sir! We can catch up with it at the next flag station which is at Demecser."

So they drove off at once, and the count arrived in time to get a ticket and get on the train. Miska drove back, but halfway to the manor one of the horses nearly collapsed. When later he led the horses into their stable, one of them went in, but the other dropped dead. As soon as the count came back home, the coachman reported to him that Lancsi, the dapple horse, was dead.

"Well, Miska," the count said to him, "let's not worry about it more than we can help, but you must tell me how it happened. One of them had been all of a sweat, but not the other horse. Could you tell me the reason why?"

"Well, sir, there's no denying it that Lancsi was as good as dead when we'd got halfway home, but I managed to bring him home."

"You brought him home, didn't you?"

"Yes, sir, I did."

"Well," the count said, "so that's that. Now listen! We're still in the early part of the year, my son; you'll get your year's wages, but mind that you keep out of the stable."

"All right, sir. It can't be helped, I must do as you wish. Tomorrow, as soon as my portion of life [wheat paid in kind to farmhands] has been measured out to me, I'll move home, and I shall never set foot on the manor again. All my life I've been a coachman, and that's the only job I mean to do. It's for you now to find somebody to drive the coach."

And so it happened. The count paid Miska a year's wages, and Miska left the manor. But what next? The count had a lot of horses. Twelve grooms had been looking after the horses, feeding and currying them. But after Miska's departure, not one of the grooms could go near the horses. Whenever the grooms appeared with hay and water, the horses would jump so that you'd think they'd hit the ceiling, and then they would bite and paw the ground and kick out in a frenzy. There was no way to get them under control, neither by using a halter nor by any other means. Finally, the steward of the manor had to be sent for, so that he could see for himself what was going on in the stable. The grooms reported to him that for the past three days the horses had taken neither a bit of fodder nor a drink of water, and that all of them would soon perish if this went on for long. They said that there was nothing else to do but to send for Miska and call him back.

Next day a man was sent for Miska. "Uncle Miska, you must come back at once."

"At whose order?"

"At the count's order."

"Well, boy, I won't take any notice of it. Go back and tell the count that you haven't found me at home."

In the afternoon a second messenger came to Miska. He fared the same as the first since Miska took no heed of the count's message. "Go back, son, and tell the count that I shan't return until I hear the same voice calling me back that ordered me to leave. Should the count take the trouble to come here in person to call me back, I might return and see what could be done with the horses."

Then the count himself went to call him back and said, "Come back, Miska, and you shall have your old job as long as you live; and when you get old, you'll get a pension, and I shall always see after your needs. Only come back at once, because all my horses will perish if you don't."

So Miska went with the count and together they drove back to the manor. Miska made for the stable. It was a mighty big stable, kept clean and in order, with the name of each horse written over his stall. When he went in he found the horses in a frenzy.

"Get me that whip, the one with the snapper." And promptly he made use of it, lashing at the horses sideways. "The plague on you! What the dickens has come over you? Here! Now let them have their feed and drink. I dare say they're not going to refuse it. It's only that you haven't been looking after them in the proper way."

And for another three years Miska was looking after the horses. When he grew old, the count gave him a pension, and there was no disgrace in his going away, and it was right to take on another man in his place. All the same, if at that time he had not been called back, all the count's horses would have perished. That's a fact, and there's no lying about it. True, I haven't been there myself, but I've heard it from men who wouldn't tell a lie.

I was there myself once when a man said to Sanyi, Miska's son, "You owe your fine horses to the magic of your father."

"There wasn't any black magic about the old man," Sanyi said. "Maybe your horses can turn out just as good."

"Then tell me the secret of your old man."

"Well, in spring when the flies and butterflies begin to try their wings and flit over the fields, go out and look for one with a red wing and try to catch it, even if you have to follow it across seven boundaries. And when you've got hold of it, cut your ax into the tongue of your cart, and push that butterfly into the split."

As a matter of fact, I have never tried it myself, because I have a fear of such things.

Lazybones

From Linda Dégh, *Folktales of Hungary* (Chicago: University of Chicago Press, 1965), pp. 142–47.

Type 902* *The Lazy Woman is Cured.*

Narrator, Mrs. József Palkó, aged seventy-four, an illiterate peasant of Kakasd, Tolna County. Collected by Linda Dégh, 1950. Dégh, *Kakasdi Népmesék* (Budapest: Akadémiai Kiadó, 1955), no. 35.

Characteristic of this type of humorous story is a tendency to point a moral concerning the proper conduct of the village girl. These amusing jests aim to show that such failings as untidiness, laziness, foolishness, and slovenliness impair the poor peasant girl's chance of getting married. In our peasant society of old, industry used to be the most highly appreciated quality of a peasant girl; she was praised for her ability to work. In the village or on the farm, a woman who has no love for work will prove a disastrous choice, and in a peasant community no lazy girl will ever find herself a husband. In her story, Mrs. Palkó emphasizes the moral of proper conduct by pointing out the place of women in a rural community.

There is evidence that our tale has some connections with similar topics in Rumanian folk-literature. Variants have been collected in Estonia, Lithuania, Yugoslavia, Russia, and Japan.

Mrs. Palkó belongs with our most eminent storytellers. She came to Hungary in 1946 with a small group of Székelys who had been living in Bukovina for over two hundred years, forming a Hungarian linguistic community in the midst of people of different languages. In the course of her strenuous life, Mrs. Palkó brought up thirteen children. She learned her stories in workers' hostels, during spells of work as a seasonal laborer in agriculture. Both her father and her brother used to be famed storytellers. Only after their death did she take up storytelling for the entertainment of others. In my collection, *Folktales of Kakasd*, I published seventy-two of her tales. For the present, her storytelling is mainly reserved for winter occasions, usually when people gather to perform some work in common, or at family meetings, especially when they gather to keep vigil at a wake. On such occasions Mrs. Palkó starts telling her tales at 6 P.M. and goes on till the next morning. Her easy-flowing style reveals an unusual depth of emotion and a fine lyric sense in the fairy tales and displays her keen sense of humor in the dramatic recital of the jests. In recognition of her storytelling talent, she was awarded the title of Master of Popular Arts in 1954.

There was a wealthy farmer who had a daughter. She was his only daughter. And though she was big and strong, she was a lazy girl, averse to taking the broom in her hand, and all the chores had to be done by her mother. Her laziness had soon become common talk all over the village, and there was not a young man who came to woo her, in spite of her father's wealth.

Her mother never stopped nagging. "You see, my girl, there isn't a single lad to hang around you as there are about the other girls. All of your friends are taken out to dances, while you're just sitting at home, because the young people don't want to have anything to do with you."

"Do not vex me, mother," she says. "Come Sunday, there'll be a dance, and I'll be going with the others."

And so it happened. She went to the dance. And while all the other girls had been asked by their young men, there was no one to take a single turn with her; and there she was standing like a proper wallflower, in lack of a partner.

Then a young man from a neighboring village appeared among the dancers. As soon as he entered he began to show interest in her, as she was quite a comely girl, if only she had not been so terribly lazy. And the young man was asking the others about her, and so he learned that she was the daughter of a well-to-do farmer with many possessions.

"Then why isn't she asked for a dance?"

They said, "Oh, she is no good at all at dancing. She never came to dance with us before. That's why she hasn't got a partner now."

Well, the young man thought it over and when the musicians struck up a tune, he asked her for a dance.

True, she did not excel in dancing, but as he was a superb dancer they did quite well and enjoyed it. When the dance was over, he asked her, "Whose daughter are you? What's your father's name?"

And she asked him, "And what's your name?"

"My name is András," he says, "and before you leave let me have a word with you, because I am going to visit you."

"What for?"

"Well, I intend to go to the spinning-house when you are there."

Happy she was that there was a young man who would come for her sake. The others were still teasing her and didn't think much about her success. So she left without talking to him and rapidly made for home. And then she reported to her mother, "Mother, a young man is coming to us to make court to me." And both the girl and her mother rejoiced at this thought.

"Well, my girl, you must put your best foot forward when he comes. Show yourself quick with your hands and busy so that you may win his affection. Don't forget how ill-reputed you are because of your laziness, so try to do your best."

And one day the young man appeared accompanied by two of his comrades. The girl's mother gave him a friendly greeting, "Welcome, sit down and make yourself comfortable." And she brought a chair for him, and put a bottle of wine and a bottle of brandy on the table and a plate with cakes.

When the visitors had done well for themselves, the young man said, "Well, I don't want to take up much of your time. I've come because I've heard that you've got a marriageable daughter. I know her because we have met at the dance. All I want to know is whether you'd be willing to give me your daughter in marriage?"

"Oh dear, I am happy to give her in marriage to you. You appear to be a handsome lad whose head is screwed on the right way. And let me tell you that you won't regret marrying her. We've made a nice fortune, and we have only a son and a girl. The two will get all we have. You'll see what dowry I'm going to give her. I'll fit her up so richly with clothes that all her life she will have enough to wear and you needn't bother about buying her a single piece. And we'll divide the land between our two children. And half of our livestock will go to her too."

On that very day they went to the priest and registered for marriage. And after three weeks they had their wedding.

And the bride got a chest as long as the longest bed, and it was packed so richly with clothes that it needed some effort to clamp on the lid. And she received all she had been promised and half of the livestock, and then her husband took her to the village from where he had come.

And he was mighty pleased about the rich dowry and was looking forward to the many good things they would be getting from her parents. But the leopard does not change its spots. Once lazy, always lazy. The girl went on the same as she used to do at home. Whitewashing and cleaning the house. Oh, no! She fought shy of both these jobs. No wonder she was of such ill-repute. On Sundays, when she changed her bodice and her chemise, she never hung them on a peg or put them into a basket, but made a bundle of the dirty clothes and threw the whole lot into the fire. And every Sunday she followed this practice. Her husband never guessed what she was doing and when after a year he looked into her chest, there wasn't a single bodice or chemise left in it.

Once an invitation came for a wedding feast from a nearby village where the relations of her husband lived. So he said to his wife, "Well, wife, I'm going to take you to a wedding."

"Where to?"

"The son of my father's brother is going to have his wedding."

"Well, I am not going with you."

"And why not? You are still young enough. And we haven't been going out much since we've married."

"Going to a wedding needs some decent clothes."

"Surely you've got plenty of clothes, even more than enough."

"I used to have them," says the woman.

"Oh, what are you telling me? You haven't sent them back to your mother, have you? Didn't you get a big chest packed with so many clothes that two men could hardly lift it?"

"Didn't you know that I've burned all of them?"

"What did you burn? Your clothes?"

"Yes, I've thrown into the fire all my garments except the soiled ones you see me wearing now."

"Don't tell me that you've been taught to throw your dirty clothes into the fire? Didn't you know that what becomes dirty by wear should be hung on a peg or put into a basket? And even then one must not wait till it grows into a big bundle, but it has to be washed and pressed and put neatly into a chest."

"Well, never in my life did I do any washing; how should I have known how to go about it? I thought it would be best if I burned what was dirty so I needn't bother about washing them."

"Well, I've had enough of that silly talk. Whatever you've got on you're going to wear, and I am going to take you to the wedding. We haven't moved out of this spot for a year, and I am not going to sit at home forever for your sake."

"Well, and I am certainly not going out in my soiled garments."

The man then went out and returned with a truss of straw and reeds which he had prepared for thatching up their roofs. Then he stripped his wife to the skin and bundled her up between the wisps of straw and reed. Then he tied it up at both ends and about her waist.

"Look here, woman" he said to her. "I'll put you on the cart and throw a rug over you so that you can come with me without being seen. And first we're going to your parents' place and there you can get yourself some garments which you can wear at the wedding."

"Well let's go then" she agreed.

"And do not fear" he said. "I will ask your mother myself to let you have some of her clothes."

When they reached the place where her parents lived, he stopped at the garden and got his wife down from the cart and, bundled up as she was, he shoved her behind the haystacks. Then he went into the house. His wife's father and mother were indeed happy that the young pair had come to visit them, and eagerly the mother asked her son-in-law, "And where's our daughter?"

"She's come too; she is in the garden by the haystacks."

They asked him, "Why didn't she come in with you?"

He said to her mother, "Just go out to her; she wants to speak with you."

The mother rushed out into the garden and called out loudly, "Where are you, my dear daughter?"

"Here I am," she said, "bundled up between wisps of straw and reed. You see, I've told my husband that I couldn't go to the wedding as I haven't any decent clothes to wear. So he bundled me up between the reed and straw he had prepared for thatching and brought me along. Now, please let me have some of your clothes."

"But what did he do with that lot of clothes I had given you for your dowry?"

"Well, mother, I've burned them all."

"And why did you do that?"

"I thought it was the best way to get rid of them once they were dirty. I simply threw them into the fire and let them burn."

The young husband went out to them and hearing her words he said, "Now you can judge yourself what sort of a wife your daughter has made. In less than a year she has foolishly done away with that lot of clothes you gave her. Well, I've brought her back to you because I don't want her any more. You'll get back every penny and whatever she had brought with her. You can please yourself with your daughter and your fortune; I do not want to have either. A fat lot do I care about her relations and the wedding feast. I'm leaving her here, and I call it a good riddance."

"But look here, son, I am willing to let her have some more clothes."

"Keep your clothes, and your daughter as well. She'll never do for a wife."

And he returned to his village and left his wife at her parents' place. There she is still with them. And he married again. And if they are not dead, they are still alive to this day.

Russia

The Sorcerer and His Apprentice

Selected by Felix J. Oinas and translated by Olga May from Mark Azadovskij, ed., *Russkaja skazka: Izbrannye mastera* ("Russian Folktales: Selected Masters") (Leningrad: Academia, 1931), pp. 390–401.

Type 325 *The Magician and His Pupil* is a famous tale known throughout Europe. Collected by M. K. Azadovskij in 1915. Narrator Natal'ja O. Vinokurova is in her fifties. Previously published in Mark Azadovskij, ed., *Skazki Verkhnelenskogo kraja* ("Tales of the Upper Lena Region"), 1 (Irkutsk, 1925).

N. O. Vinokurova was a Siberian narrator from the Upper Lena River area. She was illiterate and had spent her life in the village of her birth; only in her early youth had she served as a maid in the town. Mark Azadovskij, who discovered her and studied her tales, places her among the foremost representatives of the art of Russian fairy-tale narration. Vinokurova discards the typical fairy-tale ritual with its fixed beginnings and its threefold repetitions. Her prime qualities as a narrator lie in her penetrating psychological insights and in her humanization of the miraculous aspects of Märchen.

"The Sorcerer and His Apprentice" is one of the most widespread Russian Märchen. In this version, the old father's intoxication has been developed by Vinokurova—contrary to other narrators—into a complex scene, rich in environmental and psychological details. The narrator describes how the father's irritation, in direct proportion to his intoxication, gradually intensifies, culminating in his surrender of the bridle. This act results in the loss of his son, his frantic, unsuccessful search for him, and his ultimate despair. "This episode heightens," says Azadovskij, "the dramatic setting of the tale and seems to add one last stroke to the process of humanizing the external miraculous nature of the tale."

Literature: Mark Azadovskij, *Eine sibirische Märchenerzählerin*, Folklore Fellows Communications 68 (Helsinki: Academia Scientiarum Fennica, 1926); Felix J. Oinas and Stephen Soudakoff, eds., *The Study of Russian Folklore* (The Hague: Mouton, 1975), pp. 79–89.

Motifs in the tale-type that occur here are as follows: S212 "Child sold to magician"; D1711.0.1 "Magician's apprentice"; H62.1 "Recognition of person transformed to animal"; D100 "Transformation: man to animal"; C837 "Tabu: losing bridle in selling man transformed to horse. Disenchantment follows. (Selling horse with bridle. Horse punished by magician)"; D615.2 "Transformation contest between master and pupil"; D641.1 "Lover as bird (ring) visits mistress"; L142.2 "Pupil surpasses magician." This text does not include the episodes of the transformation and obstacle flights, and does add a prophecy of future glory (M312).

There was an old man and an old woman. They were very, very poor. They had an eight- or nine-year-old boy. Then came a time when they did not have anything to eat. "This is the end, old woman, let's send the boy out as an apprentice. Maybe he will be fed and clothed."

The father decided to take the boy to town in the morning. The old woman got up in the morning, got dressed, started the fire, and got the boy ready. "What is the use for us to keep him here hungry and naked?"

The old man and the boy started for the town. They had not yet reached the town when they met a man in a brushwood. A well-dressed man.

"Hello, Grandfather!"

"Hello, Uncle!"

"Where are you going?"

"Well, we are very poor, so I am going to apprentice my boy to someone. I just don't have any other choice."

"Ah, how much do you want for him for a year, Grandfather?"

"What can I ask for him? He hasn't been anywhere, hasn't seen anything. He is naked and barefoot. If someone would clothe and feed him. . . ."

"Well, how much do you want for him? I want to take him from you."

"Sir, I will make a deal with you. You clothe and give him shoes and whatever you give me would be fine."

The man took out a hundred rubles from his pocket and gave it to the old man.

"Sir, that boy could not earn you such money."

"Well, take what you are given. It is not your business."

The old man took the money, said good-bye, and started for home. He had just started when a thought struck him: "Oh, what a fool am I. I didn't ask his name or surname, or where he lives. To whom have I given my boy? I better go back and ask the man."

The old man turned around and yelled loudly, "Wait, wait, Uncle." The man and the boy stopped. The boy was called Mitja.

"What do you want, old man?"

"Excuse me, I didn't ask your name or surname, and I don't know where you live."

"Don't worry, old man. Why do you need my name or surname? Your Mitja will be taken care of. And when the time is up, I will bring him to you at the same place."

The old man went home with the money. On the way he went to the market, bought some bread and something to eat, and went home to his old woman.

"Well, old woman, I got one hundred rubles for Mitja. What do you say?"

They lived thriftily and had enough to get by. The year was up and the old man was to pick up Mitja on the morrow. The old woman [mother] hadn't seen her child for a whole year. She got up early and sent the old man to fetch him.

The old man went to the place where he had left his boy with the stranger. He saw the man and Mitja coming. Mitja had only been away for a year, but he looked as if he was twelve years' old. So grown and dressed, so well and clean. The old man admired the lad. He was nicely dressed and had become so strong.

"Well, Grandfather, you came for your son?"

"Yes, for my son."

"Well, here he is. Well and cared for. Wouldn't you want to give him to me for another year?"

"Well, Mitja, if you want to stay for another year."

"This year I will give you two hundred rubles. Let's go to my place. You will see where your son lives and what work he does."

The old man went along. They arrived. There was a good house. They asked him to sit down and gave him refreshments. The man had a wife and three daughters. The old man asks his son, "Well, Mitja, did you live well?"

"Oh, what do I need? Better than at home. They don't make me work hard. The clothes and keep are good."

The old man and the master made a deal. The old man received two hundred rubles.

"Well, old man, let's go. I will show you your son's work."

He took him to the back yard. A rick of chopped wood was stacked there.

"See here, your son chopped a whole rick of wood during this year." The old man thought, "What in the world did he pay one hundred rubles for?"

"Mitja, bring me the matches," said the master. Mitja went, brought the matches. "Mitja, set this woodpile on fire!" Mitja started the fire. The old man thought: "Oh, what is he doing? If he didn't like Mitja's work, why did he hire him for the second year?" The woodpile was burning bright. The master took the boy by the arm and threw him into the fire. The old man almost died from the fright, he stood there as if turned into stone.

"What are you doing? He is my only son, and you are throwing him into the fire! I will get even with you!"

"Don't worry, he will live." A little dove flew up from the fire.

"This is your Mitja. Now go home and don't worry. Now you know where I live. When the year passes, come for Mitja."

The old man comes home, brings two hundred rubles, but he does not tell the old woman what he saw, so she would not be sick in her soul. They lived the whole year without any need. To tell it briefly: the year was up tomorrow. "I'll again go for Mitja." The mother has not seen Mitja for two years. She gets the old man ready and hurries him on his way: "Go!"

The old man goes. This man comes to meet him, but he is alone, without Mitja.

"Hello, Grandfather!"

"Hello, master!"

"Did you come for your son?"

"Yes, for my son."

"Well, go to my place. I have to go some place, but I will be back soon."

The old man comes to the master's house. His three daughters are sitting at the table. The old man greets them and sits down. Mitja was not there. The old man noticed that the girls were whispering something. And about him, the old man. "Dear girls, what are you whispering about? Tell me the whole truth." He heard the youngest one begging the older girls, "Let's tell the grandfather, let's tell him."

But the oldest was obstinate. The old man began begging her and the youngest sister begged her too with tears in her eyes:

"Let's tell it to Grandfather."

"All right, old man, we will tell you, but watch out and don't tell our father. We feel sorry for you, since Mitja is your only son and you are so poor."

The old man swears that he will not tell it to their father.

"Our father is not an Orthodox Christian. He is a terrible sorcerer. Your Mitja lived with lešij [a wood goblin]. When our father returns home, he will offer you refreshments, then he will take you to that barn. There he has three hundred doves, and all of them are his workers. He will open the door and let them out and will say, "If you catch

Mitja, he will be yours, but if you catch a stranger, your Mitja will be lost."

The old man begged them with tears in his eyes, "Oh, my dearest beauties, tell me the signs of my Mitja."

"Well, Grandfather, your Mitja will come out last. And he will have a soiled tail. He will appear to be the poorest of the lot. Catch him."

When the sorcerer came, he offered the old man some tea. "Let's go, old man," and opened the door of the barn. Two doves flew out—beautiful, gay, and well fed. Another one flew after them. It was so skinny and starved. The old man said: "A crow cannot beget a falcon. As I am so worn out, my little dove—it seems—must be that wretched one." He caught the dove, hid it in his bosom, and ran from the sorcerer. He ran for a while when suddenly he thought: "Oh, what a fool am I. I did not ask how to restore Mitja. What am I going to do with a dove?"

He opened his bosom where he has hidden the dove and it flew away. The old man got frightened: he had no dove, he had no Mitja. "Where am I going now? I guess I will go back to the sorcerer." He was very gloomy. Suddenly he saw that the dove was flying back to him. It turned in front of the old man, struck itself against the earth, and became Mitja. He began to scold the old man: "You lived to an old age, but are not very wise. It is well that I myself have learned what to do. Otherwise, what would you do with a dove?"

Then they went home to mother. Well, his mother was as all mothers are, she was very glad. They slept. On the morrow they awoke and ate breakfast. Mitja asked his father to go to town. "Father, let's go to town." They walk through the brushwood. A crow sits on a bush and caws. Mitja glances at the crow and grins wryly.

"Mitja, why are you laughing at the crow?"

Mitja said this and that and answered, "Oh, it's nothing."

They walk on. Another crow cawed even louder. And Mitja grinned wider.

"Mitja, why are you laughing at the crow?"

Mitja answered again, "It's nothing."

Well, the old man pestered Mitja, "Tell me, do tell me!"

"What for are you asking me that?"

"What do you mean, what for? I am your father and such a one as you are, you won't even talk to me."

"Well, if I tell you, you will be angry."

"No, Mitja, I won't be angry, tell me."

"Well, the first crow said, 'Thou wilt be a Czar, a Czar.' And the second crow said, 'Thou wilt wash thy feet and thy father will drink the washwater.' I am ashamed."

"That's all right. After all, none of it is true. Who could imagine your being a Czar?"

"Now listen, Father. Right now I will turn into a hazel stallion and you will take me to the market and sell me. Ask for me one hundred rubles without the bridle. Watch out—don't sell me with the bridle."

Here Mitja turned a somersault and began running as a stallion. The old man caught him by the bridle and led him to the market. The buyers approach him. Some offer sixty, some seventy, but he asks one hundred rubles. One gentleman comes by: "Are you asking one hundred rubles for your horse? All right, take the hundred, but only with the bridle."

"No, I will sell only without the bridle."

Well, the gentleman decided to buy the horse without the bridle. The old man sold the stallion, put the bridle over his arm, and went home. As he was walking through the brushwood, Mitja caught up with him. In short, the next day he sold Mitja again for one hundred rubles without the bridle. On the third day he took the stallion to town again.

On arrival, he saw an open tavern. He had never drunk before.

"Well, why not? I have a few kopecks. I'll go in and have a shot."

He tied up his stallion and went into the tavern.

"Come on, barkeeper, pour me a shot!"

The barkeeper served it to him, and he drank it up. He liked it so well that he shouted, "Give me another one!" His head was already spinning from these drinks. He stayed at that tavern for a long time. A drunk has many stories to tell. Already the stallion was getting angry. He snorted and stomped his feet on the ground outside the tavern, but the old man drank some more and became drunk.

He came out of the tavern, untied his horse, whipped him, scolded him, and jerked on the reins.

"If I want to, I'll sell you with the bridle today. So you won't imagine that you are going to wash your feet and have me drink that water."

Oh well, a drunk is a drunk. He comes to the market. A buyer asks him, "Grandfather, what do you want for your horse?"

"Three hundred rubles without the bridle."

"Couldn't you sell with the bridle, Grandfather?"

"Oh, take it, and make use of it."

And so the drunk sold it, sold it with the bridle.

While he was drunk he was running around in town, but when he sobered up it suddenly struck him, "What have I done? Why did I sell him with the bridle? I will never see my son again. Why did I go to that tavern? Why did I drink vodka?"

For a long time he waited for Mitja at the place where they always met. But Mitja did not come. For the whole week he kept running to town, thinking that he might meet him somewhere. No, he did not meet him anywhere. So he began to live without Mitja.

Mitja was bought by that same master. The very same sorcerer. He brought the stallion into the barn and put him upside down with his legs tied to the ceiling by chains. He started a small fire underneath him. "That, my dove, is my punishment for you. Because you lived with me for two years and became craftier than I am."

Well, Mitja—the horse—hung there a month or two. He was smoked all over. He did not eat or drink. He hung there for the full six months, barely alive.

One day the sorcerer went somewhere. His daughters said, "Girls, let's go to the barn and see how Mitja is doing." "Sister, let's untie him and give him something to drink." The daughters began to untie him. The oldest said, "Papa will be angry with us." "No, we will tie him up again. See, sister, his skin has cracked. We'll hang him up later."

Well, they took him down. He swayed and fell down and he couldn't stand. He had his bridle on. "Sister, let's take him to the stream to water him!"

He walked swaying, faltering. The youngest sister feels sorry for him, so she takes the bridle and leads him to the stream to drink. He drinks as if through his teeth, he drinks and drinks, but all the time he looks back cautiously. Suddenly he jumps into the water and begins to swim with all his might. So strong was the jump that it caused waves. "What will Papa say to us now?"

In that moment their father returned home, but already the stallion had run away. "Papa, Papa, the stallion ran away from us!" He did not have time to scold them. He turned himself into a carp and went after Mitja.

Mitja heard the sorcerer chasing after him and became a perch. The sorcerer chased and chased after him, but could not catch him. And so they came to a strange town. On the bridge a Czar's daughter was rinsing her kerchiefs, preparing for the evening. Mitja turned himself into a golden ring and jumped into the Czarevna's kerchief. The Czarevna was so happy with her beautiful ring that she put it on her finger and could not admire it enough. But the carp had nothing to hold onto.

The Czar's daughter went to her father and says, "See father, what gifts are bestowed upon me," and all the time she admired her ring. "From where did this gift for my finger come, as though from heaven itself." Her father says, "This ring is sent to you as an omen, either of joy or a hard time."

In the evening they got together in the garden house. They had something to eat and to drink, and then the music and dancing began. Then they heard someone under the window playing the simple village balalaika. They sent a servant to see who it was. He came back and explained that it was someone who played a new music. They listened and liked that music.

"Well, call him into the house!"

They invited him in, greeted him properly. They seated him in an easy chair. "Well, sit down and play." Some laughed at his music, some cried, some were comforted, some danced. His music appeared interesting.

When the evening was over, the musician had to be paid. Now the Czar asked him, "How much will you take for the evening?"

"I don't need anything, only if your daughter would give me that ring from her finger for my playing."

The Czarevna did not want even to talk about the ring. "Let Papa give away half of his domain, but I won't give away this ring."

The musician did not want to take even a thousand rubles. They began to argue and shout. The daughter went to the porch in tears. She cried and took off the ring: "How will I part with it?"

"Czarevna, I ask a favor of you. If your father will force you to give away the ring, take it off your finger and throw it on the ground with force. It will scatter in small sparkles. Pay attention, one of them will be brighter than all the others. You step on it with your heel. I will cling to you."

In short, the Czarevna was driven to such a state that she took off her ring, threw it on the floor, and said, "If I could not have it, you will not have it either, you dog."

Then, when the sparkles scattered about, she quickly stepped on the shiniest one with her heel. And that musician suddenly fell to the ground and turned into a rooster and began to peck, to collect those sparkles. And from under Czarevna's heel flew out a falcon and attacked the rooster. The falcon pecked the rooster to death.

As soon as the falcon had pecked the rooster to death, he fell on the ground and became a fine fellow. Mitja was just as good as he was before.

"Oh, Czar, our father, allow me to burn this rooster and then to destroy his ashes."

Then Mitja began to tell them everything. He told them every detail, and the Czarevna did not move a step from his side. Mitja stayed with the Czar one week, then another. And the matchmaking began. Mitja said to the Czar: "Czar, our father, I am already betrothed. I will go and visit my fiancee. If she does not want to marry me, then I will marry your daughter."

When Mitja went to visit his fiancee, the Czarevna even got sick from such a blow. Mitja went to see the three sisters. He arrived, and they were very glad to see him.

"What's that, Mitja is alive, and we thought that our father finished you."

"Well, my dear beauties, I conquered your father at the Czar's house."

"Thank you, Mitja, that was a right thing to do."

Mitja began to court the youngest sister and the older ones became envious. Mitja arrives at the Czar's house with his fiancee. They set the day for the wedding. On the eve of the event, the Czarevna poisoned Mitja's bride. Mitja was terribly sorry. She was better than the Czarevna. Then the Czar married the Czarevna to Mitja and said, "I have become old." And so he made him the Czar.

One day Mitja decided to visit his father. He and his wife sat down in a coach and went there. When he arrived at his father's, how could his father know that his Mitja was the Czar? In the evening they sat late at his father's, talking, and then they went to sleep. Mitja's feet were burning from the heat so he washed them. And sure enough his father became thirsty at night and he drank some water from the same basin. So the prophecy was fulfilled.

Mitja took his father and mother with him. And they lived a long life and became wealthy.

Peter the Great and the Stonemason

Selected by Felix J. Oinas and translated by Nikolai Burlakoff from I. V. Karnaukhova, ed., *Skazki i predanija Severnogo kraja* ("Tales and Legends of the Northern Region"), (Moscow and Leningrad: Academia, 1934), pp. 127–28.

Type 921A *The Four Coins* is reported chiefly from eastern Europe. Collected by I. V. Karnaukhova in 1926. Narrator Dmitrij Andreevich Orekhov, forty-two, from the village of Sibovo, Zaonezh'e.

This version of the legend has come to be associated with Peter the Great (1672–1725). Peter never attached much importance to origin or rank, and many of his assistants and close associates came from the lowest strata of society. Folk anecdotes often depict him as the "peasant Czar." In this tale the cleverness of the workers is contrasted with the stupidity of the "senators," i.e., members of the Senate—the highest administrative and judicial institution, established in Russia by Peter the Great in 1711.

The teller, D. A. Orekhov, was a fisherman by profession. Fishermen in Russia used to work in groups ("artels"), often away from their homes. During the long nights their main pastime was telling tales and singing songs. Orekhov was literate. He was a soldier in Czarist times and had lived in the city, and liked to recount details of city life in his tales. In this story, he used the term "percent" without knowing its proper meaning.

Once upon a beautiful time, Peter the Great surveyed Petersburg. He drove by Putilov's mountain and saw a stonemason. Drives up to him, asks, "God be with you, fellow. How's work? Are you earning much?"

"Such trifles deserve no thanks; in a day eighty kopecks I'll earn."

"So, does this suffice?"

"It really does not suffice."

"It's a strange matter; how do you dispose of the money?"

"Twenty percent I pay to the house, 20 percent I lend out, 20 percent I throw out of the window."

The sovereign became thoughtful.

"Explain, fellow," says he, "I do not understand."

"You see, on 20 percent I feed my father and mother; on 20 percent two sons I raise; 20 percent I give to two swans [daughters]—their wings shall become firm, that's all I'll see of them. And 20 percent I keep.

"And have you ever seen the sovereign?"

"Well, no, but I would like to."

"Well, come with me. I'll show him to you. When he arrives at the village all the people will be without caps; the only one with a cap will be the sovereign."

They arrive at the village. There everybody yelled hurrah and threw their caps in the air. Peter asks, "Which one of us is the Czar? All are without hats, only we two have our hats." ·

"I don't know," the mason says. Then the fellow falls on his knees. "Forgive me," he says, "your Czarist majesty."

"I'll take you to Petersburg, and you'll tell your riddle to the senators."

They sat down in a cart and set off to Petersburg. On their arrival Peter the Great summoned the senators and said to them, "Well, mister senators, this peasant gave me a riddle I could not solve. I ask you to solve it in three days' time."

So the peasant told them the riddle. "I earn eighty kopecks: twenty kopecks I pay to the house, twenty I lend out, twenty kopecks I throw out the window, and on twenty kopecks I live."

"Mister senators, figure out where his money is going. And you, fellow, don't you dare to tell them without my presence."

The senators thought, guessed, but could not find a solution. Time is running out, but they can't solve the riddle. So one decided to trick him [the peasant].

"Let's call him and offer him anything he asks."

They called him and started to bribe him, but he wasn't slow. He had a large hat with a wide brim. "Fill my hat up, full of gold."

So they filled it up. Then he said, "Twenty kopecks—father and mother I feed; twenty kopecks—two sons I raise; twenty kopecks—two swans I raise; on twenty kopecks I myself live."

The senators see that the answer is the simplest, but they couldn't guess it alone. When the time was up they went to the sovereign.

"So this is the solution," they say.

He says, "You could not have solved it by yourselves. He [the peasant] told you."

So they confessed. How sternly he looked at the peasant. While that one says, "Your imperial majesty, just see how many of your likenesses they gave me. How could I refuse to talk?" (*You see on every gold piece there is a likeness of the sovereign.*)

They all went to dinner. The Czar sat the peasant down by his side. The senators decided to undermine him. One hit his neighbor and said, "Pass it on." So each hit in turn until it came to the peasant. He now must hit the Czar.

But he [the peasant] stood up and said, "Well, mister senators, I had this dream. The old lady and I went to the forest and saw good firewood. So we went on and started to sink. The further we go the more we sink. So maybe we should return home? Yes, I say—turn back, but the firewood is so good! Well, mister senators, what should I do, sink or turn home?"

Well, they answer, "Of course, turn back home."

He turns around and hits one [the senator who had hit him]. "Pass it on," he says.

Immediately the Czar made him the chief senator and put the others under him.

Two Thieves

Selected by Felix J. Oinas and translated by Olga May from I. V. Karnaukhova, ed., *Skazki i predanija Severnogo kraja* ("Tales and Legends of the Northern Region"), (Moscow and Leningrad: Academia, 1934), pp. 127–28.

Type 1654 and motif K335.1.2.2, *The Robbers in the Death Chamber*, reported primarily from eastern Europe. Collected by I. V. Karnaukhova in 1926. Narrator Dmitrij Vasil'evich Belousov, sixty-two, from village Padmozero, Zaonezh'e.

The tale of a man who would rather feign death than pay his debt is fairly well known in Russia. Characteristic of this version is the identification of the robbers who come to the death chamber to divide their money with the "Pans." The "Pans" were members of the Polish-Lithuanian army that, together with the Cossacks, ravaged and pillaged North Russia during the latter phase of the so-called Time of Troubles, but especially from the end of 1612 until 1615. Although the Cossacks are said to have committed the most cruel deeds, the guilt was shifted onto the Polish and Lithuanian "Pans," since Poland through her intervention was thought to be greatly responsible for the miseries of the "Time of Troubles."

The activity of the Polish-Lithuanian army included a wide belt to the southwest and northeast of Lake Onega, the area where our version has been recorded. The collector gives no details about the informant, except to say that "He is a very skilled teller."

Bibliography: Felix J. Oinas, "Legends of the Chuds and Pans," *Studies in Finnic-Slavic Folklore Relations* (Folklore Fellows Communications 205; Helsinki: Academia Scientiarum Fennica, 1969), pp. 160–77.

There were two thieves. Surely there never were such as they before. Sen'ka and Van'ka. Whatever was around they would steal immediately.

Well, once they quarreled, and what's more over a *kopejka* [Russian monetary unit, approximately one U.S. cent]!

Sen'ka yells, "Give up the *kopejka*."

While for the life of him, Van'ka begrudged the *kopejka*.

"I'll die," he says, "yet I won't give up the *kopejka*." (You see a *kopejka* was worth a lot in the old days.)

Well, so he apparently started to die. He lay down in a coffin. He was laid out and they started to take leave of him [mourners kiss the corpse before burial]. Yet Sen'ka thinks, "Oh, but Van'ka, you're lying, you didn't die, the *kopejka* you want to hide. So I'll try you." He took a needle in his teeth; began to take leave of Van'ka, and jabs him with the needle. But that one endured.

"Well, maybe he really did die?" says Sen'ka.

But he still didn't believe it. When they carried Van'ka to the chapel and lighted the candles in the chapel, Sen'ka climbed under the floor.

At that time the *pany* [*pany*—plural of *pan*, Polish landowner, honorific title, in Russia often used derisively; usually refers to Poles in general] rode among us; robbed the villages. Here we had a big battle. Well, these Poles rode with their loot, completely drunk. And they saw the light in the chapel, so they dropped in there with their loot. They drank and drank, and one of them says, "Well, I'll split this corpse in half with my saber from head to the feet."

His comrades reply, "If you're unable to do this, then we'll do the same to you."

The Pole raised the sword over Van'ka, but Van'ka stands up and bellows, "Arise, the living and the dead!"

Sen'ka rises from under the floor now, "Just a moment," he says.

The *pany* become frightened and drop their goods and run.

Well, Sen'ka and Van'ka start to divide the loot. There are many goods. But they quarreled. Over a *gros* [small coin, approximately one-half U.S. cent] the matter arose.

Van'ka shorted Sen'ka by a *gros*.

Then Sen'ka says, "Give back my *gros*!"

But the other says, "Is it possible that you won't trust me for a *gros*?"

And Sen'ka replies, "You, Van'ka, already died for a *kopejka*, so I won't trust you for a *gros*."

Meanwhile the *pany* rode off and suddenly thought, "Why did we become frightened? After all, a dead one does not yell from his coffin; it's nothing but robbers. What's more there are only two of them."

And they sent one Pole to look.

And that one arrived, opened the window, and stuck his head inside.

Those two are quarreling yet. Sen'ka is yelling, "But my *gros*, but my *gros*!"

Seeing the *pan's* head Van'ka tore off his cap and threw it to Sen'ka. "Here," he says, "is your *gros*!"

The Pole ran to his cohorts beside himself. He says, "There is an innumerable host of them. How much loot did we steal, while for them it comes only to a *gros* each, and it's still not enough. They tore off my cap to pay one."

Thus they ran away.

Greece

The Lake Spirits of Peristera and Xerovouni

From Georgios A. Megas, *Folktales of Greece* (Chicago: University of Chicago Press, 1970), pp. 198–200.

Told by Dinos Sarantis, head drover of Perivoli ton Grevenon (West Macedonia); collected by Nikolaos G. Polites in 1898 and published in *Paradoseis*, 2 vols., Athens, 1904, no. 501, pp. 270–81.

"This most beautiful legend," says Nikolaos G. Polites, "teaches us that new legends are made every day and wedded with mythical elements, remnants of ancient mythology that have been treasured by the Greek people. The imaginary world of mythical creatures is so closely united with the real, that its limits are hard to define, and a man who has up to now lived in close cohabitation with his fellow men may quite conceivably overstep the boundaries and change into a supernatural being. The young shepherd, whose help is sought by the spirit, himself becomes a spirit and, seizing the maiden he loves, bestows on her the same unearthly spirituality as his own (*Paradoseis*, p. 1123).

It is thought that each lake, just as each mountain, has its own spirit who often wrestles with the spirit of the neighboring lake. The lakes are also thought to be related by nature to the spirits that personify the winds, the battle between which, as in the preceding legend, is represented by a storm. That spirit wins which takes on a man as its ally. This idea seems to be an echo of the ancient myth of the Battle of the Gods and Giants, in which the gods win with the mortal Heracles as their ally (see Polites, *Paradoseis*, p. 1122, no. 497).

According to our legend, by tasting the spirit's heart the shepherd of Mount Peristera is endowed with tremendous strength and, upon throwing himself into the lake, becomes a spirit of great might. The belief that a man may become a hero by partaking of a food which bestows divine strength underlies many ancient myths, according to Polites (*Paradoseis*, pp. 1129 ff.). An example is the myth of Glaucus, the fisherman: it was he who ate the imperishable grass, or, in one variant of the myth, drank of the immortal spring, and became a god. Later he threw himself into the sea and became a sea divinity. This myth emanates from a very old and widely held superstition that the attributes of any body, before it becomes food, are passed on to whoever partakes of it, for it is imagined that in the tasting, the spirit that has dwelled in the food is also absorbed. Thus Achilles was fed on the entrails of the lion and the wild boar and the marrow of the bear, and in this way acquired their strength and vigor (Polites, *Paradoseis*, p. 1133, and see p. 1052 for Greek superstitions regarding spirits in general).

Mount Peristera has many peaks and on the highest of these there is a small but bottomless lake; it isn't much more than four hundred meters long, but it has water a-plenty. There is another lake on Mount Xerovouni. Here all the creatures drink the water, but the large beasts and the goats never go up to drink, for they know full well it is bewitched. And truly, in each of these there dwells a spirit.

Once—not over fifty years ago—the spirits came out to hold a contest. They agreed that each was to take whatever the other sent him. The spirit of Xerovouni hurled snowballs at the other, and he swallowed them down. But then the spirit of Peristera began to throw balls made of lamb's innards that he had first sprinkled with salt. He obtained the ingredients for these from a shepherd whom he had obliged to give him the entrails from his sheep. The spirit opened up each sheep, took out the innards, and then sewed it up, and the sheep was none the worse for it. But after he had swallowed every one of many such balls, the spirit of Xerovouni couldn't take any more and burst.

At once, then, the spirit of Peristera ran up and opened the other's breast, took out the heart and put it on a spit, setting the shepherd (who had been there all this time, looking on) to turn the spit until the roast was done. But he could not turn it, because not only was it big and heavy in the ordinary way of things, but all the heavier for being bewitched. So he ordered him to rub the heart three times with his finger and then lick it. The first time he licked his finger he felt strength enter his body, the second and third times he became as wild as a beast. And he too went into the lake and dwelled there, for now he was bewitched.

From that time forward, nothing was heard of the shepherd, none knew what had become of him. He appeared to one friend alone, and him he swore on the Holy Writ to secrecy; the friend was a dairyman, or cheesemaker as we call them. Only to him did he appear, and bade him bring him the skim (the top of the milk, I mean, that they use for making butter), and told him that if ever he wanted to see him, he should come to the lake, climb up on a white rock, play on the pipes, and he would appear. Only he made him swear to say nothing to anyone. So it often happened that the friend would come and pipe and the possessed one would appear.

After some time had gone by, the shepherd's mother, who had never given up hope that her son was alive, began to suspect. So she pleaded with him, weeping tears, till he took pity on her, and said, "Up, then, and come with me, and you shall see Ghiannis." So he brought her to the rock where their meeting place was and hid her behind him.

No sooner did he begin to play the pipes than the possessed one sprang up, and no sooner that, than the old woman fell on him and embraced him, calling out, "My son! my son!" and I don't know what all. In a rage, the possessed one turned upon the other and shouted, "Cheese curdler is your calling, cheese curdler ever be, and night and day you'll curdle cheese, and never profit see!" And they never saw him again.

Some time passed and there was a fair in a village called Tyrnavo, which stands below Nizopolis, some two hours' journey from the lake. The possessed one appeared in the fairground and seized the fairest daughter of the village, whom he had known some time before he was bewitched. He took her down with him into the lake and bewitched her too. The village folk stood as if turned to stone at her being spirited away like that before their eyes.

The maiden, indeed, had two fine brothers, fearless and brave they were. They lost no time in getting after the spirit. But when they reached the lake, the spirit leaped in with the maiden and the waters closed over them. The youths then decided to dig into the slope of the mountain and make a gully, about two men's stature in depth, and the water began running into it. Just then the earth began to tremble, and there came down an enormous rock, big as this room, and dammed the gully. (Both gully and rock may be seen to this day.) The brothers went away in despair.

Many years ago now, in 1876, an old man, by name Kazako (I don't recall his Christian name), told me that a little while before, in '73, he'd happened to go to the lake very early one morning before the sheep went to drink, and saw, so he said, the spirit's wife sitting beside the lake and combing her hair. When she saw him, she at once sprang into the lake, forgetting to take her things. So the old one went up and found her comb, looking glass, and a tress of hair, pretty as you please, all golden. The old one picked them up. But that night the spirit came to the pen where he was sleeping alongside the sheep, dealt him a blow, and said, "Take the things back where you found them." And he did.

Middle East

Turkey

Nasreddin Hodja and Tamerlane

Collected by Ilhan Başgöz in Ankara, Turkey, in 1951. Forthcoming in *Folktales of Turkey*.

Nasreddin Hodja, the hero of Turkish anecdotes, probably lived during the thirteenth century. He combines the characteristics of a trickster, fool, wise man, and saint. He is viewed by the Turkish people as a culture hero and folk philosopher. His anecdotes, which spread all over the world, first appeared in the manuscripts of the second half of the fifteenth century, undoubtedly from an earlier oral tradition. Many of the early Hodja stories were coarse, off-color, and contained broad references (as is seen in our selection), but these elements later disappeared when the stories were circulated among educated people.

This anecdote was recorded from Ali Riza Turan, fifty, an elementary-school teacher in Ankara. He was an exceptionally fine anecdote-teller, whom the Turks might call a "second Nasreddin Hodja." During a conversation of an hour's length he could include several stories, all of which were introduced into the conversation by some functional link. They were told to support an idea, to explain an opinion, or to convince the listener of the truth of the exposé with the support of a traditional story. As a teacher, he traveled all over Anatolia and taught in several villages where he learned his stories.

Hoca is another term for *Hodja*. Motif K1956 "Sham wise man."

Tamerlane had already invaded Central Anatolia and was advancing toward Aksehir, burning and destroying everything in his path. The people of Aksehir, fearing that their city too would be burned, went to the *hoca* and begged him to use all his resourcefulness against the invaders, so that the city would remain unharmed. The *hoca* was reluctant at first, due to the fact that his opponent was such a cruel and powerful sultan. But the will of the people prevailed and upon their insistence he agreed to do whatever he possibly could in order that the city be saved.

The first piece of business that the *hoca* had the people attend to was the construction, just outside the city walls, of a huge camelskin tent, inside of which he had piled fifteen odd overstuffed mattresses. The *hoca*, wearing a high, bright-orange turban, after inspecting the tent carefully, took off all his clothing save the bright-orange turban and proceeded to climb to the uppermost mattress. He then had a staff thrown up to him, and stood there, stark naked and supported by the staff, peering down upon his nervous following.

In a short while, the advance guard of Tamerlane's army arrived at the city walls and, seeing the huge tent, decided to have a look-see at what was inside. After raising their heads toward the top of the pile, their eyes came across the *hoca*.

"Who are you?" they asked.

"I am the God of Earth," he said, making sure to sound as solemn as possible.

Being afraid of misjudging this strange fellow with the huge turban and the audacity to stand naked before a crowd, the soldiers returned to Tamerlane's court and told of the fearsome character they had met.

Tamerlane expressed interest in meeting this odd fellow and had him called to his presence.

"You, my good fellow, are the God of Earth. Is that not right?"

"That's right, your Excellency."

"Well, since you are the God of Earth, I order you to produce a miracle. If you can't, I'll have your head cut off as punishment for your insolence."

Then, turning to his blind daughter, Tamerlane spelled out the miracle to be performed. "I order you to open her eyes."

"Oh, your Excellericy, I said that I am the God of Earth. And indeed I am. But in this capacity I also have an agreement with the God of the Sky. You see, he is responsible for the upper part of the body, and I for the lower. To open your daughter's eyes would be a violation of our agreement. But if your daughter has anything that needs opening below her waist, I would be most willing to render my humble services."

The Smart Brother and the Crazy Brother

Collected by Ilhan Başgöz in Ankara in 1943 and again in Sivas, Turkey, in 1961. Forthcoming in *Folktales of Turkey*.

This is type 563 *The Table, the Ass and the Stick,* one of the well-known Grimm tales. It is no. 176 in the Eberhard-Boratav *Typen Turkische Volksmärchen.* Motifs: K2211 "Treacherous brother"; D859.1 "Magic object acquired by rapping on (cutting) a tree"; D1472.1.8 "Magic table cloth supplies food and drink"; B103.1.1 "Gold producing ass, droppings of gold"; D1401.1 "Magic club, stick beats person"; D1401.2 "Magic sack (pumpkin) furnishes manikin who cudgels enemies"; D861 "Magic object stolen"; J2355.1 "Fool loses magic objects by talking about them"; D881.2 "Recovery of magic object by use of magic cudgel"; K2241 "Treacherous innkeeper (blacksmith)."

For sources of the variants and the geographical distribution of the tale see J. P. Asmussen, "Remarks on Some Iranian Folk Tales Treating of Magic Objects, Especially Th. 564," *Acta Orientalia* (Societates Orientales Danica Norvegica Svecica) 27:3/4 (1965): 221–43. The hoopoe bird is endowed in Middle East folklore with magical properties.

The tale was recorded in 1943 from Mrs. Zeyjan Başgöz in Ankara and again in Sivas in 1961, when she was seventy, by her son Ilhan Başgöz, and translated by Larry V. Clark. Although she was not an active tradition-bearer, she knew many tales and narrated them to her children and grandchildren when requested to do so.

Born in 1889 and reared in a small Central Anatolian village, Çubuk, Mrs. Başgöz was the second child of a large tribal family. The semi-nomadic lifestyle of the tribe continued until 1915, so Mrs. Başgöz spent her summers knitting in tents pitched on high mountains where the family had moved to graze their livestock. They returned to their village in the winter. In summer and in winter, Zeyjan Başgöz heard folktales from her mother, a very good teller, and from the neighboring women. She later married an educated man, an elementary-school teacher, and moved to a nearby town, Gemerek, whose inhabitants were one-third Armenian. Here she continued to listen to and narrate tales on winter evenings, but at neighbors' houses, since her husband did not like folk culture. Following her husband's retirement they went to Sivas, a city of 250,000, where she met Gül Nene (literally Rose Granny), a celebrated storyteller, in the 1930s. Gül Nene spent many winter evenings in Mrs. Başgöz's house, telling tales to her children, many of which, like the present story, entered Zeyjan's repertoire. Gül Nene's narrative style, especially her projection of individual feelings and ideas into the tale, is still apparent in Mrs. Başgöz's technique, although some aspects no longer reflect the psychological or social reality of the teller. For example, when Mrs. Başgöz says, "Like us, they lived from meal to meal," she is repeating Gül Nene's traditional complaint, but Mrs. Başgöz herself was not that poor.

Once upon a time, when creatures of God abounded, when camels were towncriers and roosters were barbers, a father had two sons. One son was smart and one son was crazy. The father was not very rich (like us, they lived from meal to meal). They had a barn and a few animals inside: a pair of oxen, a cow, a water buffalo, and one or two other animals. (But even if we live a thousand years, our end is death, is it not? May God not part us from our faith before then.) The father got sick and died. The two sons said to each other: "Come, let us divide up our property." (You know, property makes enemies of brothers.) Before the father's death, they had built a new barn. The crazy brother said: "My brother, when we bring the animals from the water, let's turn them loose. Those who enter the new barn shall be mine, and those who enter the old barn shall be yours." (Apparently a board is missing in the head of this son as in mine. Would any animal enter the new barn? Naturally, all of them will go into the old barn that they're used to.) The smart brother approved, and one morning when they brought the animals from the water, they let them loose. All the animals went and entered the old barn, except one old ox that went into the new barn. The crazy brother said: "Oh, what will I do? What bad luck this is! What can I do with a single ox? It can't be harnessed in the yoke. It can't pull a cart. As soon as it is morning I will take this ox and sell it."

When it was morning the crazy brother got up and with a staff in hand led the ox along a mountain road. He went uphill and downhill, he went for six months and an autumn, and when he turned around and looked behind, he had traveled only the length of a grain of barley. He came up a mountain and saw a tree.

A hoopoe on the tree was singing: "Hoopoopoo ibibik! Hoopoopoo ibibik!"

The crazy son said: "All right, I will sell my ox to this hoopoe bird."

"Hoopoe, I am selling an ox. Will you buy it?" (What does the hoopoe understand? All he does is: "Hoopoopoo ibibik!")

The crazy one thought the hoopoe said: "I'll buy it." So he tied the ox to a tree and said to the bird:

"If you don't have the money now, I will come tomorrow and get it, all right?"

Again the hoopoe sang: "Hoopoopoo ibibik! Hoopoopoo ibibik!"

"All right," said the crazy son, "agreed. Good-bye. I'll come early tomorrow and get my money." The next day the crazy son got up early in the day, took his ax in hand, and went along the mountain road. He came beneath the tree, where the hoopoe was once again singing on a branch.

"Hoopoopoo ibibik, hey! Where is my ox money?"

"Hoopoopoo ibibik."

"I want my money. Where is the money for my ox?"

"Hoopoopoo ibibik."

"Since you won't give me the money for my ox, I'll cut down the tree you're perching on."

The crazy brother began cutting down the tree where the hoopoe slept. He gave one blow with the ax, then another, and another. Soon, the hoopoe began to speak, and said: "Please stop! Don't cut down my tree, and I will give you a donkey. Take him and go! But take care while you're on the road and don't say: 'Whoa, donkey, whoa.' All right?"

The crazy brother said all right, and took the donkey. While returning home, he got curious. (He, too, was apparently an impatient person, like me.) Somewhere along the road he said to the animal: "Whoa, donkey, whoa." As soon as the donkey heard this, he stopped in the middle of the road, lifted his tail, and began to relieve himself. The crazy brother looked, and what did he see? The donkey had relieved himself of a handful of gold pieces. Immediately, he took the gold pieces and filled his pocket. Keeping on the road to home, his feet were kicking his rear for joy, so fast did he go. He came and knocked on his brother's door. (Oh, crazy one, you've found a nice way to make your living. Why don't you sit down and be quiet? No, he won't stop babbling.) "Look, brother," he said, "I exchanged my ox for a donkey." His brother said: "Shut up, you crazy coward! What will you do with a donkey in the city?" The crazy one said: "Wait, my donkey has a talent." And when he said: "Whoa, donkey, whoa," the donkey lifted its tail and dropped a handful of gold pieces. His brother's eyes opened this wide with surprise. He warned the crazy brother over and over again: "Please, don't tell anyone about this, or they will take it away from you."

That night, joy kept sleep from entering the eyes of the crazy son. The next day he got up early and, after getting a handful of gold pieces from the donkey again, said to himself: "Hey, this donkey doesn't have any shoes on its feet. I'll take it to the blacksmith and have it shoed." He took the donkey and came to the blacksmith's shop. He said to the blacksmith: "Usta [Master], will you shoe my donkey?" The blacksmith said, "Of course," and the crazy one said, "But take care after I'm gone that you don't say 'Whoa, donkey, whoa.' All right?" The blacksmith laughed. (Why shouldn't he say "Whoa" to the donkey? Animals don't understand other languages. You have to say "whoa" for it to stop.) The crazy one left the donkey and came home.

While shoeing the animal, the blacksmith thinks: "Why don't I say 'Whoa, donkey, whoa,' and see what happens?" And as soon as he said: "Whoa, donkey, whoa," the donkey spread his legs and left a handful of gold pieces in front of the blacksmith. The blacksmith didn't believe his eyes. He looked, he took it in his hand, he looked again. It was really gold.

Immediately he took the donkey and brought him to his own barn, and took another donkey from there, shoed him, and got him ready. Then he tied him to the shop. The next day the crazy brother came. "Usta, is the donkey ready?" "He's ready, my boy, he's tied over there. Go and get him." The crazy son took the donkey, pulled him over to the side of the road, and said in his ear, "Whoa, donkey, whoa." No action at all in the donkey. When he repeated: "Whoa, donkey, whoa," the donkey lifted his tail and deposited a huge pile of dung in front of him. The crazy one was sick at heart. He said: "Usta, this donkey is not mine. My donkey relieved himself of gold pieces." The blacksmith began to laugh: "My child, it's obvious why they call you crazy, because you say such incoherent things. Who in the world ever saw your donkey dropping gold pieces? Get out of here. I have not time to trouble with crazy ones." With a kick to the crazy brother's rear, he threw him out of his shop.

The crazy brother came home and passed that night with dark thoughts. The next day, he took his ax in hand and went again to the mountaintop. He found the tree where the hoopoe slept, and started asking: "Hoopoopoo ibibik, hey! Where's my ox money?"

The answer again: "Hoopoopoo ibibik."

"If you don't give the money for my ox, I'll cut down your tree."

He started cutting down the tree with his ax, thud-thud, and very shortly the hoopoe began to speak again. He said: "Please don't cut down my tree. I'll give you a tablecloth. But take care that you don't say 'Open, tablecloth, open, and be spread with all sorts of food.' " The crazy one took the tablecloth under his arm. While going along the road, he said "Open tablecloth, open, and be spread with all sorts of food," and the tablecloth opened up. And inside (let me tell you, gentlemen, it was worthy of your mouths), it was spread with forty meat dishes, forty milk dishes, forty wheat dishes, and forty sweet dishes. The crazy one sat down and ate what he could eat, and filled his breast pocket with what he couldn't eat, and came home.

He found his brother there. "O, my brother," he said, "I exchanged the donkey for a tablecloth." "Damn you, brother," he answered the crazy one, "you exchanged a donkey that relieves himself of gold pieces for a piece of linen?" The crazy one: "But my tablecloth is talented." And the minute he said again "Open, tablecloth, open, and be spread with all sorts of food," the tablecloth opened and was spread with every sort and variety of food, even some that are not cooked in the sultan's kitchen. The smart brother said: "O, brother, be careful that you don't talk about this with anyone. Sit down and live comfortably until the end of your life." The crazy one said: "No, I'm going to invite the Padishah to a feast. Let him come with his whole army and be my guest for dinner."

He sent this invitation to the Padishah: "My Padishah, this is what I would say to you. May you come with your whole army and be my guest one evening." The Padishah, thinking there must be some reason behind this invitation, mobilized his soldiers and came to the son's as guests. (I might say 50,000 soldiers, you might say 100,000 soldiers. Anyway, they came and camped on our threshing field.) The crazy son was inside a tent, and as long as he ordered the tablecloth to open, the food kept flowing out. The soldiers could not finish filling their plates. Everyone ate and filled their stomach. The remaining food they gave to beggars and the poor, and they too filled their stomachs. The Padishah was curious: "How does this poor crazy son make so much food?" He sent a man to look over the situation and learned that the talent was in the tablecloth. At once, he sent word to the crazy son: "Either you will give me the tablecloth, or your head is gone." (Iron is breakable, the Padishah's order is not.) They took the tablecloth and left the crazy son's. Once more our crazy one was left without.

The next day, taking his ax in hand, he came to the mountaintop. At the foot of the tree he began calling the bird again: "Hoopoopoo ibibik, hey! Where's my ox money?"

"Hoopoopoo ibibik."

"If you don't give me the money for my ox, I'll cut down your tree."

He began cutting down the tree again. In a few moments the hoopoe said: "Stop! Don't cut it down, and I will give you a pumpkin. But take care while you're on the road that you don't say: 'Come out of that pumpkin and hit so-and-so's head.'" The crazy son took the pumpkin under his arm. On the way back home he said: "Come out of that pumpkin and hit so-and-so's head." Well, he was used to having all sorts of good things come out. This time forty very tiny men came out of the pumpkin, with sticks in their hands, and made a concerted attack on the crazy son's head. They hit him until he couldn't bear any more. The crazy son said: "Please! Go back in, go back in!" And all of them went back into the pumpkin again.

The crazy one ran to his house and said to his brother: "My brother, I exchanged the tablecloth for a pumpkin." "Damn you, you bum! What's this pumpkin worth?" The crazy brother said: "You will see in just a minute. Come out of that pumpkin and hit my brother's head." Forty dwarfs came out of the pumpkin with sticks in their hands and cudgeled the smart brother's head. A worse beating would be impossible to imagine. He began to implore him: "Please, my brother, you are right. But don't do as I have done. Save me from their hands." The crazy brother said: "Go back in, go back in," and the dwarfs went back into the pumpkin.

Then he took the pumpkin and went straight to the blacksmith's shop. "Usta, why won't you give me my donkey?" "Get out, you crazy coward, what donkey?" "Usta, are you going to give me my donkey or not?" "Get out, you crazy coward, what donkey?" "In that case, the fault is not on me, Usta. Come out of that pumpkin and hit that Usta's head." Gentlemen, the dwarfs came out of the pumpkin and began to thrash Usta until he couldn't stand it anymore. (I would wish such a beating on the head of my enemy.) "Please, crazy one, stop it! In my barn is your donkey. Take it, it's yours, and save my soul." Usta brought the donkey and the crazy son said, "Go back in, go back in," and the dwarfs returned to the pumpkin. He took the donkey, laughing and playing, and came to the Padishah's palace. He went inside: "My Padishah, will you give me that tablecloth of mine or not?" The Padishah said, "You crazy coward, get out of here before I chop up your soul!" The crazy son said, "Come out of that pumpkin and hit the Padishah's head."

Gentlemen, the dwarfs surrounded the Padishah and beat him until he couldn't take any more. (Would you dare do such an injustice?) They began to give the fellow such a beating, that if he didn't return the tablecloth, he would surely die. At once, he called to his men and they brought the tablecloth and gave it to the crazy son. The crazy son draped the tablecloth over his arm, put his pumpkin under his arm, settled himself comfortably on his donkey, and you would have thought that he was a Kurd with five goats [The Kurds are generally so poor that when they have five goats they think themselves wealthy. There is a Turkish saying: "Beş keçili Kürd gibi kurulmak," "To be proud as a Kurd with five goats" = "To give oneself airs"]. When he said "Whoa," the donkey poured out gold pieces. When he said "Open, tablecloth," a thousand and one kinds of food appeared. It was enough for the crazy son, and for the smart son, and for you, and for me. Thus did the brother attain his desires. Three apples fell from the sky, one on Gül Nene, one on the teller of this story, and one on the wife of Uncle Riza [They are all three the same person: the female narrator].

Dervish Baba

Contributed by Ilhan Başgöz from the personal collection of Pertev Boratav. Forthcoming in *Folktales of Turkey*.

In Eberhard-Boratav, *Typen Turkishche Volksmärchen*, this is no. 300. That index lists two variants collected in Turkey and a third unpublished variant collected from Yugoslavian Turks in Uskup by C. S. Mundy. The tale is presented as a peasant play by E. Elçin in *Anadolu Köy Orta Oyunlari* (Ankara, 1964), pp. 73–76.

Recorded in 1964 by Hayrünnisa Boratav from a young villager, Fehmi Asker of Izmir-Bornova, Naldöken village. The entire population of the village is Alevi, a heterodox Muslim order. Clearly this narrative depends on vocal and musical effects for its humor and entertaining qualities.

Once upon time, there was a Dervish Baba who went about begging. One day he stationed himself at the door of a mosque where people would throw him maybe forty *paras*, two *kurush*, one hundred *paras*, five *kurush*—as they came out after performing the *namaz*. One man had a gold *lira* in his pocket, which he threw to the dervish by mistake.

This man was going to buy some things from the market. He entered a store, and the storekeeper asked, "May I help you?"

"Give me two yards of that cloth, five yards of that, ten yards of that." He had exactly a gold lira's worth of cloth cut. The storekeeper wrapped the material. When the purchaser was going to pay for it, he discovered that the gold lira was not in his pocket. "Oh, what did I do with it? Did I drop it?" he thought. Then he realized, "I must have given it by mistake to the dervish." He dashed outside. He searched and found the dervish walking about in the street. He was ashamed to say, "Give me my gold *lira*." So, he began to sing:

> "Dervish Baba,
>   You have yellow gold, yellow gold, yellow gold."

The dervish answered, also with a tune:

> "Oh, my son,
>   I don't have it, don't have it, don't have it."

Seeing that it was no use, the man said, "Come on, let's go to a judge. He will decide our case." And so the two of them set out. They passed through Gargara and came to Bilegi. There was a shepherd beside the road, tending his flock. The shepherd asked, "Hey, where are you going?"

"Where should we be going? Look, thus and thus . . ."

"Well, speak up and let's see," said the shepherd, who also had a whistle. The owner of the gold lira took up the tune again:

> "Dervish Baba,
>   You have yellow gold, yellow gold, yellow gold."

The dervish answered:

"Oh, my son,
I don't have it, don't have it, don't have it."

The shepherd was pleased, and taking his whistle, he adapted it to their tune:

"Duru duru duru, dut dut,
duru duru dut dut
duru dur dut . . ."

"Come friend, you are our witness," they said. And so saying they took the shepherd and set his flock moving. Over there is Emir-Agze, which they presently reach. There—pardon the expression—is a gypsy sitting with a violin.

"Hey, where are you going?"

"Where should we be going? the situation is thus and thus, we have a dispute and we are going to the judge."

"Speak, let us see, what is your problem?" They perform in order:

"Dervish Baba,
You have yellow gold, yellow gold, yellow gold."

Moving the violin stem slightly, the gypsy tries to adapt the violin scale to the rhythm of the tune. Then the dervish takes his turn:

"Oh, my son,
I don't have it, don't have it, don't have it."

The shepherd plays:

"Duru duru duru, dut dut . . ."

Immediately the gypsy violinist begins with his violin:

"Gidi giy giy giy gide giy giy . . ."

"Come on fellow, in that case you are also a witness," they said to the gypsy, and the four of them set out.

They arrive and are ready to come before the judge in the early forenoon. They say to the messenger, "We have a case and want to present it to the judge." The messenger conveys the information to the judge, and he calls them. "Speak, let us see what your problem is."

These four people—one with a violin, one with a whistle, one a dervish—began to explain their case with these rhymed words:

"Dervish Baba,
You have yellow gold, yellow gold, yellow gold."
"Oh, my son,
I don't have it, don't have it, don't have it."

"Duru duru duru dut dut . . ."
"Gide giy giy giy gidi giy giy . . ."

The judge, unable to understand this business, said, "Order! Order! You are dismissed for now. Come back tomorrow at the same time and explain your problem to me."

In the evening the judge went home. After eating, he performed the *namaz*. While performing the ritual, he thought of these men and smiled. The judge's wife noticed this and after the *namaz* she asked, "Judge, what were you smiling about while you were doing the *namaz?*"

"Oh, nothing. I just thought of something."

"No, tell me."

"Well, it is not something that can be told. It is just a case that came up today. I smiled about it."

"Tell me, what was this case?"

"Well, what can I say? Four men; one with a violin, one with a whistle. . . . The first of which went 'duru dut dut,' the other 'giy gidi giy giy,' and another one who said, 'You have yellow gold,' and another who said, 'Oh, my son, I don't have it, don't have it,' " he explained.

His wife insisted, "By all means, I am also going to hear this case."

"How disgraceful. What is your concern with other people's business?"

"No, I am definitely going. You will stretch a curtain across, and I will listen to the case behind it."

His wife also performed very well. The next day, she hung bells around her waist and went to the court. They hung up a red curtain, and the judge's wife sat behind it.

The judge then said, "Call those complainants from yesterday and let us see about them." They call them, and they enter.

"Explain, and let's see what the problem is."

They see that there is a curtain there. There must be something behind it, certainly it is not without a purpose. The violinist tightens his violin pegs. They perform in order:

"Dervish Baba,
 You have yellow gold, yellow gold, yellow gold."
"Oh, my son,
 I don't have it, don't have it, don't have it."
"Duru duru duru dut dut dut . . ."
"Gidi giy giy giy, gidi giy giy . . ."

The judge stood up quickly and said:

"In my forty years as a judge,
 Such a case I have never seen, never seen, never seen."

And immediately from the other side a jingling:

> "Childir, childir, childir, childir . . ."

The judge's wife had started to play behind the curtain. And then she spoke up, "Continue, boys." Do you suppose that the shepherd and violinist are going to stop?

> "Duru dut dut dut . . ."
> "Gidi giy giy giy . . ."

They had a merry time.

"Here," she said, "take two gold pieces." She gave them two gold *liras*. They combined business with pleasure.

Egypt

The Sure News Is Up Ahead

Collected and translated by Hasan El-Shamy. Forthcoming in *Folktales of Egypt*.

Recorded March 1969 from Darweesh Omar, forty-five, night guard at the Folklore Center in Cairo. He had learned the tale twenty years earlier in his village of Shuttureh, Suhag province, Upper Egypt, during flood (*dameerah*) times.

The main tale types here, which are usually combined in Arab cultures, are 1511 *The Faithless Queen*, Part I, "The Queen and the Loathsome Paramour," and 449 *The Tsar's Dog*. Prominent motifs are F111 "Journey to earthly paradise"; J514.3 "Greedy man keeps demanding one more thing from a complacent man, at last is magically blinded"; H1311.1 "King seeks one richer (more magnificent) than himself"; D141 "Transformation: man to dog"; C785 "Tabu: trying to save provisions for another day"; H1023.22 "Task: catching a sunbeam."

The tale reiterates numerous themes central to Arab cultural systems: contentment with one's lot in life; antifeminist attitudes; discouragement of inquiries into unknown and futuristic world views. The world as a woman is a recurrent theme in Arab folk religious literature and appears frequently as a saint's legend.

In its present frame story structure, the narrative is restricted to Egypt, mainly the Delta and Upper Egypt. Its origin may well be the familiar ten millième brochures taken from the *Arabian Nights* and sold in the marketplaces. Still the tale has its own oral folk character that sets it apart from its literary match. Type 449 is distributed in eastern Europe, Ireland, and Scotland.

State that there is no god but Allah.

Once there was a poor woodgatherer. He and his wife lived in the hills. He kept on working and selling his firewood and saving some until he saved forty piasters. What will he do with these forty piasters? He thought and thought: "What should you do with this money, boy? What should you do with money, boy?"

He said, "I'll buy a donkey."

He bought a limping donkey as good as his money allowed him.

One day while he was working, a *Maghrabi* (Moroccan) passed by him; one of those Maghrabis who discover treasures. He said to him, "Would you sell this donkey?"

He answered him, "Buy."

"A hundred pounds."

He answered, "Go, leave me alone."

"Two hundred pounds."

"May God forgive you."

"All right, be my partner."

The woodgatherer thought that the Maghrabi was ridiculing him, whereas the Maghrabi could see that the donkey was marked to lead them to a treasure. He answered the Maghrabi, "I'll be your partner."

The Maghrabi said to him, "Go get me seven or eight more donkeys and come back quickly."

He went and hired seven or eight donkeys. Instead of paying twenty piasters a day, he paid a pound a day for each and they all started out relying on God.

When they reached the place, the Maghrabi uttered some words and the earth split. He told the woodgatherer, "Go down there and start packing and carrying out. But there is a kohl container—do not touch it."

He asked, "Why?"

The Maghrabi said, "Do not ask about what does not concern you. You will find the sure news up ahead."

They filled all their sacks and loaded them on the donkeys. The Maghrabi said a few words and the earth became like it was before.

They depended on God and they hurried toward their place. At the crossroads the Maghrabi said to the woodgatherer, "Here we part. You take four of these animals, and I take four, and may safety be with you."

The donkeyman said, "Why? This way we can find a treasure every day, and what about the kohl container?"

The Maghrabi answered, "You'll find the sure news up ahead," and said, "Peace be upon you," and left.

Our friend the donkeyman went home and his condition became completely different. He built a palace with a garden and had servants and slaves and he became the richest man in the country.

One day he was looking at himself in the mirror. He liked himself very much. He looked to the Vizier and asked, "Is there anyone who is more handsome than I am? Is there anyone who is richer than I am?"

The Vizier answered, "Only God knows, King. 'No one is rich except God; no one is handsome except Mohammed [the Prophet].' "

Now the King—who was originally a donkeyman—said to him, "I want you to find me someone who is richer and more handsome than I am, and if you don't I will (may this happen to the distant one) chop off your head."

The Vizier went out "carrying all the sorrows of the world on top of his head." He kept on looking and looking but no one was richer or more handsome than the King. Finally, after "walking had made him barefooted," he sat down to rest inside a mosque (like el-Sayyida Zaynab Mosque right here in Cairo). He found an old beat-up-looking man who looked like a dervish sitting down next to him. The man said to him, "What's the matter with you? You look distressed."

The Vizier replied, "By God, I am the Vizier and today the King asked me to find him someone who is richer and more handsome than he is."

The dervish exclaimed, "Is that all?"

The Vizier replied, "My heels have been worn down. I couldn't find anyone."

The dervish said, "Take me to him and never worry."

The two of them left. When they got to the King, the King asked, "Vizier, have you found the one who is richer and more handsome than I am?"

The Vizier replied, "Yes, King. 'Our master,' the dervish here, will tell you."

The King asked, "Who, master dervish? Who, master dervish, is richer and more handsome than I?"

The dervish said, "The Lady," and the King exclaimed, "And where is she?"

The dervish replied, "Between you and her there are ten years of travel, and only you, no one else, will be able to find her" (for he wanted him to taste how bitter things can be).

The King ordered, "Prepare my horse."

He took his rations and set out looking for The Lady. "One country carried and another put him down" until he finally came to a little town. He was very tired. He got off his horse and went inside a mosque to rest. After having washed and done his prayers, he sat down to rest. He saw a man weaving baskets. He would weave a stitch and come running into the mosque and go all the way up the minaret, gaze sharply in all directions, come down, weave a stitch, come running into the mosque and go all the way up the minaret, gaze sharply in all directions, and come down and weave a stitch.

"My God!" wondered the King, "What's this man? Are you weaving a basket or looking for something in the sky?"

The man replied, "This is no concern of yours. What do you want?"

The King said, "I'm looking for The Lady."

The man replied, "You'll find the sure news up ahead. Go."

The King got on his horse and left. He kept on going until he came to another town and it was on a market day. In the market there was a blind man begging: "He who slaps me, may God reward him! And he who gives me alms, may God send him a catastrophe!"

The King exclaimed, "Oh God, what's this man? Are you begging for alms or wishing people evil?"

The man replied, "This is no concern of yours. What do you want?"

The King answered, "I'm looking for The Lady."

The beggar said to him, "You will find the sure news up ahead."

The King left. He kept on going until he came to a place where he found a man lying down under a tree. His body was crawling with worms and he was saying, "It serves me right! It serves me right!"

The King asked him, "Hey man, what's your story?"

The man replied, "This is not your concern; this is not your concern. Go get the sure news from up ahead."

The King left and after that he met a man with a she-mule. The man had a huge millstone on the mule's back and was making her go up the hill and down again, up the hill and down again. All that and beating her with a whip in his hand.

The King said to him, "Brother, I have seen enough. By God, by our Prophet, would you tell me your story?"

The man tied the mule to a tree and said to him, "Sit down. I'll tell you my story."

"This she-mule in front of you is my cousin (bint 'Aam). I was a King like you. One day as I was walking in my kingdom I heard people whisper and say, 'Our King is a cuckold, for his wife has a lover and he is sitting at home not doing anything about it.'

"I noticed that every night she gave me a glass to drink. After that I wouldn't feel anything. That night I pretended to be asleep and threw what was in the glass away, without her noticing it. As soon as I closed my eyes, I heard her shout with hate, 'May you never get up again,' and she slapped my face and went out.

"I followed her. She kept on going until she came to the hills. There was a little hut and she entered it. When I looked, I found a slave called Sa'Aeed. She was in love with him. He hit her and kicked her and threw her out, but she kept on going back, imploring, 'Oh, sweetheart! Oh, my eyesight! It was my husband—may he never get up again—he just didn't want to lie down and become breathless.'

"She kept on crying and kissing his hands and feet, and the ugly slave would kick her and insult her, and she would say, 'Whatever you do is all right with me.'

"He finally gave her a dirty piece of bread to eat and then she devoured it as if she has never seen food before. After this, they went to a little mat in the corner and then they began to have their time. When I saw that, my blood boiled in my veins. I attacked the slave and struck him with my sword and he fell down on the floor. I looked at my wife and said, 'Why is a dry morsel of bread from Sa'Aeed better for you than all I give you?'

"She was crying and shrieking and holding his head in her lap. She threw a dish of water in my face, shouting, 'Get out of your human image and assume the image of a dog.'

"I found myself changed into a dog running here and there. She tied me with a rope and dragged me home. She got all the servants and slaves to beat me and said to them, 'Whenever you see this dog, beat it. And he who does not beat it will be put in prison.' Was I beaten!

"One day I saw the door open and nobody was around. I ran away to town. I kept roaming the streets until I finally came to a butcher shop. At night the butcher took me home with him. When we entered his house, his daughter exclaimed, 'Father, isn't it a shame that you expose me to the eyes of a strange man?'

"Her father replied, 'Strange man? May God prevent that. Where is that man?'

"His daughter pointed at the dog and said, 'This.'

"The man said, 'Are you mad? Has something happened to your mind? This is a dog.'

"She said, 'I'll show you.'

"She got a dish of water and splashed it in my face and said, 'Get out of your dog image and assume your original image,' and I found myself a man again sitting next to her father.

"The butcher exclaimed, 'There is no God but God, and Mohammed is his Prophet! Who did this to you, son?'

"I told him the story. His daughter said, 'This woman will never leave you alone for you have killed her lover and she will keep on looking for you until she finds you, for you have burned her heart.'

"She said to me, 'If you want to get your revenge, throw this water on her face and hit her with this stick before she can say anything to you and make her anything you wish.'

"When I went home, I found my wife still crying. The head of the slave Sa'Aeed was in front of her. She was holding a funeral and lamenting. She was threatening, 'If I just knew where you were. If I could just get hold of you!'

"I did as the girl had told me and said to her, 'Be a mule,' and now she has to pay for what she has done to me."

He looked at the mule and asked, "Isn't that so?"

The mule nodded its head, "Yes."

Then the man said, "This is my story and do not try to find The

Lady for you will never have her. It's better for you to go back to your home."

The King went back to the man whose body was crawling with worms. As soon as he appeared the man said to him, "Have you found the news?"

The King said, "No."

The man said, "Sit down here next to me. I will tell you my story.

"I was living happily with my father. We were comfortable and had land, stock, and everything. We were happy and thanking God. One day I said to my father, 'I have to go and seek my fortune.'

"He said to me, 'Why, son? God has given us ample livelihood here.'

"I did not listen to what he said and followed my own whim. I left and kept on going until I found an apartment building ('Aumarah). Inside there was singing, dancing, and music. Seven beautiful girls came out on the balcony when they saw me. They called to me, 'Won't you come in, Clever Hasan?'

"They lowered a lace or something, and I got hold of it and they pulled me up. Whether I stayed with them for years, or months, or days, I don't know. I was very happy. There was nothing beyond that, food, clothing, laughter, no cares.

"One day they all cried and said, 'Our mother has died. We will be in mourning for three months. We have to go to our land and we will be back.'

"They told me I could open all the rooms in the house. 'You can open all the rooms except this one.'

"They put on their feather clothes, became pigeons, and flew away.

" 'Safety be with you.'

" 'May God make you safe.'

"I became alone.

"Every day I opened a room until all the days were gone except one day. I said to myself, 'Boy, why don't you open this room and see what's inside? 'There is only one lifetime, and there's only one God.'

"I opened the room. Inside I found an ogre tied down with iron chains. He said to me, 'Let me loose, Clever Hasan, and I will fulfill your wishes.'

"I said to him, 'What's your name?'

"He answered, 'My name is Ungrateful.'

"I said to him, 'Why should I set you free? I don't need anything.'

"He answered, 'The girls are coming back soon. I can hear them coming. Let me loose, for God's sake! I will grant you a wish: something you have never seen or heard before.'

"Greed possessed me, and I untied him. As soon as he became free, he said to me, 'Make your wish. How do you want to die? Shall I squash you or throw you into the air?'

"I implored him: 'May God satisfy you. May God lead your path.'

" 'Never! Make your wish as to how to die. I have been tied for a thousand years!'

"When I saw that he was determined, I said to him, 'Throw me into the air,' hoping that something would happen. Maybe a bird would pick me up or something.

"He got hold of me and threw me into the sky. I traveled up and down for twenty-four hours. As I was about to land on the ground, one of the girls intercepted me before I hit the ground and they left me here. Now as you see, my body was all squashed and it is crawling with worms. I'm living on these worms. Eating one here and one there.

"This is my story, and you will never find The Lady. It's better for you to go back to your home."

The King got on his horse and kept on going. Now to whom did he go? To that man going up and down the minaret—the man weaving the baskets. As soon as he saw the King, he asked him, "Have you found the sure news?"

The King said, "No."

He said, "Sit down next to me. I will tell you my story."

"I was a prayer-crier (*mu'azzin*) and I used to make my living from what I got from good-hearted people coming to the mosque and from making baskets. I was very happy and contented. And God gave me an ample livelihood.

"One day when I went up the minaret to call for dawn prayers, I saw a flock of birds flying over my head. Little birds that I had never seen before. I thought of catching one or two for myself and my family. I stretched out my hand and got hold of one. Instead of me pulling it down, it pulled me up. It plucked me off the minaret just like you would pluck a weed. I was like a toy rattle in its claws. It flew I don't know for how long. When it landed, I found myself in a country other than *the* country and among people other than *the* people.

"I was hungry and tired. My clothes were all torn also. An old man —a good-hearted old man—saw me going down the street and asked me, 'Where are you from, son?'

"I said to him, 'I'm from God's land.'

" 'Who's your family?'

"I answered, 'I'm from God's people.'

"He asked me, 'Who are those?'

"I answered, 'The nation of "There is no god but Allah, and Mohammed is his Prophet." '

"The man said, 'You are one of us. Why don't you go eat and change your clothes.'

"I said, 'I have no money.'

"He answered me, 'Money, what? There is no money here.'

"I asked, 'Then how do you buy and sell?'

"He answered, 'We sell for prayers upon the Prophet—upon him be God's peace—and we buy for prayers upon the Prophet, but you buy and get only as much as you need.'

"I said, 'By God, that's a very good thing!'

"He said, 'Go, get what you need, and I'll be waiting for you here in the mosque.'

"I went to the restaurant and ate chicken, *kabāb*, rice and stew, and apples and on my way out I asked how much. The man said, 'Ten prayers upon the Prophet.'

"I gave him eleven: 'Ten prayers upon the Prophet and one for you.'

"He said, 'No, we take only what's due us. Are you a foreigner here?'

"I said, 'No, I just forgot.'

"I went to the clothes shop and bought luxurious silk and cashmere clothes, went to the barber and shaved, and I became twenty-four carats' satisfied. I went back to the sheik in the mosque. He asked me, 'How did you do?'

"I answered, 'Nothing is better anywhere else!'

"He asked me, 'Are you married?'

"I said, 'No.'

"He answered, 'Then you must complete the missing half of your religion.'

"He took me to his home and said to me, 'If you find a girl that you like, just point her out and you will marry her.'

"I asked, 'Don't we ask about her family? Her origin and her nature?'

"He answered, 'Everyone here is legitimate. And all people are alike.'

"When we reached his home, his daughter opened the door for us and she had a face as beautiful as the moon. I said to him, 'This girl.'

"He said, 'This is my daughter and we will go ahead with God's blessings.'

"We got married and lived happily for maybe a year, maybe two, maybe five years or six; I don't know how long. One day I went out and bought meat. I gave it to my wife and said to her, 'Cook it for supper,' and when I left home again, I found a man selling chickens. My appetite pushed me toward the chickens. I bought all the chickens. I took them to my wife. She asked me, 'Are we having a feast?'

"I said, 'No.'

"She asked, 'Then why all the chickens?'

"I said, 'To have a surplus.'

"She struck her chest with her hand and said, '*Ya kharabi!* [How disastrous!] What about the meat?'

"I said, 'For tomorrow.'

"She started shrieking and yelling, 'A tomorrow man!' And she ran after me: 'A tomorrow man! A tomorrow man!'

"I ran out of the house and when I looked behind me, I found the whole town chasing me. I stumbled and fell. It chanced that I landed next to that white bird. I got hold of it and it flew me back to my original home and I found myself weaving baskets again. Palm leaves have slashed my fingers. One day I may eat and one day I may not. So I'm going up in the minaret and maybe I'll find that bird again to take me back.

"This is my story, and you will never have The Lady. It's better that you go back to your home."

The King left him and went on his way. He came to that first one he had met—the beggar in the market (this is the most important of all).

When he got there he found that our friend was still standing there saying, "He who gives me a piaster or a loaf of bread or something, may God send him a catastrophe! And he who slaps me, may God grant him."

The King said to him, "I have met your three friends, and now it is your turn to tell me your story."

The man held the King by the hand (like this—tightly) and said, "Sit down next to me. I was a firewood gatherer. I used to gather firewood from the hills and sell it to people to use for baking. From this God sent me three, four, maybe five piasters a day. I saved some money and bought a one-eyed donkey."

All this, and the King is wondering, for this is his story; this is how he started before God bestowed upon him what he has now.

The man continued: "One day a *khawagah* [European] came and asked me to sell him my donkey. I refused. He said to me, 'We will open a treasure and you will be my partner.' So I went with him.

"We reached a deserted spot, and the *khawagah* opened his books of magic and the earth opened. We went inside and we carried a hundred loads of gold out and loaded them on donkeys and mules. The last time we went in, I found a small kohl container. As soon as I touched it, the *khawagah* came running at me and said, 'Don't open it!' and he took it.

"On our way home I kept asking him, 'Apply some kohl to my eyes.'

"He replied, 'You'll regret it.'

"I could not see the kohl in front of me and not wear some. Finally the *khawageh* agreed and he put some on my right eye. As soon as he did, I could see all the treasures in the world. Greed possessed me. I said to him, 'Put some on my left eye.'

"He warned me, 'You'll regret it.'

"I got hold of him and said, 'By God, the Almighty, you will not leave here until you have put some in my other eye.'

"He said, 'You'll regret it.'

"I said, 'Regret it, regret it. You must put some in my eye.'

"He put some on my left eye and as he did, he slapped me on my face and said, 'Go, distant one, you are blind,' and he disappeared.

"Now my house is full of gold, but I cannot even see where my hand is going. I'm standing here; perhaps . . . perhaps the *khawagah* will come back. His slap is unforgettable. If he slaps me, I'll recognize his slap and make him restore my sight as he took it away."

The King now remembered the kohl container that he wanted to have and he knew that that was his story. The blind man then said, "This is my story, King. And you will never get The Lady and it is better that you go back to your home."

The King said, "No, I must find her, for I have to find out who is richer and more handsome than I am."

The blind man said, "Since you are, distant one, so blind, go down this road and you'll find what you are looking for."

The King left and kept on going on the road that the blind man showed him. He finally came to a huge apartment building that was so high the eye could not reach its top. And so bright that the eye could not look at it. Beside the apartment building he found some beautiful maidens. He approached them and said, "I'm looking for The Lady. Are you The Lady?"

One of the girls answered, "No, I'm the servant of the servant of The Lady."

They went inside and told The Lady that somebody outside wanted to see her. She said, "Let him in."

He went inside. Things were like he had never seen before, and The Lady had such beauty that nothing could match it.

"Peace be upon you."

"And upon you be peace. What brings you here?"

He told her his story from the beginning to the end and said to her, "I want to marry you."

The Lady said, "Since you have gone through all that and reached here, I will marry you if you can fill me this bottle with sunlight."

He took the bottle and went outside. He sat down under a tree and started thinking. He realized what the dervish had put him to. This Lady was nothing but the world itself. The more you have of it, the more you want. Everyone is fighting over her, but no one can have her.

He left them behind and went home and lived happily. And I was there and just returned.

[Comment from one of the audience: "One was blind by his eyes and the other was blind by his heart."]

The Falcon's Daughter

Collected and translated by Hasan El-Shamy. Forthcoming in *Folktales of Egypt*.

Tape-recorded in April 1969 from 'Aazeezah Mohammed 'Aeed, thirty-eight, a Bedouin, mother of a girl of three, who lived with her husband, thirty-two, and his second, younger, and favored wife in Al-Basateen, a district of Maadi bordering the eastern desert. Although living under urban conditions—the husband did odd jobs and sometimes acted as a middleman—she still wore a veil and was not permitted to leave her home alone. She told the tale in the presence of her husband, as she knew it to be his favorite and used it to entice him. Her maternal aunt "and other women" had told it to her. All ten informants of Egyptian and Nubian variants known to the collector were women. The tale deals symbolically with the domineering role of the mother-in-law in a patrilocal society.

Episodes of types 705 *Born of Fish* and 706 *The Maiden Without Hands* are joined here. Motifs present are T511.1 "Conception from eating fruit"; T578 "Pregnant man"; R13.3 "Person carried off by bird"; N711 "King (prince) accidentally finds maiden in woods (tree) and marries her"; S51 "Cruel mother-in-law"; Q451.1 "Hands cut off as punishment";T412 "Mother-son incest"; S163 "Mutilation: cutting (tearing) out tongue"; Q414 "Punishment: burning alive"; S22 "Parricide."

Basic parts of type 705 hark back to mythological contests in Egyptian antiquity. The falcon mother episode suggests the ancient Egyptian falcon-formed god Horus and goddess Hathor, believed to dwell in a holy sun tree. In the myth of Horus and Seth, the mother cuts off Horus's hand after having been contaminated by a union contrary to nature and replaces it with another totally pure.

Informant: State that there is no god but Allah.
Collector: There is no god but Allah.
Informant: Once there was a woman who did not get pregnant. A vendor went by selling pomegranates. He called, saying, "Pomegranates for pregnancy."

She was very desperate; she wanted to get pregnant. She got one from him. She put it (do not blame me) underneath a dough pot.

Her husband came and said, "I'm hungry."

She said to him, "Eat what's under the washing pan, and do not touch what is under the dough pot."

He ate the pomegranate, saying, "This daughter of a dog, she gets only one for herself and nothing for me."

So he ate it. His stomach got loaded—he got pregnant. He completed all nine months' of pregnancy and labor pains hit him. Now he wants to deliver.

His wife told him, "You can't do it here; go outside in the open away from people. And take this meter of silk and this one of cloth. If the baby is a boy wrap him in the cloth and bring him home. But if it is a girl wrap her in the silk and leave her."

It turned out to be a girl. He wrapped her in the meter of silk and left her next to a tree. A falcon came and picked her up, took her to his nest, and took care of her. He got her grain and other things and mouth-fed her until she became as big as we are, that big.

Meanwhile the Sultan's son was being begged to get married, but he was refusing. One day he took his mare to water her at the stream. When he got there, it looked as if there were a vapor lamp inside the stream. He looked up and saw the girl sitting at the top of the tree, looking just like the moon. He went home sick with love.

An old woman who used to visit his mother asked her, "Why is your son sick?"

She answered, "By God, he has been sick like that for two weeks. He's just lying down and we don't know what his sickness is."

She (the old woman) said to her, "His sickness is love."

She (his mother) said to her, "Why don't you come and see him?"

They both went to his chamber. The old woman asked him, "Why are you sick? Why are you sick, son?"

He answered, "Grandmother, I am sick. I saw something that you have nothing to do with and that you can't reach."

She said, "Yes, I can, and can bring it too. You just tell me."

He said to her, "Could you reach what is on the tree?"

She said, "Yes, I can."

He said, "All right."

She said, "Get me a sheep and a knife and come along with me. Stay away from me, but get me a sheep and a knife."

They went to that tree and the old woman held the sheep by the tail and pretended to be slaughtering it by the tail. The girl saw her from above. She said, "Not from there, old mother, not from there. At the neck!"

She said to her, "I can't see, daughter."

She held him by the back and pretended to be slaughtering him there. The girl called her again saying, "Not from there, old mother, not from there, from the neck!"

She said, "Daughter, I don't know anything else but that. Why don't you come down and show me?"

But the girl wouldn't. She pretended to be slaughtering the sheep at the leg, and said, "Come down, daughter, I cannot."

So she came. She said, "Oh tree, my tree, be as big as my little finger so that I can get down to slaughter the sheep for her and go up again."

The tree shrank, and she got down. He came fast, picked her up and went away. He took her and returned home. When he went home he married her. He gave twenty days of wedding celebration and married her.

One day he wanted to go to Hejaz. He went to his mother and said to her, "Mother, the favor you would like to do for me, do for my wife." She said to him, "That's all right, son. I've got no blessings but hers."

After he left, she (the wife) would say to her, "Mother, give me a piece of bread." She (the mother) would answer, "After I have cut off your arm." And then she would cut off her arm.

And she (the wife) would say, "Mother, give me a piece of bread"; she (the mother) would cut off her foot. She trimmed her off until she became only a lump of flesh and then threw her out of the window. She (the wife) landed on *khatim elmulk* ["the ring of kingship"]. It said to her, "I am your servant; what would you like to have before you?"

She answered it, "I wish myself to be like before, a garden and a palace next to the Sultan's son's, and to have fruit grown out of season in my garden."

The Sultan's son returned from Hejaz. His mother pretended to be his wife. His mother made herself like his wife. He asked her, "Where is my mother?"

She replied, "Your mother died."

She wore her face and he asked, "Where is my mother?"

She replied, "Your mother is dead, and we took her away."

She made herself to be his wife and he slept with her. She became pregnant from him and now she is craving. She said, "I would like a bunch of grapes from the neighboring garden."

He sent a servant, who said:

"Lady, oh Lady, whose house is next to ours,
Haven't you got some grapes for the craving that is ours?"

She answered,

"Shame, shame, my mother craved me and my father
conceived me.

The falcon and the peacock nursed me,
Now the Sultan's son has impregnated his mother,
And her craving hits nobody but me!
Scissors, cut off a piece of his tongue
So that he will not tell on me."

When he got back, the Sultan's son was asking him, "Where are the grapes?"

He (the servant) said, "Ahhhh Ahhhh ahh. . . ." Of course he couldn't speak. He (the Sultan's son) sent another one. This one went to say:

"Lady, oh Lady, whose house is next to ours,
Haven't you got some grapes for the craving that is ours?"

She answered,

"Shame, shame, my mother craved me and my father
    conceived me.
The falcon and the peacock nursed me,
Now the Sultan's son has impregnated his mother,
And her craving hits nobody but me!
Scissors, cut off a piece of his tongue
So that he will not tell on me."

When he went back, of course he could not talk. The Sultan's son shouted at them: "Sons of dog, what happens to you there? Why do you all come back stuttering? I'll go myself."

He went to her and said:

"Lady, oh Lady, whose house is next to ours,
Haven't you got some grapes for the craving that is ours?"

She replied:

"Shame, shame, my mother craved me and my father
    conceived me.
The falcon and the peacock nursed me,
Now the Sultan's son has impregnated his mother,
And her craving hits nobody but me!
Scissors, cut off a piece of the tip of the edge of his shawl
For he is very dear to me."

Then he asks her, "What did you say?"
She repeated.
He said to her, "Please tell me the story."
She said to him, "The one in the palace is actually your mother and I am your wife. As soon as you left she cut me to pieces and threw me outside."

She told him the whole story from the beginning. "She threw me out and I prayed to God. I requested of the ring to put me as I was and now she is pregnant and sent you after the grapes."

Now he went back to his mother, poured gasoline over her, and burned her up. He went back to his wife and they lived together happily.

Tunisia

The Sparrow and the King

Collected by Hasan El-Shamy in Cairo in April 1969.

Motif B171.1.1 "Demi-coq crows in king's body, when the king eats him." Narrated by Saleh Bel-Qasem, twenty-four, a student from Tunis. He had heard the tale repeatedly from his mother and other relatives.

This narrative seems to be restricted to North Africa. Three other variants are published as a booklet: 'Abdul-Hameed Al-Qustantini, *al 'usfur wa al'malik* (The Sparrow and the King) (Tunis, ca. 1968), is very similar to our text. A Berber variant is given in E. Laoust, *Étude sur le Dialecte Berbère du Chenoua* (Paris, 1912), "Le Roi et l'oiseau," p. 194, in which a sparrow has a pitcher (an erotic symbol) that the King takes away from him. The sparrow shouts, "The King is jealous of me; he took my pitcher." When the sparrow is killed another one comes out of his entrails. The brother of the sparrow drinks of the pitcher, he becomes King, and the King becomes his servant. The sparrow marries the King's daughter.

Motif B171.1 appears as a part of type 715 *Demi-Coq*, which is common in Arab countries but represents a different tradition.

I am narrating to you about that sparrow. The sparrow found a grain of barley. He put it in his mouth and flew over the King's palace. He saw the King wearing a necklace made of diamonds and gold. There is that sparrow making a necklace with a piece of string and the grain of barley and standing on a tree shouting, "What the King has, I have! What the King has, I have!"

That King heard him and said to his slaves and servants, "See where he got that barley seed."

They looked and said to the King, "He got it from your granary, Master."

The King said to them, "Beat him and take it away from him."

Those slaves beat the sparrow and took the grain necklace that he made with the grain of barley away from him.

That sparrow stood there shouting, "Where is justice! The King was unjust to me. I had what he has. He took it from me."

The King hears him and says to the servants, "Give it back to him."

They gave the sparrow back his necklace.

The sparrow started shouting, "I had what the King has. The King got jealous of me and took it away. He got scared of me and gave it back to me."

That King heard that talk. He became furious and ordered his servants, "Catch that sparrow. Slaughter it and serve it with *kuskuss* for my supper."

Those servants caught the sparrow. He shouted, "I am not afraid."

They cut his neck with the knife; he shouted, "What a beautiful red necklace."

They dropped him in hot water; he shouted, "What a beautiful bath!"

They plucked his feathers; he shouted, "Don't tickle me so hard!"

The cook carried him on a plate with *kuskuss* to the King. There is the King swallowing that sparrow in one bite!

After the evening prayers there is the King sitting in his reception room and all the ministers and princes sitting with him. There is the sparrow shouting (from the King's belly), "What a spacious palace! What a luxurious palace!"

There is the King feeling pain in his stomach. There is the sparrow breaking loose, shouting, "I found a grain of barley. I made a necklace with it. I had what the King had. The King got jealous of me. The King stole my barley seed. The King got scared and returned it to me. The King killed and ate me, but here I am. What a fat King. What a round stomach on that King!"

The King ordered his servants to chase him (the sparrow) away.

Iraq

The Cruel Mother-in-Law

Collected by Hasan El-Shamy in Cairo in June 1970.

Motifs S51 "Cruel mother-in-law" and F559.3 "Extraordinary excrements." Narrated by an Iraqi woman, forty-nine, from Baghdad while on a visit to relatives. She heard the tale from her mother and, like most female informants, was very reluctant to tell any *sawalif* or *hichayat*, for "they are only told to immediate family."

This tale seems to be restricted to the eastern part of the Arab culture area (probably as a result of limited collections among females). Three other variants are in print, all told by female informants. (1) Iraq: S. Jamali, *Folktales from the City of the Golden Dome* (Beirut, 1965), no. 7, pp. 37–45 (2) Syria: Bernard Lewin, *Arabische Texte von Hama* (Beirut, 1966), no. 3, pp. 20–27 (3) Arabia: A. Al-Juhaiman, *Asateer Sha'Abiyyah* (Folk Legends), vol. 2, no. 18, pp. 323–32.

The device by which the wife's hunger is discovered varies. At the advice of a friend, the husband ties up a white pigeon (2) or a white cock (3) and releases it in front of his wife. In variant 1 he gives a party, but the wife does not have the strength to laugh.

In place of the excrement claimed to be gold, variant 3 has the husband's friend disguise himself as a new polite wife. He drills a hole in a pot, breaks down the door, etc., and finally sits down indecently so that his privates are seen. When the mother inquires about the strange possessions of her new daughter-in-law, she (he) comments, "This is a mark of high (class) wives." The mother is grateful to have the old wife back.

A woman had an only son who became grown up and had not been married yet. She wanted to find him a bride, but he always told her, "Later, not now," and things like that. One day his mother said to him, "Listen, my son, I've grown old and become tired of household work. You must get married before I die."

He said to her, "Well! Find me a good girl from a good house."

She looked until she found him a girl from one of the most notable houses in their town and he married her.

When the wedding [party] was over and after seven days or so, he went back to his shop to work while his mother stayed with his wife. His mother said to his wife, "Listen, in this house [you] don't open what is closed or close what is opened, nor uncover what is covered or cover what is uncovered, nor unwrap what is wrapped or wrap what is unwrapped, nor unfold what is folded or fold what is unfolded. Do you understand?"

The girl, his wife, said, "Yes."

Days passed with things like that. His mother is everything in the house; his wife works all day while his mother orders her around. When the man returns home his mother would call him before he would enter his room and take whatever he had brought home with him—food, pastry, or things like that. His mother would set the dinner for him and if he would say "[Let us] call so-and-so [his wife] to eat with me," she [his mother] would answer him, "This can't be. She is still new in the house. She would get bold [fresh] with us. Wait for a few more days."

After a few more days her son would say, "Let her come and eat with me."

His mother would say, "She hasn't been broken to our house yet. She does not need to eat for she has been eating all day."

He would say to his mother, "May God extend his grace upon us. Let her eat as much as she wants," and [he] used to eat only until he was half-full and leave some of the best food to his wife. His mother would hide it and would give her only hard bread and water.

The girl was not used to that; she had been raised in a house of plenty. She grew sicker and weaker by the day. Her color faded and she became as yellow as the *curcum* [saffron]. Whenever her husband asked her, "What is the matter with you?" she would answer, "Nothing."

One day he said to one of his friends at the store, "By God, Father of so-and-so, my wife is becoming sick. Every day she is getting thinner and paler. I don't know what to do. I am afraid she doesn't want me. Ever since she set her foot in my house and she . . . , she doesn't speak to me, and she is always sad."

His friend said to him, "I'll tell you what to do to see whether she wants you and wants to stay in your house, or whether she hates you and would like to return to her father's house. After dinner swear by God that she joins you and your mother for the coffee, then break wind. If she laughs at you, she doesn't care for you and you should send her back to her father's home. If she doesn't, then she is ill."

That same day after the man ate his supper and thanked his God, he said to his mother, "Call so-and-so [his wife] to have coffee with us."

His mother said to him, "Mohammed, my son, wait! If you treat her like this, she will not have awe of you!"

He swore by God, and his mother went to call her. As they were drinking their coffee, he broke wind. His mother laughed, but his wife didn't and kept on drinking until she finished her cup.

The following day he told his friend about what had happened. His friend said to him, "Your wife is hungry. Your mother is starving your wife."

When he went back home that day, he said to his mother, "We will have guests for dinner. Cook good food for ten persons." His mother went to the market and bought everything: meat, chicken, vegetables, rice, and fruit, and made a huge dinner.

When the meal was done, he said to her, "Mother, my friends are not coming. By God, call my wife and let us all eat this food."

His mother said to him, "You eat and leave the rest; I'll take it to her later."

He swore [that his wife come]. His mother got up to call the girl, his wife, and said, "You will spoil her. No one does this. She will not respect you after that."

He answered, "That is all right."

His mother said, "If she eats too much, she will mess up the bed."

He said, "That does not matter."

His wife came, sat down and ate, and ate and ate, while his mother was [growling], saying all the time: "I told you. She will have awe for no one from now on. She will get sick from too much eating. She will do it in bed!"

After she finished eating, they went into their room while his mother stayed outside boiling with anger. When he got up for morning prayers, his mother slipped into the room and defecated in the bed and ran out. She waited. When he went back into the room, he saw what had happened. He took a golden pound out of his pocket and walked out.

His mother was waiting and shouted, "Didn't I tell you. Now what are you going to do?"

He answered, "Mother, God made us rich; this is a blessed girl. Look what she has defecated—gold! A golden pound, and there are more."

His mother shouted, "That is not her! That was I who did it in your bed. This gold is mine."

He replied, "True, mother! It is yours. Now go clean up the mess you have made."

He built a new house for his wife and moved out of the old one and got his mother a servant.

Israel

A Dispute in Sign Language

From Dov Noy, *Folktales of Israel* (Chicago: University of Chicago Press, 1963), pp. 94–97. Israel Folktale Archives 505. Recorded by S. Gabai from Shlomo Haim, born in Iraq.

This tale is a combination of type 922 *The Shepherd Substituting for the Priest Answers the King's Questions*, episode I ("The Situation"), and type 924A *Discussion between Priest and Jew Carried on by Symbols*. For a different interpretation of the signs in a Jewish version of this tale see M. Gaster, *The Exempla of the Rabbis* (London, 1924), no. 443, pp. 177, 269. For another version see A. Druyanov, *The Book of Jokes and Wit* (Tel Aviv, 1956), vol. 2, no. 2028. For a bibliography of the Arabian versions of this tale type see V. Chauvin, *Bibliographe des ouvrages Arabes au relatifs aux Arabs* (Liège and Leipzig, 1892–1922), vol. 8, no. 112, p. 125, and E. S. Stevens, *Folktales of Iraq* (London, 1931), no. 18, p. 89. Type 924A is discussed in R. Köhler and J. Bolte, *Kleinere Schriften* (Weimar, 1898–1900), vol. 2, no. 64, pp. 479–94, "Rosenblüts Disputaziones Freiheits mit einem Juden." It has crossed to Argentina in the Spanish tradition and is currently told in the United States by American Jews. Its popularity lies in its parody of the Talmudic method of debate.

Once there was a wicked priest who hated Jews. One day he summoned the chief rabbi and said to him, "I want to have a dispute with a Jew in the language of signs. I give you thirty days to prepare yourself, and if nobody appears to take part in the dispute, I shall order that all the Jews be killed."

What was the rabbi to do? He brought the bad tidings to his people and ordered them to fast and to pray in the synagogue. A week went by, two weeks, three weeks passed, but there was no one with the courage to accept the priest's challenge and the great responsibility. It was already the fourth week, and still there was no one to represent the Jews in the dispute.

Then along came a poultry dealer who had been away, bringing chickens from the nearby villages into the town. He had not heard what was going on there, but he noticed on his arrival that the market was closed, and at home he found his wife and children fasting, praying, and weeping.

"What is the matter?" asked the poultry dealer. His wife replied, "The wicked priest has ordered a Jew to hold a discussion with him in the language of signs. If there is no one who is able to do so, all of us will be killed."

"Is that all the matter?" wondered the poultry dealer in surprise. "Go to the rabbi, and tell him that I am ready to participate."

"What are you talking about? How can you understand the priest? Greater and wiser men than you have not been willing to take upon themselves this task!" cried his wife.

"Why should you worry? In any case we shall all be killed." And off they went together to the rabbi.

"Rabbi," said the man, "I am ready to meet the priest!"

The rabbi blessed him. "May God help you and bring you success."

So the priest was told that a Jew, sent by the rabbi, would hold a discussion with him in sign language.

"You have to understand my signs and to answer them in the same way," explained the priest to the Jew before a great assembly. Then he pointed a finger at him. In reply the Jew pointed two fingers. Then the priest took a piece of white cheese from his pocket. In reply the Jew took out an egg. Then the priest took the seeds of some grain and scattered them on the floor. In reply, the Jew set a hen free from the coop and let it eat up the seeds.

"Well done," exclaimed the priest in amazement. "You answered my questions correctly." And he gave the poultry dealer many gifts and ordered his servant to bathe him and to give him fine garments to wear.

"Now I know that the Jews are wise men, if the most humble among them was able to understand me," admitted the priest.

The town was in great excitement, and the people waited in suspense for the result of the dispute. When they saw the poultry dealer leaving the priest's house in fine garments and with a happy expression on his face, they understood that everything was in order, blessed be the Almighty.

"How did it go? What did the priest ask you?" all the people wanted to know. The rabbi called the poultry dealer to his home and asked him to relate what had happened.

And this is what the poultry dealer related: "The priest pointed with one finger to my eyes, meaning to take out my eye. I pointed with two fingers to imply, I would take out both his eyes. Then he took out a piece of cheese to show that I was hungry while he had cheese. So I took out an egg to show that I was not in need of his alms. Then he spilled some wheat grain on the floor. So I fed my hen, knowing it was hungry and thinking what a pity to waste the grain."

At the same time the priest's friends questioned him. "What did you ask the Jew? What did he reply?"

The priest related: "At first I pointed one finger, meaning that there is only one king. He pointed with two fingers, meaning that there are two kings, the king in heaven and the king on earth. Then I took out a piece of cheese, meaning, Is this cheese from a white or a black goat? In answer he took out an egg, meaning, Is this egg from a white or a brown hen? Finally I scattered some grain on the floor, meaning that the Jews are spread all over the world. Whereupon he freed his hen, which ate up all the grain, meaning that the Messiah will come and gather all the Jews from the four corners of the world."

A Tale of a Jew Who Bridled the Wind

From Dov Noy, *Folktales of Israel* (Chicago: University of Chicago Press, 1963), pp. 101–4.

Israel Folktale Archives 142. Recorded by Zvi Moshe Haimovitch, director of the Malben Home for the Aged in Neve Haim, from Elija David, a resident of that home, who was born in Basra, Iraq.

For another version of this tale, in which the city smoke is bridled, see A. Druyanov *The Book of Jokes and Wit* (Tel Aviv, 1956), vol. 2, no. 1995. The general motifs H500 "Test of cleverness or ability," H960 "Tasks performed through cleverness," and H1020 "Tasks contrary to the laws of nature" are popular in Jewish test tales.

There was once a King who had three Viziers: a Jew, a Moslem, and a Christian. The King venerated his Jewish Vizier above all of them because of his great wisdom; he could always find a way out of any difficulty.

The other two Viziers, the Christian and the Moslem, always sought ways to belittle the Jew in the King's eyes. The King, however, was clever and did not pay attention to their intrigues. He used to say, "The Jew is wiser than you!"

"Are we stupid in your eyes?" they asked.

"No, you are not stupid, but a Jew is wiser. The righteousness of these words will be proved by a Jew himself."

One day the King ordered his servants, "Stand at the marketplace and charge the first Moslem passing by, 'You have stolen from the King the wind and the air encircling the earth.'"

The King's servants did as they were bidden. They stood at the marketplace until they saw a Moslem. Instantly they caught hold of him, charged him, and brought him before the King. The King blamed the Moslem, accusing him of having stolen the wind and the air. The Moslem pleaded with the King for mercy, swearing that he was not guilty of this offense.

Said the King, "If you want to be forgiven, do as I bid you. I shall hand you the wind. Do as you like with it, and in four months time, let me know what you have done."

Four months passed, and the Moslem appeared before the King. He had but one request. "Forgive me, my King! I did not know what to do with the wind. Indeed," he pleaded, "I am blowing on my hands, and not a sign of the wind remains."

The King sent the Moslem away and ordered his servant to catch hold of the first Christian at the marketplace and to charge him with the same offense. The servants did as they were bidden. They went to the marketplace and waited until they saw a Christian. Instantly they caught hold of him, charged him, and brought him before the King. The King accused the Christian of having stolen the wind and the air. The Christian fell at the King's feet and begged for mercy. The King sent him off, urging him to make use of the wind and to report back in four months time.

Four months passed by, and the trembling Christian came to the King's palace with tears in his eyes. He begged for mercy, saying he did not know what to do with the wind. The King forgave him and sent him away. Then he said to his servants, "Go to the market, catch hold of the first Jew you set your eyes on, and charge him with the same offense."

The King's servants did as they were bidden. They stood at the marketplace and waited until they saw a Jew. A poor and shabby man he was, indeed. Instantly they caught hold of him. He did not seem worried at all on hearing the offense he was being charged with, and when he appeared before the King, he said, "Of course I can bridle the wind and make use of it, but I need three things. I need a written authorization. I need a sum of money for preparation and clothing, for of what esteem will I be in the eyes of the world if I am shabby? Lastly, I need a team of workers and clerks to carry out the project."

The King immediately ordered clerks to prepare the certificate and agreed to fulfill all the Jew's conditions.

In no time the Jew opened a big office with clerks and workers. Then he ordered all the houseowners and shopkeepers to come to his office.

When they appeared, he ordered them to shut all the windows of their flats and shops.

"How will we be able to breathe?" they asked him in amazement.

The Jew answered, "The wind and the air are mine, by order of the King. Here is his signed certificate. If you want to breathe, you must pay a tax." So the Jew collected a large sum of money. He also prohibited jewelers from using bellows and owners of sailing vessels from using the wind, without paying a tax.

The Jew put the money he collected into safes together with copies of receipts he had given against payments. Clerks kept the accounts and handed over reports of all the expenses and of the Jew's profits from exploiting the wind.

Four months passed by, and the Jew went to the palace with his profits. The King, arrayed in fine clothes, called his Viziers, the judges, as well as the Moslem and the Christian who did not fulfill their missions.

The King asked the Christian, "Why did you not carry out my orders?"

The Christian answered, "I could not control the wind." The Moslem gave a similar reply.

The King called the Jew and asked him, "What did you do with the wind I gave you?"

The Jew gave details of what he had done in the four months at his disposal and the large sum of money that enlarged the King's treasury from the use of the wind.

The King was delighted with the Jew's cleverness and said to his Viziers, the judges, "You see, the cleverness of a Jew is greater than yours; that is why I revere a Jew!"

The King appointed his Jewish Vizier as his chief advisor and the poor Jew as his financial advisor. From that day no one dared to talk against Jews in the whole kingdom.

Asia

India

Teja and Teji (Assamese)

Collected by Praphulladatta Goswami. Forthcoming in *Folktales of India*.

Recorded from Srimati Jnanadasundari Barua, about sixty, of North Lakhimpur in Upper Assam in 1948.

This characteristic north Indian tale begins as a Cinderella story, type 510, with the persecuted heroine theme. Motifs of type 510 present are S31 "Cruel stepmother"; L55 "Stepdaughter heroine"; B313.1 "Helpful animal reincarnation of dead mother"; B115.1 "Ear (mouth) cornucopia"; E631 "Reincarnation in plant (tree) growing from grove"; D950 "Magic tree"; D1648.1.1 "Tree bends only to heroine"; L162 "Lowly heroine marries prince."

The second part of the story brings in the motifs of the false bride, E610.1.1 "Reincarnation: boy (girl) to bird to boy (girl)"; and G61 "Relative's flesh eaten unwittingly."

In a Kachari version from Rangiya in Kamrup district a *bel* tree grows from the mother's buried bones, and the mother comes down from the tree every night to feed her children. In a Nepali version, a two-headed ewe befriends Dhon Cholecha, a girl mistreated by her stepmother. The ewe is killed and from its bones grows a tree of cakes, on which Dhon feeds. For published variants see "The Big Tortoise" in Maung Htin Aung, *Burmese Folktales* (Bombay, 1948), pp. 112–23; K. K. Vaidya, *Folktales of Nepal* (Kathmandu, 1961), pp. 1–13; L. N. Bezbarua, *Burhiair Sadhu* (Tales of a Grandmother) (4th ed.; Gauhati, 1957).

There was a rich peasant. He had two wives. The elder wife had a daughter and the younger a son and a daughter. The boy's name was Teja while his sister was called Teji. Their stepmother was not overfond of Teja and Teji. Nor did she like their mother, for she was the peasant's favorite. One day both the wives went to have a bath in the tank. The younger one asked the elder one to give her a scrubbing. While pretending to scrub her the elder wife pushed her into the tank and said, "Remain there as a big tortoise." The younger wife immediately changed into a tortoise and had to remain in the tank.

When their stepmother came back Teja and Teji asked her about their mother. She said harshly, "How should I know where she has gone?" So the day was over. Next morning Teja and Teji went out with the cattle to graze them. As they were walking along the bank of the tank a tortoise came out and addressed them: "My dears, I am your mother. Your stepmother pushed me into the water and turned me into a tortoise. I wonder if you have had enough to eat." So saying she took an arum leaf, put a little of her vomit there, and asked her children to eat it. They ate up the vomit and felt hungry no longer. Thus every morning they used to meet their mother and eat her vomit.

The elder wife now noticed that the children did not complain of hunger and were growing healthier and more attractive day by day. She had given good things to her daughter to eat, but that girl never put on flesh. Her suspicions were roused and one day she sent her daughter along with Teja and Teji to see if her stepchildren had anything to eat anywhere. Teja and Teji now thought how to give the slip to their stepsister and meet their mother. They sent her away after a straying cow and came to their mother, but as they were trying to have a hurried meal their stepsister returned and found them out. She also wanted a share of what they had taken. Teja and Teji gave her a share but urged her not to say anything to her mother. The girl promised not to report the matter.

In the evening when the children returned home the elder wife noticed that her own daughter looked quite well fed and began to question her if the children had taken anything anywhere. The girl said, "No, we did not take anything." Her mother did not believe her and began to question her further. At last, in fear of a beating, the little girl had to report everything that had occurred. That very evening the elder wife placed some potsherds under her sleeping mat and took to her bed. As she tossed in her bed the potsherds crackled and her husband asked her, "What's the matter with you?" She said, "Ah, I am aching in all my joints, I am so ill." He asked, "What would you like to eat?" She groaned and said, "I think that big tortoise in the tank—its flesh would be good for me."

The peasant arranged to have the tortoise caught. When Teja and Teji came to know of this they rushed to their mother and told her. She said, "My dears, no use weeping. Listen to what I say. When they would cast their net to catch me I won't be caught, but if you yourselves try to catch me, even with some ordinary contrivance, I will get caught. When after dressing and cooking me they will invite you to eat with them do not eat my flesh but hide it under the leaf-plate. Later find some way to bury the flesh along with the leaf-plates on the bank of the tank. There I will grow as a tree of gold and silver and help you in times of difficulty." They promised to do as she had instructed them.

Next morning when the men tried to catch the tortoise she could not be caught. When they were tired of casting their nets the children went forward and easily caught her with an ordinary fishing contrivance. But they did not eat her flesh and afterward buried it on the bank of the tank. Next morning there grew a tree of gold and silver. People flocked to see the wonderful tree, and the King also heard about it. The King came and wanted to take it away, but there was none who could uproot it. Teja was standing close by and he said to the King, "Your Majesty, I can pull it out for you, but you must promise to marry my sister." The boy spoke in this way because he had been instructed by his mother. The King agreed to his proposal, and Teja pulled out the tree. The King thanked the boy and said, "Your sister is too young, let her grow up, then I'll marry her." The boy gave the King a grackle and a pomegranate seedling and said, "Your Majesty, it is just possible you will forget about my sister. Take these two things with you, and when the bird starts to talk and the plant bears fruit come and take away Teji." The King promised to do so.

After some days the grackle started talking and the pomegranate bore fruit, but the King had completely forgotten about his promise. One day while he was resting the bird sang out:

> *Ezar nizar paril* [untranslatable]
> The pomegranate has ripened and dropped.
> How is it the king has forgotten?
> Sister Teji is grown up now.

The King was startled to hear the voice and as he looked around the bird sang again:

> *Ezar nizar paril,*
> The pomegranate has ripened and dropped.
> How is it the king has forgotten?
> Sister Teji is grown up now.

Now the King remembered his promise to marry the girl. So, without delay, he set out for Teji's village, married the girl, and started back with his new bride.

The King had seven wives he had married earlier, and they did not like that another wife should be added to their number. When the King returned in a boat with Teji and the boatmen were about to moor the boat, the eldest wife sang out:

> Do not get off here,
> O evil Teji,
> This is my ghat.

When the boatmen tried to moor at another spot, another wife sang out:

> Do not get off here,
> O evil Teji,
> This is my ghat.

In this way all the seven wives did not allow her to get off at seven places. So the boatmen had to moor the boat at another ghat or landing place.

Teji had a happy time with the King. Her stepmother, however, was unhappy that she should have such a good fortune. After a year when Teji gave birth to a boy, as is usual she wanted to pay a visit to her parental home. The King gave her leave. When she arrived her step-mother seemed very solicitous about her comfort and welfare. One morning she said to the girl, "Come, let me do up your hair." While pretending to comb her hair she pushed a thorn into Teji's head and said, "Change into a mynah." Teji instantly turned into a mynah bird and flew to the roof of the house. When after a few days the King sent a letter and men to take back Teji, her stepmother dressed her own daughter in Teji's clothes and ornaments and sent her away with Teji's child in her arms. The bird followed the litter of the false wife.

In Teji's dress the stepsister looked like her, and the King did not notice any difference. She was, however, given constant trouble by the baby, who missed his mother. When the stepsister tried to dandle and console the child, the mynah cried out:

> Whose child it is, who dandles it,
> She but leaves it making it weep all the more.

The King overheard the bird singing in that way and wondered. Teji had been weaving a netlike cloth on her loom and it had remained unfinished. Her stepsister now sat at the loom and made a show of weaving, and the bird cried out:

> Whose net-cloth it is, who weaves it,
> She but breaks the threads and leaves them knotted.

The King's suspicions were aroused, for he had noticed earlier that his wife Teji could handle her child quite well and, also, could weave ably. He took two sweet-balls and addressed the bird: "O mynah, I have in my hand two sweet-balls—one the ball of hunger and the other the ball of thirst. If you are indeed someone of my own then eat this hunger ball, if you are someone else then eat the ball of thirst." The bird alighted on his hand and pecked at the sweet-ball of hunger. As the King caressed the bird his hand felt something sharp in the head of the bird. He pulled it out and lo! there was Teji in the flesh.

He now got the entire story from her and grew furious at the perfidy of her stepmother and her stepsister. Directly he ordered his executioners to kill the impostor, put her flesh and fat in a cask, her head and hands and feet in another cask, and her blood in still another cask. When his orders were attended to he asked two men to carry the casks to Teji's stepmother. He instructed them thus: "Give her first the cask of flesh and fat and say this is venison. Leave the other casks when you depart in the morning."

So they took the casks to the evil woman. When she received the first cask she said to herself, "Excellent, my daughter went only the other day, she has already sent me presents, whereas the other girl did not have such kindly feelings." So the happy mother cooked the flesh and served it to her household and with the fat she lighted lamps. The King's men said they were unwell and did not eat anything. When the feasting was over, they began to sing:

A relative cooked it, a relative served, they all ate together,
With a relative's fat they lighted lamps, the floor was flooded
    with light.

The woman overheard them singing and asked, "What are you singing there, men?" They said, "We have got a high temperature and don't know what we are singing." Next morning she found that the men had left and there were other casks near her door. She eagerly opened them and when she saw the head and hands and feet and the blood of her dear daughter and realized what she had fed on the night before, her grief and consternation knew no bounds. She rent the air, crying loudly.

The Mother Serpent (Gujarati)

Contributed by Praphulladatta Goswami. Forthcoming in *Folktales of India*.

Supplied in 1964 by Somabhai Parekh, Baroda. Motifs B491.1 "Helpful serpent" and D391 "Transformation: serpent to person."

The recital of this tale serves a religious purpose in the ritual *vrata* performed by womenfolk in parts of India. Snake worship is not a major cult but it has a hoary tradition. The Paraskara Grihya Sutra prescribed offerings to snakes, particularly on the full moon day in the month of Sravana (July–August). The Naga Panchami day (fifth day of the dark fortnight of Sravana) is set aside for snake worship. In Assam and Bengal many people offer worship to the snake goddess Manasa or Padma in Sravana or at some other time in the rainy season.

For the cult of snake worship in Bengal see Asutosh Bhattacharyya, "The Bengali Snake-Charmers and Their Profession," *Indian Folk-Lore* 1:2 (1958): 3–10; Edward C. Dimock, *Manasha, Goddess of Snakes* (University of Chicago Committee on South Asian Studies, Reprint Series 13, 1961); Pradyot Kumar Maity, *Historical Studies in the Cult of the Goddess Manasa* (Calcutta, 1966); J. P. Vogel, *Indian Serpent Lore* (London, 1926).

A helpful serpent appears in Mary Frere, *Old Deccan Days* (London, 1929), no. 11, "A Funny Story."

Khir is a porridge of millet or rice, boiled in milk. *Lapasi* is a boiled wheat dish.

There lived an old man with his old wife. Their seven sons and their wives also lived with them. The senior six wives were well regarded while the seventh one was disregarded and hated. She had no relative at her father's place. All the persons of her father-in-law's house used to describe her as "one having nobody at her father's place."

When all the members of the family finished their meals joyously, then the youngest wife used to eat by collecting with great difficulty the scraps of food that remained at the bottom of the earthen pot. After eating, she alone used to clean a heap of pots.

Living in that way, the season for offering food to dead ancestors came. From the milk of buffaloes, sweet *khir* was prepared. The youngest wife was pregnant and desired much for *khir*, but who would give it to her? All had taken their food and, afterward, there were only half-burned crusts sticking to the bottom of the earthen pot. "Half-burned crusts of food. Well, that will do for me." Having thought so, the youngest wife tied the half-burned crusts of *khir* into a piece of cloth and decided to eat it after going to the outskirt of the village. At the time of fetching water she went to the outskirt of the village. The well was overcrowded by women, desirous of fetching water. The young wife thought of eating the *khir* at the next turn of fetching water, when there would be nobody at the well. She had once fetched water. During that time, she kept the *khir* wrapped in a piece of cloth, near the hole of a snake. Having kept the food there, and thinking that she would eat it at ease afterward, she went to take her bath.

While she was taking her bath a female serpent came out from behind. The serpent was also pregnant. She desired to have the food of *khir*. She came and ate away all the *khir* and then sat hidden in her hole. She thought to bite the owner of the *khir* if he used abusive language to her.

After taking her bath, the young wife came joyfully and quickly untied the piece of cloth; she did not find a single crust of *khir*.

"Ah! Oh! I was unlucky not to have them at my house and when I brought them here, here also I could not eat them. Well, there might be an unhappy woman like myself; she might have eaten them. Let the heart of one who ate them experience deep satisfaction," the young lady observed.

The female serpent came out of the hole at once and asked the lady, "Who are you, O lady?"

"Mother, I am an unhappy one. I am pregnant. I had desire for *khir* and when I went to take bath, somebody ate up my *khir*. Well, she must be an unhappy one like myself. It is good that the poor one has eaten it."

"O lady, your crusts of *khir* have been eaten by me. Had you used abusive language, I would have bitten you. But you have blessed me. Now, tell me what miseries you have."

"Mother, I have nobody at my father's or mother's place. The ceremony for my first pregnancy will be due now, but there is nobody of my parental relatives to perform the function." As she spoke tears came into her eyes.

The female serpent said, "Daughter, do not worry. For today, believe us to be your paternal relatives. Our residence is in this hole. At the time of celebrating the first pregnancy, please put an invitation letter for the auspicious occasion near the hole." The serpent became the adopted mother. The young wife, in an astonished mood, went home.

The auspicious day for celebrating the first pregnancy was just due. The mother-in-law spoke: "The brotherless lady has no paternal relatives; who the devil will celebrate her first pregnancy?" The young wife said, "Mother-in-law, give me one invitation letter for the auspicious occasion."

"Oh brotherless one, you have nobody at your father's or mother's place; to whom do you want to give the invitation letter for the auspicious occasion?"

"I have a distant relative of mine; please give me one."

"Look here, the brotherless one is out of her senses."

At once a female neighbor spoke: "O lady, give her a piece of paper. What do you lose thereby?"

The young wife went to the outskirt of the village and put that letter near the hole of the serpent and returned.

The day for celebrating the first pregnancy came. The wives of the elder brothers and the mother-in-law began to mock the young wife with the words "Just now, a number of paternal relatives of the young wife will arrive; they will bring big trunks full of clothes; let the earthen pots be placed quickly on the hearth, let water be boiled for preparing *lapasi*." As they were going on, cutting jokes, guests with red turbans on, resembling great Moghal grandees, were seen coming. There was a lady, looking like a Rajput, with them. The young wife at once recognized the mother serpent. The relatives on the side of the husband were astonished at the sight and began to hum.

"Where did the paternal house of the parentless one spring from? Where did these come from?"

"Welcome, welcome, the paternal relatives of the young wife, welcome!" All began to speak like that. The pots for cooking *lapasi* were placed on the hearth.

Now the female serpent called the young lady and whispered in her ear: "Daughter, please tell them not to cook anything. Put the vessels of milk boiled with spices in this room. Having shut the door, we shall drink it. We belong to the community of serpents and, as such, we cannot eat ordinary food."

The young wife went to the mother-in-law and told her not to cook anything as her paternal relatives took only milk as their food; and further added that they would drink only milk boiled with spices.

It was time for the meal. Vessels full of boiled milk with spices were placed in the room, which was shut. The guests at once assumed the forms of snakes, applied their mouths to the vessels, and drank up the milk within a moment.

The first pregnancy of the daughter was celebrated, and the snakes gave liberally gold and silver and silken clothes to the relatives. The relatives of the house of the husband were wonderstruck and exclaimed, "Oh, they have brought so much! They have brought so much in dowry!"

The guests said, "Please allow us to go and take our sister to our house for the delivery."

"Ah dear, may she accompany you! Can we refuse this? After all, this is a call on your own daughter."

"And do not send anybody for her return. We shall come and bring our sister back with us."

The relatives of the husband came out to bid good-bye to the young wife. "Now, please go back." Speaking thus, the guests requested the husband's relatives to go back. When they came to the hole, the serpents told the girl, "Look here, sister, do not be afraid. We shall assume our original forms. You follow us into the hole." The girl said, "Very well."

So the snakes at once entered the hole. The girl also followed them. As they went inside, she found rooms beautiful like the *dhatura* flower. There were beautiful beds, and swinging beds in the netherland. The mother serpent was enjoying the swinging bed with the noise "Kicaduka, kicaduka" and the snake god, with jewels on his head and with a big mustache, was found sitting on a soft cushioned seat.

The snake god kept the lady as his daughter in the netherland. The lady enjoyed the swinging bed made of silver and gold. The parents treated their new daughter with great care.

The female serpent was also due to deliver children. The serpent told the lady, "Look here, daughter, do not be afraid. We are a community of snakes. If all the children of a snake remain alive, then there will be no empty space on the earth for human beings to walk, even. Therefore we go on eating our children when they are being delivered. Do not be afraid."

The young lady, with an earthen lamp in hand, stood near the serpent. The serpent went on eating her children as she delivered them. On seeing this, the young lady was disgusted, and as a result the lamp fell down from her hand. In the darkness, two young ones of the female serpent escaped. The tails of both the escaped ones were eaten away by the female serpent, and so they both were without tails.

At the completion of nine months, the young lady also delivered a son, beautiful like the ring of a god. The son grew day by day. When he learned to crawl on his knees, the lady said to the mother serpent, "Mother, now please take me to my house." The mother serpent gave her mattresses, big mattresses, a cradle, necklaces, anklets, and other ornaments. By giving her innumerable valuable gifts, the female serpent satisfied her to the full.

Then the serpent spoke: "Look here, Daughter, put your arm into the mouth of your grandfather, sitting here. Do not be afraid. He will not bite you." With fear, the lady put her arm into the mouth of the old snake. The hand up to the arm's length was put into the mouth, but she drew it out in fear. Then she saw that her arm was covered with bracelets of gold.

"Now, put in the other arm." The lady put the other arm up to the length of the shoulder into the mouth of the snake, and the whole arm was found covered with bracelets of gold. Two brothers accompanied the lady and left her at the outskirt of her husband's village. When the young wife went to her house, both the mother and the son were surrounded by the husband's relatives and they all shouted with joy: "The young wife has come. The young wife has come. She has brought much dowry. Nobody knows the whereabouts of the village of the paternal relatives of the young wife."

The son of the young lady was now grown up. Once, the wife of the elder son was cleaning grain for grinding. The son began to scatter the barley grains by filling his fist. The wife of the elder son shouted, "Do not scatter them, dear son. Why do you scatter the barley grain of poor people like ourselves?" The young lady felt the taunt to her core and, going to the hole of the snake, wept there. And to the surprise of all, a number of bulls carrying bags full of barley grain came to her house. The husband's relatives were much ashamed.

Once the son spilled milk from the vessel and the elder son's wife taunted him: "Dear son, do not do so; your mother's paternal relatives are rich and they will send a number of buffalo for you. Please keep yourself from pouring away milk of the buffalo of poor persons like ourselves."

Again, the young wife went to the hole of the snake and wept. The female serpent came from inside and spoke: "Go, do not look behind; do not give buttermilk to a juggler; speak the word *nagel, nagel* and a herd of buffalo will come to your house." The lady, speaking the word *nagel*, returned to her house, and the herd of buffalo followed her. The young wife, after going home, said, "Dear lady! Dear lady! Please clean the buffalo shed." The husband's relatives came out and were astonished to see innumerable buffalo with white marks on their foreheads.

Now, what happened in the hole of the snake? The two young ones of the female serpent were without tails and as such nobody wanted to play with them. All used to say:

"Go away, O tail-loser, I won't allow you to play.
Go away, O tailless one, I won't allow you to play!"

Both the brothers approached the mother and asked:

"Mother, Mother, speak, who has made us without tails?"

"Sons, you have a sister on the earth. When you were born, the earthen lamp fell from her hand. Therefore, you are without tails."

"So we both shall go and bite her."

"Alas! O sons, how can you bite a sister? That sister is such that she will bless you."

"If she blesses us, we shall return, after giving her a gift of a sari and a blouse; and if she uses abusive language, we shall bite her."

Both the brothers went to the sister's house. It was evening, and one hid himself near the threshold and the other one sat hidden in the watershed. Both thought, "If she comes over here, we shall bite her." When the sister came to the threshold she stumbled and her foot dashed severely against something. She said, "May the paternal relatives of a parentless one like myself be pleased and forgive. Sesanga is the father and the female serpent is the mother, who have given silken clothes to me as dowry."

On hearing these words, one tail-loser thought, "Oh, this sister blesses me, how can I bite her?"

The sister again went to the watershed. There also she stumbled and her foot dashed against something. Again she said, "May the paternal relatives of a parentless one like myself be pleased and forgive. Sesanga is the father and the female serpent is the mother, who have given silken clothes to me as dowry."

The second tailless one also thought, "Look here, this sister blesses me. Can I bite her?"

Both the brothers assumed the forms of human beings, saw their sister, and, having given to her son golden anklets as a gift, went away to their hole.

May Mother Serpent be fruitful to all as she became fruitful to her!

The King of Cheats (Oriya)

Contributed by Praphulladatta Goswami. Forthcoming in *Folktales of India*.

Supplied by Kunja Bihari Das, Cuttack, in 1964. Tales of trickster thieves are popular in India. Type 1525N *The Two Thieves Trick Each Other* is reported 13 times from India and nowhere else; the first episode in the present tale follows the first episode in that type. Also present are elements from type 1539 *Cleverness and Gullibility*, "The youth sells pseudomagic objects and animals," such as the gold-dropping bear (motif K111.1) and type 1545 *The Boy with Many Names* who cheats people by using fanciful names (motif K602). Other motifs of deception are K148 "Cheaters sell each other valueless article"; K252.1 "Deceptive sale of another as slave"; and K846 "Trickster being attacked by ferocious animal persuades dupe to take his place."

This story reflects the philosophy of "profitable one-upmanship" found in the Sanskrit *Niti Shastras* to which belong also the *Panchatantra* and its abridged version the *Hitopadesha* dating back to 500 A.D. and 1200 A.D., respectively.

It was a dark midnight. Visibility was poor. The village cheat and the city cheat came from opposite directions and met under a tree. The village cheat had a load of limestone on his head, and the city cheat carried a big sack of ashes. The village cheat said, "Friend, what do you carry?" The city cheat said, "I carry a bag of camphor." He also inquired of the village cheat about his load. The village cheat said, "I carry a load of cowries. Are you interested?" The city cheat said, "Will you take this camphor in return?" Each agreed to the proposal, and their articles were exchanged.

The village cheat delightedly said to his wife, "Look how clever I am, I have got this camphor in exchange for a bag of limestone." The city cheat said to his wife, "There are a few clever people in the world. I am one of them. You will be surprised to know how I have cheated a fool and brought this bag of cowries. The fellow will die of heart failure when he will discover articles of no value in the bag. Let him die, what is the value of a fool's life?"

Children of both these families were waiting with anxiety to see what these bags contained. To their utter amazement, there was only limestone or ashes. The faces of both the cheats in their respective houses turned pale. The wives of both of them rebuked them, saying, "Fie on you, fool! Are you not ashamed of your silliness?"

Neither of the cheats could open his lips out of shame. In cheating each had been cheated. Whom would each hold responsible? It was possible that a clever man might be cheated under peculiar circumstances. He had to console himself somehow.

However, they had a chance meeting in a market, and they could not check laughter at the sight of one another. A cheat can be a friend of another cheat. So they made up their minds not to cheat each other any more and were tied by a mutual bond of friendship, giving *Mahaprasad* [putting ceremonial food] in each other's mouth. The city cheat joyfully said, "Who in the world can cheat us now? We can cheat the people wherever they gather in a large number. We shall invade the market, the crowded fair, and city streets. Henceforth the bathing ghat and even this sacred temple will not be safe. Not only money and golden ornaments and jewels, we shall steal away the mark of sandal paste from the forehead of brahmans, even collyrium from the eyes of ladies."

With this they went out. First they reached the house of an old woman; she was bent down with age and could hardly walk without a stick. The two cheats collected an account of her life from the village to serve their own purpose. Then they approached the old woman, bowed to her, and said, "Dear auntie, you have not visited us since your marriage. It is regrettable that you take no interest in your family affairs. But we have not forgotten you. We remember your previous affection toward us with joy. That is what has brought us here. You will be happy to know that the marriage ceremony of my son is going to be performed soon. I have no near and dear relations to look up to. You are to do everything. Please get ready and follow me."

Her father's home was at a considerable distance. She had a natural longing to see her brothers and their children. But she had had no opportunity to see them. Now she wept bitterly when she recalled the incidents of her childhood and youth. She was comforted by these welcome guests who stayed in her house for the day. They were offered oil in a cup of gold to rub on their bodies before bath. Her son accompanied them as a guide to show them the bathing tank.

The cheats besmeared their bodies with oil, hid the cup in the dense shrubs, and cried out that it was taken away by a crow. Then they took their bath, returned to the old woman's house for their meals, and said, "Auntie, please do not be sorry for the mishap. There was no help for it. We put the cup of gold on the bank. It was carried away by a naughty crow. We followed it. But it disappeared out of view within a moment." The son of the old woman had watched everything, but pretended as if he knew nothing. He did not open his lips and allowed the matter to drift. The cheats took him to be a fool.

The old woman was sorry at the loss of this valuable cup and repented much for not giving them oil in a copper, silver, or brass cup. In sorrow she refused to attend the marriage ceremony of her brother's son and sent her own son instead. The son accompanied them riding a horse.

On the way the cheats said, "Brother, we feel very hungry. You have got some valuable ornaments on your person. Why don't you sell one of them and bring some food for us?"

The boy said, "My dear brothers, why should we sell our ornaments unnecessarily? A man does this when he finds no other means. Perhaps you do not know that I am quite known in this area. I can supply you with as much refreshment as you require. But there is one condition. You should not embarrass me in any way. You should do what I say. The matter is also not very hard and will not be troublesome to you in any way. When you are asked 'one' or 'two' you will say 'two.' "

The cheats were unmindful. They did not think that the word "two" would cause any handicap in respect of their very existence. They agreed to this proposal without a second thought. The boy went to a merchant and said, "I have brought two workmen for sale. They are strong and stout and expert in farming and will give you very good service. Please pay me a good price and take charge of them." The merchant was satisfied to see these two persons of well-built body and asked them, "One or two?" The cheats as directed said, "Two."

The sale was now over. The boy went away with the money. The two slaves, now purchased, were taken to the garden to work in spite of their strong protests. But the merchant did not listen to them. The two cheats now realized that the so-called boy was the greatest of all cheats. Then they turned to the merchant, fell at his feet, and said, "Sir, we are not habituated to hard work. We rather engage laborers for cultivating our land and doing all sorts of odd jobs. We belong to well-to-do families and do not desire this sort of rough treatment at all. The boy with whom we had a little bit of intimacy invited us for some refreshment here and to our surprise has sold us to you."

The merchant said, "I do not care to know anything about you. After all, I must carry on my business. Business is business. There is no place for sentiment or emotion in it."

The two cheats begged for mercy and said, "We have been cheated. You have been cheated, too. The money paid to the culprit must be realized somehow. Please send somebody with us. We shall realize the amount and pay it back to you." The merchant was convinced of their innocence, released them, and sent a man with them in search of the offender.

The boy, however, rode a horse and reached a village in no time. There was a confectioner's shop nearby. Sweets were arranged in good order. A boy was the salesman. The cheat went on swallowing up the sweets with both hands. The boy protested against this unusual practice, and said, "Sir, ask me for any sweet you want. First pay and then eat the sweet." To this the cheat said, "Do not worry. My name is Fly. Go and inform your father that the fly is eating away the sweets. He will never grudge at all. For I am his friend."

The boy ran in and told his father about this strange fly. The father did not care to understand the implication of his complaint and angrily said, "You are a fool. How much can the fly eat? To whom have you given the charge of the shop? Go at once and guard the shop."

Meanwhile the cheat filled a bag with sweets and rode away. He came across an old woman on the way. She was accompanied by a young lady who was hardly sixteen and very handsome. Her face was moonlike and she possessed the color of molten gold. The boy stopped the horse, dismounted, caught hold of the girl, and rode away. All this happened in the twinkling of an eye. The old woman was thunderstruck. She could not for a moment realize what was happening before her and what she should do under the circumstances. At last she raised an outcry. The cheat said, "Do not worry. My name is Son-in-law."

The old woman, however, went on shouting till many people gathered. The crowd asked her the reason of her screaming. The old woman went on repeating a single sentence, "My daughter has been carried away. My daughter has been carried away. His name is Son-in-law." The people laughed and said, "What? You daughter has been carried away by the son-in-law? This is no stealing, no robbery. This is what always should happen. There is nothing unnatural in it. Why do you weep, old woman? Why do you bray like a donkey? She is now grown up. Should she not have her conjugal life?"

The cheat rode away with the girl and reached a forest. He dismounted for a rest. A bear was eating white ants on an anthill nearby. As soon as he saw the intruder the bear attacked him. The cheat was of strong physique and fearless. He gave a good account of himself. He fought till the bear was fully exhausted. Then he skillfully caught hold of its muzzle and rubbed it on the ground. But it could not be killed since the cheat was weaponless. Nor could he set it free out of fear for his life.

To fight with a savage animal was a hard task for him. All his money was scattered. He did not know how long this fight would last. He felt tired and exhausted and was also afraid that he might be killed in the end. But luck was favorable to him. A merchant arrived at the place and saw a lot of money scattered on the field. He felt tempted, as he was greedy by nature, and went on picking up the coins.

He saw the young man holding the muzzle of a bear and rubbing it on the ground. He said, "My dear friend, where does so much money come from? Why do you rub the muzzle of this terrible bear?"

The cheat said, "Sir, this is not like any other wild bear. It has got some special virtue. It purges money if you rub its nose. It is of use to a man who wants to grow rich. I have now tamed it properly like a cat so that it may not harm any person."

The merchant said, "Will you sell it?" The cheat replied, "If I get a good customer." The merchant said, "May I know the price?" The cheat said, "I shall not part with it if I get less than a thousand rupees."

The merchant thought to himself, "Business is not an easy job. It constantly worries man, ruins his health and mental peace. Who knows when it will fail? The reputed millionaire sometimes becomes a beggar in the street. But why should I trouble myself unnecessarily if this bear produces money to my heart's content? Henceforward I shall have an easy life. I shall spend lavishly, eat and drink merrily, and sleep soundly."

He counted the money he had. It was just one thousand rupees. He paid it to the cheat. The cheat also took all the money that was still spread all around. The merchant began rubbing the muzzle. The cheat rode away with the young lady and soon went out of sight.

The cheat in course of his journey saw a washerman spreading the cloths to dry under the sun. The cheat chewed sweets in his mouth. The washerman was tempted by the sweets and his mouth watered profusely. He asked for a sweet and was given one. The washerman after eating the sweet remarked that it was very tasty. He asked for one more. The cheat said, "I am glad that you like it. But you will be surprised to know that these are not sweets prepared by a confectioner. These are the fruits that a tree bears. Look, there is a hill in the distance. You will find a small lake on the top of the hill. On the bank of the lake, there is a tree laden with fruit of various kinds. Pluck as many of them as you like. There is nobody to stop you. Eat the sweets, drink the transparent water of the lake, forget the worries of hard work and the strenuous life, and live like a prince or monarch or a god in heaven."

The washerman was pleased with the idea and went on as directed to the top of the hill. Meanwhile the cheat gathered up all the valuable cloths, put them on the back of the horse, and rode away till he reached a safe place. He tied the colored cloths to the branches of a tree and said, "O my magic tree, bloom silk cloths of great value for me."

A merchant going by the tree heard this utterance and wondered, "How can a tree bear silk cloth like flowers of various colors? This is strange, really very strange. Such things may happen in heaven. But who has heard of it on earth?"

He approached the cheat and said, "What are you doing?"

The cheat said, "This is a strange tree that bears silk cloth like flowers; climb the tree, sit on its branch, and say, 'Bloom, my magic tree, bloom cloth for me.' Then you will find cloth appearing on the branches, cloth of great value, worthy of kings and emperors. Look, here is my sweet lady. She is very lucky. She never puts on old cloth. She puts on a new cloth like a new leaf but for single day. Then she throws it away like a stale flower."

The merchant had a textile shop. He thought to himself, "Why should I purchase cloth from a factory? The tree itself is a factory. The factory engages laborers, and is a constant source of trouble to its owner. But this cloth-producing tree does not incur any expenditure, will not depend on me for its food and drink, and will not worry me in any way. I shall gain a lot of money, grow very, very rich in no time."

He bargained and paid a good amount of money to the cheat, and became the owner of this magic tree. The cheat rode away with his lady. The merchant climbed the tree, uttered the words of the cheat exactly, but to no effect, and was aggrieved.

The other two cheats went in search of their fellow and reached the confectioner's shop, which had been looted. They took with them the confectioner and came on the old woman whose daughter had been forcibly carried away. They took the old woman and reached the merchant who was still fighting with the bear. They killed the bear and took the merchant with them. They consoled the washerman who was still weeping and took him with them along with the textile merchant. Now they all reached the cheat's house and demanded the articles he had stolen or cheated them of.

The cheat said, "I am not a cheat, thief, or robber. I shall return all your articles except the sweets that I have taken and wasted. But I am ready to pay the price. I am not a cheat, thief, or robber, as you think. I have done this all out of fun. I have shown how people can be guided by their nose."

All were pleased with his courteous behavior. Dainty dishes were served. Soft beds were provided. They took full meals and rested there, being assured that the articles would be returned.

In the meantime the cheat thought out a plan and tried by all means to work it out. He bribed the watchman of the village, who proclaimed before the people by beat of drums of the King's orders that anyone having a foreigner in his house as a guest must bring him to the King's court the next morning. Some of these foreigners, it was alleged, were engaged in espionage. Any man in the village failing to do so would be guilty of high treason and penalized.

The two cheats, the washerman, the old woman, and the two merchants heard this declaration with awe and fled away for their lives. One of the cheats heaved a deep sigh of relief at a safe distance from the place and said, "Brother, I am a village cheat, you are a city cheat, but our brother is the king of all cheats. He is a world cheat. All our plans will fail as long as he lives. Our cleverness is no match for his. Our families are starving. Let us work hard to maintain them. A cheat is meant to outwit others. If he himself be outwitted it is really a shame, more painful than any disease."

The king of cheats lived a happy life with the young lady of beauty. When I approached him for a message he said, "Cheating adds a color to your personality as long as you maintain it with your cleverness."

My story ends here.

The Monk Who Dueled (Kannada)

Contributed by Praphulladatta Goswami. Forthcoming in *Folktales of India*.

Supplied by R. C. Hiremath, Dharwar, and recorded from Iragappa, seventy. Motifs F610 "Remarkably strong man"; and F617 "Mighty wrestler."

Ikkeri was the capital of a small kingdom in Karnatak that flourished from the fourteenth century until the coming of the British in the nineteenth. The valiant king mentioned in this legend ruled from 1545 to 1558. In his later days he traveled in northern India and Nepal and built temples in places like Kashi, Neelakanth, Nepal, Kashmir, Hardwar, and Rameshwar.

Emperor Akbar disliked vain people. Though he was proud of the duelist of his court, he was prejudiced against Ankush Khan, perhaps because Ankush Khan was very vain. Ankush Khan's bravery and skill in dueling were supposed to be unrivaled in the whole empire. In fact, this was no exaggeration. His huge figure and piercing eyes alone could make his rivals tremble.

When once Ankush Khan knocked down all the court duelists and cried out in victory, Akbar was very much pleased and offered him a great reward. But Ankush Khan just threw a glance at it and said, "Forgive me, my sovereign, I don't want these things. My sole aim in life is to be an unrivaled duelist."

Though he could not catch the meaning of what Ankush Khan said, Akbar observed, "It has been my wish, too, that you should spread the fame of our Mogul empire."

Ankush Khan said, "For that, I will hang my sword in front of the main entrance of the capital. Whoever challenges it will have to fight with me. Please allow me to do this."

Emperor Akbar had very often longed to have in his court a duelist who could challenge the whole world. So he readily agreed.

The news went on spreading everywhere. Many Yavans, and even Rajputs, came to Delhi hoping to challenge Ankush Khan and get the royal title. None of them returned alive. Ankush Khan's victories disheartened everyone, and many had to return without challenging him. Ankush Khan found pleasure in knocking down his rivals and watching them moaning in death agony. Then he started hunting for rivals. He began to trouble even the intelligentsia of the court. He took it for granted that none could beat him. People started complaining against him. They even tried to poison the emperor's ears, saying that he went to the extent of seducing Rajput ladies. When the emperor kept quiet, people used the last possible device effectively. "Your Majesty, we can tolerate all his misbehavior, but not his vanity. Do you know what he dared say yesterday? He boasted that nobody in this world, not even the emperor himself, could defeat him."

They were expecting from Akbar nothing less than orders for Ankush Khan's assassination. Akbar too had thought of it. But he was aware of the truth in Ankush Khan's boasting. He knew he himself could not face Ankush Khan's challenge. So he fell into a dilemma. It was in a way necessary to get rid of so dangerous an enemy.

Soon afterward the emperor sent away Ankush Khan to the south with a small troop. But Ankush Khan returned victorious. Now the problem was all the more difficult. Was there none to beat this enemy in disguise?

One fine morning, some attendants appeared at the emperor's harem, saluted, and said, "Your Majesty, some monks have challenged Ankush Khan's sword, and are waiting for the orders."

"Monks? Why didn't you drive them out before they could dare do so?"

"Every subject has the right to challenge it."

"Didn't you warn them that this would be their end?"

"We did, My Lord, but they don't look like monks, they seem to be professional duelists."

Emperor Akbar thought a while and said, "All right, go fetch them hither."

Then entered a monk wearing the *Rudrakshya* garland and the holy ashes. He was followed by four disciples all of whom were strong like soldiers. The monk himself looked extremely majestic and serene. They all bowed down to the emperor. The emperor was amazed for a moment. "Who are you?"

"We are the great Lord's servants."

"You look like spies. If your behavior is found to be suspicious, you will have to be imprisoned. Speak the truth!"

"God knows we are not spies. We are the devotees of Lord Siva, on our way to holy places. Have faith in us."

"Then why on earth did you challenge Ankush Khan?"

"We heard that the emperor is worried, for there is none to defeat that devil. If you want, and if you allow, we'll knock him down."

Akbar was all the more puzzled. How did these monks come to know this? Or was it one of his own subjects who caused this rumor? He thought and then said, "It's true I was waiting for a hero to knock down that devil. But this task is absolutely impossible for you."

"Royal Sire, we are born *Kshatriyas*; we have in our veins the *Kshatriya* blood."

"You are sure you are ready to die?"

"It's our glory to die fighting."

"Very well then, you shall meet Ankush Khan tomorrow morning. Till then you shall be our guests."

It was a pretty long time since Ankush Khan had fought. He had a hot water bath, applied oil on his body, and entered the battlefield in a loincloth with his sword. The spectators shouted in excitement. His wild eyes searched for his rival. When the emperor entered, the bugles blew. Akbar took his seat. Then the monk got up and stood awaiting the signal. When Ankush Khan learned that this was the person who had challenged him, he threw away his sword and said, "My liege, it would be a disgrace to my bravery to fight this person with my sword. You shall see I will strike him to death without my sword."

Akbar stared in amazement at the monk, for the monk, too, threw away his sword. Ankush Khan was outraged. His eyes burned in anger. He burst out in impatience. "My liege, the signal, please."

The emperor raised his hand, once again the bugles blew. In a moment Ankush Khan jumped on the monk, sure to catch hold of him. But the monk escaped mysteriously, and Ankush Khan had to fall down.

Ankush Khan got up in a rage and tried again to catch the monk. A few moments passed, and at last the monk was caught by Khan. Khan thought he would knock him down presently. Suddenly the monk wriggled out and struck Ankush Khan right in his face. Khan's mouth started bleeding. He got very wild. The duel went on. All the strokes of Khan proved to be ineffective. Gradually his strength declined. Perhaps he had never met such a rival before. Having no other way to save his life and name, he desperately ran to his sword and attempted to stab the monk. The monk had no time to take his sword. People were watching them in dead silence. Suddenly the monk undressed himself, and threw his cloth on his rival's face. The devil was puzzled for a moment. The monk at once snatched the sword away from him and stabbed him. Ankush Khan cried out and fell down.

The emperor himself was confused by the miracle. People did not even have time to think over all that had happened so soon.

The emperor descended from his throne, embraced the monk, and said, "You brave warrior, you can't be a monk. Tell me who you are. Where do you come from?"

The monk answered smilingly, "Royal Sire, I am named Sankanna Nayaka. I am king of Ikkeri. I was fed up with that kingdom and so handed over my responsibilities to my brother long back and started wandering from country to country, visiting the holy places. That is all that I can say."

"O Hindu warrior, I had heard about the bravery of the kings of Ikkeri. Now I had the pleasure of witnessing it. I am very much pleased to see you. Here is a reward for you from the emperor of Delhi, do accept it."

"Sovereign liege, I willingly deserted all that I had. I don't need these things. If you want to give me something, allow me to build the holy *mutts* [Hindu monasteries] in your empire."

"All right, you can make the choice of proper places." And then the emperor granted him all possible help.

Mataru the Grandfather (Hindi)

Contributed by Praphulladatta Goswami. Forthcoming in *Folktales of India*.

Recorded by Krishnadev Upadhyaya, Gyanpur, Uttar Pradesh, from a village in the Bhojpuri-speaking area of eastern Uttar Pradesh. Bhojpuri is a dialect of Hindi. Motifs are F402.1.4 "Demons assume human form in order to deceive"; G263.1 "Witch transforms person to animal"; and G303.16.19.16 "Devil can be driven away by sacrifice."

This local tradition incorporates Aryan village and tribal beliefs concerning spirits and exorcism.

There lived a poor man named Mataru in a small village. He was a man of limited means and lived on agriculture. He had heard many stories of ghosts and demons from his grandmother in his childhood. But he always doubted their truth because he had no experience of them in his life.

One day, it so happened that he received the news of the serious illness of one of his dearest relatives. He decided to see him that very night and started on his journey. His wife implored him not to undertake a risky journey in the night, but he turned a deaf ear to her request. There was darkness all around, and nothing was clearly visible. The poor man picked his way through the dark, till he reached the bank of a river. There, to his great surprise, he saw two demons standing practically naked on each of the banks. They were as tall as the palm tree and were as black as collyrium. They spoke an unintelligible language in a nasal tone. They began running on the water of the river with slippers on their feet. They were playing *Kabaddi* on the surface of water. Mataru saw this terrifying scene. He began to tremble with fear, and the hairs of his body stood on their ends. He fell down and became unconscious. When the game was over, the two ghosts transformed themselves into two Sadhus and came to the man who was lying unconscious on the ground. They woke him up and asked him who he was and what was the purpose of his night errand. The poor man told them the whole thing. They said, "Well, your relative lives at the village nearby. If you want to go there we shall show you the way." Mataru was very much pleased and accepted their guidance. He followed them and ultimately reached the village.

In the morning, Mataru related to his relative the incidents of the previous night, and the latter thanked God for his providential escape. The villagers corroborated the story of Mataru and said they had themselves seen the two ghosts playing the game on the water of the river. After staying some days there, Mataru decided to return home, this time taking another route, which lay through thick forests, in order to avoid the demons. He started on his return journey, but after going some distance he lost his way. He did not know what he ought to do. He noticed at a distance a dim light burning in a hut. He went in the direction of the light and reached the hut.

This village was entirely inhabited by witches. They wore red *saris* on their bodies, and had vermilion marks on their foreheads. They had the power of transforming men into rams, sheep, and goats with their magic. Poor Mataru lost his memory and totally forgot about his wife and children. He was transformed into a ram by a witch who employed him as her servant. He carried loads on his back for her and kept watch at night like a dog. Thus years passed by, but there was no escape for Mataru the ram.

When Mataru did not return home for some days, his wife became impatient. She could not imagine the cause of his undue delay. So she sent her son to her relatives to inquire about him. The relatives told the son that they did not know the whereabouts of Mataru, who had left the place long, long ago. The son tried his best to find his father but failed. Thus Mataru was taken for dead and lost.

One day Muniya, the wife of Mataru, had a dream. A god descended from heaven and told her, "Muniya! do not be unhappy, your husband is alive in a far-off land, and he will come to you one day." When she awoke in the morning, she told her neighbors about the dream, but even the credulous villagers did not believe that the dream would come true. They told Muniya, "It is all wishful thinking and nothing more. How can a dead man return to life?" But she still believed in the prophecy of the god.

The witch was very much satisfied with the service of the ram. One day she took pity on his plight and transformed him into a man. She asked him to return home and restored to him his memory, which he had lost. Mataru returned to his village after years of absence. When his wife heard the news of her husband's return, she was very happy. Her joy knew no bounds when she saw him standing before her eyes. She at once called on the family priest and asked him to recite the tale of *Satyanarayan,* or *The God of Truth,* and distributed food offered to God among the neighbors. Mataru narrated his adventures to the members of his family and ultimately settled down to his agricultural profession.

One day, Mataru went to answer the call of nature in the twilight of evening and sat down under a tamarind tree. While he was returning home he felt, all of a sudden, a burning sensation in his body. He returned home and lay on a cot nearby. Within an hour he ran a high temperature, became unconscious, and in a state of delirium began to utter the words, "I cannot leave you, you have done me a great harm. I can never leave you now." Poor Muniya was stunned at the plight of her husband. She did not know what had happened to her husband, who was hale and hearty until a few hours before. Next day the village physician and medicine men were called upon to treat him. They gave him some medicine, but it was of no avail. There was no change in his condition; rather, it deteriorated. They told Mataru's wife frankly that they were unable to diagnose the disease and advised her to call for an

Ojha medicine man. The *Ojha* came, saw the condition of his patient, and came to the conclusion that he was possessed by a cruel demon. Perhaps the notorious demon that dwelt upon the tamarind tree had caught him. Poor Muniya requested him with folded hands to do his best to cure her husband. The man said, "Well, I will set everything right, but it will require a good amount of money to propitiate the demon. I will have to perform worship for months for the purpose." Muniya was at her wit's end. She did not know what to do. There was no money in the house. The only bread-earner of the family was lying unconscious on the cot. But in that hour of trial she did not lose heart. She went to a neighbor and got some money by mortgaging her old ornaments made of silver and alloy.

The *Ojha* came the next day. He sprinkled sacred Ganges water on the body of Mataru, burned a lamp of *ghee,* and muttered some charms to drive away the demon. By and by the condition of Mataru took a turn for the better. But he still cried off and on, "I will not leave you, I will not leave you until I have the sacrifice." The *Ojha* was a past master in his art, and he at once realized that the demon was a cruel one and would not be driven away unless a sacrifice was offered to him. On the following day a goat was sacrificed to propitiate him. Mataru soon was dispossessed of the demon and began to recover from his illness. The *Ojha* was given a handsome fee, and the ceremony ended with a feast offered to the Brahmanas.

Mataru lived in his village till an advanced age. His only pleasure in his old age was to recite the stories of ghosts and demons and witches, of which he had personal experience, to his grandchildren and great-grandchildren, who listened to him with awe and fear. He advised them not to visit the haunted places. He was known among the children as *Bhutaha Baba,* or "The Possessed Grandfather," who told interesting stories.

Tenali Rama and the King's Pets (Tamil)

Contributed by Praphulladatta Goswami. Forthcoming in *Folktales of India.*

Supplied in 1965 by Chandra Parameswarn, Palghat, as recorded at Coimbatore. Tenali Rama is an important figure in Tamil folklore. He was a Brahman from the town of Tennalu or Tenali said to have been blessed by the goddess Kali, who instructed him to live the life of a jester. Thereupon he joined the court of Irayur, King of Tondamandalam in southern Carnatic, and gained a reputation for cleverness. See Edward Jewitt Robinson, *Tales and Poems of South India* (London, 1885), pp. 321 ff.

Motifs H950 "Task evaded by subterfuge" and J1140 "Cleverness in detection of truth." In a Telugu version of this tale the horse is replaced by a calf: A. Jain, *Telengana Ki Lok-Kathaen* (Tales of Telengana) (Delhi, 1957), pp. 21–25.

Once the King was giving each one of his courtiers a Persian cat and a good Arabian horse. He gave them a large amount of money to look after these pets and return them fattened up when he demanded. Tenali Rama, who was watching this, thought that this was mere foolishness. The money thus spent was a waste. And he was very sure that the courtiers would definitely misappropriate this money given to them. He wanted to show the king how foolish his act was. So he begged that he too might be given a cat and a horse to look after. The King laughed at the suggestion but complied with the request.

Rama went home with the beautiful Persian cat and the strong, handsome Arabian horse. He was getting a lot of allowance for the royal pets. He bought a big cow so that the cat would have milk and bought other accessories also. Whenever the King asked him about the pets he gave very eloquent descriptions of them. The cat was very different from ordinary cats, it was a very unusual one. The horse was the most powerful one; so on and so forth. But actually he never gave anything to the poor beasts.

What he did was this. As soon as he reached home with the royal pets, he made a nice cage for the cat. Then he heated up some milk to boiling point and placed a saucer of this milk in front of the cat. The cat eagerly came to the food and lapped it up hurriedly. Oh! it got burned. It was so hurt that from that day onward the sight of a saucer of milk made it run, shrieking with fear. There was no other way of getting any food, so it started becoming thinner and thinner day by day, eating the very frugal food that was supplied to it.

Rama took the horse to his stables. He ordered a special type of stable that was built up on all sides and with only a small, high ventilator to give it air and light. Through this ventilator he threw down some dried hay every day, which was not at all sufficient for the horse. Thus a week passed.

Now the King wanted to see his pets. He asked the courtier to bring them to the court for an inspection. All the other cats looked fine and healthy, but they could have looked better, the King felt. But the worst of all was Rama's cat. It looked very thin and ill. The King got very wild and asked for an explanation. Rama put on an innocent look and replied, "Your Highness, it is none of my fault. This cat is extraordinary and unusual, I have told you. It refuses to take any milk." No one would believe this. So the King had a saucer of milk placed before the cat. The cat was put down. It just looked at the saucer and started mewing frightfully and backing away. It just ran away from the place. The King had to accept the evidence.

Then he turned to the horses. Rama's horse was nowhere to be seen. Rama reported that his horse was so strong and powerful and stubborn that he could not drag it out of the stable. The King was really pleased and surprised at this. He ordered his head groom to go and investigate the matter and bring the horse to the palace.

This head groom reached Rama's stable and was surprised to see the high walls and a small peephole. Rama, who had come with him, assured him that the horse was inside. So the groom put his head through the peephole to investigate the matter.

Now, this groom had a long grey beard. The horse was eagerly waiting for his daily ration of dried grass. When he saw the beard he thought it was the grass and got hold of it. The old man tried to pull away, but the hungry horse had the strength of ten men. He was not prepared to lose even this meager food. There was a big hue and cry.

Rama ran to the King to report the ill fate of the groom. The King came with his courtly paraphernalia to watch this strange fight. The groom was saved but for his beard. The King wanted to see this horse that was so powerful and so he ordered that the walls should be broken down. When that was done he knew what a cheat Tenali Rama was. The horse was thin and pale for want of food and air and sunlight.

Rama begged the King's pardon, telling him that he only wanted to point out to His Majesty how easily people could misappropriate money given to look after dumb creatures who can neither betray the culprits nor defend themselves. The King took his lesson and pardoned Tenali Rama.

The Peasant Thanthanpal (Hindi)

Collected by Praphulladatta Goswami. Forthcoming in *Folktales of India.*

Recorded in 1964 from Siu Mistri, an old carpenter who had left his home in northern Madhya Pradesh some thirty years before and settled in Gauhati.

Motifs T253 "The nagging wife" and J2495 "Religious words or exercises interpreted with absurd literalness." A similar story, in Assam, is in A. C. Barua, *Sandhiyar Sadhu* (Tales of the Evening) (Gauhati, 1963), pp. 1–3: the *amara* (undying) tree is seen to die; the *nijara* (untrickling) spring is seen to trickle; Mara (Dead) is seen to be alive. So Nidhani (Poor) is satisfied with his name and does not want a change. The tale can be traced back to the "Namasiddhi Jataka," given in E. B. Cowell, *The Jataka* (London, 1957), 1:237–38, in which the man Base finds Quick to be dead, Rich to be poor, and Guide losing his way, through misapplication of their names.

There was a poor peasant in a village. His name was Thanthanpal. His wife did not like this name. One day at mealtime she said, "Do you hear, I have told you so many times to change your name, but I don't know why you don't change it. All the women in the village tease me about your name. If you don't change your name by tomorrow, I won't stay here, I'll go to my mother's and not come back."

The peasant got angry, threw the platter at her, and said, "I am not going to change the name my parents have given me. If you so wish you can leave my house. But remember, don't say such things at the time of my meal. Are you going to die because of my name? It is rightly said in the *Ramayana* that womenfolk have a small mind."

So his wife left his house, not even taking her meal. Her husband tried to persuade her to stay, but she wouldn't be persuaded. On the way she saw an old woman. The old woman was stringing balls of dried-up cowdung. The wife asked her, "Mother, what may be your name?"

"My name is Lakshmi," said the old lady.

"O god, you being Goddess of Riches, you are stringing balls of cowdung!"

"It is all fate, daughter-in-law. What can you do? You have to fill your tummy, after all."

Going further the wife saw a man plowing. She asked him, "Brother, what may be your name?"

"Dhanpal."

"You are Keeper of Wealth, and you are driving a plow!"

The man said, "What can you do, it is all written by fate, you can do nothing about it."

The wife moved on. She found a man who was crying, "God is truth, God is truth," and had just returned after leaving a dead body in the cemetery. She stopped and asked him, "Who is dead?"

The man said, "Amarju Patel."

The woman hit her forehead with her palm and cogitated: This man was Immortal, and he is dead! So she returned to her husband's house and sat down at the doorsill.

In the evening her husband returned from the field. Seeing her there he said, "How is it you have come back? Didn't anyone speak to you at your mother's place?"

His wife observed:

> I saw Lakshmi stringing cowdung,
> driving a plow was Dhanpal,
> Even though Amar, he died,
> your name is nice, Thanthanpal.

Babar Deva the Outlaw (Gujarati)

Contributed by Praphulladatta Goswami. Forthcoming in *Folktales of India*.

Supplied in 1964 by Pushker Chandervaker, Porbandar, who collected these legends in December 1962 in the village of Goral, Kaira district, near the gulf of Cambay, where Babar Deva was born. He died in 1923, but his younger brother, Rama Deva, at one time chief lieutenant in Babar's gang, still lives. Babar was a Patanwadia Koli by caste.

Chandervaker heard tales about the outlaw from villagers who had seen him and had been in touch with Mahatma Gandhi, leader of the resistance to the British. Central Gujarat has known no other outlaw figure besides Babar Deva, unlike Saurastra, traditionally the land of outlaws.

Motifs Q325 "Disobedience punished"; Q411 "Death as punishment."

1. *The Outlaw Meets His Equal*

Once a social worker of the Borsad Chhavani in Gujarat was moving from village to village in the area to strengthen the morale of the people against the British government. The people had launched a movement known as the Kheda Satyagraha in 1923, and the social worker in the movement was urging the people not to pay any revenue to British officers in cash or kind. So the officers were taking possession of the land, cattle, household things, etc., and auctioning them, and the farmers were made poor in no time. This movement was headed by Sardar Vallabhbhai Patel, the "Iron Man of India."

Babar Deva, the outlaw, was also harassing the people of the area by looting and plundering them. He was extorting money and kidnapping persons.

It is said that he was inspired by Sayadu Minyano, an outlaw of Kathiawad who had plundered and looted Cambay, a town near the birthplace of Babar Deva. And Sayadu's bravery was sung by bards, and ballads were composed that were sung by ladies in the Garba dance. This inspired Babar Deva to turn outlaw.

One night this social worker was passing by a village. He knew very well that this area was much afraid of Babar Deva. And also that the area was much menaced by Babar Deva. In spite of having full knowledge of the menace of the outlaw, he left the village at night for another village, but on his way he met Babar Deva.

Babar Deva accosted him and threatened the social worker: "Oh, who are you?"

"I am an outlaw," the social worker replied.

"An outlaw? How can it be? Babar Deva is the only outlaw of this area."

"I am another one."

"Another one?" He shook his head and said, "I do not know about it. Never . . . no . . . never!"

"Do you doubt my honesty?"

"No, but you have created questions in my mind."

"Well, let us sit and discuss the problem in all its aspects."

The outlaw doubted the honesty of this man. He thought, how could he, after trusting a stranger, doubt his honesty? He thought in his mind that it was a dark night, the fellow had no weapons in his hands nor could he hide them. So there was no reason to fear him. And before he had challenged him, he was seen alone, so there was no reason to fear any danger from him.

And they sat together, and then the social worker began to talk.

"Babarbhai, I am an outlaw against this British government. We outlaws will never harass the poor, meek, and innocent people as you do. Even though we fight against the British government, we never hide anything from the government. We ourselves give information regarding our strategy to the police department of the government."

"How can it be?"

"Is it a matter to be doubted?"

Babar Deva was put into a thoughtful mood as soon as he heard the social worker.

Again the worker started talking: "Babarbhai, we are wedded to the cause of truth, and our *gurus* are Mahatma Gandhi and Vallabhbhai Patel."

"They have asked you to practice truth in outlawry?"

"Not only truth, but also nonviolence."

"Double-edged swords you use."

"But the British government dislikes you."

"Me?"

"Yes, it is of no use to harass poor people, innocent traders, and hard-working laborers."

"Oh, I see!"

"Also the tiller of the soil."

"I follow you. My good brother, I shall try my best to put your words of advice into practice."

"May the Almighty lead you on the right path." The social worker blessed him and left for the next village, leaving Babar Deva in a pensive mood.

After a few days, a letter was received in the Borsad Chhavani, addressed to Mahatma Gandhi and Sardar Patel. It was from that outlaw, saying he would be an outlaw against the British government, but his methods would be his own, for he was unable to practice nonviolence. He further wrote that when they got any news that any white officer in the district had been shot dead, they were to understand that it had been done only by Babar Deva. And thus he would prove himself an outlaw against the British government. He again confessed that he was quite unable to put nonviolence into practice.

It is said that this letter was read by Sardar Patel and was sent to Mahatma Gandhi. Gandhiji forwarded this letter to the highest authority of the state for the security measures to be taken for the white officers in the district, demanding that Babar Deva should not be victimized because of this determination.

2. Babar Deva Joins a Marriage Party

In the nearby area of Goral, where Babar Deva was born, there lived a *thakore* [landlord] having few villages under his control. The *thakore* happened to be a bosom friend of Babar Deva. He had a grown-up daughter engaged to be married. Now the *thakore* was arranging the marriage of his daughter with pomp and grandeur. A grand feast, to be given to all invitees, was also a part of the function. So he had purchased sixty tins of *ghee* [clarified butter].

The *thakore* was a very strong man and had many enemies. One night, before the marriage day, some robbers and thieves came and broke open the storehouse in which these tins were kept and took them away.

When the confectioners were called to prepare some sweets for the marriage party and asked for *ghee*, the *thakore's* servants opened the storehouse, but there was no tin of *ghee*. They all knew that sixty tins of *ghee* had been procured by the *thakore,* and none of them was found. They were taken aback. At once they reported to the *thakore* that no tin of *ghee* was found in the storehouse. Somebody must have broken open the storehouse and taken away the tins.

Now, the *thakore* had no time to pursue the matter, because the marriage party was to come in two or three days. So he at once wrote a note to Babar Deva asking to see him. The *thakore* thought that no one else but Babar Deva would stand to the test.

Babar came riding a horse and met his friend quietly. He asked: "Why do you want me so urgently?" The *thakore* narrated the event in detail. Hearing this, Babar Deva gave him solace and said that he would get sixty tins of *ghee* next morning without fail.

Next day, Babar Deva brought two carts, each drawn by four bullocks, full of tins of *ghee,* and these carts were delivered to the *thakore.*

The *thakore* thanked him and asked a promise from him that he would attend the marriage ceremony and marriage party, along with the other guests. Then Babar Deva said that he would come in disguise, since the *thakore* had also invited the government servants, police officers, the district magistrate and the collector, and so Babar Deva was not safe among them.

Babar Deva kept his word. He came in disguise, attended the marriage ceremony, but did not remain to attend the party. But when he left the marriage ceremony, a gun boomed just to inform the government that the party was also attended by him.

He left the place by crossing a river with the help of a country boat and reached the opposite bank so that nobody could pursue him.

3. *Babar Deva Attends His Own Daughter's Marriage Ceremony*

Babar Deva had shot his wife dead, sensing that she might not remain faithful to him and perhaps that she might smuggle information to the police officer about his activities.

But Babar Deva had a kept wife, a mistress, and she had a daughter. Babar Deva was out for outlawry, and the British police force was keeping watch for him with an eagle's eye. So it became necessary for Babar Deva to join his friends and other relatives to participate in the early preparation of his daughter. But he had sent word that he would definitely remain present for *Kanyadan* [giving away the bride] and *Panigrahna* [accepting the hand of the bride].

The police force was equally vigilant. They had full faith that by hook or crook Babar Deva would attend the marriage ceremony of his only issue.

On the marriage day the bridegroom with his party came and were received by relatives and friends of Babar Deva, but not by Babar Deva. But when ladies of the family went to the potter's house to bring earthen pots that are used ceremoniously in the marriage, Babar Deva came in the guise of a woman, veiling his head and mouth with a sari, and joined the party on the way to the potter's house, and he returned with the ladies of the house and family.

His arrival in the house was known only to his mistress, and when the acceptance ceremony was to be performed Babar Deva came forward, veiling his face, and he did it properly and left the house immediately afterward. After he left the house by the back door, the police force learned that Babar Deva had attended the marriage function and had escaped secretly.

4. *Babar Shot Dead His Own Wife*

Once at night Babar Deva came to his village Goral where his family lived. As soon as he entered the house he ordered his wife to cook good and sweet food. In a short while she prepared it accordingly. Babar Deva was eating sweet dishes, and his wife was serving him different dishes. When he was dining, his wife began to talk: "My good man, I have come to know that you are an expert in aiming."

"You are correct."

"Nobody's life is spared when you aim at him?"

"Unless favored by God."

"May I ask you one more question."

"Surely!"

"How do you aim?"

This question of his wife made Babar Deva suspicious of why his wife was interested in asking such questions. Why did she want to know the technique of aiming? It was never a job of women. There must be something wrong on her part, otherwise why should she ask such a question of him?

She again asked a question: "Do you hear, my brave man?"

Babar Deva finished his meal, washed his hands, and went near the wall where there was a peg on which he kept hanging his power-gun. He took his gun in his hand. He brought that near her breast and aimed at her and said: "I take an aim in this way."

And he triggered the gun and took the life of his own better half. In a second she was found in the midst of a pool of blood.

Babar Deva left her in the lurch without noticing anything, in cold blood.

She was dead and gone forever.

5. *Faithless Sister Was Shot Dead by Babar Deva*

Babar Deva had several sisters. His brothers-in-law also joined his gang like his brother and nephews. They all lived together either in fields or in forests. And their family lived in Goral together in a street that is now named after Babar Deva. From loot they had saved they built splendid houses in which lived all the members of the family of Babar Deva.

Babar Deva and his gang preferred to live in open fields. They had their huts in their fields and farms. Once Babar Deva came to his fields where the members of the family were on a farm.

Babar Deva came on the farm and he sat in the midst of his sisters, mother, and father and asked them whether they were being harassed by the police, or by the village headman, or by any other persons from his village or outside the village.

In a flattering and artificial manner his sister replied: "My brother is Babar Deva. Even God will not dare harass us. God knows his power and ability. Why should we be afraid of the police or village headman or of any other persons?"

But Babar Deva had got the information that one of his sisters was smuggling the news of his arrival to some informants connected with the police. So Babar said: "I know all about it, and you should stop flattering me."

"Who would flatter the bravest brother except his own sister?"

"Stop your talk. I know how much love and respect my sister has got for me."

"What do you say? Do you mean to say that I have no love for you?"

"I know it. Please go away from here. Get off!" With dejected face she left the place. But Babar Deva was not happy with her departure. He took his gun and aimed at his sister and shot her dead.

Afghanistan

The Romance of Mongol Girl and Arab Boy

Collected by Hafizullah Baghban in 1961 in Jindakhan and published in *Adab* (Kabul) 17 (1969–70), no. 5, pp. 1–107, no. 6, pp. 7–13.

There are elements here of type 516 *Faithful John*, especially of part I, "The Prince Falls in Love."

Motifs T15.1 "Princess so lovely that every one falls in love with her"; T11.2 "Love through sight of picture"; T92.9 "Father and son as rivals in love"; T24.1 "Love-sickness"; H1381.3.1.2.1 "Quest for unknown woman whose picture has aroused man's love"; N825.3 "Old woman helper"; H971.1 "Task performed with help of old woman"; T75.3 "Unrequited love expressed in song"; T15 "Love at first sight"; T41.1 "Communication of lovers through hole in wall"; T92.11 "Rivals contesting for the same girl"; T52.3 "Bride purchased for her weight in gold" (40 camel-loads of jewelry); N884 "Robber as helper"; P311 "Sworn brethren"; K2222 "Treacherous co-wife"; S111.4 "Murder with poisoned apple(s)"; R10.1 "Princess (maiden) abducted."

The romantic tale has been part of the Afghan oral tradition for more than a thousand years and, at times, it has provided data for romances composed by court poets. Abu al-Qasim Firdausi's "Zāl and Rudābeh" and "Bīžan and Munīžeh" at the court of Ghaznī (A.D. 1010) are two such examples. Similarly, Rudakī's "Nahr and 'Ayn," "Khingbut and Surkhbut," and "Wāmiq and 'Azrā" have prospered on the riches of the oral tradition of this area. For the same reason, mention should be made of al-Juzjāni's "Vis and Rāmīn" (A.D. 1048) and Nazāmī Ganjawī's "Khusrāw and Shirīn" (A.D. 1180) (see the collector's "An Introductory Bibliography of the Folklore of the Middle East," *Folklore Forum*, 1972, no. 9, p. iv).

Even today romantic tales are numerous and alive in the folklore of Afghanistan. Among the Pashto-speaking population, "Ādamkhān and Durkhānay" is performed on a leisurely winter evening as often as men and women can get together. Among the Dari (Afghan Persian) speakers, "Siyāmū and Jalālī" is the legend of the day and has even made its way to the radio. Although not as urbanized as this tale,

"Moghol-Dokhter and Arab-Bacha" has a large audience in the farming villages of western Afghanistan. In this romance, the oral composer has invested in the Arab and Mongol conquerors of the country, in the seventh and thirteenth centuries A.D., in order to spin a tale in a frame already familiar to him.

Muhammed Hāshim, a forty-five-year-old farmer and livestock breeder from the Bārakzay tribe of Jindakhan, told this version of "Moghol-Dokhter and Arab Bacha." He had learned the tale from Kākā Mūsā, who had passed away at age ninety, twenty years before, and who is remembered by the people of Jindakhan for his exciting narration of this and many other stories. Baghban recorded on tape a second version of the story from Juwāher, a thirty-year-old peasant housewife from Siyāwshān, in June 1967. Accompanying her husband in his dissertation fieldwork in Herat, Marcia Baghban collected a third version from Mādar Amin, the wife of the Tawberyan shopkeeper, in May 1973.

The three raconteurs listed here have pleasant voices and sing the songs interspersed through the tale. Although they had no musical accompaniment, often a lute or a tambourine repeats the melody in this romance during the performance. Musical accompaniment depends on whether the narrator can play an instrument or a willing musician is available to accompany him.

Since Muhammed Hāshim dictated this version of "Moghol-Dokhter and Arab Bacha," the collector was the only audience he had. But at other times he performed for a male or mixed audience, including children. Usually, the mood of his audience resembled the mood of the audience of a tragedy. The female raconteurs do not ordinarily perform in the presence of men, except the close members of their own families. This was true in the case of Juwāher from whom Baghban collected by sending her his tape recorder.

Elements relevant to the Afghan and Muslim culture are plentiful in this tale. Such a motif as "Love at first sight" goes back to the *Arabian Nights* and although present in the repertoire of other peoples, it has more reason to appear frequently in Muslim tradition. In Muslim society separation of the sexes overcharges the biological base of love, which may in turn inflate the emotions of the potential lovers. As a result, there is more falling in love at first sight among Muslims. Also, motif T41.1 "Communication of lovers through hole in wall" reflects the cultural distance between men and women.

In rural Afghanistan the amount of dowry symbolizes the bride's worth. The worthier the bride, the greater the dowry. This cultural fact explains why the Arab prince is required to pay forty camel loads of jewels as Moghol-Dokhter's dowry. The poisoning of the polygamous husband reinforces the condemnation of this practice in the whole body of Afghan oral tradition.

Long, long ago there was a princess by the name of Moghol-Dokhter [Mongol girl]. The fame of her beauty and good manners had reached far beyond the borders of her father's empire. She was at a marriageable age, and kings and lords from all over the world were her suitors. They had all proposed marriage to her and been rejected. No one could provide the conditions her father asked for. Some of them were disappointed and went back to their countries. Others deserted their homelands and stayed in the streets around her palace to have a glimpse of her when she went to her garden on Fridays.

Arab-Pāshā [Arab King] was one of Moghol-Dokhter's suitors. After his efforts to marry her had failed, he found a picture of her and brought it to his kingdom with him. He put the picture in a golden box and put the box in a palace called Qasr-i-Khās. Every day he went to Qasr-i-Khās alone and looked at the picture. His courtiers were eager to know what was in Qasr-i-Khās, but they never dared ask him about it.

Arab-Bacha [Arab boy], the son and heir of the King, noticed his father's visits to Qasr-i-Khās too. "What is in that palace, father?" he finally asked one day.

"Nothing, son" the King answered.

"Could I visit it?" the Prince inquired.

"No, son," the King said. "Qasr-i-Khās is my private office, and I don't want anyone to go there and see my notes and papers."

"I won't look at your papers. I promise I won't touch a single thing!" the Prince exclaimed.

"Son, it's a beautiful day. Why don't you ride your horse instead?" the King said.

"I can ride my horse any day. I prefer to see Qasr-i-Khās," the Prince replied.

Arab-Pāshā knew his son would not give up easily. He shouted at him angrily, "There is nothing for you to see in that building! Leave me alone!"

This was the first time that the King had refused his son anything, and it was the only time he'd addressed him harshly. The Prince was completely shaken. He threatened to drown himself if his father did not let him see Qasr-i-Khās.

The boldness of this idea terrified Arab-Pāshā. "He's not old enough to realize the importance of his life," he thought to himself. "I'd rather give him the key and prevent his death."

Arab-Bacha ran to Qasr-i-Khās as soon as he had the key. He opened the gate and entered the palace. There were seven rooms within, each leading to another. He walked through the first, second, and third rooms but saw nothing except furniture. In the seventh room there was a golden box lying on a desk. He opened the box and saw the picture of a Mongol girl in it. Her beauty charmed the Prince and he wondered who she was and where she lived. Except for the King he knew no one who could tell him about her. So he took the picture to him and asked, "Father, who is this girl?"

The King didn't answer the Prince's question. He grabbed the picture from him and said, "It's none of your business. Go read your lessons." Arab-Bacha understood that further questions were useless. He left the King's chamber without saying anything.

Not telling Arab-Bacha about Moghol-Dokhter did not do any good. It only increased his sorrow, and in a few months he grew listless and pale. He did not join his friends at parties any more. If they insisted and took him with them, only his body was there. His soul sought the love whom he'd met in his imagination.

The King saw his son changing. He did not want him to be miserable, but he could hardly find any solution to his problem. It was difficult for him to lose either his son or his love.

Finally his paternal love won. He called the Prince in one day and said, "Son, you're losing your health. This is all for something unattainable. The girl you love has many suitors. They've all tried to win her and they've all failed. I advise you to stop thinking about her."

Arab-Bacha listened to all his father said. But, as if he hadn't heard a word of the King's talk, at the end he asked, "Won't you tell me her name?"

"Her name is Moghol-Dokhter," the King sighed.

"Who is she?" he asked next.

"She is the Moghol Princess," the King said. He added, "Remember my advice, son."

The Prince said nothing in answer to his father. The next morning he went to his mother and said, "I need some money and a horse for a trip to the Moghol capital." The Queen tried to convince him not to go, but it was impossible. She told the story to the King. His efforts to keep the Prince had failed too. They gave him a horse and all the money he needed. Forty slaves saw him off to the border of his father's kingdom.

Now Arab-Bacha was a lonely traveler. He spent days and nights in the deserts. During the day his saddle was his seat, and at night the ground was his bed. Many weeks passed in this way and finally he arrived at the Moghol capital.

The Prince knew no one in the city. He walked aimlessly up and down the streets until he saw an old woman hurrying home from shopping. "Could you show me a place to spend the night?" he asked her sadly.

"Where are you going?" the old woman said.

"I came to the city today," Arab-Bacha answered. "I'll be here for a while."

The old woman said, "I would welcome you as my guest."

Arab-Bacha accepted the old woman's invitation and accompanied her home. He knew that she was poor and he would have to repay her kindness. "A handful of gold should be enough," he thought to himself and put the gold in her plate when she first served tea.

The old woman was happy with her present. "You don't have to look for another place," she said when she saw the gold. "Stay here for as long as you want to be in the city."

"I appreciate your offer," the Prince said. "My problem isn't only about a place to stay."

"I'll be delighted to help you in any way I can," the old woman said.

Arab-Bacha told his story, and the old woman listened to him. "You are one of the many men who love Moghol-Dokhter. However, you're young and handsome and should try your luck," she said at the end.

Arab-Bacha thought a minute and then sighed, "If only I could see her!"

"The window of my house overlooks Moghol-Dokhter's dressing room," said the old woman. "In the morning when she makes her toilette I'll show her to you."

This was the happiest news Arab-Bacha had ever heard. That night the people in the Moghol capital slept soundly, but he was awake till morning fancying the face of Moghol-Dokhter at her vanity table. Time had always gone quickly for him, but. . . .

Finally the morning came and Moghol-Dokhter sat at her vanity table combing her hair. The old woman showed her to Arab-Bacha through the window. The Prince could not resist her beauty and sang out loud.

> In that room Moghol-Dokhter
> Is combing her hair.
> She has made me insane forever.
>
> Come, my delicate Moghol.
> Come, my harvest of flowers.

Moghol-Dokhter heard the Prince singing about her. She became angry and as she stood up to see who was singing, her hair fell about her neck and came down to her waist. This scene moved Arab-Bacha, and he sang again.

> Moghol-Dokhter stood up,
> And braided her hair,
> And let it down around her waist.
>
> Come, my delicate Moghol.
> Come, my harvest of flowers.

The Princess's anger frightened the old woman, and she pulled Arab-

Bacha from the window and said, "Get away! If the Moghol King knows you are disturbing his daughter from my house, he'll punish both of us."

Arab-Bacha didn't want to lose the old woman's favor. "I'm sorry," he said politely. "I didn't do that on purpose. I was beside myself when I sang." Then he sat in a corner, very sad.

The Prince's sadness affected the old woman. "Every Friday Moghol-Dokhter goes to her garden. Go wait along the road and see her there," she said.

This news made the Prince happy. He stood up, looked around, and then counted the days of the week, "Sunday, Monday. . . . Oh, today is Thursday, and tomorrow will be Friday." Only the night was between. In the morning he would watch Moghol-Dokhter going to her garden.

The night seemed very long, but it finally passed. Early in the morning Arab-Bacha went to the door of Moghol-Dokhter's palace. Many people were waiting along the road.

"Who are these people?" the Prince asked a man.

"They are Princes and lords who are all in love with Moghol-Dokhter," the man answered. "And. . . ." He hadn't finished his sentence when a slave came out of the palace and announced, "Now, everybody cover his eyes. The Princess is going to her garden."

Hearing the announcement, everyone did as he was bidden. After a few minutes the Princess appeared surrounded by forty maidens. People peeped through their fingers and watched her walking.

Arab-Bacha's love for Moghol-Dokhter had made him impatient. He couldn't hide in a corner and wait like the others, so he started right after her.

The garden wasn't far from the Princess's palace. Upon her arrival a slave opened the door and the minute she and her maidens entered he closed it. There was no way for Arab-Bacha to get in. He walked around the wall and finally he saw a broken part that he could easily climb. It was from the top of this wall that he saw Moghol-Dokhter for the third time. He was so inspired that he forgot about her previous anger and sang this song:

> Moghol-Dokhter is a beautiful flower
> In this garden,
> And the distance between us is burning my heart.
>
> Come, my delicate Moghol.
> Come, my harvest of flowers.

Hearing the Prince's voice, Moghol-Dokhter turned around and looked at him. It was this look that caused her to fall in love with him. She hadn't yet turned back when the Prince addressed her again:

Your eyes are drunken and charming,
And you are more beautiful than a fairy.
Don't stay away from me longer!

Come, my delicate Moghol.
Come, my harvest of flowers.

Moghol-Dokhter had never admired any of her suitors, but she could not resist the Arab Prince. He'd finished singing, and his beloved was still looking at him. The expressions on the faces of both of them changed. Love replaced Moghol-Dokhter's anger, and hope took the place of Arab-Bacha's despair. She sent him a message to propose to her through her father.

Arab-Bacha left the garden and went to the old woman with the news of his success. She congratulated the Prince and said, "You shouldn't waste any time; go tell the King about your wish and the Princess's consent."

The next morning Arab-Bacha went to the Moghol King and presented his proposal.

"The Qājār King," said the Mongol King, "proposed yesterday that my daughter marry his son. I asked forty camel loads of jewels for her dowry, and he's to come back in forty days with the jewels requested. If you bring this amount in a shorter time, you'll be the one to marry her."

"I'll try," said Arab-Bacha, and he returned to the old woman's house and consulted her. "Go bring the jewels he asked and you'll get your diamond," the old woman said.

Arab-Bacha had to get the jewels from his father. He kissed the old woman's hand and headed home on his horse. He needed more speed to save time, so he drove the horse as fast as he could. He was halfway home when the animal fell dead of exhaustion.

Although he was not used to traveling on foot, he had to do it now. In a day or two his feet were sore and covered with blisters. However, he didn't lose a minute and kept on his way. On and on he went until he arrived at the border of his father's kingdom.

The governor of the province on the border heard about the Prince's arrival. He took a regiment out and received him warmly.

"I can't stay here long," the Prince said shortly after he'd seen the governor. "Please provide transportation to the capital for me."

"With pleasure," the governor said, and by the time they had lunch he had made ready everything the Prince needed for his trip.

But the trip to the capital wasn't very long. Messengers had reported the Prince's arrival to the court.

He was received by people from all sections of the capital. Arab-

Pāshā and his Queen were pleased to see the Prince back. They asked about his trip and the result of his stay in the Moghol capital.

"It was successful," Arab-Bacha said, "but I must return without delay."

"Why?" the King and Queen asked.

"To take the forty camel loads of jewels the Moghol King has asked for the dowry of Moghol-Dokhter," Arab-Bacha replied.

Arab-Pāshā and his Queen were happy to hear of their son's success. To them no amount of money equaled the Prince's happiness. They ordered the bankers to load forty camels with jewels and ordered forty slaves to drive the camels for him. The next morning the Prince set out from the capital at the head of his caravan.

This time the way was familiar. Arab-Bacha ordered the slaves to drive day and night. They slept only when they were exhausted. Day after day they traveled. On the morning of the forty-first day they entered the Moghol capital.

"Have you heard anything about Moghol-Dokhter?" the Prince asked the first man he saw.

"The Qājār King brought the jewels her father had asked for her dowry. He took her yesterday, and she'll marry his son in his kingdom," the man replied.

This sad news filled the Prince with grief. "It's impossible!" he said to himself. "I can't believe she would do that. They must have forced her to do it."

He told his slaves to take the jewels to the King's palace and tell his servants that Arab-Bacha sent them. He also told them that they should let his parents know that he would see them when he returned.

At this time, Arab-Bacha didn't feel he should see the Mongol King. He asked people the way the Qājār King had gone and set out after him. He drove his horse all day and at dusk he arrived at a crossroads. He couldn't tell which way the caravan had gone, so he got off his horse to spend the night there. He would find the way in the morning.

The Prince was overwhelmingly sad, and the dark night and the lonely desert doubled his sadness. To express his melancholy he began to sing aloud. His voice reached the mountains and echoed.

> I arrived at a crossroad,
> And sighed and cried,
> And thought of your moonlike face.
>
> Come, my delicate Moghol.
> Come, my harvest of flowers.

The Prince had a good imagination. In an instant, he recalled the past, considered the present, and saw into the future, sometimes dark and sometimes bright. Finally, he went to sleep, his thoughts whirling in his head.

This desert was the home of a notorious thief who slept during the day and robbed caravans at night. He ran into Arab-Bacha at midnight and ruthlessly thrust the point of his sword into the Prince's foot.

"Ahh!" groaned Arab-Bacha and started from his sleep.

"Give me your money," the thief said in a hostile voice.

"If I had any money I wouldn't sleep here," the Prince replied.

"Then what are you doing here?" the thief asked.

Arab-Bacha told his story, and the thief was so moved that he stopped threatening him. "Take me as your brother, and I will help you any way I can," he told the Prince. The Prince shook hands with him and said, "From now on we are brothers." They promised to be brothers until the ends of their lives.

Arab-Bacha's adopted brother bandaged his foot with a handkerchief. "Wait here," he told the Prince. "I'll bring my horse and then we'll go."

The sun had just shed its first rays when they left the crossroads. On and on they rode and the next afternoon they came near the caravan that had settled for the night.

"You should find out whether she still loves you," the Prince's adopted brother said.

"How can I?" the Prince asked.

"Sing. If she is familiar with your voice, she'll know you are here and will tell you what the situation is," his adopted brother said.

This suggestion seemed wise to the Prince. He put this message into a song:

> Moghol-Dokhter the beautiful,
> I have no food or shelter.
> Let me share your dinner.
>
> Come, my delicate Moghol.
> Come, my harvest of flowers.

Moghol-Dokhter remembered the Prince's voice and she understood the message as she heard him singing. When the dark of the night covered the land, she sent her maiden with a bowl of food and a message to him.

My faithful Prince,

I wish you to understand that the things that are happening are not due to my decision. Be patient and follow the caravan. We'll make further plans when the time comes.

Your beloved.

Moghol-Dokhter's sincere letter left no doubt that she loved Arab-Bacha. "I'll follow the caravan," he said to the messenger. "You tell Moghol-Dokhter not to worry."

Early the next morning the Qājār King's caravan left and Arab-Bacha and his adopted brother moved behind it. After a few long days on the way, setting up camps in the evening and taking them down in the morning, they followed the caravan into the Qājār capital.

The Qājār Prince, Moghol-Dokhter's husband-to-be, was the governor of a province and he and his first wife lived there. When his father arrived the Prince was notified to come to the capital for his second marriage. Meanwhile, Moghol-Dokhter was placed in a palace that had been built for her, and maidens were put in her service.

Arab-Bacha had settled in a mosque in the city and kept in contact with Moghol-Dokhter. All their plans to get married seemed in vain, but they had not lost hope and waited for a solution.

At this time the Qājār Prince was getting ready to come to the capital. His first wife was enraged by his second marriage and plotted to murder Moghol-Dokhter. She poisoned some apples and asked him to take them to her. She said the apples were her gift to his fiancée.

On his way to the capital, the Prince had dinner in the shade by a spring. After dinner, he ate a few of the apples his wife had sent for Moghol-Dokhter. He thought he would replace them with better apples when he arrived.

After he'd eaten the apples, he felt weaker and weaker every minute. Finally he lost consciousness and died. Seeing his master fallen, the Prince's horse went back alone. The officials traced its tracks to the spring and saw the Prince's body. They reported the tragedy to the King and the Queen who came to the spot immediately.

The news of the Prince's death spread around the city. Moghol-Dokhter and Arab-Bacha heard about it too. They were sad about the death of the Prince but happy for their own success. They packed their clothes with the understanding that Arab-Bacha would call Moghol-Dokhter at midnight and they would leave. Packing had made Moghol-Dokhter tired and she had fallen asleep early in the evening. When Arab-Bacha called no one was awake to open the door for him. So, he sang this song to wake her up.

> Moghol-Dokhter has forgotten the rendezvous,
> And has gone to sleep.
> Maybe she doesn't want to be my companion.
>
> Come, my delicate Moghol.
> Come, my harvest of flowers.

Moghol-Dokhter heard Arab-Bacha's voice and opened the door for him. "No delay," he said as he saw her. He and his adopted brother helped her mount the horse and the three of them set out for Arab-Bacha's home. The night was pleasant, and the sound of their horses' hooves echoed in the dark of the night. Arab-Bacha was very happy and when they were out of the city he began singing:

> I left my sorrows,
> And joined my love tonight.
> That makes me fresh like a flower.
>
> Come, my delicate Moghol.
> Come, my harvest of flowers.
>
> Moghol-Dokhter left at dawn,
> Accompanying her love
> And deserting her enemies.
>
> Come, my delicate Moghol.
> Come, my harvest of flowers.

On and on they went, and one after another beautiful scene passed in front of them. Herds of camels grazed in the valleys, and herdsmen soothed them with the sound of their flutes. Arab-Bacha felt it was the happiest moment of his life and called Moghol-Dokhter's attention to the things around them by singing this song.

> You, the newly widowed Moghol,
> Look at the camels
> Grazing between the branches of the river.
>
> Come, my delicate Moghol.
> Come, my harvest of flowers.

"Whom had I married that you call me widow?" she asked angrily.

"That was only to make my song rhyme," Arab-Bacha replied.

Everything was quiet after their talk. The click of the hooves of the horses was the only sound that could be heard. Suddenly a shepherd shouted, "Catch him! Catch him! Get the sheep from him!"

The Princess, the Prince, and his adopted brother stopped and looked around. A wolf had taken a sheep from the shepherd, and he ordered his dogs to save the sheep.

Arab-Bacha was a skillful hunter. Seeing the scene brought his past memories back to him. "Let me catch him," he said and spurred his horse. The wolf ran up and down the hills, and the dog and the horse chased him. As they got closer to him, the wolf grew frightened. He left the sheep and ran away. Being exhausted, the horse fell dead at the end of the race.

The Prince had to walk back the distance he'd chased the wolf on his horse. As he got closer to his companions, he reported the horse's death through this song.

> It might be a sign of my bad luck
> That my horse fell dead,
> Running over the mounds.
>
> Come, my delicate Moghol.
> Come, my harvest of flowers.

He still had a little distance to go when he saw herds of camels grazing on the hillsides. He wanted to show the scene to Moghol-Dokhter and his adopted brother so he sang,

> From one rock to another rock,
> Camels are grazing on *kenger*.*
> Come, see, Moghol-Dokhter.
>
> Come, my delicate Moghol.
> Come, my harvest of flowers.

Finally he joined Moghol-Dokhter and his adopted brother. His horse's death made him very sad. However, his adopted brother consoled him, saying that he would walk, and gave his horse to him.

Moghol-Dokhter and Arab-Bacha refused the ride, but he insisted that they should. "It's a shame that you walk in front of us and we ride your horse," they said. They talked, and finally he convinced them to accept his offer. Thus, the couple on horseback and the Prince's adopted brother on foot in front of them, they resumed their journey.

They traveled all day and in the evening they settled by a graveyard. Arab-Bacha was tired and as soon as they'd pitched their tents he fell asleep. His adopted brother and Moghol-Dokhter cooked pilau and when everything was ready she called Arab-Bacha, singing this song.

> Moghol-Dokhter has started a fire,
> To cook pilau,
> But Arab-Bacha is in a deep sleep.
>
> Hear my voice,
> Come, my dear Arab.

Moghol-Dokhter's voice woke up Arab-Bacha. After supper, they slept in the graveyard for the night.

At dawn, they moved on. Their destination was the border of Arab-Pāshā's kingdom. They traveled tirelessly and by noon they reached

---

* A thorny desert bush fed to livestock in winter.

the border. Wide deserts continued monotonously, but everything around was familiar to the Prince. He'd come hunting here and knew the place very well.

Herds of sheep were grazing on both sides. Arab-Bacha asked the shepherds whose herds they were.

"Arab-Pāshā's," the shepherds answered.

Arab-Bacha presented the sheep to Moghol-Dokhter through this song.

> A thousand herds of sheep
> And my soul and property
> Are all for my love.
>
> Come, my delicate Moghol.
> Come, my harvest of flowers.

After the travelers crossed the desert, high mountains drew their attention. Herds of goats grazed on the grass among the rocks. Arab-Bacha asked the herdsmen whose goats they were.

"Arab-Pāshā's," the shepherds answered.

Arab-Bacha presented the goats to Moghol-Dokhter too.

As they passed the high mountains, wide plains attracted them. Herds of camels were around and grazed on the thorn bushes.

"Whose camels are they?" Arab-Bacha asked.

"Arab-Pāshā's," the herdsmen answered.

The Prince offered the camels to Moghol-Dokhter.

> One hundred herds of camels,
> And one hundred strong herdsmen,
> By the will of the Lord,
> I offer all to my Moghol.

A little farther on horses grazed on alfalfa. When Arab-Bacha understood that they were his father's he presented them and whatever else that he and his father might have to Moghol-Dokhter.

> My gardens and my land,
> My country and my crown,
> Are all for my love.
>
> Come, my delicate Moghol.
> Come, my harvest of flowers.

Now, they were near his father's capital. A miller saw the Prince and ran to the court taking the message of his arrival. The courtiers, officials, and the people of the capital came out and received the Prince warmly. They took him and his companions to the palace.

The Prince introduced his companions and mentioned his adopted brother's kindnesses to him. "You are my son too," the King said as he drew the Prince's adopted brother in his arms and kissed him.

A week later the King held a great bridal feast. He married his daughter to Arab-Bacha's adopted brother and Moghol-Dokhter to Arab-Bacha. Lights were on for one week, and, as was the custom, Hindus were served uncooked food and Moslems were served cooked food.

The Decapitation of Sufi Islam

Collected by Marcia Baghban, American-born, from her husband, Hafizullah Baghban, a native of Herat, in December 1973.

Motifs D1641.7 "Severed head moves from place to place" and D1841.3.2 "Saint unharmed by fire."

Sufi Islam is the founder of the Karukh Sufi brotherhood that has a large number of followers in the villages and towns of Herat and the rest of Afghanistan. After his death in an Iranian attack on Herat in 1842, legends grew about the martyred war hero and mystic leader. He is glorified in the legends of the flight of his head from the presence of the Shah of Iran to Karukh, Afghanistan.

Usually the legend is told by the devotees of the Karukh order, but not necessarily in religious and ritualistic circumstances. The members of the brotherhood relate this legend with pride in ordinary conversations or in defense of their circle. Women are seen among the audience but not as active tellers.

The *mandāu* bush is cultivated for its oil.

When the Iranians attacked Herat, Hazrat-i-Shaykh al-Islam and his Sufi brothers moved to defend the province. War started in Shakīwon [the local pronunciation of Shakībān] where Hazrat-i Shaykh al-Islam fought and led his followers to fight bravely. During the second or third day of the war he was killed by an enemy conspiracy and his disappointed followers dispersed. The Iranians cut off his head and took it to their Shah, who became angry because they had killed the holy man. They put his body on a pile of *mandāu* bushes and set it on fire.

In the evening, some of the Sufi brothers went to collect his ashes to take them to Herat. They saw that the pile of bushes had burned, but Hazrat-i-Shaykh al-Islam's clothes had not even changed color. They moved his body to Karukh [in Afghanistan] and buried it in the *rauza* [garden]. One night when a few brothers were reciting the Holy Quran by his grave, they saw the grave crack and the head come down from the sky and join the body.

The Two Thieves With the Same Wife

Collected by Hafizullah Baghban in 1967 in Herat.

This is a version of tale type 1525Q *The Two Thieves Married to the Same Woman*, reported only from India. It also incorporates type 1525L *Theft Committed while Tale is Told:* "one party relates the situation in the form of a tale, to the gentleman who is being robbed," which is known in Russia and Lithuania as well as India.

In 1952 a Negro youth told a joke to Richard M. Dorson in Cleveland, Mississippi, with the same theme of the bigamous wife. Two GI's in Japan in World War II meet and exchange amenities. They discover they come from the same town, live on the same street, at the same address, and are each married to a woman with the same appearance and distinctive birthmark. One shakes the other's hand and says, "We must be husbands-in-law."

The English play *Box and Cox* by John Maddison Morton (1811–1891) hinges on a comparable situation where a landlady rents the same room, unbeknownst to her renters, to a day and a night tenant.

Baghban recorded the present text from ʿĀṣiya, a forty-year-old woman known as a storyteller, who had learned it from her mother, also a good raconteur. Later the same summer he recorded a second version from Sufi Mullāh Rahīm, seventy, of Nāwbādām, a devotee of the Karukh order, who had learned it fifty years before from a cousin, Mullāh Mammad Jān, then sixty. Rahīm's text is somewhat more revealing of the thieves' sexual relations with their wife.

Motifs H100 "Identification by matching parts of divided token"; K341.20 "The story about theft while doing the stealing"; H1151 "Theft as task"; K306.1 "The stolen and restolen ham (money)."

Once upon a time there was a woman who had two husbands. One of her husbands was a day thief and one of her husbands was a night thief. They both lived in the same house for fourteen years, but they didn't know about each other. When the day thief came home the night thief was not there, and when the night thief came home the day thief was not there.

The day thief and the night thief were both recruited for the army. The day thief came to his wife and said, "I'm going to go in the army. Make me a set of clothes." The night thief came to her and said, "I'm going in the army. Make me a set of clothes."

The woman made a set of clothes for the day thief and a set of clothes for the night thief. She baked five loaves of bread for the day thief and five loaves of bread for the night thief. She baked a *qalif* [bread baked with butter] and divided it into two parts and made two handkerchiefs, one for the day thief and one for the night thief. She wrapped half of the *qalif* with five loaves of bread in one handkerchief and the other half of the *qalif* with five loaves of bread in the other handkerchief. The next day the day thief came and took his bed pack and the night thief came and took his bed pack.

The day thief and the night thief both left and went and went and went until both of them stopped to have lunch. The day thief said, "I'll unwrap my bread." The night thief said, "I'll unwrap my bread." Finally, the day thief said, "Brother, I'll unwrap my bread and we'll eat it. When mine is finished, we'll eat yours."

When the day thief brought his handkerchief holding the bread, the night thief said, "Brother, you brought my handkerchief and my bread." The day thief said, "I got it from my own pack bag." They unwrapped the bread from the handkerchief and with more suspicion the night thief said, "Here is my half of *qalif* and here are my five loaves of bread." The day thief said, "Let's go see whether I got them from my pack bag or from your pack bag." They went and checked the day thief's pack bag. He'd taken them from his own pack bag. Then the night thief got his bread and his handkerchief. They were all like those of the day thief's. He put the two halves of the *qalif* together and they were like one whole. He asked, "Brother, where did you get these?" The day thief said, "From my house." He asked, "Where is your house?" The day thief answered, "In such and such a place." He asked, "What is your wife like?" The day thief answered, "She is short and has big eyes." He said, "The house you are talking about is my house and the woman you are talking about is my wife."

The day thief said, "She is my wife." And the night thief said, "She is my wife." They were going to have a fight and finally they told their officer, "We've forgotten something at home. Will you let us go get it?" The officer dismissed them, and they went back. When they reached the door of their house one of them was going to go in and the other one wouldn't let him. The woman looked down over the wall. They asked, "Whose wife are you?" She answered, "I'm the wife of both of you. I managed to keep both of you without one knowing about the other for thirteen years. Now that you know the story, I'll be the wife of the one who proves to be more skilled than the other in his profession."

The day thief and the night thief accepted. The day thief told the night thief, "You should go wherever I take you." The night thief said, "All right."

The day thief bought a turnip, and they went to the city. Incidentally, a merchant had come to buy wedding clothes for his daughter-in-law. He had a bag of money in his pocket. When the merchant got off the *gādī* [horse-drawn cart] and was going to enter the *tīmcha* [covered bazaar], the day thief took his bag of money and put the turnip in his pocket. The merchant went into the *tīmcha* and told a *bazzāz* [cloth merchant], "Give me so many meters of this cloth and so many meters of that cloth and. . . ." When he got the cloth he asked, "How much shall I pay you?" The *bazzāz* said, "Two thousand *afghanis.*"

The merchant put his hand in his pocket and took out the turnip. He told the *bazzāz*, "I bought some turnips. I left my money bag in the store and took a turnip instead. Let me go get it." As he was walking out of the *tīmcha* the day thief took the turnip out of his pocket and put the money bag in its place. The merchant went home and when he saw his wife he said, "I told you to give me the money bag and you gave me a turnip." His wife said, "You are mistaken. I gave you the money bag." He put his hand in his pocket and got the bag out. She said, "Isn't this the money bag?" He said, "In the *bazzāz'* store it was a turnip." He put the money bag in his pocket, sat in the *gādī*, and went back to the city.

As he was going into the *tīmcha*, the day thief took the money bag from his pocket and put the turnip in its place. When he went to the *bazzāz'* store he put his hand in his pocket and said, "Sir, here is your money." Again, he took out the turnip. He said, "Heavens, they've given me the turnip again. Let me go get the money." On his way out of the *tīmcha* the day thief took the turnip out of his pocket and put the money bag in its place.

The merchant sat in the *gādī* and went home. He told his wife, "I told you to give me the money bag and you gave me the turnip." His wife said, "So and so's father [form of address from wife to husband], wasn't the money bag in your hand? When did I give you a turnip?" He took the turnip out of his pocket and hit it on the ground. There was the money bag. He said, "In the *tīmcha* it was a turnip." His wife said, "Maybe there is something in the man's store. This time tell him to get out of his store and count the money for him."

He went to the city the third time. In front of the *tīmcha* the day thief took the money bag out of his pocket and put the turnip in its place. When the merchant went to the *bazzāz* he said, "Sir, will you come out of your store so that I can count your money here? Every time I get my money out of my pocket there it is a turnip, while outside your store it is a money bag. Maybe there is something in your store." The *bazzāz* said, "Very well." He came out of his store and the merchant put his hand in his pocket and took out the turnip. The *bazzāz* said, "Are you making fun of me?" The merchant came back, but the thief did not put the money in his pocket this time.

The day thief and the night thief went to their wife and the merchant went home with the turnip. After the day thief and the night thief had dinner in the evening, the night thief said, "You should accompany me wherever I go." The day thief said, "Fine."

The night thief took a ladder and some long nails and they left. They went and went until they reached the King's palace. He pounded the nails into the wall and tied the ladder to the nails with ropes. They climbed up and over into the palace. They opened the kitchen *dāloncha* [village kitchen] door and saw a concubine holding the King's head on her lap and rubbing his feet. She had a rooster tied to the bed leg. The night thief told the day thief, "You sit here."

The day thief sat there, and the night thief went in and saw that the concubine was asleep. He put the King's head down and lay the concubine down on one side. He took the rooster outside, killed him, set fire in the *manqalfarangī* [a grill], put spices on the rooster, and put it in a pot on the *manqalfarangī*. He told the day thief, "You come stir the rooster." Then he went into the room and rubbed the King's feet until he woke up. He asked, "What time is it?" The night thief said, "It is early." The King said, "I don't know why I can't go to sleep." The night thief said, "Maybe you are worrying about something. If you want I'll tell you a story." The King said, "It will be good if you tell me a story." The night thief said:

Once there was a woman who had two husbands. One of her husbands was a day thief and one of them was a night thief. She was married to both of them for fourteen years, but they didn't know about each other. They were recruited for the army at the same time, and the day thief went to her during the day and told her, "I've been called by the army. Make me a set of clothes and a few loaves of bread." The night thief went to her at night and told her, "I have been called by the army. Make me a set of clothes and a few loaves of bread."

She baked five loaves of bread for one and five loaves of bread for the other, she baked a *qalif* and gave half to one and half to the other, she made two handkerchiefs, one for one and one for the other and wrapped the *qalif* and the bread in their handkerchiefs. In the morning, the day thief came and took his bed pack and then the night thief came and took his bed pack. On the way they became friends and went and went and went, and at noon their officer said, "Sit here and have lunch."

The day thief said, "I'll bring my bread and we'll eat it." The night thief said, "It makes no difference. You or I will bring our bread and we'll both eat." The day thief said, "I'll bring my bread first, when it is finished we'll eat yours." The night thief accepted. The day thief brought his bread wrapped in his handkerchief. The night thief said, "Brother, you brought my bread. I know that is my handkerchief." The day thief said, "I brought my own bread." The night thief said, "You unwrap it." He unwrapped it, and the night thief saw the half *qalif* and the five loaves of bread. He said, "Brother, this is my handkerchief." The day thief said, "No, it is not. Let us go and see your pack bag." They went to his pack bag and his handkerchief and his bread were there. They put their half *qalif* side by side. It made one *qalif*. The night thief asked, "Where did you get your *qalif*?" The day thief said, "My wife baked it for me." The night thief asked, "Which *malla* [quarter] are you living in?" He said, "In . . . Where is your house?" The day thief answered, "My house is in the north. It has a *dūlakht* [dust in the air; here, a door that opens in the middle] door." He asked, "What is your wife like?" The day thief answered, "She is short and has big eyes." The night thief said, "That is my wife."

One said, "She is my wife." The other one said, "She is my wife." Finally they both agreed. "It can't be resolved here." They went to their officer and got his permission to go back home.

At this time the water in the pot had evaporated and it made lots of noise. The night thief told the day thief, "Stir the rooster so that it doesn't burn."

The day thief was first and the night thief followed him. "Stir the rooster so that it doesn't burn."

They came to the door and the day thief was going to enter the house. The night thief did not let him go in and shouted and made lots of noise. "Stir the rooster so that it doesn't burn."

The King asked, "Why do you say, 'Stir the rooster so that it doesn't burn.' " The night thief said, "In this story the storyteller says, 'Stir the rooster so that it doesn't burn.' "

The woman looked down over the wall and said, "Why do you make so much noise?" They asked, "Whose wife are you?" "Stir the rooster so that it doesn't burn."

She answered, "I'm the wife of you both. I've been the wife of you both for thirteen years. I managed to keep both of you in the same house without one knowing about the other." "Stir the rooster so that it doesn't burn."

"Now I'll be the wife of the one of you who proves to be more skilled than the other in his profession." "Stir the rooster so that it doesn't burn."

They both accepted what she said, and the day thief told the night thief, "Let us go to the bazaar." When they went to the bazaar the day thief bought a turnip and stood in front of the *tīmcha*. A merchant came to buy wedding clothes for his son. There was a bag of money in his pocket. The day thief took the money out of his pocket and put the turnip in it. "Stir the rooster so that it doesn't burn."

The merchant went in the *tīmcha* to a *bazzāz* and told him, "Give me . . . meters of . . . cloth and . . . meters of. . . ." The *bazzāz* measured the cloth and gave it to him. He asked, "How much is it?" The *bazzāz* said, "Two thousand *afghanis*." He said, "Let me give you your money." He put his hand in his pocket and took out the turnip. He said, "Heavens! I brought turnips and left my bag of money in the store and put the turnips in my pocket. Let me go get my bag of money." "Stir the rooster so that it doesn't burn."

When the merchant left the *tīmcha*, the day thief put the bag of money in his pocket and took the turnip out. He sat in a *gādī* and came home. "Stir the rooster so that it doesn't burn."

He knocked on the door and his wife opened the door. He shouted, "Damn it, I told you to give me the bag of money and you gave me a turnip!" "Stir the rooster so that it doesn't burn."

His wife said, "I swear there is no turnip in our house. How could I give you a turnip? It was the bag of money I gave you." "Stir the rooster so that it doesn't burn."

He said, "Stupid, here is the turnip," and he threw the bag of money on the ground. His wife asked, "Isn't this money?" He said, "I swear it was a turnip." "Stir the rooster so that it doesn't burn."

The merchant put the bag of money in his pocket, sat in the *gādī*, and went to the *tīmcha*. Again the day thief took the bag of money from his pocket and put the turnip in it. "Stir the rooster so that it doesn't burn."

He went into the *tīmcha* and said, "Sir, let me give you your money." He took a turnip out of his pocket. The merchant returned, and in front of the *tīmcha* the day thief put the bag of money in his pocket and took the turnip out. He sat in the *gādī* and came home. He knocked on the door and his wife came. He said, "Stupid, why do you do this? I tell you to give me the bag of money and you give me the turnip." She said, "It is not a turnip. Didn't you see the bag of money just before? Why are you doing this? Are you going out of your mind?" He took the bag of money and threw it on the ground and said, "Isn't this a turnip?" She said, "This is money." "Stir the rooster so that it doesn't burn."

The merchant said, "When I go to the *tīmcha*, it becomes a turnip, and when I come here, it becomes a bag of money. I don't know what it is." His wife said, "There must be something in the *bazzāz'* store. This time, ask the *bazzāz* to get out in the *tīmcha* and then count his money and give it to him." "Stir the rooster so that it doesn't burn."

The merchant sat in the *gādī*, arrived in front of the *tīmcha*, and got out of the *gādī*. The day thief took the bag of money out of his pocket and put the turnip in it. He walked into the *tīmcha* and asked the *bazzāz*, "Sir, will you come out into the *tīmcha*? There must be something in your store. Every time I come here there is a turnip in my pocket. When I go back home, it is a bag of money." "Stir the rooster so that it doesn't burn."

The *bazzāz* walked out of his store and sat in the *tīmcha*. The merchant took the turnip out of his pocket. The *bazzāz* started complaining, "You are making fun of me, going back and forth and bringing a turnip." "Stir the rooster so that it doesn't burn."

The merchant was embarrassed and returned home. This time the day thief did not put the bag of money in his pocket. The merchant sat in the *gādī* and went home. And the day thief and the night thief went home too. "Stir the rooster so that it doesn't burn."

In the evening, the night thief said, "Come with me now." He got a ladder, some nails, and rope, and they went to the King's palace. "Stir the rooster so that it doesn't burn."

The night thief pounded the nails into the walls of the palace and he climbed. Then he told the day thief, "Now you climb." The day thief climbed too. "Stir the rooster so that it doesn't burn."

They went into the King's kitchen, opened the door of his room and saw the King's head on a concubine's lap. The concubine was going to sleep. "Stir the rooster so that it doesn't burn."

The night thief told the day thief, "You sit here." The day thief sat, and the night thief went in. There was a rooster tied under the King's bed. He brought the rooster outside, killed him, pulled off his feathers, burned his feathers, brought the *manqalfarangī*, and made a fire. He put spices on the rooster and told the day thief, "You sit here and I'll go into the room. When I tell you, 'Stir the rooster so that it doesn't burn,' you stir it." The night thief went into the room. The concubine was asleep. He put the King's head on his lap. He rubbed and rubbed the King's feet until he woke up. The King said, "What time is it?" The night thief said, "It is still early." The King said, "I don't know why I can't go to sleep." "Stir the rooster so that it doesn't burn."

The night thief said, "Maybe you're worrying. If you want, I'll tell you a story." The King said, "All right. Tell me a story then." "Stir the rooster so that it doesn't burn."

Then the night thief asked the King, "Does this woman belong to the day thief or to the night thief?" The King said, "She belongs to the night thief. The night thief has done a lot. He's gone to the King's palace, killed the rooster, and told the King a story. The woman belongs to the night thief."

The night thief rubbed the King's feet very softly until he went to sleep. Then he put his head down and got out of the room. He and the day thief ate the rooster and went home.

The King was asleep till the sun rose. When he woke up, he told his concubine, "You *gayūburīda* [a woman whose hair is cut because of some disgrace], why didn't you wake me up?" The concubine said, "I don't really know. I just woke up." The King asked, "Where's the rooster?" She said, "He was tied to the leg of your bed." They looked around, but they could not find the rooster. The King said, "A thief came into the palace last night, killed the rooster, cooked it, ate it, and told me a story, but I didn't understand."

The King was very sad and he wore black. He sent the town crier to the bazaars to tell the people, "Whoever had come to my palace and told me the story last night should let me know who he is. I'll cover him with gold." The night thief heard the town crier and said to himself, "I'll go." He went to the palace and rang the bell. They took him to the King. The King asked, "Son, was it you who had come to my palace last night and told me the story?"

He said, "Yes, sir. I had a wife that the day thief and I shared. I did this to prove my superiority. Now, does she belong to me or to the day thief?" The King said, "She belongs to you." The King gave him prizes, and the day thief went into the army and the night thief went to his house. God gave them their wishes. May he give us our wishes too.

Khastakhumār and Bībīnagār

Collected by Hafizullah Baghban in 1967 in Herat.

The tale type 425 *The Search for the Lost Husband*, best known as the tale of Cupid and Psyche, is one of the oldest, most studied, and most widely distributed folktales in the world. The 1,100 versions collected by Jan-Öjvind Swahn (*The Tale of Cupid and Psyche*, Lund, 1955) are only a fragment of the mass of variants that could be accumulated from the living oral tradition. Scholars have traced the history of the tale to Greek mythology, Hindu Jātakā, and the Near Eastern *One Thousand and One Nights*.

The present version of type 425 was narrated by Yar Muhammad, a fifty-year-old farmer from Shāflon. Yar Muhammad's repertoire was rather large, and he said he did not remember from whom he had learned each tale.

Yar Muhammad narrated this tale to an all-male audience on a winter evening, and a feeling of sober involvement among his audience could be detected.

The particularly Afghan and Muslim adaptations of this tale are noticed in motifs H94.4 and K629.1. Because of their religious commitments, Afghan peasants do not drink wine. Therefore, the supplanted wife drops her ring in a jug of water rather than a glass of wine (H94.4). The enchanted husband and his supplanted wife bathe the ogre co-wife (rather than the servant) in boiling water in order for them to escape (K629.1.), in accord with the negative feelings against polygamy.

The following motifs occur sequentially in the narrative: B622.1 "Serpent as wooer"; B620.1 "Daughter promised to animal suitor"; L54.1 "Youngest daughter agrees to marry a monster (later the sisters are jealous)"; B604.1 "Marriage to snake"; D621.1 "Animal by day, man by night"; C421 "Tabu: revealing secret of supernatural husband"; H1385.4 "Quest for vanished husband"; Q502.2 "Punishment: wandering till iron shoes are worn out"; D474.2 "Transformation: water becomes bloody" (or turns into pus in this case); H94.4 "Identification by ring dropped in glass of wine" (in glass of water in this case); G530.2 "Help from ogre's son"; D1658.1.1 "River grateful for being praised even when ugly" (in this case a stream of blood or pus is grateful); D1658.1.5 "Apple tree grateful for being shaken" (in this case crooked tree grateful for being praised); D1658.1.4 "Continually slamming door grateful for being fastened" (in this case half-open door grateful for being shut); B391 "Animal grateful for food"; D1393.2 "Magic objects and (animals) maintain quiet so that fugitive may escape"; K629.1 "Escape by bathing guard in boiling water" (here co-wife bathed in boiling water); D1393.5 "Magic thorn attacks pursuers and helps fugitive" (here "juwaldūz"—large needle); D1039.2 "Magic salt (covers the ground)"; D454.12 "Transformation: mirror to glass mountains"; D483.1 "River expands and becomes sea" (here a little water becomes river); G512.11 "Ogre drowned."

Once upon a time there was an old *khārkash*.[1] Every day he collected thorn bushes and sold them in the bazaar. He bought bread with the money, brought it home, ate it with his daughters, and thanked God. One day he collected some thorn bushes and tied his sheaf, but when he tried to lift it up he couldn't. It was too heavy for him. He unwrapped

1. A person who makes a living by gathering and selling thorn bushes.

his rope and took one bunch of thorns, two bunches of thorns, and three bunches of thorns from the sheaf. Suddenly he saw a black snake lying in the thorns in his sheaf.

The snake said, "Don't be afraid. I won't harm you." The old man said, "I'm not afraid." The snake said, "But I'd like you to give me your youngest daughter." The old man said, "I will." The snake said, "At your daughter's wedding, wind will sweep your *takhbum*.[2] Then clouds will come, and rain will settle the dust. Then many snakes will come. Don't be afraid of them." The old man said, "I won't."

The old man took his sheaf of thorn bushes to the bazaar and sold it. He bought some bread, took it home for his daughters, and sat down, sad and depressed. His youngest daughter asked, "Father, why are you so sad today?" The old man said, "I'm not sad, my daughter." His daughter asked, "No, really, you seem sad." The old man said, "I'd tied my sheaf today and tried to lift it up. It was too heavy for me. I unwrapped my rope and took one bunch of thorn bushes, two bunches of thorn bushes, and three bunches of thorn bushes from my sheaf. A black snake was in the sheaf and he told me, 'You ought to give me your youngest daughter. On her wedding day, first, wind will sweep your *takhbom*, then it will rain and settle the dust, and then many snakes will come to your house. Then I'll marry her.'"

His youngest daughter said, "Father, it's all right." She consoled the old man. After a few days, the wind blew and swept his *takhbom*, it rained and settled the dust, and then many snakes came in his house. The black snake came too. They fed the people and recited her *khotb-i nika*[3] with the black snake. After the wedding the other snakes left, but the black snake went away and came back periodically. At night he took off his *jild*[4] and showed himself to his wife. The black snake's wife had two stepsisters. When they saw her husband, they became jealous. One day they told their sister, "When the snake comes, ask him, 'How does your *jild* burn?' Then burn his *jild* so that he can't go anywhere."

In the evening the snake came; they had dinner and sat for awhile. Then his wife asked, "How does your *jild* burn?" He slapped her on the mouth so hard that blood flowed from her lips. Her sisters were listening at the *kaj*.[5] Then he felt bad, put her head on his lap, and told her, "Foolish human being, why do you ask me such things? What if you and I have enemies?" She said, "Why should we have enemies? I just asked you." The black snake said, "My *jild* burns with garlic and

2. An open platform on the second floor.
3. A religious passage recited at the official announcement of marriage.
4. A supernatural covering that gives man a false appearance.
5. A passage for ventilation at the deep center of the oval roofs in western Afghanistan.

onion skins. If one burns my skin, I'll go. You'll have to make seven sets of iron clothes, seven pairs of iron shoes, and seven iron canes and come west till they're worn out. Then you'll find me."

As soon as the black snake finished explaining the secret of his *jild*, his wife's stepsisters ran and found some garlic and onion skins and burned his *jild*. He became a green pigeon, flew out, and sat on the wall of the old man's house. He told his wife, "Find seven sets of iron clothes, seven pairs of iron shoes, and seven iron canes and come west until you find me."

In the morning the black snake's wife had seven sets of iron clothes, seven pairs of iron shoes, and seven iron canes made. Her father begged her not to go, but she said, "I'll go." She went day and night until she saw a caravan of camels. She asked, "Whose camels are these?" The camel herder said:

> They belong to Khastakhumār.[6]
> They are the dowry of Bībīnagār.[7]

She answered:

> May Bībīnagār's luck burn.
> May Bībīnagār turn blind!

She left the camels and went and went and went day and night until she saw a flock of sheep. She asked the shepherd, "Whose sheep are these?" The shepherd answered:

> They belong to Khastakhumār.
> They are the dowry of Bībīnagār.

She said in answer:

> May Bībīnagār's luck burn.
> May Bībīnagār turn blind!

She left the sheep and went and went and went until she reached a herd of cows. She asked the cowboy, "Whose cows are these?" He answered:

> They belong to Khastakhumār.
> They are the dowry of Bībīnagār.

She said:

> May Bībīnagār's luck burn.
> May Bībīnagār turn blind!

6. The hero of the tale.
7. The heroine of the table.

She left the cows and went and went and went until she reached a herd of donkeys. She asked the herdsman, "Whose donkeys are these?" The herdsman answered:

> They belong to Khastakhumār.
> They are the dowry of Bībīnagār.

She said:

> May Bībīnagār's luck burn.
> May Bībīnagār turn blind!

She went day and night and night and day for years. Her seven sets of iron clothes wore out and she reached a spring. She sat by the water to rest when she saw a concubine come to take water. She said, "May I drink some water from your jug?" The concubine answered, "My master is waiting for me to wash his hands and you want me to give you water! He'll get mad at me."

Bībīnagār prayed, "May this water turn into pus!"   .   .

The concubine took the jug and poured the water on her master's hands. It was all pus. Her master cursed, "Gaysūburīda,[8] did you fill the jug from the pus stream?" The concubine answered, "I swear I filled it from the spring." Her master said, "Go back and fill it again." When she came back, Bībīnagār said, "Let me drink some water from your jug." The concubine said, "My master is waiting, can I give you water?" She prayed, "May this jug of water turn into blood." When the concubine poured it on her master's hands, it was all blood. He cursed, "Gaysūburīda, did you fill it from the blood stream?" The concubine said, "No, I filled it from the spring." He asked, "Why does this happen then?" The concubine said, "There is a *malang*[9] in shabby clothes sitting by the spring. She asked for water both times, but I didn't give her water." The master said, "First give her the jug to drink water and then bring it here."

The concubine brought the jug and filled it from the spring. Bībīnagār said, "Let me drink some water from your jug." The concubine gave the jug to her. She drank some water and then dropped the ring that Khastakhumār had given her in the jug. When the concubine poured the water on her master's hands, the ring fell out and he saw it. He recognized the ring and put it on his finger. Then he came out and saw Bībīnagār sitting by the spring. He said, "I can't take you with me right now. Let me go consult my parents first. I'll tell them that you are a concubine."

8. A woman whose hair is cut to disgrace her, for unlawful acts of sex and so on; here an insult.
9. Beggar, with a religious connotation.

Khastakhumār went in and told his mother, "There is a concubine waiting outside. If you promise not to eat her, I'll bring her in to do my work." She said, "No, I won't eat her."

Khastakhumār brought Bībīnagār in, and she worked for them in the house. One day Khastakhumār's mother said, "I promised I wouldn't eat her. Let me send her for my sister to eat." Khastakhumār was engaged to his aunt's daughter.

One day Khastakhumār's mother told Bībīnagār, "Go to my sister's house and get her *khamīrturūsh*[10] so that we can make some dough." Bībīnagār was going to get the *khamīrturūsh* when Khastakhumār came in front of her. He asked, "Where are you going, Bībīnagār?" She answered, "I'm going to your aunt's house to get the *khamīrturūsh*." Khastakhumār said, "As you go you'll see a pus stream. Say, 'Hurrah, hurrah. Such a stream of butter! I wish I had time to taste a bit.' As you go farther you'll see a stream of blood. Say, 'Hurrah, hurrah. Such a stream of juice! I wish I had time to drink some.' As you go farther you'll see a crooked tree. Say, 'Hurrah, hurrah. Such a straight tree! I wish I had time to sleep in its shade.' After you pass this, you'll get to the gate of my aunt's house. One side of the door is open and one side of it is shut. Open the side that is shut and shut the side that is open. When you enter the house you'll see a donkey and a dog. There is straw in the dog's trough and there are bones in the donkey's trough. Put the straw in the donkey's trough and the bones in the dog's trough.

Bībīnagār went until she saw the pus stream. She said, "Hurrah, hurrah. Such a stream of butter! I wish I had time to taste a bit." Then she went until she saw a stream of blood. She said, "Hurrah, hurrah. Such a stream of juice. I wish I had time to drink some." Then she went until she saw a crooked tree. She said, "Hurrah, hurrah. Such a straight tree! I wish I had time to sleep in its shade." Then she went until she reached the gate of Khastakhumār's aunt's house. She opened the side of the gate that was closed and shut the side that was open. She went inside the house where she saw a donkey with bones in its trough and a dog with straw in its trough. She gave the straw to the donkey and the bones to the dog. Then she went upstairs and said, "Aunt, give me your *khamīrturūsh*, we want to make dough."

She said, "Wait here. I'll bring it." She went to call her daughter to eat Bībīnagār. Before she returned, Bībīnagār got the *khamīrturūsh* and ran. When Khastakhumār's aunt came and saw that she was escaping she said, "Dog, catch her." The dog said, "You always gave me straw and she gave me bones. I won't catch her." She said, "Donkey, catch her." The donkey said, "You always gave me bones and she gave me straw. I won't catch her." She said, "The side of the door, catch her."

10. A sourdough ball used as starter when making bread.

The door said, "You always kept me closed and she opened me. I won't catch her." She said, "Stream of blood, catch her." The stream of blood said, "You always call me 'stream of blood' and she called me 'stream of juice.' I won't catch her." She said, "Stream of pus, catch her." The stream of pus said, "You always call me 'stream of pus' and she called me 'stream of butter.' I won't catch her." She said, "Crooked tree, catch her." The crooked tree said, "You always call me 'crooked tree' and she called me 'straight tree.' I won't catch her."

Bībīnagār brought the *khamīrturūsh*. When Khastakhumār's mother saw her she said, "This plan didn't work." After some time Khastakhumār's aunt told him, "You should marry my daughter and make Bībīnagār's fingers into candles on her wedding night." They got *juwāb-i arūsi*[11] and on the *haynābanduni*[12] evening he went to Bībīnagār and said, "Tonight they are going to make your fingers into candles." She asked, "What shall I do?" He said, "Bring some cotton so that I can wrap them." She brought the cotton, and he wrapped it around her fingers. Then he prayed and left her.

They lit Bībīnagār's fingers as candles and she walked in front of the henna and the bride and bridegroom. She said, "My fingers are burning, Khastakhumār!" He said, "My heart and soul are burning, Bībīnagār!" They walked around and she said, "My fingers are burning, Khastakhumār!" And he said, "My heart and soul are burning, Bībīnagār!"

They were there till midnight and then they put henna on the hands of the bride and bridegroom who then went to bed. The following night was their wedding. Before going to bed, Khastakhumār told Bībīnagār, "Boil the water and then bring it to her in the morning. She'll pour it on her head and will die. You and I will go away."

On the wedding night, they first ate and then went to sleep each one in a corner. The bride and bridegroom went to bed in another room. Bībīnagār boiled the water and took it to the *tushnūk*.[13] At midnight, Khastakhumār called his bride. She went to the *tushnūk*, sat on the brick, and poured the boiling water on herself. Her teeth came out of her mouth and she died.

Khastakhumār and Bībīnagār took a dozen needles, a *khīk*[14] of water, a dozen *juwāldūz*,[15] some salt, some glass, and left. They went and went and went until sunrise. At sunrise the ogres awoke and opened the door. Khastakhumār's aunt said, "Look at my daughter

11. The consent of the parents to a date for their daughter's wedding.
12. A ceremony in which henna is put on the hands of the bride and bridegroom before the wedding.
13. A washroom as it appears in peasant villages in western Afghanistan.
14. A processed sheepskin in which water is carried; also called *mash-kaw*.
15. A large needle with which peasants sew bags and saddles.

laughing." When they went in they saw that she was dead. They left in pursuit of Khastakhumār and Bībīnagār. When they got close to them, Khastakhumār spread the *juwāldūz* and prayed, "God, may the whole ground grow *juwāldūz*." *Juwāldūz* grew all over the land. But they merely staggered and then ran after them.

After they passed over the *juwāldūz*, he scattered the needles. After they passed over the needles, he threw some salt. After they passed over the salt, he threw the glass and said, "God, may all the ground turn into glass." They slipped and fell and ran over the glass. After they passed over the glass he poured the water and said, "God, may this turn into a river." A river came in front of them. They were on one side of the river and Khastakhumār and Bībīnagār were on the other side of the river. Khastakhumār's aunt asked, "How did you cross the river?" They said, "We crossed!" She told Bībīnagār, "I swear in the right-hand *haykal*[16] that I won't bother you. Tell me how you crossed the river." She said, "I just crossed." Khastakhumār's aunt said, "I swear in the left-hand *haykal* that I won't harm you. Tell me how you crossed the river."

Bībīnagār said, "I put some rocks in my pants and then crossed the river." They put some rocks in their pants and jumped into the water. The water drowned them.

Khastakhumār said, "Let us wait and see whether they'll drown or come out of the water. If blood and foam come to the surface, they'll come out. If black blood comes to the surface, they'll die." They waited a few minutes and saw that blood and foam came to the surface. They started crying and begged God for protection. After a while black blood came out. They were very happy and left.

They went and went and went until they reached the herds of sheep, donkeys, cows, and camels. Khastakhumār brought his herds with him and came to the old man's place. When he saw his daughter he was very happy and remarried her to Khastakhumār, lit seven cities, hit the drum on the stick and the stick on the drum,[17] gave the Hindus raw food and the Moslems cooked food. God fulfilled their wish. May he fulfill every human being's wish.

16. Literally, idol, temple, or statue; in the tale, what ogres and witches swear by when they make a promise. Left-hand *haykal* is the ogre's real worship object, so promise is kept when sworn by it; an ogre's swearing by the right-hand *haykal* is not reliable.
17. Refers to the music of the folk actors at weddings.

The Seventy-Year-Old Corpse

Collected by Hafizullah Baghban in 1966 in Herat.

Types 437 *The Supplanted Bride* (*The Needle Prince*) and 425G *False Bride Takes Heroine's Place*; and motifs M353 "Prediction by bird that girl will have dead husband"; D765.1.2 "Disenchantment by removal of enchanting thorn"; K1911.1.4 "False bride finishes true bride's task and supplants her"; H13.2 "Recognition by overheard conversation with objects."

This tale is a combination of types 437 *The Supplanted Bride* and 425G, a subtype of Cupid and Psyche studied by the Swedish folklorist Jan-Ojvind Swahn (*The Tale of Cupid and Psyche*, Lund, 1955). So far very little is known about its history and distribution in Afghanistan, Iran, and the Arab countries. Swahn suggests that it has traveled from Italy to Turkey where it changed into a novelette and spread through the Arab Near East. However, more library and field research needs to be done before an accurate assessment of the tale in the Muslim world can be made. Type 437 is reported only sporadically in Europe and is better known in India.

Baghban collected the present version from Hayāto, a thirty-year-old housewife from Herat City. In the summer of 1967, he collected another version from Madar Safiya, a forty-five-year-old housewife and mother from Tawberyan. Accompanying her husband in his dissertation research in Herat, Marcia Baghban collected a third version from Madar Amin, the fifty-year-old wife of the Tawberyan shopkeeper, in 1973.

In each of the three versions from Herat the informant is a woman. In fact, the fieldworker has not heard men narrate this combination of types 437 and 425G with the use of the formula:

> Sang-i sabūr, to sabūr-o ma sabūr,
> Chākhū-yi dasta siyā, to az hāli dili ma āgā
>
> Patient stone, you patient and I patient,
> Black-handled knife, the witness of my heart.

What does this signify? Where it is practiced more commonly than polygamy, arranged marriage also plagues the happiness of young men and women. For their part women have spun this tale as a healthy expression of their stifled feelings in a male-dominated world. The woman has to live with patience in the face of dissatisfaction, or take her life with the black-handled knife she holds. Nevertheless, since folklore functions as an outlet for her swollen emotions, her tension rarely leads to despair and suicide.

Once upon a time there was an old man who gathered thorn bushes and sold them for a living. The old man had a daughter who was home alone while her father went to collect thorn bushes. One day when the old man was gone she got her cotton *ghonda*[1] and spinning wheel and sat outside spinning the cotton. A nightingale sat on the wall and said, "Unfortunately, you'll marry a seventy-year-old corpse."

When the old man came home in the evening she said, "Father, today a nightingale sat on the wall and said, 'Unfortunately, you'll marry a seventy-year-old corpse.' " The old man answered, "My daughter, a nightingale is a bird. He said something. You don't have to worry."

The next day the old man went to collect thorn bushes and his daughter sat outside spinning cotton. Again the nightingale came and said, "Unfortunately, you'll marry a seventy-year-old corpse." When her father came back she said, "Father, today the nightingale came and told me, 'Unfortunately, you'll marry a seventy-year-old corpse.' " He said, "My daughter, how do you know what a nightingale says? Wash your clothes and hair tomorrow. I'll take you to your aunt's house."

In the morning, the old man's daughter heated water and washed her hair and herself. She washed her clothes and baked bread. When her father came they took a few loaves of bread and a jug of water and left. They went and went and went and then she asked, "Father, where is my aunt's house?" He answered, "My daughter, we have to go a little farther." They went a little farther and she asked, "Father, I'm getting tired. Where is my aunt's house?" He answered, "We'll be there soon. If you are hungry, let us sit here and eat our bread." They sat in the desert and were eating. The bread stuck in the old man's throat. He said, "I wish there were some water!"

The old man's daughter said, "I'll go look around and fill the jug." The old man said, "No, I'll go." His daughter insisted, "I'll go." She grabbed the jug and went until she came to a fort in which there was a pool. She filled her jug and when she returned she saw that the door of the fort was shut. She said, "God, what shall I do?" She sat there crying and digging the ground. Suddenly a window opened and she went in. There were seven rooms, each one's door opening from the inside to the other. Inside the seventh room there was a seventy-year-old corpse. There were needles all over the corpse. She sat by the corpse for a while. Suddenly a caravan's bells started ringing. She climbed over the roof and shouted, "*Sārwon*,[2] how much is a concubine?" The *sārwon* answered, "One *kīsi sadtamanī*."[3] She said, "I'll give you two *kīsi sadtamanī*, give me a concubine." She gave him two *kīsi sadtamanī*, and the *sārwon* tied a concubine to a rope and she pulled her up on the fort. She

1. Cotton ball ready to be spun.
2. A camel driver or camel herder.
3. A bag containing one hundred *taman* (a unit of money).

told the concubine, "I'll go make ablution and pray. You go inside and pick the needles from the corpse. Don't pick the needle on his nose until I come."

The old man's daughter made ablution and started praying. The concubine was picking the needles from the corpse. She picked all the needles and she picked even the last needle which was on his nose. The corpse sneezed and sat down. He said, "God, who gave me my wish so that I give her her wish?" The old man's daughter heard him and was upset. The "corpse" married the concubine and made the old man's daughter a concubine.

After a few days the "corpse" was going to the city to buy clothes for his wife. He asked the old man's daughter, "What do you want me to buy for you?" She said, "I want you to buy me a patience stone and a black-handled knife." When he went to the city he bought clothes for his wife and then went to a store and said, "I want a patience stone and a black-handled knife." The storekeeper answered, "I have a patience stone, but I don't have a black-handled knife." He bought a patience stone, but wherever he went he couldn't find a black-handled knife. He was very sad when he was going home and thought, "The poor concubine asked for a patience stone and a black-handled knife, but I could only find one of them for her." A passerby asked, "Why are you so sad?" He answered, "A person asked me to buy her a patience stone and a black-handled knife. I bought the patience stone, but I couldn't find the black-handled knife." The man said, "Go to such and such a store. He has a black-handled knife."

The "corpse" went to the store and bought the black-handled knife. He came back and joined the passerby who had shown him where to buy it. As they were going the passerby asked, "Whom have you bought the patience stone and the black-handled knife for?" The "corpse" answered, "It is for such and such a person." The passerby said, "If she lives in your house, watch her closely. She'll put herself in an oven and cover the top. Then she'll tell her story from the beginning to the end. At the end she'll kill herself."

The "corpse" brought the patience stone and the black-handled knife and gave them to the old man's daughter. She put herself in an oven and covered the top. The "corpse" sat near the oven and listened. The old man's daughter started from the beginning.

"Once there was an old man who made a living by selling thorn bushes. His daughter was alone in the house when he went to gather thorn bushes. She brought her cotton *ghonda* and spinning wheel out and sat spinning the cotton. A nightingale sat on the wall and said, 'Unfortunately, you'll marry a seventy-year-old corpse.' When her father came home she told him. He said, 'My daughter, a nightingale is a bird. What does he know?' The next day her father went to collect thorn bushes, and she sat outside spinning cotton. The nightingale came and said, 'Unfortunately, you'll marry a seventy-year-old corpse.' When her father came home she told him again. He said, 'My daughter, he's a bird. What does he know? Tomorrow wash your hair and your clothes, bake some bread, and I'll take you to your aunt's house.'

"O patience stone, you patient and I patient,
O black-handled knife, be the witness of my heart!

"In the morning she heated water, washed her clothes and herself, and baked bread. They took a few loaves of bread and a jug, and her father said, 'Let me take you to your aunt's house.' They left home and went and went and went and finally she asked, 'Father, where is my aunt's house?' He said, 'We have to go a little farther.'

"O patience stone, you patient and I patient,
O black-handled knife, be the witness of my heart!

"They went a little farther, and the girl said, 'Father, where is my aunt's house?' He answered, 'My daughter, if you are hungry we'll sit here and eat our bread and rest. Then we'll go.' They sat in the desert and were eating their bread. The bread got stuck in her father's throat, and he said, 'I wish there was some water to drink.' The daughter grabbed the jug and said, 'Father, I'll go find some water.' He said, 'No, I'll go.' She said, 'I'll go' and she went.

"O patience stone, you patient and I patient,
O black-handled knife, be the witness of my heart!

"She went and went and went until she reached a fort with the door open. She went in and filled her jug, and when she returned the door was closed. She sat there and cried and dug the ground and cried and dug the ground until a window opened.

"O patience stone, you patient and I patient,
O black-handled knife, be the witness of my heart!

"She went in through the window and saw six rooms opening inside each other. In the seventh room there was a corpse covered with needles. She sat by the corpse and in a while she heard a caravan's bell. She climbed on the roof and called, 'Sārwon, how much is a concubine?' He answered, 'One kīsi sadtamanī!' She gave him two kīsi sadtamanī and bought a concubine and pulled her in the room and told her, 'Pick all the needles from this corpse's body, but don't pick the one from the tip of his nose.'

"O patience stone, you patient and I patient,
O black-handled knife, be the witness of my heart!

"The old man's daughter was praying. The concubine picked all the needles and the needle on the corpse's nose. The corpse sneezed and sat up and said, 'God, who fulfilled my wish so that I fulfill her wish?'

"O patience stone, you patient and I patient,
O black-handled knife, be the witness of my heart!

"The concubine was the first one the 'corpse' saw. He married the concubine and made me his concubine. One day he was going to the city to buy clothes for his wife. He asked me what I wanted him to buy for me. I said, 'I want a patience stone and a black-handled knife.' He went to the city and bought me a patience stone and a black-handled knife. Now I have put myself in the oven, and told my story. Shall I stab him or shall I stab myself?"

When she said this the "corpse" opened the top of the oven and took her out. He asked the concubine, "Do you want a loaf of barley bread or a *bīdāw*[4] horse?" She answered, "What am I going to do with a loaf of barley bread? I want a *bīdāw* horse to take me on the mountains and deserts." He tied her hair to a *bīdāw* horse's tail and ran him until she was torn into pieces. He covered her skull with silver and made it into a glass to drink water, and married the old man's daughter. God fulfilled their wish. May He fulfill ours too.

4. A racehorse.

Japan

The Mountain Where Old People Were Abandoned

From Keigo Seki, *Folktales of Japan* (Chicago: University of Chicago Press, 1963), pp. 183–86.

Type 981 *Wisdom of Hidden Old Man Saves Kingdom*. Kata No. 329, "The Mountain Where Old People Were Abandoned." Collected in Iida-mura, Shimoina-gun, Nagano-ken, from the mother of collector Kiyomi Suzuki.

Motif S140.1 "Abandonment of aged" appears in the eleventh-century *Konjaku Monogatori* in a tale derived from India. More than 40 variants of this motif have been found in Japan; not all have the sequel of the tests solved by the rescued elder. Dorson has a text of this legend in his *Folk Legends of Japan* (Tokyo, 1961), pp. 223–25, with references on pp. 222–23 to the powerful short novel by Shichiro Fukasawa based on this theme, first translated into English by John Bester in *Japan Quarterly* 4 (1957): 200–32, and later adapted into a Kabuki play and a motion picture. Donald Keene has included his translation of Fukasawa's novel in his recent collection of three modern Japanese short novels, *The Old Woman, the Wife, and the Archer* (New York, 1961). Keene's introduction, pp. xi–xiii, contains an excellent discussion of the central motif of the tale and its relationship to past and present Japanese life. He notes that the Japanese have undoubtedly found this story a painful one but that they have never forgotten or suppressed it. He supposes that despite the respect paid to the aged in modern Japan, memories of an ancient past still lurk in people's minds.

The tale is scattered throughout Europe. Stith Thompson, *The Folktale* (New York, 1946), pp. 266–67, remarks that it is often ascribed to King Solomon. Wolfram Eberhard *Typen chinesischer Volksmärchen* (Helsinki, 1937), pp. 115–17, lists six variants from China, and S. Thompson and W. Roberts, *Types of Indic Oral Tales* (Helsinki, 1960), p. 123, give five from India.

Long ago when people had reached the age of sixty and were unable to do anything, they were thrown into a mountain canyon. This was known as "sixty canyon abandonment."

In a certain village there was a farmer who became sixty years old. Since the lord of the country had commanded it, the time had arrived for him to be thrown into the mountain canyon. The man's son took him on his back and set off for the mountains. They continued farther and farther into the mountains. As they went along, the old man, riding on his son's back, broke off the tips of tree branches in order to mark the trail. "Father, father, what are you doing that for? Is it so you can find your way back home?" asked the son.

"No, it would be too bad if you were unable to find your way home," replied the father, "so I am marking the trail for you."

When he heard this the son realized how kindhearted his father was, and so he returned home with him. They hid the old man under the porch so that the lord would know nothing about it.

Now the lord of the country sometimes commanded his subjects to do very difficult things. One day he gathered all the farmers of the village together and said, "You must each bring me a rope woven from ashes."

All the farmers were very troubled, knowing that they could not possibly weave a rope from ashes. The young farmer whom we just mentioned went back home, called to his father under the porch, and said, "Today the lord commanded that everyone bring a rope woven from ashes. How can we do this?"

"You must weave a rope very tightly, then carefully burn it until it turns to ashes; then you can take it to the lord," said the old man.

The young farmer, happy to get this advice, did just as he was told. He made a rope of ashes and took it to the lord. None of the other farmers were able to do it, and so this farmer alone had carried out the lord's instructions. For this the lord praised him highly.

Next the lord commanded, "Everyone must bring a conch shell with a thread passed through it."

The young farmer went to his father again and asked him what he should do. "Take a conch shell and point the tip toward the light; then take a thread and stick a piece of rice on it. Give the rice to an ant and make it crawl into the mouth of the shell; in this way you can get the thread through."

The young farmer did as he was told, and so got the thread through the conch shell. He took the shell to the lord, who was much impressed. "How were you able to do such a difficult thing?" he asked.

The young farmer replied: "Actually I was supposed to throw my old father down into the mountain canyon, but I felt so sorry for him that I brought him back home and hid him under the porch. The things that you asked us to do were so difficult that I had to ask my father how to do them. I have done them as he told me, and brought them to you," and he honestly told what had happened.

When the lord heard this he was very much impressed and realized that old people are very wise and that they should be well taken care of. After that he commanded that the "sixty canyon abandonment" be stopped.

The Man Who Bought a Dream

Collected by Robert J. Adams in 1967 in Nomura village, Tsugawa-machi, Niigata-ken, from Mrs. Tsune Watanabe.

Type 1645A *Dream of Treasure Bought.* Kata No. 204, "The Man Who Bought a Dream."

The tale given here is a new recording of No. 45 in *Folktales of Japan.* The storyteller is a remarkably gifted raconteur whose life and storytelling abilities were described by Adams in his doctoral dissertation, "Social Identity of a Japanese Storyteller" (Indiana University, 1972). Mrs. Watanabe's variant of the tale is outstanding in its delineation of the psychological motivation of the tale's protagonists. Her skillful use of dialogue brings the characters to life and adds a compelling immediacy to the tale. The moralistic comments made at the end of the tale emphasize the storyteller's intense involvement in the tale as a repository of cultural and personal values.

The worldwide distribution of the tale is described as follows in the headnote to the variant originally given in *Folktales of Japan:*

"*Eighteen versions of this tale are recorded in Japanese collections. It appears as a legend about a* choja *named Sanya in Dorson's* Folk Legends of Japan (*Tokyo, 1961*), *pp. 185–86.*

This tale is similar to the legend of King Guntram that is widely known in Europe. This thirteenth-century Frankish king was supposed to have dreamed of crossing an iron bridge and finding buried treasure. As he slept, his servant observed a mouse run from the king's mouth. The servant helped the mouse cross a stream on his sword and watched it disappear into a hole, then return to the king's mouth. When the king awakened, gold was found at the place the mouse had gone.

*The tale is particularly well known in Scandinavia, where King Guntram is generally replaced by a pair of laborers or traveling companions. Reidar Christiansen has assigned the story to No. 4000 in his index of Norwegian migratory legends (*The Migratory Legends,*

Helsinki, 1958). The only known variant of the tale in the United States was recorded in Maine in the seventeenth century. This version, reported in Horace Beck, The Folklore of Maine *(Philadelphia and New York, 1957), p. 37, lacks the dream about treasure but in other respects is strikingly similar to the Japanese tradition."*

There were two friends who went to the mountains to gather dead branches for firewood. They took their lunches and went to gather wood. "Well, it's almost noon, let's sit down and eat our lunch." "All right. It's a little early, but that won't hurt, let's eat anyway."

So they sat down and ate their lunches and rested a while. "It feels so good here, let's take a little nap. We've been working hard all morning, we need a little rest, otherwise we won't last out the day." "That's right, let's take a nap." And so they both lay down for a nap.

One of them went right to sleep, but the other one just couldn't get to sleep. He twisted and turned and tossed, but he couldn't go to sleep. The other one was snoring away, it sounded like thunder, he was snoring so loud. *Gooonnn goonnn goonnn goonnn goonnn goonnn,* he was fast asleep and snoring like mad.

The other one just couldn't get to sleep. He just sat there, smoking one cigarette after another, and watching how his friend was sleeping. After a while the man who was sleeping stretched and yawned in his sleep, *uhhhhhnnnnnnnn.* Just as he stretched in his sleep, a bee came out of his nose and flew off somewhere. After the bee flew away, the man woke up. "Well, that was a nice nap. I had a good dream too."

"What sort of a dream did you have, here in the middle of the day like this?"

"I dreamed that in the garden behind the mansion of the richest man in Osaka there is a jar of gold buried under the little mountain in the garden."

"Really? What's the man's name?"

"I don't know what his name is or anything like that. All I know is that he is the richest gentleman in Osaka. It was just a dream, so I couldn't ask what his name was or anything like that. All I know is that he was a very rich man, the richest in Osaka, and that in the garden behind his mansion there is a little mountain. There is a big pine tree growing beside it. Beside the pine tree there is a *nandin* [*nandina berberidaceae,* also called sacred bamboo] bush. The jar of gold is buried under the *nandin* bush. That was the dream I had."

"What a funny dream! Listen, how about selling it to me."

"What! Are you serious? How could anyone buy a dream? What would you do with it?"

"I don't know what I'd do with it, but anyway, how about selling it to me."

"I never heard of buying a dream. What in the world do you want to buy it for?"

"I don't have anything particular in mind to do with it, I just want to buy it. Come on, please sell it to me."

"I hate to go around selling dreams. I'd feel funny taking money for something like a dream."

"That's all right. That's all right. Just sell it to me. Here, I'll give you this much money, now please sell it to me."

And so finally the man who dreamed the dream sold it because the other man kept begging so hard. And so he made some money just by having a dream and selling it. [Laughs, and all laugh.] That's the way he got some money out of it.

Then the man who had bought the dream went home and told his wife what he had done. "Wife, wife, I and the neighbor went to the mountains to gather some cedar branches for the fireplace. At noon we ate our lunch and lay down to rest. He went right to sleep, but I just lay there wide awake. I tried and tried to take a little nap, but I just couldn't drop off to sleep. No matter what I did, I was just as wide awake as ever. So I was sitting there smoking and listening to him snoring loud as thunder. Then just as he was stretching in his sleep, a bee flew out of his nose. After the bee flew out he woke up and said that he'd been dreaming, and then I bought the dream from him." Then he told his wife what the dream he'd bought was about.

"What! You bought somebody else's dream? What in the world did you do that for?"

"Well, I am going to go and find that jar of gold and dig it up. But I don't have enough money to get there. Can you help me get some money?"

"Here we don't even have enough money to live on, and you go around buying people's dreams. How can you tell whether there's anything to it or not, it's just somebody's dream. And then you think we ought to borrow money so you can go to Osaka just because of what he saw in his dream!"

"Well, I want to go and see if there is anything there. I've just got to go and see. I've just got to go and dig there and see what I can find. Please borrow some money for me."

He kept after his wife until there was nothing she could do but go to her parents' house to borrow some money. She told them what he wanted, and they said, "What a fool he must be! Buying people's dreams! How can he tell if there is anything to it or not? How does he know, maybe it's not true at all. Borrowing money and going all the way to Osaka!" [From Niigata prefecture to Osaka is a distance of approximately four hundred miles.]

"That's just what I've been telling him, but he keeps saying, 'I've got to go and see, I've got to go and see, I just can't rest until I go and see,' and so there's nothing I can do."

"Well, if there had been an accident and somebody was hurt, or if he was sick or something and you needed the money it would be different, but just to go to Osaka for the fun of it, without any idea of whether or not he's going to make any money out of the trip!"

"There's nothing I can do with him. Please, just loan me the money." And so her parents finally agreed to loan her some money, and she took it home and gave it to her husband.

"Now you remember how valuable this money is. I borrowed it from my parents, you know."

And so the man took the money and set off for Osaka. The trip took many days. This was a long time ago, you know, back in the days when they had to walk all the way. [Laughs.] He would stay overnight in the inns along the way, and then walk all day. Finally he got there.

But even after he got to Osaka, he didn't know where to go. He didn't know the man's name. It was just a dream, you know, and so all he knew was that it was the richest man in Osaka. So he walked around everywhere asking, "Where's the richest man in Osaka?" [Laughs.] "Where's the richest man in Osaka? Where's the richest man in Osaka?" He kept on asking for the richest man in Osaka until finally someone told him that he was in such and such a place. "Does that man have a little mountain in the garden behind his mansion? If that's the right man, I'll give you some money to show me where he lives."

"If that's what you are looking for it must be that house over there. That's Kiibe-san's house. I think it must be him. Why don't you go and ask over there."

And so he went to that house. "Is this Kiibe-san's house?"

"Yes, it is."

"Do you have a little mountain in your back garden?"

"Yes, we have."

"Is there a big pine tree by the mountain?"

"Yes, there is."

"Is there a *nandin* bush beside the pine tree?"

"Yes, there is."

So he knew for sure that this was the right house. "Could you please let me stay overnight here?" And so they decided to let him spend the night.

"You asked so many questions about the mountain in my back garden, is there something special about it?" said the man.

"Yes. I heard that there is a jar of gold buried under the *nandin* bush there by the mountain, and I've come to dig it up. Do you have some servants who could help me dig it up? If they help me dig it up, I'll give you part of the money that's in the jar. Please give me someone to help me. I'll give you plenty of the money."

After this they all went to bed. But the master of the house said to himself, "Who does that fellow think he is, coming here to dig up that jar of gold out of my garden. I'm not going to let him do it. I'll go out tonight and dig it up myself." And so he called some of his servants, five good strong men, and took them out to dig up the jar. The ground was dry and hard to dig, but finally they came to the lid of the jar. "That's it! That's it for sure! That's the jar of gold! Here this jar of gold has been buried all this time, and I never knew it. How come that ragged old man knew that it was here, that's what I'd like to know. Well, I'm not going to let him get away with any of this money!" Then he lifted the lid off the jar. Just as he did that, *ba jaba jaba jaba jaba jaba ja*, something flew from the jar with a noise like thunder. He looked into the jar and there was nothing there. Whatever it was that had been in the jar had flown away when he opened the lid. There wasn't a thing left, just the empty jar.

There wasn't anything the master of the house could do. He had got his servants out, and they had dug up the jar, and now it was empty. All he could do was put the lid back on and bury the jar back in the ground again. So that's what they did. They put the lid on neatly just like it was before, and then they buried it again. They planted the *nandin* bush back on top of it and pretended that nothing had happened.

The next morning the master of the house told the old man, "I was given this *nandin* bush just recently and planted it there only a few days ago. But we didn't see any jar of money when we planted it. If you want to dig it up, please go ahead. I don't think you'll need very many men to help you, two ought to be enough. It'll be easy to dig, because the tree's been planted just recently."

"Oh, really? Well then, please give me someone to help me dig." So the master gave him two servants, and they started digging. Of course it was easy to dig, after all the ground had been dug up just the night before! [Laughs.] They soon got to the lid of the jar. "This is it, that's for sure! No doubt about it!" They took out the jar and took off the lid. The jar was empty! Not a thing in it! Not even a drop of water. Just the empty jar!

The poor man was just completely shocked. "What's happened? How could I have done this? What'll I do? I sacrificed everything just so I could dig up this jar. I went hungry and without clothes. I borrowed money and went in debt. And all for nothing but an empty money jar! And here I've hired these men and I can't pay them. What'll I do?"

Then he said to the rich man, "I don't have much money left. I've spent most of what I had, but I want to pay you for your help. Please take this much and forgive me for not being able to give you more. If the jar had been full of gold I would have given you a lot of money, but the jar was empty. And I have spent most of my money on the trip here to Osaka. Please take what I have left and forgive me for troubling you." So he gave him some money to pay the servants and for his board and room.

"Now I have to go home. I don't have a cent left, but I can beg for money along the way. There's nothing else to do." And so he left the rich man's house and started for home, begging for food and a place to sleep along the way.

"Here I am walking back home and begging all the way. My wife warned me not to be so foolish as to buy somebody's dream. 'There's nothing to a dream. You don't know if it's true or not,' she said, but I had to go and buy it. And I didn't even have my own money to buy it with. I had to get my wife to borrow money from her folks. Now I'm ashamed to face her again. I think I'll jump in the river and drown myself. What shall I do? Shall I kill myself? Shall I kill myself? I'm going to jump off that high bridge and drown myself in the river. But wait! I don't want to kill myself here and never tell my wife what really happened. I'll just have to go home and tell her." And so he kept on going, begging for food and lodging all the way. After many days he finally got close to home.

"What'll I do now. I am ashamed to face my wife. I'll just have to kill myself. I'll jump in the river and kill myself." But he kept on walking toward home. "I'll kill myself now," and he went a little further. "Now I'm really going to drown myself," and he walked on a little further. He kept on like that until he got all the way home. [Laughs heartily.]

He went up to the house and his wife came out to meet him. "*To-chan* [Papa]! The other night about midnight all sorts of gold coins came flying into the house! The money came flying in so thick and fast, falling around everywhere, it sounded like thunder. The noise was just deafening, *gara gara gara gara gara gara gara gara gara*, I thought that it would knock the house down. The money just kept thundering down, gold and treasures of all kinds, until the floors were shining with gold. I've left it just lying there without picking it up until you came home to see it. It's all over the living-room, and the dining-room, and the kitchen."

He went in to look and sure enough, there was gold everywhere, glistening and shining, *pika pika pika pika pika pika*. And so that's the way it is, if a greedy person tries to dig up a jar of gold, it will turn into an empty jar. And the person who is supposed to get the money, if he doesn't get a chance to dig it up, then it will get to him some way or other. A jar of gold is only meant for one person, and not for anybody else. If it's meant for a certain person, then no matter what happens, he will get it sooner or later. And so that's the story. *Zatto mukashi sageta.*

Storyteller (laughs, then cheerily): It was lucky that he didn't drown himself, wasn't it?

Collector: It was, wasn't it.

Storyteller: He was so discouraged and ashamed to ever face his wife again, and was going to drown himself, or kill himself some way. And there was all that money waiting for him! But he had lost all hope and was sure that there was nothing to do but die. If he had killed himself he would have never even known that all that money was there for him. He was lucky that he got home without dying.

Philippines

The Adulteress Rat

Contributed by E. Arsenio Manuel. Forthcoming in *Folktales of the Philippines*.

First told in Manuvù by Ayug Ammad in 1956, then about twenty-six years old, as heard from his father; translated with the help of Saddani Pagayaw and published by E. A. Manuel as *Upland Bagobo Narratives* (University of the Philippines, 1962). A second version was recorded in 1963, which is the more complete of the two and is reproduced here. A third version was recorded in 1964 from the same ethnic group, with a tragic ending for both the adulterer and adulteress, the former jumping unknowingly into the sharpened stakes below the house and the latter committing suicide. This is a very popular tale among the Manuvù and reflective of their culture.

A play entitled *Three Rats*, in English, written by Wilfrido Guerrero, is structurally similar to the tale reproduced in this collection; this is a good case of parallelism arising from two different cultures, one non-literate and the other literate.

Suggested type 1427* *Husband Cannot Forgive Adulterer, for It is Always the Latter's Fault*. Motif U110 "Appearances deceive" and suggested motif Q241.1* "Adulterer punished: jumps into stakes prepared by husband of adulteress."

One evening the fisher-rat said, "*Inayrinan* [Wifey], just stay here in the house because I am going out to fish." Then he left and upon arriving in the river, he started to catch fish with his torch.

When the fisher-rat was halfway through, he became restless. He remembered his wife left alone in the house. He said to himself, "I am going home now; I am getting suspicious that my wife is doing something bad in the house."

Earlier when the other male rat had found out that the husband was not at home, he ran up the house to see the female rat. After some time this male rat looked out of the window and saw a light. The female rat also peeped out and saw the light coming. "Jump out," she blurted, "my husband is coming!"

The other male rat jumped out. Just then the husband came up the ladder. Upon dropping his basket of fish, he asked his wife, "What was that dropping with a thud there?"

"It must be the node of a sugar-cane that fell," the female rat explained.

The fisher-rat was curious. He asked his wife, "Why is your anus wet?"

"It is the urine of our child," the female rat explained.

The following night, the fisher-rat went out fishing again. But before leaving, he sharpened some bamboo sticks and stuck them below the house where he heard the thud the previous night.

"*Inayrinan* [Wifey], I am going to fish tonight," said the fisher-rat. "I had a poor catch last night." Then he left.

The fisher-rat had not gone very far when the other male rat was already up there in the house. Then the fisher-rat immediately returned home and called as he was reaching for the ladder, "Wifey, I am here!"

There was a commotion in the house. A moment later a shriek was heard below. It was the end of the other male rat.

The Gungutan and the Big-Bellied Man

Collected by E. Arsenio Manuel in 1956 in Salaysay village, Kallinan district, Davao City. Forthcoming in *Folktales of the Philippines*.

Suggested motifs are H1212.1.1* "Quest forced upon big-bellied man because of feigned dream"; H1212.1.2* "Forced feigned dream comes true"; G512.1.1.1* "Ogre killed by spearing"; K1833* "Disguise by using monster's headdress"; D535.2 "Transformation to horse by putting on rein"; B15.3.2.1* "Deer with a golden antler"; D58* "Big-bellied man transformed to handsome young man."

Collected from storyteller Mavilaw Imbang, then about seventy-five, a minor datu of Salaysay village. Tale published in 1961; now retranslated from original text and additional parts supplied by the same storyteller in the compiler's collection.

The Gungutan is one of the best known characters in Manuvù and Matigsalug oral traditions. In Manuvù folktales he is sometimes a cannibal. In "Tuwaang Attends a Wedding" (one of the epic songs constituting the Tuwaang epic cycle summarized in Manuel's "A Survey of Philippine Folk Epics," *Asian Folklore Studies* 22, 1963), the Gungutan has the power to transform itself into a fowl.

There was once a big-bellied man who lived alone. One day the hairy Gungutan came to him. The big-bellied man asked the vistor, "What news do you bring me?"

"I came to ask you to tell me about your dream," the Gungutan said. Big-belly replied, "But I have no dream." "That is not possible," the Gungutan said, "you must have dreamed something, last night or the other night." And the big bully of the forest threatened Big-belly. Big-belly cowered, repeating he did not have any dream. "Do not fool me," the Gungutan insisted.

"All right, I have a dream," said Big-belly, who had to fabricate one. "In my dream my spirit saw a big hog and a fishtrap full of fish."

"That is good," the Gungutan said. "Let's go and see the hog and the trap." But Big-belly said that was only a dream. "Never mind," the Gungutan said. Big-belly tried to excuse himself, saying he could not carry his body, for he was too fat. But the Gungutan forced him. Now they departed until they reached a big river. They went downstream until they reached a junction where they saw a fishtrap. "See," the Gungutan said, "your dream is true."

They examined the fishtrap and found that it was full of shrimp and eel. The Gungutan told Big-belly to carry the trap of fish. Big-belly could hardly lift the trap, but the Gungutan helped him put it on his back. Big-belly complained he could not carry the load, but the Gungutan told him to stop his plaints. Big-belly carried the fishtrap, sometimes falling on his knees and bruising himself on the stones in the riverbed as they trudged downstream.

Soon they found a big trapped hog as they went up the river bank. The Gungutan said, "Carry that hog, Big-belly." "I can't," Big-belly replied. "But that was your dream," said the Gungutan, who immediately lifted the carcass of the hog, throwing it on top of the fishtrap. Big-belly dropped down on his knees and could only mumble words as he heard the Gungutan say, "That was your dream, fool!"

They followed the course of the river up until they reached Big-belly's cottage. Then the Gungutan disappeared. As Big-belly dropped his load, he staggered on the ground. He heaved a sigh of relief, and after resting for a while he singed the hog, butchered it, chopping it into pieces. He cooked much food and had a real hearty meal.

Two days later the Gungutan came again and said, "Come with me, Big-belly." Big-belly became worried because he could hardly move, his bones aching all over. He showed his bruises and explained his condition and pleaded to be excused, but the Gungutan forced him to go with him. "Come with me," the Gungutan said, "we are going to visit some neighbors."

They departed and when they had gone some distance, they came upon a thicket. Big-belly could not see a way through the thicket, but the Gungutan told him to make the way. Big-belly could not refuse and he got squeezed between the trees. Big-belly complained, "I cannot go on farther, my belly is too heavy for me." But the Gungutan said, "Even if there is no way, get going; we are going to pass through."

Now the Gungutan seized him and threw him up the tree. Big-belly nearly fell down as he took hold of a rotten branch that snapped. Then the Gungutan ordered, "Start shouting." Big-belly could only scream to show his disgust and fear, then he shouted as told until they heard a dog barking. The barking dog came nearer and they found out that it was the dog of the Avūhan, the cannibal.

The dog looked up the tree, barking. Then they heard the Avūhan coming and calling to his dog. In a moment the Avūhan arrived. He saw Big-belly up the tree and said, "What a big male hog!" Then he hurled his spear at him. The Gungutan said, "Catch the spear." And Big-belly caught it.

The Avūhan said, "He is a brave dog, this one." Then he unsheathed his bolo and threw it at Big-belly. The Gungutan said, "Catch the bolo." And Big-belly caught it.

The Avūhan now took his knife and threw it at Big-belly, but Big-belly caught it.

After that the Avūhan took his bag and threw it at Big-belly. The Gungutan said, "Catch that bag." And he caught it.

The Avūhan took off his trousers and jacket and threw them at Big-belly. The Gungutan said, "Catch them." And he caught the trousers and jacket.

"Now," the Gungutan said, "throw back that spear at the Avūhan." Big-belly cast the spear and the Avūhan was hit. The Gungutan came down the tree and slashed the Avūhan with his blade. Big-belly now came down.

When he was down, the Gungutan said, "Carry this Avūhan and take him to his wife, Uwod Talinga. Use the headdress of this monster with a golden horn, so that when you reach the house, the bad *busaws* will not be able to recognize you because you are wearing this golden horn. If you reach the place, tell his folks to singe him because you are going back to get a female hog. If you will not do that, the monsters might kill you."

Big-belly carried the Avūhan at once and departed. Soon he arrived at the house of the Avūhan. He said, "Wifey, are you there? I caught a big hog." And the woman said, "Bring it up here." And he went up and went inside the house. He said, "Singe this hog and call your brothers-in-law because I shall go back for another hog which I left behind." Then he hurriedly left.

It did not take him a long time when he was back with the Gungutan. The Gungutan said, "Take the trousers and jacket; also the spear and the bag." "See that," the Gungutan continued, "if you did not come along with me, you wouldn't have acquired those trousers and jacket, the spear and the bag." And then they left. It did not take them much time to reach home. And the Gungutan disappeared again.

After two days had passed the Gungutan came once more. Big-belly had already heard his trumpeting from a distance and had started to cry because he was worried it was the Gungutan coming again. His bruises had not yet dried up and his belly appeared badly beaten. And it was true, the Gungutan was already there before him. "Where is the rein and bit of your horse?" he asked Big-belly. "Come with me because we are joining the datu's hunting party."

The Gungutan took the rein and put the bit onto the mouth of Big-belly. Then he rode on him. And he forced him to run. Soon they reached a wide grassland and they saw many people.

A young man saw them and said, "Why is that Gungutan coming here riding on a man for a horse? It is the strangest thing that can happen!" When the two arrived, the young man challenged the Gungutan at once: "Let us have our horses fight."

"Yes," the Gungutan said; "but I am afraid your horses will be beaten."

Five horses were unleashed. They dashed on to fight Big-belly. But Big-belly fought the five horses, who all scampered away. "Look at that," the Gungutan said, "I told you so."

They got to talking of other things. "We are here," the young man said, "to catch the deer with a golden antler as a bridewealth prize for the datu's daughter, for the datu said that whoever could catch the deer with a golden antler shall be married to his daughter."

The deer with the golden antler had run into the thick grass. So the suitors set fire to the grass to flush out the deer with a golden antler. And the deer indeed came out dismayed. The young suitors, on their horses, started to chase it. The other people watched them eagerly catch the deer with the golden antler, but the young men failed.

Now the Gungutan said, "Watch me, young men, for I shall take my turn to chase the deer, the bridewealth prize for the datu's daughter." The Gungutan leaped to Big-belly's shoulders and urged him, "Run fast, Big-belly." And the Gungutan's horse ran as fast as it could. Now the people saw the deer running around the world. It was a wonderful sight to behold Big-belly running like a swift striking lightning.

Soon the deer with the golden antler was overtaken. As soon as the deer was killed, the Gungutan disappeared. The big-bellied man now turned into a handsome young man whose forehead beamed like rays.

He carried the deer on his shoulders, directing his steps to the house of the datu. And the datu greeted him, "You have caught the deer with the golden antler; now you can marry my daughter and you will be my son-in-law."

Agkon, the Greedy Son

Contributed by E. Arsenio Manuel. Forthcoming in *Folktales of the Philippines*.

A Kalingga tale as reported by Pedro Bayangan of Lobo, Kalingga province, and included in Maria Delia Coronel's collection *Stories and Legends from Filipino Folklore* (Santo Tomas, P.I.: University of Santo Tomas Press, 1967). It suggests type 766* *A Boy Refuses to Give the Angels and God Food*: "God commands Death to take his life," for which one Lappish text is reported. Suggested motifs are Z45 "Phantom eats victim gradually, with mother's approval"; E50 "Resuscitation by magic."

There once lived at the foot of a mountain a widow, Balligokan, and her son, Agkon. Every morning the rooster would wake up Agkon by crowing: "Kook-ko-ko-oook! Agkon, come and trap me."

Agkon would answer, "Wait, I'll first look for some fibers to make up my snare."

The next day, the rooster again jumped on Agkon's window and crowed: "Oo-oo-oo-o! Agkon, come and snare me."

And Agkon said, "Wait, I'll get some strings for my snare."

On the third day, the rooster flapped his wings loudly and cried out: "O-oo-ook! Agkon, when will you come?"

Agkon jumped out of his house and said, "I'm coming!"

Agkon ran out, laid his snare with care, and after a few moments it caught a wild fat rooster, which he proudly showed to his mother.

"What a nice fat rooster, Agkon! Now we shall have some nice food," his mother said happily when she saw the rooster.

Agkon burned the feathers of the rooster, cut it into pieces, and began to cook it. When it was almost cooked he dropped the ladle. "Mother," Agkon cried, "I dropped the ladle."

"Never mind, Agkon," his mother said as she quickly went out of the house, "I'll pick it up."

As soon as his mother was down, Agkon quickly drew up the ladder. Then he asked for the ladle and after telling his mother that he would eat first and call her later, he proceeded to do so.

After a while the mother said, "Agkon, please leave the wings for me."

"But the wings are delicious, mother," Agkon said and started to eat them.

"Leave me the claws, my son," the mother pleaded.

"They are just what I want, mother," he said.

"But surely, you will leave me the neck, Agkon."

"It is just what I am eating, mother," Agkon said.

Only the head was now left. "Agkon, my son, will you not give the head to your mother?"

"But, mother," Agkon answered, "you know very well that I need to eat the brains."

When nothing was left of the rooster, Agkon put back the ladder, and the mother wearily went up the steps. She looked at the pot and found a little soup left, which she took, and mashing some rice in it, ate in tears. She decided to revenge herself on her son. She went down and said, "Agkon, I'll go and look for some ripe bananas." Her son was already sleeping after his heavy meal and did not hear her.

The mother went upstream and after walking for a long time she heard loud weeping and found a family mourning over a man who had been dead three days. She moved on until further up she found another man who had been dead five days. She was not satisfied, however, because the dead man's tongue and eyes were not yet bulging out and she continued her search. In the third village there was loud crying and lamentations because no one could go near the dead man since he was very black, swollen, and distended, with his tongue out, his eyes bulging, and blood dripping out of the pores of his body.

Balligokan offered to buy the dead man, but the relatives were already happy to have someone take care of the dead so that they gladly gave it to her free. Balligokan offered to carry the dead man and said, "Apo Ladag [Sir Dead Body], I will carry you on my back." The dead man climbed on her back and she brought him to her granary where she covered him with rice-on-the-stalk. Then going to the house she called her son and said, "There are some ripe bananas in the granary."

Agkon went down and peeped inside the granary where the *Ladag* caught him and proceeded to eat him. He shouted to his mother, "Mother," he cried, "the *Ladag* is eating my feet."

"That is for the claws of the chicken that you would not share with your mother," the mother answered.

"Mother, the *Ladag* is eating my arms."

"But you did not give me the wings either, my child," his mother said.

"Now he is eating my breast, mother."

"Neither did you share the breast of the rooster with me, my son."

"He is beginning to feed on my neck, mother."

"Well, you ate the neck of the rooster, Agkon."

"Go ahead, *Ladag*," said the mother, "eat his head."

That night, Balligokan felt lonely; there was no one to talk with. The following day, there was no one to carry fuel, no one to help her. Her loneliness was worse, and, feeling sad, she went to the granary to look for any remains of her son. She found a little blood on the floor, which she took, and going to the river began to perform some ritual. She took some water and began to bathe the blood and said, "May I bathe Agkon! May I bathe his hands!" At once his hands were formed. And as she said, "Legs, feet, arms," all were formed into a man. But the crows were there flying around crying: "*Wak, wak, maburak!*" [May it be scattered!]. As they cried so, whatever was being formed of Agkon would be disengaged. The mother cried, "Go away, crows, to the woods. The papayas there are just ripe." The crows flew away but before she could finish forming Agkon they were back again, crying.

"Go away, crows," she cried, "The bananas upstream are just ripe for eating." The crows flew away and when they returned, Agkon was completely formed. When the crows began to cry, Agkon picked up a stone and threw it at them, driving them away.

Then mother and son were reconciled and both resolved to love each other truly. And Agkon said, "Mother, from now on, we shall always eat together!"

The Seven Young Sky Women

Collected by Hazel Wrigglesworth in 1972 in north-central Cotabato, on the island of Mindanao, and translated by her.

Told by Si Juanitu, an Ilianen Manobo male storyteller about thirty-five years old. Ilianen Manobo is a Malayopolynesian language spoken in north-central Cotabato.

Type 400 *The Man on a Quest for His Lost Wife* with the Swan Maiden introduction, which is often attached. This well-known

Märchen is found all over Europe in hundreds of texts and has been carried to the New World. Familiar motifs present in this version, well adapted to the Manobo culture, are D361.1.1 "Swan maiden finds her hidden wings and resumes her form"; B451 "Helpful eagle" (eel); H1233.1.1 "Old woman (man) helps on quest"; H94 "Identification by ring"; B222 "Kingdom of birds"; B223 "Kingdom of fishes."

Widely reported throughout the Philippines, the Swan Maiden tale is told among the following ethnic groups, listed in geographic order from northern Luzon to Jolo Sulu, the mecca of Muslims, in the south: Tinguian, Amganad Ifugao, Kallahan Keley-i, Casiguran Dumagat, Mamanwa, Binukid, Ata of Davao, Dibabawon, Sindangan Subanon, Siocon Subanon, Ilianen Manobo, Livunganen Manobo, Sarangani Manobo, Maguindanao, and Tausug.

The collector has recorded two other variants in Ilianen Manobo besides the present text. All three center on a different Manobo culture hero.

This is a story about the beginnings of the first people on earth—our ancestors.

Once there was a young man whose name was Itung.[1] His hobby was making ornamental knee bands. After a long while of just staying at home weaving, he found he had nothing left to make ornamental knee bands with. "What I'd better do," said the young man, "is to go and look for some *Adsam* vine[2] because I've nothing left to weave with."

And so he got busy now and got dressed. When he finished dressing, he went and got his bolo knife and left. He walked and walked, for his journey would be a long one.

After this young man called Itung had been journeying for quite some time, he realized he was lost, for he no longer remembered which direction he had come from. "Where have I come from?" he said to himself, "I'll rest here for awhile."

And so there he is, this young man called Itung, in the middle of his journey and overcome with thirst. But where can he get water? And so he looked around now to see.

A while later he was forced to stop again when his head hit the corner post of a house. This young man looked up and what he saw was a small temporary shelter there. "Ah," said the young man, "a house here!" He went up the house ladder and who should meet him but a woman. "I got lost here looking for *Adsam* vine," he told her. "Oh," replied the woman, "it's good that you happened along for I

1. A Manobo expression of emphasis roughly equivalent to the English expression "imagine that"; it occurs frequently as a literary nickname for "young men" who are especially fond of its use in punctuating their speech.
2. A black vine used for lacing and for weaving ornamental bands.

have something to tell you." And so she told the young man what she had to say. "What I want to tell you," said the woman, "what I have to say is that when it is high noon,"[3] she went on, "there is a pool over there visited by young women, but nobody knows where they come from. There are seven young women altogether." "Very good!" said the young man, "maybe I'll be able to marry one." And then this woman said, "If you don't believe me, well, just see for yourself when noontime comes."

Immediately this young man decided to stay there. And since it was already the middle of the morning the woman said, "I think, Anù,[4] that you should go; because maybe they'll arrive soon. And these young women are very difficult. What I think you should do is take along some bananas, seven pieces, because those young women have pet monkeys. And these bananas, if you're able to get close enough, you should give to the monkeys so that they'll go away."[5]

So the young man took the bananas and left. When he arrived at the pool he immediately hid himself. After a while he heard a rumbling sound. "What's this?" said the young man. And as he watched, the young women alighted in front of him; Itung could not tell them apart they were all so beautiful. He could not distinguish one from the other for there was no difference at all in their beauty.

Now the young man went closer to where the young women were. He took off his clothes so he could bathe nearby. And as they bathed, there nearby Itung bathed also.

Finally Itung took the bananas and threw them to some of the monkeys, six of them. And then he sat watching over the clothes of the youngest maiden. Again, Itung took bananas and threw to the monkeys, but it was discouraging because this one monkey wouldn't pay any attention, and it wouldn't eat the bananas. Itung would throw the banana here to the monkey, but it would not come near him. Said the young man, "What will I do now?"

After a long while, when Itung had reached the end of his bananas, the monkey finally went away. It took the very last banana thrown to it by the young man and it left. Itung snatched the clothes of the maiden there and ran. Home he went to his house.

When he arrived there the woman met him. "Anù," she said, "hide that dress of hers and return to the pool and hide yourself again." "All right," said the young man.

Hurriedly the young man returned and wasn't long in getting there.

3. Noontime is believed to be the hour when fairies and other spirits leave their dwelling places and come to bathe in pools and springs.

4. A name that everyone except other young men call a young man.

5. It is implicitly understood by a Manobo audience that the monkeys were pets owned by the young sky women to guard their winged-dresses when visiting the earth.

He got busy and hid himself again. And although he was overly tired now, what the young women were doing was playing in the water, chasing each other around.

After this young man had watched for some time, the young women began getting ready to leave. The oldest sister got dressed now. Then the others came out of the water to dress also. What should happen next but this youngest wasn't able to get dressed because she couldn't find her dress. The young man watched as these young women helped their youngest sister look for her dress. When it wasn't found the oldest sister said, "We will have to leave you here because you are no longer able to go along. You be good now!" And at that they went up, these six young women.

And there is the young woman crying now. And here is the young man still hiding. The young man only waited for the sisters to leave and then he quickly came out. "Now, princess,"[6] he said, "what's happened that you're crying?" "Oh," wailed the young woman, "who are you? Don't you come near me!"

The young man took off his turban now and threw it to the young woman. "Wrap yourself in that, princess," he said. But it was as if this young woman didn't hear him for she just kept on crying. Then the young man wrapped the young woman in his turban and held her saying, "Princess, stop your crying." But she pushed him away. Said this young woman, "Give me back my dress if you were the one who got it. You shouldn't fool me if it was you." But the young man said, "I didn't get it; I couldn't do a thing like that," he said. "But since it is impossible for you to return home, what I'd like is for us never to be separated —as long as we're both alive."

How sad this young woman felt for she did not want to agree; however, she no longer had any way of returning home. "What I have to say," said the young woman, "is that if I ever find my dress, I will return to my place. I am being forced to accept now because I cannot return home. But even though we produce offspring like the Rudsing-banana,[7] don't think I won't leave you if I ever find my dress." Then the young man said, "Princess," he said, "now I will put my words into action for I have found someone just like myself, wherever you go I am going to marry you." The young woman answered nothing, but her crying increased. And so the young man took her now and carried her home across his shoulders.

When they arrived there at the house of the old woman, they went up the house ladder. "Oh," said the old woman, "where did you come

6. The term used for a chief's wife or daughter.
7. Newlyweds are admonished by a Manobo chief and the old men of authority to multiply as the Rudsing-banana, a variety that produces very rapidly.

from?" Said the young man, "From over there." The young man came over closer to the old woman and whispered something. The young woman glanced at them and was deeply disturbed. Then the old woman said, "Anù, I want you to go home now to your father's because I'm accustomed to living alone." For this old woman was the sister of the young man's father. So the old woman made the young man and the young woman return home to their own place.

As they were arriving at their own place, how all the people looked to see him carrying such a beautiful young woman! Everyone stopped their work. Even the young men playing sipà-ball[8] stopped to watch them as they arrived. The young man's father asked, "Who is coming that everyone is so interested in?" Said the people, "It's Anù carrying a young woman." Said the chief (young man's father), "Tear down the wall so I can see Anù." The chief looked out and it was indeed his son carrying a beautiful young woman on his shoulders. This chief could hardly contain himself now and said, "My goodness, Anù, where did you find a daughter-in-law for me who is so beautiful to look at?" But the young man said nothing. He just continued on to his room and put down the young woman. His mother came over and held the young woman on her lap. Indeed, this young woman couldn't sit down because of her sisters-in-law taking turns holding her on their laps.

And there they lived now. And during those days this aunt of the young man, the aunt who lived alone, came to visit. One time this old woman came to visit and said, "Anù, tie this bag of mine up there at the rafters of the roof because it's not to be opened. Put it up high," she said. And that is just what this young man did.

It wasn't many years when this wife of the young man gave birth. The baby was a girl. Indeed the child was the image of her mother.[9] And now the mother is busy sewing and embroidering dresses for her child.

This child grew so quickly now that it was as if its body was being blown up. When she was old enough to know what she was doing, she begged something one day from her mother. Said the child, "Mother, I want that tied up there in the rafters of the roof." But it was as if the mother hadn't heard her for she just kept on with her embroidery.

Then the child began to cry. Finally the mother glanced over, saying, "We can't get it because it's too high, and also it isn't ours; the owner of it will get angry," she said. But the child kept on begging continuously for the hanging object, and she couldn't be stopped. Then the child rolled herself on the floor with her crying. Finally the mother put her in the cloth cradle and sang a lullaby to her, but she couldn't stop the child's crying. And again the mother said, "Princess, stop your

8. A game played by kicking a small ball or other object on the heel.
9. From a Manobo figure of speech: "She looked like a leaf taken from the same betel-nut tree."

crying for we will wait for your father." And at that the child stopped her crying.

And now let us return to the child's father. This father of the child is about to arrive home from a long journey. He was still there on the steps of the house ladder when the child met him.

Said this child, "Father, get me that tied up there in the roof rafters so I can play with it." The father looked where the child was pointing and indeed it was the small bag of his aunt's. "Oh, no!" said the young man, "that's not ours." Then he held her in his lap and kissed her. But the child still kept crying for it. This young man walked the length and the width of the house trying to stop his child's crying, but the child would not be stopped.

Finally the mother said, "Get it because this child has been crying too much already." Said the young man, "Princess," he said, "it's hard for me to get what our child is begging for because we were told by Aunt not to open it." So the mother of the child kept still, but the child kept on crying and would not stop. Finally she had no voice left from her crying.

After a while this young man changed his mind and said, "You can have it, but do not open it." Instantly the child stopped crying. The young man climbed up and gave it to the child, and the child laughed to show how happy she was.

Again the child said, "Father, untie the string so I can see what's inside." "Don't," said the young man, but again the child cried worse than before. And again the mother spoke, "If what's inside is not poison, then open it. Otherwise the child will start crying again, and we'll be the ones to suffer," she said.

Slowly now the young man opened the bag. And what was inside but the dress of this child's mother. The child spread it out and threw it up over her head. How disturbed the young man became because he didn't want his wife to see the dress.

Finally the wife looked up and saw it. "Oh," she said, "I didn't know it was my dress that Princess was begging for. Now that I see it is, I will go home to my kingdom. But this child of ours, I can't take her along. You take good care of her." And Anù had nothing to say. "You have nothing to say," said the wife. "Are you feeling bad because I warned you ahead of time? If you want you can visit me," she said, "there in my place where the moon rises and the sun sets."[10] The young woman dressed herself, kissed the child, and rose up into the air.

And now the wife of Anù was completely out of sight. Anù almost fainted, for his breath was like a single strand of abaca fiber that was

10. Undoubtedly a cultural adaptation of the "east of the sun, west of the moon" motif.

almost ready to snap. Anù said, "Mother, Father, take good care of Princess here because I've made up my mind to search for my wife. If I can't find that place of hers, then I will look for a way to kill myself."

And his parents said nothing now, an indication that they were truly worried. The young man went down the house ladder and continued in the direction he was already facing. Long grass or short, the young man continued. The young man walked as fast as he could, not realizing whether it was night or day. To show that this young man was completely overcome by sleep he would just topple over; then when he awoke he would continue. His body could no longer be recognized because it was so covered with cuts.

After the young man had traveled for a long time, he met up with an old man. Said the old man, "Why are you in such a hurry, Anù? Where are you coming from?" But this young man didn't answer immediately. Finally he said, "Help me, Grandfather, because I'm looking for my wife. She told me that her place is where the moon rises and the sun sets." "Oh," said the old man, "where the moon rises and the sun sets? I don't know where that is, but we will ask the fowls here in the air." The old man whistled now, and would you believe it, all the birds came near him! Because this old man, well, he's the head one over the birds. Said the old man, "Which of you knows a place called the place where the moon rises and the sun sets?" But none of the birds knew. "Now," said the old man, "that none of the birds know, we will try the fishes of the sea." So they continued to the seashore, and the old man whistled again. This old man asked, "Which of you has heard the name of a place called the rising of the moon and the setting of the sun?" They asked each other, and at last an eel stood up. Said this eel, "If it is the rising of the moon and the setting of the sun, I know where it is. You must pass through that mountain toward the west, going downhill seven times and uphill seven times, until you come to the place."

Truly this young man thanked the eel and the old man now, and he journeyed on. He traveled on until he was about to reach the place. He looked it over and saw that there were many inhabitants indeed. Finally he asked permission to go up the house ladder at a large house that he thought was the house of the chief of the place. "Can a stranger come up?" he called.

Finally a guard of the door looked out and said, "That's what the notched log is for." So the young man went up and sat down, and indeed he was as motionless as a shield leaned against the wall. Then a man managing the betel-nut container came over and served the young man; when he had finished chewing he was asked some questions. The man that served him asked, "Where do you come from?" "Ah," said the young man, "great indeed is my purpose; and so that you'll know,

I am looking for my wife here." "Now," said the man, "since that is your purpose, sit down and I will tell the chief over there." This man went into the room of the chief and told him. The young man waited, and finally the chief came out. Without even seating himself he said, "Are you the one looking for your wife here?" "Yes, it is I, Chief," said the young man. "You can have her," said the chief, "if you can recognize her from seven sisters; then you can take her back home."

So seven young women were brought out of their room, and the young man passed his eyes over each of them, but there was indeed no difference among them. Said this young man, "Am I permitted to inspect their fingers?" "Why not?" said the chief, "do your best to recognize her because if you can't tell her on your first try, then you can't have her." And so this young man kept inspecting all the fingers now of these young women and at last he said, "This one, Chief, is my wife because I recognize this tiny mark of a needle here in the center of her smallest finger." "You can take her," said the chief, "for she is indeed your wife."

And so this couple returned home to their own house, which was located near a trail.

China

The Bridge of Ch'üan-chou

From Wolfram Eberhard, *Folktales of China* (Chicago: University of Chicago Press, 1965), pp. 103–10.

The bridge of Ch'üan-chou, which still spans the Loyang River, is one of the most famous engineering works of ancient China and is the subject of many novels, short stories, and theater plays. In the form presented here the tale is obviously a composition of numerous stories, most of which are known in the literature from the late fourteenth century on. The individual parts of this tale occur in many other areas of China in connection with other bridges.

Our text contains numerous allusions to legends and other beliefs. The ruler of heaven, theoretically the highest deity of the pantheon, is here clearly identified with the deity of the north star. The tortoise and snake are his symbolic animals, and are commonly represented in reliefs or sculptures found in temples throughout China.

The rank of professor (*chin-shih*) indicates a man who has passed the highest state examination. It is believed that this high earthly honor is also recognized by spirits and ghosts. Several texts report that there were examinations even in hell and heaven.

Hsia Te-ai, the drunkard's name, means "can go into the sea." Predictions made on the basis of an explanation of a written Chinese character were a common way of reading oracles, and many literary stories in short story collections deal with this idea.

The eight workmen were, of course, the Eight Saints or Immortals of popular belief. Lü Tung-pin is one of them. Chess playing is a suitable leisure time occupation for saints; many tales contain this motif.

The use of the foot as firewood is also a common motif in Chinese tales, usually of Buddhist character. This motif appears again in tale No. 75 of *Folktales of China*, with disastrous results. The use of one's legs as firewood is found in India under motif D2161.3.3.1 "Witch burns her child's legs for wood then covers child with sheet and child is whole," but has not been reported from any other area.

If a monk like I-po died in a truly Buddhist way—while sitting with crossed legs—his body was often wrapped in burlap and covered with lacquer, producing a statue of the monk.

It is one of the duties of the earth deity to watch hidden treasures, if these have an owner. In a number of stories, a stranger is allowed to borrow from such a treasure until the real owner has grown up; then the borrower has to return the money to the owner. K'ang Chin-lung (K'ang gold dragon), in testing Li Wu, behaves as Taoist saints often do in order to find out whether an adept is really serious.

The family names of the principal heroes of this story are the family names of a group of famous Fukienese clans. These clans still identify themselves with the bridge and the stories about it.

Motifs D1258.1 "Bridge made by magic," and H984 "Tasks performed with help of saint."

Wolfram Eberhard, *Typen chinesischer Volksmärchen* (Helsinki, 1937), nos. 101 and 102; Eberhard, *Volksmärchen aus Südost-China* (Helsinki, 1941), nos. 63 and 64. Text from Ch'üan-chou in Fukien province. Lin Lan, *Sha-lung* (Shanghai, 1931), pp. 60–67.

The Loyang bridge lies twenty miles outside the east gate of Ch'üan-chou, just on the borders of the district. It was particularly difficult to build a bridge at that spot, because it is the meeting point of the sea tides and of the river rushing down from the mountains. It is said that evil spirits live in the river, and therefore not only was it extremely difficult to lay the foundations of the bridge but the boat traffic was also very dangerous. There are innumerable tales in Fukien about this bridge, but I will only relate the best known.

When the ruler of heaven wanted to dispose of his carnal body, he considered the entrails to be the vilest part of the human frame. He drew his magic sword, split open his body, and flung his entrails into the Loyang River. But the entrails of the heavenly ruler were still subject to many influences, and they immediately turned into a tortoise and a snake spirit, which were always playing cruel tricks on men in the Loyang River.

Before the bridge was built, everyone had to cross the river by boat. In the reign of the Emperor Shen-tsung (998–1022) of the Sung Dynasty, a pregnant woman from Fu-ch'ing was once crossing the river to Ch'üan-chou; just as the boat reached the middle of the stream, the tortoise and snake spirits sent a strong wind and high waves to upset it and sink it. Suddenly a voice cried out from the sky, "Professor Ts'ai is in the boat. Spirits must behave decently with him." Scarcely had the words been spoken when the wind and the waves died down. All the passengers had heard exactly what was said, but when they asked each other's names there was no one called Ts'ai in the boat; only the pregnant woman from Fu-ch'ing belonged to the Ts'ai family. All the passengers congratulated the woman, who was quite bewildered, not knowing whether to believe or disbelieve what she had heard. "If I really give birth to a son who later becomes a professor," she said, "I will charge him to build a bridge over the Loyang."

Several months later the woman named Ts'ai really bore a son, who was named Ts'ai Hsiang. Later, about 1025, he became a professor. His mother told him her experience on the Loyang River and begged him to think of ways and means of building a bridge, in order that she might fulfill her vow. Ts'ai Hsiang was a dutiful son and immediately gave his consent.

At that time, however, there was a law against anyone's being appointed an official in his own province. Since Ts'ai Hsiang was a native of Fukien, he could not become governor of Ch'üan-chou, which is in that province. Fortunately his friend, the head eunuch, conceived a wonderful plan.

One day, when it was announced that the emperor would walk in the garden, the eunuch took some sugared water and wrote these eight characters on a banana leaf: "Ts'ai Hsiang must be appointed official in his home town." The ants immediately smelled the honey and gathered on the characters in vast numbers, to the stupefaction of the emperor, who happened to pass the banana tree and saw the ants drawn up in the form of eight characters. The head eunuch watched him reading them over and over, and quickly wrote out the decree appointing Ts'ai Hsiang to be governor of Ch'üan-chou. The emperor wanted to punish the eunuch when he handed him the decree, but the man excused himself, saying, "The emperor says nothing in jest." Ts'ai Hsiang immediately received the appointment.

On his arrival at Ch'üan-chou, he turned plans over in his head day and night, but the waves of the Loyang River beat so high that no means could be found of fixing the pillars. At length, finding that despite all his learning he was completely at a loss, he decided that the only hope was to implore the help of the gods. He wrote a letter to the dragon king and then asked which of his servants would be willing to go into the sea and deliver it for him.

It happened that one of the servants was a drunkard named Hsia Te-hai, who, mistaking the words for his own name, knelt down and said, "I am Hsia Te-hai. What commission have you for me?" The magistrate nodded his head, and replied, "You must go down into the sea. You have three days in which to deliver this letter to the dragon king. If you fail, you will receive three hundred blows." Throwing the letter to the servant, he left the hall. The poor man was in despair at his plight, but it was too late to refuse and with a heavy heart he returned home.

At first he cursed his luck and cursed Ts'ai Hsiang; but since that did not help him much, he spent all his money on buying wine, and drank and drank until he was quite tipsy. Then he stumbled along to the river, where he planned to end his troubles by jumping into the water. As he arrived at the river bank a stiff breeze sprang up. No longer having proper control of his limbs, he fell down on the beach.

The next morning, as the blood-red sun slowly rose in the east, he was wakened by the crowing of cocks. Opening his eyes, he found himself lying on the same spot by the seashore. When he took the letter out of his pocket, he saw that it was quite different from the one Ts'ai Hsiang had given him. Realizing that a miracle had taken place, he rushed back to the magistrate's residence in high spirits, and told all that had happened to him during the night.

Ts'ai Hsiang opened the letter and saw that there was only the character "vinegar" written on the sheet of paper. After a moment's thought he understood from the form of the character that the dragon king had ordered him to lay the foundations on the twenty-first day at the hour "yu," and he gave orders for all the necessary materials to be ready at that hour.

Now that the time for laying the foundations had been fixed, workmen had to be engaged. On the same day eight strange men appeared and announced that they would do all the work without payment. Ts'ai Hsiang thought that they were good socially minded workers and made no further inquiries about them, but people thought it strange that only eight workmen were engaged for this enormous work.

The twenty-first day drew near. The tides really seemed smaller in the river bed, and the workmen got everything ready. For a few days they did nothing but sit on the ground and play chess. Everyone thought this too much and urged them to work, but the eight men merely replied, "It's such a small job. Why make such a fuss about it? In any case, the hour 'yu' has not yet arrived."

Soon, however, the time came and the river dried up. Suddenly a whirlwind sprang up at the place where the eight men were playing chess. Sand and stones were blown in all directions, completely obscuring the sun and the moon, and none of the other workmen were able to open their eyes. When it became quiet again, everyone saw that the stone foundations were safely laid. There was also no trace of the eight workmen who had been playing chess. It was obvious that they were the Eight Immortals who had turned into men to help build the bridge.

Although the foundations had been successfully laid by the immortals, the construction of the stonework and balustrading still remained to be done, and many workmen were engaged to complete the great work quickly.

At that time a monk named I-po, who was one of the fifteen people on Ts'ai Hsiang's council for building the bridge, gave him the greatest assistance. Most of the plans and suggestions for laying out and strengthening the construction originated with him, and with the help of this Buddhist monk the design was unusually beautiful.

I-po had one other faculty that caused the people the greatest astonishment. The workmen at the bridge were so numerous that sometimes there was not sufficient wood for cooking the food. When this happened, I-po stuck his foot in the stove and the flames shot up and cooked the food in a few minutes.

When the bridge was finished, he changed into an immortal and flew up to heaven. To this day there is a temple in his honor north of the city, where he is worshiped under the name of the monk I-po. The statue is said to be made out of his body, and for this reason the temple is called the temple of the genuine immortal.

Although Ts'ai Hsiang expended his whole personal fortune as well as the donations of the charitable, he found that funds were still not sufficient for the completion of the bridge. Then the goddess Kuan Yin turned herself into a beautiful woman, got into a boat, and sailed up the Loyang River, where she allowed men to throw pieces of money at her. The man who hit her would become her husband, but whoever failed should have their money used for building the bridge. There were many rich young men who thought her so beautiful that money rained onto the ship as thick as snowflakes, but not one single piece touched her. At this moment Lü Tung-pin flew by on a cloud and saw Kuan Yin. He thought he would play a trick on her, and by the help of his magic he caused a piece thrown by a small fruit seller to touch her dress. The little man was overjoyed at winning such a beautiful wife, but suddenly the ship and the woman vanished, to the despair of the little man, who jumped into the river and was drowned.

The money problem now being solved, and the leg of the monk I-po providing sufficient firewood, the workmen were able to return to work. But there were so many people that, although there was enough rice to feed them, there was a scarcity of fish, vegetables, and meat. Kuan Yin heard about this and, through her magic arts, turned the man who had hit her but never received her into thousands of little fishes to serve as the daily fare of the workmen. To this day there is a kind of long, thin white fish in the Loyang River which the people call silver fish.

When the bridge was finished, everyone praised Ts'ai Hsiang; but when the tides were high, the balustrades were still under water and people had to wade over.

Here is a tale about Li Wu, who later rebuilt the bridge of Ch'uanchou.

About seven hundred years after the death of Ts'ai Hsiang, in the reign of the Emperor Ch'ien-lung (1736–1796), there was a man in the district of Ch'in-chiang of the Li family, who was called Li Wu (fifth) because he was the fifth son.

In his youth he was a ne'er-do-well, always buying things and not paying for them, which made shopkeepers more afraid of him than of a tiger. But there was one butcher who not only made no objection to his debts but even encouraged him to buy more goods. When Li wanted to buy a piece of meat, he only needed to write a receipt and the butcher gave the meat to him at once. Li Wu the lazybones was naturally content with this arrangement, but after it had gone on for some time he began to wonder what the reason was.

One day he again signed a receipt for some meat, but instead of going away he hid himself and watched. The butcher took the receipt and went slowly up to the top of a small hill. There he brushed aside the grass by the temple to the earth deity and thrust the receipt into a grave, at the same time taking out a piece of silver. Then he smoothed down the grass, and went slowly and contentedly down the hill. Li Wu ran to the place and nearly jumped for joy; the grave was filled with pots of silver, one of which was only half full, the other half containing the receipts that Li Wu had given the butcher in course of time.

As he was standing there, a voice called from the sky, "This money belongs to Li Wu. Today you have come, and I, humble spirit, can give up my post." Li Wu understood at once, and carried all the silver back home.

The butcher had discovered this treasure one day when he was passing the temple of the earth deity, whom he had heard saying to his wife, "The silver under the stone belongs to Li Wu, who has still not come for it. I shall have to guard it till my death." When the butcher heard this, he looked about and at length discovered some huge pots, which, however, were only filled with pure water. He knew that the money did not belong to him, but he proposed to make use of it. He used the receipts of Li Wu to produce money from under the stone, because exactly the same amount appeared in the pot as the receipt was made out for.

Now that Li Wu had become a rich man, I do not need to tell you that he opened shops, built houses, and kept a host of male and female slaves. His chief joy was in entertaining guests, and although he may never have had eight thousand guests, like a famous man of old, at least he had a round hundred.

One day, a strange man called K'ang Chin-lung arrived from distant parts. He claimed to be able to discover buried treasures. Perhaps he was also a fabulously wealthy man, but on this occasion he came to test the habits and character of Li Wu. Li Wu was, however, a good judge of character and immediately invited K'ang to be his guest, treating him better than anyone else. He was given basins of gold to wash his face in. Although each time that he washed he threw the golden basin into the lotus pond, Li Wu never uttered a bitter or unfriendly word. After K'ang had been there several months, he disappeared one day without saying good-bye.

Li Wu, it happened, had once insulted some rogue living in the neighborhood. To get his revenge this man accused him of being a bandit, saying that formerly he had been a penniless vagabond, until one day he had become very wealthy. Now his house was always full of guests, and he was obviously planning a revolt. Li Wu's fortune and possessions were confiscated, and he was thrust into a wooden cage and sent to Peking to be tried.

When he passed over the Loyang River in the prison cart, he was soaked through by the high tide that was breaking over the balustrading. He said to the guardians with a sigh, "If I escape with my life, I will raise the Loyang bridge three feet." A stone dealer and a rope dealer that were passing laughed when they heard Li Wu's oath, and they said to him, "You will never escape! But if you return and raise the bridge three feet, we will give you the stone and the ropes for nothing." They had heard of the accusation, and never thought that Li Wu would return alive.

After they had traveled for a long, long way, they arrived at Shantung province, where on all sides they saw fields with stone notices: "Field of Li Wu." They made inquiries, and discovered that they had been bought by K'ang Chin-lung in the name of Li Wu.

When he arrived in Peking, his guilt could not be proved. K'ang Chin-lung made a golden snail for him; the shell was made of gold with a living snail inside. Li Wu presented it to the empress, who was so pleased that she harassed the emperor until Li Wu was declared innocent and sent home.

There he dug up all the golden basins out of the lotus pond, looked after the fields that K'ang had bought for him everywhere, and soon became one of the richest of men.

Then, in order to fulfill his oath, he engaged workmen and raised the Loyang bridge three feet higher. The fortunes of the two traders who had opened their mouths too wide were confiscated for the construction.

Chu the Rogue

From Wolfram Eberhard, *Folktales of China* (Chicago: University of Chicago Press, 1965), pp. 192–94.

This story has not yet been found in texts dated before 1800, but its main episode—the account of the man who defies death—can be found in earlier sources. Usually the hero in such stories is P'eng-tsu, a sort of Chinese Methuselah. The satirical beginning of our text is not unique; religious folktales are often told in a slightly mocking tone.

A P'u-sa (bodhisattva) is in Chinese folk religion a Buddhist deity. Jih-kuang (sunshine) *and* Yüeh-kuang (moonlight) are well-known figures of Buddhist religion. They have counterparts in Indian Buddhism, but in China, where they are known since at least the fourth century A.D., they are also connected with popular Taoism. Yüeh-kuang is in early folk belief a messianic figure, whose reappearance on earth was predicted by apocryphal texts.

Yü huang-ti is in folk belief the emperor of all deities, both Buddhist and non-Buddhist. This deity is more recent than the two bodhisattvas; it has become prominent only since the eleventh century.

The Wen-shen (plague deities) are very numerous, and are usually represented as triads in folk temples. Their cult is strongest in coastal central and south China. On the island of Taiwan, of four thousand temples studied, eight hundred were devoted to these deities.

The hells in folk religion are highly organized and bureaucratized institutions. Normally there are ten hells with up to one hundred thirty-five subhells. Yen-lo-wang (King Yama) resides in the fifth hell, and not in the first or judgment hell. The king of hell has many servants; one of them, Huo-wu-ch'ang (life is not eternal), has to catch the soul of the condemned person and bring the soul down to hell. Huo-wu-ch'ang can adopt different shapes; sometimes he is a one-legged creature. Belief in one-legged beings is more typical of southern than of northern China.

Niu-t'ou (Oxhead) and Ma-mien (Horseface) are two policemen in hell, standing by the main judge. Popular prints depict them with animal heads on human bodies. A raksha is another type of employee in hell.

One of the most famous punishments in hell is the caldron of oil; the ice hell too is well known. The Yin-yang River, usually called the Nai-ho River, separates this world from the netherworld. A bridge as wide as a hair goes over it, and this is the reason why Chu prefers to ride on a carp, which is a fish of good luck.

Motifs D831 "Magic object acquired by trick exchange," and B184.1.1 "Horse (mule) with magic speed."

Chu, the good-for-nothing, was a regular rascal, prepared to play pranks on all and sundry. One day the sun was blazing in the sky, and he called out, "Sunshine P'usa, I never sent for you. How dare you come uninvited into my room! I will complain to Yü huang-ti." The sunshine P'usa was very frightened by this threat, and said, "Please don't complain. There is a pot of silver in front of your house—you can take that." When Chu really found a pot of silver, he no longer shouted accusations at the sun.

The next night the moon was shining, and he said to it, "Moonlight P'usa, I never sent for you. How dare you enter my house without permission! I will complain to Yü huang-ti." "Please don't do that," said the moonlight P'usa in a terrible fright. "Take the pot of gold behind your house and say no more about it." After he went and dug up the pot of gold, Chu the Rogue kept silent.

One day he went into the temple of the plague deities. "You are jumbled together in threes and fours," he said to them. "You are certainly bad men. I will complain to Yü huang-ti." But the plague deities were not so meek as the sun and moon gods. When they heard Chu's disrespectful words, they complained to Yen-lo-wang, the king of hell.

Yen-lo-wang happened to be in the judgment hall at this moment, and he sent the bee spirit up to earth to find this wicked man. But Chu was very clever, and pasted paper over all the holes in the doors, walls, and windows. He left only one small hole, which he covered with a pig's bladder. Therefore, when the bee spirit arrived, it searched in vain for some opening until it came upon the small hole. "I've been trapped!" it cried, as it found itself inside the bladder. Chu chortled with glee.

When Yen-lo-wang realized that the bee spirit had been gone for several days without returning, he ordered the one-legged spirit to go up to earth and catch Chu. Unfortunately, Chu also knew about this, and filled his house with prickly things and sat down in the middle of the thorns. The one-legged spirit found Chu sitting in his house doing nothing, and dashed in. The thorns stuck in the spirit's foot and, being unable to run away, he was taken prisoner by Chu.

Yen-lo-wang soon noticed that the one-legged spirit also failed to return and, mounting his thousand-league horse, he went together with Oxhead and Horseface to the house of Chu. Chu knew of his coming in advance, and gave his wife exact orders about what to do. With a smile on her face she went to greet Yen-lo-wang and invited him to dinner.

After the meal Chu took an old water buffalo out of the stable. When he mounted the animal to ride down to the underworld, as he had arranged with Yen-lo-wang, his wife hung two glowing arrows on the animal's back, so that the buffalo, maddened by the sudden pain, rushed away so fast that Yen-lo-wang's thousand-league horse could not keep up with it.

Yen-lo-wang called out to Chu to stop, and then asked him, "What kind of buffalo is that? I never knew that they could run so fast." "It is a thousand-league buffalo," answered Chu without turning a hair. Yen-lo-wang was very surprised, and begged Chu to allow him to try it. Chu agreed, but warned him, "My buffalo knows only its master. It only runs fast with me." "Is there nothing to be done to make it think I am you?" asked Yen-lo-wang. "Perhaps it would be deceived if you put on my clothes," answered Chu. He gave his clothes to Yen-lo-wang, who put them on and got on the water buffalo, which refused to move a step. Chu, however, was seated on the thousand-league horse and dressed in Yen-lo-wang's clothes.

He gave the horse a blow and soon arrived in hell, where he placed himself on to the throne, and said to the rakshasas and other small servant ghosts, "Chu the Rogue is following me on a water buffalo. Beat him the moment he arrives."

The spirits did not know that the man on the water buffalo was the king of hell. They did not ask his name, but pulled him off his mount and thrashed him, until Oxhead and Horseface arrived and explained what had happened. Mad with rage, the king of hell climbed onto his throne and ordered the little spirits to heat the caldron of oil for Chu to be boiled in.

When the spirits brought the oil, Chu asked them, "Do you want to become rich?" When they all asked him how it could be managed, he continued, "You see, Yen-lo-wang is a stupid man. You need only a few pints of oil to boil one man. I suggest that you leave enough oil to roast me and then sell the rest. Won't you become rich then?"

The little spirits were very pleased at this idea, and sold the spare oil at once. Just at this moment the order came to boil Chu. Anxious to show their zeal, the spirits cast him into the caldron. But he did not cry out, because he held himself up on one side with his head and on the other with his feet; although Yen-lo-wang went on stoking the fire, he could not boil him to death. In despair he ordered the spirits to drag him to the Yin-Yang River and leave him there to freeze to death.

On the bank Chu called out as loud as he could for someone to ferry him across. There was a carp in the river, who was so sorry for Chu that he offered to carry him to the upper world himself. Chu looked at the carp, and thought, "What a fine carp! I must catch it and sell it for wine." He called out, "Brother carp, please tell me how I can cross over." "It's very simple," answered the carp. "You get on to my back, and I will carry you across." "But your back is so slippery," said the rascal. "I am afraid of sliding off. I don't think I dare go, unless you agree to a suggestion of mine. I shall tie a rope round your body and hold one end myself. Then I won't drown if I fall in."

The carp allowed itself to be bound, and Chu rode safely over the river with the rope in one hand. But when he arrived in the upper world, he dragged off the poor carp and sold it to buy wine.

Burma

The Rawang

Far up on the Tibetan border of northernmost Burma lies Putao district of Kachinland. Here live the Lisu, Rawang, and Kachin in the mountains and valleys facing peaks of everlasting snow. The Burmese city of Putao is some seven hundred fifty miles north of Rangoon. This area is extremely isolated even today, and the people continue to live in their age-old way, each tribe following its own customs and speaking its own language. Rawang is just one of hundreds of Tibeto-Burman languages spoken in Asia. The Rawang people are the last of the Tibeto-Burman migration into Burma. There are Rawang living in Tibet and China as well. The Rawang are mostly animists but in the 1950s and 1960s, due to the missionary efforts of persons such as the collector, some have become Christian. None are Buddhists.

The Rawang tales presented here represent the highly popular cycles of the trickster and his foolish sidekick and the poor orphan who succeeds in life. Mvkang Vya, or Liar Mvkang, is the trickster, and Mvsu Dal, or Foolish Mvsu, is the dupe. While the Rawang trickster reveals the same character portrayed in other Asian groups by the hare or the mouse-deer, among this people he is talked about as a man. In Rawang mythology he is half-man, half-spirit, and his lying and trouble-making brought on the flood, as in the case of the North American Indian trickster. The tiger is a dupe as well as Foolish Mvsu.

All the tales presented here were recorded in Kachinland by the writer, Suzan Lapai, between 1958 and 1964. Even young children tell a tale well, and I first heard many of the narratives from them. Adults did not believe at first that I was interested in these stories until I began writing them down.

I collected Rawang folktales in many ways. Sometimes when I took medicine to a sick person, as we talked of sickness and different customs about disease, I could get a tale. Nanghø Pong told me many stories when he was recovering from a gunshot wound.

Nanghø Pong came from a family of four orphans. Pong, which means first son, was the oldest and somehow managed to keep the children together. They had their own little house, and all the kids helped in the fields and in housework. The villagers and relatives helped them, of course, but they were independent. Each one learned to read and write, though only Dø (second son) got a chance to go to school. They endured their hard life but tragedy almost overcame them. Vchang (third daughter) was a beautiful teenager when she became ill. I gave her vitamins and malaria medicine but nothing helped. When a doctor came to Putao, I took him to her house, but he said that she was dying of anemia and that he could do nothing.

Pong was later crippled by his hunting accident and Dø was accused of killing a Burmese soldier and was jailed for awhile. Vnin (second daughter) married, but was never in good health and lost several babies. She is a good weaver and is a leader among the women. Pong and Dø were born storytellers and taught me much Rawang folklore.

Another informant, Yintang Miter, was from the eastern border area and his family was aligned with the Maran clan of the Kachin. A sensitive young man, he worried about new ways displacing the old Rawang customs. I encouraged him to collect Rawang traditions, and he has become an active folklore collector respected by the villagers. He is one of the few Rawang to hold a degree from an American college.

Perhaps my most interesting informants were the shamans. Ngvtzu Møn, already elderly when we met him, proved a living encyclopedia of Rawang tradition. When we finally got him to record for us, he chanted and talked for forty-eight hours with hardly a break. Sangdong Dø and Bangu Nøn also were shamans, and it was interesting to hear them compare the Rawang folklore as each spoke a different dialect. Though they were separated by high mountains and deep valleys, their traditions were strikingly uniform.

In narrative style the Rawang seem very conservative and always want to "tell it right." There are variations, of course, but if a story varies too much, the teller will be asked, "*Where* did you hear it that way?"

The myths have to be told almost word-perfect and no deviation is allowed. If an informant forgets or mixes up the sequence, someone will always correct him. The myths take us back to the original creation and down to the flood, when all of man was to have been destroyed. From there two orphans are saved up on a high peak and from these two the world was repopulated. This creation myth would only be chanted at a great feast, using *mvngrung ka*, or ballad speech. This feast would continue for several days and a big *mithun*, a type of cow, would be sacrificed. It is assumed that the spirits will all be listening and so the chanter is under great strain not to make any mistake. If he does, he will surely not be invited to chant the next year. It is here, in the *mvngrung* chants and in the *dumsha ka*, diviner's chants, that we get the historical records of the Rawang migration.

Note: For a participant account of the missionary experience among the Lisu and Rawang hill tribes around Putao in the 1960s, written by the then brother-in-law of the collector, see Eugene Morse, *Home to Hidden Valley* (Reader's Digest Press, 1974).

Liar Mvkang and the Rich Villagers

Collected by Suzan Lapai in 1961 in Tarrawanggong village. Told by Nanghø Dø.

Present-day Rawang society is classless in the sense that there is no industry and no landlords and no group is downtrodden by another.

The land is there for the taking, and anyone can homestead the virgin jungle. Prosperity is possible for persons who work hard and have good luck. Sickness can strike anyone and even the best fields are of no use if the family has malaria at harvest time.

The term for the rich villagers of this tale is *mvgamri*, and it seems to point to a feudalistic system sometime in the past. The ordinary elders of a village who help solve problems by customary law are called *shaqreri* and are greatly respected. The *mvgamri*, however, are fair game for our trickster, and though pity might be felt for poor Foolish Mvsu, in his encounters with Liar Mvkang, everyone is glad when the *mvgamri* get their comeuppance.

Liar Mvkang is somewhat of a playboy and ladies' man and sometimes tricks people out of their wives as well as their wealth.

Motifs: K714.4 "Victim persuaded into entering basket" (reported from China); K842.1 "Dupe persuaded to take prisoner's place suspended in air" (reported from India); K1051.1 "Dupe dives for alleged jewels" (reported from India). These motifs appear as episode V of type 1535 *The Rich and the Poor Peasant*, a very popular European tale also heavily collected in India.

Long, long ago some rich old elders made plans to kill Liar Mvkang and so they suspended him up over a stream. When he had been suspended (in a basket) for a while, there came along the path by the bank of the stream a hungry old man who was driving cattle. Seeing him, the old man spoke up to Liar Mvkang and said, "Oh, Liar Mvkang, why are you suspending yourself up there like that?" Then Liar Mvkang, answering, said, "Oh, old man, I also, like you, have sore and running eyes, and hoping for my eyes to get well by it I am suspending myself like this."

Then the old man answered and said, "Oh, Liar Mvkang, in that case, let me be suspended up there too; my eyes also are very sore." "Okay, then, I will," said Liar Mvkang. "Well, then, you let me down gently over on the shore, and then I will help suspend you," he said.

The old man then slowly let Liar Mvkang down on to the shore, and let him loose (out of the basket). Whereupon Liar Mvkang put the old man in his place (in the basket) and suspended him instead (back over the stream). Then he started driving on all the (man's) cattle and returned to his village. When he got back to the village, the rich old elders spoke to him, saying, "Oh Liar Mvkang, from where—how . . . what . . . from where did you get all these valuables?" Then Liar Mvkang spoke back to the old people, saying, "There is a great lot of treasure down in the waterhole, and I got these from down under the water in the big pool."

Then all the rich men agreed to go back with him (to get the underwater riches). Now Liar Mvkang told those whom he liked to carry the open-weave baskets, and those whom he didn't like he had carry the tight-weave baskets. When they all got down to the stream, Liar Mvkang, wearing only a wood-bark raincape, stopped and said to them all, "Now when I shout out 'Let's all dive in,' from the top of the big rock, all of you together jump in, and deep down in the bottom of the pool there will be treasures, brass gongs, and things awaiting us, and we can carry away as much as we want."

Having said this to the rich old villagers, Liar Mvkang got a man-sized log and stopped a bit upstream from the rest. Then he pushed the log off into the water *ptchhah* (splash), and yelled, "Come on, there's the place, let's everyone jump in."

Then all the rich old villagers, taking it to be the truth, jumped down into the big pool, where those whom he favored and had carried open-weave *dvhong* baskets were able to swim (back to shore), but because those he disliked had carried close-weave *vpe* baskets, when the water filled them up it pulled them down and so they all drowned in the water.

That is all.

Liar Mvkang Sells Ashes

Collected by Suzan Lapai in 1958 in Dukdang village. Informant: Mvjang Søn.

The name of this informant tells us that he is the fourth son (Vsøn) of the *mvjang* clan. He came from the Krangku area of what is known as the Triangle on maps of Burma, where it is marked "Unadministered Territory." After his father died, his mother migrated with fourth son and his two sisters into the Putao Plain where they settled in Dukdang village.

Vsøn was a schoolboy when I first met him, and I was surprised at how many folktales he knew. Later, as a teen-ager, he developed into a skilled hunter. Once he was attacked by a wounded tiger, and I took care of him. There were deep claw wounds under his armpit and in one wound on his back I had to insert a four-inch drain. The tiger died just as it closed its jaws on Vsøn's neck, and I could see the tooth impressions, though it did not break the skin.

The Rawang eat the meat of the tiger (tiger meat tastes much like cured Kentucky ham) and use the bones for medicine. The skin and the teeth are kept as trophies, but the skull is buried outside the village. The tiger's cubs sat on top of the grave and howled at night, and it was pretty scary when I had to go to Vsøn's house every four hours each night to give him his shot of penicillin.

This tale of the Liar Mvkang cycle occurs as episode IV of type 1535 *The Rich and the Poor Peasant.* Since the type is well reported in both India and Europe, the inference seems clear that the *Märchen*, or its parts, have diffused among these remote hill tribes.

Motif K941.3 "Enemies burn their houses to be able to sell ashes" (reported from central India).

One day, long ago, the rich old elders wanted to drive out the Liar Mvkang, so they burned down his house. Then Liar Mvkang spoke up to them, saying, "Though you've burned down my house, at least please keep and save for me the ashes thereof." The elders granted this wish, and having burned the house down saved the ashes for Liar Mvkang.

Then Liar Mvkang took up a load of the ashes, and carrying also about three *viss* of salt (wrapped up in individual packages with leaves), went on his way. When he had traveled and almost reached a distant village, he stopped and mixed his salt in with the ashes. Then he left his load standing propped up near the village, and entered the village.

In the village Liar Mvkang spoke to the villagers, saying, "Oh you villagers, I was carrying along a load of salt, and got so tired I couldn't carry it any farther, so left it down the trail close to the village. So please take care to pen up your cattle, else they will certainly lick up my load of salt." The villagers answered and said, "That's all right, our cattle aren't too unruly. If you have taken reasonable precautions to protect your load of salt nothing will happen." Then Liar Mvkang said, "Well, that's all right then. I took care of my load; just so you take care of your cattle. But as your guest I hold you responsible for my load of salt."

The night passed and in the morning when he went to see his load, sure enough the cattle had turned over his load, and scattered the salt and ashes, licking up all the salt. Then Liar Mvkang spoke to the villagers saying, "Hurry and pay up. My whole load of salt has been licked up by your cattle, so hurry and repay me." The elders of the village then answered him and said, "You must be able to tell which cows are responsible. You make sure which one is responsible and take the cow as replacement (for your salt.)" Since the salt was mixed with ashes, of course, every cow had a black ring around its mouth.

Then Liar Mvkang made out that every cow in the village was responsible, and drove off all the cows in the village. When he got back to his own village he met those who had burned his house, who asked him in astonishment, "Oh, Liar Mvkang, with what treasures did you purchase these cattle?" Then Liar Mvkang said, "O elders, there's a land where ashes are very valuable, and I purchased all these cattle with the ashes from my house which you burned down for me." Then the rich old elders, thinking that what he said was the truth, all burned down their own houses (in order to get ashes).

Then the elders each took the ashes from his house and went away, hoping to sell them to other villages, asking everywhere, "Oh, you villagers, doesn't your village want to buy ashes?" But in each village they answered, "We already have plenty of ashes, but nothing can be done with it—it is just useless." So the rich old elders did not get to sell their ashes, but only burned down their own houses instead.

Liar Mvkang and the Water Snake

Collected by Suzan Lapai in 1963 in Dukdang village. Told by Nanghø Pong.

In this tale the big water snake called *børin* is a simple dupe, a foil for another of Liar Mvkang's tricks, but his role in Rawang animism and mythology is considerable.

The *børin* is a dreaded water deity that can be compared to the Chinese *lung*, the Tibetan *klu*, and the Indian and Burmese *naga*. The *børin* is supposed to be a real snake as well as a spirit, and people vow that they have had actual encounters with one. To even see one is so frightening that it results in "soul loss," and this is one of the few occasions when a Rawang would call on the name of God, Gvray Gasang.

In common with other Asian beliefs concerning the *naga*, the *børin* is said to have a jewel in its head, and the owner of such a stone is considered to possess the ultimate in lucky fetishes.

Motifs: A1023 "Escape from deluge on tree" (reported only from India and from North American Indians); A2413.5 "Stripes of alligator" (big snake) (reported from India); K607.2 "Crocodile (snake) masking as a log obeys suggestion that he move upstream"; K561.1 "Animal captor persuaded to talk and release victim from his mouth" (cf. type 6); (Thompson-Roberts, *Types of Indic Oral Tales* report three variants with monkey-lion, iguana-jackal, and quail-fox).

Once upon a time Liar Mvkang went up into a grass field to get some firewood. When he arrived there he began preparing rattan strips to tie up his load of wood. The big water snake came up to him and asked, "Rich man, what are you making rattan strips for?" Liar Mvkang said, "Haven't you heard, don't you know that the earth is going to be flooded? I plan to make myself a basket and suspend myself from a tree to escape the flood. Have you planned how you are going to escape?"

Then the *børin* (water snake) said, "Ah, brother, look. You have a knife and you know how to make rattan strips. I don't know how to do anything, so could you tie me to the tree first?" Liar Mvkang made some long strips and agreed to tie the snake to a tree growing in the grass field. Then he wrapped the snake around the tree and began to tie him up. When he had tied the snake down pretty good, he asked him to try moving. Wherever the snake could move slightly, Liar Mvkang tightened the coils of rattan. Finally he had tied the snake down so tightly that he couldn't move.

When he finished, Liar Mvkang said that he would go down the hill and make some rattan strips for himself. From the bottom of the field, Liar Mvkang began lighting fire to the grass. As the wind started driving the fire up the hill, the *børin* said, "Hey, what's all that noise?" He didn't know what fire was. But then suddenly as the fire got closer, the heat was unbearable. The air was filled with billowing smoke, and the snake squirmed under the tight rattan coils. The heat seemed to suck the air out of his lungs. He fought the tight bonds with every bit of strength he had. The fire now surrounded him completely and his skin was getting charred to a black crisp. Even the tree was on fire. In desperation the *børin* strained with all his might and because the strips were half burned through by now, the coils snapped and the snake was free. Once rid of his bonds, he immediately slid down the hill into the river. As he hit the water he sizzled and steam filled the air.

It was from that day on that the big water *børin* has had stripes. When he had cooled off, he began looking for Liar Mvkang and planning how he might catch him. One day the snake came across Liar Mvkang in the river fishing. The snake straightened himself out and tried floating like a log. As he came closer, Liar Mvkang noticed him and immediately realized that the snake was trying to look like a log. He said, "If you are a log, float upstream and if you are a snake, float downstream." When the snake heard this he decided to float upstream to fool Liar Mvkang. When Liar Mvkang saw the log float upstream, he laughed and laughed, saying, "Since when did a log ever float upstream? You just gave yourself away, you dumb snake!" And he ran away from the river.

But the snake kept looking for opportunities to catch Liar Mvkang. One day he found his fish traps and decided to wait for Liar Mvkang there. He hid himself in the water and kept his mouth open by the fish trap. When Liar Mvkang came to check the trap, he stepped into the snake's mouth.

This made the snake so thrilled that he was making guttural sounds like, "Mmm mmm mmm." Liar Mvkang was barely able to suppress his agony but he managed to say, "Wow! When I was burning you on the tree, I sang out, 'Whee hoo hoo' with delight, but now that you have caught me you only say 'Mmm mmm mmm.' Can't you even express your joy properly?"

So the snake opened his mouth wide and yelled, "Whee hoo hoo!" As soon as the snake let go he pulled his foot out and ran for his life. From that day on the *børin* has always been after human beings.

That is all.

The Orphan and His Grandmother

Collected by Suzan Lapai in 1963 in Dukdang village. Told by Nanghø Pong.

This tale is typical of the highly popular orphan series. An orphan is never turned out to fend for himself. There is always some relative who will take him in, and Rawang are horrified to hear of "orphans' homes" in other parts of the world. Even so, the plight of an orphan is greatly pitied, and it is acknowledged that his lot is a hard one. An adult will say "Now I am an orphan" in self-pity when his parents die. To call someone a *dvrvt* (orphan) is an insult. Often one hears a naughty child or a noisy group of youngsters scoldingly called *dvrvt*.

There are no inns outside the cities in Burma, and in this tale we see the common hospitality that is offered to travelers in the mountains. Any stranger is welcomed as a guest for up to three days. If he stays longer than that, then he is expected to help in the chores such as carrying water and finding firewood. If his stay is extended for some reason, then he will go with the family to work in the fields. No money is ever asked.

In the tales, the orphan may face difficult ordeals, but he is always successful in the end.

Motifs: L111.4.1 "Orphan hero lives with grandmother" (reported for the North American Indian); K2150 "Innocent made to appear guilty"; K251.1 "The eaten grain and the cock as damages" (type 1655 *The Profitable Exchange*, known in southern and eastern Europe, India, Africa, and among the American Indian); K2151 "The corpse handed around. Dupes are accused of murder when corpse is left with them" (reported for India, cf. type 1537* *Corpse's Legs Left*); K443 "Money (or other things) acquired by blackmail."

Long ago there was an orphan boy who lived with his old grandmother. They were so poor that they didn't even have any spoons or bowls. The orphan grew up day by day and as he got older he realized how poor they were. One day he said to his grandmother, "Ah, grandma, it isn't good that we remain poor like this. I want to go on a trading trip to make money." But the grandmother said, "Ah, grandson, you are all that I have left, and besides, you are all alone. You couldn't go to foreign lands, you would get lost."

Still the orphan boy insisted: "Eh, I want to have things like everybody else's son, so I'm going. Fix up my food for the trip, please, and I'll go." But the grandmother was very reluctant, for he was ignorant of many things.

One day as she was looking through his hair for lice, she couldn't help crying because her grandson wanted to go off. The orphan asked, "Why are you crying?" She said, "I don't want you to go away. You are still small and can't look out for yourself." But the boy said, "Don't worry, I'll be all right and I can really handle myself; everything will be fine."

So the orphan boy pulled out a hair of his grandmother's leg and left his home without anything else because there was nothing else to take. Later he arrived at a village and entered a house there. He found a woman spinning thread. Then the boy sat down by the rice pounder and laid his grandmother's hair on the edge. A little while later a chicken came by and with a flap of the wings the hair was lost. When the hair disappeared, the boy started to cry. He made a fuss about losing the hair and blamed the family for it. Finally, when they couldn't get him to calm down, the woman said that if he could recognize the chicken that did it, he could have the chicken. So he chose a chicken and went away.

Then he arrived at another village and entered a house. It so happens that in this house a person had died and the body was laid out to one side of the room. Later that night when all the people watching over the body had fallen asleep, he killed his chicken. He pulled out all the feathers, stuffing them in the dead man's mouth and scattering them around. Then he got rid of the chicken. Next morning when he got up he made a big fuss about the dead man eating his chicken. Finally the people said, "Look, nobody ate your chicken but the dead man, right? If this dead body ate your chicken you can have it to do with as you like." The orphan wrapped the body up and took it away.

When he arrived at another village he left the dead man outside the village in a little rest hut. He covered it with leaves that the cows like a lot. Then he went into the village. He told everybody that they had just arrived and that since it was getting dark that he had left his old grandfather out in the hut. He wondered if they locked their cows up, because if they didn't it could be dangerous for his grandfather. Everyone insisted that their cows were locked up, and besides, his grandfather was an adult and could look after himself. Next day, however, some of the cows had got out and had trampled all over the body in their desire to eat their favorite leaves. The orphan took the whole village to see what had happened and cried uncontrollably. He began to sue everyone who was there. The villagers had nothing to pay, and so they said that he could take all the cows that were responsible in this tragic accident. The orphan chose this cow and that one and that one, and cleaned the whole village out. Then he led them away and returned to his own village.

On nearing his village his grandmother came outside. She thought it looked like her grandson and went out to meet him with some corn soup. But the rich people all said, "That's not your grandson, that is one of our sons coming back." In their haste they knocked the old woman down and ran out to meet him. When they got near they were surprised to see that it was the orphan and were all ashamed.

Later the orphan boy became the richest man in that area. This goes to show that no one is supposed to look down on an orphan. God helps both the rich and the poor and all have equal opportunity.

For this story, that's all there is.

Korea

Why People's Noses Run When They Catch Cold

Collected by Yim Suk-jay from a schoolboy of fifteen in 1915 in elementary school in Sunch'ang, North Cholla province. Translated by Roger L. and Dawnhee Yim Janelli.

The collector heard this scatological legend from a schoolmate. The teller was Pak Chong-tae from Taekang Myon, Manwon Kun, North Cholla province.

Motifs are A1337.0.2 "Disease caused by ghosts"; F547.3 "Extraordinary penis"; and F547.5.4 "Double vagina."

Long, long ago, there was a king who had a son, and this son had two penises hanging there. So when it came time for him to marry, his father planned to marry him to a girl with two vulvas. But although they searched far and wide, they couldn't find such a girl.

The king's son died without ever getting married, so he became a ghost who wandered around looking for a girl with two vulvas. This ghost searched everywhere and looked very hard, but he just couldn't find one. And so, since there was nothing else he could do, he began doing it to people's nostrils. From that time on, people began to catch cold. When somebody catches a cold his nose is stuffed up at first and he can't breathe, and then later his nose starts to run. That's because when the ghost puts his penises up there the nose feels stuffed up. After he's finished, he takes them out and that's when people can start to breathe again. But because he left his liquid up there, their noses run.

The Red Pond

Collected by Yim Suk-jay in 1946 in Seoul. Translated by Roger L. and Dawnhee Yim Janelli.

Collected from a professor at Seoul National University, Kim T'aek-won, forty. He came from T'aeyang Tong, Sangha Myon, Kyonghung Kun in North Hamgyong province, the area where the pond of the legend is located.

Yi Song-gye, a famous archer, was the founder of the Yi Dynasty and ruled from 1392 to 1398. The Tuman River divides northeastern Korea from Russia and Manchuria. Dragons are symbols of kingship and often appear in stories about great men. Korean fortune-telling is done by reading faces as well as palms.

Motifs: B11.2.2 "Color of dragon"; B11.3.1.1 "Dragon lives in lake"; F713 "Extraordinary pond (lake)"; D1814.2 "Advice from dream"; Q112.0.1 "Kingdom as reward"; A931 "Meander-pursuit: a fugitive's doublings cause a river's windings"; Z71.6 "Formulistic number: nine (99, 900, 999, etc.)" (reported from India, China, and the Philippines).

Long, long ago, Yi Song-gye lived in Kyonghung, and he used to fish in the big pond there. While he was fishing one day he fell asleep and an old, white-haired man appeared in his dream, saying, "I am the owner of this pond, but a villain has come and is trying to take it away from me. Please help me to get rid of him. I can see by your face that some day you are going to be the founder of a nation. If you help me chase away the villain I will help you to become king of a large territory with its capital located here."

When Yi Song-gye awoke, he thought his dream had been rather odd, but he didn't pay it any mind.

The next day, he returned to the pond to fish, and while he was fishing the water became very turbulent and huge waves erupted. On the surface of the pond appeared two dragons, one black and one yellow, their bodies entangled in combat. Yi Song-gye just stood there and watched.

That night in his dream, the old man appeared again and asked him why he hadn't helped, as the old man had asked, and shot one of his arrows into the villain. Yi Song-gye replied, "I have to know which dragon is the villain. Could I just shoot either one?" Then the old man explained that the black dragon was the villain trying to get possession of the pond.

When Yi Song-gye went to the pond to fish the next day, the same thing happened again: the water became turbulent and huge waves erupted. The two entangled dragons appeared on the water's surface, and Yi Song-gye quickly shot the black dragon.

As soon as the black dragon was hit, it ran away, twisting its body and emitting red blood from its wound. Because of the pain, the dragon was twisting and turning his body as he ran out to the sea, and the impression made by this dragon formed the course of the river there. The turns that can be seen today in the lower part of the Tuman River were made by that twisting dragon. There are ninety-nine of those curves there; if there were one hundred, Kyonghung would have become the capital, and Yi Song-gye would have become the king of a large nation. But since there are only ninety-nine, he became king of only a small country, Korea.

The pond where he used to fish is still red from the blood of that dragon. That's why people call it Red Pond.

The Kindhearted Crab and the Cunning Mouse

Collected by Yim Suk-jay in 1927 in Sunch'ang, North Cholla province. Translated by Roger L. and Dawnhee Yim Janelli.

The collector heard this tale many times from his own mother, but he did not write it down for his archives until 1927. His mother (1872–1961), a skilled narrator and prolific informant, was from Chong, North Cholla province. Her family name was Yi, and like many Korean women of her time she had no personal name. The collector was born in 1903 in Sunch'ang, in North Cholla province, where he heard this story from the age of ten on up.

Feasting a visitor is an accepted part of Korean hospitality. To go to another's house and stay for a meal is considered neither inappropriate nor uncommon. Invitations to a meal are expressed as "Come to my house today (tomorrow)."

Motifs: A2494 "Why certain animals are enemies"; K2058 "Pretended piety"; J2136.4 "Trickster pinched by shellfish (crab) (reported from India, Japan, and Indonesia); A2433.1 "Establishment of animal haunt."

A long time ago, a crab and a mouse became friends. Being kindhearted, the crab brought his friend the mouse to his home and entertained him very well, giving him delicious food to eat. The mouse was delighted and said to his newfound friend, "It's the first time for me to meet such a fine friend as you. You have treated me so well and fed me so nicely that I have enjoyed myself thoroughly." After thanking the crab several times, he told the crab to be sure to come to his own house the following day.

And so, on the next day, the crab went to the mouse's house. When he arrived, he found the mouse looking up at the sky. The crab wondered why the mouse was doing that and stood by quietly watching him. But no matter how long the crab stood waiting there, the mouse just stared at the sky. He spoke no words of greeting nor even asked the crab to sit down. After a while, the crab could stand it no longer. He spoke up first. "Mousie, I'm here." But the mouse still looked up at the sky. So the crab spoke up again. "Mousie, I'm here. Your friend the crab has come!" The mouse pretended not to hear him and simply remained as before, staring skyward. A third time the crab spoke. "Mousie, I'm here. I've come." Nevertheless the mouse sat motionless without even turning his head and just stared at the heavens. Finally, the crab shouted, "Mousie, I'm here. I'm telling you that your friend the crab is here." But the mouse still pretended not to hear him, and without even budging just continued to gaze skyward. Since there was nothing else for him to do, the crab returned home.

The following day, the mouse came to the crab's house and again expressed his appreciation for the delicious food he had been given and for the fine treatment that he had received from the crab two days before. Showering praise upon the crab, he said, "How can you treat a friend so wonderfully? There must be no one else in this world with a heart as generous as yours." The crab was really very angry, but upon hearing himself praised so lavishly he answered, "Oh, it was really nothing at all. But by the way, you told me to come to your house yesterday, and then when I got there you just sat gazing at the far heavens."

The mouse looked startled and said, "What? You came to my house yesterday? When you came, didn't you tell me that you had come? You just came and said nothing?"

"Why do you think I said nothing?" the crab answered. "Although I said 'Mousie, I'm here' you just sat gazing up at the heavens. Several times I repeated, 'Mousie, I'm here. Your friend the crab has come,' but you pretended not to hear me and just sat there staring up at the sky. And so, since there was nothing else I could do, I just came back home."

Only then did the mouse give some indication of recalling anything of the events on the preceding day. Pretending to be absolutely mortified, he asked "Oh, is that what happened? Oh, dear! I'm really so sorry. Nowadays I'm trying to cultivate my religious spirit by deep contemplation; and yesterday was the day for staring up at the sky, so that was all I did. I'm so sorry for sending you away after you had come on my invitation."

When he saw how sorry the mouse seemed to be, the crab himself began to feel somewhat apologetic. After all, since the mouse had been trying to develop his religious spirit, it was really his own fault for going and visiting him on such a day. Perhaps he, the crab, should be the one to apologize. And so, once again, the crab brought out his delicious food and fed the mouse, treating him very well.

Now that he had received another fine treat from the crab, the mouse said to him, "Crab, come to my house tomorrow. It's my turn to treat you, and I promise to treat you very well."

The next day, the crab once again went to the house of the mouse, but the mouse seemed not to notice his arrival for he just sat there staring down at the ground. This time too, the crab was the first to speak. "Mousie, I'm here." But the mouse pretended not to hear him and still sat staring down at the ground. Nevertheless, the crab spoke up again, shouting this time, "Mousie I'm here. Your friend the crab has come." But the mouse just sat there without even turning his head. And so, since there was nothing else he could do, the crab just returned home.

The next day, the mouse again visited the home of the crab and began expressing his gratitude profusely to the crab, thanking him for the fine treatment he had received and the fine food he had eaten. However, the crab felt that the mouse had been rude in his behavior and sulkily asked him, "Yesterday, when I went to your house, why did you pretend not to know me?" Acting as if he were totally surprised and feigning complete ignorance, the mouse answered, "What? Did you say you came to my house yesterday? I was completely unaware that you had come. When you came, why didn't you say anything to let me know you had arrived?"

"Why didn't I say anything? Time and time again I said, 'Mousie, I'm here. Mousie, I came. Your friend the crab is here.' But you pretended not to hear me and just stared down at the ground. And so I had to come back home."

Then the mouse seemed to suddenly remember. Apologizing profusely, he said, "Oh, now I know what happened. These days I spend much of my time cultivating my religious spirit and yesterday was the day I was to spend looking down at the ground. To think that you made a special trip to my house and then had to return home makes me feel awful. I'm really very sorry."

Upon hearing these words of apology, the crab's annoyance began to melt and he started to think of his responsibilities as a host. He went and brought out the last of the food in his house and offered it to the mouse. Having received yet another fine treat from the crab, the mouse said as he was leaving, "Tomorrow I must entertain you as best I can, so please don't forget to come to my house."

The following day, the crab went to the place where the mouse lived. When he arrived this time, the mouse was staring at a distant mountain. Instead of greeting his friend pleasantly, the mouse didn't even look up. Since he just continued to gaze at the mountain, the crab greeted the mouse first. "Mousie, I'm here." But the mouse just sat staring at the mountain and gave no response. So the crab shouted, "Mousie, I'm here. I came. Your friend the crab is here. Yesterday, didn't you tell me to come and visit you today?" Nevertheless, the mouse pretended not to hear him, and sat silently staring at the distant mountain. But the crab tried again, this time screaming at the top of his lungs, "Mousie, I'm here. Your friend the crab has come. I said I'm here. . ." But it was useless. The mouse just sat there and stared at the mountain off in the distance. And so, once again there was nothing else he could do and the crab just returned home.

The next day, the mouse again came to visit the crab. As he greeted him, the mouse began to ramble on and on about the fine treatment he had received and how much he had enjoyed himself on his previous visits. But the crab thought only of his rude behavior and said curtly, "What sort of nonsense are you trying to tell me this time?"

The mouse pretended to have no idea what the crab was talking about and just blinked his eyes innocently. "Did I do something wrong? Are you saying that because of something I did?" With a rising voice, the crab answered, "You tell somebody to come to your house and when he arrives you pretend to be completely unaware of his presence? You invited me, and then when I went you pretended not to see me. And you did it time and time again, didn't you? Only yesterday you did it again. You explicitly asked me to come, but when I did you pretended not to see me and just sat there gazing at some distant mountain, didn't you? Did you speak even one word of greeting? Did you even bother to look up at me? Is that any way to behave?"

"Oh, did I do that?" the mouse asked. "I really am very sorry, but please let me explain. Sometimes I sit in deep contemplation in order to develop my religious spirit, and when I had invited you I had completely forgotten that yesterday was the day I had to spend staring at a mountain. When you arrived, I was staring at that mountain for the sake of spiritual improvement and I had lost all awareness of what was going on around me. It was because of that that you had to return home. I'm really very sorry. The next time you come, I will do everything in my power to see that it doesn't happen again. After all, our relationship is no ordinary one. Do you think I would deliberately treat you so badly? It was by mistake that I did not receive and entertain you properly. You really needn't be so unpleasant about it. I really think you might owe me something of an apology."

Thus spoke the mouse, hoping to receive another good meal at the crab's expense. But the crab was not dissuaded so easily this time. He hated the mouse now. Rushing forward, he leaped upon the mouse and sank his claw firmly into the mouse's thigh. Vehemently he exclaimed, "You foul wretch! You have no sense of decency or justice. You go around telling lies at every chance you get, and until now I have been deceived. But my eyes have been opened. Now I see. Doesn't a wretch like you even know when to stop? You can't fool me any more!"

The mouse was shocked. "Oh, wow! I thought this lousy crab was a weak, kindhearted person; but he's so violent. Now that he knows all my tricks I won't be able to fool him and eat here any more." And then the mouse ran right out the door.

After this happened to the crab and the mouse, they went their separate ways and were no longer friends. The crab went to live in lakes and streams, and the mouse went to live in houses and fields.

The Grave of the Golden Ruler

Collected by Yim Suk-jay in 1974 in Seoul. Translated by Roger L. and Dawnhee Yim Janelli.

Told by Tok-yu Hong, forty-three, an amateur folklorist from Kangwon province, Kangnung city, Kyo Tong, employed by the government.

There were two Silla dynasties in Korea. The one referred to existed from 57 B.C. until A.D. 668 when the dynasty united the entire Korean peninsula. The reference to Silla is probably not meant literally but seems to be a device for saying "A long time ago."

The hour of the snake and the day of the snake refer to the system of reckoning time by twelve animals of the Asian Zodiac. The "snake location" refers to the system of geomancy, which uses the human body as a metaphor. One taps certain "veins" to obtain certain kinds of fortune. A snake location would indicate a fortune having to do with snakes.

Motifs: B360 "Animals (tadpoles) grateful for rescue from death (reported from India, Japan, Malaysia, Indonesia)"; B493.1 "Helpful frog" (reported from China); D1172.1.33 "Magic bowl furnishes food" (known in Buddhist mythology); E3 "Dead animal comes to life"; E64 "Resuscitation by magic object"; Q51 "Kindness to animal rewarded"; N511.1.1 "Treasure buried in graves" (reported from China).

A long time ago—I don't know where it was but I heard that it happened in Silla times—there was a drought and a farmer went to his rice fields to open an irrigation channel into his paddy land. Onto the earth banks that divide the paddies some other farmers had thrown some tadpoles because the tadpoles were drinking the scarce water that the farmers needed for their rice crop. But this farmer felt sorry for the tadpoles, so he collected them together and put them into a nearby waterhole. Without his kindness the tadpoles would have died, but because of it they were able to become frogs.

I guess these frogs wanted to repay the farmer for saving them. They went to the yard in front of his house and all croaked so loudly that the farmer's ears hurt from the noise. Several times he came out of his house and chased them away, but the frogs would return and begin making the noise again as soon as he went back inside. Finally, he decided to chase them farther away; but when he chased after them, he realized that he had only followed them to a big pond. Now that they had brought him there, the frogs jumped into the pond and began emptying it, one mouthful at a time. Since there were thousands of them, it didn't take long before the whole pond was drained. At the bottom of it, the farmer saw an unglazed earthenware bowl. He thought of his dog's dish, which had just broken recently, and figured that the earthenware bowl would make a good replacement for it. So he walked over to the bowl, picked it up, and brought it home.

When the farmer put some food into this bowl for his dog, the animal ate from it constantly even though the farmer didn't put any more food there. He thought this was kind of odd so he went to take a closer look at the bowl. He saw that no matter how his dog ate, the amount of food in the bowl remained the same. So the farmer tried putting rice, money, and other things into the bowl. Each time he did that, the amount he had put in stayed there regardless of how much he took out.

The farmer became a rich man, but he thought his neighbors should also benefit from his bowl. The word soon spread throughout the village and many people came to see him and use it. At last, the farmer became tired of the steady stream of visitors. Thinking that he had already accumulated enough wealth to live comfortably, he sent the bowl to the king as a gift.

Now in another village it happened that a man was building himself a new house, and he happened to build it on a day of the snake and in a snake location. After he had finished the house and was just about to enter it, snakes appeared everywhere: in the yard, in the rooms, on the roof—the place just became a world of snakes. However, the man had to get inside his house, so he took a club and caught and killed all the snakes with it; and then he hung them on the branch of a tree. After that, he locked the door to his room and spent the first night there.

When he awoke the next morning he found that all the dead snakes were gone. Apparently they had revived and escaped somewhere. But then, at the hour of the snake—that's to say about ten o'clock—the snakes came back and the place was full of them. So the man went out and killed them all again.

Well, this went on for several days. Each time he would kill all the snakes, somehow they revived. Wondering about this mysterious occurrence, one day he watched to see what was happening. In the early morning, at the first crowing of the cock, a yellow snake appeared carrying a golden ruler. The snake took this ruler and measured the length of one of the dead snakes with it, from head to tail. When he did that, the snake came back to life. In that way, all of the dead snakes were revived. So the man tried to catch the yellow snake, but it fled quickly, dropping the golden ruler from its mouth. After all the other snakes had run away, the man picked up the ruler and took it home.

Well, just about that time a baby in the neighborhood had died, and the man figured that if he measured the baby with his golden ruler the baby might come back to life. So he measured the baby from head to foot and, sure enough, the baby revived. So the man went around measuring other dead people with his ruler and bringing them back to life.

Word of the golden ruler spread; and when the king's daughter died, he heard that there was a man who could bring the dead back to life. The king summoned him to the palace, and the man revived the king's daughter.

So now the king had both the bowl and the golden ruler. One day, the highest of the heavenly gods appeared to the king in a dream and said, "I sent those two treasures to you as a gift because you had governed wisely and well. But isn't it time to return them to me?"

When the king awoke the next morning he thought it over and concluded that if he kept the treasures too long, there would eventually be too many people in the world and they would all become very lazy. He decided to return the treasures.

So the king had nine coffins made. He put the treasures into two of them and left the other coffins empty. Then he had nine graves dug and the place is called the grave of the golden ruler.

That's what I heard from old people.

The One-Sided Boy

Collected by Yim Suk-jay in 1930. Translated by Roger L. and Dawn-hee Yim Janelli.

Told by the collector's landlady, forty, Chon T'ae-son, at a boarding-house in Seoul.

Note the following cultural features in the tale:

Korean drills are shaped much like awls.

Yangban were the Korean equivalent of the Chinese gentry, complete with civil service exams, literacy, and special privileges.

Part of a Korean wedding ceremony consists of the groom and his party going to the house of the bride to bring her to the house of the groom. At the marriage of an eldest son, the bride usually comes to live in his house, for the eldest son inherits most of his father's land in return for the care and support of his aged parents and the performance of ancestral rituals.

The bride's family offers to pay the one-sided boy because they do not know that he is the brother of the groom. The work of a footman would be done by a hired servant, and no one would expect that the brother of the groom would do it.

A pot for steaming rice cakes has a few holes in the bottom of it, each about two inches in diameter.

The gate guard's hair: Korean men wore their hair long, tied in a knot on top of their heads until the Japanese colonial era (1910–45). Some old men can still be seen with the topknot, but the custom is now exceedingly rare.

The rich man accepts the boy's excuse because it is based on filial piety. Probably no other reason would have been acceptable.

Motifs: T516 "Conception through dream"; T511.1 "Conception from eating a fruit" (reported from India, China, and Indonesia); F525 "Person with half a body: as if body has been split in two" (reported from China and Indonesia); T550.2 "Abnormally born child has unusual powers" (reported from Japan); K2211 "Treacherous brother"; D283 "Transformation: man to water"; D250 "Transformation: man to manufactured object"; D211 "Transformation: man to fruit"; F632 "Mighty eater" (reported from India); H335 "Tasks assigned suitors: bride as prize for accomplishment" (reported from India, Indonesia, Indo-China, China, and Japan); K331.2.2 "Guards fatigued by trickster so that they sleep while goods are stolen"; K635 "Sleeping enemy's hair tied to an object prevents pursuit."

The final episode in which the one-sided boy abducts the rich man's daughter conforms to an incident in type 1525 *The Master Thief*.

This tale is very popular in Korea. Twelve variants have been collected, all containing the elements of the two and one-half pieces of fruit, the half boy who is very strong, an evil elder brother, the capture of the bride from a neighboring house on the third night when the guards and family are tired, and playing pranks on them (as in type 1525). The incident of the elder brother's wedding and the one-sided boy's overhearing the monks and guarding against them appears to belong to a separate tale type. In some versions the one-sided boy brings home a huge rock as well as a tree, and tells his mother she can use it for making rice cakes, by pounding the dough upon it.

A long time ago there lived an old, childless couple who wanted a son so badly that they would have been happy to have only half a child. One night while the wife was dreaming, an old, white-haired woman appeared to her and gave her three dried persimmons. The wife took and ate the first two, but when she had begun to eat the third, her husband reached for it. "Are you going to eat them all by yourself?" he asked. And so her husband ate half of the third persimmon.

Not long after, the woman showed signs of being pregnant and eventually gave birth to three sons. Two were normal but the third had one side missing. He was only half a child.

The one-sided boy grew up to be strong and was able to walk quite well, but the two normal boys hated him and were always planning to kill him. One day they tied him to a big tree, but he uprooted the tree with himself still tied to it and brought it home to his mother saying, "Let's chop up this tree for firewood; and if you untie this rope, you can use it for a laundry line." When his mother asked him who had tied him to the tree like that, he just told her that he had done it himself in order to carry the tree home.

The fine character of the one-sided boy mattered not to his brothers. They still wanted to kill him. Once, they ordered him to dig a very deep hole in the earth, and when he had done as he was told, the brothers heaped earth and stone upon him from the top of the hole, burying him underneath. They thought that this time they had killed him for sure, but when they arrived home, they found that the one-sided boy had got there ahead of them.

After that happened, the brothers racked their brains to find ways of destroying him. One day they sent him deep into the mountains to fetch wood, hoping that he would be caught and eaten by a tiger. The one-sided boy obeyed their command and was on his way to the mountains when he overheard the conversation of three monks. They were talking about his brothers. One monk said that the one-sided boy was a fine fellow but his brothers should be destroyed since they were always trying to kill him. He knew that the eldest brother was planning to marry soon, and suggested that his wedding day be chosen to kill him. He told one of the other monks to become water and to kill the brother if he became thirsty and drank it. In the event that failed, he told the third monk to become a big pear and to kill the brother if he ate it. In case that plan also failed, the first monk said that he himself would become a sharp pointed drill and rest on a shelf in the bride's house. When the brother entered the house, he would fall from the shelf and stab him. All the monks agreed that this was a good plan.

Although the one-sided boy had heard everything, he revealed none of it when he returned home. He waited until the wedding day of his brother and then insisted on becoming a footman in his brother's bridal party. The brother strongly opposed this, but the one-sided boy kept insisting. At last, there was nothing the brother could do but agree to it.

So the one-sided boy got to lead the horse that his brother was riding, and he led it to the bride's house as quickly as he could. When they passed a well and a small gourd along the way, his brother became thirsty and asked him to bring some water. But the one-sided boy pretended not to hear him and led the horse quickly past the spot. A little later, the brother asked him to pick up a pear that was lying nearby, but again he pretended not to hear him and quickly passed the spot. This made the elder brother very angry. He told the one-sided boy not to come with him any further, but the boy followed along anyway, making his brother even angrier.

When they arrived at the bride's house, the one-sided boy quickly went into the bride's room and took down a drill which was lying on the shelf there. This too made the elder brother furious, but there wasn't anything he could do about it. And when the bride's family brought out the food, the one-sided boy ate enough to feed one hundred people; and when they offered to pay the boy for his services as footman he refused payment and instead ate enough food to feed another fifty people. It was not until they returned back home that the one-sided boy explained to his brother about the water, pear, and drill.

And then one day he asked his mother to go to the rich man who lived opposite them and tell him that he wanted to marry his daughter. At first his mother told him that such a marriage was impossible and she wouldn't go. However, the boy insisted so much that his mother finally went to the rich man's family. But they thought it was impertinent for such people to propose marriage with a *Yangban* family. They slapped her face and told her to return home.

The next day, the one-sided boy went to see the rich man, and when the man came out of his house the boy told him that he was going to marry his third daughter. Upon hearing these words the man slapped him, saying that the proposal of marriage with the daughter of a *Yangban* by such a malformed thing like him was the height of insolence. The boy retorted that there was no law that prevented him from marrying her, but the rich man still refused. So the boy asked the man if he could have the daughter if he secretly carried her away on his back. The rich man admitted that if he succeeded in taking her away secretly, there would be nothing he could do but allow him to have the girl. The boy told the man he would come that night to carry the girl away.

The rich man set his servants to guard the gate, roof, and yard of his house; and the man, his wife, and his son surrounded and guarded the girl. The boy climbed up a nearby mountain and from his vantage point there watched the goings-on in the house. When he saw that it was well lighted and guarded by so many people, he decided not to try that night.

The next morning, the rich man came and said that since the boy had broken his agreement with the *Yangban*, he could never have the girl. The one-sided boy replied that he had intended to come on the preceding night but his mother had become ill from the slap that she had received and he had to travel to a distant place to obtain medicine for her. By the time he returned last night it was too late to come, but he promised to come that very night. To this the rich man replied, "Since it was your devotion to your parent that prevented you from coming, I will forgive you," and then he returned to his house and set his servants to guarding it as he had done the night before. When the boy saw that the house was so well guarded on the second night as well, he decided not to go there that night either.

The next morning, the rich man returned again and reprimanded the boy for attempting to deceive a *Yangban*, but the boy excused himself again by saying that it was because of his mother's medicine that he had been unable to come. But he promised to come that very night without fail.

So the rich man went home and took even greater pains than before to guard his house; but the guards who were on the roof, in the yard, and by the gate had not slept for two nights and began to doze. The one-sided boy entered the grounds and covered the head of the guard on the roof with a pot used to steam rice cakes; on the head of the guard in the yard he put a big cooking pot; and he took the hair of the gate guard and tied it to the gate. Then he spread sulphur on the rich man's beard; put a flute in his wife's mouth; and put stones into the big, flowing sleeves of the son's jacket. Then he put the daughter on his back and left the house.

The son was the first to awake and realize that his sister was gone. In the dark, he attempted to light a fire, but it soon spread to his father's beard. When the son tried to strike out the flames, his weighted sleeves hit his father's face, knocking out his teeth. His mother awoke and tried to say something but could only produce music on the flute. The guard on the roof seemed to be mumbling about the large number of stars in the sky, and the man in the yard mumbled back that the sky seemed to be very dark. Meanwhile, the gate guard was begging whoever was holding him to set him free. But nobody was chasing the one-sided boy. So he took the girl and lived with her happily from then on.

Oceania

Micronesia

The Ghosts of the Two Mountains

Collected by Roger Mitchell in Harmon Village, Guam, November 1963.

Belief in origin myths is waning in contemporary Micronesia. This particular tale maintains its popularity because of its scatological and trickster elements. Quite Micronesian are the themes that misunderstandings can be settled over a friendly meal and that statuses of individuals and groups can be clarified through public competition. This complex is still carried on through village feasts and introduced competitive sports.

See Roger Mitchell, *The Folktales of Micronesia*, published as *Asian Folklore Studies* 32 (Tokyo, 1973), tale 3, "The Displaced Island," pp. 20–23; tale 4, "The Fished-Up Island," pp. 23–26; and tale 5, "The Island Dropped from a Basket," pp. 26–29, for similar tales of island creation.

Motifs: *A955.0.3 "God kicks once and creates islands" and *A618.4 "Universe created by kicking" appear in Bacil F. Kirtley's, "A Motif-Index of Polynesian, Melanesian, and Micronesian Narratives" (unpublished Ph.D. dissertation, Indiana University, 1955). Two other motifs are identifiable from Thompson's motif index, A955.3 "Origin of island's shape and position" and A964 "Mountains (hills) from ancient contest (fight)."

The narrator of this tale was Machume Sonis, a male, age twenty-one (1963), from Tol Island, Truk Atoll, who has a degree from the University of Guam and speaks Trukese, Ponapean, and English. He is now a personnel officer in Truk District and Trukese representative to Congress of Micronesia. In addition to being an informant for this tale, Sonis acted as interpreter at other times.

Laurentius Bollig in *Die Bewohner der Truk-Inseln: Religion, Leben und kurze Grammatik eines Mikronisiervolkes* (Anthropos Ethnologische Bibliothek, 1927, p. 8) makes a brief reference to a close variant of this tale.* See also Paul Hambruch and Anneliese Eilers, *Ponape*, 2:

* Multiple references to a bibliographic item will be listed by short title in this headnote as well as in those that follow.

Teilband: *Gesellschaft und Geistige Kulture; Wirtschaft und Stoffiche Kultur* (Hamburg: Friederichsen, De Gruyter, 1936, pp. 45, 162–63); and Paul Hambruch, *Ponape*, 3: Teilband: *Die Ruinen: Ponapegeschichten* (Hamburg: Friederichsen, De Gruyter, 1936, pp. 192, 210–11), for Ponapean tales containing motif *A955.0.3. The works of Hambruch and Eilers appeared in the series edited by Georg Thilenius, *Ergebnisse der Südsee-Expedition 1908–1910*, 16 vols. (Hamburg: Friederichsen, De Gruyter, 1914–38). Other authors included in this series, cited in subsequent notes, are Augustin Krämer, Wilhelm Müller, and Ernst Sarfert.

William A. Lessa in *Tales from Ulithi Atoll: A Comparative Study in Oceanic Folklore* (Berkeley: University of California Press, 1961, pp. 275–89) has treated closely associated motifs extensively under motif A814 "Earth from object thrown on primeval water." See Mitchell Collection, variant 6, for a Marshallese variant of motif A955.3.2.1 "Primeval hero moves islands into their present position."

Similar tales have been abstracted from the Gilbert Islands by James G. Frazer and published as *The Belief in Immortality and the Worship of the Dead*, vol. 3: *The Belief Among the Micronesians* (London: Macmillan, 1924, p. 57). For the Polynesian outlier Nukuoro, Anneliese Eilers has contributed *Inseln um Ponape: Kapingamarangi, Nukuor, Ngatik, Mokil, Pingelap* (Hamburg: Friederichsen, De Gruyter, 1934, pp. 183, 298). Closely related are those stories in which land or islands are stolen and moved, as reported by Augustin Krämer in *Palau*, 4: Teilband: *Geschichten und Gesange* (Hamburg: Friedrichsen, De Gruyter, 1929, pp. 35–36); Paul Hambruch and Anneliese Eilers in *Ponape*, 2 (pp. 114–15); Ernst Sarfert in *Kusae*, 2 (Hamburg: Friederichsen, 1920, p. 408); Laura Thompson in *Archaeology of the Mariana Islands* (Honolulu: Bishop Museum Press, 1932, p. 62); Roger Mitchell in *The Folktales of Micronesia* (pp. 343–45, 557–58). See Mitchell Collection, Indiana University Folklore Archives, motif A955 "Origins of islands," variant 7 for a Losapese text of island origins.

Long, long ago on Tol Island there lived two ghosts. The names of the two ghosts were Akatop and Niepanow. Well, actually Akatop lived on the mountain called Winimur, and Niepanow lived on the other mountain called Unipot, which is now the highest mountain in Truk District as a whole. The main job of these two ghosts was building the mountains. They were competing with each other, each building his own mountain. And at that time the ghost on Winimur was leading. He had the highest mountain, maybe because he was a man, and Niepanow was a woman, and actually he was stronger than Niepanow. And all through the building of the mountain Akatop did many bad things to Niepanow. One of these things was when Akatop wanted something like if he wanted to urinate or what, he just got out from his house and called on Niepanow, and he probably stuck out his penis and urinated on Niepanow because, you know, Akatop's mountain was higher than Niepanow's, so it was very easy for Akatop to do that. And finally when he wanted to urinate he just called Niepanow and said, "Well, are you thirsty or do you want to take a shower? There, the rain is coming." So he urinated right on Niepanow.

So Niepanow had a very hard time. Day and night she kept thinking of a thing that would make her feel better. So one day she got out from her home and called on Akatop, and she asked Akatop if he could come down to her home and have supper with her that evening. Then Akatop was really in favor of what she suggested to him. So that evening Akatop got down to Niepanow's home, and they had a very nice supper, and Niepanow tried to treat him very nice. That way she wanted to play a trick on him. But before that, she tried to be real nice to him so Akatop wouldn't recognize what she was going to do later on. By that time they were starting to talk about the building of their mountains and, you know, Niepanow started to tell Akatop that because he was a man, or a very strong man, that that was why he had a higher mountain that she had, and she suggested one thing to Akatop. She told him if he agreed with her that they would try to kick their mountains off to show who was really the stronger person among them. So Akatop really laughed. He laughed at what she said because he knew himself that he was the strongest, and probably he could kick more off his mountain than Niepanow could too. Then Akatop agreed with this, what Niepanow told him, and Akatop told Niepanow that he would be the first.

Then Akatop went to his mountain, that is Winimur, and called down to Niepanow; and he said, "Are you ready?" and "See what I will do to my mountain." And then Niepanow said, "Yes." So Akatop kicked his mountain and, you know, because he was a man, a very strong man, he kicked his mountain, and almost half of his mountain broke; and that's where we now have Moen Island, Dublon, Fefan, Uman, and Udot, and those very little islands like Romonum, Falapanges, all these islands that are in Truk Atoll. So that made the other islands, but actually, according to this legend, there was only Tol Island that time, no other island besides Tol Island; but when Akatop kicked his mountain, that built up the other islands.

Then Akatop called back again to Niepanow, and he said, "Okay, let's see what you can do with your mountain, Niepanow." So Niepanow just kicked a little bit off her mountain, that is Unipot, and that's where we have these very small islands like those in Oren, very small islands. Then Akatop really laughed at Niepanow because Niepanow couldn't even kick her mountain. But by that time Niepanow was really laughing, and told Akatop that he was really stupid because he kicked off his mountain. Now Niepanow had the highest mountain, that is Unipot, and still now Unipot is the highest mountain among those mountains in Truk District because she fooled Akatop. Now whatever she wanted to do to Akatop, she just did it because she had the highest mountain. If she wanted to throw her waste materials or whatever she wanted to do to make Akatop feel bad, she just could do it since her mountain was the higher one. And that's how we got Mount Unipot as the highest mountain in Truk district. That's all.

Adventures and Death of Rat

Collected by Roger Mitchell at the University of Guam, October 1970.

Rat is the rascal of the Micronesian folktale. As this tale points out, she was once a respected member of the animal community, who had to be disposed of because of her antisocial behavior. Rat's fall from grace was not due to trickery per se, but rather because she sinned against her kin group in her inordinate greed for food. Rats are unpopular, for they cause a great deal of damage in their gnawing of food crops and household goods.

See Roger Mitchell, *The Folktales of Micronesia*, tale 13, "Rat's Canoe Trip," pp. 45–48, and tale 22, "Origin of the Rat Clan," pp. 71–73, for similar accounts of Rat's trickery.

Motifs in Kirtley's index, 1955: *B295.2.1 "Animals make voyage in canoe (usually have shipwreck)"; B222 "Kingdom (land) of birds"; *B557.17 "Turtle carries rat upon sea"; K952.2 "Ungrateful water passenger injures (kills) animal (fish) that transports him."

The narrator was Isauo James, a male, age twenty-five (1970), from Kuttu I., Satawan Atoll, who at the time of recording was attending the University of Guam. He speaks Trukese and English. In addition to being an informant, he is also a collector and a translator.

William Lessa includes a variant of this tale in *Tales from Ulithi Atoll*, pp. 245–64. The references early and late are rich, with high structural consistency. Kenneth P. Emory has published *Kapingamarangi: Social and Religious Life of a Polynesian Atoll* (Honolulu: Bishop Museum Press, 1965, p. 351). August Erdland reports about the Marshalls in *Die Marshall-Insulaner; Leben und Sitte, Sinn und Religion* *eines Sudseevolkes* (Munster: Aschendorff, 1914, p. 246) and William H. Davenport catalogs "Marshallese Folklore Types" in the *Journal of American Folklore* 66 (1963): 222. Paul Hambruch has written about Nauruans in *Nauru* (Hamburg: Friederichsen, 1914, pp. 449–51) and about Ponapeans in *Ponape*, 3 (pp. 155–56). Trukese have been described by Laurentius Bollig in *Die Bewohner der Truk-Inseln* (pp. 235–36) and Yapese by Wilhelm Müller in *Yap*, 2 (Hamburg: Friederichsen, 1918, pp. 478–79). See Mitchell Collection, motif *B295.2.1, variants 2, 3, 4, and 5 for contemporary Kusaiean, Palauan, Ulithian, and Yapese versions.

Long, long ago on Kuttu, all of the birds, including Rat, assembled in a big house. And one night they had a big meeting, and in their meeting they decided that the next day they would go out sailing on the water. So when the next day came they put down their canoe, a very big canoe, and all of the birds including the rat went on board and they sailed. They stayed in the water for about one day and one night without eating anything because they didn't bring food with them. So while they were still sailing, they saw a ripe coconut floating on the water. They went to take it in order to eat it because they were really hungry. When they got it, they bit the husk off, and at that time the rat called out from under her place on the canoe that she would like to have half of the coconut and she would like to drink the water inside the coconut. Because Rat was the only lady on the canoe, they gave her the water inside the coconut and half of the meat. The other half they divided among themselves.

Except for the hermit crab. He was bailing the water out from the canoe and so they all ate and this hermit crab didn't. He was really mad because he was hungry, and they didn't even bother to give him a piece of the coconut meat. So he decided to make a hole in the canoe so that all of the birds would fly away when the canoe sank, and only the rat would stay on the canoe because she didn't have wings to fly.

So when he made the hole, the water started to come up inside the canoe. But the birds were so involved in their conversations that they didn't see that the canoe was about to sink. So when the canoe sank, all of the birds flew away and the rat was trying to get away from the water. She went up the sail and she tried everything to make her stay away from the water. And when she was still trying to get away from the water she saw a turtle.

Then she yelled at Turtle to come and when the turtle came, she asked him if he could take her to their island. Turtle was willing to take her to the island, so he offered her his back, told her to step on his back and he would take her to her island. So the rat went over to the turtle's back, and they started on their journey back to Kuttu.

When they reached the place, the turtle kindly asked Rat to come off from his back.

But even then Rat was reluctant to come off because she didn't want to make herself wet in the shallow water. So she asked this turtle to come a little bit further. Then Turtle did. He crawled up and he was on the shore. He asked the rat again to come off his back, but she was still refusing him. She asked him again to come up in front of their house so that all of the birds would see her when she came off from the back of the turtle.

So the turtle crawled up until he reached the place where she wanted him to stop, and at that place Rat came off. She called the birds and asked them what were they waiting for? Since they had the turtle, why didn't they come out and turn it over so they would have him for their supper. So the birds came out from the house and they turned the turtle over, and after that they prepared to cook the turtle. They dug a fire hole in the ground, put in some stones and fire. On top of the stones they put a fire. They built a fire to make the stones hot. When it was ready, they took the turtle and put him inside of the hole and covered him up. When they had covered the hole, they came back to the house and they had some talk about their adventure.

At this time, Rat decided that since she was the one who had fooled the turtle, she would be the one who had the most of the meat. So when the group of birds were still talking, Rat sneaked out from the house and she went into the jungle. There she dug underground, because she wanted to make a tunnel underground where she could take the meat from underneath the firehole. Not up on top of it because she was afraid that the birds would see her. So she dug in the ground and made a tunnel leading to the fire hole. When she got there, she came back to her place and made some small baskets. She would put the meat of the turtle inside them. When she got all of the baskets that she needed, she took them with her when she went to that place underneath the fire hole. She got there and she took out all of the meat inside the turtle and she left.

The only thing that was left in the hole was the hard cover of the turtle and the head, but the meat inside was all gone. She went to her place, and she hid herself there. When the time came for the birds to uncover the oven and take out the meat, they all went to the fire hole to watch the big birds taking off the cover of the oven. They got there, and they started to uncover the thing that they had buried under the ground inside the oven. When they got to the turtle, they turned it over and they found out that all of the meat inside was gone. They were all really mad because every bird was ready to have a small share of the meat. But they just found out that the meat was gone, so nobody would fill his stomach with the meat.

They came back to their house and they had a meeting, and in the meeting they approved that they would find out who the crooked person was. So every bird was assigned to his or her place to look, and they had arranged that if anybody found the crooked guy he would make a noise so that all of the birds would come and take him. So they started their hunt. They went all around the island, and the birds who were expert in fishing were assigned to walk on the shore and those others were assigned to check in the taro patch and in the coconut trees, and all of the trees were covered by birds, those who were assigned to look in the trees.

There was a bird who was assigned to look with others on the shore, and he was *Kaukau*, Heron. He walked on the shore and he came to a place where it was not good and he decided to hunt there. He went there and stuck his bill around under the husks and leaves in order to find something that he wanted to find under the things. So when he got to a coconut husk, he stuck his bill underneath it and tried to turn it over. At that moment, he saw Rat, because Rat was using that husk to cover up her hole underground. So as soon as Rat saw Kaukau, she appealed to him to come inside and they would have something to eat. Kaukau agreed with her and so he came inside the hole. There Rat put down some meat, the meat of the turtle, and they talked. But before Rat would let him eat the meat that she had offered him, she made him promise that he wouldn't let anybody know that she was the one who took the meat of the turtle. So Kaukau promised that he wouldn't tell anybody. Then Rat put out all of the meat that she had and also her leftovers and Kaukau started to eat.

Because it was almost one day since Rat had got the meat, it was not plentiful anymore. The meat was not plentiful. She had only a little, so Kaukau could eat the rest of it. He ate and after that he decided to go out and have some fresh air outside. Then Rat asked him again not to tell anybody about what she had done. But as soon as Kaukau got outside the hole, he made a noise. He shouted that he had found the rat. When the birds heard the noise, all of them came and they stayed outside the hole. And Kaukau told them that Rat was under the husk inside the hole. When he took off the husk, all of the birds could see Rat inside the hole. She was really scared and she just stayed inside the hole.

When the big birds came, they saw the rat, and they grabbed her and they took her with them to their house. They held her there. After that they had a meeting, and the purpose of the meeting was to decide whether or not to kill Rat because of what she had done to them. They had this meeting and every bird agreed that they would kill her. But to show that Rat was a member of the group, they didn't want to stab her or use any weapons in the killing. They decided that all of the birds would come and take the rat up into the sky and there they would leave her to fall.

After their meeting they all went outside, and they grabbed the rat, and the big birds took her up high into the sky and there they left her to fall. When she fell down, she broke herself into small pieces.

After that, all of the birds came into the house, and they had another meeting to talk over things that they wanted to talk about. But the body of Rat was all scattered around the island when it broke into pieces. After the death of Rat every bird was happy. They lived together happily and enjoyed their staying with each other.

That's the end of the story.

The Maiden Who Married a Crane

Contributed by Roger Mitchell. Collected in Barrigada, Guam, in February 1971.

Ideally, Micronesian marriage weaves both the principals and their families into a lifetime network of mutual aid. Hence the importance of a productive son-in-law. As fisherman, Crane has great potential, while the sleek good looks of the others make them suspect. In his final act, Crane both avenges his kin and strikes a blow against unbridled greed.

See Roger Mitchell, *The Folktales of Micronesia*, tale 17, "The Birds' Courtship," pp. 56–60, for a Ponapean variant.

Motifs: *B602.11 "Heron weds maiden"; Q272.1 + "Greed (gluttony) punished"; T70 "The scorned lover"; Q286 "Uncharitableness punished."

The narrator was Ruthie Zackhras, a female, age twenty-six (1971), from Namorik Atoll, Marshall Islands, who had a public high school education and spoke Marshallese and English. She was a collector/translator as well as informant.

This tale agrees well with Paul Hambruch's Ponapean variant (*Ponape*, 3, pp. 174–75). A recent Trukese variant emphasizes heron's qualities as a fisherman but the girl leaves him for someone more handsome (Roger Mitchell, *The Folktales of Micronesia*, pp. 427–31). In Palau the ugly bat wins the girl (Augustin Krämer, *Palau*, 4, pp. 132–33); while in the Central Carolines a disobedient girl is carried away by a bird as a bride (Augustin Krämer, *Inseln um Truk (Centralkarolinen*

Ost) [Hamburg: Friederichsen, De Gruyter, 1935], p. 238). A Yapese girl sought out the frigate bird after being refused by others (Wilhelm Müller, *Yap*, 2, pp. 474–75). See Mitchell Collection, motif B602 "Marriage to bird," variants 2 and 4 for Ulithian and Yapese variants.

Long ago there was a girl and her parents who lived on a small island. These parents were the kind of parents who wanted to pick or select a husband for their daughter. The girl's name was Likwaliklik. One day she was on the beach, but her parents were doing some work in the middle of the island. While the girl was on the beach, the plover sailed along the beautiful beach and said to the girl, "Likwaliklik, Likwaliklik. Is there anybody else with you on this island?" And she said, "Yes, my parents and I." Then the plover said, "Where are they?" She replied, "They are in the woods." And the plover said, "What are they doing?" "They are bringing food, white and red," the girl said. "Run and tell them that there is a canoe here." The girl ran into the woods and started calling "Mother?" She answered. "Father?" He answered. "There is a canoe in the lagoon." They asked, "Whose is it?" "The plover," she answered. Then they said to her, "Go and drown him." She ran to the beach and drowned the plover as she was told.

Later came another young man there. A sandpiper came sailing into the harbor calling, "Likwaliklik, Likwaliklik. Is there anybody with you on this island?" "My parents and I." "Where are they?" the sandpiper asked. She answered, "They are somewhere in the island." "What are they doing?" the sandpiper asked. "They are bringing me food, white and red." The sandpiper said, "Run, run and tell them that there is a canoe in the lagoon." She ran to her parents and told them about the canoe. They asked, "Whose canoe is that?" "The sandpiper," she answered. Her parents said, "Go and drown him." She ran back and drowned the sandpiper.

The next day another young handsome man, the tern, came sailing into the harbor calling, "Likwaliklik, Likwaliklik. Is there anybody else besides you on this island?" "My parents and I," she answered. "Then where are they?" the tern asked. She answered: "They are in the woods." "What are they doing?" the tern asked. "They are bringing food, white and red," the girl answered. The tern said, "Then run, run and tell them that there is a canoe in the harbor." She ran to the woods calling "Mother?" She answered. "Father?" He answered. The girl said, "There is a canoe in the lagoon." "Whose is it?" they asked. "The tern's," she answered. "Then go and drown him." She ran to the beach and drowned the tern.

The next day the most handsome man, the frigate bird, came sailing into the harbor calling, "Likwaliklik, Likwaliklik. Is there anybody else besides you on this island?" "My parents and I," she answered. "Where are they?" the frigate bird asked. She replied, "They are somewhere in the woods." "What are they doing?" the frigate bird asked. "They are bringing food, white and red," the girl answered. "Then run, run and tell them that there is a handsome man in the harbor," the frigate bird said to her. She ran to the woods calling, "Father? Father?" He answered. "Mother? Mother?" She answered. "There is a canoe in the harbor," she told her parents. "Whose is it?" they asked. "The frigate bird," she replied. Her parents said, "Go and drown him." She ran to the beach and drowned the frigate bird.

The next day an ugly young man, the crane, came sailing into the harbor. This young man had a funny figure. He had a big stomach, a long neck. He had a funny-looking figure. He came with his canoe calling, "Likwaliklik, Likwaliklik. Is there anybody else besides you on this island?" "My parents and I," the girl answered. "Where are they?" the crane asked. "They are somewhere in the woods," the girl answered. "What are they doing?" the crane asked. "They are bringing food, white and red," the girl answered. "Then run, run and tell them that there is a handsome man in the harbor," the crane commanded. The girl ran into the woods calling, "Father? Father?" and he answered. "Mother? Mother?" and she answered. "There is a young man sailing in the harbor," the girl told her parents. "Who is it?" they asked. "It is the crane," the girl answered. "Go get your purse and go with him." She refused and she was crying, but her parents forced her to go with the crane.

The girl went on board the crane's canoe and they sailed away. When they were approaching the first island, the girl asked the crane, "Whose island is that with many breadfruits on it?" "Oh, it belongs to one of my brothers that you did not like." While they were approaching the second island she asked, "What about that one with lots of pandanus?" "Oh, it belongs to my younger brother that you didn't like." "What about that island with lots of coconut trees on it?" the girl asked. "Oh, it belongs to one of my brothers the one you didn't like," the crane answered. But when the girl saw the last island she asked, "Whose island is that with no vegetation on it, but only jungle?" "Oh, that is our island." "But there is no food on it," the girl said to the crane. "You are wrong. There are plenty fishes on that island," the crane said to the girl. "You will have more than you will need." They went ashore and the crane told the girl to wait for him while he went fishing because it was almost supper time. The girl said to him, "It is too late. It is already dark. You will not see any fish." "Don't worry. There are plenty fishes on the island," the crane said to the girl.

He took his basket and went into the woods. He caught lots of lizards and brought them to the girl. She saw them and screamed. She said to the crane, "I thought you were human but you are not. If I had known about you in the first place, I wouldn't have come. Please return me to my parents." The crane became angry and he killed Likwaliklik. He roasted her and the next day he returned her to her parents in a big basket. The parents were very happy that their son-in-law was bringing them food. The crane left the basket with the parents and flew away. When they were about ready to eat they found out that the food was their daughter. When they looked up, they saw the crane on a tree laughing and saying, "Eat your daughter. It is good." The parents really were furious with the crane but they couldn't catch him. The crane flew away.

This is the end.

The Exiled Sister and Her Son

Contributed by Roger Mitchell. Collected on Tanapag, Saipan, in January 1971.

Lukelang and Olofat were once gods in the Trukese pantheon. In this domestic tragedy two cultural emphases are stressed: the brother-sister bond should be greater than that of husband-wife, and brother-sister owe each other strong moral and material support. The brother compounds his sins by following the exile of his sister with the slighting of his maternal nephew, who in matrilineal Truk should have been his honored heir. Lukelang, a high god, and Olofat, his son and a trickster-culture hero, have here been demoted.

See Roger Mitchell, *The Folktales of Micronesia*, tale 61, "The Exiled Sister," pp. 174–77, for another variant to this tale. See tale 31, "Olofat and the Stolen Eyes," pp. 92–95; tale 38, "The Mosquito Larvae Pregnancy," pp. 106–8; and tale 72, "Olofat's Son," pp. 209–15, for other narratives showing Olofat in his more traditional role of trickster-culture hero.

Motifs: L111.1 "Exile returns and succeeds"; C515 "Tabu: touching (plucking) flowers"; D1030.1 "Food supplied by magic"; A814.2 "Earth from sand strewn on primeval water"; D1273 "Magic formula (charm)"; D2125.1 "Magic power to walk on water"; D2136.6 "Island magically transported"; H151 "Attention drawn and recognition follows"; K2212.2 "Treacherous sister-in-law"; Q431 "Punishment: banishment (exile)"; S371 "Abandoned daughter's son becomes hero"; S33 "Cruel brother."

The narrator, Pia, a female, age seventy (1971), from Saipan Island, Mariana Islands, is a descendant of Trukese-speaking immigrants who came to Saipan in the nineteenth century. A housewife and gardener with no formal education, she speaks Trukese and some Chamorro. Isauo James was the collector and translator of this narrative.

This tale needs a special motif or perhaps even a type number, for over and over again a woman is exiled or cast away and through her son returns victorious. Laurentius Bollig reports this tale with little change in *Die Bewohner der Truk-Inseln* (pp. 227–28); and two other variants were collected on Satawal and Namonuito Atolls by Hisataku Hijikata and published in *Dittilapal-Satewal* (Tokyo: Sanseido Publishing Company, 1953, pp. 58–71); and by Augustin Krämer in *Inseln um Truk* (pp. 242–43). See Mitchell Collection, motif L111.1, variants 1 and 3, for a variant from Losap Atoll and one from Palau Islands.

Drift away, drift hither, there lived Lukelang and his wife. They had two children, Olofat and a daughter. They lived on the island and when the children grew up, their mother and father died. However, before they died, while they were dying, they asked Olofat to take good care of his sister. Therefore, right after their death, Olofat started to see to it that his sister was happy. Their father was the chief of the island. When he died, the title passed down to his son who was Olofat.

Olofat wanted to get married, so he picked a woman of his choice and they stayed in his house. His wife didn't like her sister-in-law to stay in the place. She not only didn't want her to stay there, but she really didn't want to even see her. Because of this, she tried everything to get rid of her sister-in-law.

Olofat happened to have a spider lily outside his house. He loved the plant very much and he made it clear to the people of the island that anybody who touched it would be punished. He would go and look at the flower before he left to work. That was how important the plant was to Olofat.

This couple had a baby. They really loved the baby. However, Olofat still felt that even his baby should not touch the flower. One day when he was about to leave his house, his wife told him that she would go and wash their dirty clothes in one of the far away streams. So he sent a messenger to tell his sister to watch the baby. Then he left the house before his sister arrived. His wife went outside the house and picked the flower and came back and hid it under the baby's small pillow. When her sister-in-law came, she told her what to do and then she left. Olofat's sister put the baby to sleep and then she started to clean up the house. She stayed there almost the whole day.

Olofat and his wife came back at the same time. As soon as they stepped inside the house, his sister was on her feet to leave. She left them and went back to her house. She didn't know that there was something terrible back at her brother's house. She prepared herself and was ready to come back to the house again. She always visited them before she went to sleep.

Olofat took a bath and went outside to see his flower. However, when he got there he found that his flower was gone, and he was very upset. He rushed inside and asked his wife who had picked his flower. His clever wife told him that she left right after him. She explained further that since she was away for the whole day she could not possibly know what happened to the flower. She suggested that they ask his sister because she was there. However, Olofat knew that his sister could not do it. He saw her when she left, that she did not have anything with her. He was also confused because he believed his wife. He knew she was not there the whole day.

Confused by what had happened to his precious flower, he demanded his wife to help him look for the missing flower. His wife pretended to look around and then she went inside the house and took out the flower from under the baby's pillow. She took it and showed it to her husband. She explained to him that it might be his sister who did it because she was with the baby. Her sweet talk convinced her husband. He believed that his sister had done it. So he decided to kill her, no matter how precious she was to him. He had said earlier that anybody who picked the flower would be punished. Although he loved his sister, he could not possibly permit her to do this.

Olofat sharpened his knife to use in killing his sister. His knife was so sharp that if a fly sat on its edge, it would be cut in two pieces. That was how sharp his knife was. When he was finished sharpening it, he took it with him. He went down to the men's house and sat there. He waited for his sister to come.

His sister, after finishing up everything in the house, left to visit her brother and his wife. She walked to the men's house and saw that her brother was sitting there. So she dropped down on her knees and started to walk on them. But Olofat told her to stand up. He was so very angry he did not want to listen to her. He ordered her to stand up and walk to him. His sister could not do that even if she knew that he was upset. She continued to walk on her knees. Finally she was about to reach the house when Olofat rushed out and grabbed her head. He had her head in his left hand and in his right hand was the knife. He raised it up in the air and then he was about to chop her head off. He could not. He let go of her head and left her sobbing there. He returned to his house.

The woman was crying outside the men's house. She was crying because she was really afraid of her brother and his knife. She knew that there was something wrong in the house when she was there. She thought to herself that the best way for her was to leave the island. She stood up and headed to the shore. There she took some grains of sand with her and started to walk. She walked and walked until the water was too deep. Then she reached for some of the grains and dropped them there. When she did, a new beach was formed. That enabled her to walk again. Also during this trouble, she was in her early months of pregnancy.

When she was far away from the island, she threw down the grains in the water and made a small and beautiful island. There she built a house for her. There were coconut and breadfruit trees on the island. She lived there for a few months. Then she gave birth to a son, and she took care of him and raised him to grow up.

The baby grew up on the island and he found that they were the only people on the island. He asked about it from his mother, but she never told him the truth. Then one day her grown son decided to have a trip. He wanted to go around and see whether or not there were other places and people on these places. He told his mother about his plan and his mother agreed to it. She took him inside the house and applied some magic to his feet. The power of the magic would make him be able to walk on the water. So when she finished the magic, she told him to go. He left the small island and came to the island where his mother used to live. When he got there, his uncle was working on his canoe. He came inside the men's house and sat down. He watched his uncle while he was busy working on his canoe. Those who were in the house did not like him. However, some of them had the feeling that he was related to Olofat, but nobody had the courage to come and ask him.

The boy sat there until noon. Then some relatives of those who helped on the canoe came to the house. They brought food for the workers. When the food came, everybody except the boy ate. The men divided the food among them so that everybody would eat. But nobody called the boy to join them. When they all finished, they gathered the bones of their fish and their coconut husks so they could give them to the boy to eat. They knew that he was hungry. The boy took the things they gave him and piled them up near his mother's post. And late in the afternoon, he left the island.

When he came home, his mother asked him about his uncle's canoe. She wanted to know whether or not it was ready to be used. But the boy told her that it was not ready yet. Therefore she told him that next time he would use her adze in the house in order to help finish the canoe. She told him everything about the different things used to make the canoe. He was instructed to get or use only those things that belonged to his mother. So the next day the boy left his small island. He went to the same place he had visited. When he got there, his uncle

The Exiled Sister and Her Son   317

had just started to work on the canoe. There were other people in the house, but they were there to help. They were not allowed to work with Olofat on the canoe. All they had to do was to help turn the canoe to one side and then another. Their work was also to take the heavy things out of Olofat's way.

When the boy got there, he went straight into the house. He went over to the other end of the house and took down his mother's things. He took them with him. Then he went on the other side of the canoe and started to work. Everybody was curious about him. They wondered how come he picked out the things that had belonged to Olofat's sister. Some of them felt he was related to Olofat's sister. But nobody asked him that. They just watched him. He finished the side he was working on and then he moved to the other side that his uncle was on. When it was about to be finished, he took back the things where he took them from. Then he came back and sat down.

It was now mealtime for them. Women were coming in and out of the house. These women brought food for the men. When the food was prepared, the men were divided up into groups and so was the food. But the lone boy did not join them because they did not want him with them. They ate their food and again gathered up the bones and took them to the boy. The boy took them and piled them up with the others that he had before. He then left the people there. He went back to his island. When he got there his mother asked him about the canoe. He told her that it would be ready by the next day. That day would be a special day for Olofat and his people. They would be celebrating the completion of the work on the canoe. Olofat's sister knew that there would be a lot of people coming to the house. She also knew that her brother would be needing some assistance in the preparations for the day. So she told her son that they would help Olofat.

When the special day came, Olofat's sister made her magic. The magic was intended to produce people, all female, and food. It worked out fine. There were many, many women on the island and the food was already cooked. The only thing left was somebody to eat the food. However, that was not the plan. She told the women there that the food was for her brother, so they would take it to him. The women obeyed what she commanded. They took the food on their canoes and set sail. When they got there, everybody was ready to eat, but they stopped and looked at these beautiful females.

The women tied up their canoes and started carrying in the food they brought. They took it into the house where the canoe was. Then they were about to leave when the boy stopped them. He told them that they had to get his food from Olofat and the people there. This was the coconut husks and the fishbones. The women gathered this trash, put it on their canoes, and left for home. They reached home and unloaded their cargo. They showed the mother what the islanders had for her son. Although she was mad, she did not show it. After all, it was her brother. She knew that her brother was a good man. He would have welcomed her son if he knew who he was. Besides that, she knew also that Olofat realized who the boy was and he would be looking for him.

Olofat was very surprised with the food. He realized that the boy might be his sister's son. So he asked the men around the house to distribute the food among the people. Everybody was satisfied with the food they ate. They also enjoyed some dances performed in honor of the celebration. When everything died down, people were beginning to leave.

A few days had passed, and Olofat decided to use his canoe to sail around. He also planned to search for the boy. He prepared his canoe and sailed away with a few crew members. They were quite a way away from the island when he told the crew to look for an island. He knew they would finally come to it because he was sailing in the direction the boy and the woman took. Everybody was on the lookout for an island.

Olofat's sister after the trip in which the women delivered the food knew that her brother would follow them. She knew how he must have felt after they left because it was very obvious to know what was going on there. Anybody who was there during the celebration would have concluded that the women were sent by Olofat's sister. After all, nobody else would be that generous to give away so much food to him. With these feelings in mind, she had cautioned her son to be on the lookout there. She told him that while he was playing on the island, he should be on the lookout because somebody was coming to visit them. But she did not want anybody except her son to be on the island. So if there should be somebody coming, she would move the island to another place.

One day her son was playing on the shore. It so happened that while chasing his ball he stopped to take a rest. Then there was something moving out there in the far away distance. He was not sure whether or not he was really seeing a moving object or if he was just imagining that he saw an object. He took a rest and when he tried to have a good look at the thing he saw that it was a sailing canoe. Then he forgot about his fun with the ball and started to run to his mother. When he got there he told her his story about the canoe. His mother sent him back to look for it, whether it was coming to the island. He left the house because he wanted to check on the canoe. When he returned, he saw that the canoe was coming toward the place. So he ran back and told her.

She asked him to stay with her in the house. She had planned to make the island invisible and then move it some place else. Therefore she waited and waited for the canoe to come closer. And when the canoe was pretty close, she turned the island invisible and at the same time removed it.

The people on the canoe were surprised at the sudden disappearance of the island. They turned back and headed for home, and they did not see Olofat's sister any more.

The Mistreated Stepson

Collected by Roger Mitchell on Ponape Island, Kolonia Town, in April 1971.

Food and its fair distribution are matters of prime concern in Micronesia. To receive less than one's just share can be interpreted at best as a sign of neglect and at worst a calculated insult. It is also widely held that revenants can appear in the form of birds and that a dead mother's spirit will continue to evince concern over her children's welfare.

See Roger Mitchell, *The Folktales of Micronesia*, tale 58, "The Mistreated Stepson," pp. 165–68, for a Marshallese variant to this tale.

Motifs: E323.2 "Dead mother returns to aid persecuted children"; E423.3 "Revenant as bird"; E732 "Soul in form of bird"; F1041.1.2 "Death from grief for death of lover or relative"; S51 "Cruel mother-in-law"; F942 "Man sinks into earth."

The narrator was Ishmael Edward, a male, age twenty-eight (1971), from Pingelap Atoll at the time of recording. He is now a resident in Sokehs, Ponape Islands, where he is a Protestant minister. He speaks Pingelapese, Ponapean, and English and is a teacher at the mission school. Edward served both as informant and interpreter. Kohne Ramon translated the text.

This tale is broadly represented in the literature, with variants from the Marshalls to Yap. A Ponapean variant in which the child flies away with birds has become widely disseminated because of its inclusion in Eve Grey's *Legends of Micronesia* (2 vols, Honolulu: Department of Education, Trust Territory Pacific Islands, 1951, book 2, pp. 57–59). Many variants were collected by the Germans: Ernst Sarfert, *Kusae*, 2 (pp. 459–60, 481–82); August Erdland, *Die Marshall-Insulaner* (pp. 255–57, 280–82); Paul Hambruch, *Ponape*, 3 (pp. 173–74, 418); Wilhelm Müller, *Yap*, 2 (pp. 485–86). Three post-World War II variants are recorded: John Fischer, "Language and Folktale in Truk and Ponape: A Study in Cultural Integration" (unpublished Ph.D. dissertation, Harvard University, 1954, pp. 244–49); Roger Mitchell, *The Folktales of Micronesia* (pp. 571–73). See Mitchell Collection, motif E323.2, variants 1, 2, and 4 for variants from the Marshall Islands, Woleai, and Palau.

Long, long time ago on Pingelap there was a couple who had a son. They really loved their son and they took care of him very well. They worked for their son and they really respected him very much. After awhile the mother got sick. She was really weak and was going to die. The mother told her husband, "Please, if I die, don't marry another woman, because if you do the other woman would not take care of our son." So the man promised his dying wife, saying that he would not marry another woman. The husband told his wife, "I will stay single until our son gets married; then I will get married." After awhile the mother died. The son and his father stayed together. They were living for quite awhile. Then the father asked the son, "Son, can I marry a lady so that she can help us, cook our food, and wash our clothes?" The boy said, "Yes, father. It's all up to you. If you want to bring a woman here, it's all up to you. If you want to stay single, you can stay single. If you want to marry, you can get married. It's all up to you." So the father brought a woman, and they got married. They stayed together for a long time, and after awhile the woman sort of got tired of the boy. They stayed together for awhile, and the woman got pregnant and gave birth to a child, and the father loved the new child very much.

After awhile he started hating his own boy and the woman also hated the boy now. Both of them hated the boy, and the boy was sad because his own father and his stepmother were not treating him very well. During this time, every time they ate, the father, the mother, and the other child, they would eat and throw the peelings and the bones and the garbage at him. That was what he ate. He ate garbage. They would do this every time they ate, just throw him garbage to eat. The father was a very good fisherman and he liked to go out fishing quite often. One day he took his son with him and they went out fishing and when they returned from fishing, the father jumped out of the canoe and walked straight to the house and washed himself. He left the whole canoe and all the fish in the canoe for the boy to take care of. The boy would take the fish up to the house, go back and pull up the canoe alone. This happened for a long time. The father would go home, wash, and sleep. The boy would stay, take all the fish to the house, come back, and would take the canoe all by himself up to the house. After he pulled up the canoe by the house, he would cook the fish; and after he had finished cooking the fish, they would eat. The father, the stepmother, and the other child ate first, and after they were all through eating they left the garbage for him. This kept on, time after time. And the ghost of the mother would come and watch how her boy was being treated and she didn't like it. She was really sorry for the boy who was being treated really badly, who was being mistreated, treated like a nobody, and all such bad things. Then one day the father called the son and said, "Let's go fishing." So they went out fishing and they anchored outside the reef. The father got off the canoe and he started spear fishing. He would dive down, get one fish, and throw it into the canoe, and dive down again. The father would come up and the boy was crying. The father said, "What's the matter?" The boy said, "I thought I'd like to eat fish and I was going to fix *sashime* [raw fish, often prepared with lime juice or soy sauce], and I touched it and it bit my hand." The father said, "Who told you to touch the fish? They are not for you. They are for the woman on the land." After awhile the father would dive down and catch a fish and as he came up, the boy would be crying. He would ask him why and the boy would say he was trying to fix the fish and the fish bit his hand. The father would say, "These fish are not for you. They are for the woman in the house." At the same time the ghost of the boy's mother, who had changed herself into a bird, was flying over the canoe and she watched the treatment the father was giving her son. The spirit in the form of a bird would fly toward the canoe and talk to the boy. She would say, "Come, come with me. We will leave this place, because I don't want you to be mistreated like this." So the boy started crying and his father surfaced again and asked him why he was crying and he would say the fish had bitten him. Then he would say the same thing, that the fish didn't belong to him. They belonged to the woman in their house. After awhile the man was suspicious about why the boy kept on crying and crying. So he went under the outrigger and he hid there and he watched. As the father watched from under the outrigger, the bird came down and started talking to the boy. The bird said, "Come with me, son, come with me. I don't want you to stay in this place. They are mistreating you." The boy started crying and the man witnessed this. He got up on the canoe, and they left for home. When they got to the shore the man was changed all of a sudden. He helped the boy with the canoe and he was treating him really nice. He also helped with the canoe and the fish, because he had seen that his former wife, the boy's mother who had died, had talked with the boy and he was really sorry. As they brought the fish to the house, when the boy started cooking the fish, the father offered the boy some fish, but the boy wouldn't accept it. The father insisted that the boy take the fish, but still the stepmother was not very kind to him. But the father was telling the stepmother to be good to the boy, but she wouldn't change. So one day the boy started walking away from their house and he started walking toward his mother's grave. As he got there, the mother told him that she would soften the earth so he could join her. She did. She softened the earth and the boy started sinking in the ground. He was disappearing, and finally a man came by. The man saw only the head. So the man went and told the boy's father. The father went to the grave and all he saw was the hair on the head. He started grabbing at it but then he missed and the boy disappeared. As the father saw his son disappear and go under the ground, he was crying and he was sad. He was crying and struggling all over the place. He admitted what he had done to the boy. So he went home and beat up the stepmother and he chased her away from the house. The father was really sad. He went home and chased the woman away and after that he went to his room and he slept. He just lay there day after day and he never ate. He lay there and thought of the wrong he had done his boy. He just lay there and he didn't eat. He grew weaker and weaker and skinnier and skinnier every day. Finally he died.

This story tells us that if a mother dies, the father shouldn't bring another woman in, because then the stepmother would start hating the daughters and sons. This is a good example of this. That is why when a father is widowed he will not marry again, because then another woman will start hating his daughters and sons.

And that concludes the story.

The Spirit Who Swallowed People

Contributed by Roger Mitchell. Collected on Mangilao, Guam, in January 1971.

Malevolent, cannibalistic spirits are more than a dramatic device to the average Micronesian. Many locations on land and sea are avoided by juvenile and adult alike as the haunts of such threatening creatures. This tale also illustrates a cultural truth: despite the culpability of one's behavior, he can nevertheless expect the firm support of kin if disaster strikes.

See Roger Mitchell, *The Folktales of Micronesia*, tale 80, "The Deserted Woman and the Giant," pp. 237–39, for a Kusaiean tale of another mother who rescues her disobedient son from the clutches of an evil spirit.

Motifs: F912.2 "Victim kills swallower from within by cutting"; C614.1 "Forbidden direction of travel"; C610 "The one forbidden place"; *F402.6.7 "Spirits dwell on island" (Kirtley, 1955); F911.5 "Giant (spirit) swallows man."

The narrator was Merko Louis, a female, age twenty-nine (1970) from Ngatik Atoll at the time of recording, but now a resident of Madolenihmw, Ponape I. She attended public elementary schools and mission schools, and speaks Ngatikese, Ponapean, Trukese, and English. Her husband, Minoru Louis, collected and translated this tale.

Close variants are reported from Yap Islands by Wilhelm Müller, *Yap* 2 (p. 585) and from Kusaie Island by Ernst Sarfert, *Kusae*, 2 (pp. 458–59). The major motif, F912.2, is a common one in many tales and is recorded by Paul Hambruch in *Ponape*, 3 (pp. 244–45); from Ulithi Atoll by William A. Lessa in "Discoverer-of-the-Sun: Mythology as a Reflection of Culture," *Journal of American Folklore* 79 (1966): 21, and from Losap Atoll by Roger Mitchell, *The Folktales of Micronesia* (pp. 441–43).

Taimwan was very young and one day he asked his mother to go out fishing with him in the deep water. They went out and his mother taught him how to fish. On the next day he went out by himself. He was instructed by his mother that there was a spirit on the other end of the island of Ngatik. Therefore it was very dangerous for him to go there because the spirit was very harmful. It could eat him. So he was informed about the spirit and then he went out. He went out and used his spear. He fished with a spear. He was fishing around their area, nearby their house. But he couldn't catch any. Then he decided to move further up toward the place where the spirit was. He was fishing along and finally he came to the place where the spirit lived. Then the spirit saw him, and it sang a song in order to attract Taimwan's attention and then make Taimwan come closer to him. The song went like this:

"Taimwan is spearfishing toward me.
I'll grab him and swallow him."

So then Taimwan also replied:

"But when you defecate,
I'll come out."

They kept telling each other about what they wanted to do. Finally the spirit caught Taimwan and then ate him. Taimwan went down into the stomach of that spirit, but when the spirit felt like he wanted to defecate, he went. Then Taimwan came out with the waste material.

Taimwan got out and ran back to his place. The next day Taimwan thought that this type of a thing was sort of a fun game. He came back and the spirit said again:

"Taimwan is spearfishing toward me.
I'll grab him and swallow him."

And Taimwan also replied:

"But when you defecate,
I'll come out."

Then the spirit caught him and also ate him. But the same thing happened. He went to his toilet place, and Taimwan also came out with the waste material. Then he ran back to his home. Now the spirit began to think of a better way of swallowing Taimwan and then really making Taimwan stay in his stomach. Before Taimwan returned on the next day, the spirit took a big piece of plank and swallowed it. Then as Taimwan came back on the same day, the spirit grabbed him and swallowed him. Taimwan's hand was caught on one of the spirit's teeth. This tore Taimwan's hand and blood was on the lips of the spirit. So Taimwan went in and got stuck there, because the plank plugged the opening where he used to get out on previous days. Taimwan was there in the stomach, still alive. His mother was wondering, "How come Taimwan is so late to return?" She was thinking, "Maybe Taimwan went to the place where the spirit is. Let me go and find him." She started out and began to search for Taimwan along the shore of the island of Ngatik. As she went along, she found the spirit sitting in his house. Then the woman asked the spirit, "How come you have blood all over your mouth?" The spirit said, "Because I just finished eating a lizard." But she replied, "A lizard couldn't make your mouth bloody like that. Maybe you ate something even bigger than a lizard." The spirit insisted, "No, I ate a lizard. Not anything else but a lizard." They were in an argument. Finally the spirit got angry and said, "I ate a boy who came around my place. I caught him and ate him." Then the woman knew that that was her boy. She went in and fought with the spirit. They were fighting, but the woman had a shell hidden in her dress. She found it on the shore and put it in her dress. When they were fighting, she forgot all about that shell. Finally the spirit also grabbed the woman and swallowed her. He didn't chew her. He just put her in his mouth and swallowed her. Then she went down and met with her boy in the stomach of the spirit. They were there sitting, wondering how could they come out. The piece of plank was plugging the way for them to escape or come out. Then the lady remembered that there was a shell she had put in her dress. She pulled it out and started to use it to cut the spirit's stomach. She did this and made a big hole in the stomach and really killed the spirit. Then both of them got out and escaped from the spirit. He was lying there dead, because the woman had killed him with that shell.

The First Getting of the Way to Cultivate Cyrtosperma

Contributed by Katharine Luomala. This origin myth was written out in Gilbertese in 1951 by Tuia Atanuea for Katharine Luomala, who rendered the English translation.

The narrator came from the island of Arorae, which is still regarded as the home of the most expert cultivators, and the myth tells how his island first learned to raise taro, i.e., *Cyrtosperma chamissonis*, referred to in the tale as *babai*. This plant, with umbrella-sized leaves and long stalks, yields the most prestigious food in the Gilbert Islands. The corms are laboriously tended and raised in pits, and pulled and eaten on special occasions. *Cyrtosperma* corms, or puddings made from them, are the most highly valued foods presented in the village assembly house.

In the myth a giant from a neighboring island threw his spear at a black cloud hiding the sun. But the cloud was actually a mass of very tall leaves of two male and two female *Cyrtosperma* plants growing and mating on nearby Tarawa Island. Cleaved and knocked down, one plant stayed on Tarawa, while the other three fled to the ocean as porpoises and swam south to Arorae. There another giant, informed in a dream by his goddess that the porpoises were plants, lassooed, planted, and fertilized them. This was the beginning of *Cyrtosperma* cultivation on Arorae.

During general ethnographic fieldwork in 1948 on Tabiteuea Island, Luomala collected other *babai* myths. See her "Humorous Narratives about Individual Resistance to Food-Distribution Customs on Tabiteuea, Gilbert Islands," *Journal of American Folklore* 78 (1965): 28–45.

Motifs: A523 "Giant as culture hero"; F531.4.5.5 "Giant has enormous spear"; F628.4 "Strong man's mighty spear cast"; D441.4 "Transformation: plant to animal"; H975.1 "Tasks performed by aid of goddess"; A2684 "Origin of cultivated plants" (reported among the Tonga).

Long, long ago. Arorae people tell the story that the way to cultivate was the work of the people of the northern Gilberts, but it did not remain exclusively with them until the present. And the thing that they cultivate as their food, the *babai*, is very truly the principal work of the Gilbertese people every day so that their food, the *babai*, will flourish.

The way of its being obtained in Arorae: people of Arorae tell the story thus. Formerly on Tarawa there were four *babai*, and these are their names: 1. Te Waka Baurua, a male; 2. Te Wa-n-o, a male; 3. Nei Taima [Nei means "Lady"], a female; and 4. Nei Boakinna, a female. These cultivated plants grew up, indeed, on Tarawa. And there is a certain land lying near Tarawa that is called Maiana; and there was on Maiana a certain giant—a very strong man—whose name was Te Toa ma I-Matang [probably correctly Te Toa mai Matang, "The Giant from Matang"], and he indeed lived on his land, Maiana. And on a certain morning that giant waited and waited for the warmth of the sun, but it did not rise as usual, for the face of the sun was in a black cloud, like a rain cloud, and the sun's warmth could not then be shed on the land. And that giant was sick at heart when the warmth of the sun was not shed. And this giant had a weapon that was called Te Koro ma I-Matang [probably Te Koro mai Matang, "The Javelin from Matang"], and when the sun did not shed its warmth he took that weapon of his and he cast it at the thing that obscured the face of the sun, and it completely cleaved that thing apart, which was not really a cloud at all but really the leaves of several *babai*, for those things when they mated yonder obscured the face of the sun. And they cleaved apart and they ran away to the ocean to become several porpoises. And they skipped from the north inside the ocean. Those porpoises were sought to be snared, but were not caught, by the people of the land where they arrived [approached]—there were three of those *babai* together that cleaved apart on Tarawa, and one stayed behind in Tarawa—and when those porpoises hurried from the north the people of the lands in the central Gilberts did not snare them [although they tried]. And they continued going from the north, for they were going to Arorae.

And there was a certain giant on Arorae who lived at the southern end of Arorae, and the name of that place of his was Tenangiruku [meaning "The Cloud, or Abundance, of Beach Morning Glories"]. That giant's name was Sir Takoto. When those porpoises were nearly at Arorae, there was a certain ancestral deity, Lady Tituabine, who came to tell Takoto, "Make yourself a very strong rope [either the type *an ni* or the *taboa*] and get it ready for the morning. They will be skipping from the north, those porpoises, which are not really porpoises but are really *babai* coming from Tarawa. You will snare them, and, as for me, I am going to help you by cutting their roots in order to get cultivated plants for you, and I shall tell you the ways of their being fed"—their cultivation.

When it was morning it was signaled that the porpoises were skipping near Arorae from the north. And the giant Takoto puts his canoe in the sea and he sails those porpoises in and he snares them. And the ancestral deity Lady Tituabine helps Takoto, the giant, by cutting the roots of the several *babai*, which are porpoises. When all are caught and drawn up near the place that is Takoto's place called Tenangiruku where he stays at the southern end of Arorae—and when those *babai* had all arrived ashore—that ancestral deity told Takoto the ways of cultivating those several *babai*. And when the ways of the food of the plant Te Waka Baurua were obtained he [Takoto] planted it and he fed it in the way in which he was told by that deity, and that *babai* developed very well. He then was told the ways of the food of Te Wa-n-o, and he planted it, and he fed it, and it also grew exceedingly well. He also obtained the ways of feeding Lady Taima and he planted it and he fed it that *babai*'s food, and it thrived also. They remain skillful even to this day on Arorae; the people of Arorae are cultivators of the food, the *babai*, in which they are skillful because they got their skill from their ancestor, Sir Takoto, and his ancestral deity, Lady Tituabine.

Polynesia

Maui of a Thousand Tricks

Contributed by Katharine Luomala. First printed in her article, "A Dynamic in Oceanic Maui Myths," *Fabula* 4 (1961): 155–58.

Maui is the great Polynesian hero-figure, alternatively demigod, culture hero, and trickster. He mediates between the gods and men, he impudently overturns social customs and established codes of behavior, sometimes he upholds conventions and magically punishes their violators. Because he is only a demigod, he dies, violently, often through pressures from an encircling structure into which he has wandered, such as a cave that magically compresses, or the vagina of the goddess of death.

The following cycle of Maui's mythical adventures from East Maui (the island may or may not have been named for the demigod) appeared in the Hawaiian newspaper *Kuokoa*, 27 June 1863, as written down by Puaaloa, "Ka Mo'olelo o Maui." A translation from Hawaiian into English by Mrs. Mary Kawena Pukui was deposited in the Bishop Museum Library, Honolulu.

Katharine Luomala's article calls attention to the function of visual illustrations in perpetuating the myths about Maui. A narrator invites his listeners to look, with himself as the guide, at anything or anybody associated with his narratives about the demigod who fished up islands, snared the sun, raised the sky, stole fire from the gods, and performed other marvelous feats. He may take visitors on sightseeing tours to view the places, artifacts, natural phenomena, people, creatures, or customs that are related to Maui's career.

The four mythical tales here presented all refer to places in East Maui, although they contain well-known deeds of Maui localized in a number of other Polynesian sites.

Motifs: *The Origin of Maui* T510 "Miraculous conception"; cf. T531.1 "Conception from having licked semen-stained loincloth." *The Theft of Fire* A2320.3.1 "Origin of mudhen's red head" (reported from Hawaii); A2741 "Plant characteristics from accident to original plant"; A1414.1 "Origin of fire-rubbing sticks"; cf. A1415 "Theft of fire. Mankind is without fire. A culture hero steals it from original owner" (reported generally throughout Oceania); A1414.7.1 "Tree as repository of fire." *Snaring of the Sun* A728 "Sun caught in snare" (reported for Oceanic, American Indian, and African myths); A1150 "Determination of seasons"; N825.3 "Old woman helper." *Earth-Fishing* A955.3.2 "Origin of island's position"; A955.8 "Island fished up by demigod (hero)" (reported for Hawaii, Tonga, New Zealand, the Marquesas, Tuamotus); D2074.1.2 "Fish or sea animals magically called" (reported for Tonga, Hawaii, Tuamotus); C331 "Tabu: looking back."

The Origin of Maui

Maui was the son of Hina and Malo, that is, Ka'anomalo [sic]. The place where he lived was at Kipahulu, here on Maui. It was on the beach. Malo was not the name of Hina's real husband; he was just a person she met when she went to scrape seaweeds. The name of Hina's real husband was Akalana. Hina and Akalana already had three sons who were named Maui-mua, Maui-hope, and Maui-ki'iki'i. Maui-akalana was the hero of this tale we are hearing about. This was how that Maui was conceived.

Hina made tapa in a cave under a precipice called Oheo. There she remained to beat tapa. And having a longing for seaweeds, she grasped the stick she used at the beach, a shallow dish and a beach bag, and went. This was the very first time the chiefess went herself for seaweeds. Whenever she had a longing for seaweeds, her attendants went to get them. That was the custom but now she longed for seaweeds and went herself. As she went along the beach she did not go where the seaweeds were numerous or to a place that was near. She went right on to a place called Keanomalo [sic]. When she arrived there, she peered over and saw a red loincloth (*malo*) lying there. She went down, picked it up, and draped it over her skirt. Then she fell into a deep sleep. There she remained until afternoon and when she awoke she saw that the sun was moving westward. She arose but did not have the thing she had longed for, seaweeds, before she had fallen asleep. Her attendants came to seek her and found her going home. They asked her, "Where have you been all day?" Hina told them what had happened, as we had described it before, and Akalana replied, "We shall have a lord." They remained until the child was born and named him Maui-akalana. They reared him until he grew up.

The Theft of Fire

Their food was uncooked, and their food was fruits ripened in the earth. There was no fire then to cook their food, and there was no means of

cooking taro, sweet potatoes, yams, ti roots and other things that Akalana could get. Maui asked Hina, "What can be used to cook our food?"
His mother replied, "Fire is the thing that is used for cooking." "Who
has the fire?" inquired Maui. His mother answered again, "The mudhens have the fire." Then her son declared, "I shall go and fetch the
fire." She said, "Are you strong? You must be very strong and swift,
then you can obtain fire." "Yes," replied Maui. Then Hina instructed
him just what to do, "If you are going to fetch fire, you must not go to
any of the birds except the smallest. It is the smallest of the mudhens."

Then he started off to get fire. He went to Waianae on Oahu. The
mudhen's fire was lighted when he arrived but only the large mudhens
were there. They said, "Say, the redheaded mudhen's food is gone, for
here is Hina's swift son." The reason for their talking this way was that
Maui had often pursued them and they knew how fast he was. When
he tried to snatch the fire they picked up everything, fire, bananas,
ashes, wood and all, and flew away. He was left disappointed. This occurred again and again until he found the smallest starting a fire and
laying bananas on it. Maui grasped wood, bananas, and bird, and held
them fast. He bent down to strangle the bird because he was angry
with it for withholding the fire. The bird said, "Say, don't kill me or
you will not obtain fire." He asked, "Then give me some." The bird
replied, "Then go and rub a taro stalk; there you will obtain it." He
went to rub it and not a spark was found. Thus did the taro stalk become furrowed as we see it to this day. Maui begged again, "Give me
some fire. If you do not, I shall kill you. You will find no escape." The
bird answered again, "Go fetch a ti leaf." Maui fetched a ti leaf and
rubbed it but it did not light. The furrow made by Maui's rubbing remains to this day. Maui went back to kill the bird, and it replied as it
did before. It told Maui to rub water (*wai*). This was a riddle and did
not refer to real water but to the tree called *waimea*. He went to rub the
water but obtained no fire. He returned and gave the bird a beating.
Then it said, "Go fetch the wood of that tree standing there, the *waimea*." He rubbed it and fire was lighted. He burned the forehead of the
bird with it and that is why the foreheads of the mudhens we see are
red. Thus fire was gotten for us to this day.

Snaring of the Sun

After Maui obtained fire he told his mother about it. She answered,
"Where is the help from you? You may think that I am doing well with
my work. I beat my tapa but before even the pieces can be welded the
sun has set. Weeks and months go by before a tapa is ready to trim.
When it is put out to dry it does not dry at all before the sun sets. It is
thus all the time, and the only thing that helps in drying a tapa is to

light a fire." The youth Maui replied, "Would it not be well if I went to cut off the sun's legs?" His mother asked, "Are you strong enough?" He said, "Yes, I am strong." Hina asked, "What have you that will conquer the sun?" He answered, "My own strength will prevent his escaping me." Hina agreed, "Go then but here are some things that will hold the sun for you." Hina gave him fifteen sennit ropes and told him, "This is not the only thing you will need. Go to your ancestress and she has the other things that you'll need to conquer the sun. She will give you explicit directions, for it is she who feeds the sun. The name of the ancestress is Wiliwilipuha (Hollow Wiliwili). When you come to a large growing *wiliwili* tree you will find your ancestress there. The name of the house where the sun is fed is Haleakala (House of the Sun)." Hina instructed him carefully, "Wait until the first cock crows, then the second and the third. Watch until a large old woman comes out. That is your ancestress. She will start a fire and put some bananas on it. Reach down and steal the hand of bananas. When she sniffs this way and that and then sniffs upward and asks the question, 'Whose mischievous one are you?' tell her, 'Yours.' If she asks again, 'Mine by whom?' answer, 'Yours by Hina.' " The mother taught him all he was to do and then he started off to Kaupo. From a place directly above Nu'u, Maui ascended to the place Hina pointed out to him.

He sat at the foot of the *wiliwili* tree until the first crow of the cock and the second and the third. The name of the crowing rooster was Ka'auhelemoa. When it crowed for the third time he peered and saw an old woman creeping along to cook bananas for the sun. She lighted a fire and placed a hand of bananas on it. Maui stole the hand of bananas. When the old woman reached to turn it over she found them gone and grunted, "Humph! Where did the bananas of my sun go to?" The old woman was blind and that was why she had not caught him stealing. She went to fetch another hand of bananas to roast and again it was taken. This happened again and again to the old woman's bananas. The old woman thought to herself, "This must be the work of a mischief-maker." She sniffed this way and that and then upward. She asked, "Whose mischievous one are you?" Maui answered, "Yours." "Mine by whom?" she questioned. "Yours by Hina," replied Maui. Then he leaped down and sat in the old woman's lap. She asked, "What purpose brings you here?" He answered, "I have come to conquer the sun because it goes too fast and the tapas that Hina makes have no time to dry. Therefore I have come to conquer it." Then the old woman gave him a stone and a single sennit rope. When put with the others he had sixteen in all. The stone made the seventeenth article and that was to be used in beating the sun. The day had begun to dawn and the sun was hungry for bananas. The old woman instructed him what to do, "Stay at the foot of this tree and when the first ray appears snare it with a sennit rope and tie it to the tree. Do that until all the ropes are used. Then take the stone and use it for the body of the sun."

She stopped instructing the youth who went to dig a pit at the foot of the tree. He sat in it and he wasn't there long when the first leg of the sun appeared. He snared it fast with a sennit rope, and he continued with the second leg until fifteen were tied fast. The other leg was worked below and he waited for it to come up. It kept struggling below and then as it came up he snared it fast. When the sun saw that Maui had bound all of its legs it began to fall back. He tied the legs fast to the trunk of the tree and it was unable to retreat. It was tied fast. The body came up and he grasped the stone at once and raised it threateningly, then put it down again. The sun said, "Spare me." Maui answered, "Why should you be spared, for you are unkind. You shall not be spared by me." "No! Spare me," pleaded the sun and they made an agreement between them. After that they talked about the time that the sun should hasten, and agreed that for six months it might go fast and for six months it was to go slowly. It was agreeable to both. That is why the sun remains long in the summers and for a short time in the winters, and mankind is benefited thereby.

Earth-fishing

This was another of Maui's deeds in his youth after he had snared the sun and had obtained fire. He used to follow his brothers when they went fishing and sat at the stern. His brothers were angered and said, "Why do you persist in filling up the canoe?" He answered, "How can I fill it when I have a small body?" His brothers replied again, "You can see that the canoe, the only means of getting out to sea, is very small." They took him and threw him overboard. He waited until they were ready to go again and persisted in wanting to sail to sea with them. Maui was vexed because all the fish his brothers brought back were sharks. He chanted for no reason at all, "If I were to sail to sea, the great *ulua* (Caranx) fish Pimoe will take my bait." Because he said that his brothers took him on board when they sailed again.

They went to the fishing ground frequented by *kahala* fish. It was named Po'o, and is located directly outside of Kipahulu. The landmark is Ka Iwi-o-Pele, a place in Hana. After they had let down their stone anchor, he tossed in his fishhook named Manaiakalani. His brothers also let down their hook and said, "Let the *ulua* grope for it," meaning, "Let the fish take the hook." Maui replied, "Let the shark grope." Thus they did on the canoe. It was just as he said, for a shark kept taking their hook until a fish took his. He chanted, "The *ulua* has groped." His brothers exclaimed together, "A shark has groped." He denied this, "No, an *ulua* has groped because I have let down my hook Manaiakalani. The great *ulua* fish Pimoe has taken it and there it is struggling to cling to the sea floor." He said to his older brothers again, "There is nothing we can do but to cut your line and let the fish pull us along." They consented and cut their line. The *ulua* pulled them swiftly along. It pulled out his line until it was restrained by a gourd, that is, the line (kept in the gourd) had all given out. The fish towed them swiftly for days before it came up to the surface. He (Maui) said to his brothers, "This is the thing to do, if you would listen to what I have to say. You paddle our canoe and none of you look behind you. I shall pull in the line with the fish. If you look back the fish will break away." The brothers agreed and paddled the canoe while he pulled in the fish. It was almost at the back of the canoe when the brother at the stern turned to look. The line broke at once and the fish disappeared. The canoe and fish were widely separated. The breaking away of the fish was the reason the islands remained separated.

Perhaps there is more (about Maui) left but I am putting an end right here . . . Puaaloa.

Melanesia

The Myth of Fuusai

Collected by Elli Köngäs Maranda on Fou'eda Island in April 1968, translated from the Lau, and printed in the *Journal of American Folklore* 86 (1973): 4–7. Reprinted by permission of and arrangement with the American Folklore Society.

If the biblical story of Paradise is about a man, a woman, and a snake, the following is about a snake, a woman, and a man. The similarity ends with the set of actors, and I mention it only because the contrast brings into relief the fact that meanings are not universal and that our triads are not everyone's triads.

The story cited and analyzed here was written down from dictation during a period of intensive myth collecting from one man, the chief of Sikwafunu clan, Timoti Bobongi of Kwalo'ai, Malaita, British Solomon Islands.* Bobongi had agreed that I should write down his myth repertory, and he was willing to work full days to that end. I had known Bobongi for almost two years then, and we spoke Lau in all our conversations. All questions that I posed were asked in Lau. After writing down a myth, I regularly read it back to him to check for the accuracy of the recording. At that time I also tried to spot problems in understanding the text and asked for clarifications. Our cooperation was a source of delight for both, and at times people would gather to listen to the storytelling.

Bobongi is an acknowledged singer of tales and is often invited to sing myths in the memorial feasts of different clans. He has also mastered genres other than myth (*'ai-ni-mae*) and is a competent performer of songs (*nguu*) presented at weddings (*faalua*). Further, he is an accomplished carver and had just prior to our arrival completed a decorated temple in honor of the ancestors of his clan. On top of all his other achievements, Bobongi was at one time a political leader, one of the nine chiefs of the Marching Rule, an independence movement that

* I have briefly discussed Bobongi and his repertory in Elli Köngäs Maranda, "Towards the Investigation of Narrative Combinatorics," in Elli Köngäs Maranda and Pierre Maranda, *Structural Models in Folklore and Transformational Essays* (The Hague, 1971), pp. 11–15.

united Malaita in the mid-forties. Whatever the task at hand, Bobongi is a very ambitious man and sets himself high standards. In singing, he prides himself on his skill at setting words into verse; in storytelling in prose form, he can convey shades of meaning in a skilled manner. For example, the reader will notice that the anger of the husband in this myth is expressed by the terms with which he refers to his wife. When his suspicion grows, he moves from "my wife" ('afe nau) through "this woman" (ngwela geni na), to "that old woman of mine" (kukue nau ba)—the last a term a Lau man would never use about his young wife.

Bobongi tends to blow up descriptions of young marriages. He will then enumerate in some detail the duties of the wife and the decisive events that for the Lau mark the consolidation of a marriage (a man builds a house for his wife; the wife makes a garden for him; she bears a child for him). He is aware of using repetitious uniform passages at those times. There is a statement in this text, inserted by Bobongi as an aside, where he directly says, "Here it is like Abunamalau," that is, like another myth he had recited to me previously.

This storyteller is preoccupied with personal appearances, and he devotes space in his narration to youth, beauty, and pleasing physical characteristics; he is moved by the sight of a beautiful girl and allots time in the singing or reciting of a myth to lengthy descriptions of her charms.

The myth of Fuusai is one of the shortest related by Bobongi. Lau mythology, and Malaitan mythology on the whole, is quite complex, and the texts, even when recited in prose form, are long; when sung, they will last several hours. There is a repetitious quality to the style, which in itself is a subject of study. Mainly, repetition serves as a unit marker, so that one unit ends and another begins with the same word.

Culturally, the Lau are a sea people, distinct from the rest of the inhabitants of Malaita in the Solomon Islands, who are hill people.

In Malaita, men are the important half of the world. In this myth, however, it is the child, the wife, and the mother-in-law who determine the fate of the man. What the myth presents is a set of basic social relationships. The reactions of the first husband are those of mistrust and aggression, and he loses; those of the second are trust and acceptance, and he wins all the power, prosperity, and authority that are the lot of a wise man.

If Afubora is taken as the key character, then the message of the myth gains depth. For as long as Afubora is tied to her origins, she is unable to function as a wife and mother. Only when her mother is dead can Afubora contract a marriage that functions. She must be freed of her origins. When she is freed, she is able to transmit her inheritance, all the riches of the snake, the power, the material success; and in Malaita spiritual and material success are coexistent.

Although Abunaili commits a murder, his child will still transmit the powers of the snake to the clan of Fuusai—"the mana of that snake is in Fuusai." Abunaili may not enjoy it, but his descendants will.

Motifs: B145.2 "Prophetic snake"; B176.1 "Magic serpent"; B211.6.1 "Speaking snake (serpent)"; B535.0.14 "Serpent as nurse for child"; C162 "Tabu: marriage with certain person"; E761.1 "Blood as life token"; F721.1 "Underground passages"; F942 "Man sinks into earth"; F942.3.1 "Earth opens at woman's bidding to enclose her"; N340 "Hasty killing or condemnation (mistake)"; S118.1 "Murder by cutting adversary in two."

The Myth of Fuusai.* It starts with the snake, the snake. That lady lived in a rock, lived on, and she gave birth to a child. She gave birth to a girl. And then she heard of—the girl was already a maiden—and she heard of the dance in Fuusai. She heard of that dance, and she wanted to go and watch it. And she went, went and watched the dance. Watched the dance of panpipes. She went like that. When she was almost there, she stole in, hiding herself as she went. The women of Fuusai wondered, "But where is that beautiful girl from that stands here? Why has this girl come?"

Still another day it went again like this. Two watchings of the dance were finished, her mother, that snake, asked her, "Where did you go? I missed you." And her daughter spoke, told her, "Oh, I watched that dance in Fuusai." And that snake said to her daughter, "You were not born of any man. You were not born of any woman. If you still go, you will crush me." And she spoke to her daughter, "Should a man see you, and if he marries you, when he sees me it will not be good. For I am not human, I am a thing of the ground."

That snake spoke like this to her three times. Her daughter did not take heed. When it came to the sixth visit to watch the dance, Abunaili saw her and said, "I will just take a look at that girl. A girl like this I did not see in the village of Fuusai, I did not see in this Abualakwa. A woman like this I did not see in the area of this village." And Abunaili said, "Tomorrow I will look for that woman, that girl." [Whispering: "Afubora is the name of that woman."]

And Abunaili stood waiting, when the panpipes were being danced. That girl watched the dance, the dance was about to start. That girl went. She hid herself.

Abunaili watched her movements. He looked and saw the girl ap-

---

* The title of the myth is pronounced as part of the text. Variants of the same myth, although with quite different outcomes and general development, are to be found in two works by Ian Hogbin, *The Island of the Menstruating Men: Religion in Wogeo, New Guinea* (London, Toronto, 1970), pp. 34–35, and *A Guadalcanal Society: The Kaoka Speakers* (New York, 1964), p. 79.

pear. Abunaili walked ahead, held her hand. The girl said, "Let me free. I was not born of any man, I was not born of any woman."

Abunaili spoke, "Nobody is born of nobody. One is born of people."

That girl said, "Oh, me, of a thing of the ground I was born."

Abunaili said, "Never mind, you are my wife. Never mind if you were born of a thing of the ground."

And Abunaili married Afubora. Married her to Fuusai. And Afubora spoke thus, "In the future, if you see my mother, will it be well? If you see my mother and it is well, you shall dwell with riches."

She spoke only like this, she did not utter the name of her mother, she spoke guardedly.

And Abunaili built a house for his wife. And those two lived on. And a child was born. Those two had a child, and then they went to the garden, taro garden. Afubora waited for Abunaili to go before her, and she deceived him: "Go on ahead, I will go and gather the bamboo for the digging."

Afubora followed after, Abunaili went before her. She took her child, gave it to her mother, gave it to the snake in the rock. And her mother coiled around it.

Coming back to the village, she deceived her husband: "Go on ahead, I will collect things, then I will go." And Abunaili led the way. Afubora went off, passed by the opening of the rock, took her child.

Three times she had given her child to her mother. The fourth time arrived. And Abunaili wondered, "To whom does that woman give my child?" And Abunaili was digging in the garden, and, at noon, Abunaili lied to his wife, lied to Afubora: "Oh, stay where you are, I will just go for a walk. I will look for an areca nut." Abunaili lied thus to his wife. Abunaili happened to take a stone ax in his hand, and he went to Fuusai. When he came to Fuusai, he asked the women of Fuusai, thus: "But to whom does that old woman of mine give my child?" He asked, and the married women of Fuusai all denied: "Oh, we do not look after this child. Should a woman of Fuusai look after him, she would not hide him, we would see him."

Abunaili went back, searched. Abunaili passed by the rock, heard the crying of a child. The snake was coiled around it. Abunaili walked to the rock. He looked and saw his child embraced by the snake. Abunaili was startled and amazed. "Oh, that woman, she gives my child to a strange creature. She lies to me that a woman of Fuusai is looking after him."

Abunaili walked forth, reached for the child to get it from the snake. Took the ax, cut the snake to pieces. Cut her to two pieces. The snake collapsed inside the rock.

Afubora worked on, prepared the garden. Blood gushed forth from her nostrils. It ran to the top of her breasts. And she said: "Oh, now my mother is dead. My husband has killed my mother. A sign of that has come to me."

And Afubora stood up. She wailed. She did not take bundles of things, she did not cut a bundle of taro, she reached for her rainwrap and for her bag, and she left the garden. She came, arrived, looked into the rock, and saw her mother prostrated. Those two pieces of the snake. And her mother spoke, that snake: "My daughter dear, I told you, when you went to the dance in Fuusai. I forbade you, and you did not obey. You have crushed me. I told you. Your husband, Abunaili, had he seen me and had it been well, if he had accepted me, shell strings would have poured in, food would have grown like anything. Had he killed a man in these eight sites of bravery, no man could have killed him. His word would have been supreme, had he accepted me. He has finished me like this, and his word will have no power."

The snake spoke thus to her daughter Afubora, "Bring the dark cloth and wrap me in it. Bury me." The snake spoke to her child. Afubora wrapped (*afu*) her mother in the dark cloth (*bora*), took her, and buried her. After burying her, she returned to Fuusai.

She went and arrived in their house and sat down at the housepost. Abunaili was carrying the child. And Afubora wailed, wailed to her husband: "Dear husband of mine, dear Abunaili, what did I tell you? That time when you held my hand, the day when the panpipes were danced in Fuusai. I told you: 'Let me free, I was not born of any man, I was not born of any woman, I was only born of a thing of the ground.' And you did not heed me. You pressed on to marry me. Had you seen my mother and had it been well you would still have me as your wife, but today you killed my mother, you spoiled everything. Had you accepted my mother, your word would be supreme in these eight sites of bravery. Had you asked for shell strings, for dolphin teeth, they would have come to you. Food would have been abundant. But you cut my mother, all these things will never be yours." Afubora spoke like this, wailed. She wailed thus, and her legs were hidden by the ground. [—Here it is like Abunamalau.—] Abunaili did not look at her, he only sat straight. She wailed, and it reached her waist. She wailed, and it reached under her breasts. She wailed, and the ground reached her armpits.

And Afubora spoke to Abunaili: "Dear husband of mine, dear Abunaili, you will live on in Fuusai. You will marry again a woman in this Fuusai, in this Safangidu, in this Abualakwa. You will again build a house for her. She will again feed a pig for you. She will again make a taro garden for you. She will again make a yam garden for you. She will again bear a child for you. You killed my mother, I am leaving you."

Abunaili was startled, looked, the ground hid Afubora. And she spoke from underground. And she withdrew following an underground passage. A passage that they call the cave of Lilibu. She followed it. She went and came up again. She came up in Langane.

That man of Ofahao saw that girl, her coming up, her coming into daylight. He looked, went to her, and saw. "Where is this beautiful woman from?" He walked forth, Filihau. And he came and asked that girl, "Where are you from?"

And Afubora spoke, "I am a woman of the ground. Therefore I do not live in any village. I do not live in any house. I was born of a thing of the ground."

And Filihau said, "Never mind. I will marry you anyway." And Filihau married that girl Afubora. He married her to Ofahao. And they call her the Lady of Langane. She started as the Lady of Fuusai. Many things follow from her, from this woman. Many words. Many holy things, traditional. They follow her words, they follow her name.

Her names are many: Afubora, the Cut Woman, the Woman Who Withdrew into the Ground, the Quick Woman. These all are her names.

[—This story is too sacred to tell into the tape recorder.—]

She gave birth to eight men in Ofahao. These eight men are: Amasia, Etifonu, Maoma'iluma, Biru'ilalo, Kafa'igou, Suulaola, Maesiana, Ruru.

These eight men originated the lineages of Langane. These are in the genealogy of Belo. Ofahao lineage, Maanakao lineage, the third man's lineage Malililiboso, the fourth man's lineage Lower Bina, the fifth man's lineage Upper Bina, the sixth man's lineage Acleade, the seventh man's lineage Arue, the eighth man's lineage Afuafua.

Question: What about the child she left behind?

Answer: He lived in Fuusai, the lineage of Fuusai. He was Gounakafogwarea. Today those things he started are in Fuusai. The mana of that snake is in Fuusai. When she arrived in Langane, there is her second mana.

Africa

Liberia

The Two Brothers

Collected by John Milbury-Steen in Loffa County, Liberia, in 1971.

Told by a female elementary school student. The collector was present in a classroom with many students who held the microphone, recorded themselves informally, and provided audience participation. The informants were members of the Gbande tribal society, a Mande-speaking people living in northeastern Liberia.
Motifs: H1333.5.0.3 "Quest for Gold Flower"; T685.1 "Twin adventurers"; T685.2 "Hostile twins"; N271 "Murder will out"; E632.1 "Speaking bones of murdered person reveal murder" (reported from the Ibo, Yoruba, and Fang); S73.1.4 "Fratricide motivated by love-jealousy."

Once upon a time, two twins got up. One said, "This girl and I will marry"; the other said, "No, she and *I* will marry." It was the small brother and the big brother who were arguing.
    Then the girl's father said, "Anyone who brings a gold flower will marry my daughter." So they went to look for gold flowers. They found two roads, one cleared and the other overgrown. The big brother said, "I'll take the one overgrown." So they each took a different path and went. Then the small boy went and picked a gold flower. The big brother picked a flower of a different color. Then they came and met. The big brother said to his small brother, "Give me that flower." He wouldn't give it to him. He said, "You'll have to kill me first." Then the older brother took out a knife and killed him. He carried that flower. After he carried it to the girl's parents, then they asked him, "Where is your brother?" He said, "I don't know where he is, because we each took a different path as we were going."
    That boy who had been killed was in the bush. They were looking for him. They kept looking for him. Then a soldier went and saw a skeleton on the ground. They went and asked about it all over town. They asked the older brother. He said, "I'm not the one who killed him." Then the bones sang a song and sang it and sang it:

It was for the sake of a gold flower
That my brother killed me.

How the Society Can Get Back Its Medicine

Contributed by John Milbury-Steen. Collected in Loffa County, Liberia, in 1971.

Narrated by an uneducated woman. A native speaker borrowed the tape recorder and recorded story sessions in town at night. This is a formulaic chain tale, on the model of type 2034 *The Mouse Regains Its Tail* (motif Z41.4), known, oddly, among the Berbers and in England and the United States. It has been thoroughly adapted to the Gbande locale. A proposed new motif number is Z41.4.3* "How the society can get back its medicine (magic). Dog swallows medicine (magic) and will give it back only after drinking oil of a cow. The people go to cow, cottonwood tree, eagle, old woman, man, horse, chicken, cockroach, rat, rice." Also present is motif D1337.1 "Magic object beautifies." Note the following terms employed in the tale: *society* = the Sande society, the women's secret society; *Kwi* = Western, i.e., American or European, as opposed to tribal and indigenous; *iron country money* = iron money in the form of rods, also called "Kissi money"; *medicine* = equivalent to magic; *soup* = a thick gravy poured over rice.

Once upon a time there was a town that was very big. There was no equal to it. All of the people had children. They were there and put them into a women's society at the same time. All of the people made a big farm because the beginning of the Sande society was near. All of them agreed to make the farm with one voice. The rice grew well. When it grew they harvested it. Then they said, "The time has reached for the beginning of the Sande society. All of the women said, "We agree. It's a good thing."

At that time, no one would see anything *Kwi*, no one would put his eyes on it. No one would see salt; the country salt made from ashes was their salt. No one would see money, except iron country money that they would thank dancers with.

After the society went into the bush, it stayed there three years.*

* An extremely long time for a society to be in session. Nowadays the society meets for a matter of weeks. The narrator is setting the scene in the remote past.

Then the society came out. Then they sat down. They told the society members, "Come and sing a song." All of the people were seated listening. They were very happy.

Then the people got up and went and killed one cow. They cooked it for them. When they cooked it for them, the most outstanding thing in it was the medicine to make the girls beautiful. The society girls didn't know anything about it. The people put it under the rice. Then they put the soup on top of it. They were listening and said, "We brought rice to the society girls to eat." They put the particular rice in a large pan. The girls ate it and all of them were satisfied. The people who were taking care of them ate some and they were satisfied. Then they said, "The dog is sitting here," but, as for this dog, he was always with them. The remainder of the rice they gave to this dog. Well, their hands didn't reach the beauty medicine. The dog ate it and swallowed it. He didn't talk. He was quiet.

Then the people said to them, "You may give thanks to us, but we haven't heard the name of the medicine." Then they said, "Oh? We haven't seen the medicine." The dog was just sitting down listening. Then they said to him, "Dog, you haven't seen the medicine?" He said, "No."

When they troubled him, he said, "All right. I have seen it. I swallowed it." They said to him, "Give it back." He said, "Before I give it back, I must drink the oil of a cow. That will make me give it."

As for the cows, they were standing there, those they were about to kill. They were standing there. The people said to one, "It concerns you." He said, "Oh! You mean I have to give some oil for the dog to drink before the dog gives the medicine to give to the young society girls before they send them to be married? I have to eat a cottonwood tree leaf first. When I'm full, I'll give oil for the dog to drink."

They said to the cottonwood tree, "It concerns you." He said, "Oh! You mean the cow has to eat my leaves before he gives oil for the dog to drink before the dog returns the medicine to give to the society girls before they send them to be married? An eagle has to sit on me first."

They said to the eagle, "It concerns you." The eagle said, "Boy! You mean I have to sit on the cottonwood tree before he gives leaves for the cow to eat before the cow gives his fat for the dog to eat before he gives the medicine to give to the society girls to send them to be married? I have to eat an old woman's eye first."

The old woman said, "Give my eye? I would have to eat flying bug-a-bugs first and a man would have to bring them."

The man said, "Catch flying bug-a-bugs? I would do that if I could hold a horse's tail."

The horse said, "You mean it will only rain if the man shouts for it to rain while holding my tail so that the flying bug-a-bugs will come out so he can catch some to give to the old lady in order for her to give her eye to the eagle so the eagle can sit on the cottonwood tree so the tree can give some leaves for the cow to eat so the cow will give some of its oil to the dog to drink to get the dog to return the medicine to the society girls so they can be sent to be married? I will not let the man hold my tail unless I step on a young chicken."

The young chicken said, "I am just standing here and haven't done anything. You mean the horse has to step on me before the horse lets the man pull his tail and shout for rain so the flying bug-a-bugs will come out so he can catch some to give to the old lady before she will give her eye to the eagle before the eagle consents to sit on the cotton-wood tree before the cottonwood tree will part with any of its leaves to give to the cow before the cow will give its oil to the dog to drink before the dog returns the medicine to the society girls before they send them to be married? Unless I eat a cockroach, the horse may not step on me."

So they said to the cockroach, "This is it. It concerns you." The cockroach said, "Oh! But I'm lying down here minding my business. No one eats me unless I eat the tail of a rat."

The rat said, "Oh! After all of this, you're ending with me?" They said, "Yes." The rat said, "I will not give up my tail for the roach to eat so the roach will let the chicken eat him so the chicken will agree to being stepped on by a horse so the horse will let the man shout for rain while pulling his tail so it will rain for the flying bug-a-bugs to come out so he can catch some to give to the old lady to persuade her to give her eye to the eagle so the eagle will sit on a cottonwood tree so the tree will part with some of its leaves to give to the cow so the cow will contribute some oil to the dog so the dog will return the medicine to the society in order for the girls to be married—I say I will not give up my tail so all this will happen, unless I tell my friend Bongorli and he understands it."

Bongorli said, "I will put down my head to think about it." As they said it, he put down his head. After they said it all, he came out of thinking and began putting down his head to think again. This is no other than rice. When it ripens it will be bending down its head. When it bends down its head, then they harvest it after a lot of work.

Bush Fowl and Turtle Build a Town

Contributed by John Milbury-Steen. Collected in Loffa County, Liberia, in 1971, from a young man attending high school. A native speaker borrowed the tape recorder and recorded story sessions in town at night.

Trickster stories told by high school students are usually directed against authority figures rather than peers. This consummate trickster tale, however, affirms conservative values of family unity and community. Bush fowl and turtle refuse to support their families and instead move out of town into the bush. This act of desertion, along with their gluttony and breaking of their oath, makes their downfall seem just. Each deceitful character takes advantage of the other, and mutual treachery leads to the death of both.

Motifs: K171 "Deceptive division of profits"; K231.2 "Mutual agreement to divide food. Trickster eats other's food and then returns to divide his own"; K1601 "Deceiver falls into his own trap" (reported for the Hottentot); M101.3 "Death as punishment for broken oath"; Q582 "Fitting death as punishment" (reported for the Duala and Wakweli); S112.1 "Boiling to death."

The hungry season is the period—September and October—just before the harvest when the old rice has been eaten and the new rice is not yet ripe. A bug-a-bug hill is a termite mound.

Once upon a time Bush Fowl and Turtle were in one town. Then the hungry season came. The two of them sat down and said, "Since the hungry season is so troublesome and getting food is so hard, let's go and set up our own village and be there. Whatever we get we can eat. There are too many people in this town we have to share with. That's what makes getting enough food hard." So the two of them agreed and went. They went out of town and went to set up their village.

The place where they set up their village was level ground. A big bug-a-bug hill was standing there, very tall. Bush Fowl didn't like Turtle too much. So he climbed up on top of the bug-a-bug hill and built his own house there. That bug-a-bug hill was standing on a level place. As for the turtle, he had no strength to climb it. He built his own house on level ground.

One of them would go and pick wild yams. He would come and cook them. The other would go and pick yams and also come and cook them. The turtle first called the bush fowl. "Bush Fowl!" He said, "Yes?" Turtle said, "Come, let's eat." The bush fowl would be on the top of the bug-a-bug hill and would fly and come down to Turtle's house. He ate the turtle's yams. He flew back and went up on top of the bug-a-bug hill to his own house. Then he cooked his own yams and he called Turtle. He said, "Turtle!" Turtle said, "Yes?" He said, "Come and eat yams." When Turtle would go climbing up to Bush Fowl's house, you know, it was on the bug-a-bug hill, and, you know how Turtle climbs a hill—it's very hard for him. He tried to climb and gave it a good try, but he would just get his hand on the door sill and then slip back and fall down, turning over and over. Then he would find himself lying at his own house. The bush fowl called him again, "Hey, Turtle! My stomach is full!" Turtle would be bitter. He said, "This is why this man built his house on the back of a bug-a-bug hill, so that I can't go up there to eat his rice, but he comes and eats my own rice."

The next day they looked for yams again and brought them and cooked them. The turtle called the bush fowl again. The bush fowl came again and went down to the door of Turtle's house to eat the yams. He knew Turtle was unable to go to him. He called Turtle again. Two times Turtle failed. When they had gone to build this village they had taken an oath the two of them had sworn between them, "When we come here, neither of us should do anything bad to his friend." The oath would catch anyone who did something bad to his friend. They made the oath properly. Both of them agreed to it.

Oh! This business was really hurting the turtle. The bush fowl was eating Turtle's food and the hungry season was hard. Turtle was unable to go eat his own food. He said, "Since the bush fowl is doing this to me, I'll kill him."

Then he went and set a trap right at the door of his house just where the bush fowl would come down when he moved from his house. The trap was at his doorsill. It was a trap made with a bent stick. Then they went again and picked all the yams and brought them. Turtle cooked his own first. He said, "I'll kill Bush Fowl today and cook him and eat him. No one can act this way to his friend." The oath was still binding on them, but he forgot it.

So he cooked yams and called Bush Fowl. He said, "Bush Fowl! Bush Fowl!" He said, "Yes?" He said, "Come!" He didn't know about the trap. He just flew and came down into the trap and it caught him. He said, "Turtle! Something has caught me! What did you lay down at the door of your house?" Turtle said, "Let me just finish eating my yams. Your mischief is at an end today. I'm going to kill you today." He said, "What! Man! Don't do that to me! Have you even forgotten the oath we swore?" He said, "That's your business." The turtle sat and ate the yams and finished completely. He brought a cutlass and cut Bush Fowl's head off.

He sat down and took the feathers off and cut him in pieces and put them in a pot. When he put them in the pot he set it on the fire to cook. The fire wood was very short and the pot was very tall. The turtle couldn't even stand on the ground to see the inside of the pot. Ah! He just wanted to see inside the pot. He wanted the cooking to go all right. He climbed up to see the inside of the pot. [What about the oath they took!]* He stood and stretched out his head to see the inside of the pot, the short wood slipped under his feet and he fell into the pot where the bush fowl was cooking. He turned over. When Turtle turns on his back, he can't do anything. He stayed like that and was also cooking. The water was enough for the bush fowl because he (Turtle) wanted to cook him well to eat him. He stayed there and the two of them cooked together. That's how the oath caught Turtle.

So, taking an oath isn't good. But if you take an oath, beware of breaking it: it'll always remain with you.

* The narrator here interjects his own comment.

Nigeria

Jọmọ, Guardian of the Great Sword

Collected by Deirdre La Pin in October 1972 in Ilè-Olú'jí, near Òndó, and translated from the Yoruba.

Chief Bàálè Akínlàjà is a semi-retired cocoa farmer who divides his time between his plantation and the political duties associated with his title. One evening he joined a group of other Yoruba storytellers in Ilè-Olú'jí. His performance was highly acclaimed by an audience of twenty-three friends and neighbors. A few observed that it had been many years since they had heard this *itàn* or "true story" told with such accuracy and detail.

Jọmọ is a Gargantuan warrior who is part human and part divine. Some people say that he came from Benin to the Òndó-Okìtìpupa area in the remote past. Others claim that he hails from Òyó. Among his superhuman features are a bulbous nose with a remarkably keen sense of smell and two fan-like ears that hear noises and conversations over great distances. He spares himself and others the embarrassment of eavesdropping by inserting into his ear an *agìṣaṣa*, or feather of the Clock Bird, guardian of all winged creatures.

Behind this uncommon exterior is a hero of extraordinary strength and willingness to serve. Praised as the "Guardian of the great sword . . . ," he is also said to have brought the Yorubas one of their favorite foods: okra. Jọmọ's usefulness, however, is offset by his "protruding teeth" or greed, and his neighbors ask Orúnmìlà, the god of Ifá divination, to suggest a way to curb his unfettered appetite. Three types of cowries mentioned are associated with Ifá practice in Òndó: cowries "from under the mat" are given as payment to the priest; *adìbò* signal Orúnmìlà's response to "yes and no" questions according to whether they land face up or face down when tossed into the air; *gégélèsé* are single cowries strung together in bunches and given to the priest as sacrifice.

Jọmọ's disappearance into the ground near the *ẹ̀ẹ́dẹ́n* or *ẹdọn* marks his transformation into an *umọlè* or earth spirit, protected by the Ògbóni Society; *ẹdọn* brass figures are central to the society's ritual communion with the spirits of the earth.

In essence, the *ìtàn* is a serious warning against the abuse of power. Jǫmǫ abandons his personal exercise of force; but when he submits to community control he learns that the townspeople are no better able than he to limit his warrior's strength to wise and useful ends. Such indiscretion will eventually cause the aggressors themselves to die by Jǫmǫ's sword.[1]

Motifs: F614.10 "Strong hero fights whole army alone"; D169 "Transformation: woman into bird"; D1311 "Magic object used for divination"; B143.1 "Bird gives warning" (reported for the Benga); K735.1 "Mats over holes as pitfall" (reported for the Fiort and from Angola); K1601.1 "Pitfall arranged but victim escapes it"; F942 "Man sinks into earth"; D1960.2 "Kyffhäuser. King asleep in mountain will awake one day to succor his people" (but here he is falsely aroused by a quarreling woman).

> Jǫmǫ "Guardian of the great sword,"
> He who stretched his mighty hand to grasp the cudgel
> At the dawn of time.

It was·war he fought . . . war. How he fought! One day, Jǫmǫ went to battle. He set out, he reached the enemy, he fought and he killed. He killed with his right! He killed with his left! Then he went away. When he returned home he went to the council meeting. Now at this meeting he seated himself in the middle of the group and acted as chairman. When the others had seated themselves, Jǫmǫ addressed them: "Greetings; may I have your attention!"

Even if a thousand lumps of pounded yam were there, no one would have the courage to take one until Jǫmǫ arrived. One day, he was on his way to the meeting. The members were telling each other, "He hasn't come yet, he hasn't come yet!" When he approached the group, he took the pounded yam and unwrapped it. For his followers, he took just a single lump, broke it in two, dipped it in soup, and held it out to them. And there was no ǫba who dared to say, "Why are you behaving like this?" Before he served the rest, he would take whatever he wished and help himself. When he was at the palace, there was no one who dared to take exception to what he said. Such a person could not be found there.

The next time for battle came. When he left for the fight, the townspeople said, "What shall we do with this man who won't let us breathe,

1. I am grateful to Túndé Ayándòkún of Ilè-Olújí for his assistance with the transcription and translation of this narrative. Sekoni Oluropo kindly provided additional information on the tradition of Jǫmǫ. This narrative is part of a collection funded by the Foreign Fellowship Program during 1971–73.

Jomo who doesn't allow anyone to breathe freely?" They made up their minds. They took the kind of cowries one keeps under the mat, they took two *adìbò* cowries, and they took three *gégélèsé* cowries tied on a string. They went to Orúnmìlà. They said, "This man oppresses us and won't let us be free in our town. Whenever we go to a council meeting, he takes enough pounded yam for ten people and gives it to his children. He won't let us eat. If he speaks, we have to agree to whatever he says."

Orúnmìlà said, "All right." He said there is no way they can physically overpower him. However, he has a throne—a throne that he sits on. He said that they should dig a hole there, a hole. He said they should buy a sword, they should buy a sharp iron spear and a bit of broken bottle. They should put all of it into the hole. They should make it look exactly the way it did before; they should look for an imported mat, buy it, and spread it over the hole. He said that when he comes back from battle and gets ready for the council meeting (it was usually held on market day) they should clear the way for him so that he might sit down there.

As Jomo was coming from the battle (his mother had died by that time, about twenty years earlier), his mother changed herself into a bird. She went to meet her son. She had heard all the plans that they had devised and she went to meet her son. As Jomo was coming along, she beat his right ear with her wing; she beat his left. She smacked him several times and began to sing to him again and again. Jomo didn't answer. She sang. He didn't answer.

After a time he neared his house. The soldiers behind him called out, "Greetings, Jomo!" He continued to march along. The bird flew after him. She brushed his ear . . . and again she brushed his ear. She sang:

> O Jomo Tàràko*
> O Jomo Tàràko
> Greetings, Jomo
> O Jomo Tàràko
> When you arrive at the meeting
> O Jomo Tàràko
> They have spread a mat of fiber,
> They have spread a mat of grass.
> O Jomo Tàràko
> A hole is there!
> O Jomo Tàràko
> Thorns are there!

---

* "Tàràko" is a praise name for Jomo, suggesting his massive size and superhuman strength. The word is principally valued for its euphonic function in the chorus of the song.

O Jọmọ Tàràko
A sword is there!
O Jọmọ Tàràko
Do not sit there!
O Jọmọ Tàràko
Call your dog
O Jọmọ Tàràko
Call your Loghoye
O Jọmọ Tàràko
Throw pounded yam there
O Jọmọ Tàràko
Then call "Loghoye"
O Jọmọ Tàràko
Jọmọ my son
O Jọmọ Tàràko
Don't sit there!
O Jọmọ Tàràko.

He did not heed her. His ears were deaf. When he got to the town gate, the bird flew up in front of him. She brushed him with her wing, she beat him and took up the song she had sung before.

A man called "Wise One" was following and called out, "Hey there, Warrior! Take the *agiisasa* feather out of your ear!" He took it out. He looked to the right, he looked to the left. He took it out. The man said, "There was a bird singing today, but you didn't hear it." Then Jọmọ told him to let the bird come and sing, he told the man to let her sing. The bird flew up and perched on his shoulder. She put her beak into his ear like this. She went:

O Jọmọ Tàràko
O Jọmọ Tàràko
O Jọmọ my son
O Jọmọ Tàràko
When you have got to the meeting
O Jọmọ Tàràko
They have spread a mat of fiber,
They have spread a mat of grass.
O Jọmọ Tàràko
A hole is there!
O Jọmọ Tàràko
A sword is there!
O Jọmọ Tàràko
Break two lumps of pounded yam
O Jọmọ Tàràko
Call your Loghoye

O Jọmọ Tàràko
Call your dog
O Jọmọ Tàràko
Jọmọ my son
O Jọmọ Tàràko.

He said, "What?" The friend who had heard the song before explained it and told Jọmọ the sense of what the bird had sung. Jọmọ said, "Oh! in the meeting!" The friend said that they had spread a mat where the throne stood, that thorns were there and a sword was there. He said that he should take a piece of pounded yam, dip it into the soup, and throw it on top of the mat. Then he should call his dog. Jọmọ said, "Fine, all right, I understand." He put the feather back into his ear and went on his way. The bird rose and flew off.

When he reached the house, he bathed. People greeted him, "Hello there, Warrior! Welcome home!" The whole town crowded around to greet him. The meeting was two days away. Dawn broke on the following morning.

In the Warrior's house some people brought palm wine, some brought palm gin. The next day was the day on which they were going to perform a ceremony like the annual feast of chiefs today. That day came when they were bringing palm wine for the assembly, the very day of the meeting. They brought yam, they pounded it, and finished pounding. Palm wine, beer, and good things filled the meeting place. They began saying to each other, "The Warrior. . . ." They waited, but he didn't come. They sent people and told them to call him and say they had been waiting since morning. Jọmọ answered, "Ahhhhhh . . . well, all right. I am on my way."

Then the Warrior got himself ready in his house. He took the stool he sat on at home and told one of his children to carry it. He picked up his cloth and tied it around his waist. He reached the palace and told them to bring his stool and put it there. Everyone cried, "Warrior, *this* is the place for you to sit down!" He told them to be quiet. He brought the stool to a different place and sat down. He said, "Now! Where is the yam!"

They pulled off a small lump of yam and brought it to him. He looked to the right, he looked to the left, he looked all around. He took the pounded yam and broke it neatly. He took the cover off the pot, divided the piece into two and dropped it into the soup. With a great whirrrrr he threw it and it landed where the mats were spread. He called, "Loghoye!" Loghoye sprinted over to the yam, running with great speed. He fell into the hole.

When he fell into the hole, Jọmọ said, "Hey! What is this?" Everyone began to look at one another fearfully. Where could they escape?

He jumped up brusquely and called a soldier. He told him to bring his feather and his sword. The soldier ran off and came back. As for the townspeople who were there, some dashed through the backyard and some scaled the wall.

Jọmọ took his sword and unsheathed it. Then he shut his eyes. He had already wounded one person when an elder came running out, an old man. [Ọlọ́rùn,* don't let old men die out in the town. Amen.] He said, "Hey there Jọmọ, 'Guardian of the great sword, the one who spread his mighty hand to grasp the cudgel,' what are you doing?" He answered that he wanted to kill them, that they had dug a hole under his throne, that he had thrown a piece of yam there and it fell into the hole and so did his dog. That dog was his only dog. Because of what happened to him, he would kill a thousand persons.

Ah! The old man told him to first look into his face. He soothed him and sang the praises of his family. He said, "Warrior! Look into my face! I am one who gave birth to you. I am an old man. War doesn't make a forest disappear. War cannot wipe out a whole town. Was it good, what the town did to you? It is true that they plotted against you. But if you kill them now, you will soon find when your ear turns deaf that you have killed your children along with them. This is well enough!"

Jọmọ gazed upward for a long time. He turned his back and set out for home. As soon as he reached his house, he looked in front, he looked in back. He said, "It is the hour to leave the world." He took his sword, the very sword he fought with, and carried it into the open yard in front of the house, the place where what we call èédèn spirit is located. He thrust his sword into the ground and went in. He cried out, "My fellow townsmen, if war ever comes again, if war comes along and you are fighting, you must call me!" They said, "Fine." Then he disappeared into the ground and out of sight.

Not more than three days later, a woman and her husband were quarreling furiously. He took a stick and was poised, ready to beat her. She quickly stepped outside and called, "Jọmọ ooooo! 'Guardian of the great sword'! Save me!" Jọmọ rose bit by bit from the ground where he had entered. He took his cudgel. Swish! Clash! He didn't give a thought to the people he was fighting. The elder of the previous day came running out and spoke: "Have you forgotten that this is your town?" He said they had called him; he had told them that if war broke out they should call him. "Isn't this war?" He told Jọmọ that he didn't seem to care at all whom he was killing. There was no outbreak of war in the town, it was just an ordinary woman who had called him.

Jọmọ said, "Ah! This is too much!" He said the town should assem-

* Ọlọ́rùn is the principal Yoruba deity.

ble and they should call the ọba. The ọba gathered everyone together. Jọmọ addressed them and said, "Never, henceforth and forevermore," if war broke out in the town should they call him. He would never come again. Jọmọ thrust his sword into the ground and disappeared.

And ever since that time, when we have a person with protruding teeth in our house, we do not dig a hole to trap him, nor do we hide in order to kill him on the sly. But he gave us a law that if war breaks out, no one must call him. Even if the fighting continues until tomorrow, he will not heed our call again. It is women who will bring about a war simply because someone beats them. If there is a spirit who says we should not call him, then we should not call him. This is as far as I have journeyed and returned this day.

Audience: "Thank you, Baba."

He-Who-Meets-Problems-Alone and He-Who-Seeks-Good-Advice

Collected by Deirdre La Pin in June 1972 in Aiyégúnlẹ̀ village near Ibàdàn and translated from the Yoruba.

The teller of the following òwe (proverb, parable) is James Ọlá. Ọlá, chief arbiter in his small farming community, frequently employs parables to settle village disputes. The tale of Anìkàndágbón and Afọgbọn-ọlọgbọn-sọgbọn is one of the most commonly known in Yorubaland (from Ekìtì to Kẹtu) and is most often heard in the shortened proverb form that concludes the narrative here: "To seek good advice is best; to try to solve problems by oneself is not good."

In his interpretation, Ọlá has skillfully fashioned the òwe into a statement about the clash of priorities between traditional and modern modes of education. Each philosophy is represented by one of the tale's contrasting characters. Anìkàndágbón is portrayed as an egotistical intellectual who has passed beyond the need to rely on the wisdom of his associates. Afọgbọn, on the other hand, prefers to make decisions collectively, thereby safeguarding harmony in the community and preserving continuity with the past. Ọlá's characterization of the young educated ọba relates directly to present-day politics in which traditional rulers are selected according to their inclination toward or away from "progress." The emphasis on the ọba's open-mindedness (despite his education) serves to reinforce the suitability of his choice between the two characters for the chief's title.

Motifs: H501 "Test of wisdom"; H506 "Test of resourcefulness"; H1023 "Tasks contrary to the nature of objects."

In a town there were two friends. They were very close. One was called Anìkàndágbón or "He who Meets Problems Alone"; he knew how to read. The other was called Afọgbọ́n-ọlọ́gbọ́n-sọgbọ́n or "He who Seeks Good Advice." These two spent many years together making jokes about their names.

Then the old ọba died. His son, who was next in line, was well-educated. When they had gathered to appoint his chiefs, he heard them greet one of his relatives, "He who Meets Problems Alone," and he answered "That's right!" And "He who Seeks Good Advice" he answered "That's right!" The ọba who had just been installed said that he wanted to design a test for the men known by these names. He told the town that he wanted to know if it was possible to reach the solution to a problem without help from others. This he wanted to find out.

One day the ọba said that he wanted to hold a feast at the palace in honor of his dead father. He invited the whole town. Then he bought a cow. The ọba instructed them to kill it and afterward to cut off its two hind legs. "He who Seeks Good Advice" arrived and they greeted him; he answered saying that to be amenable to good advice was best. Then "He who Meets Problems Alone" arrived and he said there was no knowledge that he didn't possess, that he could make intelligent decisions unaided, that all the wisdom he needed was in his own head.

The ọba told them to sit down. When they had finished feasting, the ọba called his messengers. He instructed them to summon "He who Seeks Good Advice." They called him and he said, "Take this hind leg with you. In one week you should bring it back in perfect condition. It must not be spoiled. Bring it exactly one week from today. These bearers will carry it to your house. Now "He who Meets Problems Alone," take this leg that remains. One week from today you will bring it to the palace in perfect condition."

When they got home, "He who Seeks Good Advice" put his piece down. His family demanded, "Where did you get a-hold of this cow—this cow leg?" He asked the whole household to come over and help him solve a problem: the ọba gave it to him, saying that he should take care of it for a week and then take it back in perfect condition. He couldn't figure out a way to do it.

"Ah!" the people said. "There is a solution!" They said they would call the butcher to come and weigh the leg. Then a week later they would bring them a similar piece so they could take it to the ọba. They took the leg and the beef sellers came to examine it. They said they would cut a piece exactly like it and bring it back in a week. That way

he could take the ǫba a leg that was in perfect condition. He thanked
them.

When "He who Faces Problems Alone" took his leg home, his relatives asked, "Where did you manage to get this?" He said that the ǫba
had given it to him. He didn't discuss the matter with anyone. He took
it into his room. Then he cut down a big tree and built a fire. He made
a drying rack over it, took the meat and put it on top, and roasted it so
that it would stay fresh. After five days the meat fell from the bones.
It spoiled, and maggots infested it. He tied it again and again with a
rope, but it was no use. He tried over and over again, but to no avail.
When a week was up the bone had slipped out of the meat and a rotten
smell filled their whole house! The only thing left to do was to ask for
his family's advice. His relatives said, "What do you want our advice
for?" When he told them they merely expressed surprise that he had
failed to find the solution within his own head.

When the week was up, the people who took the cow leg away for
"He who Seeks Good Advice" brought back one that was in perfect
condition. The time had come when the ǫba was expecting them to return the meat. The townspeople gathered. "He who Seeks Good Advice" put on fine clothes and his followers also put on fine clothes. The
bearers came and they carried away the cow leg that was in perfect
condition. He arrived at the palace. They told "He who Meets Problems
Alone" to bring his. When he tried to carry it into the palace, he had
to leave it behind; he couldn't find anyone to help him. How it smelled!

When they appeared at the ǫba's palace, they called for "He who
Seeks Good Advice," and he answered, "Here I am." They said he certainly deserved his title, that he was a person who took good advice.
When "He who Meets Problems Alone" came up, they turned away
from him. His clothes were a mess, and the ǫba told him, "Move away,
back over there . . . far away!" He put the meat down.

Then the ǫba addressed the townspeople. " 'He who Seeks Good Advice' has brought his leg here today. Have you looked at it closely?"
They answered that they had seen it. "As for 'He who Meets Problems
Alone,' this is his. Is this like the one you took away from here a week
ago? Is this how it looked last week? Wasn't it in perfect condition
when you took it away? Why has it become like this?" He humbly explained that he had really taken a lot of trouble, but that it didn't seem
to make any difference. He had made a fire and roasted it, but the meat
didn't stay together. The ǫba said, "You have tried to solve this problem without any help, it is true. You, 'He who Seeks Good Advice,' how
did you do it?" He answered that people had made suggestions, that
he took their advice and it worked. He left the meat with them (the
butchers) and they brought one back.

The ǫba took "He who Seeks Good Advice" and said, "My townsmen, this man is a chief, for he is useful to the community because he solves his problems collectively. This one, they should kill him because he is a 'Scourge on the Town.' Anyone who tries to be clever in this way is a blight on the town. He is a selfish person, an evil person."

They begged the ọba not to kill him. His relatives said they would pool their money and pay for the cow. They brought another cow, and the ọba drove him out from the town, saying that he didn't want him to live in his town any more.

This is where the story ends. To seek out good advice is best. To try to solve problems by oneself is not good.

Cameroun

Wanto and the Shapeless Thing

Collected by Philip A. Noss in August 1966 in Bétaré Oya and translated from the Gbaya.

The narrator, Abel Wah, was a Gbaya farmer and teacher who lived in the country about thirty-five miles northwest of Bétaré Oya in central Cameroun. He was about forty-five years old, a man of minimal school training but one highly respected for his knowledge of Gbaya tradition.

The Gbaya are a Sudanic-speaking people who inhabit eastern Cameroun and the Central African Republic. Agriculture, supplemented by hunting and fishing, provides the Gbaya with their main means of subsistence.

Tapes of Noss's tales, together with the original transcriptions and translations, are on deposit at the Indiana University Archives of Traditional Music. In the translations given here, items enclosed within brackets are audience comments.

There is a strong likeness in this narrative to type 555 *The Fisher and His Wife*, the well-known Grimm tale in which a monster transformed into a fish grants a poor fisherman all his wife's wishes, which become increasingly extravagant, until the couple is returned to their original poverty. In the present story the monster suggests the wishes to hunter Wanto, and to fit the tribal mores the wife's questioning is suppressed. Wanto errs, like the poor fisherman, in lusting for power. Tape II, No. 48.

Motifs: D1761.0.1 "Wishes granted without limit"; C311.1.5 "Taboo: observing supernatural helper"; C423.1 "Taboo: disclosing source of magic power" (reported also for the Fang); C905 "Supernatural being punishes breach of taboo"; C930 "Loss of fortune for breaking taboo" (reported also for the Loango).

> Young men, listen to a tale, a tale for fun,
>   listen to a tale, a tale for fun;
> Young men, listen to a tale, a tale for fun,
>   listen to a tale, a tale for fun;
> Elders, listen to a tale, a tale for fun,

listen to a tale, a tale for fun;
Rrrrrr, kpinggim!

Okay, there was Wanto. He bought some rope for duiker snares, sharpened his machete real sharp, by God, took his spear, and was off into the valley. He went on and on setting snares until suddenly the rain came. There was no chance for him to make a shelter. He looked around and saw the roots of a large tree and ran quickly to get in among them, but when he got there, something big and shapeless was already there! He spun around to escape, but the thing said, "Don't run! Stop! Come here! Don't run away!" So Wanto edged forward a bit. [The big shapeless thing, was it the corpse of an animal?] No, I'll tell you, I'll explain it. It was something—one wouldn't know what it was. One wouldn't know where its tail was or where its head was. It said, "Wanto, what are you looking for?" Wanto answered that he was setting snares, and the thing said, "Okay, but what do you really want?" Wanto said he wanted duikers and buffalo and bush bucks to kill.

"Oh, those are the things you get because you have to, but there's more than that," the thing urged. "If you were like a king, what nice things would you want?"

But Wanto answered, "I don't have any children, I don't have any brothers—what would I do with all those things?"

"Okay," the thing said, "Wanto, come. Go find a nice high dry piece of land and build yourself a house there." Wanto went up and looked around for a good piece of land; he went back into the valley and cut some stakes and then built himself a house. Next the thing told Wanto to build a house for it beside Wanto's house, and he shouldn't make a door to it or any opening, so Wanto built the second house too. Then it said that Wanto should go and bring his wife, so he went and led Laaiso back. She thought her husband had killed an animal, but it wasn't an animal. She brought her little baskets and her big baskets; she thought maybe her husband had found the corpse of a buffalo and was going to cut it up, but when they got there it was nothing but a little grass hut! Laaiso asked him what was going on, but he just told her to be quiet.

Then Wanto went to tell the thing that his wife had come. It said he should tell her to come so that it could see her, but when she came, it had already seen her from inside its doorless house, and Laaiso didn't see it. She asked Wanto, "What kind of thing is inside the house that it doesn't have any doors or openings?" But Wanto said, "Shhh, don't talk. You're just a woman. You can't understand this," and he told her to go back to the house he had built and stay there. So she went back and sat down. Is a woman greater than a man? [No, the tortoise's tricks are in its stomach!] Yes, the tortoise's tricks are in its stomach!

Then the thing talked to Wanto again and said that he should ask for anything he wanted because it had the power to give it to him. "Don't you want to have children?"

"We've been married a long time and don't have any children yet; where am I going to get children?"

"No, just ask! Don't you want lots of wives?" Wanto agreed, and it asked how many he wanted.

"I want nine more wives, and Laaiso is the tenth," Wanto said. But the thing told him not to ask for wives yet, he should ask for houses first, so Wanto agreed, "Okay, I'll take houses." So the thing said some words and the houses were there. After a while Wanto said he wanted a wife for each house, and the thing said some more words and there was a wife in each house. Then he said he wanted a compound around him, and the thing made a compound appear. Next Wanto decided it wouldn't be too good if he was just there alone with a lot of women, so he said he wanted lots of people in the compound too. The thing spoke and people appeared and filled the compound. There were people in all directions, a whole town, and in the middle was Wanto the chief.

After some time Wanto went on tour and was given all sorts of gifts. He told the people that when he came back after four months they should all gather and have a festival for his kingship, and the word went out to all parts of the kingdom. Things were well established by now, you see.

After a while the thing spoke again, and Wanto's hut turned into a house with a metal roof. It spoke again and its own house turned into a house with a metal roof beside Wanto's palace, but it still had no opening. The only one who saw the thing was Wanto, for it had given orders that Wanto shouldn't let any wife, any child, or any of his great men see it. That was the command it had given. No one would see it, only the two of them would see each other. And that was the way Wanto lived.

Now you know how people are. Wanto gathered them all together for the festival, they made a lot of beer, they made all sorts of preparations, and then the dancing started. Wanto gave food to everybody, and they all danced, it was a real dance! The town rocked, *hidi hidi hidi hidi*, and Wanto was King.

Wanto slept, and the next day they held court and the people filled the courtyard, *pang-tang*. Everyone sat down, and Wanto's throne was brought in. He sat down, and all you could hear was greetings, greetings, greetings, greetings. Wanto got up and went into his house for a bottle of beer, he drank it all, yes all of it, and he got to feeling pretty good. He came back, sat down, and then told them the reason that he had called them together—they should go into the house for a little taste first. He invited all the leaders in and he entertained them well. Now, of course, for a man tasting means drinking, so they drank and drank and drank. Then he told them all to come and everyone stood up together. They had just been sitting in the courtyard doing nothing, but now Wanto opened a door and led them through, he opened another door and led them through, and then he asked, "All right, do you know how I got all this power?" And they answered, "No, King, we don't know yet, we don't know yet, we don't know yet!"

"Okay," he said, "I've been King a long time. It's time for you to see where I got my power. [That's the way to kill himself!] Do you see that house over there with no door? Go throw it away!" And when a King speaks, who can refuse? So they rocked it, *hiki hiki hiki,* and sent it flying, *kpang!* They caught a quick glimpse of the thing and they turned away horrified. It chuckled and then it laughed and then it started singing:

Wanto, the town is ruined, inangere, inangere,
Great King, the town is ruined, inangere, inangere,
Wanto, the town is ruined, inangere!

Oh Wanto's red leather sandal, the town is ruined,
    inangere, inangere,
The good things have come apart around you, inangere, the wives,
Wanto's kingdom, I'm going home, inangere, inangere!

Great King, the town has come apart, inangere, inangere,
Towal, the town is ruined over you, inangere,
Oh Wanto's red leather sandal, I'm going home,
    inangere, inangere,
Wanto, I'm on my way, inangere, inangere!

The thing sang like that, then it got up and when it called the red leather sandal on Wanto's foot, the sandal shot off his foot, when it called out the name of one of Wanto's wives saying it was leaving, the woman disappeared. Wanto's children, his power, everything that he had named into being, everything disappeared, it was all gone—[Was the thing still singing?] There was still the song. [Do it again!] Okay:

Wanto, the town is ruined, inangere, inangere,
The good things have come apart around you, inangere,
Oh Wanto's red leather sandal, the town is ruined,
    inangere, inangere!

Towal, the town has split, inangere, the cattle,
Wanto's kingdom, the town is ruined, inangere, inangere,
Great King, the town has left, inangere, the young men,
Wanto's kingdom, the town is ruined, inangere, inangere.

The good things have come apart around you, inangere, inangere,
Great King, the town is ruined over you, inangere, inangere.

Everything was on its way, the cattle, the goats, the palace women,
the young men he had commanded, everything he had ruled, it all disappeared, everything went into the sky, leaving just Wanto and Laaiso
the way they had been before. When morning came the cord for snaring bush bucks returned to Wanto's waist, the loincloth was back
around his middle again. And Laaiso, too, leaves covered her rear again.
When she saw what had happened, she picked up her pestle and beat
Wanto almost to death! But what could he do? What is gone, will it
come back again? [No!] So the place was empty and silent, *selelele*.

Sometimes if you're somewhere and you're fortunate, you get something but you don't know how to keep it because your lips blab it, *lɛp
lɛp lɛp lɛp*, all away. And when it leaves your hand, you don't know
what you did to get it in the first place. That's my tale! Break a little
dried bullhead, break it in two *lup*, and that's the end!

Wanto and the Success-by-the-Stump People

Collected by Philip A. Noss in August 1966 in Bétaré Oya and translated from the Gbaya.

André Yadji was the pastor of the Lutheran congregation when he told
the tale of Wanto and the Success-by-the-Stump people. He was about
forty years of age, a leader among the Gbaya community, and a well-
known teller of tales. He invited neighbors and friends to his home for
a session of tales and then before his audience of about twenty children and adults he told about Wanto.

Wanto is the hero of Gbaya tales. He is a fictitious character similar
to Everyman, a comic figure doing what comes most naturally. A major
part of this performance is the song that the audience enjoyed singing
because of its rhythmic cadence and catchy melody. The song is
Wanto's plea for help and his wife's remonstrance that he should have
known better, for in Gbaya tradition it is she who symbolizes responsibility and virtue. Throughout the song the cadence of the pendulum
continues, most clearly in the ideophones *kɛyɛm kɔyɔm*, as Wanto
swings on the vine. The audience sings along while the narrator leads
with the main lines of each verse, in between quoting Wanto's cries for
help and explaining the meaning of the words. In some versions Laaiso

is able to rescue her husband, but in this version he is left to swing apparently forever. Tape II, No. 34.

Motifs: J2411 "Foolish imitation of miracle (magic)" and F517 "Person unusual as to his legs."

The tale that we will hear now—there was a certain clan called Success-by-the-Stump. Those Success-by-the-Stump used to follow a big river upstream, and at the head of a certain valley there's a great big tree where they would swing. The Success-by-the-Stump people were a people that came from downriver. They would hang on the vines and swing back and forth, back and forth.

Before climbing up they would remove one leg and put it on the ground. Then they would climb up with their stump of a leg and dance. They would dance a long time, until dawn when they would climb down, each would take his leg and put it on again, and then they would go their way. Nobody understood them.

Then one day Wanto went hunting, setting snares along closer and closer and closer to where they were. Suddenly he noticed where they had put their legs to one side and were swinging back and forth until dawn. Wanto took his own leg—the medicine that they tapped their legs with to take them off, Wanto tapped it against his own leg. Wanto tapped it against his leg, took off one leg, and climbed into the tree with his other leg. He held the vine tightly against his leg and began swinging back and forth, back and forth.

After a while they had covered quite a distance and he began to sing. He saw that things were about to end but his leg was stuck fast, *kpak kpak*, to the tree, he was swinging and the stump of his leg was stuck fast, so he began to sing:

> Success-by-the-Stump,
> My shoulder is broken,
> Send a message for Wanto,
> My shoulder is broken.

> Father, Success-by-the-Stump,
> My shoulder is broken,
> Send a message for Wanto,
> My shoulder is broken.

> Laaiso, Warn-doesn't-listen,
> My shoulder is broken,
> Send a message for Wanto,
> My shoulder is broken.

> Yes Father, Success-by-the-Stump,
> My shoulder is broken,

Kɛyɛm kɔyɔm,
Kɛyɛm kɔyɔm,

Success-by-the-Stump,
My shoulder is broken,
Send a message for Wanto,
My shoulder is broken.

Father, Warn-doesn't-listen,
My shoulder is broken,
Send a message for Wanto,
My shoulder is broken.

Maidens here, Warn-doesn't-listen,
My shoulder is broken,
Send a message for Wanto,
My shoulder is broken.

Father, Success-by-the-Stump,
My shoulder is broken,
Send a message for Wanto,
My shoulder is broken.

Maidens here, Warn-doesn't-listen,
My shoulder is broken,
Send a message for Wanto,
My shoulder is broken.

Father, Warn-doesn't-listen,
My shoulder is broken,
Kɛyɛm kɔyɔm,
Kɛyɛm kɔyɔm,

Success-by-the-Stump,
My shoulder is broken,
Send a message for Wanto,
My shoulder is broken.

Father, Success-by-the-Stump,
My shoulder is broken,
Send a message for Wanto,
My shoulder is broken.

Father, Warn-doesn't-listen,
My shoulder is broken,
Send a message for Wanto,
My shoulder is broken.

"Buddy, toss me a hook,
toss me a frame to get
down on!"

Warn-doesn't-listen,

My shoulder is broken,
Send a message for Wanto,
My shoulder is broken.

"You, cut a forked stick
and bring it!"

Warn-doesn't-listen,
    My shoulder is broken,
    Send a message for Wanto,
    My shoulder is broken.

"Just take me so I can
get down from here,
won't you?"

Success-by-the Stump,
    My shoulder is broken,
    Send a message for Wanto,
    My shoulder is broken.

He was trying to find
someone to take him down,
but there was no one.

Father, Success-by-the-Stump,
    My shoulder is broken,
    Send a message for Wanto,
    My shoulder is broken.

Father, Warn-doesn't-listen,
    My shoulder is broken,
    Send a message for Wanto,
    My shoulder is broken.

That's his wife saying
that she warned him in
vain, he didn't listen.

Warn-doesn't-listen,
    My shoulder is broken,
    Send a message for Wanto,
    My shoulder is broken.

Father, Success-by-the-Stump,
    My shoulder is broken,
    Send a message for Wanto,
    My shoulder is broken.

Maidens here, Warn-doesn't-listen,
    My shoulder is broken,
    Send a message for Wanto,
    My shoulder is broken.

So, father! they sang on and on and on, wow! He tried to think of something to do, but he couldn't think of anything. What he was saying there, he was saying that his wife, his wife Laaiso should throw a rope, a rope that she could pull hard and tear him, *mgbodok*, loose so he could get down. But since his leg was already stuck, there was no way for him to get down any more.

They danced on and on and on, and then the Success-by-the-Stump came back upstream to the foot of his tree. They said, "Well, you Wanto, when you came and found us dancing like that, if you had asked us, 'Say, tell me, how is it that you take off your legs and then are able to climb down again?' we would have told you, and when you understood everything you could have joined us. But in this case where you just arrived and saw us and joined in and got your leg stuck, what will you do? You'll just have to figure a way out of this yourself! As for us, the way we did it our legs didn't get stuck, so we'll just take our legs and be on our way. But you go ahead and find your own way to get loose. We don't know anything more that we can do for you."

Chameleon Wins a Wife

Collected by Philip A. Noss in Kaladi shortly before Christmas 1967 and translated from the Gbaya.

Adama Elsie was a twelve-year-old living in the Cameroun town of Kaladi when she told this to her own family. Her performance was animated and dramatic as she moved about the room playing the parts of each of her characters.

In this tale Chameleon appears as the culture hero who returns from the land of the dead, outwits the other animals seeking to kill him, bests Wanto, and marries the beautiful girl. Tape X, No. 16.

Motifs are H336 "Suitors assigned quests" (reported from the Fjort); F136.1 "Otherworld in east"; and K850 "Fatal deceptive game." Suggested motifs are K515.7* "Escape by hiding in hollow fruit" and K859* "Fatal game: impaling with spear."

> Elsie: Okay, listen to a tale! Listen to a tale!
> Audience: A tale for fun, for fun!
>   Your throat is a gong, your body a locust;
>   bring it here for me to roast!

There was a certain woman and she had children. She gave birth to a very beautiful girl and to a boy. The girl's name was Dekere. Now her mother had planted her calabash seeds in the East that belonged to Death. One day the mother gave a command to the animals that they should all gather. The animal that would go, she said, that would set out from here and go and get the calabash there in the East and bring it and set it down here would marry Dekere.

So one animal went and died along the way. Another went and became emaciated along the way and came back, another went and died along the way. Then Chameleon said, yes, he would go. But they said,

"Oh, Chameleon! For all the animals that have gone and died, are you going there?" But he said, "No, I will go. What's it to you?" Chameleon put his spears on his shoulder with a rattling sound, *wokoro wokoro*, and began to sing:

> Oh Ɗekere, mother, bid me farewell,
> My wife Ɗekere, mother, bid me farewell.

> I'll marry Ɗekere, mother, bid me farewell;
> My wife Ɗekere, mother, bid me farewell,
> My wife Ɗekere, mother, bid me farewell,
> My wife Ɗekere, mother, bid me farewell.

> I'll marry Ɗekere, mother, bid me farewell;
> My wife Ɗekere, mother, bid me farewell.

> Oh Ɗekere, mother, bid me farewell,
> My wife Ɗekere, mother, bid me farewell,
> My wife Ɗekere, mother, bid me farewell,
> My wife Ɗekere, mother, bid me farewell.

> Oh Ɗekere, mother, bid me farewell;
> I'll marry Ɗekere, mother, bid me farewell.
> My wife Ɗekere, mother, bid me farewell,
> I'll marry Ɗekere, mother, bid me farewell.

On and on, and then he arrived in the East of Death. He went and got under the great big father calabash, *yarr*, and set it on his head, *ɓet*, and all the little calabashes followed, *'urrr*. And he began singing:

> Ɗekere, mother, bid me farewell,
> My wife Ɗekere, mother, bid me farewell.

> I'll marry Ɗekere, mother, bid me farewell;
> Oh Ɗekere, mother, bid me farewell,
> My wife Ɗekere, mother, bid me farewell,
> I'll marry Ɗekere, mother, bid me farewell.

> Oh Ɗekere, mother, bid me farewell,
> My wife Ɗekere, mother, bid me farewell.

> I'll marry Ɗekere, mother, bid me farewell;
> My wife is Ɗekere, mother, bid me farewell,
> Oh Ɗekere, mother, bid me farewell,
> My wife Ɗekere, mother, bid me farewell.

> I'll marry Ɗekere, mother, bid me farewell;
> My wife Ɗekere, mother, bid me farewell,
> My wife is Ɗekere, mother, bid me farewell,
> I'll marry Ɗekere, mother, bid me farewell.

Hoo D̂ekere, mother, bid me farewell,
My wife D̂ekere, mother, bid me farewell.

On and on, and then he arrived. D̂ekere's little brother happened to come outside and he whispered, "Hey, Mother, Chameleon is coming back!" But his mother pounded his head to the ground, *rot*, "Chameleon? You just found Chameleon's spirit, Chameleon who died back there on the road! What's wrong with you?" But then Chameleon's wife herself came out, "Mother! Chameleon *is* coming back!" But she said, "Oh, what is this that's gotten you onto Chameleon, Chameleon who became thin and has already died? All the other animals went and died along the way, to say nothing about Chameleon!"

But then Chameleon arrived in town. He took the great father calabash and set it down with all the others alongside, and then they said, "Okay, you have married your girl. Now go home." He went and picked up a dry *kabo* fruit and hollowed it all out. Now all the other animals were waiting in ambush to kill him so he got inside it with his wife and closed the opening, *rukut*, and then started singing:

Kpikiri kpikiri, kabo shell,
we who are a kabo shell,
let's hurry quickly to find them.

Kpikiri kpikiri, kabo shell,
we who are a kabo shell,
let's hurry quickly to find them.

Kpikiri kpikiri, kabo shell,
we who are a kabo shell,
let's hurry quickly to find them.

Kpikiri kpikiri, kabo shell,
we who are a kabo shell,
let's hurry quickly to find them.

Kpikiri kpikiri, kabo shell,
we who are a kabo shell,
let's hurry quickly to find them.

On and on they went rolling along, *kpikiri kpikiri*. They said, "D̂ekere who? Hey, the way they're honoring D̂ekere back there, when she comes the earth will quake, it goes *dîrrr*. But us, we're just a kabo shell. Take us and throw us over to the other bank. And Chameleon that they're honoring back there you'll find them without difficulty!" But in fact, it was D̂ekere and Chameleon who were saying that. Now the water there was a hot spring that was boiling, *sua sua*; if you fell into it you would die, your skin would all peel off. And so they took Chameleon and tossed them onto the other bank, *tos,* and Chameleon stepped out of the shell, *dengen,* with his wife.

But Wanto was waiting up ahead to kill them. As they were going along Wanto burst out of hiding, *heyem,* and said, "Hey, Chameleon! We'll fight and the one who throws the other will take the other's wife!" So they fought and he threw Chameleon, *gubak,* and took his wife.

A long time passed, and there was a festival. Chameleon put his spear in the back of his head and pulled it out his rear, *fal.* When Wanto tried to do it, he ended up stretched out, *kangingingi,* dead. Right! and so Chameleon took his wife.

That is what happens when one person has done something and you say you will do it, you will copy him. When he has done it, you say you will do it. That is how it began. But if Wanto and Chameleon had not been around to do that kind of thing, a person wouldn't take another's wife. Wives wouldn't leave their husbands for this to happen.

Eagle, Python, and Weaverbird

Collected by Philip A. Noss in September 1966 in Bouli and translated from the Gbaya.

The tale of the weaverbird was told by Dɛng Wan, a young married woman. She is a sister of Ngozo and she told it to the same group of about twenty-five children and adults to whom Ngozo told the tale that follows. Through the formulaic opening song, the performer addresses her tale specifically to the children. It is a well-known tale that has many versions, some aetiological like this one, others continuing into a second episode in which the chameleon destroys the python, rescues the eagle's child, and wins her as his wife. Tape VI, No. 12.

Aetiological motifs: A2332.5 "Color of animal's eyes" and A2433.4 "Haunts of birds." Also present is Q285 "Cruelty punished."

> Children, listen to a tale, a tale for fun, for fun,
>   listen to a tale, a tale for fun;
> Children, listen to a tale, a tale for fun, for fun,
>   listen to a tale, a tale for fun;
> Children, listen to a tale, a tale for fun, for fun,
>   listen to a tale, a tale for fun.

There was a certain bird, an eagle, whose name was Mbulɛ, and there

was a tall kapok tree above a deep pool. The eagle laid an egg in the
tree. Now in the pool there was a python. One day the python sharpened its ax and came to the foot of the tree. Time was passing for the
egg, it was soon to hatch, and one day it did hatch. A little while later
the eagle defecated a little drop of shit, *biyāk*, into the water—the python swallowed it. It defecated a drop of shit into the water again—the
python swallowed it.

Then the eagle went off a little way, as far as Sananga, to look for
some food for the child that had just been hatched. And the python
brought the axes it had just sharpened and put them at the foot of the
tree. Then it put its mouth to singing:

> Tɛlɛm tɛlɛm, the shit is so good, what must the real thing be like?
> Tɛlɛm tɛlɛm, the shit is so good, what must the real thing be like?
> Tɛlɛm tɛlɛm, the shit is so good, what must the real thing be like?
> Tɛlɛm tɛlɛm, the shit is so good, what must the real thing be like?

And that song ended.

After a bit the eagle got Sumbula the weaverbird to come and guard
its egg. So the weaverbird got ready to call the eagle, it put its mouth
to it:

> Mbulɛ has gone off down there, look at 'Mbula red red red;
> Mbulɛ has gone a visiting to make a kill,
>   look at 'Mbula red red red.
> Oh Mbulɛ has gone off down there, look at 'Mbula red red red;
> Oh Mbulɛ has gone a visiting to make a kill,
>   look at 'Mbula red red red.
>
> Oh Mbulɛ has gone off down there, look at 'Mbula red red red;
> Mbulɛ has gone a visiting to make a kill,
>   look at 'Mbula red red red.
> Oh Mbulɛ has gone off down there, look at 'Mbula red red red;
> Mbulɛ has gone a visiting to make a kill,
>   look at 'Mbula red red red.
>
> Oh Mbulɛ has gone off down there, look at 'Mbula red red red;
> Mbulɛ has gone a visiting to make a kill,
>   look at 'Mbula red red red.

The eagle heard and here it came, it had only killed two red duikers,
so it brought them flying, *fiiiii*. The python heard the wind from the
eagle's wings as it approached and with a gurgling sound, *wɔlɔk wɔlɔk
wɔlɔk*, it slipped under the water. Mbulɛ dressed the antelope, giving
the meat to its child and the bones to the weaverbird. The weaverbird
pecked at the bones, it pecked at the bones here, it pecked at the bones
there; meanwhile, Mbulɛ took a sun bath.

The next day Mbulɛ went hunting again. Having gone as far as Sananga, it wasn't far from the Pangara, right?* [Right!] So from Sananga it went straight to the Pangara. There on the banks of the Pangara it speared two water buck. Ɓiyāk, its child defecated a drop of shit into the water again, and the python had a little taste. When it tasted how sweet it was, it took its axes and called, "Children, bring the axes and let's put them to the bottom of the tree! This really tastes good! We've got to get at it!" So they chopped as they put their mouths to it:

Tɛlɛm tɛlɛm, the shit is so good, what must the real thing be like?
Tɛlɛm tɛlɛm, the shit is so good, what must the real thing be like?
Tɛlɛm tɛlɛm, the shit is so good, what must the real thing be like?
Tɛlɛm tɛlɛm, the shit is so good, what must the real thing be like?
Tɛlɛm tɛlɛm, the shit is so good, what must the real thing be like?

"Hey, what is this?" the weaverbird asked. "The eagle is a great ruler and now he's gone hunting—what is it that's always doing this?" So Sumbula got up, shook itself, and put its mouth to song:

Mbulɛ has gone off down there, look at 'Mbula red red red;
Mbulɛ has gone a visiting to make a kill,
  look at 'Mbula red red red.
Oh Mbulɛ has gone off down there, look at 'Mbula red red red;
Oh Mbulɛ has gone a visiting to make a kill,
  look at 'Mbula red red red.

Oh Mbulɛ has gone off down there, look at 'Mbula red red red;
Oh Mbulɛ has gone a visiting to make a kill,
  look at 'Mbula red red red.
Mbulɛ has gone off down there, look at 'Mbula red red red. . . .

The eagle heard. By this time the kapok tree was just about ready, gɛrɓɛlɛng, to fall. The eagle heard and here it came, fiiiii. The python felt the wind from its wings—wɔlɔk wɔlɔk wɔlɔk they all gurgled under water again. So Mbulɛ came and dressed the animals and gave nothing but bones to Sumbula. The weaverbird pecked at them for a while and then started thinking, "What's the great ruler doing to me? Why, I'm guarding its child and when it goes way off like this, it wouldn't come back to find its child, if it weren't for me! And then it just gives me bones to peck at. Is that right? Well, okay, it's all right. It's all right, let the eagle go. It'll go again and now that it's already crossed the Pangara, what must it be thinking? Now that it's crossed the Pangara it'll head straight on, lɛkip, to where there's big game to kill!"

* Sananga was a village about three miles from Bouli; the Pangara is a large river about twelve miles beyond Sananga.

And so the next day Mbulɛ left again. When Mbulɛ was far away the python came to the opening of its hole, and then, "Children, get the knife ready!" By now it had opened its eyes, Mbulɛ's child had opened its eyes, it defecated a little shit into the water again, they ate it, they tasted how sweet it was, and they started sharpening the axes again. They approached the foot of the tree, they came close, and by now the kapok tree was teetering to fall:

Tɛlɛm tɛlɛm, the shit is so good, what must the real thing be like?
Tɛlɛm tɛlɛm, the shit is so good, what must the real thing be like?
Tɛlɛm tɛlɛm, the shit is so good, what must the real thing be like?
Tɛlɛm tɛlɛm, the shit is so good, what must the real thing be like?
Tɛlɛm tɛlɛm, the shit is so good, what must the real thing be like?

There went the kapok, there it went, there it went, *wimm!* it splashed into the water, *pungem,* the python were on top of Mbulɛ's child!

Meanwhile, the weaverbird flew off, it flew off, and then began to wonder, "Now that I didn't sing, and Mbulɛ's child fell into the water, when Mbulɛ comes back what will it do to me?" Finally it made up its mind, "Okay, it's all right. It's all right. There's still God, and he'll help me." So it sat a bit, then it shook itself, it shook itself, it shook itself, it sat a while longer and then it decided to go out back, to go out on the path to Mbulɛ's toilet to have a look. As the weaverbird went along, what should it see but smoke rising, *ndɔrr!* "What's this smoke from?" it wondered. As it turned out, it was smoke from Gbaya fires. The weaverbird waited a little while longer.

Now Mbulɛ began to get worried. Before when Mbulɛ would go on a trip it wouldn't be long before it would hear a song, but this time it didn't hear the song and it got all upset, all upset, all upset. That day it had only killed two animals and it came flying, *fiiiii,* thinking it would soon see the top of the kapok tree, it would soon see the top of the kapok tree, it would soon see the top of the kapok tree—*yaa,* there was no kapok. "Haa, what has Sumbula done to me?" Of course, now that the tree had fallen, its child was gone too. The pythons had taken it for their own purposes. So the way Mbulɛ used to be able to see the kapok tree from halfway across the earth, now it couldn't see it any more. It threw down the animals, it was heartbroken. When it got to the place, there was nothing all the way down to the ground. With its head down it followed the path toward the toilet and there it saw where the weaverbird had gone, and that's where it went.

The weaverbird had seen the smoke and had decided that it wouldn't have anything to do with Mbulɛ again for Mbulɛ had done it wrong. It was he the weaverbird who had guarded Mbulɛ's child, but Mbulɛ had given it nothing but bones and it had pecked at them so long that its eyes were all bloodshot, its eyes were all bloodshot. Well, if its eyes had

Europe

Ireland
Peig Sayers of Blasket
Islands, 1946, narrator of
"Fionn in Search of His
Youth" (see Introduction,
p. xxii). Contributed by
Sean O'Sullivan.

Hungary
Zsuzsánna Palkó of
Kakasd, Tolna county,
1963, narrator of "Lazy-
bones" (see Introduction,
p. xxiv). Contributed by
Linda Dégh.

The collector for the Israeli Folktale Archives, Zvi Moshe
Haimovitsch (second from right), with four storytellers
in the Malben Home for the Aged in Neve Haim. Tales
from three are included in *Folktales of Israel*: Menashe
Mashlad, with hand outstretched, narrating, born in
Baghdad, 1890 (No. 68); Joseph Schmuli (left), born in
Basra, Iraq, 1877 (No. 26); and Elija David (center), born
in Baghdad, 1895 (No. 42, reprinted here, "A Tale of a
Jew Who Bridled the Wind"). Contributed by Edna
Cheichel, Israeli Folktale Archives, for Dov Noy.

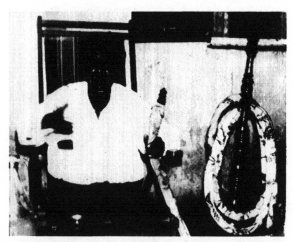

Yefet Shvili, an itinerant silversmith, born in Yemen in
1918, narrating, with his narghile (water pipe). Dov Noy
included one of his tales in *Folktales of Israel* (No. 29)
and published his repertoire in *Yefet Schwili erzählt*
(Berlin, 1963); see also by Noy, "The Universe Concept
of Yefet Shvili, a Jewish-Yemenite Story-Teller," *Acta
Ethnographica* 14 (1965): 259–75. Contributed by Edna
Cheichel, Israeli Folktale Archives, for Dov Noy.

Yefet Shvili with his mother, wife, and children.
Contributed by Edna Cheichel, Israeli Folktale Archives,
for Dov Noy.

Meir "Mirko" Ezra, born
in Barazan, Iraqi Kurdi-
stan, in 1887, sixteen of
whose tales are in the
Israeli Folktale Archives,
and one (No. 33) in
Folktales of Israel.
Contributed by Edna
Cheichel, Israeli Folktale
Archives, for Dov Noy.

Asia

Afghanistan
Asia, a Herati storyteller,
1968. Contributed by
Hafizullah Baghban.

Meriam (far right), a Herati, telling tales in a domed mud hut in
Tawberyan village, 1973. Contributed by Hafizullah Baghban.

Japan
Mrs. Tsune Watanabe of
Tsugawa, Niigata, 1967,
narrator of "The Man
Who Bought a Dream."
Her life and repertoire
are described in Robert J.
Adams, "Social Identity
of a Japanese Storyteller"
(Indiana University
doctoral dissertation,
1972). Contributed by
Robert J. Adams.

Burma
Wadamkong Kwin,
twenty-six, a Rawang
storyteller, and his wife
in traditional dress,
Bangjutag village,
Kachinland, 1957. Con-
tributed by Suzan Lapai.

Asia

Philippines
Saddani Pagayaw, a Manuvù storyteller from Basyaw village, western
Davao in central Mindanao, 1960,
wearing Manuvù traditional costume
of beaded abaca cloth, with poniard
at his side. Contributed by E. Arsenio
Manuel.

Oceania
Timoto Bobongi, a Lau, of Kwalo'ai
Malaita, British Solomons, in 1968;
narrator of "The Myth of Fuusai."
Contributed by Elli Köngäs Maranda.

Macheme Sonis, twenty-one, of Tol
Island, Truk Atoll, in 1963; narrator
of "The Ghosts of the Two Mountains." Contributed by Roger E.
Mitchell.

Republic of South Africa
Nongenile Masithatu Zenani, a Xhosa, telling a *ntsomi*
in her homestead in the Transkei, 1972; narrator of
"Mbengu-Sonyangaza's Sister Prepares to Undergo
Purification Rites" (see Introduction, p. xxiv). Con-
tributed by Harold Scheub.

Asilita Philisiwe
Khumalo, a Zulu,
telling a *nganekwane*
near her home in
Nongoma District,
kwaZulu, 1972. Con-
tributed by Harold
Scheub.

Cameroun
André Yadji, a Gbaya storyteller, gesturing while telling
a tale, in Meiganga, 1974; narrator of "Wanto and the
Success-by-the-Stump People"; the last picture shows
him with Abel Wah, narrator of "Wanto and the
Shapeless Thing." Contributed by Philip A. Noss.

"These two spent many years making jokes about their names together"

"He (the ọba) instructed them to summon 'He Who Seeks Good Advice' "

"These bearers will carry it (the meat) to your house"

"He tied it again and again with a rope, but to no avail"

"'He Who Meets Problems Alone' went away and put the meat down"

Nigeria
James Olá, a Yoruba, of Aiyégúnlè village near Ibadan, narrator of "He-Who-Meets-Problems-Alone and He-Who-Seeks-Good-Advice"; he is photographed telling this tale in 1972. Contributed by Deirdre La Pin.

"To try to solve problems alone is not good" (the bow signals the close of the narration)

North America
French Canada

Adolphe Duguay, eighty-three, narrator of "The Sword of Wisdom," with his wife at Petite-Lamègue, Lamègue, Ile Shippagan, Gloucester county, New Brunswick, in 1955. Contributed by Luc Lacourcière.

Joseph Bouliane, eighty-seven, narrator of "The Tub of Butter," at Les Escoumains, Saguenay, Québec, in 1954. Contributed by Luc Lacourcière.

Florent Lemay, sixty-seven, narrator of "The Scalping of Pérusse," at Sainte-Croix, Lotbinière county, Québec. Contributed by Luc Lacourcière.

Mrs. Daniel Poirier (née Delia Gallant), fifty-seven, narrator of "The String of Trout," at Egmont Bay, Prince county, Prince Edward Island, in 1957. Contributed by Luc Lacourcière.

South America
Peru

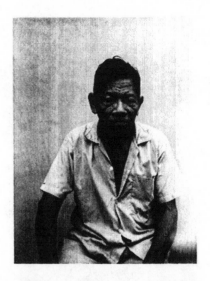

Laureano Mozombite, sixty-seven, a
Yagua, narrator of "The Twin Cycle,"
founder of the Catalán community
of Yagua in Peruvian Amazon, in
February 1975. Contributed by
Paul Powlison.

Juana Berroa Pinto, forty-five,
narrator of "Treasure, Envy, and
Witchcraft," in Pampa Chica, a
neighborhood in the squatter settlement of Independencia in Arequipa,
1972, with her children Juan, Doris,
Deri, and Wilmer. Contributed by
Jean MacLaughlin.

Jaime Rodríguez Huillca, thirteen,
narrator of "The Mouse and the Fox,"
in Independencia, Arequipa, 1972.
Contributed by Jean MacLaughlin.

become all red, it wouldn't be stupid enough to suffer like that for someone else's child again. It would be much better to leave. Now that it had seen the smoke of the fires of the Gbaya, it would go to live behind their houses. That way when they threw out the scrapings from the cassava pot or when they threw out cassava crumbles, it could eat them and maybe, just maybe, its eyes would get a little better. But as things turned out, the weaverbird's eyes weren't going to get better— they were red for good!

You agree, don't you, that bones are dangerous things? [Right!] Bones are hard things! And from all its pecking, its eyes became red. So the weaverbird went and built its nest where the Gbaya live. It is because of the eagle that the weaverbird follows the Gbaya. In the bush, wherever you go, the weaverbird knows your smell and it will be there the very same day to build its nest. If Mbulɛ hadn't been so cruel as to give bones to Sumbula to peck and peck without getting anything from them, without getting anything at all, the weaverbird's eyes wouldn't be red and it would be a real good-looking person. But instead of that, its eyes are red. That's why the weaverbird builds its home in the same place as the Gbaya, that's why the Gbaya says the weaverbird is a flea-type person, the weaverbird is a parasite like a flea. Mbulɛ is to blame. My tale is finished. Take my spear and strike the shade tree, take the dried hawk and break over it, *kɛyɛm*.

The Ant and the Termite

Collected by Philip A. Noss in September 1966 in Bouli and translated from the Gbaya.

The tale of the ant and the termite is a formulaic narrative that purports to explain why the large black ant eats termites. It was told by a teenager named Ngozo in the home of his uncle. The *zio* fruit referred to in the tale is large fruit that grows in gallery forests. Tape VI, No. 26.

Type 2042C* and motif Z49.6.2 *Bite (Prick) Causes Series of Accidents* to people and animals, reported from India.

Listen to a tale! [Yes!] The tale that I'm going to tell has no song. It's like a parable, but it isn't a parable.

There was a certain mother who had a child, she had only one child, and her child died. She went and buried the child. After a long time grass and brush grew thick over the grave. She decided to go and clear off the grave, but a termite had eaten off some grass stalks and as she swept off the grave the grass cut her hand. When she flicked her hand to shake off the blood, a drop of blood landed in the eyes of a fly.

The fly flew blindly trying to get away and bumped its head into a drum, and the drum sounded, *ding*. Now in the town of the genet, the genet wasn't well and the colobus monkey thought that since the genet wasn't well, now that the drum had sounded, it must have died. So the monkey tried to run away, it ran carelessly and stepped on a zio fruit. The fruit fell, *bɛdɛk*, and hit the back of an elephant. The elephant ran a long way and stepped on the back of a tortoise in the grass. The tortoise defecated fire! So, the fire burned all the grass, it burned the ant's eggs.

The ant thought, "How is this? I've lived here a long time, the grass has never burned, nor have my eggs ever burned. So what caused my eggs to burn up today?" The ant became angry, it set out and asked the fire, "Fire, what made you burn the grass so that all my eggs got burned up?"

The fire answered, "Me, fire, the way I used to be, if nobody set me to the grass, I wouldn't burn the grass." So the ant was asking the fire how come it burned its eggs, and it said the ant should ask further, because it didn't like to burn. The ant asked the fire, and the fire said it should ask the tortoise. "It was the tortoise that squeezed me out onto the ground as fire. Go ask the tortoise why it defecated me onto the ground."

So the ant went and asked the tortoise, "Tortoise, what happened to you?" And it answered, "Ant, a person like you, if a huge object stepped on you, wouldn't you shit on the ground?" The ant agreed. And who stepped on the tortoise's back? It should go talk to the elephant instead.

So the ant went and asked the elephant, "Elephant, what caused you to step on the tortoise's back?" The elephant answered, "If a big fruit fell on your back, wouldn't you run blindly?" Yes, it agreed that it would run blindly. Well, then the way the elephant ran blindly, it wasn't trying to be mean, the ant should go and ask the zio fruit instead.

So the ant went and asked the fruit what caused it to break off and fall, and it said, "Oh, if nothing touched me, would I fall? Ask the colobus monkey, the colobus that stepped on me and knocked me down, go ask it instead."

So it went and asked the colobus monkey, and the colobus answered, "Well, the way things are in towns, if you heard that someone was ill, and then if you heard a drum, *ding*, wouldn't you run to see if the sick person had died? That's why I ran blindly and knocked down the fruit, I didn't do it to be mean. Ask the drum."

So the ant asked the drum and the drum said the way it acted, if no one hit it, it wouldn't make any sound. The ant should ask the fly why it came and hit it, the drum didn't know why.

The ant went next and asked the fly, "Fly, what is the reason for hitting the surface of the drum?" The fly answered, "You, ant, if blood got in your eye, you would run wildly too. And so I ran wildly and struck the drum, *ding,* and it made a sound. Go ask the what-cha-ma-call-it, go ask the woman instead."

So the ant went and asked the woman what caused the blood to come out. The woman said, "Oh, by nature I don't like to lose blood, ask the grass that slit my finger instead."

So the ant went and asked the grass what happened to cause it to fall down. The grass answered that by nature it stood upright, it didn't like death, but when the termite ate it down, wouldn't it naturally fall? It wasn't that it was trying to be mean. The ant should ask the termite instead.

"Termite, why did you cut it down?"

The termite answered, "Baaa!"

"Termite, what was it?"

The termite said, "Baaa!"

That's why the black ant has fought the termite and captures termites up to this day. It is I, Ngozo, son of Ngol Banda, who tells this tale today. Mine is finished.

The Boy and the Buffalo

Collected by Philip A. Noss in January 1967 in Bouli and translated from the Gbaya.

Bɛr Poro was a ten-year-old Gbaya boy when he and his seven-year-old brother visited my home and told several tales. One of them was an old Gbaya folktale that Bɛr Poro retold as though it had happened to himself. In the song *kpongo* is the sound of his fist as he pounds on the door. The image "the neck of the cob" here refers to his own handsomeness, while in other versions it describes the beauty of his sister. Tape IX, No. 4.

This is a catch tale, type 2202 and motif Z13.2 *Teller is Killed in his own Story.* Baughman lists a number of United States examples; the bear eats the storyteller, in texts from New York, Pennsylvania, and Texas.

Listen to a tale!

My father had died, my mother had died, all my people had died. The only ones left were my sister and myself. I found a place in a valley and went and lived there, I lived by myself with my sister.

A long time passed, and then I took my bow and arrows and went off to hunt. I hunted a long time, I didn't find any buffalo. I came back and lay down. I went back and hunted again. When I came to a certain place I noticed that the buffalo had gone by there. I tracked them a long time and then came upon them eating. I shot one, *mgbut*, and it started to chase me, *but*. I ran and ran and ran, I crossed the stream and started singing:

> Kpongo-ye, kpongo iron,
> > Open the door for me!
> Kpongo, my neck is the neck of the cob,
> > Open the door for me!
> Kpongo, kpongo-ye, kpongo iron,
> > Open the door for me!
> Kpongo, my neck is the neck of the cob,
> > Open the door for me!
> Kpongo, kpongo-ye, kpongo iron,
> > Open the door for me!
> Kpongo, my neck is the neck of the cob,
> > Open the door for me!
> Kpongo, kpongo-ye, kpongo iron,
> > Open the door for me!
> Kpongo, my neck is the neck of the cob,
> > Open the door for me!
> Kpongo, kpongo.

When my sister heard the way I was singing, she opened the door and I rushed into the house and shut the door, and the buffalo circled around our house there and fell over and died. The buffalo fell and died.

Then I went again. We cut that one all up, put it on the fire. We chopped it up, it was really fat, she chopped the bones and filled a pot, she chopped the bones and filled a pot, and then I took my arrows again to go hunting. Here she ate the buffalo fat and it made her fall sound asleep, *keteng!* When I came to a certain place, the buffalo had gone by. I trailed them a long time and when I came near, here they were eating. I shot a buffalo cow, *pup*, I shot her with an arrow, and she started to chase me. I ran and ran and ran and I started singing again:

> Kpongo-ye, kpongo iron,
> > Open the door for me!

Kpongo, my neck is the neck of the cob,
  Open the door for me!
Kpongo, kpongo, kpongo-ye, kpongo iron,
  Open the door for me!
Kpongo, my neck is the neck of the cob,
  Open the door for me!
Kpongo, kpongo, kpongo-ye, kpongo iron,
  Open the door for me!
Kpongo, my neck is the neck of the cob,
  Open the door for me!
Kpongo, kpongo-ye, kpongo iron,
  Open the door for me!
Kpongo kpongo, my neck is the neck of the cob,
  Open the door for me!
Kpongo, kpongo-ye, kpongo iron,
  Open the door for me!
Kpongo, my neck is the neck of the cob,
  Open the door for me!
Kpongo, kpongo.

And then my sister—the buffalo fat had made my sister fall sound asleep, *kengeleng,* and she was sleeping, and I went around the house and the buffalo went around me and gored me to death. That's the end of it. When she got up, I was already dead. Here was my body, there was the body of the buffalo, after it had gored me to death. That's the end of that one.

Zaïre

Origin of the Enmity between Dog and Leopard

Collected by Daniel P. Biebuyck in 1955 in Manyema village and printed in Nyanga and French translations in Biebuyck and Kahombo Mateene, *Anthologie de la Littérature Orale Nyanga* (Brussels: Académie Royale des Sciences d'Outre-Mer, 1970), pp. 87–93. Translated from the French by Brunhilde Biebuyck. The narrator was She-Rungu of the Nyanga tribe.

Motifs: A2494.215 "Enmity between dog and leopard (reported for the Benga) and K1847 "Deception by substitution of children."
   Translator's note: The following translations derive mainly from the French texts translated from Nyanga. On difficult passages D. P. Biebuyck was consulted for direct translation from the Nyanga texts.

The Nyanga live in a forested area that is rich in its diverse species of fauna. Wild animals, as well as a few domesticated animals, play an important role in the Nyanga diet, economy, material culture, ceremonies, rituals, value system, and oral literature. Animals in Nyanga tales are cast both as principal and as secondary actors. Whereas some animals may be mentioned vaguely and snakes, insects, and fish never appear as generic categories, other animals (Duiker [*nteta*], Leopard [*nkoi*], the terrestrial turtle [*nkúrú*], Elephant [*ntsuu*], Chameleon [*koú*]) become dominant actors in the tales.
   In general, all animals figuring in these tales act and think as humans, and operate within a human setting. Yet, however strongly these animals may be personified, they are never confused with humans. Aside from the dog, none carry proper names, but rather appear in the texts under the generic name of their species. (The leopard assumes both the name of his species, *nkoi*, and his praise-name, *minebusara*, Master-of-the-Forest.) Often, however, morphemes that in Nyanga culture designate kinship or status may be affixed to these generic terms. Within the tales, animals may interact with other animals, or they may interact with men, divinities, and celestial elements.
   It is not enough to say that these animals serve as symbols behind

which human characters can be substituted. In these tales, the Nyanga express a certain interpretation of their universe that justifies the causes and reasons for certain conflicts between animals, for certain animal habits, and for the attitudes men hold about animals. This idea is well expressed in the following tale, which has as its dominant character Beni, the dog.

The dog, particularly the well-trained hunting dog, is the object of multiple prescriptions, rules of conduct, and rites. In Nyanga thought, the dog is the culture hero who stole the fire from the God of fire (*nyamuraîri*); the one who brought the banana tree from faraway lands; and the one who taught men the secret techniques used to understand the language of animals. The following tale demonstrates not only the perpetual enmity between dog and leopard but also accounts for the origin of that enmity. In his quarrels with Leopard, Beni usually emerges as the victor, though this victory is more complete some times than at other times. This relationship reflects Nyanga thought concerning the opposition between the village and the forest. Though Leopard is lord of the forest (*minebusara*), he is necessarily weaker than Dog who is an animal of the village.

The Lord of the Forest (Leopard), Monkey, Civet Cat, Dog built [their houses] together, Dog having the name of Beni, his companions having no other names. When they were established over there, Leopard complained of not being married to one of the daughters of his maternal uncles, whereas his companions were married. Leopard said that he was about to go ask a young girl from his uncle. They went, all four of them; they set out, they arrived at Leopard's maternal uncle's. Leopard arrived there and told his uncle that he came to ask him for a young girl. His uncle said that he could not refuse him a young girl. "Go fetch goods, the young girl is here."

Leopard and his friends returned home; arriving there, Monkey's wife asked her husband: "What is the news over there to where you went?" He said that a young girl was given to Leopard in marriage and that there only remained the goods [to be found]. The following morning, Leopard goes into the forest with Beni. Arriving in the forest, Leopard caught a gazelle, he placed her "like there" still alive. He took another gazelle, and did not kill this one either. He took a *mukaka* antelope and [left it] in the same manner. Again, he took a gazelle. Having taken the four animals, whole, he said to Beni: "Let us return." They returned.

Arriving at their place, his companions thought that Leopard owned goats in the forest. They locked up the three gazelles and the *mukaka* antelope still alive. They established themselves in the men's house. The next morning they said to one another, "Let us go and give the marriage goods." All together, they went to the maternal uncle of Leopard. They went along, leading the goats. Arriving at the place of Leopard's uncle, they said, "Maternal Uncle, these here are the marriage goods." The maternal uncle said: "May you be blessed, you my sororal nephews. Now then, make the choice among those young girls there." Leopard chose a young girl for himself. They returned, they arrived home, they established themselves.

Two days later, Leopard said to Beni: "Let us go into the forest to search for other goats." Beni said that he planned to go and do another job. Leopard asked Monkey and Civet Cat, and they also refused, saying that they were going to do their own work. Each one went into the forest with his wife. And they were accustomed to leaving their children at home. Indeed, all of them had children. And the wife of Leopard, she also had children. When all had left for the forest, Leopard took two puppies of Dog, one young of Monkey, and a young of Civet Cat. He placed them in three small baskets. In one of the small baskets, he put the two puppies of Dog, in another one he placed the young of Civet Cat. Late in the afternoon Monkey and Civet Cat and Beni with their wives returned to the village. Each one on his side, arriving in his house and looking there where he had left his children, said, "Where has my child gone to?" Beni said to himself, "I have left eight puppies there, and there remain only six; where then have the other two gone?" They stayed there. Night fell. They went to sleep.

In the early morning, Leopard said, "Let us go then to take the marriage goods." All go, whereas their wives remained there. Leopard made Beni carry the basket where his own puppies were, Monkey the basket where his young was, and the same for Civet Cat. They take the road. When they had covered a distance equal between the place of departure and the place of destination, Leopard said, "I often make people carry something that they do not know." Beni said, "What one man knows, another also knows." As far as Civet Cat was concerned he said, "It is I who only have one intelligence who will perish." Monkey said, "It is I who am climber, my dwelling is above." Having spoken in that way, they left.

When they were in the village, Leopard said that he was going to defecate. Dog said to him, "It is after having gone as far as two times seven hills that you must defecate because if your mother-in-law sees your excrements, she will make fun of you, saying that you defecate beside the trail." Having heard that, Leopard went.

When he was in the forest, Beni said to his companions, "Let us first open these baskets so that we may know what is in them." They opened the baskets. Looking inside: Lo! It was their children who were there. Beni said, "That is the reason why he has said that he often makes people carry what they do not know." They asked themselves who among them had feet so fast that he could return home and come back before Leopard would be back. Beni said, "It is I." Beni ran very quickly. He made the road, running very quickly. At the end of two efforts, he was already in the village. He said to the wife of Leopard, "Give me your children so that they may go and eat the food that we have been unable to finish there where we have gone." The wife of Leopard carried out [of the house] all of the children; Beni placed them in the baskets since he had already given his children to his wife, as he had already left the children of his companions to their [respective] wives.

Having finished packing the children, Beni made the road, running very quickly, he ran, he ran. He arrived there where his companions had remained. He asked them, "Isn't he back yet?" He sat down, he gave the news to his companions: "I bring his children, but I have told our wives to be ready to flee, that the wife of Monkey will have to climb on a high tree, that the wife of Civet Cat will have to hide, that my wife will have to flee far away where I will rejoin her." His companions said, "You have done well." Having waited a long time, they heard Leopard say, "Good! Good!" They said to themselves, there he comes. Leopard came and said, "Let us go then."

They left and went to the maternal uncle. He said, "My father, here is another [part] of the marriage goods: three goats for you and one for my aunt." His maternal uncle said: "Be blessed, you my nephew. Now go find two additional hind legs so that you can carry off your wife." Leopard said, "Yes, it is the women of my house who will come to bring them."

The following morning they returned; they proceeded down the road, Beni and Monkey and Civet Cat treading cautiously. They appeared at their houses. Beni remained on a little hill, and Monkey settled himself near a tree, saying to himself that when Leopard would emerge from his house, he would climb this very tree. Civet Cat also installed himself on a little hill, saying that when Leopard appeared "I will try to run, and it is there where he will await me that he will eat me." When Leopard arrived within his house, he asked his wife, "Where are the children?" His wife responded, "How can you ask for the children when yesterday you sent Beni here so that I would send you the children so that they could eat the food that was offered to you in hospitality?" Hearing this, Leopard appeared in the middle of the village. Seeing him thus, the Dog fled, and Monkey climbed a tree. Having climbed the tree, he cried, "*Kico, Kico!*" Leopard chased Civet Cat, he caught it and ate it. Since then, Leopards have always eaten Civet Cats. After that Leopard went to chase Dog; they proceeded down the road chasing one another. Leopard was unable to catch up with Beni. It is for this reason that Leopard is always chasing the Dog.

Having left the danger safely, Beni settled himself with men. He said, "My work is to always chase the other animals, but I cannot chase the Leopard because one day I tricked the Leopard." It is from there that has come the name of *Mbibi* (dog), whereas previously he (dog) was called *Beni* (host).

That is the reason why Dog is never in accord with Leopard, even though long ago he was the servant of Leopard.

Trapper, Gatherer-of-Honey, and Cultivator

Collected by Daniel P. Biebuyck in 1952 in Manyema village and printed in Nyanga and French translation in Biebuyck and Kahombo Mateene, *Anthologie de la Littérature Orale Nyanga* (Brussels: Acadé-mie Royale des Sciences d'Outre-Mer, 1970), pp. 173–75. Translated from the French by Brunhilde Biebuyck. The narrator was Kabonganya of the Nyanga tribe.

The following text puts into perspective the prototypes: Trapper (*shé-kitéi*), Gatherer-of-Honey (*shé-bŭki*), and Cultivator (*shé-kihíngi*). The first two attempt to trick the Cultivator. However, the latter succeeds in breaking up their friendship pact, thus forcing them to accept a pact that includes all three of them. This is a rare tale that implicitly stresses the original synthesis of these three economic activities in Nyanga so-ciety. In addition, it correctly reflects the late introduction of agricul-ture into Nyanga.

Specifically, the text can be placed in the wider category of tales dealing with "characters." The characters in these tales appear under teknonymic or otherwise rarely used personal names. Sometimes they occur in couples illustrating binary opposition (for example: the man of the forest versus the man of the village).

Motifs: M246 "Covenant of friendship"; A1471 "Origin of com-merce" (reported for the Benga); K1832 "Disguise by changing voice" (reported for the Fang).

Three men went into the forest: one was the Cultivator, [the other] the Trapper, [the third] the Gatherer-of-Honey. Arriving in the forest, they asked themselves: "How shall we build [our houses]?" They said: "You, the Cultivator, build your house in the middle of the three hills." The Trapper built his house on a hill, the Gatherer-of-Honey built his on a hill. No sooner had they finished building [their houses] than the

Cultivator had already finished growing plants behind his house. The Trapper asked the Gatherer-of-Honey to make a blood pact [with him], saying that they should not make such a pact with the Cultivator. Having finished making friendship, and having killed game, the Trapper went with the meat to his friend. They did not show it to the Cultivator. The following day, the Gatherer-of-Honey passed with a jar of honey to bring it to his friend the Trapper. They did not give anything to the Cultivator. And so it was every day; they made things pass at the entrance of the village of this one [the Cultivator]. He said to himself that his children alone would die of hunger.

This Harvester, this Cultivator, went to sow discord between the two friends. He called in a loud voice, "You man of the rodents *Mikii*, you the Trapper, it is you who will kill my children, never again bring rodent *Mikii* here [at my house]." The Cultivator also set out to the village of the Gatherer-of-Honey calling, "You Gatherer-of-Honey, it is the flies that you bring here that cause my children to be sick; also it is my rodents *Mikii*, which you eat, that make you fat." On his side, the Trapper reflected much, saying that so then his friend had just insulted him; on his side the Gatherer-of-Honey also thought that his friend had just insulted him. Having heard that, the Trapper and the Gatherer-of-Honey, one left from his [house], the other left from his house, they met in the valley at the Cultivator's. Arriving there, they questioned each other.

One said, "You yelled to me that it was my rodents *Mikii* who are the reason why your children have caught the kwashiorkor, yes my rodents *Mikii!*" And the other said, "You yelled that because of me your children have their throat obstructed by larvas of bees." The one denied and the other denied, both at the same time. At this time, the Cultivator was dancing, while his wife beat the drum for him. This instigator, the Cultivator, took to dancing and singing:

> I the instigator Cultivator.
> I just finished placing in discord those
> who are two.

The two friends understood, having heard the manner in which this Cultivator had placed them in discord, one against the other. Having considered that, they made a pact of friendship with the Cultivator. As such, the three became friends among each other; they began to give meat, honey, and agricultural products, all of them giving to one another mutually.

That is why a man should never refuse the mark of friendship because the mark of friendship is a thing capable of saving the family group.

How Nturo Rejected Mpaca

Collected by Daniel P. Biebuyck in January 1952 in Usumbura village
and printed in Nyanga and French translation in Biebuyck and Kahombo Mateene, *Anthologie de la Littérature Orale Nyanga* (Brussels:
Académie Royale des Sciences d'Outre-Mer, 1970), pp. 187–89. Translated from the French by Brunhilde Biebuyck. The narrator was Shé-
Muranda Nkúbá of the Nyanga tribe.

Motifs: G311 "Burr-woman: ogre who jumps on one's back and sticks
there magically" (reported for the Luba) and G521 "Ogre made drunk
and overcome" (reported for the Yoruba).

The following text belongs to the Nyanga category of tales dealing
with fabulous beings. Though there are several types of such beings,
those that play a dominant role in Nyanga tales are: *Kirimu* (a dragon
of many heads, which inhabits the virgin forest), *Mukiti* (represented
either as a fabulous serpent or as a giant iguana that lives in deep or
troubled waters), and *Mpaca* who figures as the dominant being in
this particular tale. Though *Mpaca* is of male sex, he is often presented
as a woman of the following appearance: dirty, with a mass of hair,
very long nails, and very thin (since he does not eat). This enigmatic
specter, however, has the ability to metamorphose himself into a young,
beautiful girl. In addition, he possesses a keen sense of smell, and usu-
ually has the snout of an animal. *Mpaca* is generally jealous and powerful and of evil intentions. He attacks women alone in the forest,
though this attack is never of a sexual nature. He attaches himself
firmly onto women's backs, forcing them to execute various tasks; he
kidnaps children and "eats" men; he sows discord between husband
and wife. However, for all his cunning, *Mpaca* is usually overpowered
through his love of beer and song. As is shown in this tale, one rids
himself of *Mpaca* quickly by making him drink large amounts of beer.
In other narratives, songs exert a magic power over *Mpaca;* thus, his
intended victims who are good singers are victorious over him. Though
this particular text treats *Mpaca* with indifference, other tales may describe him in either a sympathetic or antipathetic manner.

There was a woman named Nturo. After her marriage, she quarreled
with her husband. Having felt the blows of her husband too long, Nturo
said that, as far as she was concerned, she would hang herself. She
went. When she was at the point of "from where do you come, and
where do you go," she went to appear in a small village.

Now, it so happened that the specter of the forest, Mpaca, was the
lord of that village. When she entered [the house], the specter of the
forest, Mpaca, pronounced her name: "E! Nturo!" This one said, "So

then, someone just recognized me!" When the two were already in the house, Mpaca jumped; he placed himself on the back of Nturo. This Mpaca had a long nail; he advanced it and introduced it into Nturo's neck. While she was doing all the work in this house, and Mpaca was always established on her back, she told him: "One day you must descend [from my back]; I do work, and I am always with you. I go to the river and I carry you on my back!" [Nturo being] totally worn out [by the complaints], Mpaca finally removed his nail from her neck. The next morning, this Mpaca went to fetch wood for Nturo. While he was gone in the forest, Nturo fled. During her flight, Nturo entered into a snail's shell.

When Mpaca returned, in arriving there, he saw that there was no one there. He extended his nail; he did not find the place where the woman had gone. He retracted his nail. That nail searched here and there; it came upon Snail Shell, it made her come out. He advanced the nail [again], dug it into that woman there, and she wore herself out [with complaints]. Her aunt appeared to her in a dream [entered within her], saying that she should prepare some beer. She prepared it. [The beer] was ready, she went to tempt the specter with that beer. He drinks it. He removes his nail from her neck so that he can drink it [the beer]. The beer goes to Mpaca's head; he is drunk from it. He falls asleep. While he was asleep, she [Nturo] slashed his throat with his knife and returned to the village of the people of her family.

That is the reason why one must not hang himself, nor even think of hanging himself, one must not cut off one's life when God is still withdrawn. As such you must not threaten yourself in your life if God is still withdrawn.

South Africa

The Xhosa

The Xhosa are an important member of the Nguni language group of southern Africa, a group which also contains the Zulu, Swazi, and the Ndebele (the latter, of Zimbabwe). About half of the fourteen million Africans in the Republic of South Africa are Nguni-speaking. Of the approximately four million Xhosa in the republic, about one and one-half to two million live in the Transkei, a semiautonomous "homeland" area of South Africa; a smaller number reside in the Ciskei, another "homeland"; and the rest are scattered throughout the country, mainly in such urban areas as Johannesburg, Cape Town, East London, and Port Elizabeth.

Traditionally, the Xhosa are a pastoral, cattle-raising people, with considerable cultural focus on the cattle. The political organization is patriarchal, involving a system of leadership that moves from headman to sub-chief to chief. Xhosa religion emphasizes kinship relations. The basic kinship unit is the homestead, an extended family under one patriarchal head. Family residence is patrilocal, with patrilineal extended families. Marriage is exogamous and polygynous, and involves complex contractual arrangements under a system of *lobola* (see headnote to final story in this section, Mrs. Zenani's narrative). A central characteristic of the homestead "is the overwhelming stressing of the bonds linking the adult males and all the children, through the emphasis put on descent from a patrilineal ancestor" (A. Winifred Hoernlé, "Social Organization," *The Bantu-Speaking Tribes of South Africa, An Ethnographical Survey*, ed. I. Schapera [London, 1937], p. 75).

Patriclans are divided into Great House and Right Hand House lineages (see headnote to final story), and each of these lineages is in turn composed of Great House and Right Hand lineages. This tendency towards fission has resulted in a large number of minor chiefdoms among the Xhosa, since sons in both of the lineages would proceed to establish their own lineages.

For general background see *The Bantu-Speaking Tribes of South Africa*, ed. I. Schapera (London, 1937); Gwendolen M. Carter et al., *South Africa's Transkei* (London, 1967); *African Societies in Southern*

Africa, ed. Leonard Thompson (London, 1969); Philip Mayer, *Towns-men or Tribesmen* (Cape Town, 1963); Monica Hunter [Wilson], *Reaction to Conquest* (London, 1961); *The Oxford History of South Africa, Volume I, South Africa to 1870,* ed. Monica Wilson and Leonard Thompson (New York, 1969); J. Van Tromp, *Xhosa Law of Persons* (Cape Town, 1947); S. M. Seymour, *Bantu Law in South Africa* (Cape Town, 1970); Audrey I. Richards, *Hunger and Work in a Savage Tribe* (New York, 1964); John Henderson Soga, *The Ama-Xhosa: Life and Customs* (Lovedale, 1931).

A Girl is Cast Off by Her Family

Collected by Harold Scheub in September 1967 in a kraal overlooking a deep valley in Mboxo (Nkanga) Location, Gatyana (Willowvale District), in the Transkei and translated from the Xhosa. The narrative was performed at a party celebrating the emergence of young initiates who have just completed their circumcision rituals and accompanying seclusion.

Water spirits interact with human beings and shape their destiny in the oral narratives of southern Africa, where ponds, lakes, and rivers play an important part in the ecology. In the present instance, an old woman water-spirit rectifies the injustice done to the persecuted younger sister and protects her from her hostile parents. The sacrificial ritual of the dun-colored ox to appease the water-spirit represents an earlier social reality.

Motifs: L52 "Abused younger (here elder) daughter"; S10 "Cruel parents"; K2212 "Treacherous sister"; B491.2 "Helpful lizard"; N815.0.2 "Helpful water-spirit"; F133 "Submarine otherworld" (reported from the Gold Coast and among the Sotho); F153 "Otherworld reached by diving into water"; F166.11 "Abundant food in otherworld"; F932.1 "River pursues fugitive" (reported from the Xhosa); N825.3 "Old woman helper" (common in Africa); Q285 "Cruelty punished"; V12.4.4. "Ox (bull) as sacrifice"; F420.4.9 "Water-spirit controls water-supply" (reported among the Shangang in South Africa); C420 "Taboo: uttering secrets"; *F932.13 "Water cannot be dipped from river" (suggested motif).

The performer was Mrs. Noplani Gxavu, a Gcaleka woman about thirty-five years old. She is a fine performer, very demonstrative, a highly contemplative woman. Her performances are animated—a lot of body movement, very poetic use of the language, much gesture, facial expressions, vocal dramatics, a close relationship with each member of the audience. Her narratives are usually quite lengthy, and her audiences most frequently composed of women of about her own age. The narrative is related in Xhosa. The audience is quite large—about forty women, twenty children, a half-dozen men. All are Gcaleka. The narrative lends itself to gesture and body movement, and there is a considerable amount of each in this performance.

Notes: *ochre*—is used for dyeing garments and as a cosmetic; *the fat congealed*—a Xhosa idiom: she is getting her just desserts; *amasi*—fermented milk; *mvubo (umvubo)*—boiled maize, mixed with *amasi; tyhini!*—an expression of surprise.

Now for a *ntsomi*.

There was a man who fathered two children—daughters, a young one and an older one. But he did not love the older one; he loved the younger instead. This younger daughter was quite ugly, especially her eyes, which were turned upwards. And the elder of the two girls was very lovely.

Time passed, and these girls grew up. When they reached marriageable age, it was the proper time for them to go and dig ochre. Because they hated their elder daughter, her parents found a means whereby they might kill their child.

First, they spoke to the girls of the village, the girls who were going along with their daughters. Then they said to the daughter whom they loved, "You must help! As soon as she enters the clay pit over there, bury her in the hole in which you'll dig the ochre."

They went then, and when they had come fairly close to the ochre pit, a girl from another homestead, a neighbor of her parents, turned around as if she were going to urinate, and she said to this girl, "Watch out! I'm warning you because we're friends, because you're my agemate. Don't go into that hole over there! We have been ordered by your parents to bury you in the hole!"

Well, the girl heard this; she heard it clearly.

The other girl added, "Now, don't worry. We'll share our ochre with you, even if your sister gives you none. Do you see how happy she is? She's pleased because we're going to destroy you today in the ochre pit!"

They took that journey, and came to the ochre. The younger sister immediately threw herself into the work; she was the first one into the pit, already grasping the garments of her sister, throwing them down over there, saying, "Let's go inside, Child of my father! Let's not waste time!"

Her sister said, "No! I'm not going in!"

She said, "What do you mean, you're not going in? Do you have servants to dig clay for you, that you refuse to enter? You won't go in despite the fact that *we're* going in?"

"No!" she said, "No, I'm not going in. I'll go away even if I have no clay. I'm lazy, that's the reason! Who cares?"

She said, "You're not lazy! You just want to take advantage of us! You want us to dig clay for you!"

She said, "All right, don't give me any clay if that's what you want! What I say to you, I'll say to the others too. Whoever does not want to need not give me any ochre. I'll go on my way, even if I don't have any ochre. And I won't feel left out!"

Well then, the girls went into the pit without answering her. The two sisters had already discussed it, so there was no use pursuing the matter any further. And one of the other girls had already whispered to her, warning her.

The other girls went in and dug clay, continuing to throw it outside on their blankets, throwing the clay out on their blankets. She sat there, and she kneaded the clay that the other girls were throwing out. She continued to knead the other girls' clay.

Her sister said again and again, "I don't care if you knead the clay! You'll not get even a fragment of it!"

She said, "It doesn't matter. I'll go just as I am."

Well, friends, the clay was dug, and then the girls came out of the hole. The loads were fastened and they prepared to set out. Conversation now dried up for the younger sister, the one who had been happy when they were about to kill the other one and bury her in the clay pit. There was no pretense of joy any more.

Conversation ended, and she saw that "*Tyhini!* People are folding their things up, and we haven't buried her yet in this hole! These others cannot bring themselves to force her, they seem unable to drag her forcibly when she refuses to go in—even though they had been asked to do so by her mother and father." And they had agreed to do so! They had even been promised a reward: they were to be given much sheep, much money! Now, out of pity, they are unable to fulfill that request. Now they do not want to kill this sister, "And I had hoped to become the only child in the house!" And so she became a person who did not converse.

They fastened their loads, and they apportioned out to her parts of their ochre that, because each of the girls (other than her sister) provided her with a share of her ochre, amounted to even more than theirs. Her share of the ochre was large compared to those of the other girls of the village; they gave her a lot of clay. Then she was so burdened that the others said, "If you're overburdened, you can take some of your ochre and give it to us now while we're still far from home. Then, when we're almost there, we'll give you back your clay, and it'll again amount to more than ours. After all, you did knead the clay for us, and our hearts were loosened by the work that you did for us."

Well, then, they traveled, and when they were on the way, the girl said, "*Kwek!* I'm really weighed down!"

They said, "All right!"

They loosened their loads, then lessened hers. When they were fairly near to their homes, then, they took her load and added to it again, and hers was bigger once more than theirs.

But where is her sister now? Where is her sister? There she is! a person who is friends only with herself, up there in front. She has no one to chat with because she has concluded that "All these people who were asked to do something by my parents are not trustworthy! Look at this! I'm returning home with my older sister. And I was gleefully hoping to have buried her in that clay pit!"

The father was milking in the cattle kraal, and when he saw his daughter—*ntla!* he hastily pulled the kraal post from the earth. He didn't even pick up the bar that was lying on the ground; he pulled the kraal post up from the earth, he was so upset. And he threw himself at that girl, the girls of the other homesteads already having turned to go to their own homes. He threw himself at this daughter of his now, and he beat her. The load fell to the ground; the girl picked it up, and as she was putting it down on the upper side of the house, her mother was stirring the food here on the hearth. When she saw that her daughter was still alive, the mother no longer stirred purposefully, she only stirred absentmindedly. And she went straight at her daughter with that stirrer still covered with bubbling hot food. She hit the girl on the head with the stirrer. The girl fell near the door, then she got up and ran. She realized that "I cannot go to the village, because my family will just go there and bring me back." She ran, then, to a large river in which, in those olden days, water used to be dipped. She hurried by that place and went on to the spot where they dip water now. She went to this place; she arrived and cried, she cried while sitting above this river.

While the girl was crying, a monitor lizard appeared. The lizard asked, "What's the matter, Girl?"

The girl reported, "I'm not loved by my mother and father!"

"Why not?"

"There's no reason. Even you, Lizard, would know the reason by now if there were a reason, because you too belong to the village. You wouldn't miss the news because you're a part of the village. When the women of the village come to the river to dip water, you would overhear them gossiping about this matter. There's no reason."

The lizard said, "Just watch me as I enter the water, then come in yourself. You won't drown." So saying, the lizard went into the water. The girl also entered; she threw herself in, crying.

When she had entered the water, and when she got over there, "*Tyhini!* This is a homestead! And where's the lizard?"

Here is the lizard, sitting behind a door, already explaining to and being listened to by an old woman who was sitting over there near the door. The lizard was recounting to her the journey of this girl, and the mercy that the lizard had paid to her.

Then the lizard turned to the girl and said, "No, the assistance that I gave you is not mine. I am merely a messenger of this home. There's my mother at the door. Just go on, Girl, explain."

The girl explained immediately, hurriedly, anxiously, as if her parents and sister, those who had been beating her with kraal bars and stirrers, might come in at any time and drag her off. So she pushed on, the girl pushed on with her story, and then a sound was heard over there on the upper side of the house. When that sound occurred, the old woman got up; she carried a small club—not really much of a club, actually, more like a twig. She beat, she beat in that place where the sound came from, a sound that was like thunder. Then there was silence—*cwaka!* As soon as the old woman beat with this twig, there was silence—*cwaka!* This old woman beat in a dark place over there on the upper side of the house, she beat there and then there was silence—*cwaka!*

Then, when it was quiet, the old woman came toward the girl and said, "Well, my girl, you're welcome here at the Great Place, because we already know the reason you have left your parents. We asked you to explain, but this was only because we wanted you to be heard by these people here in the Great Place; we wanted them to know how it happened that you came to be here. We knew the reason while you were still leaving your home; we knew the reason when you were still going to the clay pit; we knew when you were experiencing the harsh treatment; we knew of the conspiracy to kill you by your parents; we knew when they were planning your burial in the wilderness, in the pit. We knew about the conspiracy. You're welcome here at the Great Place. As for your parents and sister, we'll give them a little punishment and, if you so desire, we'll make it possible for you to be reunited with them. But if you desire, you may determine to remain here with us."

Well, friends, that's how it happened. This girl remained there. They prepared something for her to eat; thick milk poured over boiled corn for her, and she ate. There was happiness at this home, it was very pleasant here. The girl ate.

Then, at dawn, after people had slept, very early in the morning that sister of hers came to dip water here in this place, because this was the place where people dipped water. She came there and just put the bucket down. She sang as she went along, happy because she was now alone at home. She did not care where her sister might have gone to die. She felt that her sister would surely die, because she had seen how severely she had been beaten by her parents. She had seen her run away, to go and die in some unknown place. At least she was hopeful that she had gone somewhere and died there. She *must* have died, because she had never seen anyone beaten by a cattle post or a stirrer clogged with hot smoking food who survived such treatment; she could not believe that anyone could have survived such beatings. Well, then, she dipped with a dish. She dipped and dipped, and eventually the pail was filled. When the pail was filled, the girl took it. She was full of dreams, well-fed, because she was now alone at her home. But then, the pail would not lift from the ground! That was a mystery! That was the mystery that confronted this girl. The fat congealed! And the songs of joy stopped in her mouth. The pail would just not lift up from the ground!

Time went on, and the pail continued to refuse to be lifted from the ground. So she got up and went hurriedly to report this fact at home, that the pail would not lift. Her father, angrily, took his great club, a club that he had not even finished cutting properly yet (he had barked it with an ax, but had not finished it). The father took this club and hit her on the neck with it. And the girl fell. Her mother, who had been sweeping, took the broom and turned it backward, and she also hit the girl on the head. The daughter ran as they said, "You're a lazy bum! It's a shame that we killed our other child! Now we're left with the likes of you! These children! It's as if we had given birth to children who had died immediately, at birth! as if all our children had died in infancy! At least we were satisfied with the work that the other one did. It's just that we didn't love her. It was an irrational dislike, an intense dislike that we felt for her. Our very blood, our flesh resented her. Go, Dog! Go and sleep wherever you like!"

Her mother got up in a fury, and she quickly snatched up another pail, the one that remained there at home; it was a leaky pail. And she traveled, she went and half filled it with clay, trying to patch it so that she might dip some water with it. She dipped in a hurry; she did not even use a dish as might have been expected. She just dipped the whole pail in the river. Well, the woman yanked it angrily—and the pail did not move from the ground! The woman tugged it, she struggled with it, but the pail would not move. She spilled the water, and the pail did move when it was empty. "Now what is this? I'd better go and report this to my husband!" She went off then, she left the pail there and went to report to her husband.

The man said, "What kind of disease is this that you people have? you and your progeny? Was there ever such a thing as a pail that refused to be lifted from the ground?"

She said, "Well, it just doesn't lift from the ground!"

Then the man threw himself furiously at the woman with his fist, he was that angry. He didn't even have time to pick up a stick; he plunged at her with his fist. They both fell over there, behind the lower portion of the door. As they got up, the man did not bother to take anything with him, because there was no pail anymore. He leaped to that milk pail over there. He went hurriedly, saying, "I'll drink this water myself, alone! It's impossible! Never has a pail not got up from the ground! It must be something that your boy friend told you, that you should bring me nothing to drink! that there should be no eating here at home today! Your boy friend must have put you up to this!"

The man went off, shouting in anger, and he came to the river. He arrived there, infuriated, and he dipped the entire pail into the river. When he had dipped the entire pail, that pail would not even budge. It was filled with water, and it remained on the ground and threatened to pull the man in as well. He spilled the water from the pail, and dipped again, and that too refused to be taken up from the ground. He spilled most of that water from the pail, he left just a little in the pail so that he could have at least one swallow as he stood there. But no, even this little drop of water would not leave the ground. He lowered the pail, he knelt down to the pail, hoping to drink with his mouth, and he felt that his entire body would go right into the pail. He realized that "I'll sink here at this rate! I'll dip with my hand, that's better!" But he had the same sensation again, that he would disappear. He took just a little bit of water—*cwe!*—even less than a cupful, so that he could have a mouthful; he was tired now, he had been here a long time. The sun now was about to set. But even that little bit just would not come to his mouth! He gave up, and turned the pail upside down and it became dry. Then the man took his pail and went home, cursing as he went. "What kind of judgment is this, oh God, which you have made on me and my family?" He walked on then and arrived at home. His wife peeked out at him while he was still on the way, because she had heard from her daughter that he was coming. She could see that he seemed to be carrying nothing but the pail—no water, just the empty pail.

Well, then, this man arrived and said, "I've given up! Please go to the neighbors and ask for just a drop of water so that we can go to sleep having drunk."

They went to the neighbors to ask for water, and that is how it was that they had water in that homestead before they went to bed.

The next morning, the girl was sent out again: "Do go, because this matter of the pail refusing to get up from the ground started with you!"

The girl went then, and as she prepared to go, she said, "I won't even bother to take a pail this time. I'll just try with this big billycan."

They said, "Travel, you dog! You've always been very lazy! You were the reason that the pail did not get up from the ground! We've been dipping from that place for a long time, we've grown old dipping water over there!"

She traveled, she went, and she dipped with this billycan. But the billycan would not leave the ground. She tried again and again: she dipped, then spilled the water out, dipped again, and finally she put the billycan down and cried. She cried and cried. Then the girl who was her sister appeared. She just appeared; she did not speak. She stared at the girl, then disappeared again. The other one was still crying, and she cried the more when she saw that her sister was still alive, and here, in this place!

She said, "Maybe that's the reason for these problems we've been having with the water! It might be because she was expelled in such an ugly way by her parents! If that's the case, then I have even more reason to cry. Why is it that she appeared so healthy just now?" This girl cried the more, and then the lizard appeared.

The lizard asked, "What's the matter, Girl? Why are you crying?"

She said, "I'm not wanted by my mother and father!"

"Why is that?"

"Well, they said that I must dip water here, but it refuses to be dipped!"

"Oh? What happened to the water that it refuses to be dipped?"

The girl said, "It's a mystery, Lizard, that I've never seen before! It all began with me. And now my parents are holding me responsible for it. 'It was because of you that dipping became impossible, so it will be with you that the dipping will start again! Go, until the end of the year!'"

"Is that what they said?" It is the lizard speaking.

The girl said, "That's what they said."

The lizard said, "Kwek! That's really a civilized punishment that they've given you! I think that I too should contribute to your punishment!" So saying, the lizard threw itself at the girl, beating her with its tail. It bruised her, it flogged her with its tail, as the girl cried. It was painful. She cried, and ran to her home.

When her parents saw that she was coming and carrying nothing, they went out to meet her with sticks. So she disappeared and secretly went off to sleep in other homesteads. When she got up the next morning, she thought of home. And she went home.

Again, it was said, "To the river!"

She went to the river, she arrived and dipped. But the water again refused to be dipped. And so she sang a song. A little plan came to her mind, that she should sing a song here above the river. The lizard waited there below, and listened to the efforts that were being made by the girl above the river. After a while, the girl was heard saying, "Kwek!

I'm tired! I must just rest for a time." The girl sat and rested, she rested and rested, and then her sister appeared.

She said, "What's the matter, Sister?"

The girl said, "It's this water! It won't be dipped! From the time you left home, we have not been able to drink water. And the people in the village are tired of us asking for water."

Her sister said, "Should I help you? Won't you tell on me?"

She said, "No, I won't tell on you!"

So she helped her sister to put the billycan on her head, then, when she was leaving, she kicked her and said, "If you tell on me, you devil, I'll hear you before you even go to sleep!"

The girl went, and then she appeared carrying the water. Her mother told her father, and her father peeked out—*kwok!* It was a good thing! They went out to meet her, admiring her now.

"How did you manage to dip it?"

"Well, it just happened."

All was well then.

"Now you must go there regularly," and the next day she went. The same thing happened: when she got there, this girl sang her songs, joyful now, as she hoped that the water would again allow itself to be dipped.

She sang her song:

> "Won't you help me, me, me, me?
> Won't you help me, me,
> Child of my mother, Thintwayo?
> Won't you help me, me,
> Child of my mother, Thintwayo?"

Gqi! Thintwayo suddenly appeared.

She said, "Did you tell about me?"

She said, "No, I said nothing about you!"

She said, "All right, dip!"

She dipped. Her sister helped her to put the water on her head, and she went off.

She said, "But if you tell about me, I'll hear you—even if I am this far away!"

She went.

As soon as she appeared at the homestead, her mother saw her coming with the water. And her father was full of kindness. The girl was smiling, and she continued to smile, looking to the side to hide the smile.

Her mother asked again and again, "How did you manage to dip this water, my child?"

"Well," she said, "I just dipped it"—continuing to smile, looking to the side to hide the smile.

Well, her mother knew that she should really press this child. Why does she always look to the side after she has dipped the water? She wasn't smiling the day before yesterday! or yesterday, for that matter! She pressed her: "Now, how did you manage to dip it?"

"No, I just sat there at the river and cried. When I got tired, I cried. I cried; and then a lizard appeared. That day that you beat me when I had come home having left the pail over there, the lizard beat me too. It beat me as I cried at the river. And you added to the beating! Thintwayo is alive! She's not dead! We didn't know it, but she's been living over there, and she's very healthy! She says that she eats *amasi* over there!"

"What? She is there?"

"Yes!"

"Oh, our child! What can we do to see her?"

"Please, Mama! Don't tell on me! Please! She has warned me gravely. She said that she would hear me!"

"No, no, we won't talk about that! Now, this is what you must do, my child. Amazing! to think that our child is the chief of the river! When you go there next time, put this dish of *mvubo* in the pail. Then, when she's about to help you to lift it to your head, you must say, 'Let's eat a little *mvubo*. Don't you crave *amasi* from home?' "

"All right, Mama. *Kwek!* It's as if dawn will never come today!"

They slept then. In the morning, she poured the *amasi* that was there into a dish, then seized a pail and said, "Well then, Mama, I'll go off on that errand now, the one we decided on yesterday."

She went to the river then, walking and singing. She arrived there, and sang. She was very happy today, there was no crying. But then she stopped smiling when a time had passed and her sister had not yet appeared. She stopped smiling now, but she did not stop singing her song:

> "Won't you help me, me, me?
> Won't you help me, me,
> Child of my mother, Thintwayo?
> Won't you help me, me,
> Child of my mother, Thintwayo?"

Thintwayo appeared and said, "You told on me! I warned you! I said that I would hear, even without your telling me! You told your parents about me! All right, dip!"

She said, "No, I didn't tell on you! I didn't tell on you! You're mistakenly accusing me!"

She said, "No, you told on me!"

"Oh, please, Thintwayo!" She coaxed her. Then her sister came out of the water to help her to put the pail on her head. When she was beginning to help her, the other girl said, "No, please wait! Here's some *mvubo* here in the pail! Let's just eat a little."

The other one said, "*Yu!* No, I've had enough here at the Great Place. I'm almost tired of it! It's even eaten by pigs here, it's so plentiful!"

She said, "Oh, please! It couldn't be as good as that from your own father's cows! Let's just eat a little, Child of my mother!"

Her father had come together with other men from the village, and their plan was to lie in wait, surround the pool, then ambush her. They planned to seize her, to lasso her and go home with her. The men had now surrounded the pool, only the tops of their heads showing above the bushes, so that when the sisters were eating the *mvubo*, this girl could be circled, then caught and taken home.

Thintwayo dipped some *mvubo*, and as she was about to dip the spoon a second time, she said, "I just don't feel like eating any more. I ate the *mvubo* only to please you. I've had enough. And anyway, my body feels as if something is creeping on it, my body tells me not to eat, because when I'm on the outside of the pool, I'm vulnerable."

Her sister said, "No, go on and eat. You feel that way because it's been some time since you've been away from home. There's nothing in the *mvubo* that can harm you! You can see that I myself am still eating. What do you think I've put in it? Do you think I'd be eating it myself?"

While the sisters were chatting like this, the men closed in.

Someone said, "Move in!"

She was seized, and they departed with her and her sister. But that deep pool followed them, it heaved in such a way that there was no avoiding it. It was like high tide in this place!

Someone said, "Let's try the ancestors! Let's see how it was dealt with in the past, and do that!"

"We're going to have to shout, because there's no way for us to go and get the cattle that are needed to satisfy these angry waters! There's no way to get out of the door!"

And indeed, the pool moved in. The homestead was now right in the pool!

The men called out, "We'll offer a red ox!" But the pool remained. "We're offering a black ox!" The pool did not move. They mentioned all the colors of cattle, but the pool did not recede. And here she is, the good sister, shut up in a house! *Kwok!*

"What's the solution to this?"

"We've gone through all the colors of oxen!"

An old man, an age-mate of the father of this owner of the homestead, said, "Please point out a dun-colored ox. In the old days, the homestead of the Great Place, the river, used to prefer that kind of ox."

Someone said, "We offer this dun-colored ox, Homestead of the Great Place! And we're asking that you give us this girl as a loan."

"You've punished us. We'll never again treat her in that way!"

"We're asking for her as a loan from you, we're asking that she remain here with us, that she not return with you."

"But we want you to know that we're not claiming her in any aggressive way. Loan her to us! We're pleading with you."

"Take that ox, the dun-colored one! We give it to you, Homestead of the Great Place!"

Then this dun-colored ox came out of the kraal on its own. No one brought it out, because the people were trapped in the house because of the pool. The ox came out on its own, and the water of the pool reached up to its belly. And so the pool departed with its ox.

The girl who had just been taken from the Great Place of the river was loved greatly now, the one who had been driven away from home because she was hated there but who had been loved at the Great Place of the river.

The other sister, the younger one, lived in sorrow. She became a servant. But the older girl never paid her sister back in kind. She was generously disposed toward her, even though they had gone through all those unhappy experiences. She loved her, and the parents' hearts also loosened up in the end, and they came to love their children without partiality.

The *ntsomi* is ended, it is ended.

A Zim Steals a Duiker's Children

Collected by Harold Scheub in November 1967 in Nyaniso Location in Matatiele District, the Transkei, and translated from the Xhosa.

The performer was a Hlubi woman, about thirty-five years old. The audience consisted of eighteen women, three teenagers, twenty children and two men. She was a good performer, with a fine blend of gesture and body movement on the one hand and narrative development in its verbal aspects on the other. There are few details here; her major concern is with action, and most of the action takes place off the written page—with body and head, with playful relations with a responsive audience.

Note: *Zim*—the most common of the villains in Xhosa and Zulu oral narratives. It usually has but one leg (it had two at birth, a sweet one and a bitter one, and its parents immediately ate the sweet leg), and is able to travel at great speeds on that one leg. It is not exceptionally bright, and its hunger for human flesh seems insatiable.

This story recalls the popular nursery tale of the big bad wolf trying to get into the houses of the three little pigs.

Motifs: G413 "Ogre disguises voice to lure victim" (reported for the Sotho); G441 "Ogre carries victim in bag (basket)" (reported for the Sotho, Xhosa, Zulu); G556 "Recognition of captive's voice brings about rescue from ogre" (reported from the Xhosa and Zulu); R10.3 "Children abducted"; R110 "Rescue of captive."

It happened in a *ntsomi*.

There was a duiker that gave birth to some children. One day the duiker traveled, she left the children behind in the house and went to find some food for them. She said, "My children, you must close this door! Don't open it for anyone!"

The children remained in the house. The duiker traveled, and when she returned, she said,

> "You! Children of the duiker!
> Please throw a small rope to me,
> And then I'll comfort you!"

The children said, "That's Mama!" They opened the door. The duiker entered, and gave the children some food.

Again, the duiker traveled the next day. She said, "My children, you must close this door! Don't open it for anyone! No one should come in here!"

The duiker traveled. Again she returned, and said,

> "You! Children of the duiker!
> Please throw a small rope to me,
> And then I'll comfort you!"

The children opened the door. Their mother entered, and she gave the children some food. Their mother remained there.

Again the next day, their mother went out, she journeyed. She said, "Children, don't open the door!"

Their mother traveled, she traveled, she went to seek food. Then a Zim arrived, and it said,

> "You! Children of the duiker!
> Please throw a small rope to me,
> And then I'll comfort you!"

The children said, "No, that's not Mama!" They did not open the door. The Zim ran off, it traveled.

It said, "*Kwo!* I didn't get them!" It departed, and their mother returned.

She said,

> "You! Children of the duiker!
> Please throw a small rope to me,
> And then I'll comfort you!"

The children said, "That's Mama! It's Mama!" The children opened the door. Their mother entered, and she gave the children the food. She slept.

Again, the next day, their mother journeyed. The Zim took an ax at its homestead and heated the ax in the hearth until it was red-hot. It completed this work, and then it swallowed the ax. The ax made its voice small, dainty.

The next day, the Zim arrived and said,

> "You! Children of the duiker!
> Please throw a small rope to me,
> And then I'll comfort you!"

The children opened the door, they said, "That's Mama!" But the Zim entered the house!

It said, "*Kwo!* I've got you now!" It took the children and put them into a sack. Then it went off with them.

The mother of the children arrived, and the children were gone! She said,

> "You! Children of the duiker!
> Please throw a small rope to me,
> And then I'll comfort you!"

She arrived, the children were not in the house. Their mother went out then, she traveled. She traveled, asking for her children. But she did not find them. Then she came to a homestead where a party was going on. She arrived, and sat down there. This mother was downcast.

The Zim passed by this homestead, it arrived and requested some beer. It was given beer, and it drank. Then it took its bag and put it over there, on the side. The bag spoke!

The bag spoke, and the children were heard, crying, over there in that sack!

There were some important men here—this man, this Zim, this beer. They took the bag outside, they took that bag. They hid it. They put it into another house.

When the Zim got there, it arrived and the sack was gone! The mother was given her children, and she went off with them. The Zim had not yet got the children!

The *ntsomi* is ended, it is ended.

Hlakanyana Does Mischief but is Caught

Collected by Harold Scheub in November 1967 in Nyaniso Location, Matatiele District, in the Transkei, and translated from the Xhosa.

The performer was a Hlubi woman, about fifty years old, and the audience consisted of fifteen women and five children. She was a calm and experienced performer, with accomplished use of gesture and vocal drama. She had very close relations with the audience, which delighted in the antics of the trickster in this narrative.

Hlakanyana is the major trickster character in the Xhosa narrative tradition, sometimes female, sometimes male, with magical powers of the European witch, the tail of the Devil, and a propensity for deadly tricks.

Motifs: K851 "Deceptive game: burning each other. Dupe burned (boiled) to death" (reported for the Iba, Thonga, Xhosa, Zulu, and Sotho); G61 "Relative's flesh eaten unwittingly" (reported for the Iba, Thonga, Fjort, Benga, and Sotho); D231 "Transformation: man (woman) to stone" (reported for the Sotho and the Xhosa); D2143.4 "Hail produced by magic" (reported for the Sotho and Nyanga); K891 "Dupe tricked into jumping to her death"; suggested motif: H1555.2* "Test of honesty: jumping over pit filled with milk to reveal milk thief."

A *ntsomi* goes like this—
There was a girl called Hlakanyana. One day she traveled and came to a homestead. An old woman was there, alone.
She said, "Old woman, let's cook each other!"
The little old woman said, "All right, Child of my child!"
Hlakanyana dipped out some water and filled the pot. When the pot became warm, Hlakanyana got in.
Then she said, "Old woman! Old woman! Take me off the fire, I'm burning!"
The old woman took Hlakanyana off the fire. Then Hlakanyana put the old woman in. She made a fire.
The old woman said, "Hlakanyana! Hlakanyana! Take me off the fire, Child of my child! I'm burning!"
She said, "No, Grandmother, it's not yet time!"
"My child, my child, take me off the fire! I'm burning!"
"No, Grandmother, it's not yet time!"
The little old woman died, the little old woman died.
Hlakanyana took her off the fire then and put her into a dish. Her two sons were not there, they were out hunting. When they came home, Hlakanyana was already wearing the little old woman's clothing. She took some meat out for them, and they ate, they ate.

In the midst of this eating, one of the sons said, "Oh, what's this? It seems to be a hand! It's good, this!"

Hlakanyana went out. She went, she went, and when she had gone a distance, and was standing alone, she said, "Yeeeeeeeere! They're eating their mother!"

Then these two ravenous men went out. They took some sticks, and made her run. They went, they went, they went, they went—and look! a river, and it was full! When they got to the river, Hlakanyana turned herself into a black rock. Then, when the sons arrived, they were unable to find her.

One of them picked up the black rock and said, "If I could find her, I'd do this!" And he hurled the rock to the other side of the river. Then the rock changed, and it became Hlakanyana!

She said, "Yeeeeeeere! You ate your mother!"

She went. She went, she went, she came to a homestead. When she arrived, some men were stitching the thatch on the roof of a house— one was inside, one outside. Hlakanyana got rid of the man who was on top, and then she climbed up. She stitched, she stitched, she stitched, then Hlakanyana went inside. The man who had been inside went to the outside. She stitched, she stitched and stitched—but Hlakanyana was actually stitching the foot of the big man to the roof!

When she had finished doing this, a huge hailstorm came up. Hlakanyana went out.

She said, "Hey! Come down from there!"

There were only the two of them at the house! The hailstorm arrived and pulverized the man.

Hlakanyana started, and she ran and ran. She came to a homestead. When she got to this homestead, Hlakanyana got married. Hlakanyana got married, even though she had a tail! She was dressed in clothes, so that she was beautiful to look at.

Then one day someone said, "What's this? Since the bride came here to our home, the milk has been disappearing! There's no milk here at home! Let a contest be held!"

He dug a deep hole outside and put some milk into it. The hole became full. Then it was said that all the people of this homestead should jump. All jumped over this hole, all jumped over this hole. Hlakanyana tarried, not jumping.

Someone said, "Jump!"

She said, "No, I'm afraid!"

Again, someone said, "Jump!"

She said, "No, I'm afraid!"

When she did jump, her tail dipped down into the milk. They beat her, they threw her to the dogs! And the dogs fought her, and killed her.

The ntsomi is ended, it is ended.

Mbengu-Sonyangaza's Sister Prepares to Undergo Purification Rites

Collected by Harold Scheub in September 1967 in a kraal in Mboxo (Nkanga) Location, Gutyana District, in the Transkei, and translated from the Xhosa.

Performed by Nongenile Masithathu Zenani, age fifty-five. The audience grew to over fifty Xhosa men, women, and children. Mrs. Zenani is a Xhosa doctor of considerable ability, a talented oral historian, and a highly accomplished narrative artist. See Harold Scheub, "The Art of Nongenile Mazithathu [sic] Zenani, a Gcaleka Ntsomi Performer," in *African Folklore*, ed. R. M. Dorson (New York: Doubleday and Company, Anchor Books, 1972), pp. 115–42.

This extended tale contains a considerable amount of ethnographic detail on Xhosa puberty rites and marriage customs. The adventures with cannibals and ogres, the abductions and the rescues, are set in the midst of customs that are a part of the fabric of Xhosa life. Indeed, the imaginative elements of the narrative are the means of communicating cultural values and patterns.

The "Great Place" (*komkhulu*) is the home or kraal of a king or chief at which live the most important of the king's wives.

Intonjane refers to the strict rituals observed by a Xhosa girl when she reaches puberty. She lives secluded in a house for a period of time, up to three months, and is attended during the day by women companions and their chaperones. In the house, the *ntonjane* girl lies concealed behind a rush mat with her attendant. All her activities and contacts during this period are rigidly prescribed, and she is addressed as *Intonjane* (cf. John Henderson Soga, *The Ama-Xhosa: Life and Customs* [Lovedale, South Africa, 1931], pp. 216–18).

When the husband says, in the narrative, "I wasted my cattle," he is referring to *lobola*, a custom whereby the family of the bridegroom compensates the family of the bride by presenting them with cattle. More important, as Van Tromp has pointed out, "Through the medium of *lobola* . . . a relationship of mutual affinity between two people and their families is created." *Lobola* involves religious, social, and legal as well as economic elements. If the husband rejects or mistreats his wife, he forfeits the *lobola*, or the wife's father or guardian may dissolve the marriage by restoring the *lobola* to the husband (cf. Albert Kropf, *A Kafir* [sic] *English Dictionary* [Lovedale, South Africa, 1915], p. 219; S. M. Seymour, *Bantu Law in South Africa* [Cape Town, South Africa, 1970], pp. 142–43; J. Van Tromp, *Xhosa Law of Persons* [Cape Town, 1947], pp. 48–49).

The allusion to "my right-hand wife" refers to the second wife married by a Xhosa commoner. His first wife is known as his "great wife." Each wife establishes a house within the homestead. The third wife is the *qadi* (support) to the Great House; the fourth wife is the *qadi* to the right-hand house, and so on.

According to Xhosa history, two chiefs of different culture groups sent their daughters and bridal parties to Phalo (1702–75) to marry the young chief. They arrived at the same time and, in perplexity, not wishing to insult either of the chiefs, Phalo consulted his most trusted adviser. This expert assembled both wedding parties in the courtyard, before King Phalo, and asked him, "What is this between the arms of the chief?" Phalo replied that it was his head. Next, the expert took the king's right arm, and asked what that was. Again, Phalo replied. Then the expert pronounced that one of the wives should be the head, or the brain; and the other the right arm, or the strength. The head came first, but both were important and of high status, and the right hand could help the head (cf. Van Tromp, pp. 88–92; Seymour, pp. 120–21).

Motifs: D1402.7.2 "Magic spear kills"; F510 "Monstrous persons"; F511.2 "Person unusual as to his ears"; G11.18 "Cannibal tribe"; G441 "Ogre carries victim in bag (basket)" (reported for the Sotho, Xhosa, and Zulu); R111.1.4 "Rescue of princess (maiden) from giant (monster)" (reported for the Kpelle); G556 "Recognition of captive's voice brings about rescue from ogre" (reported for the Xhosa and Zulu); R156 "Brother rescues sister" (reported from Liberia and Sierra Leone); Q421 "Punishment: beheading"; E723.7.1 "Wraith speaks."

Note: *Intsomi* (or *ntsomi*)—the imaginative oral narrative of the Xhosa. All imaginative oral narratives fall into this category. Historical narratives and occurrences are called *amabali* (sing., *ibali*); factual stories generally are called *iimbali* (sing., *imbali*), and histories sometimes fall into this classification also.

Now for a *ntsomi*.

At the homestead of the Great Place were two girls. They had a brother, a little boy who was the last born. And the girls had chaperones—one of the sisters was chaperoned among the young men, the other among the boys.

Then it was announced, "The elder sister must be initiated into womanhood!"

She hesitated for a time, then decided that she would go through the purification and initiation ceremonies during the following year. "I don't want to be initiated this year!" And things were left at that.

One day, she said to the other girls, "Let's go and gather wood in that distant forest, the one that people don't usually enter! Let's go there and see this thing that's so feared in that forest! There's a lot of firewood there. I tell you, wood is really plentiful in that forest!"

Twelve girls went, two of them from the Great Place, the other ten from the village. They traveled, they went to gather firewood. They carried provisions with them—cooked maize. (In those days, people cultivated with digging sticks, they cultivated with their hands. There were no plows then, and no oxen were yoked. People cultivated with their hands in those days.) Maize and millet—the girls made some loaves of millet, and some maize. They carried these with them, and they journeyed. The forest was a long way off.

They walked, they walked and walked and walked, they traveled and finally came to the forest. When they got there, they took the provisions down from their heads and put their equipment on the edge of the forest. Then they went into the forest and gathered firewood. When they had penetrated that forest, they found great amounts of wood. They gathered it up, they gathered it, they gathered it, and then put it outside, on the edges of the forest. They stacked it there. When they had finished doing this, they saw some beautiful gardens. And the gardens were twelve in number—the same number as the girls! They were indeed elegant plots.

The chief's daughter said, "Do you see what I see?"

The others said, "What is it?"

"Do you see this? Such beautiful gardens! All arranged in order! Count them!"

They counted the gardens; they were twelve.

Someone said, "How did they come to be equal in number to us?"

"Well, I don't know. My guess is that it's a gift to us—a gift from the ancestors!"

One of the girls agreed. "These gardens are a gift to us from the ancestors!"

"Well, let's go home now."

The girls carried the firewood and went home. On the way home, the chief's daughter said, "We've got to steal some seeds from home. Each one of us must steal some seed-corn, some pumpkin seeds, and sugar-cane seeds. Then we'll wait for the rains to come. We'll also have to hide some hoes—digging sticks." (That's not a hoe with a metal head, the kind we have today. In those days, the hoes were made of wood. They were like wedges, and plowing was done by putting these wedges into the ground.)

Well then, they agreed to this plan, and they moved on. When they got home, each of the girls went in the direction of her own home—one went that way, one went this way, another went that way. When they got home, they all stole seeds and hid them.

Time passed.

Time passed, time passed, and then the rain fell. And it really rained! The rain dropped like teeth! The girls came together again and again after the rains began to fall.

"Hasn't the princess noticed that the rains have begun to fall?"

Another said, "Surely she's seen it."

They came together again, and when they had done so the chief's daughter said, "It's rained. We've got to go and cultivate those gardens. Do you have the seeds?"

One girl said, "We hid the seeds as soon as we got home!"

She said, "Now don't tell anybody about this at home! I, too, I don't mention the subject at my home!"

"Well, we haven't talked about it!"

"We don't talk about it either."

They went off then one day; they again made their provisions and went over there to the gardens, carrying the things that they would use to cultivate. They arrived at the forest. When they got there, they gathered firewood; they gathered firewood, they gathered firewood, they gathered firewood. Then they came out of the forest and stacked the wood; they put the firewood on the edge of the forest. Then they turned from where they had stacked the wood, and began to cultivate. Each one plowed her own garden, each one plowed her own, each one plowed her own. They plowed, they plowed industriously so that they could finish quickly. They plowed, and then finished. When they had finished plowing, "All right, then, let's go home!"

They went home; they walked and finally arrived at their homes. Time passed.

Time passed, time passed, time passed at their homes, and after a month had gone by, during the second month after they had returned, the chief's daughter again brought the girls together. "Let's just go out there and inspect those gardens. Let's go and see if those plots of ours are in need of weeding."

"All right."

"Be sure, now, not to talk about this!"

"No, we won't mention it!"

"I, too, I don't talk about this matter at my home."

Well then, time passed, and again they traveled. They arrived over there. Oh! they arrived and found their corn thriving. They arrived and hoed, they hoed and hoed. When they had finished hoeing, they went into the forest. They gathered firewood there, they piled it up, they ate their provisions, they carried the firewood, and departed.

When they got home, they stayed as before at their homes, and time passed.

Time passed, they remained at home, and it happened just as before: after a time, "Hey!" the girl said again. "Let's just go and inspect those gardens. Let's see what's happening over there."

Mh! Again they made their provisions, and they walked, they walked and went to inspect their gardens. They arrived there, and the corn was now in the stage of forming little ears. They arrived, and the cane was in the blossoming stage. Well, they looked around as they had before, and they gathered firewood in the forest as they had previously. Then they carried the firewood again, and went home.

Time passed, and they remained at home for a long time. Finally, they estimated that the garden must be at such-and-such a stage now.

Time passed.

Time passed, time passed, time passed, and: "Oh! Let's go again!" the chief's daughter reminded them. Provisions were prepared, and they went off.

When they got there, they found that the corn was thoroughly ripe. They arrived, and the cane also was perfectly ripe. They gathered firewood, they gathered firewood for a short time, and then they kindled a fire. Each one plucked an ear of corn from her own plot, each of the girls plucked an ear of corn from her plot, and the corn was roasted. When the corn had been roasted, it was eaten. And when they had finished eating the corn, some of the sugarcane was picked. Each one picked cane from her own garden, each one picked cane from her garden, and they gathered then in one place and ate the cane.

While they were eating the sugar cane, *thu!*, a huge yellow dog suddenly appeared! When this dog had appeared, *thu!*, they said, "Where did this dog come from?" The dog came on, on and on and on it came. It went right up to this chief's daughter; it went to her, and was affectionate, wagging its tail, beating its tail, wagging its tail against her, climbing up on her again and again, beating its tail, wagging its tail, wagging its tail against her.

Someone said, "Hey, this dog! This dog must be the dog of a friend of yours! Because it certainly seems to know you!"

"Besides, your friend's dog is just this size!"

The girl said, "No, it's not this one! I don't know this dog!"

"Then why?" said the other girls.

"How is it that this dog is so friendly to you?"

"How can you say you don't know it?"

"Well, my friend, I don't know this dog! I don't know this dog at all! No! And besides that, I'm afraid of this dog!"

They hurried away. The girls got ready, they fastened their skirts. They were still fastening their skirts when they heard stalks breaking —*krwaba! krwaba! krwaba! krwaba! krwaba!*—stalks breaking there in the garden. And when the girls went to look—*kraaaaawo!*—there were people there! people they did not know! and these people had very long ears! These people—"Oh! they're *oogonggonggo!*"—fantastic beasts, people who eat other people!

The girls ran, and while they were running, they were being pursued. They ran very fast, and while they were running, they were being pursued.

Among these monsters was a leader, and he said, "Leave them alone!

Leave all of those girls alone! Just grab thaaaaaaaat one who's in front!" referring to that girl over there, the one for whom the dog had wagged its tail—that girl over there! the one who had urged the others on. It was because of her that they had all come over here.

The monsters passed the other girls by, all all all all the other girls; they passed them by, and finally they caught up with this other girl. They seized her. The girl cried out, but by that time she had been kidnapped. The other girls were left alone, and they ran on. They finally got to their homes.

They arrived, and said, "So-and-so has gone off with the monsters! They attacked us while we were roasting meat! We had planted some gardens out there!"

Someone said, "*Kwo!* No one would even dare go there!"

"We must just accept the fact that she's gone, friends!"

"Our child is gone!"

Time passed, time passed then.

The girl cried as they took her home to their kraal. And as they returned, all of the monsters were staking claims to this girl, thinking that she would be slaughtered.

One of them said, "I get a foreleg, Chief!"

Another says, "Me, too, I get the other foreleg!"

"Well, *I* have a breast!"

Another said, "I'll have a leg!"

"Chief, I'll take the other breast!"

"I claim the head!"

"I want the viscera!"

. . . until the end.

The chief said, "Noooo! She's not to be touched! This girl will be my wife! She will be Nojikolo (She-of-the-waist-band). She'll be the wife of the Great House, she's going to make a fine breed of children for me. If any one of my offspring is not a thoroughbred, then he'll be eaten!"

The monsters were disappointed; they had been anticipating devouring the meat that they had found that day.

A house was built for the girl, and she lived in it together with that monster who was now her husband. Time passed for her, and ultimately she became pregnant and gave birth. She bore a beautiful child, a child who resembled her mother.

When she had given birth to that child, the monsters said, "Chief, give us the child! We want to eat her!"

He said, "No, I can't eat her! This child is loved by Nojikolo! My wife would feel terrible!"

So they left this child alone, even though they were ravenous for her flesh. Whenever the child cried, they would leap at her; they would lick her tears, they would swallow her tears. But then the chief would scold them: "No! No! Don't do that to Nojikolo's child!"

They would leave the child alone then and run off. But even when the child was in the company of others, whenever she cried, the monsters would leap on her and lick her tears from her face.

"Ffffff! Mnca! Kwo! If only we could taste the girl herself! Ffffff! Mnca! Kwo."

Time passed. Time passed, and Nojikolo again gave birth. This time she bore a child who was a boy, who resembled his father, whose ears reached to his shoulders.

And time passed.

This girl grew up, she developed breasts. She would sometimes go to the river with the other girls to dip water, but she was so loved by her father that she did not work at all. One day, she wanted very much to go to the river, so she took a tin and went to the water. When she got to the river, the others were dipping and hoisting the water to their heads.

As for her: "This tin is weighing me down! What's the matter?" Her tin pail would not leave the ground! "Help me, someone! Help me to lift it!"

Someone said, "Yo! You're too soft!"

"You're spoiled! We all know that you never do any work because you're so spoiled!"

"You're so loved!"

"Now how could that thing weigh you down?"

"Too soft!"

"Spoiled!"

They left her there. The child sat down. While she was sitting there, struggling with the tin, something in the water bubbled to the surface—vumbululu! A beautiful person rose to the surface—vumbululu!

When this person came out of the water—vumbululu!—the child ran.

But the person said, "Don't run! I won't do anything to you! Come here, I have some questions to ask you!"

The child returned.

This person said, "Whose child are you?"

She said, "I'm Nojikolo's child!"

He said, "Now, what does Nojikolo say when she swears?"

The child said, "She says, 'I swear by Mbengu-Sonyangaza that I will punish you!'"

This person said, "Do you see me?"

The child said, "Yes."

He said, "Do you know me?"

The child said, "I don't know you. But I can see that you resemble my mother."

This person said, "How do I resemble your mother?"

She said, "You resemble her because of your gat tooth. And the point of hair on your forehead. You also have the same color that she has."

This person said then, "I'm her brother! I'm the very one she swears by! I'm this Mbengu-Sonyangaza about whom she always speaks! Now, then, this is what you must do, my child. Go home, but carry these two reeds along with you. Put them down in the doorway of your house. Your mother will come to help you take the tin of water down from your head. Don't let anyone else do that! Then you must throw the reeds into disorder, so that your mother steps on them. When she has stepped on the reeds, you must cry for them, say that you want them replaced with fresh ones! But again, don't agree that the reeds be picked by anyone else! Demand that they be picked by your mother!"

Well, the child did that. She took the reeds and went off with them. She got home, she arrived and put the reeds in the doorway. She crossed the reeds, one over the other, in that doorway.

She said, "Mama! Come and take the pail of water down from my head! Mama! Come and take it down!"

"No, take it down yourself! Don't be so silly!"

"Mama! Come and take it down!"

"Take it down yourself! What is this, that your things have to be taken down by me? What are you carrying?"

"I said, 'Mama, come and take it down!'"

"*Kwok!* This child is really naughty! I'm going to have to give you a beating!"

The girl's father spoke: "No, Nojikolo! Please take the water down for the child. She's been standing there in the doorway for a long time!"

Nojikolo got up then and went to the child, scolding her. "This child is silly!" She went to her angrily, and in her anger she smashed some of the reeds. Then she helped the child to take the water from her head.

The child cried, "*Yooooooooo!* How could you smash my reeds? I want my reeds! I want them! How could you smash my reeds? Go!"

"No, stop it, child!"

Her father said, "Stop, my child. I'll pick some more reeds for you. I'll pick them myself."

"No! I don't want them to be picked by you, Father! They must be picked by Mama! I don't want them to be picked by anyone else! *She* must go and pick them! She crushed my reeds on purpose!"

This happened: the child cried, the child went to bed still crying because her mother had not gone to get more reeds. Her mother angrily scolded the child for her antics. "She's naughty!"

In the morning the child woke up and continued insisting that her mother get the reeds. She cried and said that she wanted the reeds, that they should be picked by her mother.

"No, Nojikolo! Go, finally!" so said the husband. "This child will get thin if you don't go and pick the reeds for her! Go and pick them, satisfy my child!"

So the mother got up and went, and the child followed. When they were close to the river, the child said, "Mama, you who did not agree to pick reeds for me, do you think that I'm pushing you to this river just to get some reeds? I'm not pushing you for reeds at all! I saw something at the river!"

"What did you see?"

"You'll see it, Mama. Please go on. I saw a handsome person, handsome! handsome! handsome! He resembles you, this man! This person has a gat tooth, he has a hair point, and he says that he's your brother! the one by whom you swear! He says that he's Mbengu-Sonyangaza!"

Kwo! Her mother hit her. She slapped her with her open hand.

"You're silly! You're naughty! What Mbengu-Sonyangaza? I'll beat you!"

"Oh, please go on, Mama!"

She went on. When she got to the river, *thu!*, he appeared. She saw her brother. *Kwo!* she cried. Her brother cried. His sister also cried, and the child cried too. They all wept a little over each other. Then they went up the river, moving away from the usual dipping area. They went to sit in another spot.

Her brother asked, "What happened to you, Sister?"

"Well, I was kidnapped by those monsters! But I wasn't eaten. It was declared that I should produce a thoroughbred, and so I became the chief's wife."

"How can I help you escape?"

She said, "Well, I'll work out a plan, I'll work out a plan."

"Do you want to come home? to come home with me now?"

"Yes, I want to come home."

"All right, then, please think of a plan."

She took his garment and trampled it with mud; she dirtied it, it became muddy. She tramped on it, she trampled it. She took some mud and smeared his whole body with it, from head to feet. His clothes oozed with mud, and she put them on him; they were dripping wet.

Then she said, "You must crawl, crrrrrrrrawl! Walk on your knees. And you must walk ahead of me, I'll walk behind you. I'll say that I've made you my servant. No one will do anything to you."

He went then, he went with her, Mbengu-Sonyangaza crawling

ahead of his sister, creeping along, dirty. He was oozing with mud and water. His sister walked behind him.

They suddenly appeared at the monsters' place—*thu!*

"*Halaaaaaaaaala halala!* It has appeeeeeeeared! My servant is here with me! *Halaaaaaaala!* See! See!"

The chief came out of his house, and said, "*Tyhini!* Nojikolo has a servant! Well, what shall we do about this? Get the bad things from off the path, so he won't be hurt! Clear the way! Everything must be clean! Remove the doctored herbs! The little beast of the chief's wife is here! Remove the doctored herbs from the path! Clear the way for them! Bring a mat!"

A mat was put down, a new mat.

The chief's wife was pleased because of her little beast. She went around, saying, "Little beast of miiiiine! Little beast of mine! Little beast of miiiine! Little beast of the chief's wife Nojikolo!"

Mbengu-Sonyangaza went into the house, and when he had entered, she made a bed for him, a bed fashioned from a mat. She made a bed for him behind the door. He remained there, and his garment was still oozing because it was so wet.

They slaughtered for the "little beast" then. A beast was slaughtered for Nojikolo's servant.

Time passed, and they were happy.

Then, at dawn, the monsters went out to hunt people. They would return later with a dead person who would be cooked here at home. But an animal would be brought for Nojikolo, the woman, because she did not eat human flesh. They went off, they hunted, and then they returned. They brought an animal along for Nojikolo, saying, "Here it is! Here's your animal, Nojikolo!"

She said, "Thanks! This little beast of mine doesn't eat human flesh either, so don't come in here with human flesh!"

The "little beast" was cooked for, then, and he ate with his sister. Again they went off to hunt; the monsters went off to hunt.

The "little beast" asked, "Well, Sister, do you have a plan for our escape? How will we do it?"

"We're going to escape today! I want us to leave this place today!"

There was a little old woman there who did not know how to walk. She had been left behind at home, this little woman, already old; she was left alone in this homestead. And everything, everyone else departed—even the child of the chief's wife departed. The other child, the boy, went along with the hunters. The one who remained behind was the girl, Nojikolo's daughter.

Time passed, and when time had passed, Nojikolo gathered all the stock together; she brought all the livestock together, and all the goods and property were tied on a wagon. All valuable property was brought together, everything that was attractive, everything that was beautiful, all of it. Everything was gathered together—sheep and that sort of thing, goats and that sort of thing, cattle and that sort of thing, horses and that sort of thing—and they were gathered in large numbers behind the wagon. Then the wagon was hitched up, things tied on, and then they climbed up. Mbengu-Sonyangaza was carrying a spear. They climbed up, and then they journeyed off.

When they had departed and were far in the distance, the old woman of the house heard the wagon rattling far off—*goqo goqo goqo*—and she slid along the ground, she slid along the ground and appeared at the door.

"*Tyhini!*" She got to the door just as the others had gone to the other side.

She said, "Hey! All the property of this home! There are no people here, so who could be taking it all away? Everything's gone! Why have the goats and sheep and cattle and horses all been brought together into a single group? Who's driving the livestock? And who inspanned the wagon?" She shouted, "Nojikolo! Nojikolo! Where are you? Where are you, my friend? Nojikolo! Who'll do something about this theft?"

No sound from Nojikolo.

The old woman slid along the ground, she slid along the ground, and finally got to Nojikolo's house. Oh! even the door of Nojikolo's house had been taken!

The old woman called out, "The homestead has been robbbbbbbbbed by the beast of Nojikolo!"

That occurred just about the time that the monsters were turning back.

"Heey! What's being said over there? It sounds like Grandmother! She seems to be shouting to us! Just wait a minute!"

"The homestead has been robbbbbbbbbbbed by the beast of Nojikolo!"

"Heeeey! She says that the homestead has been robbed by the beast of Nojikolo!"

Kwo! They hurried then, climbing up the hill to the homestead. When they got there, Mbengu-Sonyangaza and his sister had already moved out of sight; they had disappeared, they were no longer visible. They simply could not be seen.

The little old woman pointed: "Over that hill, over therrrrrrrre!"

The monsters, as numerous as an army, pursued them, they pursued them.

When she saw the monsters in the distance, Nojikolo said, "Oh, I wonder, Mbengu-Sonyangaza, Child of my father, what will become of us now? Because look! over therrrrrre are the monsters! Not even I will be safe today!"

He said, "Don't worry. It'll be all right!"

He had been driving the oxen, but now he said, "You drive them, Girl!" And he stopped as his sister continued to drive the livestock. Mbengu-Sonyangaza stopped, and he hurled his spear at the first monster who appeared. The spear hit the monster, and down it went. And when it fell down, all of the monsters fell! They died as one! all of them died, even those who had not been stabbed by the assegai. They all died! Then Mbengu-Sonyangaza climbed up on the wagon, and he drove on. They went on their way, and finally arrived at home.

When they got home, he said, "There she is, Father!" He was speaking outside: "I've come with her, I've brought the child and her spoils. I have returned today!"

They all came outside, and thanked him. They gave thanks for their safe return. An ox was slaughtered, as a ritual washing of the girl's stigma of being married to a monster. They knew that this was the girl of whom it had been said, for a long time, that she should be initiated into womanhood. And she had responded for a long time, "I don't want to be initiated into womanhood yet!" and now it was said, "Well, she must be initiated."

She said, "I want to go to the clay pit first. I want these chaperones of mine"—she was referring to those who had been girls at the time of the first adventure; they had been ten, and now they were married and living in their husbands' homesteads. It was arranged that these women should return; they should return because their leader was now here. And so, when they were asked to do so, they returned from their homesteads.

They journeyed then; they went to the clay pit to dig clay. When they got to the pit—this daughter of the chief was carrying a spear. When they got to the pit, they began to dig clay. They dug. She took off her apron (a thing that is tied around the waist) and put it down on the ground. They dug, they dug for the clay, they dug. Then they departed. They carried the clay and went home. They crossed a river.

When they had crossed the river, the chief's daughter said, "Yo yo yo yo yo yo! Kwo! I left my apron over there at the pit!" Oh! What should she do about that? They were far from the pit, and the sun was already setting. "No, I can't leave my apron behind. Other people might go over there and take it! I must go back, even if the sun is setting! Nomavo, please come with me!" Nomavo was her sister.

"Mh! No, friend, I won't go. I can't go over there now! It's too far!"

"Oh, what's the matter, Child of my mother? Why won't you come with me? Is it true that even *you* won't come with me?"

"No, I won't go back there with anyone! At this time of night, I'm afraid!"

"Well then, if you won't come with me, I'll just go by myself! But all of you must sit down here and wait for me. I'll plant my spear here in the ground. You keep your eyes on this spear. If I should happen to stumble, it will fall, then rise again. If I die, the spear will fall and not get up. In that case, you should go home."

"We understand," and the girls sat down.

She went back, having planted her spear in the ground. They watched the spear. After a time, when she neared the pit, she stumbled and fell. And the spear fell too.

They said, "She's dead! Let's go!"

They got up then, and the girls traveled. After they had gone, the spear rose because the girl got up.

She went into the pit, and when she had entered, she found that it was bright inside. It was all lit up.

She said, "Hey! Why is the pit all lit up?" But what had made her think that the pit was all lit up was actually a pair of eyes! She saw the eyes of something here in the pit! She took the apron—it was lying there in front of the thing with the eyes. When she had taken the apron, this thing seized her and put her into a sack. It went out with her, it took her home. It arrived at its home, and hung her on the upper side of the house, away from the door.

Those other girls had gone home—but this girl they had left behind was due to be initiated into womanhood that very day! What should they do? What should they say? When they had crossed a stream, the girls discussed the problem of what they should do.

"We should appear at home singing a *ntonjane* song."

"And we can help to begin the ceremonies over there at home!"

"But what should we do about *her*? She's not here!"

"Well, let's just take this crab," the others said. "We'll initiate this crab!"

"Crab, come here!"

"We're going to initiate you!"

The crab: "No, I have my children to think of! I don't attend such things!"

They traveled on.

"What'll we do about this problem?"

"Let's get a raven!"

"A raven likes meat!"

"The raven just can't refuse!"

"How shall we deceive it?"

First, a frog was caught. When the frog had been caught, it was held in the air, and someone said, "Come, Raven! Here's some meat!"

The raven came and then it too was seized.

One of the girls said, "We're taking you to a place where some meat is being eaten. You're to be initiated into womanhood! You'll get to eat meat—the small intestines! You'll eat the liver! everything, even the duodenum! You'll remain in seclusion, behind a screen."

"Don't make a sound! Just stay there!"

The raven agreed, and they all went off. The girls wove a screen of reeds that would become the *ntonjane* screen.

When they got home, the girls went around to the rear of the homestead, singing a song of initiation into womanhood. The song went like this:

> "You, Nongabe-ungezanga-ngena!
> *O yooooo wewowe!*
> *Yee-e yee-e yee-e yee-e!*
> This is not *ntonjane,*
> It's just a little wound!"

The mothers of the girls also sang this song when they heard that the girl was beginning her initiation. "She" was made to enter one of the houses, and they put up the screen that they had woven; the raven remained behind the screen. The bird was hidden from the girls who were not involved in this affair. The other girls would not allow others to go behind that screen and see the raven; only the ones who knew about it were allowed to go there.

Time passed, and that *ntonjane* girl was cared for; that *ntonjane* girl was cared for. At dawn, a beast was slaughtered for the *ntonjane* girl. The beast of the ritual-entry-into-the-*ntonjane*-house was slaughtered, and then the beast of the second stage of the ceremony, the wormwood stage, was killed. The mothers of the girls were also slaughtered for.

Time passed, the time of the *ntonjane,* and beer was brewed. Now the *ntonjane* would have a coming-out ceremony, an emergence-at-marriageable-age ceremony. As the beer was about to be strained on the day of that ceremony, an ox was slaughtered for the boys, an ox was slaughtered for the young men, an ox was slaughtered for the place of the *ntonjane,* an ox was slaughtered for the men, an ox was slaughtered for the women. The boys ate below the kraal, the young men ate in the courtyard, the men ate inside the kraal, the women ate in the sheep kraal, and there was eating too inside the place of the *ntonjane.* A great amount of smoke was caused by all this roasting of meat, and there was joy throughout the homestead because the chief's daughter was being initiated into womanhood.

On the day that this feast was taking place, that noxious creature who had seized the girl over there in the clay pit took the sack in which he had hung her and carried it on his shoulders. He went off with the bag. As he traveled, he happened to see the homestead where all the smoke was, and he smelled the meat in the air for the wind was coming from that direction. He sought the place where the smell of meat and the smoke were coming from, and then he headed in that direction. When he got there, he first went over to the boys below the cattle kraal.

He said, "Boys! *Tyhini!* You take on the whole cow! Please throw me some of the fat! And some of the lean meat too! If you do, I'll make the Bird of a great one sing for you!"

The boys threw some meat—lean meat, fat meat. He ate it, he ate and ate and ate, he ate the meat. Then he picked his teeth, he picked his teeth, he picked meat from his teeth and threw the tooth-pickings over there into the sack, so that the girl inside the sack might eat. The girl had not eaten since the last time she had been home. But she refused to eat the food that had been picked from teeth.

When he finished eating, he took a big stick and hit the girl. "Hnnnn! Please sing, Bird of a big one!"

The girl sang:

> "What should I say? What should I say?
> I traveled and got hurt!
> You, Bentsel'-esangweni!
> Noluhlu, won't you help me?
> *Tshiiiiiii! Ngantshooooooooo-ooo!*
> Nomavo, won't you help me?
> *Tshiiiiiii! Ngantshoooooooo-ooo!*"

When this girl sang like that, she was heard by a little child, the child who was the last born of this home. He was here with the other boys. He recognized that the voice was like that of his sister, and he called another of his brothers. He ran, the child ran over there to the young man in the courtyard.

He arrived and said, "Brother! Brother! Brother, please come here! Here's the voice of the *ntonjane!* I heard it in that bag over there! It was the *ntonjane!* She was calling out to you. And that *ntonjane* was calling for Sister too! Yes! She's over there! Yes, she was calling for this one, the one following her in age! She was calling her by name!"

"Oh!" the young man said. "No, don't shout like that! Please stop. Be quiet, I hear you."

The young man stayed where he was, and this other man was coming closer, carrying his sack. He approached the young men in the courtyard, and this boy was sitting at his older brother's side.

The other one said, "Young men! You take on the whole beast! Please give me some of the fat! And some lean meat! I'll make the Bird of a great one sing for you!"

The young men cut off some of the meat for him and threw it to him, both the lean and the fat. He ate it, he ate and ate, this thing ate; and when he had finished eating, he picked his teeth, he picked his teeth, he picked his teeth, throwing the tooth-pickings to the girl inside the sack. But the girl refused to eat the tooth-pickings; she just stayed there in that sack.

When he had finished eating, he took his stick and hit her—*mku!* "Sing, Bird of a great one!"

The girl sang:

> "What should I say? What should I say?
> You, Bentsel'-esangweni!
> I traveled and got hurt!
> Noluhlu, won't you help me?
> *Tshiiiiiii! Ngantshooooooooo-ooo!*
> Nomavo, won't you help me?
> *Tshiiiiiii! Ngantshooooooooo-ooo!"*

She stopped then.

When she had stopped, he departed, taking his bag with him. He went to the kraal where the fathers were eating. When he came to the fathers, he said, "Hello, gentlemen!"

"Yes!"

"Please give me some lean meat! And some fat! I'll make the Bird of a great one sing for you!"

That young man got up and went over to his father. He said, "Father, I wonder what we have put into the *ntonjane* house? Because the *ntonjane* is there in that sack! You'll hear her in a minute. That *ntonjane* calls me by name! She even calls my sister's name! You'll hear her, it's the real *ntonjane*. The one we slaughtered beasts for here at home. Now, I wonder what it is that we slaughtered for here? I wonder what it is that we slaughtered so many cattle for?"

That person was given fat and lean meat by the men, and he ate and ate. When he finished eating, he picked his teeth, and again poured the tooth-pickings into the sack. Then he took his stick and beat the bag—*mku!* and said, "Sing, Bird of a great one!"

She sang,

> "What should I say? What should I say?
> You, Bentsel'-esangweni!
> I traveled and got hurt!
> Noluhlu, won't you help me?
> *Tshiiiiiii! Ngantshooooooooo-ooo!*
> Nomavo, won't you help me?
> *Tshiiiiiii! Ngantshooooooooo-ooo!"*

Well, he got up and went off, carrying her on his shoulder. He went to the women in the sheep kraal.

The father of the *ntonjane* got up there among the men, this thing having already been heard by all the people. "Well, it *is* the girl in that sack! How could this have happened?" He went over to the yard and called his wife.

"Come here!" Then he said, "You mustn't cry when you hear this! The girl for whom we have gone to such expense to initiate here at home —here she is! in this sack! Now you mustn't show that you recognize her—not even a little! You mustn't show that you know what's going on! Just look on and pretend not to be concerned about her. We'll try to solve this in some way."

Well, then, the wife sat there. Because she was a woman who easily broke into tears, she took some time to go off and attempt to control herself. Then she went back and sat down.

The other one went to the women. He came to the women and said, "Women, please throw me some fat! And some lean meat! I'll make the Bird of a great person sing for you!"

The women threw him some meat. He ate and ate, and then picked his teeth. He threw the tooth-pickings to the girl; he threw her the pickings. Then he took a stick and beat her—*mku!* "Sing, Bird of a great person!"

The girl sang,

> "What should I say? What should I say?
> You, Bentsel'-esangweni!
> I traveled and got hurt!
> Noluhlu, won't you help me?
> *Tshiiiiiii! Ngantshooooooooooo-ooo!*
> Nomavo, won't you help me?
> *Tshiiiiiii! Ngantshoooooooooo-ooo!*"

"Oh, all right. We thank you, Great person! You've pleased us! Now please go and eat your meat in the kraal. Go on!"

Well, then, he went. While he was eating that meat, he put the sack next to him. He was given a lot of meat, and he ate it now, not paying attention to anything else, not caring about anything now, letting his guard down. After a time, it was said, "Now, when a person visits us here, he must customarily go and fetch some water for the chief. That's the custom, the tradition for everyone who comes here. The visitor must go and dip water for the chief. This is particularly the case if the visitor happens to be a man."

"All right," he said. A cask was brought, a cask that leaked. The container was very old, and they gave it to him.

They said, "Go and dip some water! But don't dip water in a place where frogs croak! Don't dip the water in any place that has crab holes! Dip in a place where the water is clear, where nothing stirs!"

This person went off then. When he had gone some distance, he turned and said, "My bag! You're not going to tamper with it!"

"No, we're not going to touch it. Tie it up!"

"Mm!" He fastened the bag to a post in the kraal; he tied it tightly. He tied it tightly, he tied it tightly, he tied it tightly, he tied it tightly, and then he went. When he had gone some distance, he turned again. "Don't tamper with that bag!"

"No, we haven't touched a thing! It's not the kind of thing we would do! We don't handle things belonging to strangers! It's not the kind of thing we would do—tamper with a visitor's bag!"

"Oh!" He went on his way, he went on, he didn't turn around again; he went down to the river. Throughout the day, he would arrive at a place, then while he was dipping he would see a frog, so he would spill the water. Then he would find that the cask leaked, and he would try to patch it. He would dig some clay and patch the cask with it. Then he would go further down to other places along the river and dip. He would see the hole of a crab! And so he would again spill the water and go further down the river. The cask would again begin to leak and he would patch it. Then this person, this thing, would go to work again and fill the cask with mud, trying to patch it.

Finally, he came to a deep pool in the river, a pool that was calm: he saw nothing. He dipped the water, then carried it. He traveled with it.

In the meantime, this girl was taken out of the sack; she was set free over there at the kraal post. She was put into a room, and it was locked. When she had been set free, this sack was put down on the ground.

They said, "Let all the animals of earth come here!"

Quickly then, quickly quickly quickly quickly the animals came, all of the animals of the earth. When the animals were there, someone said, "Will you be able to say the thing that you must say?"

They said that they would indeed be able to do so.

It was said, "Snake! Snake, what would *you* say?" There were even snakes there! Nothing was missing!

A snake said, "I'll just get up and bite the man, on the heel or ankle or calf!" So the snake was put into the sack.

It was said, "You, Wasp, what would *you* do?"

The wasp said, "I'll just get up and sting him, I'll pierce him with a sting! I'll stick it right in!" The wasp was put into the sack.

It was said, "You, Hornet, what will *you* do?"

The hornet said, "What will I do when what is said?"

"When it is said, 'Now sing, Bird of a great person!' because that's just what's going to be said!"

The hornet said, "I'll say,

'What should I say? What should I say?
You, Bentsel'-esangweni!
I traveled and got hurt!
Noluhlu, won't—' "

They said, "Stop! You know what to do! Put him in the sack. You must say that when the proper time comes, Hornet!"

They were all put into the sack, all the things—including black biting ants, everything that bites. What was *not* put into the sack were the things that do not bite. Only things that bite were put into the sack, and when that sack reached the size it was when the girl was in it, it was left alone. It was tied over there in the same way that it had been tied previously, to that kraal post.

Time passed then, and after a time had passed this thing arrived. He took the water down from his head, and the chief dipped it and drank.

It was said, "But did you dip the water in a place where nothing croaks?"

Some meat was given to him then, he was given meat and he ate it.

Then it was said, "Well, you have performed satisfactorily."

And he said, "I must now ask your permission to depart, gentlemen."

"Yes."

He took his sack, then he put it down and said, "But did you touch this?"

It was said, "No no no no! Nobody would tamper with it!"

He said, "Please sing, Bird of a great one!"

"What should I say? What should—"

"Stop! It's obviously you!"

He carried the sack on his shoulders and departed with it. He disappeared as he went toward his homestead. He arrived there and hung the sack up in that very same place he had hung it on the previous day, away from the door, on the upper side of the house.

After a time had passed, there was a discussion about "What should be done to that thing that's in the *ntonjane* house?"

The chief spoke with the fathers of all the girls who were being initiated into womanhood, all of them. There were eleven of those girls—twelve, counting the girl who was actually being initiated. One of those eleven girls was her sister, the other ten were girls of the village. The fathers of all ten of those girls "must speak up and say what they wish to say about their daughters."

"Well, Chief, I am offering a heifer to buy the life of my daughter."

All of them made similar offers; one after another offered the chief a heifer.

But the chief indicated that he did not want the heifers; he would not accept them, because his child was not saved by anything that they had done. She was saved by her ancestors, because she was despaired of as being dead. And the chief himself had lost so many cattle, thinking that he had been slaughtering them for his child. He did not want cattle now. In any case, this child of his had returned with such a great amount of booty when she had fled from the monsters.

"What do you propose to do about your daughters? That's all I want to know." The chief went on, "Each one of you must cut off his daughter's head! Each person, each father must do that himself!"

"All right."

They went, then, to the *ntonjane* house. When they got there, the door was barricaded. When he found the door barricaded, Mbengu-Sonyangaza entered—the brother of the *ntonjane* went in and broke through the screen. The raven fled, it flew off. It was not touched. Nothing was done to it.

He asked, "Where's the *ntonjane* that you're initiating here?" and there was nothing anyone could do now.

Mbengu-Sonyangaza began with his own sister. He seized her and cut off her head and threw it aside.

It was said, then, that each father should go in and cut off the head of his daughter. The men did as they were told, each one entering the house, each one cutting off his daughter's head; the heads were then thrown outside. All of the heads of those daughters were cut off and thrown away. Now the *ntonjane* was left without a sister, whose head had been cut off because of her part in the conspiracy.

It was necessary that Mbengu-Sonyangaza's sister enter the *ntonjane* house once again. She was to be brought into the *ntonjane* house by those girls who had had nothing to do with the conspiracy. She began from the beginning, as an initiate.

As this was going on in the homestead of the *ntonjane*, over there in that thing's home, he was saying, "My wives! Go and gather some firewood!" He had three wives. "Today my bird will be cooked!" He meant this girl, because he thought that she was still over there in his sack. The three wives went out and gathered firewood. They came back and put the bundles of wood down. When they had done so, he said, "Put the pot there!" They put the pot in the place he indicated.

"What should be done now?"

The women had put the bundles of firewood down, and now they came with a great pot.

"Kindle a fire! Make it big enough to heat this pot until it's red-hot! I want to eat this bird today! It'll be baked. Bake it, so that its fat comes out of it."

Well, the women kindled the fire, and they put that pot on the hearth. The pot became very hot. When the pot was hot, he said, "My great wife, please take that sack of mine down! The pot's hot now."

The great wife went; when she arrived there, she seized the sack and her hand was pricked. She said, *"Shu shu shu! Sobani!* This sack of yours bites!"

The big fellow got up and beat her vigorously. He said, "Get out of here, you fool! I wasted my cattle when I married you! Now you do nothing for me! Come, my right-hand wife! I *lobola*-ed you with red cattle only! You take that sack of mine down for me. It's on the upper side of the house. This pot is red-hot now!"

The right-hand wife went, and when she grasped the bag, it stung her. She said, "*Shu shu shu!* Sobani! This bag of yours bites!"

He beat that wife too. He said, "Go, you fool, go! Go to the other fool outside! I wasted my cattle on you! Come, then, my little wife of the *qadi* of the great house! the one in whose house I spend most of my time! You take my sack down. This pot's red-hot now!"

This one went over there, and she took the sack. The sack stung her. When the sack had stung her, she also returned, saying, "*Shu shu shu,* Sobani! This bag of yours bites!"

He beat her also. He said, "Get out! Go to the other fools!" Then he told them, "Now I want all of you to mix up some mud! Then take the mud and close this house up tight. Lock me inside! Take the mud and plaster all the holes and cracks in the house! Then close the door and plaster over it, so that there's not even any evidence of the place where the door is! Cover it up completely! Plaster the whole thing evenly, make the door even with the wall! Let there be no hole that the wind can seep through!"

The wives did that; they locked the door, they mixed the mud, then they plastered and covered all the doorway. They completely covered it, there was not even a tiny space through which the wind could seep. When it was completed and no wind could get into the house, he said, "Have you finished?"

They said, "Yes!"

"Well, go and sit somewhere!"

He went then and took his sack down. The sack did not bite him, not even a little! He took the sack, and when he had done so, he removed the rope from the sack's mouth. He covered the pot. He grasped the sack by its bottom, and covered the pot. When he had done so, not even one creature fell out of the sack into the pot! All of them came rushing out—all over him, over his body! They tore into him, they ripped into him!

He cried out, "*Yooooooo!* Open the house! Open the door for me! I'm dying! What husband will you have if you let me die? Open for me!"

But the three women said, "Eat your bird, wise man! Leave us alone! We'll just remain steeped in our foolishness! Please, please, eat that wisdom of yours!"

He said, "Oh, what is this? These things have all but finished me! I'm being eaten alive! They're eating me! They're eating my flesh! Please open up!"

The great wife called out, "You said that we're fools! *You're* the wise one! Now you please just be eaten by that wisdom of yours! That's beautiful!"

The women sat there laughing, they laughed at him. The beasts ate him, they ate him, and left behind only some white bones. Before his spirit left him, he threw himself, he flew out through the grass thatch of the house. He ran, he ran naked, and threw himself into a pool and got stuck head-first: his head in the pool, his ass directed into the air. And he remained like that! he remained frozen in that position. Some bees came along and went inside there, they made honey in his ass.

It happened on a certain day that while some men were walking along, going about their business, they saw these bees coming out of the buttocks.

They said, "It's just a stump in the pond."

They went there and took out the honey. They took out the honey. Well, friend, it happens that bees tend to have cells in their honey-combs, and these cells are far back in the hive, the last ones; they are usually white, and they usually contain the honey.

While they were taking the honey out, "Well, what's the matter?"

"My hand can't reach back far enough!" one of the men said. "It's too big."

One of the other men had a smaller hand, and he tried it. He took out some honey, and he reached back then to that last honeycomb. But then, the buttocks contracted! they squeezed! they trapped that hand!

"*Tyhini!*"

"What shall we do about this? My hand won't come out!"

"Well, maan, it must be pulled!"

They pulled it then, they pulled the man's hand, but no!

"The bones of the ass of a grown man locked!" The dead man was speaking! the dead man was speaking and saying, inside there, "Lock, bones of the ass of a grown man! Lock, bones of the ass of a grown man!"

"What'll we do?"

"Well, friend, his hand must be cut off."

One of the men took a knife, and the hand was cut off. It was left inside there, in that ass—together with the honey. When this hand had been cut off, the dead man began to force the hand out of his buttocks. "Eeeeeeeenh!" The hand flew out! it was flung out!

Well, then, that man was now maimed. And they went on their way, in that condition.

The *ntsomi* is ended, it is ended.

New World

Canada

The Duck-Dog (Le chien-canard)

Collected by Luc Lacourcière (recording no. 4234 in the folklore archives of Laval University), in November 1969 from Mrs. Amédée Lacroix (née Maria Fradette), aged sixty-seven, of La Durantaye Bellechasse county, Québec, Canada. Translated by Margaret Low.

Type 652 *The Prince Whose Wishes Always Come True: the Carnation.* Of the nine French-Canadian versions of type 652 only one contains the motif of the enchanted girl as a flower, which characterizes the Grimm tale, and even in that version the flower is not a carnation but a fleur-de-lys, the emblem of old France.

Mrs. Lacroix, who is a very vivacious taleteller, learned all of her tales before the age of seventeen, at which time she left home to become a servant and later marry.

Motifs: N811 "Supernatural godfather" (= F311.1 "Fairy godmother"); D1761.0.1 "Wishes granted without limit"; K2250.1 "Treacherous servant"; K2155.1 "Blood smeared on innocent person brings accusation of murder"; N856.1 "Forester as foster father (nurse as foster mother)"; Q455 "Walling up as punishment"; D2105 "Provisions magically furnished"; D141 "Transformation: man to dog" (assigned *D141.0.3 "Transformation: man to duck-dog" in Motif-Index of the Archives de Folklore, Quebec); S451 "Outcast wife at last united with family."

Although a Grimm tale, type 652 has not been reported in depth. Sporadic versions are known in some fifteen European countries, with Lithuania in the lead. The special French-Canadian element is the magical evocation of the sequence of beautiful girls from France who make a play for the boy in preference to his father.

Once there was a man and a woman. They were awfully poor. They were like us; they were brought up farmers. They were farmers and they had to hire someone to live on the land to help them because they had too much land to work themselves.

The woman, they hadn't been married too many years, had had a little boy. And so (in those days, they didn't have a godfather and a godmother like nowadays; as long as they had a godmother it was enough) so they took the godmother who was nearest and she was a fairy.

So the fairy said, "In the first place, we'll call him Little John. (In those days, the first name wasn't Joseph,[1] it was little John.) What will I give him?" she says. "I don't have much to give him. (You know that a fairy has power.) For his present," the fairy said, "I'll grant him that everything he says will happen, everything he desires will come true. I have nothing else to give him," she says, "so I'll give him this gift."

So the man who had been hired to work the land, he'd been there for at least ten years, knew all about the little boy's gift. He stayed there all the time and they loved him as much as their son, just the same as their child. He was loved frightfully. They never would have thought anything could happen.

So the man started to make plans. "If I were to steal that child," he says to himself, "I could become rich later on."

The man and the woman never thought for a moment that he'd play a nasty trick like that. You needn't ask.

So anyway, one day he goes off to the village to look for a nurse and asks her if she wouldn't keep a small child until he was twelve years' old.

"When he's twelve, though," he says, "and I come to get him back, you'll have to give him to me whether you want to or not."

"You know very well," the woman says, "that I'll give him to you. He's your child. Of course I'll give him to you. Only it will be hard to give the child up then."

"I'm counting on you," he says. "On a certain night, you'll come to the door with a carriage—it'll have to be about midnight," he says, "when the mother's asleep—and then I'll give you the child and you'll take care of him. He mustn't ever go outside. I'll come to see him from time to time."

You needn't ask. He had it all planned. Anyway, he was to slaughter some animals that day. He takes a blood sausage, what you call a tripe, and empties it out and then fills it with blood, the blood of a pig, and he hides it, all carefully wrapped up in a box, under his mattress so they wouldn't see it.

"I'm going to try to play a trick on them with that," he says. He had it all planned. He wasn't the craziest of the bunch, that one!

So he goes to his room and goes to bed and sleeps; well, he doesn't sleep, but he pretends to sleep.

1. Until recently, Joseph was given as the first name to every male child in French Canada since Joseph is the patron saint of Canada.

The man and woman go to bed and they sleep. After a moment, he hears them snoring.

They had put the little baby to bed. He was six months old. He had waited until the baby was old enough to take him out of the house and until he was sure he could steal him.

It was a nasty trick and he knew it would bring a lot of grief to the woman and that there would be pure misery in the house. He knew all that. He understood.

He had hidden a special knife.

"I'll have to smear her shoes with blood to make them think that she was the one who did away with her child," he said. There was no one else in the house and the door was locked. Anyway, he said, "I'll go and steal him tonight and I don't think I'll have any trouble."

So they were asleep and he got up without making any noise. First he makes sure that the carriage has arrived. The good woman was there waiting for him. She had brought a big shawl to wrap around the child.

He goes and silently takes the baby out of his cradle and carries him out. They had agreed on which door.

"Here, I'll give him to you," he says. Then he gives her the child, and she bundles him up and he tells her to take good care of him.

"I'll come and see him from time to time," he says, "not often but often enough so he recognizes me and doesn't forget me."

"That's fine," she says, "and you can count on me. I'll never tell on you." She was happy; he had paid her.

"You'll be well paid," he says. "You'll be paid more than it's worth. You'll see. You'll have a good salary to raise him."

He goes back in the house. "What will I do now?" he says. "I'll use my tripe right away."

He gets the knife and smears it with blood and puts it under the good woman's pillow. He takes her shoes, which were under the bed, smears them with blood and puts them back under the bed to show that she had got up and walked in the blood. He had cut the tripe and had poured blood all over the cradle and had put a large blanket and a pillow there to show that it's the baby and then he fixes up the cradle the way she would have to show that she killed him. Then he goes back to bed.

You needn't ask. He didn't sleep all night. But the others slept like princes and didn't wake up at all. They slept well. They weren't expecting anything like that.

The next morning, they sit down to the table to eat and the man says, "It seems that our little baby isn't here. He isn't awake yet."

"That doesn't make sense," the mother says. "What's wrong with my little baby then? He usually wakes up earlier than this." At nine o'clock the baby still wasn't awake. "Well, I'm going to wake him," she says. "My poor little baby is sleeping too long. It's time he was fed." So she got up and went to see.

The other guy didn't say a word. He acted as if nothing was wrong. "Let's go to work as usual." He takes his cap and starts to go outside.

The mother gets there. You needn't ask what sort of a state she was in. When she took off the cover of the little cradle, there she saw, my friends, a pool of blood.

"My little baby's dead!" she says. "Hurry, come quickly, my baby's dead. Ah, it's awful to look at," she says. "I don't know who killed him."

She had an awful fit. She pulled her hair and cried murder!

The goodman says, "It doesn't make sense. Could it be you? Who came here during the night? Did you hear anyone come in during the night? The door was locked."

The hired man says, "I didn't hear anything. I slept well and when you sleep soundly, you don't think about things like that."

"I didn't wake up all night," the mother says, "I usually wake up once or twice but I didn't wake up all night."

"I don't understand it at all," the man says. He began to get irritated and angry. "The door was locked, so who came in here? It doesn't make sense," he says. "He's not there. Someone has killed him, but he isn't there. He has been taken away. Who came during the night?"

Then he started to have his doubts about his wife, and started to look at her sideways and started to shout at her.

Ah, she cried. She was brokenhearted. Her little baby, six months old! She loved him so much.

"It has to be you," he says. "There's no one else here. And look!" he says. "Your shoes are covered in blood. You walked somewhere and you threw him somewhere. You got rid of him. I suppose you burned him."

"That doesn't make sense," the woman cried. "You know that I could think the same thing of you but it's someone else. It doesn't make sense that you would come and take him."

"Never!" he says. "I didn't even get up. I didn't hear anything."

Then he got good and mad. He looked all over the place and found nothing but the shoes and then the knife under the woman's pillow.

"You're the one," he says. "It's no one else. You'll pay for it. I loved my little baby," he says. "I loved him as much as you. I loved you too, but since you're as stupid as that, my hussy, I tell you that you're going to suffer for it."

She threw herself in the fire and all over the place. Accused of a murder she didn't commit! It was terrible.

"I don't want to ever see you again. Take her and put her in that room and give her water and peas. She'll have nothing but peas and water for the rest of her days!"

The hired man looked after her; her husband wouldn't even go to see her. The hired man took her her food.

"That's the end of it," the husband said. "You'll never get out of there; you'll die there."

You needn't ask if the hired man wasn't sorry deep down. He was sorry to have done an awful thing like that and to see the woman locked in a dark room and miserable for the rest of her days and the man just as miserable. But he had his mind set on getting away from there and becoming rich with the little boy.

So he said to himself, "I had to do it and now that I've done it, it's done." He was sorry, but it was too late.

He still worked there. It was better not to even mention leaving. So he worked there and tried to cheer up the man who almost regretted putting his wife away. But he had said it and in those days, when the boss, whether king or not, said something it had to be done.

Anyway, many years went by and, of course, the woman had been locked up for many years. He had to let the boy grow up from six months to twelve years. He didn't want to take the boy away until he was twelve years old and educated. But he was anxious to get away. He found the time long. He went to see the boy though, from time to time, as if he were his own and he had him brought up and educated at the same time since the nurse was a schoolteacher as well.

He had told her to take care of him and teach him as much as she could and that later he'd come and get him and she wouldn't bother about him any more.

He came often. The boy knew him, but he didn't like him at all, he didn't like his father. He said all the time, "I don't like him and I wish he wouldn't come." That's nature, eh? Of course the little boy couldn't love him.

Then at the end of twelve years, he said to the fellow, "You needn't be surprised. You're older now," he says, "and your wife is almost dead. If I were you," he says, "there's only one thing I'd do. I'd sell all this and I'd get the heck into town. If you don't want to take her, get someone to look after her. That's what I'd do. I'm going away. I'm leaving you."

The goodman was awfully sorry. He was just like his son. That aged him ten years. To begin with no wife and now this!

"I'm going away and I won't be back. I'm going far away to forget about all this."

"You're not my son," the man says. "I can't stop you. Go where you like. I can't stop you. I'll stay here by myself."

So he goes and gets his things ready, he didn't have much, and left.

"I'll go and get my little boy and try to live with him for a bit. If he has the gift the fairy promised him, we'll be happy." But he wasn't sure. He hadn't lived with the boy at all and he hadn't told anyone else about it.

He arrived there. "I've come to get you, my boy."

"Ah, I'm not going," the little boy says. "I'm staying here. My mother's here, and I'm staying. You go back where you came from." He said all sorts of things, but it was no use.

"You're my little boy and you're leaving today. You'll come with me and if you are a good little boy you'll be happy. If you're not good," he says, "I'll put you away where you'll be massacred and beaten. I'll put you in reform school. So you'll need listen to me and be a good little boy."

Ah, he hugged his nurse and cried. He didn't want to leave.

"Get him ready," the guy says. "I'm taking him. He's my boy, and I'm taking him."

Well, she got him ready and prepared his clothes. The little boy had to say yes.

"You'll be fine with me. You'll see. We'll be happy if you do what you're supposed to. Come along with me. I don't have a house or anything but, you'll see, we'll build a beautiful house." He had some good ideas.

They leave and set out on foot. They came to a beautiful, big mountain. Oh, it was high, high, high, and beautiful. There was nothing missing but a castle.

"Aren't you hungry, Father?" he says. "I'm awfully hungry."

"Well, when we're at all smart," he says, " 'Ask, and it shall be given you.' Didn't you learn that in your catechism? 'Ask, and it shall be given you.' "

"I was taught that it's no good asking. When you don't have any money, you don't eat."

"Well, I have hardly any money in my pockets," he says, "but I think we're going to have enough to eat. In the first place," he says, "you're intelligent and anything you ask for, you'll get it."

"Well, that's the first time I've heard that. You can see I've never stayed with you. My nurse never ever told me that, and she is nice and brought me up well."

"Yeah, but it's not the same thing. I'm your father and I've got different ideas. You're intelligent and educated and perhaps you've got a gift the good Lord gave you. Myself, I'm not worth much. I'm a father who's almost hard-hearted. But you're not like me; you're a little saint. You'll see," he says. "You'll get everything you ask for. Try it then, my boy. Say 'I'd like to have a nice table here, with a heap of bread on it and butter and all sorts of things to eat.' Try it then and see if it happens."

"You're making fun of me," the little boy says. "That sort of thing doesn't make sense. I've never asked for anything like that. You know very well that people will laugh at you if you go about saying things like that."

"Well, try it anyway," he says. "You're intelligent. Perhaps the good Lord will hear you and grant your wishes. You're a little saint."

"Well, I know it won't happen, but I'll say it. I'd like to have a table here with a nice cloth and good food on it to make us a good meal."

He'd no sooner said it, my friends, than a table is set up with food on it, heaping dishes and all sorts of things.

"Good Lord!" the little boy says. "I don't know what I'm doing, not at all. What does it mean? Do you know, Father? I've never heard of anything like it in my life. All of a sudden there's a table set in the middle of a field, on top of a mountain! No one has ever seen that before."

"You see," he says, "it's a small miracle. God granted your prayer. It's a miracle."

"A miracle! In any case, it's frightful."

So they ate up, and the goodman didn't say a word. He was waiting for his chance. After they finished eating, he says, "This table can't stay here. The food will get dirty and be wasted. The good Lord doesn't like anything to be wasted. So say 'I want the table to disappear and we'll begin again another time.' "

"Ah, it's awful. I have to say that?"

"Yes, you have to say it or it will stay here and it would be a shame to waste it."

"I want the table to disappear so there's nothing left to eat."

No sooner said, my friends, than the table and food disappear.

"Ah, that's awful. I'm all confused, Father. It doesn't make sense. Something's wrong. It's either a miracle or the good Lord is laughing at us."

The little boy was so intelligent that he didn't understand that at all. He didn't know he had a gift.

"Well, since you're as smart as that," he says, "and since everything you ask for comes true, you'll see how happy we'll be. We'll begin by building a house."

"Building a house! That's awful! We need tools and all sorts of things. We don't have any wood or anything."

"You remember the table?" he says. "There was no wood or food."

"That doesn't make sense," the little boy thinks to himself. "That doesn't make sense at all."

"Say 'I'd like to have a beautiful castle here with gold and everything all shining, with beautiful rooms, with beautiful tables all set with food to eat as soon as we arrive.' "

As soon as the boy says that, my friends, they hear an awful noise. Bang! Snap! Everything cracks around them. My friends, it's awful, but there's a castle built right there!

"Ah," the little boy says, "I'm going mad! I'm going mad! I've never heard of such a thing."

The other fellow was surprised himself. He knew but he was still surprised.

They go inside, my friends, and everything was beautiful. Beautiful rooms. It was beautiful and shining all over. Everything was there. There was nothing missing. A piano and everything. The table was set, and there were roasts, chickens, bananas, oranges, everything you can put on a table.

"Ah, it's awful," the little boy says. "Now we are rich. It doesn't make sense."

"I told you. You're a little saint. God loves you. Everything you'll say, when I tell you to say it (he takes care to see that he doesn't make wishes when he's not there), when I tell you to say something, you'll listen to me and we'll be rich. We'll be happy and have everything we want. That's not all," he says. "Now we've got all kinds of food and everything we need but there's no woman here. If we had a woman here this evening, we'd have a lot of fun but we won't have any fun by ourselves."

"Yes, but we're too far away to get a woman here."

"Well, we'll do what we did before. Say 'I want the most beautiful girl in France to be here this evening.' "

"Ah," he says, "the most beautiful girl in France! That's far away. It doesn't make sense."

"Yes, but your castle a moment ago? Just think about it. You had no wood, but it was built."

The little boy says, "I'd like the most beautiful girl in France to be here tonight—and well dressed."

No sooner said than the door opens and Mademoiselle appears, and a beautiful girl at that, you needn't ask, and well dressed, the most beautiful girl in France. She flings her arms around the little twelve-year old boy and she loved him an awful lot.

"You're my wife," the man says.

"Hey!" she says. "Not so fast. I just got here and I've just met you."

"We have to move quickly. You're my wife. I brought you here to be my wife, and you know you can't go back home. It's too far away."

"I can see that," she says, "and it doesn't make sense. But you've got an awfully nice place here. How did you get it?"

"Well, it came by itself," he says. "It's a gift from God. Here, everything works by gifts from the good Lord."

"You're lucky," she says, "to have gifts from the Lord. I've never had any in my life."

"Yes, that's true," the little boy says.

So that ends there. She changes the subject right away and begins to tell him what a handsome little boy he has. "Is he your little boy?" she says. "He doesn't look like you at all. And he has an air of intelligence about him."

"He has the air," he says, "but he doesn't know the song!"

He wanted to make the woman hate the boy from the start and like him more than the boy. He was already jealous. It doesn't take long. But the young woman made a fuss over the boy.

"Come and sit at the table. The table is set." She sits down with them. They had everything they needed on the table. They had a bit to drink. They had perhaps fifteen or twenty bottles. They didn't count them, you needn't ask, there were too many of them. So they ate until they were full. They had an awful lot of fun. There were only the three of them, but it was as if they were as many as we are here tonight.[2] They had an awful lot of fun.

At nine o'clock, he says, "Well, it's nine o'clock, wife."

"Hey!" she says. "Don't call me that. I'm not your wife yet."

"Oh, but you are," he says. "I brought you here to be my wife, you're here, and you're going to serve as my wife."

"Not so fast," she says, "I'm not your wife yet. And why are you sending your little boy to bed so early? He's so handsome and smart. I haven't been with him long but I like him already." Just like that. Right away. She wasn't shy. She tells him that right away, meaning, 'I like him a lot better than you.' She doesn't say it, but he understands. Eh? He's jealous.

"He's going to bed. I only have to tell him," he says, "and he does what he's told."

"If I were you, I wouldn't send him to bed. We can chat and have a lot of fun with him."

"You'll see. We'll have fun," he says. He was beginning to get a bit heated. He'd been drinking. "Go to bed, my boy. It's getting late, and you're used to going to bed early."

"I'm going, Father," he says. "I don't mind at all." He goes to bed and sleeps. He wasn't spoilt at all.

The fellow starts to make a fuss over the woman. At ten-thirty, eleven o'clock, they go to bed. She had to sleep there. At the bottom of that high rock was a big river so he knew she wouldn't jump in the water.

Once they're in bed and he's made a fuss of her and all that, he says,

2. This was recorded at the collector's home during a pleasant gathering of the students of the Folklore Department and folk narrators.

"You'll see how happy you'll be. You'll stay here with me always and we'll never go without anything. But," he says, "there's a job you'll have to do for me. If you don't," he says, "you'll die in his place. At nine o'clock tomorrow morning, you'll get the boy up and then you'll have to kill him."

"Kill your little boy! Are you mad? I think you're crazy. That boy's smart and intelligent. Do you think I'd kill him? No way!" she says.

"Listen," he says. "If you don't kill him, you'll die at six o'clock tomorrow night. I get home at six and if you haven't killed the boy, I'll kill you. You have to kill him. He'll give us a lot of trouble. He's crazy. He seems nice but he isn't. He's a loafer and a good-for-nothing." He attributes to him every defect a boy can have.

"Ah, that's awful," she says. "I wouldn't have thought it but if it's true—I'll see him tomorrow morning—he'll die. I'll get rid of him, and it won't take long. But I wouldn't have thought it of him. He looks so nice."

"In any case," he says, "if you haven't done the job by six o'clock, you'll die."

You needn't ask; she didn't sleep all night. She only thought about that.

In the morning she had breakfast with him. "I go on a trip every day," he says. (He only pretended to, eh? He had no work or anything to do.) He goes off.

She thinks about that. "I have to kill that little boy. It doesn't make sense. There's no way I'm going to kill him. And he won't kill me either. He's just saying that for a joke. I'll go and wake him."

"Get up, John. If you want to have a bit of fun today, it's time you were up. Otherwise I'll be lonesome by myself." The little boy gets up. "I can't see what your father's got against you," she says. "Did you do something to him?"

"No. I've not been with him long. I don't like him," he says, "but I didn't do anything to him."

"Well, he gave me a job to do this morning. He told me to kill you."

"Is that true? That's awful. Kill me! He comes and gets me so I'll stay with him to have some fun and then what does he want now? He wants to kill me. Do you understand that?"

"I don't know what's wrong," she says, "but I know it doesn't make sense. I won't kill you," she says. "You're smarter and better looking than he is. We'll stay together and try to get rid of him some day."

They spend the day together. The boy had a little glass of wine from time to time. She had some gin from time to time. There was some whisky there, but they didn't bother with it. They didn't mix their drinks.

The day went by quickly. At six o'clock, the guy opens the door. The little boy was there with the girl, and they were having fun, my friends.

"Hello," she says. "You're not very polite. You've been gone all day and you don't even say hello."

"You didn't do what I told you to," he said. "We'd have been happy, but you won't be happy much longer. You're going to die. I said I'd kill you."

She wasn't expecting that. He grabbed her by the scruff of the neck and shoved her into an empty dark room. He kills her and hangs her up there on a hinge and closes the door.

The little boy doesn't really understand, but he thought when she screamed that he had killed her.

He [the man] closes the door to the room, locks it and puts the key in his pocket. "She won't bother us any more," he says. "We'll get a prettier one than her. You'll see, my boy. She didn't do what I told her. She would rather have fun with you than work. She's going to spoil you so I locked her in the room." No more was said about it.

"Now that the table is set, we're ready for another girl. Say, my boy, 'I want the most beautiful girl in London to be here this evening.'"

No sooner has the little boy said it than the door opens and a girl who is one hundred times more beautiful than the other one comes in. She was well dressed and smart and not too old. A young girl of sixteen or seventeen. She comes in and flings her arms around the little boy. She had gone right by the other one and that made him jealous again. He was awfully jealous.

"I didn't bring you here for nothing," he says. "That's my child, and I'm the boss here and I brought you here to be my wife."

"Take your time," she says. "Don't get excited. Listen, I just got here. We aren't getting married right away."

"You're going to be happy here," he says, "and well treated. You'll be happy to be married to me, and I need a wife. I brought you here from London and you can't go back."

"How did I get here?" she says. "It doesn't make sense. Traveling through the air," she says. "I don't understand that."

"I know what it is," the little boy says. "It's a miracle."

"A miracle?"

"Yes, a miracle from God."

She could see he was a nice boy. She kept her eyes on him all the time, my friends, and seemed to like him a lot.

Anyway, they sit down to the table and start to eat and drink.

At nine o'clock, it's the same thing. "Go to bed, my boy."

"Yes, I'm going. I'd rather go to bed than stay up." He goes off to bed.

"That doesn't make sense," she says. "The first night I'm here, you send him to bed. He's smart and handsome and good." She was all for him and didn't pay much attention to the other fellow.

"In any case, he's used to going to bed at nine."

"It won't be as much fun," she says.

It's just like the night before. When it's time to go to bed, it's the same thing. He's nice to her and takes her into the bedroom, and "You're my wife," but she doesn't want to be.

"Want to or not, you're my wife and that's final. You'll be happy with me, but only if you do what I tell you. I'm going to give you a job and you have nothing else to do but that. The work is all done here."

"What do I have to do that's so important? I've just got here."

"There's a good-for-nothing here, my son. I didn't raise him," he says, "and he's really a bad lot and he runs about all night long when I don't keep an eye on him. I took him away from the city. He's really unbearable. He's a liar and he's got every possible vice."

"I don't understand what you want me to do."

"Tomorrow morning, you'll have to kill him."

"Well, if you hate him so much and he's as hateful as all that, I could kill him. But if he's smart and I like him, I won't kill him. I couldn't. Anyway, I know this is just a joke."

"If you don't kill him," he says, "you will die at six o'clock tomorrow evening."

"Well, if it's like that, don't worry, I'll kill him. If you don't like him, I won't like him either."

She didn't sleep all night. She thought about that, about what she had to do.

Anyway, in the morning he has breakfast with his wife and sets out. "I'll be gone all day. I'll be back at six."

At nine o'clock, she goes and wakes him. "Get up, John," she says. "You've slept enough."

"Yes, I slept well. I'm happy," he says. "Since you've been here, life hasn't been the same. You're beautiful and nice." He pays her all sorts of compliments.

"It doesn't make any sense what I'm going to do."

"What are you going to do?"

"He gave me a job that doesn't make sense," she says. "I can't do it."

"It must be the same as yesterday, but she didn't do it." The boy doesn't say more than that.

"In any case," she says, "I can't do what he told me. We're going to have some fun."

Then they have a lot of fun. They sing and dance and drink a little. Anyway, they turned the house upside down. They had a lot of fun.

At six o'clock it wasn't so funny. The door opened. The little boy was still sitting at the table with her and having fun. The man comes in.

"Is that what I told you to do?" he says.

"You're very polite," she says. "I've just arrived and you go off all day and leave me alone and instead of saying 'hello, wife,' 'hello, son, I missed you. . . .' "

"No, I didn't miss you," he says. "You didn't do what I told you to. Now I'll have to do what I said."

He grabbed her by the scruff of the neck and took her into the same room. He had a sword and he cut her neck off and hung her up on the other hinge.

The little boy heard her scream. He found it awful, but he didn't say a word. He was terribly afraid of his father.

"Well, we got rid of those two trollops."

The little boy didn't say a word. He was afraid the same thing would happen to him.

"Now that everything is in order," he says, "you are going to say 'I want the most beautiful girl in England to be here tonight.' " England is pretty big.

"Do I have to say that? I don't like it. That makes two evenings that I've said it, and you know what you've done with the women. If I knew you were going to do the same thing, I wouldn't make her come."

"Oh, no," he says. "This one is going to be smart and she's going to do what I tell her." He tells his little boy all sorts of things to make him do it.

Anyway, the little boy says, "I'll say it. I want the most beautiful girl in England to be here tonight—beautiful and nice and smart."

No sooner said than the young girl opens the door and runs into the little boy's arms.

"Oh, you're nice and good-looking and hello, hello."

Anyway, they have a pleasant evening together. At nine o'clock, well, it was the same thing.

This was the third woman, and she was a lot more intelligent. When she went to put the boy to bed, she made certain inquiries.

"Have you been here a long time?"

"No, not long," he says.

"This is a beautiful castle. I've never seen one like it. Have you had it a long time?"

"No, it's a gift from God," he says.

"A gift from God! How's that?"

"I'm the one who made it come. I said a few words. And if you're here tonight, it's because I asked for you."

"Not another word," she says. "Go to bed. Go to sleep. Good night."

She had guessed what had happened. She could see from talking to him that it was the little boy that brought it all about. Anyway, when she talks to the man, she says that she has never seen so many lovely things, beautiful rooms and beautiful beds, everything.

"My parents left me the wood," he says, "and I used it all for this."
He cuts it as short as possible, eh?

When it came time to go to bed, it was the same story. "You're my
wife." And then, "Take your time. I've just arrived and I'm not going
to be married right away."

"I brought you here for that reason and you'll have to do the same
as if you were married."

"Well, in any case, I'm not married," she says. Meaning that she'd
do what she liked.

They go in the bedroom and chat a bit before going to bed. He gives
her the same job, to kill his little boy. She didn't know about the others
but she suspected something.

Anyway, she says, "Since your little boy isn't nicer than that, nor
smarter than that and since he's so stupid, it will be a pleasure to kill
him. But I'm afraid," she says, "if I kill him you'll kill me."

"Don't worry," he says, "we'll be happy. Anyhow," he says,
"there'll be no one but you. You're the most beautiful and the nicest.
Get rid of him and we'll be happy. We'll have everything we need and
if you want children, we'll have them and we'll be happy."

She handled it well and didn't get nervous. The next morning, they
had breakfast and he went off for the day.

She went and woke him. "Get up, John. We've got a lot of things to
talk about today. I only said three or four words to you yesterday. I can
see that there's something miraculous here."

"It's a gift from God," he says. "I don't ūnderstand it. My nurse
taught me well but. . . ."

"What, a nurse? Don't you have a mother?"

"No. I was raised by a nurse." And then, poor thing, he tells her his
story. Then, he says, "My father arrived all of a sudden. He came to
see me from time to time," he says, "but when he came to get me, he
said, 'You'll have nice presents and you'll do this and you'll do that.' I
didn't understand it at all."

"Listen," she says. "There's a marble there on the sideboard. Say 'I
want the marble to fall off and to roll as far as the door.' "

"I'll say it," he says. "I want the marble to fall to the floor and to
roll as far as the door."

No sooner said than the marble falls to the ground and rolls to the
door.

"We're saved!" she says. "I won't kill you. Don't worry. We're
saved. He said to kill you."

"That's what happened to the others," he said. "He told them if they
didn't kill me, they would die and they are there in that room."

"Is that true?"

"It's only too true. I'm sure they're dead. He locked the door so I didn't look in the room."

"Say 'The lock will fly off,' " she says.

"The lock will fly off."

No sooner said than the lock falls to the ground. They open the door and it's really something, my friends. Ah, Lord! She closes the door. She's had enough. Two women hung in there.

"I knew it. I told you," he says. "He got angry and killed them because they hadn't killed me. I'm the one who brought them here from London and France."

"Well, we're going to laugh at him tonight," she says. "You'll see."

They had a wonderful day. She would rather be married to the boy than stay with the other fellow. She already loved him an awful lot.

"We're going to have fun. You'll see. We'll get rid of that character," she says, "tonight when he gets home. But I'll have to tell you what to do ahead of time so you know it by heart. You'll hide under the bed in that room there," she says, "and when he comes in, before he gets too far, I'll be in the kitchen, and you'll say, 'I want Dad to be a duck-dog, to turn into a duck-dog who can't take more than three steps forward and three steps backward.' He mustn't be able to move further than that. Don't make any mistakes or he'll kill me right away. He'll grab me and cut my throat. I won't have enough time to escape and you will die as well."

"Don't worry," he says. "I'll go over it a few times and keep it in my head. Becomes a duck-dog, a duck-dog. Can't take more than three steps forward and three steps backward." He says that a few times. "I've got it. Don't worry."

In the evening, she says, "Hide under the bed, he's coming!"

He opens the door. "Ah, we're going to be happy," he says.

"You'll be happy, all right. He's dead."

He goes to kiss his wife but the boy doesn't even let him take three steps.

"I want Dad to become a duck-dog who can't take more than three steps forward and three steps backward!"

No sooner said than there he was on the ground, a duck-dog! Now, my friends, he didn't have such winning ways!

The little boy came out from under the bed and ran up to the girl he loved.

"There, my old rogue," she says. "You killed two women, but you didn't kill me."

"Forgive me," he says, "and tell my little boy. . . ."

"He's not your little boy," she says. "You'll remain a duck-dog and everyone will laugh at you. We are going to go and find his father and mother and you're going to start talking, my old rogue. You'll pay for everything you did and all the sorrow you've caused."

  You needn't ask. He can't say a word.

"We have a nice castle here," she says, "but it's not for us. The good Lord will come and get it when he wants to. Get your clothes and come out on the veranda with me and say, 'I want us to be on the veranda of my real father and mother and the duck-dog with us.' We're taking our duck-dog with us," she says.

They go out on the veranda with the duck-dog and the boy says that. No sooner said, than they're on his father's and mother's veranda.

"Good Lord!" he says. "It looks so poor and sad." He found it poor after the castle.

"Yes, but this is everyday life," she says, "and there is no end of suffering here."

The little boy knocks on the door and he was as polite as anything and so was she. The goodman opens the door. He was old. He had aged twenty years! He was old and almost on all fours.

The little boy throws his arms around him. "You're my dad! Hello, Dad."

The man almost faints. "You can't be my son. No, no, no, it doesn't make sense. My little boy was taken away, killed twelve years ago."

"No, I'm you're little boy. I wasn't killed. Where's my mummy!" he says.

"Your mother is almost dead. I half killed her on account of you. Is it really you? It doesn't make sense."

"It really is your son," the young woman says. "I came with him and we brought our duck-dog along. We'll bring him in soon."

"What duck-dog?"

"Your hired hand. He's a duck-dog now and when we're finished with him he'll make a good fire."

He didn't understand it at all.

"I want to see my mummy before anything else."

"She's not easy to look at. Open the door there, but she's a terrible sight. I ask God that I might die right away."

"It's not your fault, Dad."

"It's not your fault," the young girl said. "Your wife will live and you'll have happy times. You'll start life over again and your little boy will stay with you and so will I. We'll all live together."

They open the door, my friends, and there in the darkness they take a candle to see if she's alive or dead. She had an inch of moss on her head and as much on her face and she was old, old, old, and skinny, nothing but skin and bone. This poor old lady—and she was still young, eh? She hadn't been married many years.

The husband was crying, my friends, and pulling his hair. "Forgive me. It doesn't make sense that I could do that to my wife. Forgive me. Forgive me."

The little boy had never done it by himself but he says, "I want mummy to be the same as she was when I was born, and I want her to love my father as she did then and I want my father to be twenty-five years old again."

In saying that, they're no longer the same father and mother. Everything is changed. They embrace one another and kiss one another.

After that they burn the duck-dog!

Then they had a big party. They had no trouble setting the table; the table set itself. The little boy had only to ask and there—for me, the house couldn't have been in antiques[3]—I think it was all new because the boy was there to set up a beautiful shiny castle.

The young girl married the lad and they had thirteen beautiful little children. I don't know if they are still alive—I didn't live with them—but in any case, I think they are still living.

Excuse me!

The Tub of Butter (La tinette de beurre)

Collected by Luc Lacourcière (recording no. 2093), in September 1954 from Joseph Bouliane, aged eighty-seven, of Les Escoumains, Saguenay region, Québec, Canada. Translated by Margaret Low.

Type 15 *The Theft of Butter (Honey) by Playing Godfather,* and type 1 *The Theft of Fish.*

Type 15 is one of the best known animal tales in the French folklore of North America. Thirty-six versions of this theme have been collected to date: 20 versions from French Canada (Acadia 11, Québec 9) where the protagonists are the fox and the wolf; and 16 versions (the largest number of Franco-American variants of any animal tale) from Franco-America (Louisiana 13, Missouri 3), which are based on the rivalry between Lapin and Bouki.

Type 1 is somewhat less widespread and is almost always combined with one or more themes from the fox-wolf (or Lapin-Bouki) cycle.

Our informant was an extremely amiable old man who was particularly loved by young children. After school, the children would take

3. A reference to the collector's home, which was an early eighteenth-century stone house.

Mr. Bouliane's hat as he walked down the main street of his village —and, of course, he always just happened to pass that way at the close of school—and they would refuse to give it back to him, in spite of mock threats from his cane, until he agreed to tell them a folktale.

Motifs: K372 "Playing godfather"; K341.2 "Thief shams death and steals"; K371.1 "Trickster throws fish off the wagon"; K1026 "Dupe imitates trickster's theft and is caught."

Type 15 is also highly popular with New World Negroes, independently and in conjunction with other types. See the first four texts in Richard M. Dorson, *American Negro Folktales* (Greenwich, Conn., 1967).

They had gone for a little stroll along the beach and had found a tub of butter, a big tub of butter. So the wolf began to eat it right away.

"We'd better save that for Lent," the fox says. "There's fasting during Lent. Let's not eat it now." So he stops the wolf from eating it. "Let's go," he says.

So they go on their way. They build themselves a cabin and after that they both stay inside. Then after a few days, the fox goes outside one evening and begins to shout and he shouts.

"What are you doing then?" the wolf says. "Who are you shouting at?"

"Don't tell me," he says, "they're calling me to go and be godfather."

"Yeah? Go ahead then," he says.

"I hate to go."

"Oh, go ahead," he says.

The fox leaves and goes down to the beach. He goes to his tub of butter and he eats quite a bit of it. Then he goes back up to the cabin.

"What'd you call him, your godson?" he says.

"I called him Begun."

"Yeah, that's a nice name."

So things go on like that for a while but after another few days, the fox goes outside again and begins to yell.

"Who are you shouting at then?" the wolf says.

"Ah, don't tell me," he says, "they're shouting at me to go and be godfather again. It's awfully tiresome."

"Go ahead," he says. "I'd go if I were you."

"Well, I'll go then."

He goes out, goes down to the beach again and over to his tub of butter and he eats quite a bit of it. Then he goes back up to the cabin.

"And this one," he says. "What'd you call him?"

"I called him Begun-Half."

"Begun-Half!" he says. "That's a nice name."

So a few more days go by and the fox goes outside and starts to shout again.

"You're shouting again," he says. "Are they calling you again to be godfather?"

"Yes," he says. "Don't tell me they want me to be godfather again!"

"Oh, go ahead," he says.

So the fox goes out, goes down to the beach, eats all the rest of the tub of butter, and goes back home.

"What'd you call this one?" he says.

"I called him Begun-Half-Finished."

"Listen," the wolf says, "Now that Lent has started, it's about time we went and ate our butter. We'll go tomorrow."

So the next day the wolf sets off and he takes the fox with him against his will. The fox followed behind at a distance. The wolf goes down to the beach and finds that the whole tub of butter has been eaten. Well, now he's awfully mad at the fox.

So the fox turns around and goes up to the lake and the wolf follows. "If you'll make a bargain not to be mad," the fox says, "I'll make you laugh all you like."

"Oh, all right," he says.

"Sit down here and I'm going to jump and do somersaults and you'll laugh as much as you like."

So he makes him sit down there on the ice and he runs on the ice and jumps forwards and sideways and the wolf laughs and laughs. Then when they were tired, they went back to their cabin and stayed there.

The wolf was still mad so the fox says, "If you stop being angry, I'll let you eat as much fish as you like. You'll come with me."

They go down to the shore and there was a man who was coming along with a horse and a whole wagon full of smelt.

So the fox says, "Don't move. I'm going to get some smelt. Hide here and don't budge."

Then the fox goes and lies down in the road where the horse has to pass and he pretends he's dead. So the man, the wagoner, he goes and has a look.

"There's a dead animal here," he says.

He takes him and throws him on his load of smelt. His wagon was just full of smelt. Soon the fox starts pulling at the smelt, pulls away, and he drops them all along the road for quite a distance.

When the fellow gets back home, he looks and his fox is gone!

"That's really awful!" he says. "I guess he wasn't really dead."

The fox calls over the wolf. "Come and eat some smelt." He lets the wolf eat as much as he wants to, and the wolf wasn't mad at all after that.

The wolf wanted to send the fox back to get some more smelt but he didn't want to go. "It's your turn," the fox says. "You go." So he sent the wolf in his turn. "Lie down on the road," he says, "and pretend you're dead."

The wolf goes and lies down in the road and then he closed his eyes but he kept opening them from time to time.

So when the man comes he says, "What's that there? It's a wolf." But the man sees him open his eyes. "You're pretending you're dead, but you're not dead at all!"

He grabs the wolf and knocks him over the head and carries him home.

The fox was in the clear then.

The String of Trout (La brochée de truites)

Collected by Luc Lacourcière (recording no. 3388), in July 1957 from Mrs. Daniel Poirier (née Délia Gallant), aged fifty-seven, of Egmont Bay, Prince county, Prince Edward Island, Canada. Translated by Margaret Low.

Type 1832 E* *Good Manners*, and Type 1832 J* *Choice of Apples*.

The answers of a young boy to a priest or another superior have given rise to a whole series of short tales and anecdotes in the popular tradition of French Canada. Stith Thompson added about a dozen of these tales from the manuscript *Catalogue of French Folktales in North America* as T. 1832* and subdivisions.

Our informant was an indefatigable taleteller. On our first visit to Prince Edward Island, Mrs. Poirier told us 74 folktales in four days and many more on successive visits! Her repertory included as many *Märchen* as fabliaux and she knew as well some 300 folksongs.

Her tales were well loved by those in her community. "One winter," she said, "I visited in turn every house in the entire village to tell my tales. I went out three nights a week. I would have gone more often, but I didn't want people to think I was a gadabout."

Once there was a man and he had a little boy. He lived near the church. There was a small river there and he loved to fish for trout, especially so he could give some to his parish priest. Every time he caught some lovely big trout he would send his little boy to take a string of them to the priest.

One day he says to his little boy as usual, "Here, go and take these lovely trout to the priest."

"No, I'm not going," replied the little boy.

His father was surprised since the boy never ever answered him that way before. "What did you say? Go and take the trout to the priest."

"No. I'm not going."

"Why?" the father says.

"Just because I'm not going."

Well, the man says, "If you go just this once, since they are so beautiful this time, I'll never ask you to go back again."

The boy doesn't answer. He takes the trout and sets out angrily for the priest's. He gets to the door, knocks and opens the door. The priest was seated on the far side of the room, furthest from the door. The boy takes the string of trout and throws them down on a chair, closes the door, and starts to go away.

The priest runs to the door. "Come here," says the priest. "Come here, my little boy. I'll show you that that is not the way to bring a string of trout to a priest."

The little boy was a bit ashamed.

"Come here. Come here, my boy."

Well, he had to go back. He goes back to the door and he's all ashamed.

"Come in," the priest says. "I'll show you how to bring a string of trout to a priest. Sit down in my big chair and you'll be the priest and I'll be the little boy."

The priest picks up the trout and goes outside. He knocks at the door.

"Come in," the little boy says.

He comes in and goes up to the little boy who is supposed to be the priest. He bows and says, "Here, Monsieur le Curé. My father sent you a string of trout."

The little boy isn't a bit slow. He puts his hand in his pocket and takes out twenty-five cents and gives it to the priest. Then, imitating the priest, he says, "Here, little boy. This is to pay you."

The priest was surprised and a little ashamed. "I can see now," he says, "why you did what you did. You want to be paid for your trouble. Very well, I will pay you."

There was a small table there. The priest takes twenty-five cents and puts it on one corner, puts fifty cents on another corner and a dollar on another corner.

"This is to pay you," he says to the little boy. "If you take the twenty-five cents, you will go to heaven when you die. If you take the fifty cents, you will go to purgatory and if you take the dollar, you'll go to hell when you die. Now, choose."

The little boy doesn't waste time. He uses both hands. "Well," he says, "I'll take them all and then I'll be able to go where I want to." The little boy goes out the door and on his way.

The Sheep and the Ram (Les moutonnes et le bélier)

Collected by Luc Lacourcière and Félix-Antoine Savard (recording no. 888), in October 1949 from Pierre Pilote, aged fifty-five, of Les Eboulements, Charlevoix county, Québec, Canada. Translated by Margaret Low.

Type 471 *The Bridge to the Other World.*

The French variants of this tale have been the object of a computer study in France by Philippe Richard, Francis Lévy, and Michel de Virville (*Essai de description des contes merveilleux,* in *Ethnologie française* 1:3–4 [1971]: 95–120). However, there are many interesting motifs and episodes in the eighteen French-Canadian versions that have not been found in France and therefore have not been included in this computer study.

Our informant, like many French-Canadian taletellers, learned his tales in the lumber camps. Mr. Pilote told his tales primarily during Lent. At this time, young boys and girls in the region would set out from home after the daily family prayer and gather at his house to hear one or two folktales each evening.

Motifs: H1385.6 "Quest for lost sister"; H1251 "Quest to other world for samples of magic animals' food"; H1242 "Youngest brother alone succeeds on quest"; F152 "Bridge to otherworld"; E171 "Extraordinary sights in otherworld"; F171.0.1 "Enigmatic happenings in otherworld, which are later explained (in religious terms)."

Motifs special to this version follow: H331.14 "Suitor contest: trial of strength"; D300 "Transformation: animal to person (ram as priest)"; D42 "God in guise of mortal"; G303.3.1 "The devil in human form"; *G303.16.11.6 "God intervenes to save a person from the devil" (number assigned by the Motif-Index of the Archives de Folklore, Quebec).

This tale type is well distributed throughout Europe and popular in France as well as in French Canada. It is reported in the New World in Spanish, Negro, and American Indian traditions as well as the French. The religious interpretation and moral injunction at the end give it a didactic flavor.

Ah, it's worth telling you that once there was a man, his wife, and his four children, three boys and a girl.

When the children grew up into four big youths, they were pretty good, especially the girl. She was a real pretty girl. When she was about twenty years old she had some suitors, as they say, but that girl was hard to please. She couldn't make up her mind and she was pretty independent.

One day her father says, "I'm sick of this business," he says. "You keep turning down good matches. You'd probably be happy," he says, "but you seem to despise everyone. Well, if you can't make up your mind, I'll make it up for you."

This incident took place at the time of year when they were cutting the hay. The man loaded a wagon with about seventy-five bundles of hay. He put it in front of his house with a sign on it: He who pulls this load of hay the furthest will have my daughter in marriage.

So the load is placed there with the sign, and all the boys in the area there have a try at it. No one was able to budge the load of hay.

The load of hay was to be there for two weeks. After four or five days had gone by, a young man called on him, a man he didn't know. He ties his horse up by the road and goes into the house.

Well, he says, "Are you the man of the house?"

"Yes," he says.

"The sign that's there on that load of hay," he says, "is that true?"

"Yes, my young man," he says. "Yes, it's true."

He pulls off his coat, harnesses himself up, and drags the load five acres. Then he brings back the load.

"Well, my man," he says, "you're the only one to date who has moved the load of hay. At the end of the two weeks," he says, "if no one has done better than you have, my daughter will belong to you. You'll marry her and do what you like with her."

"Fine, sir."

He wanted his name and the address where he lived.

"I'm a traveler. I'll be back at the end of the two weeks."

The days went by. Ten days, twelve days, thirteen days. The morning of the fourteenth day, a man arrived there, a young man who was delicate, not tall nor heavy, and he didn't seem very strong.

He comes into the house and says, "Are you the boss here, the owner?"

"Yes," he says.

"The sign on your load of hay," he says, "is that true?"

"Yes, sir."

"Ah, we'll give it a try," he says. Pulls off his coat, harnesses himself up, drags the load of hay ten acres, and brings it back.

"Well, sir," he says, "there's still one day to go and if no one else does better than you did, my daughter will belong to you. You'll marry her and do what you like."

Takes his address.

"I'll be back tomorrow afternoon," he says.

And so the day goes by. No one else moved the load of hay. So the girl belonged to the young man, the last John that came there.

They prepared the wedding and they were married and then had a nice celebration.

The young man was a farmer, so the next day he says, "I can't stay away any longer. Get your daughter ready. Give her her goods, what's coming to her. We'll come back to see you next year," he says. "Can't come back before then. I'll tell you where I live and those who would like to come and see me during the year, well, don't hesitate, you'll be welcome."

Goodby. It's over. They've disappeared, gone.

Things went on like that for three months. They had no news. They'd been warned about that, of course.

The oldest boy, there were three boys, the oldest boy says to his parents and his brothers, "I miss our sister," he says. "We had a good time together, and she left so suddenly. She wasn't a disagreeable person when at home. I'm going to go and see her."

That makes sense. He gets ready and leaves. Takes to the road. In those days, one traveled on foot. Walks three days. The third day, he reached his brother-in-law's in the forest, a pretty little house, well-built and clean. They say hello, but he didn't see his sister.

"Where's my sister?" he says.

"Oh," he says, "she's there in her room."

"What's she doing there?" he says. "Can I see her? She isn't sick?" he says.

"Not sick at all," he says. "You'll see your sister," he says, "if you're able to do the work I'm going to give you to do."

"That's mighty strange."

"Well, that's how it is," he says. "You have to earn a thing in order to get it. Don't you know that?" he says.

"Well, yes," he says. "I'll do it if it can be done."

"We'll spend the evening together," he says, "and in the morning I'll tell you what to do."

They smoked until a certain time, half-past ten, and then they went to bed.

The next morning after breakfast, he says, "Well, today," he says, "I've ten sheep that leave in the morning and come back in the evening, and if you can bring me back what my sheep will eat today, you'll see your sister this evening."

"Not more difficult than that?" he says.

"Well, no."

"That's easy enough."

"You'll bring me what they eat today."

He set off with nine sheep and a ram. The sheep took to the forest, followed a little footpath there, and the guy followed them. They walked for about an hour. Then they came to a big river. The ram stepped aside and the sheep went ahead and started to swim across and reached the other side.

The ram went all around the guy but he just stood there. Then the ram didn't waste time. He jumped in and swam across. On the other side, he led his sheep and they disappeared.

Our guy stayed here on this side. At three o'clock, the sheep appeared and crossed back over the river. My guy's there, and he sets out in front of the sheep.

Then before leaving the woods, he says, "What did they eat? My brother-in-law told me to bring back what the sheep ate. They usually eat clover and vetch, I suppose." He put some clover and vetch in his handkerchief.

They got back to his brother-in-law's house.

"How'd it go?" he said.

"Oh," he said, "it went fine."

"It went fine?" he says. "Did you bring me what I asked for?"

The guy says, "Yes," Takes his handkerchief and unfolds it.

"Here's your clover and vetch," he says.

"Ah, you're far too stupid," he says. "Go on back home. You're far too stupid to see your sister. Get out."

Ah, he's terribly insulted, but what can he do? He's outside. He goes on home.

Ah, there's nothing more urgent when those fellows see him arrive. "Come on, our sister, our daughter, how is she?"

"I didn't have a very pleasant trip," he says. "I tell you he's an awful brother-in-law. I didn't see my sister. He threw me out. Talk about an idiot!"

"Is she sick?"

"He said she wasn't sick. I didn't see her."

The second boy, he says, "I'm going to go. You're too stupid, you are. You're starting to get old. I'm going to go."

The next day, he got ready and set out. He took the same route his brother had. He arrived there.

"Hello." And then he asked how his sister was.

"Your sister is fine. She's in her room," he says. "You'll see your sister," he says, "if you're able to do the work I'm going to give you to do."

"Well, if it can be done, I'll do it."

They went to bed and the next morning it was the same story. He went off with the sheep.

"If you bring me back this evening what the sheep eat today, you'll see your sister this evening."

"Well, that's awful easy," he says.

He did the same thing the other idiot had done; he stayed on this side of the river. He brought back some clover, some vetch, and some rice.

"That's not it at all. Get home."

Anyway it's an awful business. What does he expect? What sort of a guy is that?

When he got back home, his mother asked, "How's my daughter? How's your sister?"

"Don't talk to me about that guy," he says. "He's the worst guy I've ever seen on earth. I didn't see her. I don't know. He threw me out."

The youngest says, "I'm going to go myself." He's a young man of eighteen. "You're both idiots," he says. "You know you're both a bit simple. I'm going myself."

The next day he gets ready. He takes the same route and reaches his brother-in-law's.

"Now you are a young man with common sense. Your sister's in excellent health," he says. "She's in her room there. I've got a bit of work for you to do. If you're able to do it," he says, "you'll see your sister tomorrow evening."

"That's fine."

They spent the evening together, and the next morning after breakfast he says, "Look here. I've got ten sheep here. You're going to follow them today and if you bring me back this evening what they eat today, you'll see your sister."

Ah well, they took the same little path in the forest. When they got to the river, the ram stepped aside and the sheep swam across. The ram walked all around the young man.

"Now you," he says, "you look as if you want me to get on your back."

He jumped on the ram's back and crossed the river. On the other side, the ram led the sheep and they continued on for quite some distance.

They came to a chapel there. The sheep went into the church, the little chapel, and the ram went around by way of the little sacristy that was there.

Then the ram appeared as a priest. He said Mass. The sheep listened to Mass. When it came time for communion, they all went up to the communion table. The young man followed along. He went to the communion table with the sheep and they all took communion. He took the Holy Wafer and wrapped it up in his handkerchief. Mass ended.

After Mass they left the chapel and stayed there for a part of the day. At three o'clock they started down the little path. The young man crossed the river on the ram's back and reached his brother-in-law's house.

"Ah, how was it?" he said.

"Ah, it was extraordinary! I saw things I'd never seen before in my life," he says.

"Did you bring me what my sheep ate?" he says.

"I'm pretty sure," he says. "In any case," he says, "they didn't eat anything else. I watched them pretty closely."

"Well, show me it," he says.

He undid his handkerchief. "Darn it!" he says. "In any case, I put something in my handkerchief and I don't see it now."

"What did you put there?" he says.

Well, he tells his story. "The sheep took communion and I took the Holy Wafer and put it in my handkerchief and now I don't have it."

"We know," he says," that the Holy Wafer couldn't stay in your handkerchief. The Holy Wafer went back where it came from. You brought me what my sheep ate," he says. "I'm going to show you your sister."

He saw his sister and she was the same as when she had left home.

"Now, my young man," he says, "go back home with your sister. I'll tell you that I am God. The one who came and pulled the load of hay before I did was the devil. This girl was in the clutches of the devil, and I came to save her. Take this child, your sister, back home. She is as she was when she left home. Tell your father not to make any more arrangements to marry off his daughter. She's pretty enough to find a nice sensible man without putting a load of hay with a sign on it."

That's all.

The Sword of Wisdom (Le Sabre de la vertu de sagesse)

Collected by Luc Lacourcière (recording no. 2364), in July 1955 from Adolphe Duguay, age eighty-three, of Petite-Lamèque, Lamèque, Ile Shippagan, Gloucester county, New Brunswick, Canada. Translated by Margaret Low.

For this type, which is not classified in Aarne-Thompson nor, although it is an Irish tale, in *The Types of the Irish Folktale* of S. O'Súilleabháin and R. Christiansen, the late Paul Delarue suggested the number 305.

But, since this number has been used for a different theme in the 1961 edition of the Aarne-Thompson type index, this tale has been classified as type 305A in the *Catalogue of French Folktales in North America*.

This Celtic tale has taken root in the oral tradition of North America where it has been recorded in French 13 times: 11 times in French Canada and twice in Maine. There is also an English version from a Miramichi informant of Edward Ives and Helen Creighton.

Our informant communicated a large number of folktales, at first almost against his wife's wishes, but fortunately the latter was quickly won over and later proved to be herself an excellent informant and as prolific a taleteller as her husband.

Motifs: H942 "Tasks assigned as payment of gambling loss"; M1219.1 "Quest assigned as payment for gambling loss"; H901 "Tasks imposed on pain of death"; H1235 "Succession of helpers on quest"; H1337 "Quest for sword of light"; H825 "Old person as helper"; D112.1 "Transformation: man to lion."

The motif of the quest for the sword of light, a key motif in this tale, is reported only for Irish myth.

Once there was a lord. He had become rich by playing cards. He went and played cards and he always won large sums of money.

He had a boy. Well, his son noticed that his father played since people often came to their place to play cards.

When the son was about fifteen or twenty years old, his father said, "Now that we are fairly rich, I won't play cards any more."

"Well," the boy said, "I'm going to take your place. I'm going to play cards too to make money."

"No," his father said. "If you start playing cards, you will meet with misfortune."

"Not at all," he said. "I have to play cards."

One day the son took his deck of cards and went out to a small island. He was all alone there. "I'll play cards with anyone at all who comes here," he said.

He looks out toward the water and he sees a boat coming, a boat with six oars. Well, it comes into shore and the oars are pulled in.

There is only one man. He walks up to the young man. "Are you here to play cards?" he says.

"Yes."

"I'm going to play with you," he says.

They start to play and they played from morning until noon. At noon, they fixed themselves lunch and then played from noon until evening. Well, when evening came, the young man had won. They were playing for wishes.

So the other fellow says, "What do you wish to have?"

"Well," he says, "I wish to have one hundred steer with gold horns and gold hoofs in my father's stable."

"Well," he says, "you're asking for a lot but you'll have it."

He goes back home and his father says, "How did it go? Were you playing cards?"

"Yes," he says.

"Ah," he says, "my child, you'll meet with misfortune soon."

"Listen," he says. "I have to play cards too."

The next morning the father goes out to the barn, to the stable. There were one hundred steer in the stable all with gold horns and hoofs.

"Ah," his father says, "my poor child, you're playing for wishes. You'll meet with misfortune in the end."

"Ah, no," he says. "I'm lucky."

They were to start at six o'clock in the morning. So at six o'clock then he was there. The other fellow arrives. They start to play. They play and play and play. They play right up until noon. At noon, they have a little snack and then they play until six o'clock in the evening. The young man had won again.

Well, he says, "What do you wish for?"

"I wish to have one hundred horses, all with beautiful gold plaques on their harnesses, in my father's stable."

Well, when he gets home he says to his father, "I won again."

"Yes?" he says.

"Tomorrow morning, go and look in the stable and you'll find horses there."

The next morning then the father goes out to the stable. He finds a hundred horses there, all decked out good and proper with gold plaques on their harnesses and bridles.

"Ah," his father says. "You mustn't do it!"

"We have three days to play," he says, "and I'm sure I'm going to win. I'm lucky," he says.

Well, the next morning they go there to play and they play, play, play. In the evening, they begin to count up to see who won the most. Ah, the stranger had won.

"Well," he says, "this time I'm the one who is going to make the wish and you'll have to give me what I wish for. You don't know who I am," he says. "Well, I'm Death of the State."

"Yes?" he says.

"At six o'clock Christmas morning, I want to have the Sword of Wisdom here and if I don't, I'll cut your neck off with it. If you don't have it," he says, "I'm the one who'll have it. So you have to have it here," he says.

Ah, well, the young man is pretty sad then. He goes home with his head bent low. He gets home. Not a word!

"How was it?" his father says.

He doesn't say a word. He goes to his room and sits there brooding about the Sword of Wisdom. He'd never heard of it. Well, he stays in his room.

They had a servant there. She takes him something to eat. He doesn't eat, and when she speaks to him he doesn't answer.

She says to the lord, "Your boy is sick," she says. "He doesn't eat, doesn't talk. You should go and get the doctor or something."

"Ah," he says, "I know what's wrong with him and he doesn't need a doctor."

The servant takes the boy something to eat. "Well," she says, "what's wrong? Are you sick? I talk to you but you don't answer; you don't eat."

"Nothing," he says. "I think I'm going to die."

"Well," she says, "tell me what's wrong."

"Well, we played cards," he says, "and I lost. Now I have to find the Sword of Wisdom and I don't know where it is. I've never even heard of it," he says.

"Well," she says, "I'm going to write a letter for you. There's a witch here, not too far away, and you're going to go there and give her this letter. She'll know if there is a sword and where it is."

So the next morning, he sets off. He gets there in the evening. He knocks at the door.

"Good evening, Grandmother."

"Good evening, young man."

He gives her the letter.

"Ah," she says, "my daughter is at your place. She's a servant there."

"Oh, I've never known where she's from," he says.

"You're looking for the Sword of Wisdom?"

"Yes," he says.

"Well," she says, "you'll have your supper, then you'll go to bed, and I'll go through my books tonight. If there is one," she says, "I'll find it for you."

At night, he goes to bed and she reads until morning. In the morning, she hadn't found it. She couldn't remember where the Sword of Wisdom was.

Well, she says, "There's one of my sisters who's further on here. It'll take pretty well all day to get there. She is even more knowing than I am. I'm going to write a letter for you, and you'll go there and give her the letter."

So in the evening he reaches the sister's place.

"Good evening, Grandmother."

"Good evening, young man. You slept at one of my sisters' last night."

"Ah, I don't know," he says. "She didn't tell me who she was."

"Anyway, you'll go to bed," she says.

Then she takes a big dictionary. "It must be in here," she says. She went through it all night long. In the morning, nothing. It didn't mention the Sword of Wisdom.

"I have a sister who's much further away," she says. "I'll write her a letter. She should know. She's ten times smarter than I am."

Anyway, the next morning she writes him a letter. There's the fellow off on his way then. He gets there in the evening.

"Good evening, Grandmother."

"Good evening, young man."

He gives her the letter.

"Ah," she says, "you slept at one of my sisters' last night."

"Yes?" he says. "I don't know where I slept."

"So you're looking for the Sword of Wisdom?"

"Yes," he says.

"Well," she says, "you'll have your supper, then go to bed. I'm going to look it up."

She looks through all her books, then looks through her dictionary. Ah, when day comes, to be sure, it did exist, the Sword of Wisdom.

The boy wakes up. "Did you find it?" he says.

"Yes," she says. "There is one, but it is hard to get. You're not nervous?"

"No."

"The other side of the river there, there's a big house, a big two-story house. I'm going to give you a goat and a small boat. You're going to put the goat in the boat, and I'm going to tie the goat with a piece of rope to keep it there. When you reach the other side, you'll shout, 'Come to me, Sword of Wisdom.' A man is going to come out of the house. He'll come and cut the goat right in half with a sword. Don't be afraid. That sword won't hurt you. He's going to grab the end of the goat he cut and take it away. When he gets back to the house, he'll go in the house and you'll shout, 'Come to me, Sword of Wisdom.' He'll come out and come down and cut the goat's neck. When he goes back into the house, you'll shout again, 'Come to me, Sword of Wisdom.' He'll come and cut the rope right close to your hands. But don't be afraid. When he starts to go back to the house, you follow him. He'll stick the sword in a big tree there. Don't be slow grabbing it. Once you have it," she says, "the sword cuts ten yards in front of the point. Well, then he'll ask for it and you'll say, 'No. You have to tell me where you got this sword.'"

He does what the old woman told him, gets the sword, and asks the man to tell his story.

"Well, sir," the man begins, "my story is a little bit long, but I'm

going to tell it to you. Me," he says, "I was a man who drank. I lived
in the city and I drank an awful lot. I drank almost everything I earned,
and that didn't please my wife," he says. "One day she said, 'That won't
do. You drink away everything you earn. So,' she says, 'we're going to
go and live in the woods.' 'Ah, well,' I said to my wife, 'we'll go there
then.'

"Anyway," he said, "after some time, a couple of years, my wife
got sick. She said, 'Go to the city then and bring me back a flask of gin
to make some poultices. It will do me good.'

"Ah, me who was so used to drinking, and I hadn't been back there
since, so I was glad to go. I set out, reached the city, and went to the
inn. When I got in there, well, all of my friends were there. So they said,
'How are things going? Come and have a drink.' I was glad to have
a drink so I went. I had one drink and then another and all that. There
I was a bit drunk," he says. "I was mean and strong. When I had a bit
of gin in me, I got excited. I hit a man who was there and knocked him
down. Bang! Well, I got scared. I stepped over him and went home.

"My wife says, 'Did you bring me a flask of gin?' 'Oh, well,' I said,
'I forgot it.' Then there was more trouble over that. 'You're going back
there,' she says the next day. 'Won't do any good to put it off.' 'Oh,
that's no problem,' I says.

"I reached the city and went to the inn. There were more friends
there. Shake hands with this one, shake hands with that one. Since I
liked it, I didn't refuse. I drank and then I got angry. When I had been
drinking," he says, "I didn't know what I was doing. I hit one guy, hit
another, and flattened them both. Then," he says, "I was frightened, so
I set off for home.

"When I got home, my wife was moaning. 'Well, you surely must
have brought me a flask of gin this time,' she said. 'Ah, I forgot it.'

" 'Well,' she said, 'it would be just as well if you were a lion.'

"Then I saw that I was a lion, that I had become a lion! 'Ah, well,' I
said, 'if I'm a lion, I'm going out into the woods and find the other lions.
There must be some. What would I do here as a lion?'

"I went out into the woods and wandered about the woods. I met
fifteen lions. I stayed with them. I had the intelligence of a man," he
said, "I could think. We wandered about the woods, then we came to a
city where the king had set up a trap to catch lions, a gate it was. When
the lions went in, it closed, and they weren't able to open it. Ah, well,
they were near this thing. There was something to eat in there, and the
gate was open so they started to go in.

"I would be able to fix it," he says. "I had the intelligence of a man. It
wouldn't take long to open the gate. We go in, and the gate closes. We
start to eat. When I go to open the gate—nothing doing! I couldn't
open it!

"Well, the next day three men came with rifles to shoot us. The king had sent them to see if there were any lions in the trap, and there were fifteen of us. The men came closer. 'Ah, look at the bunch of lions here,' they said. 'We'll have a whole load.'

"Me," he said, "who had the intelligence of a man, I began to make all sorts of gestures with my paws. I bowed. I knelt down. 'There's one who's well trained,' they said. 'He's trained, that lion.'

"They went and told that to the king. 'Go and kill the others, but bring that lion to me,' the king said. Well," the young man said, "they had guns, and I wanted to escape but they opened the gate and took me to the castle. Well, when I saw the king, I started to make all sorts of gestures with my paws and all that. 'I've got a nice lion here,' the king said. 'He's a nice lion and he's well trained.' So they put me in the courtyard and went into the castle and I walked up and down in there.

"The king had a prince and the prince was married. He has a baby, not him but his wife has a baby. 'We'll put the lion to rocking the cradle tonight,' the king says. So he said to the lion, I understood everything, he says to me, 'You'll rock the baby if you like.' Yeah.

"To be sure," he says, "all of a sudden, a hand appeared! It goes and grabs the baby and takes the baby away. Then I began to cry and howl.

"They all got up. The prince, his wife, and the king. They come and look. The baby was gone!

" 'The lion has eaten my baby!' the prince said. I was making all sorts of gestures in the air and all that. 'It isn't the lion that ate the baby,' the king says. 'There's something else, and we'll find out what.'

"Then I stayed in the courtyard all the time. Well, things went on like that. Anyway, at the end of the year, there was another baby.

" 'We'll put him to rocking the child,' the king said, 'and if anything happens to the child, we'll know it's the lion. Well, big lion,' he says to me, 'you're going to rock the child. You'll have to be careful.'

"So I was rocking the cradle with one paw and I saw the arm coming. To be sure, the same hand was coming to grab the child. I grabbed the hand and pulled off the arm. Then I began to howl.

" 'Ah,' they said, 'this time he ate him, he ate the child.' They go and look. The child was there asleep. 'You see,' the king said. 'If it hadn't been for the lion, they would have taken this child away as well.' I had the hand there. 'He's well trained, this lion,' the king said.

"Well, things went on like that. They let me go outside and they gave me enough to eat. Well," he says, "one day I went to take a walk in the woods and when I got to the edge of the woods, there was a meadow there. When I reached the edge of the meadow, I noticed that I was a man! That sort of flabbergasted me for a while.

"I walked about in the meadow. I saw two young children, a little girl and a little boy, who each had a basket and they were picking something in the meadow. I thought to myself, 'What are they doing, those little children?' In any case, I went to see. I crept up quietly, quietly, quietly, and they didn't see me. I got quite close to them.

" 'Ah, my little children, what are you doing here?' I said.

" 'We're picking herbs to make a poultice for our grandmother who broke her arm.'

" 'Yes? Well, where does your grandmother live? Where is she? I could go with you. I'm a doctor. If I could see her, I could help her.'

"Well, they said, 'Come with us.'

"They walked a good distance. They came to a hole in the ground and went down into it. It was dark under the ground. It was awfully dark. I followed them. Well, we began to hear someone wailing. 'What's that?'

" 'Here's where our grandmother is,' they said.

" 'Yes, your grandmother is in there, but I can't see any light. If there was some light, I could give her some medicine to heal her arm.'

"Well, the old woman there says, 'There's a door there. Open that door, and the Sword of Wisdom is there on a table. It lights everything up like daytime. It sheds as much light as the day. Bring it here. You'll see.'

"Well, I took the Sword of Wisdom and went over to the old woman. I started to examine her and saw that her arm was torn off. To be sure, she was the one who came and grabbed the first child and she was coming for the second. So I took the sword and cut off her other arm."

"And that is how I got the Sword of Wisdom."

"Well, now," he says, "you played cards with Death of the State. It's tomorrow, Christmas morning, at six o'clock, that you have to be there like he told you with the Sword of Wisdom. And if you don't have it, he'll be the one who has it and he'll cut your neck off with it. But shortly he's going to come and he's going to ask you for the Sword of Wisdom. You'll say, 'Yes, I've got it here. Is this it?' He'll say yes. He's going to say, 'Give it to me.' Don't give it to him. Just pretend. Then you'll go up fairly close to him but don't strike right away. When you think he's just five or six yards away from the point," he says, "you'll cut his neck off. That's all you have to do. You'll be rid of him and you'll go back to your father with the Sword of Wisdom."

And that's what the lad did.

That's all I want to tell you. I've reached the end.

The Big Dog (Le gros chien)

Collected by Luc Lacourcière (recording no. 2295), in June 1955 from Pierre Pilote, aged sixty-one, of Saint-Pascal, Les Eboulements, Charlevoix county, Québec, Canada. Translated by Margaret Low.

Motifs: D141 "Transformation: man to dog"; *D141.0.4 "Wer-dog" (cf. D113.1.1 "Werwolf"). Eyewitness accounts of persons transformed into animals told by French-Canadians in upper Michigan are in R. M. Dorson, *Bloodstoppers and Bearwalkers* (Cambridge, Mass., 1952, repr. 1972), pp. 74–78, known as *roup-garou* (from *loup-garou*) tales.

There was a farmer who was alone with his wife, and he needed some help. "I'm going to look for a man to cut my hay," he says.

So he goes into the village and he comes back with a big, young man, a young man about twenty years old, a big man. So he hires him. "That's your room," he says. "I'll pay you two dollars a day. The work isn't too hard. You'll be well off here."

So they started to work Monday, then Tuesday. They noticed that the young man never ate breakfast in the morning. He was never hungry. Things go on like that for about two weeks but they, the farmer and his wife, had noticed that the young man never ate in the morning.

One fine night he says to his wife, "I've got my doubts about that guy. I don't know what he's up to," he says, "but I'm going to hide so I can see what's going on."

So they had put a load of hay that wasn't dry in the barn that afternoon. So the fellow gets up on the load of hay. The door was open and it was a nice moonlit night. So he stays there.

Around eleven o'clock, what does the farmer see entering the courtyard? A big dog with a big leg of beef in his mouth!

The dog goes under the wagon in the barn and then the man can hear bones crunching. He ate the whole thing. Then when he had finished eating his beef, the dog came out into the courtyard and licked his paws all over.

All of a sudden, he turns into the young man, the hired hand!

My man plays dead there, you can imagine. So he lets about half an hour go by, and then goes back to the house and goes to bed without making any noise.

Next morning he gets up as usual. My guy comes to the table.

"Ah," he says, "I'm not hungry this morning. It's awful."

"Listen," the fellow says. "You never eat in the morning?"

"No, I'm never hungry."

"You can well not eat. If I had eaten what you ate last night, I wouldn't be hungry either."

"What!" he says. "You saw me? How?"

"Yes," he says. "You got back at eleven o'clock and went under the wagon loaded with hay with a leg of beef in your mouth. You ate the whole thing and then when you finished you went to bed. You can well not eat!"

"You saw me?" he says. "How?"

"Well," he says, "I was lying down on the load of hay."

"You were lucky that I didn't see you. You would have ended up like the leg of beef. I would have eaten you too!"

"Well, since that's the way it is, my boy, take your rags and get out!"

So the young man beat it.

They used to say in those days that if a man didn't take the Sacrament at Easter for seven years he could be changed into an animal.

The Scalping of Pérusse (Histoire de Pérusse)

Collected by Luc Lacourcière (recording nos. 2217 & 2218), in June 1955 from Florent Lemay, aged sixty-seven, of Sainte-Croix, Lotbinière county, Québec, Canada. Translated by Margaret Low.

Motifs: S110 "Murders"; S163 "Mutilation: cutting (tearing) out tongue"; S165 "Mutilation: putting out eyes"; *S177 "Mutilation: scalping."

This narrative is one of many still told in Canada of local characters who met a brutal death at the hands of Indians. It can be compared to one of the best known historical legends of French Canada, the tale of Cadieux, a Canadian voyageur.

Cadieux, with a small group of trappers and their families, was surprised by an Iroquois war party. Cadieux remained behind as a decoy while the others escaped by canoe. After being tracked for days by the Indians, Cadieux died, but before his death, he dug his own grave, planted a small wooden cross, and composed the lament of his death, which he supposedly wrote on a piece of birchbark. The legend contains elements of the miraculous as well as the heroic since as the canoes shot the huge rapids, an almost impossible feat, there appeared a Lady in White hovering above the canoes and guiding them to safety.

The lament of Cadieux is more widely known than that of Pérusse and was long sung by Canadian voyageurs. See Marius Barbeau, "La Complainte de Cadieux, Coureur de bois" in the Journal of American Folklore 67 (1954): 163–83.

Our informant, a retired farmer, has given us to date, besides legends more than 65 songs and 50 folktales and his repertory is still not exhausted. At the age of eighty-five, he is still telling tales, with a marked predilection for fabliaux.

My grandfather, when he was a boy they called him Peter Boy Lemay, set out at the age of seventeen to work in the lumber camps of Ottawa. He went up to Montreal by boat and then there, well, he went into the woods and on to Ottawa by foot.

He stayed in the woods for eleven years. When he came out of the lumber camps after his eleven years, since the wages weren't much in those days, he had three thousand dollars in silver. That gave him enough to buy himself a bit of land and to marry and raise a family.

At that time though, other young men, his friends, had left to go up to join him in the lumber camps. There was a certain Pérusse from Saint-Eustache in Lotbinière county. He had left in the autumn, in the month of November, to go and join my grandfather. Anyway, it took them two weeks to go by foot through the woods from Montreal to Ottawa.

There were savages almost all the way along the route. Well, they were armed; they had rifles, but in those days they were flint rifles. When the weather was nice, they fired but when it rained they didn't. During eight days, they had freezing rain. They slept at the foot of trees. The first one to get out of the ice in the morning got the others out.

One night, it had been raining for three or four days and they were soaked through like ducks, Pérusse says to his friends, "Tonight, I'm going to light a fire to get dry."

"Ah, that's awful dangerous," his friends told him. "We just met up with some savages there."

"Thunder take everything!" he says. "Die or not, I'm going to dry myself tonight."

Anyway, he lights a fire. It was a night when it was really dark. They began to see savages near the fire. An arrow flew by them from time to time.

"We shouldn't have done it," they said.

They had their flint rifles there. It had rained for eight days. They try to fire their rifles; not one would go off! They had all rusted.

The arrows were flying around Pérusse. Suddenly, he was fatally wounded.

"Leave me here. Get away from the enemy and leave me here."

The savages had a big celebration.

The next day, his friends, his three friends came back. They had scalped him. His scalp was pinned to a tree and his body was stretched out at the foot of the tree. (They had taken out his eyes, pulled out his tongue.)

They made a hole and buried him.

They continued on their way up to the lumber camps. They told their story to their people from the Lotbinière region when they reached the camp, as you can well imagine.

In those days, when a man was killed, it wasn't like today. Today, no one takes any notice of that. People are killed three or four at a time and they're dead and that's that. But in those days, it wasn't like that.

One of their friends who had been in Wisconsin went back home. He told them about the terrible night they had spent. He told that to a certain Auger, who was the grandfather of Baptiste Auger who is a carpenter here in the village. When someone told him an event which had happened—he was a guy something like myself who couldn't read or write—he composed a song while working. So he composed a lament. [The melody of this version of the "Lament of Pérusse" was transcribed by the late Marius Barbeau from the composition by Joseph Auger. The informant, Florent Lemay, commented: "Je l'ai apprise de mon père; j'avais 8 ou 9 ans. J'entendais chanter une chanson, j'avais l'air. L'air me revenait le lendemain."]

Complainte de Pérusse

1

Triste départ d'un enfant agréable
Dit pour un temps adieu à ses parents,
Ayant l'espoir, les yeux baignés de larmes,
De revenir au bout de quelques ans.
Mais ce départ doit finir sa carrière;
Par l'ennemi tu dois perde la vie.

2

Cher voyageur, sur une terre étrangère,
Tu dois mourir dans peu de jours ici,
La triste nuit qui termine sa course
Environnée de trois cents assassins,
A coups de flèches des sauvages farouches,
Sans épargner trois autres Canadiens.

3

Ces coups mortels par leur blessure profonde
Font inonder son sang de tout côté.
Cher voyageur, il faut quitter ce monde;
Tu dois mourir dans ce bois étranger.

. . . .

Lament of Pérusse

1

Sad departure of a pleasant child
Says good-bye for a while to his parents,
Hoping, his eyes bathed in tears,
To be back at the end of a few years;
But his departure must end his career,
Through the enemy you must lose your life.

2

Dear voyageur, on strange soil
You must in a few days hence die
By arrows shot by wild savages.
The sad night runs its course
Surrounded by three hundred assassins
Without sparing three other Canadians.

3

These mortal blows by their deep wounds
Spill his blood all about.
Dear voyageur, you must leave this world;
You must die in this strange woods.

. . . .

[This lament contains, in all, eighteen stanzas.]

Selling Toilet Paper in the Subway

Collected by Barbara Kirshenblatt-Gimblett in March 1968 in Downsview, Ontario, and included in her doctoral dissertation, "Traditional
Storytelling in the Toronto Jewish Community" (Indiana University,
1972).

Previous to 1880, few Jews lived in Toronto. By 1934 they numbered
over 34,000 and by 1961 they reached 88,600. The high point of immigration was the period between the two world wars. Where the first
Jews came from England and Germany, the later wave came from
eastern Europe.

This and the following two tales were told by Martin Shanoff, known
as Motl, his Yiddish name, to his family and friends. Motl was born in
Brest-Litovsk, Poland (now Russia), in 1925 and arrived in Toronto,
Canada, in 1929, his home ever since. He was raised in the Jewish
immigrant neighborhood of downtown Toronto in an Orthodox Jewish home and spoke Yiddish as his first language. Motl married while
still in his teens and made his living as a salesman in the ladies' garment
trade. Today he runs his own successful sales agency and lives in an
old and established affluent Jewish neighborhood of Toronto, Forest
Hill, with his wife and children.

Motl is known in his community as an outstanding narrator. His
friends say of him: "You know who tells jokes? It's Motl. He can
rhyme them off." "He's about tops. You can't beat him." Motl himself
distinguishes between the comic narratives of immigrant misadventures given here, which he calls "classics," and jokes. The humor of
the classics lies not in the punch line so much as in "the way you tell
it." Therefore these stories can be told over and over again and retain
their appeal, whereas jokes that rely solely on the punch line are only
funny once and hence are called "oncers."

The present narrative contains the lengthy introductory preamble
characteristic of Motl's immigrant classics. In the preamble, the narrator is explicit about the background necessary for a full appreciation of
his tale. Through his preamble he insures that his use of Yiddish in the
story will successfully convey the special cultural associations that are
essential to the humorous effects he wishes to create. We see how the
narrator himself thinks about his language and culture. These long ex-
planatory preambles, the use of glosses in the course of narration, and
the substitution of immigrant English for Yiddish in some contexts are
all ways of rendering a cultural experience intelligible to those who did
not live through it themselves.

Again in this anecdote the toilet theme is prominent. Having finally
comprehended the washroom, the immigrant, who in other anec-

dotes is relieving himself in milk bottles and on pieces of newspapers, now wants to go into the toilet paper business.

Shanoff told these three tales in the home of the collector's family. The collector was not present, but used a technique now occasionally being adopted (see Milbury-Steen for the Gbande) of instructing the narrators how to record themselves. This method has the advantage of removing the possibly distracting presence of the text-hungry folklorist and permitting a more natural situation, although of course the tape recorder is there. The collector, then a doctoral candidate at Indiana University in Bloomington, knew the Toronto Jewish community and its stellar narrators sufficiently well so that she could instruct her sister by mail how to make a social evening and to invite particular people to come together, chat, and tell jokes, to set up the tape recorder inconspicuously, and to subtly encourage narration. In her letter the collector listed a number of favorite stories of the narrators and suggested that if there were a lull, particular tales might be requested. The session produced 61 stories, of which Motl told 19.

Note on Transcription and Transliteration of Yiddish: The transcription of Yiddish here reflects the basic features of the speaker's dialect pronunciation. The Hebrew-Aramaic component of Yiddish is rendered according to the east European pronunciation. Translations and glosses are based upon Uriel Weinreich's *Modern English-Yiddish Yiddish-English Dictionary* (New York: McGraw Hill, 1968). The Yiddish transliteration system used here is consistent with the one used by the YIVO Institute for Jewish Research, the Library of Congress, and Weinreich's *Dictionary*.

When the Jewish people first came to Canada, or to America for that matter, everybody was looking for a job. A man who could sew carried a sewing machine on his back and would carry it up eight or ten or twelve flights of stairs into a loft and he would ask for a job and if they didn't have a job, he'd walk down the ten or twelve flights of stairs with the little sewing machine on his back and he'd go to another place until he found a place where he could work for a day and they gave him a quarter for the day or whatever he could get. It was better than nothing. And he took it home and this is the way he went and he lived.

In those days there were many sweatshops. Labor was taken unfair advantage of. People worked twelve days a week. They worked seven days a week, twelve, fifteen hours a day, and the pay was very poor. The working conditions were very, very bad. And if anybody was lucky enough to get into some business where they could make a half-decent living, where they didn't have to feed a horse to support them and have a stall and buy oats and where did they get the money for the oats.

Everybody was supporting everybody else. Everybody was trying to help everybody else. So somebody was lucky enough to get into a business where he was making a nice living, he always had fifty people who wanted to become partners with him because everybody wanted to be a partner in a good business, which reminds me of a story I once heard about a fellow who was in New York. He goes into the subway and there are millions of people going into the subway in New York. He suddenly finds he has to go to the washroom.

He says, "*Reb yid* [Mister], I was in da vashroom and dey heven't got any toilet paper."

The man says to him, "I know. I sell it here."

He says, "How much is it?"

The man says, "Three pieces for ten cents." What can he do? He buys. He goes. While he's in the washroom he starts to think. Millions of the people use the subway every day in New York. Millions of people. Three pieces for ten cents. He walks out.

He says, "Tell me, *reb yid*," he says, "how many pieces on a roll?"

The man says, "Three hundred and sixty."

The little man starts figuring out. He says, "Three hundred and sixty pieces divided by three. That's a hundred and twenty times ten. That's twelve dollars. Tell me, *reb yid*," he says, "how much is a roll all together?"

He says, "*Se kost zibetsn sent a rol* [It costs seventeen cents a roll]."

He says, "*Zibetsn sent a rol?* [Seventeen cents a roll?] You get twelve dollars. Millions of people in the subway every day. *Siz dokh take a gite biznes. Efsher zikht ir a partner* [It is really a good business. Maybe you're looking for a partner]."

The man looks at him and says, "*Gi nor a kik. A gantsn tug geyen pishers. Kimt eyn kaker, vil er shoyn zayn a partner* [Just give a look, all day long pissers come and go. Comes one shitter, right away he wants to be a partner]."

The Laughing Hyena

Collected by Barbara Kirshenblatt-Gimblett in March 1968 in Downsview, Ontario, and included in her doctoral dissertation, "Traditional

Storytelling in the Toronto Jewish Community" (Indiana University, 1972).

Told by Martin Shanoff ("Motl"). Again the lengthy informative preamble, so typical of this immigrant genre. Also typical is the subtle, almost imperceptible, shift from either first-person narration or the description of a historical reality—"This is how it was"—to the anecdote proper.

The importance of educating one's children and encouraging them to pursue prestigious and lucrative professions is a demographic fact as well as a leading theme in the anecdotes. Martin tries to explain the emphasis on a university education as the continuation of the traditional Jewish value placed on study, a point that he elaborates in his preamble to a traditional jest thoroughly adapted to the immigrant situation. There are, however, also discontinuities. Tradition-oriented Jews value religious study and many modern Jews value a secular education. Also, in religious circles, learning is seen as an end in itself as well as a source of social prestige, whereas a modern education is usually put to work and brings in money as well as social status. Nonetheless a serious note in the jokes emphasizes how hard the immigrant parents worked to make enough money to send their children to a university so they could become professionals and make a good living.

Annotation: J. Mortimer Hall, ed., *The Unexpurgated Anecdota Americana*, vol. 2 (North Hollywood, Cal.: Brandon, 1968), no. 370, p. 143 (a barker in a one-ring circus tours the south and presents the laughing hyena to onlookers); *Jewish Jokes for the John* (New York: Kanrom Inc., 1967), unpaged (Yankl takes his immigrant grandfather to the zoo in Central Park to see a laughing hyena); *Bibliothèque Erotique*, vol. 2 (London: Society for Sociological and Psychological Research in Literature, 1920), pp. 506–14, under "Wild West Show"; Harry Morgan, *More Rugby Songs* (Aylesbury, Bucks, England: Sphere Books, 1968), pp. 101–3, "The Wild West Show" (non-Jewish); Indiana University Folklore Archives (Michigan Collection, Folder JF6.2.4), collected by Joe Rose, East Lansing, Mich., 1951.

Now you remind me a little bit of the Jewish humor and tradition and how Jewish people always want that their children should have something a little bit better and a little bit more than what they had. They live for, have always lived for, a better life.

Like when I heard a rabbi say in *shul* [synagogue] just recently that the Jewish people have always been losers and for a change they don't want to be losers any more, not since the Arab-Israeli War, not since they woke up, and they want to be a winner. But in the old times they were always losers, for two thousand years.

Jack Stern: The rabbi sounds like Stokely Carmichael.

Martin: No, he was Rabbi Mostel. He says we have been losers. He says we have been losers for two thousand years and he says it's about time we were winners.

However, in the old days, the Jewish people always wanted, if they had two cents, let their children have three cents. And they wanted to have their children, that they should have a better education because they felt that in education, in learning, because even in the Torah it always said, you know, to learn and no matter what you learned, it was important. You were a better person for learning because there is nobody worse off than an uninformed person. So they wanted their children to learn and be knowledgeable.

Lola Gold: If a daughter got married, they even kept the son-in-law for *kest* [room and board, offered by a family to its new son-in-law to enable him to continue his studies without financial worries] in order that he should be able to learn.

Martin: So people wanted their children to learn.

So a man came to this country and he had a tiny little hot dog with a bun and he used to go around with a little wagon like they sell popcorn and he used to sell a hot dog on the street with the bun. And he made a few dollars and he saved a few and he wanted to send his son to college and to a university, so he made a few more and he worked days and Sundays and nights and finally he opened up a little hot dog stand and he served a bigger hot dog and a bigger bun and put on mustard and relish. And these were in the early nineteen hundreds and nineteen fifteen just before the war and after the war into the twenties. And he made money to send his son to university, to college. First he went to high school and then to university.

There was visiting day. The father couldn't speak English too well, so he came to the college on visiting day and he said, "*Vus makhsti zinishi. Ikh bin zeyer tsefridn a di lernst do azey git* [How are you, my son. I am very satisfied that you are learning so well here]."

And he goes with him to the class and he sits in the same seat with his son and the teacher gets up at the blackboard and he says, "Ladies and gentlemen, welcome to the class. We are very glad to have the parents here enjoying this session with the children and we want to show you how your children are learning at this college." And he continues to say and he says, "Today we are going to take up the subject of the laughing hyena."

And the father says to the son, "*Zinishi, vus zugt er dortn, der lerer?* [Son, what is he saying there, the teacher?]" *Lerer* is a teacher.

"*Er zugt, tate, az haynt vet men lernen vegn di lakhedike khaye* [He says, Father, that today we will study the laughing animal (Hyena)]."

So the father thinks, "For this I send my son to college to learn about *lakhedike khayes* [laughing animals]? Well, let's see."

And the teacher goes on. And he says, "First you must realize that the laughing hyena has three characteristics."

The father pokes his son in the side and says, "*Zinishi, zug mir, vus zugt dortn der moyre* [Son, what is the teacher saying there?]" *Moyre* [fear] is also a Jewish word meaning teacher.

"*Er zugt, tate, a di lakhedike khaye hot drayerley mayles* [He says, Father, that the laughing hyena has three virtues]."

Well, the father says, "*Aroysgevorfene gelt. In drerd mayn gelt. Far dus hob ikh dir geshikt lernen in kaledzh? Tse lernen veygn a lakhedike khaye mit dray mayles? Aroysgevorfene. Eh!* [Thrown out money. My money is wasted (literally: in the ground). Is this what I sent you to college to learn? To learn about a laughing animal with three virtues? Thrown out. Eh!]" He sits and he listens.

"The first characteristic," the teacher says, "is that the laughing hyena eats once a week."

"*Zinishi* [Son]," the father says, "*Vus zugt er dortn der bok mit di gleyzer?* [What is he saying there, the he-goat with the glasses?]" *Bok* [he-goat] is not a word meaning teacher. It means idiot and *gleyzer* [glasses] means with glasses, because the father was getting a little perturbed. He says, "*Vus zugt er dortn der bok mit di gleyzer?* [What is he saying there, the he-goat with the glasses?]"

"*Er zugt, tate as di lakhedike khaye est eyn mul a vokh* [He says, Father, that the laughing hyena eats once a week]."

Well, the father started to holler and *shelt* [curse] and he says, "*Aroysegvorfn mayn gelt. Ikh hob dir geshikt in skul zolstekh kenen lernen* [My money thrown away. I sent you to school to enable you to learn]. You should be able to help me in the hot dog stand. I'm getting a big business. I'm going to open up a second stand. And he is teaching you about *lakhedike khayes* [laughing animals]?"

So he sits there, and the teacher says, "And the second characteristic is that he moves his bowels once a month."

"*Di lakhedike khaye, zinishi, vus zugt er dortn?* [The laughing animal, Son, what is he saying there?]"

"*Er zugt, tate, as di lakhedike khaye kakt eyn mul a monat* [He says, Father, that the laughing hyena shits once a month]."

"*Aroysgevorfene gelt, in drerd mit di beheyme, in gantsn aroysgevorfene gelt, in drerd mit di beheyme, in gantsn aroysgevorfn. Ni, meyle, lome shoyn hern vayter vus zugt er* [Thrown out money, to hell with the animal, completely wasted. So, anyway, let's hear already what more he has to say]."

"And the third characteristic is that the laughing hyena has sex once a year."

"*Zinishi, der bok mit de gleyzer, der moyre, der lerer, vus zugt er dortn mit mayles dortn?* [Son, the he-goat with the glasses, the teacher, the teacher, what is he saying there about virtues?]"

"*Er zugt, tate, a di lakhedike khaye trent eyn mul a yur* [He says, Father, that the laughing hyena fucks once a year]."

"*Far dus hob ikh dir geshikt lernen in kaledz in aza instetushn in nortkerolayne? Zolst zikh oyslernen vus tit zikh oyf der velt, tse lernen veygn lakhedike khayes? Zug mir eyn zakh zinishi. Ikh vil epes visn. Di lakhedike khaye, esn est er eyn mol a vokh. Kakn kakt er eyn mol a monat. Trenen, trent er eyn mol a yur. Vus lakht er derfun?* [For this I sent you to study in college, in such an institution, in North Carolina? You should learn what goes on in the world or about laughing hyenas? Tell me one thing, Son. I want to know something. The laughing hyena, he eats once a week. He shits once a month. He fucks once a year. So what does he have to laugh about?]"

An Unexpected Donation

Collected by Barbara Kirshenblatt-Gimblett in March 1968 in Downsview, Ontario, and included in her doctoral dissertation, "Traditional Storytelling in the Toronto Jewish Community" (Indiana University, 1972).

Told by Martin Shanoff ("Motl"). Once more the long preamble and the first-person narration suggesting that this is indeed a true story and then the subtle slip into the fictional tale. The punch line is a traditional formula customarily used to thank one who has given charity. A similar story, though not close enough to be a variant, is in *Jewish Jokes for the John*, where a man on his way to console a widow enters the wrong apartment by mistake, makes love to the woman there, and upon leaving bids farewell using the traditional formula for taking leave of a mourner.

The Jewish language is not really a language. It's unique because it is a slang. It was picked up in the Warsaw ghettos and in years long ago as a jargon type of language and over a period of years it was kept up by the Jewish people in the old country and it became very dear to their hearts and they referred to it as *mamelushn* [mother tongue; esp. the Yiddish language]—the language of their mothers, or their mothers and fathers. And in the last few years, here in Canada and North America, the Jewish language has been dying out to a degree because it has not been used by the new generations and even in Israel they talk Hebrew and not Jewish. So it is unique in its own right, and it is a language that many people want to keep up and support because it is really a beautiful language and has a lot of very good humor because Jewish people always wanted to laugh at situations even at times when they should have cried. They found, uh, solace in the fact that they could laugh and enjoy life even though they had much pain.

Now, there are many stories that are told, that could be told if your father would stop shaking the glasses and stop drinking so much.

Now in the old days when Jewish people came to this country, everybody was poor. And, no matter how poor you were, you always had a few pennies, a few *groshn* [grosz; penny, small coin] a few cents that you could give to somebody who was not as well off as you. You know the old story that used to go around about the poor person who had no shoes who felt very bad until he met someone who had no feet and then he didn't feel so bad anymore. So, Jewish people always felt that no matter how bad it was, there must be somebody worse off, and they took salvation in this thought at times, and they tried to help other people by giving *tsdoke* [charity, alms], by doing a good deed. And they'd give donations to just about anything under the sun, and there used to be men coming around that said they were from Palestine, . . . from anywhere. And they were collecting money and they used to put it in little *pishkes* [alms boxes] or boxes that you had on the back of the door. There was for the Jewish National Fund. There was for the Home of the Orphans, the Home of the Widows. They had more homes than I could count. But . . . we . . . donated. Nu, there's always pennies. And sometimes they'd give—like people have a tendency to gamble on seven, and eleven is a lucky number—well, in Jewish, eighteen, which means *khay* [alive], is very lucky, and you'd always put eighteen cents into the *pishke* [alms box] and if you were lucky enough to have thirty-six cents, which was a multiple of eighteen, you put in twice eighteen, or three times eighteen. And even today, people continue to put in multiples of eighteen when they buy, um, Israel bonds or when they . . . do anything good or give gifts or multiples of thirteen for bar mitzvahs [a boy's coming of age and assumption of religious responsibility at the age of thirteen].

Well, in the old days they—as I said—they collected money, and there were men going around. And most of the Jewish people, who were very fine people, they wanted to give donations, they felt it was a good deed done, that something good for them to pile up these *mitzvahs* [good deeds] to draw on, on a rainy day when they really needed something, when they were really down and out, they felt they'd have a big pile of *mitzvahs*, like my mother used to say, so that they could draw on them.

For when they needed it.

So this was fine, and we gave money, but some of the fellows got a little fed up with, in the business world, with all of these guys keep coming to the doors and asking for money. So one day, a fellow, Ben Rosenberg, living, eh, working in the place, next door to us comes in and says, "Look. I can't speak a good Jewish. You talk to this fellow, and tell him that there's a new Jewish district opened up on Jarvis Street." Well, Jarvis Street happened to be a red light district.

But he was tired of the same guy who came by and told him he hadn't been here for two years but he was just here last month.

So, the guy came in, and we said to the man, "*Reb yid, Sitsakh [es hot zikh] geofe . . . giefent a naye yidishe gegnt af dzharvis strit* [Mister, a new Jewish neighborhood has opened on Jarvis Street]."

So the man went over to Jarvis Street. He knocked on the door. And the madam of the house of ill repute answered the door, and she said, "What are you doing here?"

And the man with the long beard looked at her and said, "*Ikh bin an uremer yid fin ertsisroel gekimen zamlen gelt far di yesoymim vus viln khasene hubn* [I am a poor Jew from the land of Israel come to collect money for the orphans who want to get married]."

The woman didn't know what he said, but she thought she knew what he wanted so she took him inside. She introduces him to a girl. He looks at the girl and says, "*Ikh bin an uremer yid gekimen fin ertsisroel zamlen gelt far di yesoymim un almunes vus viln khasene hubn* [I am a poor Jew come from the land of Israel to gather money for the orphans and widows who want to get married]."

Well, she doesn't know what he's saying, but she assumes she knows what he wants. So she takes him upstairs to her room. She goes in the door. As she goes in the door, the man turns around and looks on the back of the door for the little *pishkes* or boxes, to see if there's any money there, if it's a good Jewish home, and as he turns around she's already got her clothes off.

Well, not wanting to seem ungrateful, he partook.

Silver: Of what?

Martin: She had to actually [laughter of audience] undress him and she took off his *paltn* [overcoat]. Then she took off his *mantl* [coat]. Then she took off his *hemdl* [shirt]. Then she took off his *talis* [*taliskutn* four-cornered tasseled undergarment worn by Orthodox Jews]. Then she took off his *gartl* [belt; esp. belt worn during prayer]. The *gartl* was the strap they wore around the waist to separate the *milkhiks* [dairy foods] from the *fleyshiks* [meat foods] [audience laughs]. Then she took off his *hoyzn* [trousers]. Then she took off his *intervesh* [underwear].

To make a long story short, he got dressed and put on his *intervesh*, his *hoyzn*, his *gartl*, his *taliskutn*, his *hemdl*, his *laybserdak* [the undergarment worn by Orthodox Jews which covers the chest and upper part of the back, and which has an opening for the head and tassels on the four corners]—that's the *taliskutn* again—and the, uh, *rekl* and the *paltn* and the *mantl*.

He got dressed, and, the girl held out her hand. He took her hand very graciously and said, "*Me zol derlebn iber a yur zolt ir vayter gebn aza sheyne neduve* [May we live to see another year, may you again give such a nice donation]." [Audience laughs.]

United States

Winabijou (Nanabush) Brings on the Flood

Collected by Richard M. Dorson in the summer of 1946, the first text in the wilderness hamlet of Hessel, the second in the forest reservation of Watersmeet, in Michigan's Upper Peninsula. Reprinted from Dorson, *Bloodstoppers and Bearwalkers* (Cambridge, Mass.: Harvard University Press, 1952, 1972), pp. 43–47.

The first text was collected from Mike Sogwin, an Ojibwa, about forty. The second text was told the same summer of 1946 in Ojibwa by John Pete, in his seventies, and simultaneously translated by his companion, George Cadotte.

In *Tales of the North American Indians* (Cambridge, Mass., 1929), Stith Thompson reprints a Menomini text of "Manabozho's Wolf Brother," pp. 10–11, and notes, p. 277, "This myth is common to the entire Central Woodland group of tribes."

Motifs: F420.5.2.1.3 "Hero drowned by water-spirits"; D651 "Transformation to defeat enemies"; A1010 "Deluge"; A811 "Earth brought up from bottom of primeval water"; A812 "Earth diver"; D482.1 "Transformation: stretching tree"; A2200 "Cause of animal characteristics."

The Flood story is the Chippewa classic, which I heard six different times. The main incidents always remain the same, but details vary. George Pine of L'Anse—so old and tottery he can rise to his feet only with a supreme effort—said that when the wolf jumped over the little stream, he landed in the middle of the Pacific Ocean, and the big animals in the ocean killed him. George ends up the history saying, "We're on four lengths of a big pine tree." Rose Holliday ends with Winabijou grinding the sand between his palms until he had a large handful, then throwing it over the water saying, " 'Let there be land.' A bunch of islands grew up. Was it the Apostle Islands or the Thousand Islands?" Mike Sogwin documents the growth of Winabijou's island with his own Hessel shoreline, which has steadily expanded in his lifetime.

The Sogwins localize the serpent shooting in their own neighborhood. Nanabush knelt down on the beach at High Rollway and shot his arrow twenty-seven miles across the Straits to Cross Village (an Indian reservation) in the Lower Peninsula. You can see the prints of his knees in the sand today, in two large hollows. John disagrees with brother Mike, saying they are the marks of his buttocks—which shows how tradition can vary even within one family.

At certain points in the narrative the tellers and listeners always break into laughter. They do so when Winabijou plunges the arrows deeper into the Serpents, while pretending to pull them out, a description accompanied by graphic gestures of twisting and prodding; when the bear claws and the snake squeezes the stump into which Winabijou has changed himself; and of course when Winabijou sits helplessly on top the pine tree puffing at his own excrement. But toward the text *in toto* they are devout and serious fundamentalists.

Winabijou (Nanabush) is both serious culture hero and comedian, endowed with considerable power, and he belongs to a legendary antiquity. He lies at the heart of Ojibwa mythology, and his adventures provide explanations of the world's creation, the traits of animals, the properties of plants, and other facts and forces in nature. On another plane his escapades provide the family with surefire humorous entertainment. Winabijou is a regular rascal, always hungry, scheming, greedy, and an old "letch" to boot, not above seducing his own daughter. The Indians know his character, relish his predicaments, and applaud his come-uppances.

Some of his scrapes are laughable for any audience. In the flood story Winabijou takes refuge on top of a pine tree, and there sits with his face barely above water. I could not quite understand the point of the situation. Dainty Mrs. Holliday finally told me the point, for she had expurgated the story in the first telling. It seems that when she reached that episode she looked around at the others in the group, nodding and winking and tacitly asking, "Shall I tell the professor?" They shook their heads in a strong negative. I had my head buried in my notebook scribbling down her words, and saw none of this. Later in the evening our inhibitions somewhat relaxed, and she added the omission. The flood waters eddying around the treetop kept floating Winabijou's excrement back in his face as he tried to blow it away, while holding desperately on to the submerged branches with his hands. Thus was Winabijou punished for his mischief-making.

All North and South American Indians know the trickster, under varying names. Even with one tribe, like the Ojibwa, the generic name changes slightly in nearly every village. Longfellow spelled it Manabozho, which, accented on the first syllable, sounds much like Winabijou, the form I found most prevalent.

The Flood

Listening to a living tale of the Deluge and Creation gives one a queasy feeling. Here is Genesis before anyone wrote it down. While this myth does not come first chronologically in the Winabijou cycle, it leads in popularity. The plot hinges on Winabijou's search for the killers of his chum, the Wolf, his vengeance, and the reprisal the gods then visit on him. I give here two versions, since the first has details on the killing of the Wolf not in the longer account.

The Wolf is Killed (Mike Sogwin)

In the early days the Wolf came to live with Nanabush, like a dog, you know. Every day the Wolf would go out with his bow and arrow to bring in the meat, to "bring home the bacon." Maybe he'd get a deer. So the other animals got jealous because the Wolf wasn't doing any work; he'd just bring in the meat and then take it easy while they fixed it up. So they decided to kill him.

Next morning Nanabush wakes them up and the Wolf goes out as usual. (This was some time in the winter.) He sees a pretty spotted white deer. Nanabush says, "Why don't you get it, it would make a nice hide." But when the Wolf gets close, the fawn starts to run away. It stops and turns around to look, and when it sees the Wolf coming it runs some more. (The fawn was in the plot, you see.) The deer runs to the lake where the trap was; it was ice covered with snow, but with some watery holes under the snow. The Wolf falls in and gets drowned.

Nanabush is ready for breakfast, and wonders where his chum was. He waits four days, and has no eats. So he gets mad and says he is going to kill all the animals. So they decided to give him back the Wolf —they knew he was dead, of course. Nanabush says to the Wolf, "You're just a ghost, you know; you take care of the dead people and I'll take care of the live."

That's why people die now. It's the same thing as Adam and Eve. If the animals hadn't killed Nanabush's chum, people wouldn't die today, and the world would be overcrowded.

Winabijou Looks for the Wolf (John Pete)

The Wolf was Winabijou's adopted brother, and killed meat for him, always moose. The other animals had to dry it, hang it up, and smoke it, and that displeased their friends the gods. So one day the gods thought they'd get him. They enticed him to take a trail across the river, he fell through a hole in the ice and was swimming near the entrance of their cave down below, and they grabbed ahold of him. They kept him captive quite a while, then killed him.

Next morning Winabijou started out to look for him. The trails of the previous hunts led home, but he finally struck one which led to the hole in the ice. Then he started to cry, and tears fell down his cheeks. Now he wanted revenge, so he wished that the Thunders (the good gods) would send the summer warmth right away, to bring the Serpents (the bad gods) up from their cave. In four days the ice melted and the river began to flow.

Then he started searching the river for likely remains. He looked up and saw a kingfisher sitting on a sharp cliff, looking down at a pool of water. Every once in a while he'd see the fragments of the Wolf and sneak down and get them. Winabijou asked the kingfisher why he was looking so intently. Finally the kingfisher told him that he was eating the Wolf who had been killed by the gods in a cave close by, underneath the ground. Winabijou wanted to know if they ever came out of there to travel around. "Yes, they come out to bask in the sun in a clearing, but they are closely guarded by snakes and birds and turtles, so it is hard to surprise them." Winabijou said he would pay him for that information, and he gave him a necklace of shells which had belonged to the Wolf. That is why the kingfisher has a white band around his neck today.

But Winabijou was angry because the kingfisher had been eating part of his brother. So he asked him to come down and sit beside him, so he could ask some more questions. But Winabijou really wanted to twist his neck. When he grabbed at him the kingfisher flew away, and Winabijou just caught a tuft of hair. So now the kingfisher's head has a tuft sticking up.

Next day Winabijou asked for good hot weather to bring the gods out. He was at the pool way ahead of daylight, and started making a bow and arrow and spears. He wanted the water boiling hot, and sure enough it started to steam. But the gods have many sentinels, and they showed up first—lizards, snakes, crocodiles. They stretched out on the grass: "We'll have a good sleep here." Winabijou turned himself into a charred stump, an old hemlock stump, quite high. Pretty soon the gods came up, in the shape of bears. One was a big brown bear, the other was a white one. The sentinels said to them, "Everything is prepared for you to bask here." Brown bear looked around—"I never noticed that stump before." "Oh yes, that's been there." "Oh no, I'm going over to see." So he walked over there and clawed the charred stump from the top down, scraping the bark off. After the fourth time the bear walked off, saying "No, that's a stump." Winabijou was afraid he couldn't stand that clawing and would scream out. He kept his bow right against his body, so it wouldn't be seen. The sentinels kept arguing back and forth. "That's a stump." "No, it isn't a stump." Finally the big black boa constrictor walked over and wrapped himself around it three or four times, and started to tighten up. Winabijou didn't dare make a move, but he was just about choked up when the snake let go. The boa constrictor said, "That's a stump."

"Well, we're all going to have a sleep." But one little turtle wasn't satisfied, kept looking at the stump to see it move. Finally he went to sleep too. So Winabijou came over and shot the brown bear with the speared arrow, right under the forepaw, in the vitals. The bear went "Poh." Then he shot the white bear, saying "You're the ones that ate my brother up." All the animals jumped into the river, afraid, and dug for their cave. The bears went with them, the arrows still sticking in them; they weren't killed outright.

Winabijou goes off on his wanderings again. He put a reed around his head to disguise himself. An old toad-lady comes along, carrying a lot of basswood bark. She was inquisitive and accused him, "You are Winabijou." "No, I'm not Winabijou," he said in a singsong voice. "Don't you know what would happen to us if I were Winabijou?" He was trying to trick her into answering, he wanted to find out all she knew. She began singing, "Winabijou shot the Ogema (the gods), I'm going to draw the spears out of their sides." He tried to find out more and asked her, "What are you going to do with all that basswood?" She said, "We're going to tie up the earth with it, and string it around the world like telephone wires. When Winabijou touches the strings, the gods will know where he is and ask for water, to flood him out."

She kept suspecting he was Winabijou, and turned to go. So he picked up part of a root, hit her on the head, and killed her. (The blow knocked her swelling down, so the toad is little today; he used to be big like the other animals.) Then he cut the inside out of her and put on her hide and clothes, and went on to the kings' place. They lived in a regular wigwam now, above ground, for the summer. The sentries saw him and thought he was the old toad, and told him the kings were in bad shape, and he should come along right away. Winabijou sang a song like the old woman, "I'm going to draw out the arrows." Then he said, "I'm going to do it different this time. Everybody get out, I'm going to do it all alone. It's getting serious now."

When he was alone with the kings he grabbed the arrows and pushed them further inside, tearing and twisting until he had killed them. "You are the ones who killed my brother!" he said as they lay there dying.

He noticed the Wolf's hide over the door so he took it along with him. When he came out they all knew right away who he was. The flood started. Winabijou kept running on higher land, but the water followed him. He saw a badger and asked him to dig a hole where they could hide, and promised to paint him up nice. (Like with lipstick. The badger has stripes across his face today, you know.) But in the hole the badger made a vile smell, so Winabijou got mad and killed him. Then he had to go on again.

Every time he got to a higher level the water rose some more. Finally he reached the summit of a hill where a big pine tree was standing. He asked it if he could find refuge there, by sitting on the branch. The tree said, "That's what you get for all your wrongdoing. Now the gods are mad at us and we'll all perish." But he let Winabijou climb up the branches to the top. The water rose up to his mouth. He asked the pine tree, "Can't you stretch a little?" The tree stretched four times its own height. "That's all I can do for you." The water rose again till it came up to his mouth, and stayed there. Winabijou sat on a branch holding on to the treetop with his hands, just able to breathe above water. He had to evacuate, and an evil current floated his stuff back to him, so he had to keep blowing it away as it swirled around the tree. That was part of his punishment for his killing of the gods.

Now the water animals showed up. They had nowhere to go, because the land was all covered with water, and they were tired swimming around. So Winabijou asked the loon to dive down and bring him up some earth. The loon went down and stayed a long while; then his body came up feet first, drowned. Winabijou blew on him to revive him. Next to go down was the otter. He was gone quite a little while, and drowned too. Winabijou brought him to life by breathing on him. Next to go down was the muskrat. He was the longest of any. All he could do was grab with both paws and feet on the bottom, and was lucky enough to hang on to some earth. He floated up drowned, but still had the earth in his paws and feet. Winabijou blew on him too to bring him back. Then Winabijou took the earth, dried it out in the sun, and threw it out over the water. It turned out to be a little island.

All the water animals went there to make their home. In order to reward them he told them what they could eat—the muskrat could eat rushes, the loon could eat muck from the bottom, the otter could eat fish. Then he sent the fox around the island to see how big it was. The first day he came back early in the morning. The second day he came back a little later. After a week or so he didn't come back until late in the afternoon. On the tenth day he didn't come back at all. (That's why you often see a fox trotting alongside the shore today.) Then Winabijou knew the world was ready for living. He called to the gods above and below to come down and live on this earth. That's Christ and the Devil. He wanted them to be in trouble.

The Mermaid

Collected by Richard M. Dorson in Calvin, Michigan in 1952. Printed in Dorson, *Negro Folktales in Michigan* (Cambridge, Mass.: Harvard University Press, 1956), pp. 147–48, and Dorson, *American Negro Folktales* (Greenwich, Conn.: Fawcett, 1967), pp. 251–52.

Told by James Douglas Suggs. A gifted Negro raconteur, then sixty-five, Suggs related 170 oral narratives in many genres. For his songs see Dorson, "Negro Songs from the Repertoire of J. D. Suggs" (music transcription by George List, headnotes by Neil Rosenberg) in *Folklore and Folk Music Archivist* 9 (Fall 1966): 3–39.

Although I have collected eight Afro-American variants of this well-structured legendary tradition, it has never been reported in print by other collectors. The most I can locate are a couple of incidental mermaid motifs: B81.13.4 "Mermaid gives mortals gold from sea bottom," which turns up in only one of my texts; B81.9.1 "Mermaid's hair reaches her waist"; and B81.2 "Mermaid marries man" (all cited in Baughman's index), but they belong to quite different tales. Most tellers place the mermaid's home in the mid-Atlantic, but Sarah Hall localized it near the mouth of the Mississippi, while Sarah Jackson actually saw the mermaid's hole by the bank of the Alabama River.

For the life of Suggs see *American Negro Folktales*, pp. 59–64, and for a discussion of his narrative art see Dorson, *Folklore: Selected Essays* (Bloomington: Indiana University Press, 1972), "Oral Styles of American Folk Narrators," pp. 99–146 passim.

Before they had any steam, ships were sailing by sails, you know, across the Atlantic. The Atlantic was fifteen miles deep, and there were mermaids in those days. And if you called anybody's name on the ship, they would ask for it, say, "Give it to me." And if you didn't give it to them they would capsize the ship. So the captain had to change the men's names to different objects—hatchet, ax, hammer, furniture. Whenever he wanted a man to do something, he had to call him, "Hammer, go on deck and look out." The mermaid would holler, "Give me hammer." So they throwed the hammer overboard to her, and the vessel would proceed on. The captain might say, "Ax, you go on down in the kindling room start a fire in the boiler; it's going dead." Then the mermaid says, "Give me ax." So they have to throw her an iron ax. Next day he says, "Suit of furniture, go down in the stateroom and make up those beds." And the mermaid yells, "Give me a suit of furniture." So they had to throw a whole suit of furniture overboard.

One day he made a mistake and forgot and said, "Sam, go in the kitchen and cook supper." The mermaid right away calls, "Give me

Sam." They didn't have anything on the ship that was named Sam; so they had to throw Sam overboard. Soon as Sam hit the water she grabbed him. Her hair was so long she could wrap him up—he didn't even get wet. And she's swimming so fast he could catch breath under the water. When she gets home she goes in, unwraps Sam out of her hair, says: "Oooh, you sure do look nice. Do you like fish?" Sam says, "No, I won't even cook a fish." "Well, we'll get married." So they were married.

After a while Sam begin to step out with other mermaids. His girl friend became jealous of him and his wife, and they had a fight over Sam. The wife whipped her, and told her, "You can't see Sam never again." She says, "I'll get even with you." So one day Sam's girl friends asked him, didn't he want to go back to his native home. He says yes. So she grabs him, wraps him in her hair, and swum the same fastness as his wife did when she was carrying him, so he could catch breath. When she come to land she put him onto the ground, on the bank. "Now if he can't do me no good he sure won't do her none." That was Sam's experience in the mermaid's home in the bottom of the sea.

Then he told the others how nice her home was, all fixed up with the furniture and other things. There weren't any men down there—guess that's why they ain't any mermaids any more. Sam said they had purple lips, just like women are painted today. You see pictures of mermaids with lips like that. In old days people didn't wear lipstick, and I think they got the idea from seeing those pictures.

Sam told the people the mermaid's house was built like the alligator's. He digs in the bank at water level; then he goes up—nature teaches him how high to go—then digs down to water level again, and there he makes his home, in rooms ten to twenty feet long. The mermaid builds in the wall of the sea like the alligator. Sam stayed down there six years. If he hadn't got to co'ting he'd a been there yet, I guess.

The Legend of Yoho Cove

Collected by Richard M. Dorson in Machias, Maine in July 1956 and printed in *Western Folklore* 18 (1959): 329–31.

"Uncle Curt" Morse, a celebrated humorist of Kennebec, Maine, suddenly turned serious when he related the following local legend. It turns out to be an example of the mysterious story Rudolph Altrocchi searched for as an ancestor of Tarzan plots, and uncovered in remote corners of literature, including a Persian manuscript of 1830. But he could find no contemporary traces (*Sleuthing in the Stacks*, Cambridge, 1944, pp. 95–101). Archer Taylor, knowing Altrocchi's quest, spotted an American folktale replica in Leonard Roberts' *South from Hell-fer-Sartin* (Lexington, 1955, p. 162), "Origin of Man," and supplied an introductory note to two more Kentucky texts collected by Roberts and printed in *Western Folklore* 16 (1957, pp. 48–51), under "A Long-Sought Parallel Comes to Light." Roberts refers to two others he recorded.

Uncle Curt's text resembles pretty closely the story outline given by Altrocchi and Roberts: the wild man, his mating with a civilized girl, her rescue after some years, and the wild man's tearing in two their baby and throwing one half after her. An element unmentioned by Altrocchi appears in four of Roberts' texts and that of Morse, the naming of the wild man as Yeahoh (in Kentucky) or Yoho (in Maine), from sounds uttered by the creature himself. It should be noted that Roberts' tales, although told in the Kentucky hills, all contain mention of ships, shore, and water as the avenue of escape for the captive woman (or man); Curt, living on the Atlantic coast, could report the episode as having occurred down the next cove. Altrocchi cites a French-Canadian version, where the girl also escapes via the ocean from her gorilla-mate.

For a discussion of Curt Morse as a master folk teller, see Dorson, *Folklore: Selected Essays* (Bloomington: Indiana University Press, 1972), pp. 99–146 passim.

Motifs: F567 "Wild man. Man lives alone in wood like a beast"; T471.2 "Wild man as ravisher of women"; R11.1.1 "Abduction of girl by half-bestial man"; S11.1 "Father mutilates children."

[*Tape Recording*]

DORSON: This is July the 13th, Friday the 13th [1956], a very good day to record folklore, and I am again in Machias with Curt Morse the famous storyteller, in the hospitable home of his daughter, Mrs. Eva Hall, and Curt is going to tell some of his yarns. Now there's one about how Yoho Cove got its name. How does that go, Curt?

CURT MORSE: Cove about two mile below where I live called Yoho Cove and the old fellas years ago allus said there was some kind of wild man lived there, and all they could understand he holler, "Yoho, yoho" all the time, especially at night. So he kinda slacked off and there was some of the natives down around the shore, don't 'cha know, and took kinda of a dugout canoe I call it, dug out of tree, went across there raspberryin'. Well they got about ready to come home and they heard this Yoho hollerin'—they call him a Yoho. So before they reached the boat this fella, this man, ran out and grabbed this girl and took her back in the woods with him and left the rest screechin'. So they went home and a little while afterwards why they . . . it kinda died out, don't 'cha know? They missed the girl a lot. Well they thought she was dead and about two years afterwards or about a year and a half afterwards they had kinda forgot about it and they was over there raspberryin' or blueberryin' again and they heard this screechin' and they looked up and this girl there, their relation, was runnin' and screechin' for help. So she had a baby with her chasin' along—a year old—some little year-old baby, somethin' like that. And she—they got her in the canoe anyway, started off from the shore. And the Yoho come down on the shore and caught the baby, or took the baby, tore it apart, tore it to pieces, throwed one part at the canoe as it was leavin', and took the other part back in the woods. So it's been called Yoho Cove ever since. That's all of it that I know about. It's always been called Yoho Cove.

DORSON: Mrs. Eva Hall, you've heard that, you say?

EVA HALL: I've heard it since I was a little girl, I've heard that story.

DORSON: Who'd you hear it from?

EVA HALL: Oh, I don't know, uncles, father, people who lived around there. We always heard that story. Whether it was true or not, I guess it was handed down from way back years ago when people were quite uncivilized.

CURT MORSE: Probably about a hundred and fifty years ago.

Paree at the Carnival

Collected by Richard M. Dorson in Sault Sainte Marie, Michigan in April 1946. Printed in the *Journal of American Folklore* 61 (1948): 121–23.

Told by Burt Mayotte, an auto mechanic of French-Canadian extraction.

The genre of American dialect stories has not been noticed by folklorists. A floating joke or anecdote in standard English may be adapted to the dialect, or an overheard saying or relation in immigrant English may be picked up by the "dialectician," as expert tellers of these stories, like Mayotte, are sometimes called. He avers that the present narrative, one of the most popular in his repertoire, developed from Burt's own account of his visit to the carnival when a boy, which was then repeated by his grandfather, who spoke English in the French-Canadian style, whereupon Burt then mimicked his grandfather's rendition.

For a description of Burt Mayotte as a storyteller see Dorson, *Folklore: Selected Essays* (Bloomington: Indiana University Press, 1972), "Oral Styles of American Folk Narrators," pp. 99–146 passim.

Hi get up very very hearly and walk four, five, nine mile, till Hi pass hon de cittay where is de carni*val*. Before time is come for djiné, Hi have fin' de place, and Hi hear de musik, and Hi see all de pipple pay de fi' cents and pass in de carni*val*. Before long time some feller Hi know is come dere too and pay de fi' cents for Paree to pass in de car-ni*valle*, an' Hi see de most beautiful ting Hi never have see before. Dere is much musik an' manee strannge ting wich you never believe have been make an' put hall in won place for fi' cents. Hi see won of de most wonder*ful* ting is called de merry-go-horse. She have many horse wat galloop roun' and roun', and make one hell of a hurree, to get no place fast. Hi would like veree much for galloop hon dem horse but Hi don't have de fi' cents.

So Hi pass over hon annudder strannge ting which is call de hup-go-weel. Hi don' know from w'ere she's get hall de buggee seat, or who have a buggee w'at can spare such big w'eels, but Hi see dat wid my hown eye. Great big w'eel wich roll all de time in one place, an' manee manee buggee seat is hook on de run. De pipple is sit on de seat—de w'eel is go roun', an' heveryone get a chance to pass hon de sky an' pass down to go hup some more. Hi would love for to do, such a won-nerful ting, but hagain Hi don' have de fi' cents. Seem like heveryting, from de time Hi have buy my tickette, she's want fi' cents.

You know Hi have see so many ting, de sun is go down, an' de first ting Hi know, is time for suppay. Hi ham veree much hongry, as Hi don't have no djiné eider. But dat's because Hi still don' got fi' cents. So Hi listen on de beauti*ful* mu*sik*, an' Hi pass around in de carni*valle* to manee odder beautiful tings until is pass on my nose a grande beeg butiful smell. Hi foller dat smell an' wat do you tink Hi fin'? A nice beeg place wid manee tings for heat, an' nothing is cost more dan fi' cents. Hot puppay, you should see dat! She's a ground up meat, all squeeze in a swim suit, an' wrap hup in a bun wit' leetle bit moustarde hon de top. Honlee fi' cents! Et Maudit! De popnuts, de peacorn, de hass-crim, some more honlee fi' cents. An' Paree is have no monee. Dat make me feel too hemptee on de bellay, so Hi pass hoff dat place.

An' den Hi hear de most butiful musik wat have never pass on de hear of man. Some crazee buggaire, he's holler hout loud, so hevery-bodee hear, "Twenty-fi' dollaire for ten mi*noots*." Et Maudit, Hi fin' dat place fas'. Dat's too mooch monee for ten mi*noots*. You should see wat Hi fin', small square floor midout a roof an' a rope all haround for a wall. Manee manee peeple is dere an' can see dere is four *coin* hon dat floor. An' won dam' fool hon de meedle is try for tell heverybodee h'it h'is a reeng. Moost a be, Hi'm crazee, han heverybodee helse h'is right, she look more like ha square dan a reeng, but Hi'm get away from de main ting, Hi don' come dere for argu*ment*, Hi come dere for de twenty-fi' dollaire. Hi got lots of min*oots*. She's tol' me, eef Hi stay ten min*oots* hon dees reeng square, wit' nudder man who is sit dere, he pay me de twenty-fi' dollaire. Maudit hell, Hi ham mos' happy man hon de hirt'. Wid twenty-fi' dollaire Hi can buy dat sapré merry-go-horse, Hi can ride on dee hup-go-weel, Hi can h'eat heveryting wat please my heye. Twenty-fi' dollaire, she's ha lots of monee for ten min*oots*. So Hi clim' hover dee rope and says, "Hi'll stay dee ten min*oots*."

She's have hanudder man hon dat reeng square. He seet hon dee cornaire, wid his head hang down, han he is all wrap up in a carpette. She don' look like much of a man. Sapré! Wat a commosse*eeion*. Heverybodee she's commense to hollaire. Some h'is hollaire "Hooray," some h'is hollaire for raspberray, wich hain't veree funnee, h'as Hi don't see henny raspberray dere. But heverybodee hollaire hennyway. An' den de man wat make beeg noise hon de first place, h'is make dem stop, and commense to spik on de pipple, "Ladees an' gentle*mans:* Hover hon dis cornaire, we have dee man for wich we pay twenty-fi' dollaire hon hennybody wat stay wid him for ten min*oots*. Stan' up, Tigaire." Han dees man is trow away de bat'robe, han raise hup hees head, han stan' hon dee meedle wid two hans hover de head. Et Maudjit—heverybodee tink, she's look prettee dam tough dis man. She's got hon de small shoes, an' de small boy's pants. He have much hair on dee bellee, han he look like dee Tigaire for w'ich he is call. Den he go back and sid down. Han dee beeg noise, wat hollaire so much, he's look hover h'at me, han holler some more, "Han hon dees cornaire, ladees an' gentle*mans*, we have dee man wat wants twenty-fi' dollaire."

So Hi trow away my jackette, Hi pull hoff my chemise, Hi stan' hon dee meedle, han Hi look prettee dam tough too. We shake dee hand, de bell is ring, an' Hi commense to see dat twenty-fi' dollaire. Dat's gonna be prettee heezay. But vait a min*oot*. Dis maudjit tigaire, she's grab won han', han den first teeng you know, halmost Hi don't be there hatall. But you know, a good French*man*, he don't stan' for dat. Han Hi poosh heem hoff, Hi heet heem hon dee floor, an' teenk for myself, maybee she don't come back alive in ten min*oot* for pay me my monee. So Hi ben' down for shake heem hup, han' dat maudjit two-time cross buggaire, is ketch won foot, han' hudder harm, han' tie hon greet beeg knot. Maudjit hell, dat hurt. Before Hi can undo dat, she's have dee hudder h'arm 'n foot, han make some more knot, han' Hi ham all in won piece on dee floor. Before Hi can roll ovaire, she make more knot hon my hair. Han den she find someting helse, han tie anudder knot too. Paree, Paree, Hi cry like ba*bee*. Oh, dat hurt. De wataire pass hoff my heye, han almost Hi teenk Hi don't leave for ten min*oots*.

But Hi don't give hup. Wid hall dee cries han dee knots, Hi see my chanse. Oh, Paree does see his chanse. Wen dis man is try for tie more knots, Hi have see my chanse. Hi see won great big red behin'. Hi see won great beeg brown harsehole. Oh, Paree is see his chanse. Oh, Paree bite dat harsehole. Et Maudjit, Paree. You know, twenty-fi' dollaire is too much monee for ten min*oots*. Hi have bite my hown harsehole!

(It must be told with motions. One can describe sideshows, and so on. I told this all over the Green Bay zone with Standard Oil, told it at service men's clubs, at the Coronation Banquet for King George on his visit to Canada at the Windsor Hotel.

The dialect is my own grandfather's. He razzed me, said if I wanted to bite the wrestler back I would have to bite my own behin'. Lots of fellows lay claim to it. I heard a fellow tell it in Manistique ten years after I made it up, with the same punch ending.)

Miracles of Saint Spyridon

Collected by Richard M. Dorson in September 1955 in Iron Mountain, Michigan. Printed in *Fabula* 1 (1957): 121–22.

Told by John Corombos, a restaurant owner, like so many Greek-American immigrants, who had come to the United States in 1903 as a youth from his home in Bambakou. John and his younger brother George related to me a host of national, local, and religious legends, along with *Märchen* and memorates, illustrative of their Greek inheritance still vividly remembered in the New World. The saint's legend loomed large in their repertoire and embodied deeply held beliefs in the powers of the saint. The Corombos family and their traditions are discussed in my *American Folklore* (Chicago: University of Chicago Press, 1959), pp. 156–65. These instances show Saint Spyridon upholding the cause of the Greeks against the Turkish oppressor.

Motifs: V229.2.8 "Saint's body remains unspoiled in the earth for a long time"; D1841.4.3 "Walking upon water without getting wet"; D2089.4 "Saint causes mill to turn backwards (to break down)"; Q558.18 "Saints bring about miraculous death (paralysis) because of desecration of sanctuaries"; V221.1 "Saint cures palsy."

So this Saint Spyridon, now of course he was a bishop. But he was a bishop, which of course he was a fanatic with his religion, which the Turks they were trying to keep it from expanding any farther. So they finally murder him, they throw him in the water outside Constantinople. So when there was a ship come along happens to see the body float on the water, he pick her up, and bring it to his home town, in the Corfu, where the owner of the ship has his home town. And then he built a church there, and put him in the casket, and put that body right in the church. And that body remains there untouched and undisturbed ever since. And that was the year 314 after Christ. That's about 1700 years ago. Now that body that stood remains there whole, just as it was put in there at that time.

And so the Greek people they proclaim him as a saint, and they celebrate his birthday on the twelfth day of December every year. And there's thousands going there every year to worship him. And some of them they bringing him you know lot of donations, bringing him gold candles or gold things or gold ships, because some of them they claim they were saved by the saint while they were in a rough sea voyage. Well, they pray and call him for help and they saw him just like an ecstasy walking on top of the waves. And all of a sudden the wave come down, and the boat was saved.

So they have a lot of those experiences that happens. And when you go there worship him, you can go there any time, outside his birthday. Now if you go there, there's a key there to open that casket. And they claim that Saint Spyridon is not there all the time. That is, he must do a lot of traveling. That's the belief of the people over there, see. And they try the key, the same key which this attendant has. And he gives them the key to open, and the casket does not open. And then at times again, when the body is there, or they claim the Saint is there, why the casket opens, and you can view the body of the saint. And also they have a belief in there, that this fellow he wears a pair of shoes every year. Every year when they open this casket on the 12th day of December, they find out this pair of shoes they put in there is all wore out, and just look like an old pair of shoes remain on his feet. So they believe he's doing a lot of walking for the year time. Now that's one of those miracles which they claim happen.

And also we have a story about the Saint Spyridon when Turkey enslave Greece when the holiday comes in, on 12th day—you know the Greeks didn't believe in working on holidays—so when the holiday comes in, this Turk boss of that small factory they have there which crush the olives, to produce the oil—you see it was something like handmade machinery with stones, rolling stones, and crush olives and squeeze 'em to get the oil out. So this pasha—pasha means you know Turkish head guy or boss. He said, "Come on boy," he said. "No," the boy said, "no we can't work today, it's a holiday, it's Saint Spyridon's day, it's a big holiday, we're not supposed to work." "Well," he said, "forget about that Saint Spyridon. That don't mean nothing. Let's go to work." Well then, all right. Then as soon as started to work, then all of a sudden, on the second turn, all the machinery broke down. So from then on, this pasha, when it comes again season to crush olives, he said, "When is that dirty Saint Spyridon, now we're going to have all the day." So from then they began to believe that the saints in the Greek faith, then have whole lot to do, and they will believe in miracles in those saints. And that thing helps in that way, the Greeks of that day, to preserve the religion, because the Turks then never attempt to do anything to hurt any saint, which of course they claim is gonna come back again and give us revenge.

There was also another story in the church by Saint Spyridon. There was one great big oak tree in front of the church, which the church was named Saint Spyridon Church. So this another fellow by the name of Bey—Bey means also the district, like we say the governor of the district—so the Bey he wants, he sends his boy over there to cut this oak tree down, to use the timber. It was a great big tree, of course, it was enough to build a whole house out of it. So the people they said, "Oh Mr. Bey, don't destroy that tree, that's Saint Spyridon's tree, you ain't supposed to destroy that." "Ah," he said—of course he wasn't the same, he was another Bey you understand—"ah," he said, "I don't believe in St. Spyridon," and so forth. So his boy went over there and took the ax, and tried to chop the tree down. After the second hit with the tree, then his hand's paralyzed, of this boy. And then the Bey he laid down and prayed. His boy was crippled for a week. He couldn't hardly move his hands. And then finally this Bey lay down and prayed. "Oh, Saint Spyridon," he said, "cure my boy and I never will touch your tree any more." And then they claim in a week's time the boy he started to move his hands again and he get well.[1]

1. These miracles of St. Spyridon fall into the general patterns described by C. Grant Loomis in *White Magic* (Cambridge, Massachusetts, 1948), although the medieval saints' legends he analyzes are attributed to the living saints rather than to their tombs and churches.
Four Greek items in the Indiana University Folklore Archives (Michigan section) describe a saint with an uncorrupted body, who travels during the year doing good. A skeptic at the tomb was knocked across the floor, and on looking up saw the saint's body back in the casket. All four informants mention the replacement of the shoes; one said they were made of iron, another that they were covered with seaweed (John Demetrakopoulos, Thomas Nicholas Papathanasious, Tom Pappas, from Lansing; Anthony Glavas from Chicago Heights, Illinois).

The Two Brothers

Collected by Richard M. Dorson in September 1947 in Crystal Falls, Michigan. Printed in *Western Folklore* 8 (1949): 50–53.

There are some similarities with type 834 *The Poor Brother's Treasure*, in which the poor brother tells his rich brother his dream that a gold treasure lies in a certain spot. When the rich brother goes there to pick it up, he finds dung. In anger he throws the dung into the poor brother's house, where it turns to gold. But the present tale is told on the level of realistic plausibility and contains no magical motifs. Recognizable motifs are K1044 "Dupe induced to eat filth (dung)"; N478 "Secret wealth betrayed by money left in borrowed money-scales"; N511.1.9 "Treasure buried under tree"; D1273.5 "Magic oath"; J1170 "Clever judicial decisions."

I have published "Polish Wonder Tales of Joe Woods" and "Polish Tales from Joe Woods" in *Western Folklore* 8 (1949): 25–53, 131–45.

I met Joe Woods in June 1946 in Crystal Falls, a polyglot mining town in the Peninsula sitting crazily on a hill, and heard him uncork a few stories. But on a later date we missed connections, and I didn't see him again until September 1947, when I revisited Crystal Falls. He was the man I most wanted to see in the Peninsula, for some hunch told me he had a store of *Märchen*. He did, and for two days I wrote down his long, circumstantial narrations.

Joe is stocky, arthritic, and cross-eyed. He can no longer work at any job, but he saws wood in his garden and with his wife and daughters picks blueberries in the woods. He must live meagerly on a pension, and his dingy house shows it. Joe is a little bitter, and his wit is sharp rather than pleasant. He left the Roman Catholic Church and sneers at its dogmas. Although Joe has physical failings, he is mentally sound and razor-keen. He claims to speak, read, and write seven languages—"Polock, Russian, Croatian, Bohemian, Serbian, Slavish, English"—although he has had little schooling.

Joe Woods was born Joseph Wojtowicz in the town of Csanok, province of Galicia, in Austrian Poland. Csanok, with about six thousand people, was no peasant village; besides farm lands it had an oil refinery, a car factory, a railroad station, an army barracks, and a big high school. Joe came to the United States in 1904, when he was twenty-one, to make a better living.[1] His brother, a fresco painter in Milwaukee, had written him letters of encouragement. Joe had not, however, been

---

1. He was thus part of the great Polish emigration movement that reached its height in the opening years of the present century and took the Great Lakes cities for a main target. See *Our Racial and National Minorities*, ed. F. J. Brown and J. S. Roucek (New York, 1939), p. 222.

badly off. His father was a government commissioner on the roads, getting 125 kronen a month. "You can live like a millionaire in old country on that." His grandfather owned thirty farming acres, on which the family had lived for generations. Unlike Joe, he never went ten miles from the house.

After leaving regular school at the fourth grade, Joe went to a Hungarian trade school to learn to be a carriage painter and upholsterer. For one year he worked at concrete roofing. Then he ran away from home because he had nothing to do. This itch seems a part of the man, for he traveled widely throughout the States as well. Joe's family followed him to Milwaukee in 1910, his father selling everything he had. But when Mrs. Wojtowicz died in 1912, her heartbroken husband returned to Poland and died the same year. Joe remembers his father's grief the night of her death.

"He never had one gray hair—it turned white that night. He was lying on the bed with me and my sister crying, and the iron casting broke, and he fell to the floor. He said, 'Mother came and pushed me and told me not to cry. She said I'd be with her in a year.' She died February second. He died before Christmas."

In America, Joe kept on the move, although he spent most of his time in the Upper Peninsula. He began working in a blast furnace in Milwaukee and then moved to Amasa in northern Michigan, where the iron mines offered jobs. "I've been all over the country—Montana, Missouri, Pennsylvania, Minnesota, Wisconsin, Michigan, North Dakota —working in the mines, on the harvest, in the woods. Whenever I make fifty, sixty dollars, I go see the country. Then I have to walk back."

He married in 1908. At the time, Joe was boarding with Albert Yugba, who couldn't write, so Joe wrote his letters for him. But Joe wrote other words than those Albert dictated, and asked his daughter Rose to come to America. The Yugbas had nothing in the old country, not even a house. They came over, Joe met Rose at the station, recognizing her by her photograph, and married her the next day. (Joe told this straight, but this was storytelling license; he did not marry for some months.) "She was pretty then, not like she is now," said Joe, jerking his thumb at a tall, stringy, ever-shouting woman, scurrying around the house. Rose had never gone to school; she worked as a servant at seven.

When I asked Joe how many children he had, he had to think a minute and count. "Seven daughters—Celia, Adella, Chester, Lilian, Josephine, Caroline, Gloria. No, six daughters and one boy. Three are married—no, four. One is in Milwaukee, one in Princeton, Indiana, one in Canton, Michigan, one in Chicago. The boy is in the state hospital —he has fits." Two girls still lived with the parents.

Some years ago Joe lost the power in his legs, contracting rheumatism from mine dampness, and took treatments at Ann Arbor and the state hospital at Newberry, where he stayed from 1930 to 1936. In 1944 he became an American citizen.

Where did Joe get his stories? I asked.

"There was a beggar with a wooden leg goes from house to house, singing songs—Cossack songs. At night he come to our house—we had a nicer house—and he tell stories to everybody. I wasn't supposed to listen, but I opened the door a crack and listen. And I always remember. He have a lyre, like a violin, with a wooden box you wind up. He had a voice too. His name was Andrew Bakus. Somebody give him eggs, some potatoes, some money—not much. For a couple years he didn't come; they find somebody kill him in the woods. They find twelve hundred thousand kronen sewed up in his coat under the lining.

"We used to go to the fair, and stay all night and watch the horses, and the men would tell stories there. I hear it once and I remember it. I was hungry for stories.

"When I was night shift at Balkan mine at Alpha, I used to tell stories to the trammer boss—easy job. When I got tired working in the mines, I went in the lumber camps and told stories there. Wouldn't finish one night, so next night the boys would put cigarettes, tobacco in my mouth, ask me to finish. I told them in Polish and Slavish. In the Sawyer-Goodman camp here, in Flannegan's camp at Sagola."

He had told stories in the family circle too, when visitors came, and Mrs. Woods showed herself familiar with them while he talked to me, occasionally interrupting to suggest something he had overlooked, although Joe always squelched her summarily and picked up the threads unerringly. "Way back when he was younger he could tell stories all night," she said. Joe can still tell them all night—*Märchen, Sagen, novelle,* jests, riddles, experiences.

What impressed me most about Joe Woods's folktales was their power to entertain, a point always sidetracked in academic discussions of origin and distribution. They brim with life and movement, humor and graphic detail. The plots in their full dress possess symmetry and suspense. Joe's everyday language and snappy dialogue salt the narratives that turn so flat and stilted in the printed collections and translations, no matter how vociferous the claims to fidelity. His interspersions clarify the peasant point of view. The great tragedy in the Grimms' method, repeated by the innumerable collectors who followed them, lies in their obsession with the text and suppression of the speaking human being.[2]

2. In the following text I give Joe's exact words, but not his pronunciation—its literal rendering would, I think, serve no useful purpose. He does not pronounce *th;* he substitutes *v* for *w,* and *f* or *w* for *v;* short *i* and *u* become long; and some words get wrong accents. Examples in these respective

There was two brothers live in the same village. One was very rich, bachelor. He wouldn't marry anyone because he was too stingy to support any children. His name was Alexander.

The other brother was name Steve. He was so poor he didn't have nothing to eat. And he had twelve children.

So it happen on a Easter Sunday, when everybody had a full table, he had only a few potatoes, baking potatoes, for his family. So he went to his brother Alexander, and went to the knee, and ask his brother for give him something to eat, not for himself, but for his family. But the brother Alexander get mad at him, say: "Get out, you should work for money like me. Not getta married and getta drove of kids."

"Well, you told me that good many time, my dear brother, but that don't help me. Can't you give me but half a loaf of bread?" [plaintively].

"No, I won't give you any crumb. Get out the house!" [gruffly].

So he went home. They eat them few potatoes what they have, and in the evening went to bed with the empty stomach.

But still he can't sleep. He was figuring get up and kill that brother —kid brother. So he going to the shack, take the sledge hammer, and sneak to his brother park—orchard. He was figuring climb through the window and kill his brother when he sleep. But the light was in his brother Alexander bedroom. So he gotta wait till light went out, and brother fall asleep.

But in a couple minutes, he heard a door squeak. And he see in the moonlight his brother was coming, had a shovel and a pick in his hand, and a big bag on his shoulder.

So Steve was thinking: "What he going try to do? What he gonna do?"

His brother Alexander was walking to the big apple tree, put the bag on the ground, take off his coat, roll his sleeves, and starta dig the hole. He was digging for half hour. When he had a hole above his knee, he jump out and say to himself, "That deep enough." So he take the bag, and open up, and dump what was in. The Steve brother he didn't know what was there, but when he dump them out there was jingling like steel coins—steel washers.

"Now," he says, "I gotta get rest." So he went back to the house, twice again. That was three load. And dump in the hole, put the bag over, and fill up with the earth. Then he tamped it with his foot, and he say, looking at the moon: "O moon, you see me; you my witness. Nobody can touch this money, just the man who eats the number two."

---

categories are: de, dem, fadder, brudder, t'ink, t'rone, eart', mont', fedder; vat, vorl', vid (with), veendow, sveet, vun; leaf (leave), giff, woice, willage, adwice; droogstore, bankroopt, heem, keesing, mineester, mirackle, castull, pendoolum.

He takes down his pants and shits on the place. Then he went back. And light went out. Alexander was in the bed.

Then the brother Steve come out on the gooseberry bush where he was hiding himself, where he was listening to that funny ceremony. Then he come and scoop that number two in his hand, and he carried it that way back to his home ('cause he had nothing to carry it with— he had to carry it that way), put it in the frying pan, put it on a hot stove, and burn that to the powder. Then he went to a neighbor, and he stole some garlic and some onions and some carrots, and mixed up together with that powder, rolled them in some pills like aspirin, like medicine, like marble, and take glass water. Then one by one he swallow that with the water. (Then it wasn't so bad, huh?)

Then after that he went to the brother orchard, with the shovel and pick, uncover the hole in the ground, take the bag from the top, load him up with the money what was in the hole, and carry home.

Brother Alexander hada three load, but Steve was weak. Take him seven times to bring money back. So on the last trip he put some rock in the hole, and cover it with the earth. And went home.

For three days he was figuring how much money was there. They hada measure it then, by the quart, the bushel—because they can't count. So third day he went to the brother to borrow a bushel basket. And brother Alexander was wondering: What the dickens he gonna measure, that poor thing? So before he give him the measure he stuck some beeswax on the bottom.

"All right, here's the basket, but bring him right away back."

And he measure him and he have five and a half bushel, gold and silver coin, some copper. When they was through measuring they take the basket back to his brother Alexander. He didn't know that one coin was stick to the bottom, to the beeswax. So when Alexander find that coin in the basket, you know what happen? "Well then, brother, I bet he stole my money." He run to the orchard, under big apple tree, he find his number two gone, disappeared. Went to get his tools, open up; no money, just rock.

So he went to his brother Steve and accused him of stealing the money. But Steve told him: "You're wrong, my brother, I didn't steal your money. Remember your oath, and you took moon for witness, who eat your number two 'get your money. So I do that."

"But how can you prove you eat it? I didn't see you do that." So Alexander didn't believe him; he take him to the court.

When the case come to the jury and the judge, the brother tell his story. So the judge told them: "That's all I can see by my judgment; the Steve got make a number two, and Alexander brother can eat that, then he get money back. Are you both satisfied?"

"Well," he says, "yes."

So the judge giva them two witness, to watch how Alexander gonna eat Steve's number two. Steve went to the creamery, order two gallon one-week-old buttermilk, put on the top half a gallon sour milk, then drink two ounces castor oil, and mashed potatoes, 'bout half a peck, on top of that. Then they went to the orchard—Alexander orchard. And Steve felt like he had big storm in his stomach, everything boiling together. When they come in that place where the money was buried, Steve take his pants down and make number two. But when he was through with that dirty trick, there wasn't a handful, there was a wheelbarrowful. They had to take shovel and shovel it in wheelbarrow to take it home.

When Alexander was looking on that, he pretty near fall down. He say, "Keep them damn money, I wouldn't eat that for kingdom."

So that stingy bugger lost his money. It [would] take him year to eat that.

Mexico

Kondoy

From Américo Paredes, *Folktales of Mexico* (Chicago: University of Chicago Press, 1970), pp. 7–11.

Collected by Walter S. Miller in San Lucas Camotlán, Oaxaca. Told in Spanish by José Trinidad, sixty-two, who also gave the collector a Mixe version. Miller considered this informant one of the best narrators in the community. The informant, however, tended to simplify his Spanish versions, adapting his style to the collector's writing speed. Miller, *Cuentos mixes* (Mexico, 1956), no. 6.

Hero legend with resemblances to type 650A *Strong John*. Principal motifs: A511.1.9 "Culture hero born from egg"; A526.7 "Culture hero performs remarkable feats of strength and skill"; A571 "Culture hero asleep in mountain"; A901 "Topographical features caused by experiences of primitive hero"; A1145.1 "Earthquakes from movements of subterranean monster"; B877.1.2 "Giant serpent exorcised by clergy."

Miller gives other variants for parts of this narrative, showing its currency among the Mixes. Another informant, for example, stated that the eggs from which Kondoy and his brother were born were "laid by the earth" (p. 108). As to Kondoy's serpent brother, the Mixes explain earthquakes as caused by a supernatural being in the form of a snake (pp. 205–6). According to Miller, Kondoy was still very much alive as a legendary hero at the time of collection.

In *to'oxykyopk*—the Woman Mountain—there was a cave where people used to store their unshelled corn. That's the place where they found two eggs and took them home.

Two people went there one day, a man and his wife; there is a well there. In that place the woman saw the eggs. She said to her husband, "Give me a stick. I'm going to take the eggs out of there."

So he cut a branch off a tree for her there, and he gave it to her. But she couldn't reach the eggs. She fished and fished for them, but she couldn't get them. They were still there exactly as before.

Then she turned around, and there they were on top of the rock. So she said to her husband, "Go bring them down. They're up there. They're not in the water." And the man went and took them down.

So they took them to their house. Three days later the eggs burst open. When they burst open, out of one came Kondoy, who was people; and from the other one came his brother, who was a great snake.

Kondoy grew fast. In two, three days he was already grown up. His food agreed with him. They brought it to him in baskets, and he finished everything off.

One day he told his mother, "Mother, I'm going to Tehuantepec."

"What will you do there?" his mother asked.

"Oh, I'll see. I want to see the sights there. Don't worry; I'll be back soon."

He left one day and came back the same day, and brought his bundle.

Another day he told his mother, "Mother, I'm going to Oaxaca."

"But what will you do there?"

"Oh, I'll see. My soul is full of emotion. I want to see what there is in the place they call Oaxaca. Don't worry; I'll be back soon."

He left one day and came back the same day. He brought three great jars full of money for his mother. He told her, "Mother, here is this money for you to use. I'm going on my travels now. I want to see everything as it is."

"No, my son. Why must you go wandering about? Stay here."

"No, mother. I'm going now. I'm already grown. I thank you for taking care of me; you gave me everything. Now I am leaving you this money. You will not lack anything."

Then he set out on his travels through all the region of the Mixe. When he passed through Camotlán, there in *wokkats*—Cliff Gully—he left a pot of money. Since the people were very tall, he put it away just about this high. [Informant raises his hand to the level of his head, or a little higher.]

Then he went into a cave at Trapiche de Chusnabán. There he left a chest of money. But they say the people of Cacalotepec have already gone and taken it all out. They went in a big crowd. That is why Kondoy used to say, "The people of Camotlán are good people. The money I put away when I passed by there still is in its place."

Beyond Santa Cruz, on the road to Trapiche, he had a great battle with one who called himself King Moctezuma. The signs are still there today, the musket balls they shot. Do you remember I showed you that when we were going to Oaxaca? Right there on the road there are many even today. I picked up some of them right there and showed them to you. They are rusty by now, it is true, after so many years, but these are the balls fired by Moctezuma's men when they were fighting against Kondoy.

Kondoy was over here close to Trapiche. But Moctezuma's soldiers were away over there, higher up. Around San Isidro or higher up, that was where he was. He had many men with him, thousands upon thousands. Yes, indeed! Kondoy was all by himself.

Then Moctezuma's soldiers began to fire these musket balls.

All Kondoy did was pick up big rocks; that is what he was going to throw at them; that is what he threw. When the rocks landed way up there, they killed many men. And so they fought for a long time; I think it was more than three days that they fought. Nothing happened to Kondoy; he paid no attention when Moctezuma's bullets came and hit him. Nothing happened to him, the bullets just fell to the ground. And there they still are; those were the ones we picked up. But when Kondoy threw a rock, Moctezuma's men surely died. Those poor men couldn't hold out against him; nobody could hold out against him. All those poor men died there. The rocks are still there. Did you notice how rocky it is around there for more than half a league?

So then Moctezuma left and went back to Mexico once more. That is the way things ended. That is how the old people told it to me.

There in Trapiche, Kondoy sat down to rest after the battle; the signs are still there today. When he got up, he put his hands on the ground and pushed himself up to his feet. The prints of his hands are there. Even the fingers can be seen quite clear.

Then he went on till he came to Mitla. There in Mitla this Kondoy put up his castle, but he set it on solid rock and it was made of nothing but rock. Haven't you seen it? It is still there, they say. The ground is soft in that place. They found out the ground was soft because he was wearing his crown, which weighed more than five *arrobas* [5 × 25 lbs]. His feet began to sink into the ground. This same is true of Tlacolula and Tule; all the ground is soft.

A short distance from Tlacolula, in a place that is now called Caballito Blanco, he wrote upon a rock telling his people where he was going. It cost him no trouble, though he wrote it way up high. He was three meters tall, you see? His machete weighed more than three *arrobas,* and his staff more than five. He stood on top of a big rock at the foot of the boulder, and he wrote just like that, raising his hand a little above his head.

In Tule it was Kondoy who planted that great tree. The ground there is very soft; it isn't firm; there's too much water underneath. Kondoy stuck his staff there, just like this. He stuck it in deep. And then the staff took root and grew, just the way *zompantli* posts take root. So that staff of his became a great tree.

Then he came to Oaxaca, and this was firm ground. He made his capital there. He said, "Even if there is war, and they shoot off cannon, nothing will happen. This is solid ground."

When Kondoy was in Oaxaca, his brother the great snake said, "I am going to Oaxaca. I'm going to see what my brother is doing there."

So he went into the earth there close to Coatlán. He left a trail there; it was a big hole he made when he went in. There under the earth he traveled, the earth trembled where he passed. He was coming into the flat land this side of Mitla when the priest and the bishop went and blessed the place. That was the end of him there.

Kondoy went from there to Mexico and left his crown there. He said, "When someone comes who can wear this, then the government will change."

But nobody has been able to wear it because it weighs a lot. It still is there now, they say. When you go to Mexico, go look for it and send me word whether it is true that it still is there.

Then Kondoy returned. He went in with all his soldiers near a town called Comaltepec. He didn't die. He went into the mountain there, the one called *Ipxyukp* or Twenty Peaks—Zempoaltépetl. He is still there.

On Holy Week

From Américo Paredes, *Folktales of Mexico* (Chicago: University of Chicago Press, 1970), pp. 179–80.

Collected by Américo Paredes in Matamoros, Tamaulipas, September 1962. Told by I. V., mestizo male in his sixties, born in Guanajuato. Informant comes from a devoutly Catholic background as do most narrators of tales of this type.

Tales like the following belong to a class of European jests satirizing the naïve interpretation of Catholic ritual. In Europe the principals in the stories usually are peasants. In Mexico, where Catholicism has taken on pre-Conquest accretions, the characters most often are Indians. In jests I have collected along the Texas-Mexican border, the characters are likely to be Americanized migrant workers or Anglo-Americans. In Europe the point of the jests is the ignorance of the peasants, a socially inferior class. In Mexican tales with Indian characters, there is both social snobbery and ethnic bias, since the Indians are peasants and also people with strange customs and a special way of speaking Spanish. In the border Mexican jests, the butt of the joke is the Anglo-American and his strange, Protestant culture, which the Mexican migrant worker sometimes apes.

Principal motif: J2495.3* "Religious exercises given absurd or obscene turn: Christ in the Passion Play."

Cf. types 1678* *In Passion Play the Christ Says, "I Am Thirsty,"* and 1829 *Living Person Acts as Image of Saint.* See also Howard T. Wheeler, *Tales from Jalisco, Mexico* (Philadelphia, 1943), no. 16, in which a drunk accidentally substitutes a pig for the image of Christ during a festival.

In southern Mexico they also have the custom, on the day the body of Our Lord Jesus Christ is taken down from the cross, to hire a man to dress in the clothing of Our Lord Jesus Christ, with his crown and all, and they lay him out in the coffin. And they pray around the coffin with candles, all of them there in chorus, and they sing psalms and what have you.

And one time they couldn't find anybody, and they kept looking around. So some friends told a fellow who had got up with a terrible hangover that morning and didn't have any money for a drink, "Go on, man; the priest will give you five pesos for the job. All you have to do is play the part of Our Lord Jesus Christ, and you have enough for a drink. And you can buy us one, too."

"So what do I have to do?"

"Nothing. Just lie there in the coffin for about half an hour, while all of us pray around you."

"All right."

So they laid him out, and they all began to walk around the coffin, praying and singing psalms. But suddenly he began to break wind—phew! A drunkard's farts, you know—terrible stink!

And these guys, friends of his, would go by the coffin and say,

> Here lies the body of Christ,
> What an odor comes from it!
> What can we do but surmise
> That our Redeemer has shit.

Bahamas

Ordeal by Water

Collected by Daniel J. Crowley in 1952 in Grant's Town, Andros Island.

Motif: H222 "Guilt or innocence shown by ability to swim." This traditional African method of testing the truth of a person's statements is a popular theme in the Bahamas, having been collected by Elsie Clews Parsons in 1917 (see *Folk-Tales of Andros Island, Bahamas, Memoirs of the American Folklore Society* 13 [1918] and "Spirituals and Other Folklore from the Bahamas," *Journal of American Folklore* 41 [1928]: 453–524), and in six versions (including this one) by Daniel Crowley in 1952–53. Parsons also found examples in Antigua, Nevis, Saba, the Saintes Islands off Guadeloupe, and in Haiti, and refers to earlier African versions from Sierra Leone, the Ndau, the Sotho, and Zambia. Water ordeal tales are also known in India, Greece, Ireland, Scandinavia, Lithuania, and elsewhere.

The informant, Paul Rolle, thirty-eight, was a day laborer from Behring Point, Andros Island, but had worked in Nassau for five years. His brother Harford "Joe" Rolle, their sisters, children, and extended family from Andros were a major source of tales and songs.

The story is that most popular Caribbean form, the *cante fable*, wherein each person tested must sing a song as the river rises, and at the denouement when the guilty person is discovered, the river rises inexorably to stop the song. In characteristic Bahamian fashion, where every plot is widely known and often repeated, the narrator is casual and inexact, more interested in amusing his audience than in providing a logical narration. At the same time, he moralizes about the unwisdom of theft and selfishness, and the injustice of playing favorites within a family, two basic Bahamian values. The formulaic opening and closing mark off the narration from ordinary speech, and the sung sections have a haunting melodiousness lost in print.

Once upon a time, was a very good time, Mondey chew tobacco, he spit white lime. Cockero jump from bank to bank, he ten quarter never touch water [till] the sun has set. Bunday! Eh!

Now this was woman had five daughters. She woiking out in the country. I doesn't mean just leaving over the hill and going Bay Street to woik, I mean to say she have to drive miles and miles to woik. Then she has, of the five daughters, she has one which you say was a pet; her heart was a heartstring. Although she was love this one so much, this particular daughter do all the bad things in the home, and the other four carry the blame. So, this day more en all—he ain't come a contest some time ago, I ain't know rightly, but we get down to that shortly. So this day, the mother was going to work that morning. She said, "Now here's some beans, I want you to put this bean on the fire for dinner." Well, they put the bean on the fire, this pet daughter goes to work and eat the bean. When the mother come, ask where the beans. Say, "Mother, there no bean here, there's nothing to cook." Well, it's run up, about for five or six days.

The mother say, "I get tired buying beans, because beans is so dear now, I can't afford the money to give you the clothes, and buying the beans like this, and eating the beans like this, and cause we can't get my little beans soup to eat one time. Anyhow, I going make a decree. I know river down there is enchanted river, does make people who's a tief [thief] does talk the truth."

Well, anyhow, the mother decides, "I going take the five, the four daughters down to the river." She don't want the pet because she too loveys the pet because she don't want to do nothing to this pet who doing all the damage. But these other four, they's going take this fault. Well, things is moving on. When she get home, she said, "There's no beans, beans is out. Well, I decide take you all down to the river." Well Brother, when she get to the river, well, in those days anything you call then is answer. Don't answer now.

When she get to the river, the bank is very dry. She went aside. She give a little short prayer on the sly, but she knew she was doing it, anyhow, but they don't know. Then the first daughter said—started singing. Now the river got to answer. "Go to river, go to river, go to river, oh; if I eat the beans, if I tell a lie, if I eat my mother beans, go to river, going swallow me." The water never come for that one, that jump out. She put the next one, the next one say the same thing. So now is run on for that day the four went, they ain't nothing happen. Well, then she supposed to carry the five. But this one who do the damage she don't want to carry that, she love that one so much she feel that this one ain't going to do them kind of things, ain't going to tief, but that the one doing the tiefing. You see?

Well, oh well, anyhow this day she say, "I going give them one more trial." The same thing happen again. She say, "Wait a minute. I got to try the five daughters." So, I mean, after all some the folks may know the old story better than me, but since after all I talking the old story what I know. So Brother, now, I want you remember this poem now, I mean, this a great man talking old story now. Well, here we goes again, beginning from where I say I was a great man, eh? So then [savors phrase] the times run on, the beans still was eaten.

Well, the mother said, "I really have to find out who eating the beans." At last she decide to take this pet daughter down to the river. This river will tell the truth who eating the beans because who eat the beans, she got to drown in the river cause the water going to overflood her. So this day mother and all, they start back to the river again. The first one go in the river, started singing, "Go to river, go to river, go to river, oh; if I eat the bean, if I tell a lie, if I eat my mother bean, go to river, going to swallow me." Dri [drive] back. She come out. The next one went in. Well, the last daughter now, who eat the beans now, she had to go into the river. When she get in the river, she start, "Go to river, go to river, go to river, oh; if I eat the bean, if I tell a lie, if I eat my mother bean [man in audience joins in], go to river, going swallow me."

The water come to her ankle. Damn, she ain't feel so good, because the water start springing. She start singing again, "Go to river, go to river, go to river, oh; if I eat the bean, if I tell a lie, if I eat my mama [change from "mother"] bean, go to river, going swallow me." The river come to midway, of her leg. Well, he perceive then that she eatin' the beans, 'cause the water growing now, because . . . and she can't come out the river. She got to stay there until she . . . till the truth come, 'cause the water going tell the truth. So then . . . and she got to sing. Ain't nobody telling her to sing, but she got to sing. "Go to river, go to river, go to river, oh; if I eat the bean, if I tell a lie, if I eat my mama bean, go to river, going swallow me." The water come up, you know, way up and, I mean to say, way up there, Bulla, anyhow you know where I mean, Bulla. [He sniffs expressively, while Josh says "Yeah." Chuckles through song.] "Go to river, go to river, go to river, oh; if I eat the bean, if I tell a lie, if I eat my mama bean, go to river, going swallow me."

The water come up to her navel. Damn, now she start crying, because she can't beat the river. [Sung in hoarse, low voice.] "Go to river, go to river, go to river, ho; if I eat the bean, if I tell a lie, if I eat my mama bean, go to river, going swallow me." The water come up on her arm. Now she start, now she start afloating, she got to float because she can't stay there. [Hoarse but louder.] "Go to river, go to river, go to river, oh; if I eat the bean, if I tell a lie, if I eat my mama bean, go to river, going swallow me." Now the water get up under her throat, until now he start to stop her breath.

She can't talk no more, because when your breath stop, you can't talk. So she kind of hoarsy now. [Slowly, very hoarse and poorly enunciated, like a stock idiot. A shriek of laughter and guffaws are heard from the audience. Strangles, chokes, strains out the words in realistic but still funny effects.] "Go to river, go to river, go to river, go to river, oh; if I eat my mama bean, go to . . ." [song ended by rising water]. And the woman say [falsetto and loud], "Oh Lord, look at my daughter going, can't you save now, oh Lord." [Laughter.] That time she started floating, she say Bunday!

I pass by, and I saying, "Woman, you's a fool, you know your daughter eat the beans, and you carried her. Bunday!" The kick she kick at me, damn, a goose see me, he say [falsetto] "Peep!" I say, "Ya goose, that's right." That's all, Bunday!

Cuba

Little Cockroach Martina

Contributed by Daniel J. Crowley. Collected by Berta Bascom in 1947 in Pinar del Rio. Forthcoming in *Folktales of the West Indies*.

This amusing little animal tale has been frequently collected in Cuba. See examples in *Archives del Folklore Cubano*, as reported by Fernando Ortiz, 1 (1924): 62–75, and "Personajes del Folklore Afro-cubano," 4 (1929): 97–112; and by A. Fernandez, "Cuentos Afrocubanos," 5 (1929): 265–69. Other versions of the tale are found in F. Henius, *Stories from the Americas* (New York: C. Scribner's Sons, 1944), pp. 42–45; and Pura Belpre, *Perez y Martina* (New York: F. Warne, 1961). In a general way, motifs H310–H359 "Suitor tests," plus B281.2.2 "Wedding of mouse and cockroach," reported only from India, fit here, but, as is so often the case, are widely known elsewhere. The present example collected from Pascuala, the wife of a sugar laborer, is little more than an excuse for the narrator to show off his skills as an imitator of animal sounds. The animal tale is nicely localized too, with a very Cuban lady cockroach plying her coquetry with rouge, powder, and a fan during the five o'clock promenade. The theatrical nature of Caribbean narration is exemplified here, not only in the "imitations" but also in the onomatopoeia ("zas" as the mouse falls in the soup) and the mournful song that completes the tale.

This is type 2023 *Little Ant Finds a Penny, Buys New Clothes with it, and Sits in her Doorway:* "Various animals pass by and propose marriage." See the close variants from Italy, "The Tale of Sister Cat," *ante*, pp. 72–74, and in A. Paredes, *Folktales of Mexico* (Chicago, 1970), no. 77a, "Pérez the Mouse," pp. 188–89, and note, p. 236.

Once upon a time Little Cockroach Martina was sweeping her house and she found two pennies. She was very happy and said to herself, "How can I spend these pennies? For candy? . . . No, no, no, no! I will eat the candy and it will be gone too soon. For flowers? . . . No, no, no, no! They will die too soon. For meringues? . . . No, no, no, no! They will be gone too soon. For face powder and rouge? . . . Yes, in that very thing!"

Little Cockroach Martina bought face powder and rouge, she put on her most beautiful dress, she put on all the powder and all the rouge that she had, and she stood at her window to watch all the animals go by at five o'clock in the afternoon.

Lion passed by and said to her, "Little Cockroach Martina, how beautiful you look today! Do you want to marry me?"

Little Cockroach Martina waved her fan and said, "What noise do you make at night?"

"Roarrrrrrrr, roarrrrrrrrrrrr . . . ," growled Lion.

"No, no, no, no. . . . How you frighten me!" said Little Cockroach.

Goat passed by, and said to her, "Little Cockroach Martina, how beautiful you look today. Do you want to marry me?"

Little Cockroach Martina waved her fan and said, "What noise do you make at night?"

"Be, be, be," bleated Goat.

"No, no, no, no. . . . How you frighten me!" said Little Cockroach.

Horse passed by and said to her, "Little Cockroach Martina, how beautiful you look today. Do you want to marry me?"

Little Cockroach waved her fan and said, "What noise do you make at night?"

"Neigheeeeeeeeeeeee, neigheeeeeeeeeeeeee," neighed Horse.

"No, no, no, no. . . . How you frighten me!" said Little Cockroach.

Dog passed by and said to her, "Little Cockroach Martina, how beautiful you look today! Do you want to marry me?"

Little Cockroach said, "What noise do you make at night?"

"Bow, wow, wow," barked Dog.

"No, no, no, no. . . . How you frighten me!" said Little Cockroach.

Then Cat passed by and said to her, "How beautiful you look today! Little Cockroach Martina. Do you want to marry me?"

Little Cockroach Martina said, "What noise do you make at night?"

"Meow, meow, fu, fu, fu," said Cat.

"No, no, no, no. . . . How you frighten me!" said Little Cockroach.

As soon as the Cat went away, Senor Little Mouse Perez came along.

"Milady, Little Cockroach Martina. How beautiful you look today! Do you wish to marry me?"

Little Cockroach waved her fan and said, "What do you do at night?"

"Yi, yi, yi, yi," cried the Little Mouse.

Little Cockroach said, "Yes, sir!"

Soon they were married, and many people came to the wedding, though Cat did not. But on Sunday morning, Little Cockroach Martina went to church. She said to Little Mouse, "Be careful, there is an onion in the soup, keep away from the pot until I get back." As soon as Little Cockroach left, the Little Mouse began to smell the onion.

He wanted to eat the onion, and the smell was very strong, and he went near the pot, climbed the pot and, "zas," fell into it.

When Little Cockroach came back, she knocked at the door; nobody opened it; then some neighbors came and helped her open the door. Inside the house she found Little Senor Mouse Perez dead inside the pot. Since then Little Cockroach Martina cries and says:

> "Ay poor Little Mouse Perez
> Who fell inside the pot
> For the delicacy
> Of the onion."

Trinidad

The Poor Brahmin

Collected by Daniel J. Crowley in Curepe and printed in *The Caribbean* (September 1955), pp. 28–41. Forthcoming in *Folktales of the West Indies*.

Dilemma tales, while common in Africa and Asia, are much less so in the Caribbean. The redoubtable Elsie Clews Parsons recorded one for type 653 *The Four Skillful Brothers*, in Guadeloupe in 1924 (*Folklore of the Antilles, French and English, Memoirs of the American Folklore Society* 26, part 3, 1943, no. 149). The present example of a resolved dilemma tale comes from one of the West Indies' most numerous and prominent minority groups, the East Indians who were brought out from India as indentures to work in the sugar fields after the end of African slavery in 1838. Now numbering nearly half a million in Trinidad alone, the Indians have struggled hard to preserve their identity and ancestral culture. Three-quarters remain Hindus, but the caste system and the Hindi language are moribund in the islands. The narrator, the late Basdeo Sharma Maraj of Curepe, was a practicing Brahmin pundit and religious leader who made a living for his eight orphaned children by working as a taxi driver. Although he spoke and read Hindi, he chose to tell the story in the local Creole English made famous by calypso singers. The result is a piquant tale of taking full advantage of a unique opportunity. The scenes of the fighting mother and daughter-in-law, and the taxi driver setting his tale at a traffic roundabout, with a police sergeant (whose name indicates he is of the educated scribe caste) as solver of the dilemma, are fine examples of a folk narrator's genius at adapting the universal so that it has immediate local meaning and bite.

A pertinent motif is H620 "Unresolved problem: enigmatic ending of tale," reported from India, Indonesia, Zaïre, and the Cape Verde Islanders, although in this case a decision is rendered.

Once upon a time there was a Brahmin, and he have an old mother, was blind, and he had his wife. He was very poor. He said what he must do for a living. Then he go to Mahadeo [a popular designation of Siva, destroyer god of Hinduism] to the temple, and start a prayer to him. It takes him twelve long years, praying to Mahadeo. After twelve years Mahadeo appear and ask him, "What you want? What is your desire?" Then he has study that he has his mother and his wife. Say, "Let me go home and consult my mother and my wife. Then I shall come back and ask." Then he get the permission from Mahadeo, and come to his home. His mother was blind. The mother said, "Son, if you shall go and ask Mahadeoji that he shall give me my eyes my sight, so I can do something for you, and you'll be undebted to me." He thoughted, "That's the best thing. Nobody never undebted to their mother, but I shall be undebted to my mother."

So then after he leave he mother, he went to his wife. He tell his wife that "I have worshiping Mahadeoji for twelve long years, and Mahadeo had appear and ask me to ask what is my desire. He shall fulfill my desire." So his wife said that "Your mother is old and she's blind. What she will do with sight? If you will ask for a son, perhaps by your son we shall become rich and we shall enjoy best of health. So therefore you should go and ask for a son." While talking to his wife, his mother hear that his daughter-in-law want a son, come from there with a broomstick and start to beat this daughter-in-law, saying that "You want son, and I want my eye." Well, the two of them hold on, the mother-in-law, and daughter-in-law, hold on, and they start fighting, but they did not hear Brahmin at all.

The Brahmin leave there, went in a roundabout [traffic circle], and start begun crying. Sat by the roundabout and start crying. Everybody passes there asking, "Brahmin Deota ["divine priest," a very polite form of address], what you crying for?" Never answer. After Lalaji ["esteemed Lala, surname of scribe caste] was a sergeant, he passes there on his duty. He says, "Brahmin Deota, what you are crying for?" Brahmin did not answer. Three times he ask him, three times he didn't answer. Now the sergeant sit down with him and start to cry too. Both of them start to cry, they cried for near half an hour. After then Brahmin Deota say, "Sergeant, what you have crying for? What trouble you have?" Sergeant said, "What trouble you have? You tell me your trouble, I'll tell you mine."

Brahmin Deota say, "Well, I have worship Mahadeoji for twelve long years and he had appear, and he tell me that he will fulfill my desire, but one thing I should ask him, only one thing." Then he come to his mother. "The mother wanted an eye, wife wanted a son. Wife and mother start to fight, so I leave them fighting and come here and start to cry. That's my trouble."

The sergeant said, "Brahmin Deota, that's very small. What you make me cry so long, and you have the two of them fighting there. Let us go home and see if one of them is dead or living. Let us part them from fighting."

Now sergeant and the Brahmin Deota leave there and come to his home, see them still fighting, and sergeant part the two of them and tell them, "What you all fighting for, this small little thing, small little word, so two all you killing all yourself for, and you have this Brahmin Deota crying in the street." No, the sergeant say, "Well look, Brahmin Deota, is one word he want, and here is three words come. No, you must go to Seuji [another term of address for Siva] tomorrow and worship him, and when he appear you just tell him that you don't want nothing and your wife is a half of the body, she don't want nothing. Your mother is blind. Her desire is to see her grandson eating milk and rice in a gold bowl." Here the story end.

Brazil

Cases

Collected over the course of his illustrious career by Luis da Camara Cascudo of Natal, Rio Grande do Norte, Brazil.

A *case* is a small folktale synopsized in a pithy saying. The story, usually in the form of an anecdotal legend, is understood rather than told, although it has in the past circulated orally. A speaker applies the *case* at an appropriate conversational opportunity to make his point and press home the moral of the tale. Throughout the Moslem world hundreds of such concentrated sayings recall historical or legendary events. The best known *cases* in Brazil derive from Europe through Portuguese transmittal, and become adapted to the Brazilian environment. Others originate in Brazil. All examples come from the personal memories of Luis da Camara Cascudo.

Between Heaven and Earth, like Saint Peter's Mother

Saint Peter's mother was arrogant, avaricious, and selfish. During her lifetime she never gave alms. Once when she was washing a sheaf of onions, a leaf blew away and, being unable to catch it, she exclaimed, "Go away, for God's sake!" When she died she was taken to hell or to purgatory. Her son obtained from Our Lord a release from her punishment by throwing to her the leaf or stalk of the onion to enable her to come to heaven through it. The old woman began to rise up, but on seeing other suffering souls trying to take advantage of the same conveyance, she threw them off, shouting angrily and shaking the stem, which was then broken. She has not returned to purgatory because Our Lord had sent her away from there, and as she had not reached heaven yet, she has remained between heaven and earth, wandering endlessly.

This is type 804 *Peter's Mother Falls from Heaven*, and number 221 in the Grimms' *Household Tales*. It is well known throughout Latin America. See the text "Santa Catalina" (Spain), pp. 64–66.

Neither Always Queen nor Always Hen

An important personage (a king, governor, general, wealthy man) is caught in the act of making love with a rustic woman, and defends himself by alleging the necessity of changing his food or sexual affections.

Obstinate Like the Woman of the Louse
Obstinate Like the Woman of the Scissors

In a stormy discussion with her husband, the wife insists that she has found lice on his head. She continues to defy all his reasoning, until, enraged, he throws her into the water. As she sinks for the last time she raises her thumbs in a gesture of cracking the louse.

In a variant of the type, the wife insists that cheese is cut with scissors and not with a knife.

This is type 1365 *The Obstinate Wife* in its subforms 1365C *The Wife Insults the Husband as Lousy-Head* and 1365B *Cutting with the Knife or Scissors*. Brazilian texts are published in Gustav Barroso, *O Sertao e o Mundo* (Rio de Janeiro, 1923), and João Ribeiro, *O Folk-Lore* (Rio de Janeiro, 1919).

The Cock must be Killed the First Night

The damsel—chaste, beautiful, rich—was avoided by suitors who feared her rough, violent, ferocious temper. Even though aware of her disobedience and arrogance, a young man fell in love with her and married her. After the wedding ceremony they went to bed, and when the lamp failed to extinguish itself voluntarily, the young husband shot it to pieces. In the morning when the cock started to crow and did not obey the husband's orders to be silent, he pierced it with his spear. The frightened wife, now alarmed, became as placid and sweet as an angel.

The bride's father, wishing to know the secret of the young couple's happiness, listens to his son-in-law's confidences, and tried to repeat the taming procedure with his aged wife. He shoots the light and murders the cock. The old woman made fun of him, and said that he should have killed the cock on their wedding night.

This form adds the comic episode of the father-in-law's failure to the well-known formula of type 901 *Taming of the Shrew* (motif T251.2), which has taken root in both North and South America. The incident of shooting the cock is not known in any of the numerous European versions. Luis da Camara Cascudo has studied the tale in *Anubis e Outros Ensaios* 27 (Rio de Janeiro, 1951).

May the Order from the Government be Achieved!

Returning home, a young man tells his sister there is a law from the government ordering the old women to be married before the youngest girls. The sister objected: "It is an absurd law." Then the elderly mother gave her opinion: "Shut up, girl. He who is powerful is the ruler. May the orders from the government be achieved!"

Luis da Camara Cascudo has published Brazilian versions and commented on the variant given by Luisa Freire in *Trinta Estorias Brasileiras* (Porto, Purtugal, 1955), no. 11a. [A North American form has a tittering old woman in an occupied country ask a sentry, "Pray when does the ravishing begin?" Or an old woman sits calmly in a train being held up by Jesse James. A man rushing out calls to her, "Don't you know Jesse James robs all the men and rapes all the women?" "Jesse James is running this show," she replies. Duffy Daugherty the ex-football coach of Michigan State University, gave a modified version of the Jesse James story during a broadcast of the Oklahoma-Texas football game on national television in the fall of 1973. Ed.]

Are You Going to Set Your Father Free From the Scaffold?

This saying refers to an episode in the life of Saint Anthony of Lisbon or Padua, Fernando Bulhoens (1195–1231). He was preaching a sermon in Padua, Italy, when he received a supernatural message saying that his father was in risk of dying. Through a miracle he was taken to Lisbon and appeared in court where his father had been condemned to die on the gibbet for committing a murder. Saint Anthony led the people and judges to the cemetery, brought the murdered one to life again, and asked him, "Has this man killed you?" "No, he is innocent," the victim replied. The judges freed the accused one, and the dead one returned to his grave. Saint Anthony returned to his sermon where the worshipers had been waiting for him.

This *case* is used ironically on hurried, restless, distressed persons. A long Oriental and European bibliography on the theme is given by René Basset, *Mille et un Contes.* (Paris, 1927) vol. 3, n. 293, which omits the Portuguese tradition that was transmitted to Brazil.

Peru

Treasure, Envy, and Witchcraft

Collected by Jean MacLaughlin in July 1972 on the outskirts of Arequipa and translated from the Spanish.

This legend is properly grouped with "hidden treasures" (R. Christiansen, *The Migratory Legends* [Helsinki, 1958], 8010 ff., "Stories about Hidden Treasures and the Search for Them"), because most informants shift back and forth between describing this type of encounter and other more standard "finds" of buried treasure. In many respects, this legend is closer to the tales of lost mines than to those of buried treasure caches, because many of the Peruvian legends make explicitly clear that the llama's burden is the general wealth of the mountain, whose veins of ore have been transformed into bullion or other portable form. Details of the approach to the llama's cargo and subsequent discussion of other treasure sightings and hunts are standard for most western treasure lore.[1]

Treasure acquisition through an encounter with a mysterious llama pack-train is a legendary motif widespread in Peru.[2] It differs in two major respects from European legends involving mountain spirits and mysterious ghost trains.

(1) The Andean supernatural donor is not so personified as in Europe. Rather than a specific supernatural creature or god of the mountains, the Andean donor is one of various tutelary spirits associated

1. Peruvian references to the belief in throwing one's hat or other personal object to immobilize the treasure include: Juvenal Casaverde Rojas, "El mundo sobrenatural en una comunidad," *Allpanchis Phuturinqa* (Cuzco) 2 (1970): 143; and *Monografía de la provincia de Parinacochas* (Lima: "Tipografía Peruana," S. A., for the Centro de Colaboración Pedagógica Provincial del Magisterio Primario de la Provincia de Parinacochas [1950–51], 2: 333).

2. The closest parallels I have found for the legend given here occur in Hildebrando Castro Pozo, *Nuestra comunidad indígena* (Lima: Editorial "El Lucero" [1924] pp. 406–7) and Casaverde Rojas, "El mundo sobrenatural," pp. 142–43 (two legends). Other published references specifically stating that the llama [or deer] pack-train carries the mountain's own minerals include *Monografía de . . . Parinacochas*, 2: 311; Arturo Jiménez Borja, *Leyendas del Perú* (Lima: n.p., 195?), no. 8 "Los auquis".

with mountain peaks.[3] These spirits may occasionally be described as appearing in more or less human form, yet many features of the belief system and associated legends indicate that the mountain itself is considered animate. In many legends, mountains talk to each other aloud at night, discussing the fates of men wavering in their faith about making the customary propitiatory offerings to the earth or the place during travel or a hunt. In others, mountains bet with each other about performing certain feats. In the legend given here, the informant refers not to a personified deity, but to "the place," no individual being seen. Incidentally, it is significant that August is the most auspicious time for hunting buried treasure, because in that month the earth is especially "alive," and an annual offering is made to the earthmother, Pachamama, preparatory to planting.

(2) The llama train is not ghostly, but is composed of living animals who are the sacred pets and messengers of the mountain. When a mysterious or invisible herdsman is involved, it is not clear whether he is a personification of the mountain or merely another attendant spirit, but there is no implication that he is a specific human ghost, as is so often the case in Europe and America.

Other Peruvian treasure lore deals with hidden caches (especially of Incan gold), lost mines or veins of ore, mysterious golden churchbells, and an important cluster of legends connecting bulls with treasure or mineral wealth. In some of these legends, bulls represent veins of ore (a red bull personifying copper, a white bull being silver, a black bull being coal, etc.). In others, the bull itself is made of gold and is a mysterious creature dwelling at the bottom of a lake. José María Arguedas and Francisco Izquierdo Ríos felt that the European-introduced bull had replaced the indigenous supernatural being known as the *amaru* in many of these legends.[4]

A careful historical study of treasure legends in Peru would be of great interest, considering the pre-Columbian Andean economic system. Gold had privileged ornamental value as adornment restricted to the Inca and royalty, but did not acquire its use as money until the coming of the Spaniards. Even today, there are relatively isolated areas along the traditional foot-trail barter routes in Peru where food and

3. Two of the best and most recent descriptions of the range of Andean spirits and supernaturals are Casaverde Rojas, "El mundo sobrenatural," pp. 121–243; and Juan Víctor Núñez del Prado, "El mundo sobrenatural de los quechuas del sur del Perú a través de la communidad de Qotobamba," *Allpanchis Phuturinqa* 2 [1970]: 57–119).

4. José María Arguedas and Francisco Izquierdo Ríos, eds., *Mitos, leyendas y cuentos peruanos* (2d ed.; Lima: Casa de la Cultura del Perú, 1970), pp. 261–68.

other necessities are virtually unobtainable with money.[5] With the introduction of mining for profit, many Indians met their deaths in forced labor in the mines. Under these circumstances, the theme of the lost mine or the dried-up vein of ore is usually viewed as beneficial for the Indians and punishment for the white men. It is usually seen as the result of a deliberate act by the mountain. When Indians are shown in the role of making an accidental find of a rich vein or an old, lost mine, they either obliterate all traces of it and maintain strict silence about its existence, or they are followed, exploited, or murdered for their knowledge.

The principal characters in Sra. Berroa's legend are not Indians, and the only mention of "Indian" is in reference to the mysterious herdsman, it being assumed that only an Indian would be performing such menial labor as herding. Nevertheless, her account is a synthesis of highland Quechua Indian tradition and point-of-view and European-derived tradition.

In the basic story, two traders are resting overnight during a trip hauling fruit by mule-train from Arequipa to Omate, Peru, when they hear a pack-train of llamas pass by at midnight. They hear the voice of an Indian llama-herdsman, but never see him. One of the llamas is about to lose its cargo and they decide to steal it, but are afraid of being caught in the act by the Indian, who still has not appeared. The llama's cargo is money in the form of gold units called "sterlings" (as opposed to "white silver" or regular silver). The traders decide to get rid of the fruit and take the money home instead. Townspeople believe their sudden wealth is ill-gotten, and have witchcraft worked against them. The traders consult a folk curer and then a diviner, discover the cause of their illness, and return the witchcraft. A new type of witchcraft against the traders is then attempted by the children of the original evildoer, who died from the first counterspell.

In the pre-Columbian belief system of the Andes, the earth is animate and sacred. High mountains and peculiar rock formations often bear individual names, are considered to have individual personalities, and are addressed as "lords." This is "the place," which is "like a Christian," or like a human being. Many Andean legends tell of the earth and mountains moving their mineral veins about at will, causing mines suddenly to dry up to punish the white man's greed, or showing deserving Indians where to find veins of ore or caches of hidden Inca treasure. Vicuñas and llamas are the sacred animals of the mountains.

5. Based on personal conversation with Rod Burchard, who carried out field research in 1969–70 in Huánuco, Peru, studying the use of *coca* in traditional economic barter, in partial fulfillment of his Ph.D. in anthropology at Indiana University.

In the treasure legends, these animals are often depicted as hauling the mountain's treasures to a new location in the middle of the night. A mysterious herdsman may or may not be seen. Other legends tell of disasters following the animals' being hunted or harmed. Note that in this particular legend, the traders do not attempt to keep the llama itself.

In the narrative, notice the image of prosperity depicted as the culmination of good fortune, and the envious reaction of neighbors not sharing it. The lucky finders want land, underlings to do their labor, fine clothes and houses, stores, and a liquor business. In Arequipa, the crudest hut is built with rough lava rocks, unmortared. A better house may use shaped (or "worked") stone, but the dream is to use "noble material," which is bricks and mortar. The point is that rocks are free, but bricks are usually bought. Anyone who can build himself a brick house tries to make it big enough to use the front or downstairs part as a small neighborhood general store. To have enough capital to enter the liquor business is the sure road to further riches, since alcoholic consumption is tremendous among the working classes of Peru. This is prosperity.

The neighbors' envy and subsequent use of witchcraft are a classic example of a worldview George Foster called "the image of limited good."[6] Foster based his study on Mexican peasant society and treasure legends, making the point that in a social system that does not permit true economic and social advancement through normal individual effort, people come to believe that material prosperity exists only in a fixed, limited amount, and that one person can acquire it only at the expense of another, or from some source completely outside the system. Sudden wealth can only be the result of something like the supernatural (as in finding a treasure) or the malicious appropriation of another's goods (as in theft or murder). This particular legend contains both ideas.

Suspicion and mistrust are supposedly rife in such a society. Notice that in this legend the wife hedges even when talking to the curer and the diviner, refusing to tell all she knows, giving only the sketchiest details of the treasure find. Note also that the later gift of food is suspect and is immediately given to the dog (indeed, it is poisoned). The informant later comments that her grandfather told her of this incident, and always used it to make his point that she should never accept anything free, given for no apparent reason. The informant still follows that advice to the letter. Although exceptionally poor, she never

6. See George M. Foster. "Treasure Tales, and the Image of the Static Economy in a Mexican Peasant Community," *Journal of American Folklore* 77 (1964): 39–44; and "Peasant Society and the Image of Limited Good," *American Anthropologist* 67 (1965): 293–315.

accepted the smallest favor or gift of food from the collector without making a return gift, be it a single egg, or one orange left over from her day's sale of fruit, or ordering her children to sweep my sidewalk, and so on. The informant is exceptionally scrupulous about observing ritual courtesies of exchange, but she seems typical in her underlying suspicions. For instance, another neighbor, who had eaten eggs in my house and later discovered that they had been an unexpected gift to me from a neighbor who was her enemy, was convinced that we had all been hexed. The idea that "you don't get something for nothing" carries dangerous overtones here.

The basic vision is positive, however, at least with this informant, for she firmly believes that the poor and deserving are rewarded by luck and by gifts from the supernatural. Many of her narratives reflect this, and in this legend she points out that "the place already knows who is poor" and should receive riches. When the collector heard of her uncle's own treasure find, and said, "What luck!" the informant quickly noted that the treasure had "maintained them. They've been poor." She herself is poor, and can still hope for similar luck. In the meantime, she is a folk curer and midwife, she occasionally feeds her family cat flesh to protect them against witchcraft, has Masses said and keeps vigil for a guardian skull that is ensconced in a niche in her wall, and generally combines European and pre-Columbian Andean belief in her daily life, just as they are combined in this legend.

Motifs: N555.1 "Between midnight and cockcrow best time for unearthing treasure"; A418 "Deity of particular mountain"; F750 "Extraordinary mountains and valleys"; F755 "Living mountain"; F1006 "Extraordinary activity of mountains"; A165.1 "Animals as attendants of god"; A155 "Animals of the gods"; B259 "Miscellaneous religious animals"; F982 "Animals carry extraordinary burden"; B583 "Animal gives treasure to man"; N554 "Ceremonies and prayers used at unearthing of treasure"; A1337.0.3 "Disease caused by witchcraft"; D1712 "Diviner"; N543 "Certain person to find treasure"; Q111.6 "Treasure as reward"; Q60 "Other good qualities rewarded"; Q64 "Patience rewarded"; Q81 "Reward for perseverance"; D1385.13 "Charm prevents witchcraft"; K527.1 "Poisoned food (drink) fed to animal instead of to intended victim"; N553 "Tabus in effect while treasure is being unearthed"; N532 "Light indicates hidden treasure"; N511 "Treasure in ground"; N511.1.4 "Buried treasure wanders from place to place, indicated by a light"; N551 "Who may unearth a treasure"; N538 "Treasure pointed out by supernatural creature"; N555 "Time favorable for unearthing treasure."

Collection Data: July 1972; squatter settlement "Independencia." Recorded inside informant's two-room house, built of unmortared volcanic rock with corrugated tin roof and earthen floor. Audience: None except collector.

Circumstances: Collector lived directly across street from this informant during her eight-month residence in Independencia, and knew this neighbor as well as any. This legend and subsequent discussion of belief are response to collector's asking for information about treasures and whether any had been found in this vicinity.

Translation Comment: The translation is very literal, except for a few minor changes necessary to convey the *meaning* of what was said. The following deletions were made from verbatim transcript: (1) elimination of most false starts and trail-offs; (2) two instances of brief, phrase-length deletions due to unintelligibility of tape; (3) elimination of frequent *"dice"* ("he says") meaning "the person who told me the story says" or "the story says." This narrator uses this type of "he says" automatically, in unstressed form, almost as a stall-word or crutch, and although it does not hinder the oral performance because of its lack of stress, it draws unreasonable attention in written transcript and makes following the story thread very difficult for the average reader. *Tape Location Number* (in Indiana University Archives of Traditional Music): Tape 24 (#14 of cassettes), Arequipa, Peru, "Independencia," CHILDREN, Side A, #700?–end, Side B, #1–205.

Informant Data: Name: Señora Juana Berroa Pinto; age: Forty-five; education: Primary school; birthplace: Omate, Moquegua, Peru; occupation: Independent, small-scale vendor of fruit, customarily selling from a sidewalk position at the Arequipa jail; also a folk curer and midwife; languages: Monolingual Spanish speaker (speaks no Quechua).

Comment: Sra. Berroa has nine living children, and is the sole support of the four small ones still at home. Her income is precarious, and they are very poor, even in this squatter settlement. Her total daily income approximates the Peruvian price of two pounds of meat. Nevertheless, she is proud, insists on absolute respect from her children, and carefully observes social courtesies. Very strong-willed, she is outspoken and has a quick temper. She is literate, unusual in this neighborhood for women in her economic position. Sra. Berroa narrates dramatically, using great expression in face and voice. Although she believes this story to be fact, she told it in a very polished manner, as though she has often told it before and fully recognizes its dramatic potential. Tale learned from grandfather.

Once there were some men who formerly liked to go out with mules, no? go *far* away, more or less here to Arequipa. And then, they'd gotten tired [because of] the animals, the weight they were hauling here. Then they'd taken shelter under a tree, unloading all their animals, the load. And since it must've been more or less twelve at night, then they heard someone saying in the night—

"Go on! Go go go go *on!*" he [the voice] was saying. "Ssssss! Go go go go *on!*"

"What *is* this?" they said.

How the llamas were *walking,* they say! *Loaded* with their boxes! Then they said, "What will be coming in the boxes? But where's the *Indian,* that he doesn't pass? The llamas pass pass *pass,* and that ass the Indian doesn't pass," he [one of the traders] says.

Then, "Go go go *on!* Go *on,* llama!" he [the voice] was saying. The llamas, *well* loaded! And what was it? It was the place, that was transferring riches to another spot.

Well, there's still no *Indian!*

"This llama's about to throw off her two boxes! What do we do? Listen," he told him [one told the other], "what're we going to do?"

"We'll unload the box for ourselves, the two boxes. And we'll let the llama go on."

"Ready."

They unloaded the two boxes.

"Ay! I heard another llama! But if he [the Indian] catches us! And the other boxes?"

"No, we'll just bury it in some place or other."

"Ready."

They got set to bury.

"It must be *al*cohol!"

He [One] said, "The alcohol doesn't matter. Since it's so salable, we'll sell it. We'll put water in it and we'll fix it up to sell as a type of liquor."

"OK," he [the other] said.

Then, they unloaded everything. And the Indian *didn't* pass! *All* the llamas finished passing. Then they buried it there.

Already day cleared, but in spite of this they said, "He's [the Indian] coming! How'll we do this? Listen, better that we urinate on the boxes."

"Ready."

Now they urinated on the box. And next, when it was time to open up, they found themselves with pure *money!* Gold *sterlings!*

"Ah, *caray!* It's been *luck* for us then, the devil and . . . and we've won. Listen, we're in luck! yes? Let's not carry the fruit back from Arequipa. Let's take it back to Arequipa, even if it has to be for the pigs."

"Sure!"

All of it was money. They got set, they carried, they carried, they just carried it like that, little by little, to the house. There they knocked down the price of all the fruit, *cheap*, yes? [so they could fill the saddle-bags with money].

Then, they took hold of the situation, they bought lands besides, and preferred to have their work done [by others]. They got themselves their good stores, each as much as the other. And now soon their wives were well-dressed, their children well-outfitted. And the rest of the capital profited them enough [?] to do business in alcohol, in every class of drinks. Then, from being poor, these became rich. They had a *lot* of money. Now then they made *vineyards*, now they made *wine*. And they had money, finally they made themselves their two houses. Well-made! Formerly, well, they used to use worked stone. *Very* pretty, their houses!

Then, people were envious.

"*Why* do they envy us?"

"Where have these [traders] gotten so much money? Surely they've robbed, because they went to Arequipa. Who've they murdered? That's why they've come with *so* much money."

"What do we *do* with these people?" they [the traders] said. At last, they [the traders] fell sick, the others as much as they. Then, one said, "Why *us*?" Until they [the traders] spent, spent, spent [money on medicines]. But they didn't know that they'd had evils done against them.

Well, then, in this case, already the wife of one had gone out asking, telling what had happened, that the husbands had fallen into a state of touch-and-go.

"Maybe . . . they've had . . . Tell the truth! We're not going to talk to anybody!" he [the *curandero*] told her.

"You know that they've found a . . . a treasure, and . . . in boxes on the slope. And, curious, they went to open them and found money. And to summarize, they've brought it with them in their . . . of course, they went to work, they haven't gone out to rob! They haven't gone out to assault anybody! And here the people . . . I see that they envy us."

"Let's go, lady. There I have a woman who's a diviner. She'll tell you!" he told her.

"Yes!" she said.

They went. Then this woman told her fortune. Her husband, well, they've found it—the *mini*mum facts suitable—they'd found the money. All this she'd [the wife] told her [the diviner].

"It was the place," she'd told her [the diviner told the wife]. "The place has given them these riches because they were long-suffering in their work. And God has helped them, and the place also. But what happens? People are bad, they've had witchcraft made on them. But you're going to do these things. You're going to go, lady, and bring your husband here, and *I'll* cure him."

"How much are you going to charge me?"

"We'll charge you some three thousand *soles* [about $69.00], but we'll leave them good and well."

"All right. It doesn't matter," they [the wives] said.

Then they cured them, and some of these other men fell sick, and the evil that they did to them [the traders] returned to *them*. Well, then they began to sicken, to sicken, until they died. Yes.

MacLaughlin: This *happened*?

Sra. Juana Berroa P.: Yes, it happened. Then, not content with this, these women—to the *children*!

"My mother has died in this fashion, and she's . . ." They [the children of the envious neighbors] knew that their mother had had it done, and they [the traders' families] returned it to her. Then they [the children] went, they paid a woman whose specialty was to give "white skin." Then she [the witch] sent them [the traders] some platters of *chicharrones* [crisp-fried meat or skin] for them to eat with potatoes, corn on the cob—for them to eat. Then, since this [first] witch already told them that she was going to send this, "You're not going to eat," she said. And, "Let's give it to the *dog!*" she tells him. They gave the *chicharrones* to the dog, and they say the dog just [began] to peel away, to peel away, to run up and down like crazy.

"You look how they did these evils!" Well, the dog died. It didn't fall on them because they already put a counterspell against the witch.

Now here this story has ended, miss.

MacLaughlin: But it was . . . it was true?

Sra. Juana Berroa P.: It was fact, yes.

MacLaughlin: And where did it happen?

Sra. Juana Berroa P.: This happened in Omate. Yes. In a place they call San Francisco.

MacLaughlin: Has it been a long time ago?

Sra. Juana Berroa P.: Already a *long* time ago, he says. My grandfather has told us. That [the dog] shed himself away. And he said, "You should *never* receive anything from anybody." He used to tell us. It happened so, miss.

MacLaughlin: One thing I didn't understand. When they found the boxes, why did they decide to urinate on the boxes?

Sra. Juana Berroa P.: Because they thought that maybe it was the place. Already it came to their heads that it was the luck of the place that they had there. Then immediately they'd urinated because it was a secret. That is, to urinate or throw your hat with your left hand is good. The money, or that is, the treasure that one finds won't remove itself. Because when one doesn't do it, then the place *quickly* removes it to another place when one sometimes has . . . better said, is greedy.

MacLaughlin: Ah, yes?

Sra. Juana Berroa P.: Yes.

MacLaughlin: How, for example?

Sra. Juana Berroa P.: For example, you see fire burning blue like this around here, and then, of course, they come near. Already they know that it's the place. Since formerly the Incas—well, in the *sierras* that they've passed, they've thrown all their treasures around here, and since the great rain came, it buried them. Then these are, of course, changing their location, or the place moves one to another. Because places like a Christian move it from one side to another. Also the place already knows who is poor, *this* one it causes to find it for himself. Yes.

MacLaughlin: Ah. And it shows itself also by the blue flame?

Sra. Juana Berroa P.: Yes, yes. You see the fire burn at a place and you go, it disappears, or at least also, sometimes a lamb appears.

MacLaughlin: Ah, yes?

Sra. Juana Berroa P.: Yes. Around midnight when everything is silence, and get hold of yourself and throw a little urine, or at least throw your hat, just right there the money is piled up.

MacLaughlin: And is it true what they say that in August there's more luck in finding [treasure]?

Sra. Juana Berroa P.: Yes, yes.

MacLaughlin: And are there those from here too who've found, from Arequipa?

Sra. Juana Berroa P.: Yes. At . . . wait! well, here in Characato they've found one, also in a church.

MacLaughlin: Ah, yes?

Sra. Juana Berroa P.: Oh, no no no! In a *mill* they've found it. It's coming out in the newspaper and everything.

MacLaughlin: Yes?

Sra. Juana Berroa P.: Yes. Haven't you read it? It's come out in the newspaper.

MacLaughlin: No.

Sra. Juana Berroa P.: I don't know *where* that newspaper is!

MacLaughlin: Mmmmmm.

Sra. Juana Berroa P.: They were taking out and they've found *veins* of gold.

MacLaughlin: And you yourself have friends here who've found [treasures], or not?

Sra. Juana Berroa P.: Ah, here I don't. In my land yes, yes. There also, other uncles who told me [things] like that, and other things that, I don't know, in *fact* have happened to them. They've already found.

To be precise, an uncle of mine has also found a hidden treasure like that. In a field that has a vineyard, he'd gone at night. He says that the fox was coming, was eating the grapes, and he went armed with his shotgun to kill her. And he says that he finds a little *light,* but *blue.* Afterward it turned a gold color. He says that he told his mother-in-law about it. Then, "It must be *some*thing!" he says she said. Then one day, well, my uncle got up his nerve, he threw his hat there. And it's gone. Afterward they've been digging, digging, they've found a little pot like this.

MacLaughlin: Ah, yes?

Sra. Juana Berroa P.: They've found [gold] *sterlings. Nothing* of "white silver." They've found nothing but pure sterlings. And with this my uncle has sold it, and then [*you* know] with this he's had his field worked, he's bought lands.

MacLaughlin: What luck!

Sra. Juana Berroa P.: But it's maintained them. They've been poor. My uncle was quite *poor.* Now if you'd just see them outside, I wish you'd go! They've *got!*

MacLaughlin: Mmmmmm.

Sra. Juana Berroa P.: They've *got!* Many fields!

MacLaughlin: What luck!

Sra. Juana Berroa P.: That's *luck.*

The Mouse and the Fox

Collected by Jean MacLaughlin in June 1972 on the outskirts of Arequipa and translated from the Spanish.

In Peru, the trickster-hero of many animal tales is the guinea pig or, as in this tale, the mouse. In many Spanish-speaking areas, this trickster cycle involves the clever rabbit and the stupid fox. But the Spanish word for "rabbit" is *conejo,* and the common term for "guinea pig" is *conejo de Indias,* usually shortened to the identical *conejo.* "Rabbit" is usually distinguished as *liebre* ("hare"). In the southern Andes, hardly a household does not keep a cage or a yardful of the indigenous guinea pigs, and this animal is usually understood to be the cycle's hero. Occasionally, use of the Quechua word *quwi* (in Spanish spelling, *cuy*), meaning "guinea pig," removes any doubt.

These episodic humorous tales circulate separately, or linked, as they appear in this text. Scattered texts have been published in Peru with some frequency, although rarely reflecting true oral style. Most published Peruvian texts of this cycle are some combination of the tale types included here, plus types 8, 34, 34B (see also Hansen **67D and E), 66A and B, and 74C*. Other stupid fox tales exist, featuring different protagonists, and several seem to be indigenous Peruvian tales. Peruvian studies of these fox and rabbit-mouse-guinea pig tales are Victor Navarro del Aguila, "Cuentos populares del Perú: el zorro y el ratón (y sus variantes)," *Revista de la Sección Arqueológica de la Universidad Nacional del Cuzco* 2 (1946): 118–43; Efraín Morote Best, "El zorro y el ratón" in *Elementos de folklore (definición, contenido, procedimiento)* (Cuzco, Peru: H. G. Rozas, 1950): 468–80; idem, "Cuento tradicional: Pascual y Diego: Las conexiones de nuestros cuentos," *Tradición* (Cuzco) 1:1 (1950): 38–49; idem, "El tema del viaje al cielo," *Tradición* 8:21 (1958): 20–31.

The rabbit-fox cycle is widely popular throughout Latin America, and good comparative notes can be found in most of the major collections. Stanley L. Robe's *Index of Mexican Folktales* (Berkeley: University of California Press, 1973) gives extensive and current references for these tale types for the Mexican culture area. For southern South American references, Terrence Leslie Hansen's *The Types of the Folktale in Cuba, Puerto Rico, the Dominican Republic, and Spanish South America* (Berkeley: University of California Press, 1957) and the collections of Yolando Pino Saavedra (Chile) and Susana Chertudi (Argentina) are a good beginning.

The particular text given here includes the "Tarbaby," the deceptive exchange "To marry your daughter," "Holding up the Rock," "The Rain of Fire," and "The Jug as Trap," combined with the unindexed incident of a hidden animal's lick mistaken for urine or for the presence of a hidden lover. In Arequipa, Peru, the "Rock" and the "Rain of Fire" episodes were usually linked, and were one of the most widely known animal tales. The "Tarbaby" introduction and "The Jug as Trap" were less frequently encountered in Arequipa, but seem to be quite common in the Cuzco area. This particular informant's father is from Cuzco, and taught him the tale.

The "Rain of Fire" episode requires some comment. Although obviously related to type 78A and Hansen **82, this episode does not exactly fit into either type, yet seems quite standardized throughout highland Peru in the following form. The mouse convinces the fox that a rain of fire is coming (the end of the world is implied, and the fox is praying), and the fox is tricked into entering a hole, which the mouse secretly stops up with thorns. The mouse asks the fox to feel the fiery rain, and the fox mistakes the pain of the thorn-pricks for the supposed "burn" of the fire. Only after a long while does the fox dare crawl out, then discovering the deception.

This text prompts one observation about "completeness" and "fragmentation" in taletelling. Of legends, Linda Dégh notes, "the greater the popularity of a legend within a group, the more functional it becomes, and the more and more conspicuous its incompleteness becomes. As it spreads almost like a rumor from person to person, it cannot reach a consistent form but often remains incoherent. Those who pass it on do not need to tell it in detail, since the essentials are generally known.[1]

I collected the "Rain of Fire" many times, and the occasion of this text was probably the most successful as a narrative event, with delighted audience reaction. Yet in working with this text, I found it elliptical as far as the actual plot. Being very familiar with the tale myself, at first I thought it quite clear, but discovered that several knowledgeable scholars did not really understand what was happening from the unedited, starkly literal transcript. This humorous tale has suffered the same transformation as the well-known legend—the tale action is *assumed to be known*. This version is not "fragmentary" but *elliptical*. It is "incoherent" only to an outsider. Here, the narrator stressed the humorous, dramatic aspect of the tale, and that was the basis of his narrative success: vocal theatrics, gestures, comical facial expressions. That this process happens frequently is clear in the existence of our joke about the convicts who had heard each other's jokes so often that they all laughed just from hearing the punch line (or the code number) of the joke.

The point is: (1) more care should be taken to distinguish those texts that are "incomplete" or "fragmentary" due to ellipsis of known content from those that are "incomplete" due to limited knowledge; and (2) the short, anecdotal or humorous tale should be further explored as a narrative form capable of being reduced to almost schematic proportions and yet considered "well-told."

Tale Types: Aarne-Thompson 175 *The Tarbaby and the Rabbit*; 1530 *Holding up the Rock* [K1251]; cf. 78A *Animal Allows himself to be Tied so as to Avoid Being Carried off by Storm* [K713.1.1] (Hansen **74A); cf. Hansen **82 *Puma is about to devour tiger but latter persuades him to help dig deep hole because world is coming to end*; Aarne-Thompson 68A *The Jug as Trap*.

Motifs: K741 "Capture by tarbaby"; K842.3 "Tied animal persuades another to take his place"; K842 "Dupe persuaded to take prisoner's place in sack: killed"; K1251 "Holding up the rock" (type 1530); K567 "Escape by pretending to perform errand (do work) for captor"; K550 "Escape by false plea"; K1022 "Dupe persuaded to steal food: cannot

1. "The 'Belief Legend' in Modern Society: Form, Function, and Relationship to Other Genres" in *American Folk Legend: A Symposium*, ed. Wayland D. Hand (Berkeley: University of California Press, 1971), p. 62.

escape"; K1022.6 "Fox eats cake: gets brass pot caught on neck"; J1762 "Animal thought to be a person."

Collection data: June 1972; squatter settlement "Independencia" outside in schoolyard of primary school, with collector, informant, and audience seated on rocks and ground. Audience: schoolboys. Circumstances: Boys were released from class to go outside with me and record, which they always regarded as a great event, because they loved my tape recorder. Those not interested in stories being told were playing, talking, etc. *Tape location number* (in Indiana University Archives of Traditional Music): Tape 21 (#11 of cassettes), Arequipa, Peru, "Independencia," CHILDREN, Side A, #386–509.

Informant data: Name: Jaime Rodríguez Huillca; age: Thirteen; birthplace: Neighborhood of Miraflores, city of Arequipa; length of time in Independencia: Ten years; parents' occupations: Father—construction laborer; also is a folk curer (as was his own father); Mother—takes in laundry; languages: Both parents are native Quechua-speakers who also speak Spanish. Jaime understands Quechua and can speak "only a little" (according to himself), but his dominant language is Spanish. His stories show certain stylistic features typical of Quechua and not Spanish (probably learned directly from his father's imperfect Spanish). Contact with parents' home region is one visit to Cuzco in 1966.

Comment: Jaime is very popular, a natural group leader, and this seems closely tied to his narrative skill. His face and voice are very dramatic while narrating, and he almost invariably holds his audience. He enjoys being in the limelight. His repertoire includes a high proportion of humorous tales and Märchen. Tale learned from Jaime's father, Jesús Rodríguez E. (age fifty-one), born in Cuzco.

They say once there were two *compadres,* the mouse and the fox. Then they say *every* night the mouse was eating a gentleman's flowers, an owner's flowers. Then the owner, well, "Who can be stealing my flowers for himself?! Maybe these are the ones who are carrying them off, my caretakers. What can it be?" Then they say [the owner] goes, then [the caretaker] tells him. "Every night a mouse comes to steal," he says. Then, "Now I'm really going to set a trap. But *what* trap can I set?" [the owner] says.

Then he goes to the cheese factory. "What can you make a trap out of?" [the owner] says to him. "Only traps of wood," he says. "But I think he might not fall into this trap." Then, "I'm going to give you a piece of advice," a man tells him. "Make yourself a tar doll. And you put this on the water pipe, the mouse comes, and when he gives it a whack or something, he gets stuck there." Then, saying, "Thanks!" [the owner] went off.

He makes himself a tar doll, very pretty, and puts it on the water pipe. Then in the night the mouse comes with *lots* of mice. Then he looks, saying, "Ah, *caramba!* So he's put a *caretaker!*" like that. Saying, "You have to know how to *think!*" the mouse said. Then, "I'll go in first. I'll greet him. I'll just greet him. He wants to hit me, you all come, and we'll hit him and we'll get in easily," he said.

Then [the mouse] goes off *slowly, slowly.* Saying, "Good evening, sir! Good evening, sir! Ah, *caramba!* What *is* this? He seems *dumb!* Listen, old man, right now I'm going to knock you over the cliff with a fist! Listen, old man!" Then, "Ah, *caramba!* You want to try yourself?" he says. "Last time! Good evening, sir!" Pum! He got himself stuck. "Let go! Let go! Let go! Let go! Let go! This left hand's stronger! Let go!" Pum! He got stuck. Then, "Let go!" It sticks tighter. "Let go!" They say it sticks tighter. Then, "[I'm going to give you] such a kick, I'm going to make you see stars!" he said. Then, "Let go! Let go!" Pum! He gives him the kick and he gets stuck. Now he was hanging, with one foot on the ground. Saying, "Let go! I've told you the left is *stronger*, see! Let go! Let go!" Pum! He gets stuck. Then, "I've got lots of things to defend myself with, but with these you're going to have to let go," he said. "Let go! Let go!" They say it sticks tighter. Then, saying, "[I'm going to give you] such a head butt, I'm going to knock your brains out!" Pum! He gives him the butt and he got stuck. "Let go! Let go! [I'm going to give you] such a belly smack, I'm going to make you disappear!" he said. Pum! He gives him the belly smack and he gets stuck. Saying, "Let go! Let go! Here I've got the tail end of this black whip." Sssss, he begins to just grind his tail around. Hunnnnnn! He gives it to him and he gets stuck, just completely all balled up. He goes to sleep there. Then, "Compa-a-a-a-nions!" Then the companions are *afraid*, well, uhh! So they run off.

Then at dawn, well, the owner comes. Then, "Let's see. Maybe they've caught something." And the mouse had been *sound* asleep there. Then [the owner] said, saying, "Ah, *caramba!* So *this* little mouse was the one, the stealer of my flowers," saying. Then [the mouse] saying, "Ah, *caramba!* The *owner's* caught me!" He's there thinking. "Look how he's hanging! After lunch we'll kill you, because we don't want to get our hands dirty" [the owner] says. Then, they go off to have lunch.

Then his companion the fox comes. "*Compadrito*, what's *happened* to you?" "Ah, *caramba, compadrito!* Don't you *know?!* Uhhh! It's a *long* story that I can't finish telling you about," he says. "You know, I'm going to marry the daughter of this owner. I'm little, and she's *big.* I *can't* get married. Maybe she'll *step* on me!" saying. Then, "Tie *me* up," said the fox, his *compadre.* "Ah, *caramba!* You, since you're big, you can get married," [the mouse] said. Saying, "Of course!" [the fox] tied himself up.

Then, at twelve the owner comes, with a stick behind [his back]. Then, saying, "Ah, *caramba!* This mouse has *grown!*" He beats him and beats him. "No! No! No! I'm going to marry your daughter! I'm going to marry your daughter!" saying. "Ah, *caramba!* My *daughter* yet!" saying, Pum! harder. All of a sudden he hit the rope and the rope broke. Uy! [The fox] ran off any which-a-way. Then, "My *compadrito* mouse has betrayed me. Now I'm going to eat him," he said.

Then [the fox] is going along hunting, and he finds the mouse holding onto a rock, saying, "Aaaaaaackk! Aaaaackk!" Then, "What's the matter, *compadrito?* I'm going to eat you now, even if you put up a fight!" right? Saying, "No, *compadrito!* You can eat me later. Hold onto this rock. It's going to *flatten* me. If you don't hold it up, the town's going to be destroyed by this rock." "Really?" "Really! Ay!" saying then. Well, [the fox] puts himself to it. Saying, "Since I'm bigger," he also grabs the rock firmly. Then, "I'm going to go bring you a wedge, OK?" [The mouse] climbs up on top of the rock and throws his weight against it. Then it seemed that it was moving itself. "Ah, *caramba!*" Well, [the fox] gripped it harder, saying, "*Compadrito! Compadrito!*" Not any *more!* He begins, then, he lets go, he lets go—*nothing!* The rock doesn't move, *nothing.* It's *very* firm. "Two betrayals! Now I'm *really* going to eat him, no matter *what* he gives me!" saying.

Then he's *going* along, right? He sees the mouse, scratching out a little hole. Then, "Now I'm *really* going to eat him, no matter what!" "Ttt! If you eat me, you die too," [the mouse] said. "Now it's going to rain fire," he said. Saying, "Because if you eat me, tomorrow you die." "Ah, *caramba!*" thought the fox. "It's going to rain?" "Yes, it's going to rain, rain with *fire*," [the mouse] said. Then, "Better I make this hole for *you*, and I'll get myself into this little rock," he said. "Of course," [the fox] says. They scratched it out and got themselves in. There on top [the mouse secretly] put thorns.

"*Compadrito!*" "Yes!" "It's started to rain already, it's already gotten cloudy," [the mouse] said. "But it's just *red* clouds!" Saying, "Ah, *caramba!* What! Maybe it's not going to pass me by!" The fox is already *praying.* Then, "*Compadrito!* Now it's beginning to fall in drops," said the mouse. Saying, "See? Feel!" "Ouch! It sure is, isn't it!" Then, "*Compadrito*, it's just [pouring down like a] *river!* You're under a *river.* See, feel, pure *fire!*" "Ouch! Blood!" [the fox] said. Then, "*Compadrito!*" said the fox. Then, "*Compadrito!*" Now there's no *compadrito.* Then, "That *compadrito!* Maybe it's still raining? Ouch! It's raining." He scratches out a hole at another spot. Mounds of thorns were there. "*Three* betrayals! Now I really eat him, even if he tells me something now! I don't forgive him any more," he said.

Then the mouse had gone into a house at night. Then,

was a clay pot, just full of *mazamorra* [a dessert made of corn flour and sweetened with honey or sugar]. The mouse had eaten up what he could, and had brought *mazamorra* on one little finger, had carried it to the fox. He was going along, standing straight up. Then, "*There's my compadre!*" [The fox] goes running, "*Now* I really eat you!" He'd grabbed him by the little neck. Then, "No no no! Wait wait! Look! Take this, this *mazamorra*. See what a flavor it has!" "Ah *caramba!* Where *is* some?" [the fox] said. Then, "In a house. Shhh! Shut up, then! Don't be so envious, so greedy," [the mouse] said. Then, [the fox] went, he was already just opening his *mouth* there. Then, "I'm going to pass you the key. You eat up." Then, "Carrr! Carrr!" [the mouse] said. Then he reached the key, he opened the door for him.

The fox went inside then. He's *licking* and *eating* and *eating, eating*. Until he got himself into the clay pot by the neck. Then he couldn't get out. "*Compadrito!* Bring me a big rock." Then the mouse brings him a little tiny rock this size. Then, well, [the fox] couldn't break it with this little rock. "A bigger rock!" he said. Then, "Shh! Shh! Listen, there's a big *round* rock, you hear? You can break your head there," [the mouse] said. "Where? Where?" he said. Then [the mouse] brought him near it, and it was the head of an old man. "Sssss! Here! Here you're going to bust it." Pum! "*Ayau!*" the old man said, the old man shouted. Then, "Ah *caramba!* So it was the head of a *man!*" [the fox] said. And then, well, from *fear* he got himself down, just down under the bed.

Then, there was the fox. Well, the mouse was *licking* his mouth, right? Then the old man, "*Ayayau!* I don't know *who* hit me. *Ouch!*" he said. On licking, [the mouse] touched the leg of the old man. Saying, "Old woman! You've *pissed!* What's the matter with you!" Then, and the old woman, "What's happened to *you?*" "I don't know. I think somebody's come. He's almost busted my head!" he said. "It must have been the *fox!*" she said. "Ah *caramba!* So you have another *husband!*" saying.

There it ends.

The Condemned Lover

Collected by Jean MacLaughlin in October 1972 on the outskirts of Arequipa and translated from the Spanish.

Efraín Morote Best has published an extensive study of Hansen tale type **775A & B (often told as "true," that is, as a legend), "La huída mágica: Estudio de un cuento popular del Perú,"[1] based on a representative fifteen versions from highland Peru. This tale type has rarely been printed, despite the fact that it seems widely known in oral tradition. Morote Best's study includes only two previously published texts, both from Pedro S. Monge's collection published as part of José María Arguedas' study, "Folklore del valle del Mantaro, provincias de Jauja y Concepción."[2] Actually, that same Monge-Arguedas collection contains two more tales that begin identically and change only at the point where the "obstacle flight" (D672) begins.[3] Two other versions have been published by Emilio Barrantes and Marcos Yauri Montero.[4] In an urban squatter settlement of migrants from Puno, Cuzco, the department of Arequipa and various other areas, I collected this tale with some frequency, sometimes believed as factual and sometimes not. This particular text was believed to be true.

In this tale type, the "obstacle flight" has become attached to the legendary figure of the "condemned soul" or *condenado*, the malevolent revenant. Peruvian oral tradition abounds with legends about the *condenado*, who has many ogre-like characteristics of possibly pre-Columbian extraction, as well as identifying features typical of the "condemned" as he is known in Catholic European lore. José María Arguedas' outstanding 1953 collection includes many *condenado* tales. It was one of the very few Peruvian works consulted for Hansen's *The*

1. Efraín Morote Best, "La huída mágica: Estudio de un cuento popular del Perú" in *Miscellanea Paul Rivet, Octogenario Dicata* (México: Universidad Nacional Autónoma de México, 1958 [1959]), *XXXI Congreso Internacional de Americanistas* 2: 797–848. This is a very important article for Peruvian folklore, giving good references for other legendary topics (the *karkar*, the *mula*, flying heads, the *condenado* in general), as well as synopses of tales as diverse as the Transformation Flight (D671; see type 313), The Children and the Ogre (type 327A), Strong John (type 650A), The Fox and the Condor in Heaven (type 58*), and some comment on mouse (guinea pig or rabbit) and fox tales. No references are given to the Hansen index.

2. José María Arguedas, "Folklore del valle del Mantaro, provincias de Jauja y Concepción," *Folklore Americano* (Lima) 1 (1953): 101–236. Morote Best does not provide specific page references, but these two texts are nos. 18 and 19, on pp. 150–53. This Arguedas collection and study is one of the most important works extant on contemporary Peruvian oral tradition and belief.

3. Arguedas, "Folklore del . . . Mantaro," texts nos. 16 and 17, on pp. 146–49. Note: Arguedas has since published another tale including the "Obstacle Flight," but with a different introductory plot, in "Cuentos religiosos-mágicos quechuas de Lucanamarca," *Folklore Americano* 8–9 (1960–61): 169–75.

4. Emilio Barrantes, ed., *Folklore de Huancayo* (2d ed., Huancayo, Peru: Tip. "La Industria," n.d., p. 72); and Marcos Yauri Montero, *Warakuy: Nuevas leyendas peruanas* (Lima: Ediciones "Piedra y Nieve," 1967), pp. 40–41.

*Types of the Folktale in Cuba, Puerto Rico, the Dominican Republic,
and Spanish South America*. Hansen invented many new tale type numbers to accommodate the *condenado* tales, and summarized the plots
In the 1964 edition of Aarne-Thompson's *The Types of the Folktale*,
most of these types were unfortunately re-collapsed under type
760*, *The Condemned Soul*, although many do exist as stable, quite
diverse types. Unfortunately, not even Arguedas' collection is reliable
for true oral style, although it is much closer than most published in
Peru.

At the most basic "episode" level, Morote Best divides this tale into
three parts: (1) fraternal incest; (2) condemnation and its consequences;
and (3) the "magic flight." At a more detailed level, based on a wide
knowledge of the type, he breaks it into nine basic motifs, which
roughly comprise: (1) fraternal incest, (2) flight from social disappro-
bation, (3) the youth's return to rob his father, (4) unwitting murder by
the father, (5) return to the beloved in a condemned state, (6) a journey
with the beloved and an encounter with a woman (often the Virgin)
who reveals the secret of the condemnation and (7) bestows magic objects (usually soap, comb, mirror and needle), (8) the "obstacle flight,"
and (9) the girl's salvation. In the versions I collected in Arequipa, I
found the greatest variation in the circumstances under which the girl
learns of the condemnation, details of the magic flight, and final disposal of the *condenado*. Not one version I collected specified the incest
theme, nor do the Arguedas texts, and although Morote Best's study is
excellent, I think he has overstated the case for incest.

The text published here is somewhat unusual in its inclusion of the
following episodes:

(1) Tying the *condenado* to a tree. I have recorded this tale from two
children of the same family, and both include the tree episode, but in
a faltering way. Most stumbling hesitations have been edited out of
the text published here, so this faltering is not as evident in the printed
text as it is on the recorded tape. I have heard the children's mother tell
a separate *condenado* legend that includes tricking the *condenado* into
letting himself be tied to an oak. In that legend, the incident is coherent,
and I believe that she has occasionally faltered and blended the two
tales in narrating to her children. Two of the Arguedas texts include
some motif of the couple being temporarily tied together, however,[5]
and I have collected a *condenado* tale including escape by deceptively
volunteering to be tied by the belt while absenting self to urinate (belt
is then tied to stone, etc.), so perhaps the informant's mother substi-

5. Arguedas, "Folklore del . . . Mantaro," p. 149, and idem, "Cuentos . . .
de Lucanamarca," pp. 170–72, 174–75.

tuted the oak motif for another tying episode which did form part of the tale as she herself learned it.

(2) The magic speaking blood drops (D1611.6). Although a mobile motif, none of my informants other than this one family included it in this tale, and Morote Best does not mention it either. It *does* frequently appear in versions of Juan Oso (type 650A *Strong John*).

(3) Carrying the *condenado* halfway across the river and leaving him on a rock. This is not commonly included in Hansen **775A & B as studied by Morote Best and collected by me. It is a mobile motif, however, and I have seen it in a *condenado* legend in which a man kicks a corpse or a black dog and later encounters a beautiful woman who seduces and then pursues him, saying she was the corpse (or dog). He is forced to carry her on his back, and eventually escapes by leaving her in midstream in this manner.[6]

(4) The magic rose that grows into a rosebush. Morote Best believes the magic objects to be quite standardized as mirror, comb, soap and pin or needle, occasionally being replaced by sash, scissors, thread, or a few other items not including the rose.

I do feel I need to point out that the text published here is virtually a verbatim transcript of an oral narration, whereas Morote Best provides only detailed schematic synopses of the versions he himself collected from oral tradition. With each version (from various geographical areas), Morote Best says that he has heard this tale several times, and it is to be supposed that he has chosen the most complete, the best rendered, and has avoided those which might show crossing with other tale types, although this is a process which happens frequently in actual oral tradition. The reduction to schema is valuable in many ways, but certainly has its pitfalls. For instance, Morote Best takes the position that fraternal incest is to be assumed as the original reason for elopement, even in those tales where it is not made specific. In his schematic synopsis, one of the Arguedas texts is then paraphrased as "there exists a couple . . . whose love relations are not approved by their families."[7] In the original Arguedas text, the case is concrete, "Once there was a twenty-four-year-old man who had his beloved named Godilia, about whom the young man's father had come to discover certain ties with another man and for this reason had both lovers mortified. To avoid this bother, they resolved to go away. . . ."[8]

Nevertheless, in most other respects, the text published here *is* typi-

6. Arguedas, "Cuentos . . . de Lucanamarca," pp. 169–75. A variant of this tale is to be found in Hildebrando Castro Pozo, *Nuestra comunidad indígena* (Lima: Editorial "El Lucero," 1924), pp. 392–96, and I have also collected it. Neither the Castro Pozo version nor mine includes the stream escape.

7. Morote Best, "La huída mágica," p. 802. Translation is mine.

8. Arguedas, "Folklore del . . . Mantaro," p. 151.

cal. Two of its typical features might be misunderstood or pass un-
noticed by one not familiar with the type: (1) the llama, and (2) the
girl's dog.

(1) The *condenado* comes back to the girl pulling a llama loaded
with what appear to be babies' bones. Most of the versions I collected
in Arequipa included this llama, and its cargo was usually bones.
Morote Best cites two versions containing the llama motif, and identi-
fies this as the soul of the llama ritually sacrificed as part of funeral
ceremonies in parts of the Andes, meant to accompany the young man's
soul to the otherworld (motif V67.5).[9]

(2) The girl's dog howls and cries, and the next action is the couple's
going to bed for the first time after the *condenado*'s return. The orally
recorded version shows great hesitation at this point, and I believe a
motif has been omitted due to an error of memory. In other versions I
have heard in Arequipa, the dog jumps into bed between the couple,
and prevents the *condenado*'s approaching the girl for sexual relations
(E472, E439.3, B785). One of Morote Best's versions includes a spirit-
sighted dog, but no mention of bed.[10]

In general this is a well-known but infrequently printed tale, often believed, which combines European beliefs and narrative motifs with
Andean ones. It is part of a large body of legends about the "condemned," who acquires a particularly grisly, monstrous character in
Peru. This tale type is not found in the new Stanley Robe *Index of Mexican Folktales*,[11] and in the Hansen index, the only reference is to Peru.
José María Arguedas found these *condenado* tales in the Quechua-
speaking highland areas,[12] but it is too early to make any solid conclu-
sions about their distribution, since accurate legend collecting is in an
early stage in the Andean area, and indexing and typing have been almost nil.

Tale Types: Aarne-Thompson 760* *The Condemned Soul*; Hansen
**775CB *Lover killed by father. Magic flight. Boy returns home for pro-
visions and is accidentally killed by father.*

Motifs: T97 "Father opposed to daughter's marriage"; R225 "Elopement"; R315 "Cave as refuge"; N320 "Person unwittingly killed";
E210 "Dead lover's malevolent return"; E422 "The living corpse";
E422.4.2 "Ghost with bonnet pulled down over her face"; E259 "Bloodthirsty reverants—miscellaneous"; E436 "Ghost detected by strewing
ashes"; B733 "Animals are spirit-sighted"; E434.9 "Candle light protection against ghost"; D1819.2 "Deception revealed in dream"; E266

9. Morote Best, "La huída mágica . . . ," text synopses on pp. 813 and 816,
comment on p. 829.
10. Morote Best, "La huída mágica," p. 807.
11. (Berkeley and Los Angeles: University of California Press, 1973).
12. Arguedas, "Folklore del . . . Mantaro," pp. 127–28.

"Dead carry off living"; D1814.2 "Advice received in dream"; D1610.16.1 "Speaking blood drops"; D1611.6 "Magic blood-drops impersonate fugitive"; K551.16 "Woman escapes by ruse: must go to defecate"; D812 "Magic object received from supernatural being"; D855.5 "Magic object as reward for good deeds"; E434.3 "Ghosts cannot cross rapid stream"; K710 "Victim enticed into voluntary captivity or helplessness"; D672 "Obstacle flight"; D454 "Transformation of manufactured object"; cf. D941.1 "Forest produced by magic"; D921.1 "Lake (pond) produced by magic"; D454.4 "Transformation: needle to other object"; D932.0.1 "Mountain created by magic"; D975.2 "Magic rose"; cf. D482.2 "Stretching lily plant: miraculously quick growing"; D965.3 "Magic rosebush"; R251 "Flight on a tree which ogre tries to cut down"; cf. E446.4 "Slain ghost carried off by other ghosts."

Collection Data: October 1972; squatter settlement "Independencia." Recorded inside informant's two-room house, built of unmortared volcanic rock with corrugated tin roof and earthen floor. Audience: Informant's sister Nery (age thirteen) and youngest brother (age ten months), plus collector.

Circumstances: Collector had previously recorded this legend from informant's sister Nery at the Independencia primary school, and was trying to obtain a block of narrative from this particular family. This was the first time that the collector had met this particular informant, but he and Nery were happy to record, and both contributed to this taping session. Many narratives offered at this time were spontaneously given, but the interview was only semi-open, since the collector deliberately solicited certain items, including this one. *Tape Location Number* (in Indiana University Archives of Traditional Music): Tape 27 (#17 of cassettes), Arequipa, Peru, "Independencia," CHILDREN, Side A, #303–423.

Informant Data: Name: Juan Velarde Alvaro; age: Fourteen; education: Currently in third year of "Media" (high school); length of time in Independencia: Three years; prior residence: Huancarqui, Castilla, Arequipa; parents' birthplaces: Father—Huancarqui, Castilla, Arequipa; Mother—Cotahuasi, La Unión, Arequipa; parents' occupations: Father—chauffeur; Mother—at home; languages: Parents and children are monolingual Spanish speakers (do not speak Quechua). Comment: Juan and his sister believe this tale to be true, and it was narrated without exceptionally dramatic use of face or voice. Tale learned from informant's mother, Justina Alvaro (age thirty-two), born in Cotahuasi, La Unión, Arequipa.

Once there were two lovers here just in the *sierra*, you see? a young man and a girl. And their parents hated each other, eh? The families hated each other, and they didn't want them to marry. And then they escaped, the two of them. And the girl's taken her little dog along. They went *far* away to a cave in a mountain. And there they were living.

Now they were running out of meat, of food, and the young man said, "I'm going to go to my parents' house to steal, to get me some money—just *something* in order to live," he told her. "All right. Go ahead," she told him. "But be very careful. Come back soon," she told him then. The young man left. He arrived at the house at night. Since there in the *sierra* they have the custom of keeping the money there in the middle of the corn, in the sacks, the young man already knew about it. Then he began taking it out.

And the father heard the noise. Then the father said, "A thief!" He took an ax, then he went very quietly and found him stealing and he gave him an ax blow, without seeing that it was his son. So then he killed him. And he told his wife, "Bring the light! Now I've got him!" Then when she came, it was his son. And *now* they couldn't do anything, because he was already dead. Then they had the funeral and everything, and they buried him.

And the girl was dying of hunger, eh? with the dog and all, and he *didn't* come back. Every day she had to look toward the road. And one day she was looking at the road, and saw that *way* in the distance a man was coming, with his head covered, his head covered up with a big hat, eh? He didn't look up. And [he was] pulling a llama. Then the girl waited, and the young man arrived. He *wouldn't* allow his face to be seen.

Then the girl said, "How are you? Why've you just now gotten here?" "It's that there was a party at home and they've kept me from coming, and I'm just now getting here. Unload the stuff. I'm going to go to bed," he told her. She unloaded it, and when she unloaded, in all the bags that he brought on the llama, there were *bones*, people's *hands*— like from little babies. Don't you see? He was condemned.

Then the girl got scared. She didn't eat anything. The dog howled, he *cried*. No *more!* As if he would die howling! Then that night . . . he went to bed . . . and she told him to light the light, and the young man told her no, because it bothered him because there was something wrong with his eyes. Then they went to sleep.

And in the middle of the night she dreamed that a lady, or rather, the Virgin, told her that her husband, he was dead. He was a *condenado* who was going to carry her off to death. Then she [was] afraid. And [the lady] told her that if she woke up she was going to find him keeping his own wake vigil. And she told her to tie him to an oak, a thick tree that he had beside his bed where they were sleeping, with a leather whip. "Tied up tight by the waist," she told her then.

The girl tied him up, and the Virgin also told her to leave three drops of blood near the cave. And she told her to go away with her little dog. And she went off.

And the man asked, "María, when are you coming?" "In just a minute!" a drop of blood answered him. Then, again, "I'm urinating. I'm coming in a minute!" it told him. Afterward, no *more!* "OK! I'm coming right now!" it told him. Then, "No *more* of this!" Then he realized and began . . . he got up and started to pull on the thing. No, he couldn't pull away. Then afterward they say he just broke the oak. Then he began to follow the girl.

The girl was *running*, running. Now she just couldn't any more. Now he was going to catch up with her. Then, he got there, when *way* in the distance she saw a little house. She kept on *running* and got there. And then, in this little house there were a man, a lady, and a little child, who . . . or rather, well, it was the Holy Family, the Lord Jesus Christ, yes?

She begged [the lady] for help, and then she told her, "Wash the diapers for me, and I'm going to help you," the Virgin told her then. She washed everything for her, and [the Virgin] gave her a mirror, a rose, a comb, a little piece of soap, and a needle. But before that she told her, "When he's about to catch up with you at that river, he's going to tell you to take him across because *condenados* can't cross water. Then, you leave him on a rock in the middle and you go on."

Then, he caught up with her there at the . . . well, at the bank of the river. Then the girl carried him, she left him there in the middle of the river, and she escaped. Then the *condenado* shouted to her, "María! Don't go! Get me out of here!" She didn't pay any attention, she kept on running. Then the *condenado, suffering,* got away from there. He started to follow her.

Now he was going to catch up with her and the girl dropped the little piece of soap. And it became completely . . . *very* slippery, all soapsuds —very slippery, and the *condenado* couldn't cross over. He was sliding around, sliding around. Then afterward, he crossed over.

Now he was going to catch up with her. She let go the comb, and it changed itself into lots of thorns. And the *condenado* couldn't pass through, and afterward he got through again.

And afterward, he was just about to catch up, she let go the mirror and it turned into a lake. He *couldn't* cross. Then, he did cross, and afterward she had only two things left, the needle and the rose.

Then he kept on and she threw the needle and it changed itself into some mountains, *big* ones. And the *condenado couldn't* cross over, and later he did cross. Then the girl began to run.

Now he only lacked . . . now he was going to catch up with her, she threw the rose and a great rosebush grew up. It was *big*, and the girl climbed up with her little dog. *Way* up there to the top. And the *condenado couldn't* climb up since there were lots of thorns, and he began to cut with his teeth. He began to cut, and now it was just about to fall and *again* the thing became thick. Again and *again*.

Then he went off to ask for help and he came with other *condenados* and they started to cut. Now he was going to cut, it was about to be cut. Now it was going to fall, and *more* grew up, again it just turned into more trunk. So, a *long* time passed—*hours*, eh? And the devils came, these, the *condenados*, and they carried him off. And he screamed for them to leave him alone. And then they carried him off.

Then he went, the girl climbed down with her little dog. She began to walk, and she fell now fainting—from hunger, from tiredness. And some mule drivers came along, they gave her soup, and later water, everything. Afterward, she was saved, and they carried her to her mother. And she lived there with her parents. She told them about it.

And there it ends. [This happened] in the *sierra*, but I don't know where, eh? I don't know what the little town's called. But in the *sierra* like that. My grandmother's the one who knows.

Quevedo Works as a Cook

Collected by Jean MacLaughlin in January 1972 on the outskirts of Arequipa and translated from the Spanish.

In Peru, Quevedo becomes the trickster-rogue hero of a cycle of internationally-known, humorous episodic tales often attributed to Pedro Urdemales or Juan Bobo elsewhere in Latin America. Américo Paredes has published two Quevedo tales in *Folktales of Mexico* (Chicago: University of Chicago Press, 1970, pp. 33–34), and he notes that "the Quevedo involved is Don Francisco de Quevedo y Villegas (1580–1645), Spanish poet and satirist who has become a legend as a trickster both in folk and sophisticated literature. There is a whole cycle of Quevedo stories, known wherever Spanish is spoken" (p. 205).

Few of these Quevedo tales have been published in Peru, due to their characteristically obscene nature. The only one frequently seen in print is *Holding Down the Hat* (type 1528), which circulates in oral tradition as well as in sources like school textbooks.

Although Paredes considers the Quevedo tales to be legendary anecdotes, and classes them with his legends, my own field corpus of Quevedo and other humorous tales shows that in Arequipa, Peru, Quevedo appears in two separate cycles: (1) obscene, humorous traditional tales based on sexual or anal themes; and (2) modern urbañ "contest" jokes casting Quevedo as the Peruvian (usually competing against an Argentine, and a Chilean or Bolivian) in an absurd braggadocio comparison of athletic feats or national products. In the traditional tales, Quevedo never plays the role of the fool (that being left either to the *Camanejo*, or person from the rival coastal town of Camaná, or to the fox in the animal tales). Nor are Quevedo's pranks often motivated by financial gain (cf. many of the Chilean tales of Pedro Urdemales). Some of the latter's deceptions and pranks (such as type 1530 *Holding up the Rock*; K842 "Dupe persuaded to take prisoner's place in sack: killed"; and the role of the salesman in type 1319 *Pumpkin Sold as an Ass's Egg*) do not usually appear in the Quevedo cycle in Arequipa, perhaps because of their asexual nature. These episodes are attributed to the rat or guinea pig trickster-hero of the animal tales, or belong to an unnamed sharpster in the fool cycle.

The present version of *The Boy with Many Names* (type 1545) is much more typical of Quevedo, and widely known. At an adult dinner in the laboring-class neighborhood where this text was collected, boiled beans had been served as an appetizer and the hostess laughed and made the elliptical comment, "And she thought it was the beans!" Everyone present understood the joke, with no preceding or following reference. The "nudity race" escape, incidentally, circulates independently in the Quevedo cycle as a motif.

Admittedly, I collected in a restricted area, and most of the Quevedo tales were from children and young adolescents, which may account for the preoccupation with sex and anality. But young children (ages five through seven), trying to tell Quevedo tales sometimes invented rambling stories showing an anal-sexual interpretation of his character. In one such invention, the entire plot consisted of Quevedo tripping and wallowing in excrement. A jingle collected from sisters ages five and seven translates as "*Comadre* Anuncia doesn't play with her underpants any more, because Quevedo comes along and sticks his penis in" (the term *comadre* indicates a woman to whom one is related through the godparenthood system).

This anality-sexuality seems to be the link with the urban contest-joke cycle, in which the punch line usually shows Quevedo not only deflating other participants' egos and bringing things back to reality with a jolt, but also mouthing an obscenity. In the most frequently collected joke, each brags about how his father jumped from a high building (each successively higher) without being hurt and received a trophy. Quevedo, last, says his father jumped from two stories up (very low compared to the others), and when all ask expectantly, "And what happened to him?" the answer is, "It took the shit out of him!" I have heard type 1176 *Catching a Man's Broken Wind* told as part of this Quevedo contest joke cycle. Quevedo goes out of sight, defecates, and brings it back in his hand, saying the fart ran into something and fell.

Tale Types: Aarne-Thompson 1545 *The Boy with Many Names;* Hansen 1940*B *Student poses as fool or man disguises as woman and obtains employment in house of man with pretty daughter or in king's palace.*

Motifs: K1831 "Service under a false name"; K1399.2 "The unusual names. Assuming unusual names, the servant deceives the girl, her mother, and her father"; K1315 "Seduction by impostor"; K550 "Escape by false plea"; J2300 "Gullible fools."

Collection Data: January 1972; squatter settlement "Independencia." Recorded in front room of collector's house. Audience: Group of thirteen young adolescents and children, almost entirely male, including a group of seven friends who came in a bloc, specifically to tell stories and record. The informant was one of these seven.

Circumstances: Word had recently spread that a *gringa* was living in the settlement and recording stories, and a steady stream of children began coming to the collector's house wanting to use the tape recorder. During this particular session, a long string of spontaneously offered Quevedo stories and other semi-obscene jokes and tales were narrated. This tale was well received, with much laughter.

Translation comment: As Quevedo thinks up more and more false names, the narrator began to pause and correct himself, and the audience began to laugh in anticipation, causing the narrator to say, "Wait!" or "No!" and so forth. Very little has actually been deleted, however. In the original Spanish, the last two names given are "Pendejitos" and "Pichilitas," which are obscene slang words for "cunt hair" and "penis," but which do not constitute the puns that I've put into the English translation. *Tape Location Number* (in Indiana University Archives of Traditional Music): Tape 9 (#4 of 5" series), Arequipa, Peru, "Independencia," CHILDREN, Side B, #420–548.

Informant Data: Name: Fredy Palacios Bustamante; age: Fourteen; education: Currently in "Media" (high school); birthplace: Cuzco, Cuzco [not certain, but all other older children in this family were born in Cuzco]; length of time in city of Arequipa: [not certain, but probably eight to nine years, because a ten-year-old sister was born in Cuzco, but a seven-year-old sister and all succeeding children were born in Arequipa]; length of time in Independencia: Three years; parents' birthplaces: Father—Anta, Cuzco; Mother—Yaucat, Cusipata, Cuzco; parents' occupations: Father—white-collar worker in Ministry of Agriculture at Majes Irrigation Project; Mother—at home; languages: Both parents are native Quechua-speakers. Informant speaks Quechua also.

All also speak Spanish, and both languages are used at home. Comment: The informant seemed to be functioning as a leader of his group of friends. The story was well-told, with a moderate amount of dramatic inflection in the voice, and considerable interaction with the audience. It was considered very funny. Tale learned "from friends."

They say there was once Quevedo, who was unemployed, or that is, he didn't have work. And he goes to look for work and finds it in a house where a lady had three daughters, and with the mother they were four. And he employs himself then, here in this house. And his first job that he had to do was to cook.

Then they say one, the oldest of [the daughters], they say she enters the kitchen and says to him, well, she says to Quevedo, "What's your name?" "Well, my name is a somewhat incredible name, that you aren't going to believe," Quevedo tells her. Then she says to him, "Just tell it to me. I want to know your name. What's your name?" she says to him. "Well, I'm called Little Green Peas," he tells her. Quevedo tells the oldest then. Well, now the oldest already knows.

Then the one that follows the oldest goes to the kitchen and says to Quevedo, "What's your name? What are you called?" she says. Then, "Well, my name isn't . . . I couldn't tell you." "Well, just tell me then, so I'll have the pleasure of knowing the name, your name," she says. Then Quevedo tells her, "My name is Beans." And the youngest enters. Well, she says to Quevedo, "What's your name?" she says to him. Then, "My name is *Rodajitas*" [lit., small, little, round things].

And the mother comes, she says to Quevedo, to the boy, then she says, "What's your name?" she says to him. "I'm called a . . . a *very* bad thing, madam," he tells her. "Well, what are you called then?" "I'm called Bush, madam," he tells her. Comes the husband of the lady and says to him, "Well, son, what's your name?" he says to him. "No, what am I going to be able to say to you, sir?" "You have to say!" "I'm called Little Dick," Quevedo tells him.

Then the first night, it's his turn to make the dish that he told to the oldest. He makes little green peas. Then, in the night they say Quevedo goes then to the oldest one's bed. Then they say, in the night the oldest complains and says to him, "Little Green Peas! Little Green Peas!" Then the mother says, "Ay, daughter! Why have you eaten so many peas? That's why it's hurting you." And she didn't know what he was . . . well, then, you all know already, no?

And the next day, for the one who follows the oldest they say he made the food that he told her, the beans. Then, the same, the younger one complained, "Beans! Beans!" "That's because you've eaten so *much!*" For the other, the same thing. He makes her the same dish, no? And she says to him, "Ay, ay! *Rodajitas! Rodajitas!*" "Why have you eaten so *much* then?"

Then, the next day, now all were already pregnant. And the mother is, well, is surprised to find out that all her daughters are pregnant. "And why . . . why are they pregnant?" the mother wanted to know.

Then the next day he had to go. He had to go to the bed of the mother. Then, the mother, since she wouldn't let him, turned on the light and caught him. Then they say that there was Quevedo, naked. Then they say Quevedo wasn't finding any place to escape, then the mother says, "Grab my Bush! Grab my Bush!" she says. Then they say the husband goes out, begins . . . they begin to pull her pubic hair, they say. They begin to pull the lady's pubic hair.

Meanwhile, they say Quevedo is just *running*. Then the man says to [the lady], "Grab my Dick! Grab my Dick!" And the lady thought that he was telling her to pull on him. Then Quevedo kept right on just escaping.

Then, the policeman was on the corner. Since Quevedo went out naked, then the policeman says to him, "Why are you going out naked?" "No, it's that there's a nudists' race!" Then the policeman, on learning this, undresses, and the two naked men begin to run.

And there it ends, Miss.

The Lake of Langui

Collected by Jean MacLaughlin on the outskirts of Arequipa in 1972 and translated from the Spanish.

This legend is associated with many Peruvian lakes, and Efraín Morote Best discusses ten variants (about different lakes) in his comparative study, "Aldeas sumergidas."[1] In a final footnote, Morote Best notes that he knows of three more locales where the legend is known. I myself have collected the Langui legend, and a variant from the coastal area of Omate, Moquegua (not included in Morote Best). The basic tale of inhospitality, destruction of the town, tabu against looking back, and turning to stone is also told about a few towns *not* associated with lakes. Scattered texts continue to be published, though not reflecting true oral style.

1. Efraín Morote Best, "Aldeas sumergidas," *Folklore Americano* 1 (1953): 45–81. For parallels from Spain see Joan Amades Gelats, "La leyenda de las aldeas sumergidas en Cataluña," *Tradición* 5:16–18 (1954): 5–21. Other references are contained within these articles.

Morote Best's article includes two Spanish chronicle accounts of this legend in Peru (from Phelipe Guaman Poma de Ayala, 1615, and Joan de Santacruz Pachacuti Yamqui, 1613), as well as a comparison with the Genesis account of Lot's wife and the pillar of salt (Genesis XIX:1–26). Morote Best concludes that the contemporary legend is a synthesis of: (1) the biblical tale spread by missionaries; and (2) existing pre-Columbian traditions recounting punishment for inhospitality to gods, and wrathful destruction by petrification, water, or fire. Given the frequency of seismic activity in the Andean chain, such oral history of destruction may not be without foundation in some areas. The major earthquake of 1970 obliterated the town of Yungay (Ancash), completely burying it beneath mud. It is worth noting that hospitality continues to be an important ideal social norm among Andean peasants, although travelers in isolated areas have sometimes found themselves desperately unable to purchase food (for various diatribes on the subject see Harry A. Franck's *Vagabonding Down the Andes* [New York: Century Co., 1917]).

Of those legends treated by Morote Best, only an Amazonas version published by José María Arguedas and Francisco Izquierdo Ríos contains the motif of the egg and snake in connection with the ensuing flood,[2] although this motif was specified in both Langui versions and the Omate version I collected. The Arguedas-Izquierdo version shows interesting relationships with the Langui text published here. In it, the mythical "mother" of the lake appears floating in a gold platter on the surface of the rain-caused flood. The old man also appears, and throws a duck egg, which is immediately struck by lightning and split open to loose ducks and gulls that populate the lake. In pre-Columbian symbolism, lightning is usually represented as a serpent. The other Langui version I have, and the Omate one, both refer to a snake and an egg appearing in the sky, with no explanation of how they got there. Thus the snake seems to be a mythical representation of lightning, and it does not seem to be stretching a relationship to term the egg a Cosmic Egg. Interestingly, Hildebrando Castro Pozo has noted a belief that when lightning strikes, "no one dares look where it has fallen for fear of being punished by death; 'It's good to close your eyes, if you're on the road, and go away from that place without turning your face backward.' "[3]

Another curious connection between the Arguedas-Izquierdo version from Amazonas and this one involves the "mother" of the lake itself. In Peru, there is widespread belief in lakes having supernatural

2. José María Arguedas and Francisco Izquierdo Ríos, eds. *Mitos, leyendas y cuentos peruanos* (2d ed.; Lima: Casa de la Cultura, 1970), pp. 147–50.

3. Hildebrando Castro Pozo, *Nuestra comunidad indígena* (Lima: Editorial "El Lucero," 1924), pp. 224–25. Translation is mine.

"mothers," in post-Columbian legend often taking the form of a bull or a siren living at the bottom of the lake.[4] It is interesting that Vega continued his history of the destruction of Langui with the account of the Virgin's escape and subsequent shrine. He clearly considered it all part of the same narrative, and that the Virgin is "the Patron of Water. From the lake, she's called 'Juana.' It's a woman, because the lady who changed into stone was also named 'Juana.' And from this, they gave the name 'Juana' to the lake" (see text). I must confess to not knowing the Langui area or its traditions well enough to explain this, and it was only after returning from Peru that I realized the parallel with the Arguedas tale. Nevertheless, this connection seems to be worth an investigation.

Tale Types: cf. Aarne-Thompson 750B *Hospitality Rewarded;* cf. 750* *Hospitality Blessed.*

Motifs: T150 "Happenings at weddings"; K1811.1 "Gods (spirits) disguised as beggars. Test hospitality"; H1564 "Test of hospitality"; Q45.1 "Angels entertained unawares. Hospitality to disguised saint (angel, god) rewarded"; Q1.1 "Gods (saints) in disguise reward hospitality and punish inhospitality"; Q292 "Inhospitality punished"; Q151.6 "Life spared as reward for hospitality"; C331.3 "Tabu: looking back during flight"; C961.2 "Transformation to stone for breaking tabu"; D231 "Transformation: man to stone"; Q551 "Magic manifestations as punishments"; Q552.2.1 "Land sinks and lake appears as punishment"; A910.2 "Waters created as punishment"; cf. M475 "Curse on a city"; D921.1 "Lake (pond) produced by magic"; F713 "Extraordinary pond (lake)"; A920.1.0.1 "Origin of particular lake"; D478 "Water changed to other substance (or vice versa)"; cf. A641 "Cosmic egg"; V111.3.2 "Divine person points out site for church"; D1620 "Magic automata. Statues or images that act as if alive"; V126 "Image of saint speaks"; D1654.7 "Statues that cannot be removed"; F960.4 "Extraordinary nature phenomena at anger of saint"; Q552.14.5 "Hail as punishment"; D902.3 "Magic hail"; F962 "Extraordinary precipitation (rain, snow, etc.)"; D935.1 "Magic sand"; A920.1.8 "Lake bursts forth to drown impious people"; F934 "Extraordinary occurrences connected with lakes."

Collection Data: October 1972; squatter settlement "Independencia." Recorded in large front room of informant's three-room house, built of unmortared volcanic rock with corrugated tin roof. Two rooms have a cement floor, and the front room has an earthen floor. The house has electricity but no plumbing. The yard is well-swept and there is a

4. Arguedas and Izquierdo Ríos, *Mitos,* see pp. 261–69, 271–72. Other texts and collections also show examples of this belief, but this work is one of the best legend collections extant for Peru, and is relatively easily obtainable, due to its recent republication.

flower garden. Audience: Informant's wife and five children, who all listen intently, and collector.

Circumstances: Collector had previously recorded from informant's daughter Vilma (age eleven) and son Simón (age thirteen) at Independencia primary school, and arranged this interview to record from the father. The informant seemed pleased to record his tales and legends. This particular legend was solicited, having been previously collected from the informant's son Simón. *Tape Location Number* (in Indiana University Archives of Traditional Music): Tape 27 (#17 of cassettes), Arequipa, Peru, "Independencia," CHILDREN, Side B, #1–158.

Informant Data: Name: Asencio Vega Esquivel; age: Thirty-two; education: Primary school, incomplete; birthplace: Langui, Cuzco; length of time in city of Arequipa: Twenty-two years; length of time in Independencia: Eleven years; occupation: Gardener; languages: Native Quechua speaker; also speaks Spanish, with a Quechua accent. Comment: Sr. Vega says that he was the first grandchild in his family, and was a great favorite of his grandfather's. He accompanied his grandfather frequently, and learned most of the Langui traditions that he knows from this grandfather. Notice that Sr. Vega left Langui at age ten. Sr. Vega's two oldest children have learned a large body of narratives from him, and Vilma is especially fascinated and interested in acquiring his repertoire. His eight-year-old daughter has not yet learned any narratives, "usually being sleep already" when they are told. Sr. Vega is a meticulous narrator, rather than a dramatic one. His narratives tend to be long and include minutiae. This particular legend is brief, but notice that he dates the events. His children recite his tales relatively accurately. Tale learned from grandfather in Langui, Cuzco.

The town was an environs of the jungle slopes of Cuzco, in this town. And there was a wedding. It was a wedding in the month of August— August fifteenth, in the year 1801. This happened in this period.

And when there were these wedding festivities, a man came in, a little old man, all *ragged, dirty,* like that. He entered this house where the wedding was. And at this, a lady said to the man, "My children come first, to tend to them before you. Better get yourself outside." She threw the little old man out. Then the little old man left. He left—in a little while, well, he came back, within ten minutes or so, now that the man cleaned himself up. Then he said to this woman, "I come here for you to give me some lunch in a little can." Then the lady answered him, "Still no, son. First I'm tending to my children."

Then a lady got up her nerve—there were quite a few volunteers, this kind of thing—and handed him a little bit of soup in a little plate. "Sir, take this little bit of soup," she told him. Then, "Thank you, daughter. You're very good to the poor, not like the lady who's thrown me out of the kitchen." Then he called her some twenty paces from there and he said to her, "Lady, come. When you go away from this house, don't turn back for anything."

Then the wedding *fiesta* ended, after she'd taken care [of him]. The lady took a road . . . what's it called? a bridge, Mayupata. From Mayupata she took it to the bridge of . . . well, all right, I don't remember the bridge. So she took the direction for the *Apacheta*.

Then when the lady was climbing, she forgot what the man had advised her, the little old man. And the lady had been pregnant. She was hauling something in her little carrying shawl, carrying a spindle in her hand, and with her hat in her other hand. And so it is that the lady sat down to urinate, and she didn't remember what the man told her. When she turns around toward the side below, she sees her companions being knocked down, and the water filling up. Then the lady changes into stone. And this rock exists at the present. It's like a statue, that exists on a mountain called "Apacheta." Apacheta is where the souls are buried.

And from this town, from Langui, one passes to another town. It's named Fortalencia. Then the man took two eggs, a serpent, to where he's brought this thing, the water, by another road. It's called Lahualahua. It's a very ugly road. Lacking twenty meters to reach the bridge, he threw this, an egg, and it changed into water, and the same with the serpent. Then the town began to fill up. And all those who were in this town were escaping, on burros, like that. Others escaped on top of doors, windows.

And a lady left, full of jewels, and she saved herself. The lady said, "I want you all to make my house here at the next turn, looking to the side of the mountain." And this lady is the Virgin, that exists at the present time. This is the Patron of Water. From the lake, she's called "Juana." It's a woman, because the lady who changed into stone was also named "Juana." And from this, they gave the name "Juana" to the lake. And the lake has some twenty-five kilometers in length, and it has fifteen in width—in kilometers. It's a great lake, it has quite a depth.

And at this time, two, three years passed. They took the Virgin down from the main altar to feast it, to do its cleaning, to change its mantle. Then the Virgin said that no, "Don't move me from here for anything." It began to rain colored hail and sand. Then all the town got scared, and the lake also wanted to overturn. Then again they suspended the Virgin in her place. Now until this day, they don't touch her for anything. She has an altar behind, it completely disappeared. So she remains on a normal wall. Now no altars exist, nothing any more. This happened in the year 1801, in this period. All this happened. In this same month, fifteenth of August.

The Yagua

The Yagua live in a section of the Peruvian and Colombian Amazon roughly two hundred miles wide by three hundred and fifty miles long extending southward from the second to the fifth parallel and westward from the seventieth to the seventy-fifth meridian. They number about three thousand, and are now merging into the mestizo population. Most communities consist of three or four houses of typical Amazon River frame construction, built on stilts several feet above ground with a palm bark floor and a peaked woven leaf roof. Yaguas practice a burn and slash economy, planting manioc, plantains, bananas, and other domesticated jungle fruits and vegetables. The men hunt with shotguns and blowguns for birds, monkeys, and smaller ground animals, and both men and women fish with hook and line, poisons, harpoon, and bow and arrow. Transportation in this area of abundant waterways is mostly by dugout canoe. Everyone in the community is related to everyone else by blood or marriage. Social life revolves around drinking native beer made from fruits or manioc. Religion is an admixture of animism and theism. Political organization is practically nonexistent, except as provided by the Peruvian government.

The most serious work on the Yagua, although somewhat dated, is Paul Fejos, *Ethnography of the Yagua* (New York: Viking Fund Publications in Anthropology, No. 1, 1943; repr. Johnson Reprint Corp., 1968).

In 1952, ten years after Fejos left, the writer, Paul Powlison, and his wife arrived in Peru to work through the Summer Institute of Linguistics with the Yagua tribe. We began our contacts with a small group of Yaguas from the mestizo settlement of Vainilla near the mouth of the Yanayacu River. In our second year we relocated in the newly forming all-Yagua village of Catalán two hours farther up the Yanayacu River. This village has been the locus of our tribal contacts except for a brief visit to three other tributaries in 1956 and a three-month survey trip in the fall of 1967 in which thirty-four communities of Yaguas were visited.

The trip in 1956 was made by myself in company with my Yagua informant, Laureano Mozombite, in a canoe with a small outboard motor. The second trip was made in a houseboat with my wife and three-year-old son in company with Laureano Mozombite and his wife, Victoria. Our travels took us along five hundred miles of river front in the southeastern eighth of the Yagua area. This time we carried a battery-operated tape recorder provided by the Folklore Institute of Indiana University to record what we could in the way of tales and songs from the Yaguas in these other communities.

Laureano Mozombite was about fifty-three years of age when we first recorded from him in February 1960. A member of the Red Macaw Clan, he was born on the Pumayacu, tributary of the Ampiyacu River, and grew up at Iguanacocha.

As a young man Laureano traveled far and wide with his patron, Benjamin Albán. He worked balata latex (a form of rubber), worked lumber, carried heavy loads up mountain trails. Eventually he settled on the Samiria River with his wife, son, and mother. He had been there three months, long enough to clear and plant a garden, when his mother said, "We can't just leave the rest like this. We must go back and say good-bye to my sister Agrippina." So they returned to Portugal, leaving some of their belongings at their new location. He was never to see those possessions again, for while at Portugal, his Aunt Agrippina's husband took him dragnet fishing in a nearby shallow lake at night and while working in the water he was bitten on the foot by a poisonous snake. The snake bite would not heal and became a running sore which extended up his leg to the knee. One of his metatarsal bones came out. He was inactive so long that his leg muscles began to atrophy and contract. His leg was drawn up and he could not straighten it. Every suggested remedy was tried. Finally mothballs were used and the wound healed. His mother patiently applied physiotherapy daily, rubbing his shrunken leg with warm ashes. He regained the use of it and slowly began getting around again. One day while he was helping to cut cane, a cane stalk severed by his machete fell point first onto the poorly healed snake-bite wound and black blood gushed out. The wound healed again, this time for good, but a long two years after the snake bite. Laureano still has a slight limp and there is a sunken spot on his foot where the bone came out, but he has been active and has worked just as hard as the rest of the men until five years ago when his health began to fail.

Laureano remained in Portugal two years after recovering from the snake bite before moving to the Yanayacu of Marupa near where the community of Catalán was to be established. We came as it was getting started in 1954. Laureano deserves credit as the community's real founder. He has been a help to us all through our sojourns at Catalán, as well as the times he accompanied us to our base at Yarinacocha to act as our informant, and finally on our three-month river journey in 1967 when he acted as guide, adviser, liaison man, and faithful companion.

The Twin Cycle

Collected by Paul Powlison in February 1960 at Yarinacocha and included in his dissertation, "Yagua Mythology and Its Epic Tendencies" (Indiana University, 1969).

As Alfred Metraux has written, "A pair of brothers, generally twins, are among the most important protagonists of South American folklore."[1]

The Yagua Twin Cycle consists of a series of episodes that are sometimes told as independent tales but more often as a connected series. It chronicles the origin and exploits of the twin culture heroes, Elder Brother and Placenta. The narrators are not in agreement about the roles played by the older brother and Placenta in these tales. Most depict Placenta as the transformer who changes himself at will into whatever guise meets the need of the moment, and back again. He also transforms other things. But one narrator has him appeal to his older brother to transform him by blowing on him each time. Another depicts the older brother as the transformer. Some do not distinguish between the brothers in the narration, so the listener doesn't know which of the twins is doing what. Whichever twin is depicted as doing the transforming is also depicted as the more intelligent. For instance, the older brother, when sent to invite people and when told not to let go of the flute, is not able to perform successfully and so becomes a foil to the transformer. There is not, however, any bungling that has to be corrected as in the case of some Amazon basin twin mythologies. The transformer is instructed by his brother what to do, so they really work as a team, but the transformer gets the credit for creation, most of which is really transformation.

Powlison transcribed seventeen versions of this cycle. The present tales were told by Laureano Mozombite.

The Twins' Origin

Motifs: A512.1 "Culture hero's grandmother"; Z356 "Unique survivor"; A510 "Origin of the culture hero"; A511.1.6 "Culture hero posthumous child"; T584.2 "Child removed from body of dead mother"; S301 "Children abandoned (exposed)"; S351.1 "Abandoned child cared for by grandmother"; T549.4.1 "Child born from placenta"; T670 "Adoption of children"; A511.4.1 "Miraculous growth of culture hero"; A515.1.1 "Twin culture heroes—one foolish, one clever."

1. "Twin Heroes in South American Mythology," *Journal of American Folklore* 59 (1946): 114–23.

He was formed, the Creator (God). God was formed. His parents were drinking beer. Her daughter says to a dear little old lady, "While you go cultivate under the manioc plants, we'll be drinking here together yet. I see you don't drink with us anyway." She goes, and they drink in her absence. A long while later suddenly they are quiet. Not a sound. She [old lady] listens and listens and listens. "What on earth has happened to them. They're not laughing at all any more and they're not drumming any more either."

When it's getting late, she goes at last. She sees on arrival, "Groan!" the house ruins are smoking. The savages have burned it. "The savages have killed them! That's why they weren't drumming any more. They had killed them all off!" She goes wandering all around there. She hears someone crying on the garbage heap, "Cuwa! Cuwa! Cuwa! Cuwa!" "Groan! Was it *here* the savages threw away my daughter's son?"

She goes. "I'll get him first to be my companion. I can at least raise him to be a companion to me." She gets him, she is going, she hears someone else crying. "Who [else] was there?" She returns again. It is his placenta that has been transformed [into another child]. She takes him also. She goes then to her little shack again. She washes them on arrival there.

After two days they are sitting up; after three days they are walking around. They don't delay in growing. After five days they are almost full grown. He now asks his grandmother, "What did my deceased father die from, and my deceased mother?" "Savages killed them, of course!" "Really?" "Yes."

The Twins Make Water Available by Felling the Water Tree

Motifs: A1111 "Impounded water"; B11.7.3* "Creator-grandfather controls water supply"; D169.5* "Transformation: man to hummingbird"; B437 "Helpful wild beasts—rodentia"; B461.1 "Helpful woodpecker"; B571 "Animals perform tasks for men"; D2192 "Work of day magically overthrown at night"; D1602.2.2 "Chips from tree return to their places as cut"; D642.5 "Transformation to escape notice"; G661.2 "Ogre's secret overheard by masking as bird"; D181.1* "Transformation: man to scorpion"; E149.4* "Resuscitation by blowing"; A2181 "Origin of snail"; A1610 "Origin of various tribes"; A2435.6.1 "Food of tortoise"; A934.13* "River system from felling of water tree."

God [*Risu*, from Spanish *Dios*] has caused the water to subside from them until it is all gone. There isn't any water any more. From then on they get it [by the potful] from their grandfather. The next day from there [the same place] again, the next day and the next and the next, "Groan," until they are sick and tired of it. "I'm sick and tired of this!"

They ask one who lives there with their grandfather, "How on earth does he get water?" "I don't know." "Doesn't he bathe where you can see?" "He always goes bathing yonder. He bathes at noon." He says to his placenta again, "Go see where. This fellow says he bathes at noon." "OK." He goes to the edge of the woods and watches patiently from there. At last he [Grandfather] speaks: "Ugh! It's [too] hot for me! I'm going to bathe first." The sun is directly overhead. He [Placenta] goes then and changes himself into [something] like a little humming-bird and flies after him. He [Grandfather] opens [a spigot] when he gets there in his [Placenta's] sight. "Spew! Gush!" Their grandfather stands under it. The hummingbird is flying along, "Flit! Flit! Flit!" He hits at him, "Hummingbird, hummingbird! Why are you being a nuisance?" He returns, "Chee! Chee! Chee! Chee!" He returns and as soon as he arrives back at his brother's he tells his brother, "It's in that whatcha-ma-call-it water tree, which is standing, that great big tree standing [there]!" "Really!" "Yes." "What shall we do?" "I don't know unless we cut it down." "I suppose!"

They rise and go early the next morning to their grandfather's again. They say to their grandfather when they get there, "Granpa?" "What?" "Uhh, we're going to cut down this which is standing." "Go ahead and cut! It isn't forbidden to cut it down." They invite all [to work] with them. They cut it. They begin cutting and cut and cut and cut, as far as its center. They cut and cut until the woodpecker is into its heart. "No soap!" It's getting late. It's late. They give up on it. It is quite thin [when] they leave off. "Tomorrow we'll fell it!" "Yes."

It dawns, and they go again. It stands there intact again. "No doubt he put its chips back again!" They cut again. "No soap!" They cut and cut and cut until it isn't very thick any more. At last he sends his pla-centa again, "Go listen, transforming yourself into the likeness of a little bird, to what Grandfather speaks." Their grandfather is sitting in the yard. He is smoking. He [Placenta] goes. He transforms himself. He lis-tens. He [Grandfather] smokes, he blows it around. He speaks and he hears, "Those two children will never fell the whatcha-ma-call-it water tree! They'll never be able to fell it—unless they should make a scorpion bite the tip of my little toe. It would fall then."

Placenta returns then again and tells his elder [brother] when he gets there, "Grandpa just spoke thus, 'Only if we were to make a scorpion bite the tip of his little toe, then it would fall.' " He says to him, "Trans-form yourself then!" "Into what?" "Transform yourself into a scor-pion." He transforms himself again. He has gone again. He [Grand-father] smokes, and smokes, and blows it around on its vines [that hold up the tree]. There he bites him on the tip of his little toe when he gets there, "Tch!" "Hey!" It begins to crack immediately, "Yikes! Ouch!

What smarties these two kids are!" It stays, it stays just a little bit on the lean now.

He says to him again, "Who on earth is the most painful biter?" "The red scorpion, I suppose." "Transform yourself into a red scorpion." He transforms himself into a red scorpion. He goes again and bites him the same way on arrival again. He was indeed a very painful biter, "*Tch!*" he falls prostrate, "*Blum!*" It falls then, "*Zoom, blum!*" [When] it falls his grandson runs at the same time to him, "What happened to you, Grandpa?" He is not alive any more. He had died. He blows around on him, "Phew!" He sits up, "Ha! What gives with you two? No doubt you've cut it down, too!" "Why not? What is our posterity supposed to drink?" "OK. Let it be so!"

A little snail comes running for a leaf [from the tree] and grabs it for his door plug. He handles [it]. In his view, it makes a pretty sound. Water Snail Ancestor comes running to him. He says then to him, "You just got that?" He asks him for it. "Let me see!" He gives it to him then, "Go ahead and look at it." He handles it with his hands. "How very pretty it is!" He gives it back to him, "Here it is!" He asks for it again. He gives it to him again. He rubs it in his hands. At last he says to him, departing, "I have it now!" He runs away from him to the water. He jumps with it away from him into the water. The owner of the taken object follows him for it. He has jumped with it into the water ahead of him. He jumps in after him. "No soap," he can't submerge. He just floats around.

The land snail speaks then, "Why did you impoverish me?! Now the *isulillo* [ants] will always bite my exposed, fleshy parts." Another comes running, too, "I'll be a water tortoise." When he jumps into the water, "Splash!" "Bob!" he bobs back to the surface. "No soap! You can't be a water tortoise!" Another comes running, "*I'll* be a water tortoise!" and jumps in likewise, "Splash!" Gone! He sinks, to [become] the water tortoise as he said. He glides down [into] the Amazon. "I'll be the water tortoise, you be a land tortoise." That one remains as the water tortoise. "I'll be the water tortoise, *you* be the land tortoise." "What will I eat?" "Well, fungus and tortoise fruit. You'll eat tortoise fruit that ripens red." "OK." The umbrella tree caterpillars transformed themselves one by one and just paddled away. Some just paddled away as whites, some as blacks, some as Cocama Indians— all kinds. The chips all are transformed into fish, the umbrella tree chips that were to become living creatures. All its leaves transform into what they call mojarra fish, a large variety of mojarra fish. He transforms them all then—gamitana fish, arapaima. The leaves are all transformed into fish. It [the tree] has become the big Amazon River then.

The Twins Make Corn Available

Motifs: D657 "Transformation to steal"; D1601.9 "Household articles act at command"; F1034.5 "Other parts of person's body as hiding place"; D965.8 "Magic corn"; F815.1 "Vegetables (plants) that mature in miraculously short time"; A1423.7* "Acquisition of corn"; A2723.2 "God changes nature of plant to punish wastefulness of man."

After that corn was lacking. For a long time they keep asking their grandfather for corn also. He doesn't want to give it to them. At last they say to Grasshopper, "Steal a seed for me?" "OK. [I'll try]" He is toasting coca leaves [for cocaine]. Grasshopper is toasting them. Their grandfather is sitting there outside. At last he [Grasshopper] stands up. The coca leaves stir themselves in his absence, "Stir! Stir! Stir!" When he is starting to shell some [corn], it all falls, "Splatter!" "Grasshopper, Grasshopper! You are stealing there also!" "Not at all, I happen to be right here toasting this bit of coca."

He [Grandfather] goes in after it [corn] and puts it back in its place. He puts it back where it was grain by grain. "But exactly one grain is lacking! You have stolen one grain!" "Not at all! Never!" He goes to him and looks him over completely, his mouth, his nose, everything. He looks everywhere—in his ear—"Well, did you find what you were looking for?!" He had inserted the grain of corn in his penis.

His [Grandfather's] grandsons arrive then. He takes it out for them. "Here's the grain of corn you asked for. Plant it." They return home again and plant it also when they get there. They invite their grandfather again, "Grandpa, you must go drink corn beer [at our house]." "I suppose, just like I said the other day, that Grasshopper stole corn for you also." "Naturally. What is our posterity supposed to eat?" "OK. Let it be so. But it will not grow this fast for them any more. It will take three months to grow for them."

Chile

The Witranalwe Who Guarded Sheep

Reprinted from L. C. Faron, *Hawks of the Sun, Mapuche Morality and Its Ritual Attributes* (Pittsburgh, 1964), pp. 72–73, by permission of and arrangement with the University of Pittsburgh Press.

The Araucanian or Mapuche Indians in southern Chile intermarried with the lower Chilean classes but retained their own culture and traditions. Many of their memorates and legends deal with evil spirits, such as the *witranalwe*, a ghoul seen only in outline, at night and on horseback, giving off a whitish hue and leading benighted travelers astray. Often these belief tales are told in a laughing mood around the fireside to relieve tension created by these feared beings.

In the present narrative the *witranalwe* wears a Spanish poncho and spurs as worn by the cowboys. Like a good Mapuche he requests *nāchi*, a favorite dish prepared by stringing up a sheep by its forelegs and slitting its throat, then turning the main artery into its windpipe, while salting and peppering the bloodstream. The sheep rapidly suffocates and from its intestines is drawn a highly relished blood pudding. The human actors also reflect the culture. Envy of their rich paternal uncle by the two brothers, and the desire to acquire his animals, are emotions fitting the realities of the Mapuche.

Motif: F470 "Night-spirits."

In the environs of Pitrufquén, there lived a rather wealthy man who had many animals. He also had a *witranalwe* to guard them in his absence. Near this wealthy man lived two of his brother's sons, who were poor.

One day, the rich man visited his nephews' house. They all began to drink a lot of wine and became a little drunk by late afternoon. They began to feel hungry, but the nephews had nothing to serve the old man. They decided to steal a couple of sheep from the corral of their uncle. One said to the other that he was a rich old man and that stealing one of his sheep, perhaps even two, did not matter much. They went to the uncle's corral together, leaving the old man in their house drinking.

When they arrived, they saw a huge figure on horseback. The man wore a very large black hat. He had a large mouth and long, sharp teeth, and a big, penetrating set of eyes. He wore a Spanish poncho, also large and black; and he had a set of silver spurs with great rowels. Upon seeing him, one of the nephews ran away, but the other, who had a sheep under his arm, stood still before him. He fearfully asked, "Who are you, caballero?" The answer came in a very low and deep voice: "I am the partner of the owner of these sheep." The nephew then said that the owner of the sheep was his uncle and, therefore, "Señor, we are like kinsmen."

After this, the young man took a little more courage and spoke further to the *witranalwe:* "Señor, why not let me take this sheep for the fiesta in my house? My uncle is a very wealthy man, and the loss of one little lamb, which he himself will eat part of, will not matter to him." The *witranalwe* answered in a very deep voice, "All right, but I want a bowl of *ñachi* [blood] when you kill the animal."

The young man assented to this demand, at the same time asking the *witranalwe* to help him carry the sheep back to the house. As soon as they arrived at the young man's house, he told the *witranalwe* to return in a little while for the blood. He set both the bowl and a pitcher of wine outside the house for the *witranalwe*. The *witranalwe* approached at a gallop, drank the *ñachi* at one gulp, and then tossed off the wine. When he finished, he galloped off to the uncle's corral to keep watch over his master's sheep. He never revealed the secret to his master.

Pedro Urdemales Cheats Two Horsemen

From Yolando Pino-Saavedra, *Folktales of Chile* (Chicago: University of Chicago Press, 1967), pp. 219–23.

Types 1528 *Holding Down the Hat;* 1539 *Cleverness and Gullibility;* and 1535 *The Rich and the Poor Peasant.* Motifs: K1252 "Holding down the hat"; K112.1 "Alleged self-cooking kettle sold"; K113 "Pseudo-magic resuscitating object sold"; K119 "Sale of other pseudo-magic objects"; K842 "Dupe persuaded to take prisoner's place in a sack."

Collected on tape on April 21, 1962 in Parral, Linares, from Amelia Quiroz.

Type 1528 *Holding Down the Hat* is told in Europe, especially in the Scandinavian countries, Lithuania, and Russia. It has not been listed in the Iberian peninsula but, on the other hand, exists in North, Central, and South America. In Spanish or Portuguese areas of America it appears in independent form or in combination with other types or motifs. A British variant is given as No. 69, "The Irishman's Hat" in *Folktales of England* (Chicago: University of Chicago Press, 1965), pp. 125–26. A variant related in Japanese was told by Austin Bach, a German raised in Japan, to Joseph L. Sutton in 1946. Richard M. Dorson recorded it from Dean Sutton of Indiana University in 1966. An old Korean gentleman tricks a Japanese policeman.

Types 1535 *The Rich and the Poor Peasant,* and 1539 *Cleverness and Gullibility* are widely dispersed in Latin America. The famous trickster Pedro Urdemales enters the Iberian and American versions of these tale types. Known in Spain as Pedro de Urdemalas, the Spanish American counterpart exceeds the characteristics of the Spanish rogue and takes to himself the role of other popular characters.

For the Spanish and Portuguese versions, see Terrence Leslie Hansen, *The Types of the Folktale in Cuba, Puerto Rico, the Dominican Republic, and Spanish South America* (Berkeley and Los Angeles, 1957); Aurelio M. Espinosa, *Cuentos populares españoles,* 3 vols. (Madrid, 1946–47), 3, pp. 158–59; Yolando Pino-Saavedra, *Cuentos Folklóricos de Chile,* 3 vols. (Santiago de Chile, 1960–63), 3, pp. 363–65; and Pino-Saavedra, *Chilenische Volksmärchen* (Düsseldorf and Cologne, 1964), pp. 279–80. Riley Aiken gives two Mexican variants of type 1535 ("The Two Compadres," pp. 29–36, and "Pedro de Urdemalas," pp. 49–55), and one of type 1539 ("Charge This to the Cap," pp. 41–44), in his collection, "A Packload of Mexican Tales," *Publications of the Texas Folklore Society* 12 (1935): 1–87.

Once upon a time there lived a gentleman named Pedro. As he could think of no way to earn some money, he set out on the road one day to wander. When he had walked a good bit, he had a need to do his duties, and promptly covered them afterwards with his hat. Just as he was finishing this, two men came along mounted on horseback.

"Good morning," they called to Pedro. "What are you up to there?"

"Good morning," said he politely. "I have a golden partridge and I can't take it out because I'm all alone."

"Really, man?"

"Yes. Why don't you lend me your horse to go for some help?"

One of the riders gladly dismounted and gave Pedro his horse, after which the rogue galloped away, never to return.

"I'm just going to uncover this little bird myself," said the horseman, rubbing his hands in glee and watching Pedro fade from sight over the horizon. He stuck his hand very carefully under the hat and pulled out the treasure. Ugh! He flung it away against a rock and wiped his hand in disgust. [The narrator laughs.]

Meanwhile Pedro had taken the horse to sell in town. With this money he bought clothing and still had some pocket money left over. Now, what should he spot next but a hawthorn bush! He promptly pierced all his coins and hung them on each thorn on the tree. When it was well loaded down, he stretched out on his back to guard it. Very soon two horsemen rode along.

"Isn't that Pedro Urdemales over there?" asked one.

"It sure enough is," answered the other as the two galloped over to the hawthorn bush.

"Hello, boys," said Pedro. "I'm just taking care of this tree until the fruit is ripe enough to pick."

"Humph," responded one, "really?"

"That's right. It's the nicest little money tree anybody could wish."

"Won't you sell it?" asked one of the riders.

"How could you think of such a thing? Not on your life!"

"Oh, come on and sell it to me," urged the other. "I'll give you three hundred *pesos* cash."

"What!" exclaimed Pedro. "For three hundred *pesos* you expect me to sell a tree that I can pick every year? No, sir!"

But the man pestered him so much that Pedro finally gave in. He took the money and hightailed it out of there. The two men lay down beside their tree to watch over it. But the hawthorn bush didn't yield any more. It just stood there without even flowering, the money dangling from the thorns.

"Well, we might as well pick it," said one to the other. "I've got a hunch that something is fishy here." They picked the tree of what there was and set out in pursuit of the vanished Pedro Urdemales. "We're going to nab this scoundrel and make him pay for such a dirty trick!"

In the meantime, Pedro had bought himself a little clay pot and made a hole in the ground. He placed a tin can in the hole, covered it, and lit a fire underneath. Not so long after, the irate horsemen came galloping up on him. When he saw them in the distance, Pedro began whipping the pot and chanting,

> "Boil, little boiling pot,
> I'm going to eat you piping hot.
> Boil, little boiling pot."

It boiled away merrily as the two horsemen rode up at breakneck speed.

"All right," they said, "what the devil are you doing now?"

"Good day, sirs. Why, I'm making some broth to eat, for I've got a wicked appetite."

"How do you think you're going to make broth there, man?" asked one of the riders. "You don't even have a fire."

"Boil, little boiling pot," chanted Pedro again, and away it boiled. He uncovered it and stirred up the broth. The potatoes were well done, so he took it off the hidden fire and sat down to eat lunch.

"Sell me that pot," exclaimed one of the wide-eyed horsemen.

"Now it's the same old story," said Pedro, trying to eat his lunch, "pestering and bothering around so I'll sell you the pot, and afterward you come chasing me. I won't sell a damned thing."

But the other man insisted and made such a fuss and bother that Pedro finally sold him the pot. The two of them rode home and proudly set the little pot, full of water and potatoes, out on the patio. And how they worked, whipping and beating it!

> "Boil, little boiling pot,
> I'm going to eat you piping hot."

But it was all to no avail. The pot wouldn't even simmer the least little bit.

"Let's move it over to my house to see if it works there," suggested one of them. But it was the same old story: the little pot simply wouldn't boil.

"Now we're really going to catch him and finish him off for good!" they roared, thoroughly enraged with this latest trick.

Pedro had taken the money from the sale of the pot and bought himself a young lamb, which he took home to his wife. Then he slaughtered the animal and filled its intestine with the blood, meanwhile carving himself a little hemlock whistle. Eventually he spotted the two horsemen coming on the double and called to his wife, "Here they come, my dear. I'm just going to drape this intestine around your neck and then stab you there. When the lamb's blood spurts, you'll play dead."

Up came the riders. "Now we've got you on the spot, Urdemales. What a nerve to sell us that fake boiling pot! You'll pay for this."

Pedro turned to his wife and shouted, "You, woman! You're to blame for all my fooling around!" With that, he snatched up his knife and stuck his wife in the back of the neck. The blood gushed out all over, and she fell dead to the floor. Immediately Pedro seized his hemlock whistle and blew: "Pirulí, Pirulí, Pirulí, Pirulí!" Slowly she moved a foot. "Pirulí, Pirulí, Pirulí!" Gradually she moved a hand. "Pirulí, Pirulí!" he blew again. Then and there, his wife came alive and sat up.

"Ay, Lord God, what has happened to me?" she moaned.

"You see?" said Pedro to the two men. "Thanks to you, I had killed my wife. That's how much you bother me, pestering me the livelong day."

"Sell me the whistle, old chap," burst out one of them.

"No, sir! I'm not selling any whistle."

"But you've got to. Look, I'll give you three hundred *pesos*."

"Again?" exclaimed Pedro. "For God's sake, how long will this go on? And afterward you always come back to make my life miserable."

Eventually the men insisted so much and were such a nuisance, that Pedro sold them the whistle and they left, full of contentment. One went home and started strutting about in a rage with his wife.

"You don't do what I tell you," he yelled, and—BOOM!—he stabbed her in the back of the neck with a long, sharp knife. She died, of course. Right away he began to pipe in her ear. "Pirulí, Pirulí, Pirulí!" ("Pirulí," my eye! She was stone dead.)

"I'll take her to my house to see if anything happens there," suggested the other when the husband had about given up. But it was the same story—"Pirulí, Pirulí, Pirulí!"—all over again. The poor woman never got well. They had to bury her.

Now the men were at their wit's end. "We're going to kill this guy for certain. We'll take him to pieces the minute we lay hands on him."

Pedro had already scampered away from his house. The men, however, were not to be put off, and eventually came upon him.

"Now, Urdemales, your game is up. You won't be fooling anybody any more."

"Oh, yes?" he answered. "Well, I suppose you know best."

Nearby there was a tremendous precipice, and down below a river flowed through some meadows where there was a large flock of sheep grazing. The men took Pedro to the edge of the cliff. But then they simply tied him hand and foot to a tree, for it happened to be twelve o'clock and they had to go home for lunch.

"After we have lunch," they said, "we'll be back to throw you into the river."

But what do you suppose happened? A poor old man chanced by while the others were gone and asked Pedro what he was doing tied to that tree.

"Oh, it's because I'm not capable of eating a tray of *empanadas* [a Chilean meat pastry] and of marrying the king's daughter. They're going to throw me off the cliff, and I'm a married man to boot."

"Well, I'm a bachelor and I want to marry," said the other. So he untied Urdemales from the tree, and Pedro bound the man in his place. After lunch, the two horsemen arrived to finish the job.

"No, no, sirs," begged the old man, "Don't throw me over! I'm going to marry the king's daughter. Don't you see? Listen to me!"

"Ah, you're going to marry the king's daughter, eh? That's a good one." And down he went.

Meanwhile, Pedro had hidden at the bottom of the cliff in the little inlets of the river. The poor old man sunk straight to the bottom like a stone, and out popped Pedro from the water, carrying a long switch.

"Hey, hey, look at my flock!
If you'd thrown me a little further down,
More lambs and sheep I would have found."

"There's that devil again," said the two men, looking down at the river. "And look at that flock he has! Come up here, you."

"There you go again with that foolish pestering," shouted Pedro.

"Are there a lot of sheep down there?"

"Pooh," he answered, "of course there are. I got them, didn't I? If you'd thrown me a little harder, I'd have gotten even more."

They were both so full of envy that they begged Urdemales to tie them up to the same tree and find out what good herdsmen they were. But since it was twelve o'clock again, Pedro merely bound them and left them while he went to take lunch. When he returned, the two men put up a great ruckus. "No, sir, don't throw us over, we're going to marry the king's daughter. Please!"

"Hah!" said Pedro, "the old story about the king's daughter, eh?" And—*poom!*—over and down went both of them forever.

Index of Motifs

All references are to Stith Thompson's *Motif-Index of Folk Literature*, 6 vols. (Bloomington, Indiana, 1955–58) unless otherwise indicated as follows. Motifs from other indexes: B = Ernest W. Baughman, *A Type and Motif-Index of the Folktales of England and North America* (Indiana University Folklore Series, No. 20: The Hague, 1966); and K = Bacil F. Kirtley, "A Motif-Index of Polynesian, Melanesian, and Micronesian Narratives" Ph.D. dissertation, Indiana University, 1955). Suggested motifs: m = Arsenio Manuel for the Philippines; n = Philip A. Noss for the Gbaya of Cameroun; p = Paul Powlison for the Yagua of Peru; and s = Harold A. Scheub for the Xhosa of South Africa; and st = John Milbury-Steen for the Gbande of Liberia.

Motif Number	Motif Title	Tale Title	Country
A155	Animals of the gods	Treasure, Envy, and Witchcraft	Peru
A165.1	Animals as attendants of god	Treasure, Envy, and Witchcraft	Peru
A418	Deity of particular mountain	Treasure, Envy, and Witchcraft	Peru
A511.1.9	Culture hero born from egg	Kondoy	Mexico
A526.7	Culture hero performs remarkable feats of strength and skill		
A571	Culture hero asleep in mountain	Kondoy	Mexico
A641	Cosmic egg	Kondoy	Mexico
A811	Earth brought up from bottom of primeval water	The Lake of Langui	Peru
A812	Earth Diver	Winabijou Brings on the Flood	United States
A814.2	Earth from sand strewn on primeval water	Winabijou Brings on the Flood	United States
A901	Topographical features caused by experiences of primitive hero	The Exiled Sister and Her Son	Micronesia
A910.2	Waters created as punishment	Kondoy	Mexico
A920.1.0.1	Origin of particular lake	The Lake of Langui	Peru
A920.1.8	Lake bursts forth to drown impious people	The Lake of Langui	Peru
A931	Meander-pursuit. A fugitive's doublings cause a river's windings	The Lake of Langui	Peru
A934.13* (p)	River system from felling of water tree	The Red Pond	Korea
A955.0.3 (k)	God kicks once and creates islands	The Twins Make Water Available by Felling the Water Tree	Peru
A955.3	Origin of island's shape and position	The Ghosts of the Two Mountains	Micronesia
A955.3.2.1	Primeval hero moves islands into their present position	The Ghosts of the Two Mountains	Micronesia
A964	Mountains (hills) from ancient contest	The Ghosts of the Two Mountains	Micronesia
A1010	Deluge	The Ghosts of the Two Mountains	Micronesia
A1023	Escape from deluge on tree	Winabijou Brings on the Flood	United States
A1111	Impounded water	Liar Mvkang and the Water Snake	Burma
		The Twins Make Water Available by Felling the Water Tree	Peru
A1145.1	Earthquakes from movements of subterranean monster	Kondoy	Mexico

Index of Tale Types

All references are to Antti Aarne and Stith Thompson, *The Types of the Folktale* (Helsinki, 1961) unless otherwise indicated as follows. Types from other indexes: H = Terrence L. Hansen, *The Types of the Folktale in Cuba, Puerto Rico, the Dominican Republic and Spanish South America* (Berkeley and Los Angeles, 1957); and L = Luc Lacourcière, *Catalogue of French Folktales in North America* (*Catalogue raisonné du conte populaire français en Amérique du Nord*, forthcoming [Québec: Presses de l'Université Laval]). Suggested types: m = Arsenio Manuel for the Philippines.

Contributors

ROBERT J. ADAMS wrote his doctoral dissertation in folklore at Indiana University in 1972 on "Social Identity of a Japanese Storyteller." He was on the faculty of the Folklore Institute at Indiana University until 1975, and currently teaches at Miyasaki Medical College, in Miyasaki, Japan.

HAFIZULLAH BAGHBAN is a doctoral candidate in folklore at Indiana University from Afghanistan. He is writing his dissertation on the traditional theater in Herat.

ILHAN BAŞGÖZ is professor of Uralic and Altaic Studies and Fellow of the Folklore Institute at Indiana University. He is preparing a volume of folktales of Turkey for the Folktales of the World Series and has published, with Andreas Tietze, *Bilmece: A Corpus of Turkish Riddles*.

CARLA BIANCO took her doctorate in folklore at Indiana University in 1972. Material from her dissertation formed the basis for her book *The Two Rosetos*. She is on the faculty of the University of Siena in Atezzo.

DANIEL P. BIEBUYCK is Rodney Sharp Professor of Anthropology at the University of Delaware. Together with Kahombo C. Mateene he published *The Mwindo Epic from the Banyanga* and *Anthologie de la littérature orale nyanga*. His daughter Brunhilde, who translated the Nyanga tales from his fieldwork in Zaïre, is a doctoral candidate in the Folklore Institute of Indiana University.

KATHARINE BRIGGS is past president of the Folklore Society in England, and coeditor of *Folktales of England* in the Folktales of the World series. Her publications on English folklore include the four-volume *A Dictionary of British Folk-Tales*.

LUIS DA CAMARA CASCUDO, dean of Brazilian folklorists, was born in Natal in 1898. He is professor emeritus of the Universidade Federal do Rio Grande do Norte. His works include *Contos Tradicionais do Brasil* and *Dicionario do Folklore Brasileiro*.

REIDAR CHRISTIANSEN, who died in 1971, held the chair of folklore at the University of Norway until his retirement. He edited *Folktales of Nor-*

way in the Folktales of the World series and published *The Migratory Legends* and *Studies in Irish and Scandinavian Folktales.*

DANIEL J. CROWLEY is professor of anthropology and fine arts at the University of California in Davis. He is preparing a volume on "Folktales of the West Indies" for the Folktales of the World series and has published *I Could Talk Old-Story Good: Creativity in Bahamian Folklore.*

LINDA DÉGH is professor of folklore at Indiana University and editor of *Indiana Folklore.* She has published *Folktales and Society: Storytelling in a Hungarian Peasant Community* and edited *Folktales of Hungary* for the Folktales of the World series.

RICHARD M. DORSON is distinguished professor of history and folklore and director of the Folklore Institute at Indiana University. He is general editor of the Folktales of the World series.

WOLFRAM EBERHARD is professor of sociology at the University of California, Berkeley. He edited *Folktales of China* in the Folktales of the World series and has published *Typen chinesischer Volksmärchen* and *Studies in Chinese Folklore and Related Essays.*

HASAN EL-SHAMY is assistant professor of folklore at Indiana University, where he took his doctorate in 1967. He is preparing a volume on "Folktales of Egypt" for the Folktales of the World series.

PRAPHULLADATTA GOSWAMI is professor of folklore at Gauhati University in Assam, India. He is preparing the "Folktales of India" volume for the Folktales of the World series and has published *Ballads and Tales of Assam: A Study of the Folklore of Assam.*

HAMISH HENDERSON is on the staff of the School of Scottish Studies in Edinburgh. Together with John MacInnes he is preparing a volume of "Folktales of Scotland" to be included in the Folktales of the World series.

BARBARA KIRSHENBLATT-GIMBLETT took her doctorate in folklore at Indiana University in 1972, writing her dissertation on "Traditional Storytelling in the Toronto Jewish Community: A Study in Creativity and Performance in an Immigrant Culture." She is on the faculties of the folklore and folklife department at the University of Pennsylvania and of the Yivo Institute for Jewish Research, New York.

JULIAN KRZYZANOWSKI has held the professorship of Polish literature at the University of Warsaw since 1934. He compiled an index of Polish folktales, *Polska bajka ludowa w ukladzie systematycznym.*

LUC LACOURCIÈRE is professor of folklore and director of the Archives de Folklore at Laval University in Quebec, Canada. Margaret Low, translator of the French-Canadian tales, is a doctoral candidate in folklore there under his direction.

SUZAN LAPAI is a candidate for the master's degree in folklore and the doctor's degree in Uralic and Altaic Studies at Indiana University. She lived in Burma from 1948 to 1968.

DEIRDRE LA PIN is writing her doctorate in the department of African languages and literature, University of Wisconsin at Madison, on "Styles of Performance in Yoruba Oral Narratives."

KATHARINE LUOMALA is professor emeritus of anthropology at the University of Hawaii in Honolulu. Among her works on Polynesian folklore are *Voices on the Wind: Polynesian Myths and Chants* and *Maui-of-a-Thousand-Tricks: His Oceanic and European Biographers.*

JOHN MACINNES is on the staff of the School of Scottish Studies in the University of Edinburgh. He is preparing with Hamish Henderson a volume on "Folktales of Scotland" for the Folktales of the World series.

JEAN MACLAUGHLIN is a doctoral candidate in folklore at Indiana University, writing her dissertation on "Traditional Oral Disparagement Humor among Quechua-Spanish Bilingual Children in Arequipa, Peru."

E. ARSENIO MANUEL is professor of anthropology at the University of the Philippines, Manila. He is preparing a volume on "Folktales of the Philippines" for the Folktales of the World series, and has compiled *Philippine Folklore Bibliography* and *A Survey of Philippine Folklore.*

ELLI KÖNGÄS MARANDA is professor of anthropology and sociology at the University of British Columbia in Vancouver. She took her doctorate in folklore at Indiana University in 1963. Together with Pierre Maranda she has published *Structural Models in Folklore and Transformation Essays* and *Structural Analysis of Oral Tradition.*

GENEVIÈVE MASSIGNON edited *Folktales of France* in the Folktales of the World series and published *Contes de l'Quest* and *Contes corses* from her own fieldwork. She was on the staff of the Centre Nationale de Recherche Scientifique in Paris until her death in 1966.

GEORGIOS A. MEGAS was until his retirement director of the Folklore Archives at the Academy of Athens and Professor of Folklore at the University of Athens. He edited *Folktales of Greece* in the Folktales of the World series and has published *Greek Calendar Customs* and *Griechische Volksmärchen.*

JOHN MILBURY-STEEN received a master's degree in creative writing from Indiana University in 1974. He served in the Peace Corps in Liberia from 1968 to 1972 and while there made a collection of Gbande tales from Bolahun.

ROGER E. MITCHELL is professor of sociology at the University of Wisconsin at Eau Claire, Wisconsin, and received his doctorate in folklore from Indiana University in 1967. He has published *Folktales of Micronesia*.

PHILIP A. NOSS was on the faculty of the department of African languages and literature at the University of Wisconsin at Madison until 1974. He presently resides in Cameroun, where he is attached to the Centre du Traduction Gbaya.

DOV NOY took his doctorate in folklore at Indiana University in 1954, and teaches at the Hebrew University in Jerusalem. He founded the Israeli Folktale Archives, edited *Folktales of Israel* in the Folktales of the World series, and has published *Moroccan Jewish Folktales*.

FELIX J. OINAS is professor of Slavic languages and literatures and Uralic and Altaic Studies and a Fellow of the Folklore Institute at Indiana University. He has published *Studies in Finnic-Slavic Folklore Relations* and, with Stephen Soudakoff, *The Study of Russian Folklore*.

SEAN O'SULLIVAN was the archivist of the Irish Folklore Commission from its founding in 1935 until 1970, when it became the archives of the new Department of Irish Folklore in University College, Dublin. He was archivist and college lecturer in the department from 1971 until his retirement in 1974. His published works include *Folktales of Ireland* in the Folktales of the World series, *A Handbook of Irish Folklore*, and *The Folklore of Ireland*.

AMÉRICO PAREDES is professor of English and anthropology at the University of Texas in Austin. He edited *Folktales of Mexico* in the Folktales of the World series and is the author of *"With His Pistol in His Hand": A Border Ballad and Its Hero*.

PAUL POWLISON took his doctorate in folklore at Indiana University in 1969, writing on "Yagua Mythology and Its Epic Tendencies." He is on the field staff of the Summer Institute of Linguistics working in Peru.

YOLANDO PINO-SAAVEDRA is director of the Instituto Investigaciones Folklóricas "Ramón A. Laval" at the University of Chile. He edited *Folktales of Chile* in the Folktales of the World series, a selection from his *Cuentos Folklóricos de Chile*.

KURT RANKE has held the chair of Volkskunde in the University of Göttingen, and is editor of *Fabula* and the *Encyclopädie des Märchens*. He edited the *Folktales of Germany* volume in the Folktales of the World series. His major works include *Die Zwei Brüder* and *Schleswig-Holsteinische Volksmärchen*.

PIRKKO-LIISA RAUSMAA is researcher in the Finnish Folklore Archives in Helsinki. She has published *Catalogues of Finnish Anecdotes and Historical, Local and Religious Legends*.

HAROLD SCHEUB is on the faculty of the department of African languages and literature at the University of Wisconsin at Madison. He is preparing a volume on "Folktales of Southern Africa" for the Folktales of the World series and has compiled a *Bibliography of African Oral Literature*.

KEIGO SEKI is on the faculty of Gagukei University, Tokyo. He edited *Folktales of Japan* in the Folktales of the World series and has published a six-volume classification of Japanese folktales, *Nihon Mukashibanashi Shusei*.

MERLE E. SIMMONS is professor of Spanish and Portuguese and Fellow of the Folklore Institute at Indiana University. He is the author of *The Mexican Corrido as a Source for Interpretive Study of Modern Mexico, 1870–1950* and *A Bibliography of the Romance and Related Forms in Spanish America*.

RUTH L. TONGUE is coeditor of *Folktales of England* with Katharine Briggs in the Folktales of the World series and author of *Somerset Folklore* and *Forgotten Folk-Tales of the English Counties*.

ROBERT WILDHABER was longtime director of the Museum für Völkerkunde in Basel, Switzerland, and is editor of the *International Folklore and Folklife Bibliography*. He is preparing a volume on "Folktales of Switzerland" for the Folktales of the World series.

HAZEL WRIGGLESWORTH is a doctoral candidate in folklore at Indiana University, writing her dissertation on "The Manobo Folktale: Its Teller and Audience in Ilianen Manobo Society." She is a member of the field staff of the Summer Institute of Linguistics working in the Philippines.

General Index

Abandonment: of infants, 553; of old people, 243

Abduction: children carried away in a sack, 402; of girl by ogres, 410; of girl by unidentified creature, 417; of girl by wild man, 486, 487

Accidents, series of, 375–77

Adam and Eve, 480

Adultery: culturally unacceptable, 252–53; punished, 252–53

Advice: given by father, 244–45; given by mother, 330, 331, 353; given by neighbors, 357; given by old man, 355; given by old women, 261; sought from neighbors, 357

Aesop, xx, 106

"The Altarpiece in Ringsaker Church," xx

Ancestors: snake as, 183; worship of, 182. See also Deities

Anecdote (mentioned in headnote), xix, 41, 41–42, 42–43, 56, 137, 468, 471

Anger: as cause of death, 313, 443; as cause of revenge, 307; at bird for withholding fire, 330; caused by discovery of murder plot, 355; caused by drunkenness, 460; caused by hunger, 307; caused by murder of child, 432; of ant at fire, 376; of spirit, 324

Animals: ant, 375–77; badger, 482; bee, 247, 275, 426; boa constrictor, 481; buffalo, 377–79; bull, 8–9; calf, 106; cat, 72–73, 509; chameleon, 368–71; civet cat, 381–84; cockroach, 346, 508; cow, 57, 58, 72, 345; crab, 289, 307; deer, 29, 256; dog, 73, 106, 235, 380–84, 409, 509; donkey, 106, 141–42, 144, 150; duiker, 401–2; elephant, 376; fly, 377; fox, 74–77, 446–48, 528, 530–33; frogs, 294; goat, 72, 509; grasshopper, 556; hornet, 422; horse, 111, 275, 509; laughing hyena, 472–74; leopard, 381–84; lion, 106, 460–61, 509; lizard, 392; loon, 483; monkey, 376, 381–84; mouse, 72–73, 245, 509, 528,

530–33; muskrat, 483; otter, 483; ox, 91, 106, 399–400; python, 372, 373; ram, 453–55; rat, 72, 252–53; sheep, 5, 452–55; snail, 273, 387, 555; snake, 181–87, 231, 232, 267, 295, 422, 502; termite, 375–77; tortoise, 267; turtle, 347–49; wasp, 422; water buffalo, 275; wolf, 60–62, 76–77, 446–48, 480–81. *See also specific animals*

Animals, characteristics of: food-providing, 57, 58; long-lived, 7–9; prophetic, 238, 240–41; talking, 7–9, 72–74, 74–77, 141–44, 231, 232, 235, 238, 239, 240–41, 265, 275, 283, 345–46, 446–48, 481, 508, 555. *See also* Magic animals

Animal tales (mentioned in headnote), 445, 508, 528, 542

Ant: angry at fire for burning eggs, 376; why ant eats termites, 377

Arabian Nights, 149, 210. See also *A (One) Thousand and One Nights*

Asbjörnsen, Peter (folklorist), xix

Auger, Joseph, composer of "Complainte de Pérusse," 466

Badger: why badger has stripes on face, 482

Banishment. *See* Punishment

Baptism. *See* Religious rites

Barbeau, Marius (folklorist), 466

Bargains and promises: between giant and sun, 332; honored by secret society, 54; if saved, victim promises to raise bridge, 273; made with devil, 98; not to remarry, 320; ogre swears by left-handed *haykal*, 237; to await birth of male child, 11, 22, 23; to divide food, 347; to get chalice, 94; to give newborn child to devil, 82; to keep secret, 309; to keep secret of friend's enchantment, 133–34; unborn son will build bridge, 269

Baughman, Ernest W. (folklorist), 33, 34

Index of Bibliographic Items

618   Index of Bibliographic Items

Index of Collectors